HAVEL

HAVEL
A LIFE

MICHAEL ZANTOVSKY

Atlantic Books
London

First published in hardback and trade paperback in Great Britain in 2014
by Atlantic Books, an imprint of Atlantic Books Ltd.

1 2 3 4 5 6 7 8 9

A CIP catalogue record for this book is available from the British Library.

Hardback ISBN: 978 0 85789 849 4
E-book ISBN: 978 0 85789 851 7

Printed and bound by CPI Group (UK) Ltd, Croydon, CR0 4YY

Atlantic Books
An Imprint of Atlantic Books Ltd
Ormond House
26–27 Boswell Street
London
WC1N 3JZ

www.atlantic-books.co.uk

For David, Ester, Jonáš and Rebeka

All my life I have simply believed that what is once done can never be undone and that, in fact, everything remains forever. In short, Being has a memory. And thus even my insignificance – as a bourgeois child, a laboratory assistant, a soldier, a stagehand, a playwright, a dissident, a prisoner, a president, a pensioner, a public phenomenon, and a hermit, an alleged hero but secretly a bundle of nerves – will remain here forever, or rather not here, but somewhere. But not, however, elsewhere. Somewhere here.

Václav Havel, *To the Castle and Back*

Contents

Illustrations

24. Re-elected. © Karel Cudlín.
25. Without the goose step. Reviewing the honour guard.
© ČTK/Karel Vlček.
26. The president and his spokesman. © Oldřich Škácha.
27. At breakfast. © ČTK/Libor Hajský.
28. Speaking to the joint session of the US Congress.
© ČTK/Jaroslav Hejzlar.
29. Goodbye to red ties. © Vitaly Armand/AFP/Getty Images.
30. The Stones in the Castle. © ČTK/Michal Doležal.
31. Communist leader Antonín Zápotocký makes room for Winston
Churchill. © ČTK/Michal Kalina.
32. The federal conundrum. © ČTK/Stanislav Peška.
33. The abdication. © ČTK/Michal Krumphanzl.
34. With Tom Stoppard at the Czech premiere of *Travesties*.
© Ondřej Němec.
35. 'Welcome, Your Holiness, among us sinners.'
© ČTK/ Martin Gust.
36. 'Ma'm, let me present Gyula.' © Alan Pajer.
37. Dancing with Hillary. © Alan Pajer.
38. With Bob Dylan and Dáša. © Alan Pajer.
39. The presidents and the first ladies, Madeleine Albright and author.
© The White House.
40. 'The man of my life.' © Ivo Šilhavý.
41. With the Dalai Lama. © ČTK/ Michal Kamaryt.
42. The premiere of *Leaving*. © Alan Pajer.
43. The Mourning. © ČTK/René Fluger.
44. A step too far. © Tomki Nemec.

Prologue

THREE QUESTIONS SHOULD BE ASKED, at least implicitly, and answered, at least tentatively, before another small forest of trees falls victim to the idea of writing a book. Is the subject of any interest to anyone but the author? Have there been other treatments of the subject, which could satisfy such interest? Is the author the right person to write about the subject?

Václav Havel was one of the more fascinating politicians of the last century. His unique riches-to-rags-to-riches life story is easily given to simplistic accounts, but there is no doubt that he played a prominent role in finally putting to rest one of the most alluring utopias of all time, and oversaw one of the most dramatic social transitions of recent history.

Although many people, including Havel himself, often marvelled at the fairy-tale nature of his sudden elevation to the highest job in the country, there had been in fact nothing miraculous or accidental about it. As this book will aim to show, the ambition to 'repair the world' had been present in Havel's life ever since, at the age of ten, he envisaged a factory manufacturing 'good' rather than goods. Equipped with a hypertrophied sense of responsibility that led him to stand his ground and persist in the face of adversity, and with the less than conspicuous but all the more real discipline and industry with which he applied himself to the tasks at hand, he emerged in November 1989 not just as the most likely, but as the only plausible candidate for the leader of the revolution.

Even so, Havel cannot be simplistically reduced to a dissident or politician. He was also a formidable thinker, who consistently attempted to apply the results of his thinking process, as well as the moral precepts, which were at its core, to his practical engagement in the realm of politics. Some would question whether he was an original thinker of lasting significance. Although well read, he lacked the formal education, broader erudition and systematic discipline of a real scholar, and he was often wont to remind his readers and listeners of this handicap. His moral philosophy can be reduced to three concepts, which are inseparably linked to his name. The first, the 'power of the powerless', also the title of his best-known essay, is almost slogan-like in its simplicity. It makes for a great rallying cry, but at first sight it appears not to be applicable to most day-to-day situations, where power rests with the powerful, and the powerless are just that. Paradoxically, it is even harder to apply when the powerless suddenly find themselves in positions of power. And yet, this concept found an indelible expression in perhaps the only revolution in history that left no victims. The second, 'living in truth', has an almost messianic tinge, and exposes its author to charges of being starry-eyed, hypocritical or worse. By most ordinary definitions of 'truth', Havel can sometimes be caught in contravention of his own teaching, and yet few can fault his determination to live up to the principle as best he could. The concept of 'responsibility', rooted in the 'memory of being', completes the triad. The rest, as they say, is commentary. Havel left behind no comprehensive work, and no formal philosophical system. In some of his metaphysical thinking, especially during his presidential days, he balances perilously on the brink of new-ageism and pop philosophy. For the most part, however, there is a crystal-like moral clarity and consistency to his thought.

Next to, but not second to his role as dissident, politician and thinker, Havel was a wonderful, witty and original writer. His success in that arena owed nothing to his public status and renown as a dissident or a politician; in fact, it came into play a long time before he became the best-known Czechoslovak prisoner of conscience, and an even longer time before he became a president. Quite to the contrary, it could be argued that Havel's public career imposed severe constraints on his writing. The high points of his creative work came in the mid-1960s with plays like *The Garden Party* (1964) and *The Memorandum* (1965). Although never embraced by the Communist art commissars, Havel enjoyed considerable artistic freedom and numerous opportunities during this period. *Leaving* (2008), his last play, begun before he embarked on the presidency and finished only after he left it, is a telling reminder of his writing potential. The intervening period contains little gems, such as the one-act plays *Audience* (1975) and *Private View* (1975), powerful moral dramas like *Temptation* (1985), intriguing exploits like *The Beggar's Opera* (1972) and *Largo Desolato* (1984), and some arguable failures like *Conspirators* (1971) and *Mountain Hotel* (1976). The two autobiographies masked as interviews with Karel Hvížďala, *Disturbing the Peace* (1986) and *To the Castle and Back* (2006), attest to both Havel's unique power of introspection and his subversive humour. His prose writings at the height of his dissident era, including some of his most memorable essays and the unique piece of epistolary work that is the *Letters to Olga*, are hybrids of creative writing, philosophy and political prose, best appreciated in the context in which they were written; nevertheless, some of these have clearly passed the test of time and changing circumstances.

Finally, there was Havel the person, someone who achieved his impact on others through means as unique as was his life. From his teens onwards, he was a leader, setting agendas, walking at the front, showing the way. Yet none of this was in any way associated with the monomania of a true visionary, but was conducted rather with a diffidence, kindness and politeness so unwavering (and often unwarranted) that Havel himself caricatured it in some of his plays; moreover, these traits were graced by an all-encompassing sense of humour and the absurd, which was mostly kind, sometimes wicked, but never cruel. A man thriving on company, the heart and soul of the party, winning friendship easily and returning it in abundance. A lovely man, the English would say.

Still, there was the other Havel, 'a bundle of nerves',[1] depressed, ill, raging at his own impotence, escaping into drink, prescription drugs, sickness and sometimes ill-considered sexual adventures. His confidence never wavered when he stood at the head of millions and pondered the possible crackdown by tanks surrounding Prague in November 1989. Yet when he did become president, with all the trappings of power, he was rarely sure he was up to the task; by his own admission he became suspect to himself. Trying to live in truth, he measured himself, though never others, by this impossibly high standard and by his own judgement he invariably failed. An imperfect man, like the rest of us.

---

1   *To the Castle and Back* (*Prosím stručně*). Translated by Paul Wilson (London: Portobello Books, 2008), 330.

The only way to explain and understand Havel's enormous and lasting popularity and significance – as the aftermath of his death made plain – is thus to consider not just the individual areas of his work and activity, fascinating and valuable as they are, or to explore the individual aspects of his complex personality, but rather to see how the pieces fit together in a coherent, enduring and mutually reinforcing, though paradoxical, whole, which was so much greater than a sum of its parts. He was the ultimate WYSIWYG, authentic, genuine, real in a way most people can only aspire to and most politicians would kill for. Even his flaws were real, not the peccadilloes of some media-concocted caricature of a celebrity.

As it happens, there exist several previous biographical studies of Havel from various perspectives and angles, in Czech, in English and in other languages, all – with one exception – written before Havel's death.[2] They all contain valuable insights into multiple aspects of Havel's life, work and personality. Obviously, they are fragmentary: no account of a life can be complete until that life is over; but they are also fragmentary in the sense of focusing on a particular component of the Havel myth, be it his lifelong perspective as an outcast and rebel, his ambivalent attitude to politics in general – and to his presidency in particular – his moral philosophy, his artistic creativity or his free-wheeling lifestyle. That said, there is of course no such thing as a definitive biography, and this work is therefore destined to be regarded as a mere stepping stone on the path towards discovering the true Václav Havel.

Finally, why me? I was close to Václav Havel but I could not claim to be the closest person to him, or to have known him the longest. I knew of him for two thirds of his life, but knew him well only for the last third. We were close for most of that time, but due to the vagaries of the very history he had helped to make, and the obligations that it entailed for both of us, we did not see each other for long periods at a time. In fact, one of the mysteries of Havel – and one on which this book can only shed some partial light – is who really were

---

2   The three most interesting, in this author's view, are Carol Rocamora's *Acts of Courage: Václav Havel's Life in the Theater*, Martin C. Putna's *Václav Havel: A Spiritual Portrait in the Framework of the Czech Culture of the Twentieth Century* and Jiří Suk's *Politics as Absurdist Drama, Václav Havel in the Years 1975–1989*, the last two unfortunately only available in Czech. Three general, though incomplete biographies, Eda Kriseová's *Václav Havel, The Authorized Biography*, John Keane's *Václav Havel: A Political Tragedy in Six Acts* and Daniel Kaiser's *Dissident, Václav Havel 1936–1989*, are also worth reading for their wealth of detail and for interesting, albeit sometimes disputable perspectives. This author was grateful to be able to draw on all of them.

the people closest to him. Apart from his two wives, and his brother Ivan, who between them comprised the family he had as an adult, and perhaps the late Zdeněk Urbánek, who alternated between the roles of Havel's *alter ego* and *superego*, there were a large number of people with whom Havel was intimate, and yet there was no one who could claim to be his closest friend without being challenged for the title. There was, mixed with the warmth and the friendliness, a certain remoteness to his personality, a sense of detachment, an inner impenetrable core that you could never enter.

This also accounts for a certain asymmetry in Havel's personal relationships, including our own. No matter how important various people were to him at various times, there was always the sense that they needed him more than he needed them. There was, as far as I could tell, no deliberate effort on his part to dominate or to engage in one-upmanship. On the contrary, he tended to be modest to a fault, self-deprecating, even apparently submissive towards friends, and yet he somehow always came out on top. I believe that this was the secret key to his unique but strangely effective leadership style, and for that reason I will deal with it at more length later in this work.

There is no question that Havel and I felt good in one another's company, and that we shared many laughs, moments of sadness, quite a few drinks and some incredible moments together, both before and after he became president. My proudest moment with him was not when the two of us 'jointly' addressed the joint session of the US Congress as I will describe later on, or when he presented me to the Queen. Instead, it was when he allowed me to carry his personal effects in a string bag on 17 May 1989, as he emerged from the side entrance of the Pankrác prison on his release from his last imprisonment.

During the first two of his four terms as president (from 1989 to 1992), I probably spent more time with Václav Havel than any other person, including his wife. This was not a mark of my importance, but of the nature of my job: as his spokesman and press secretary I had to be present at each foreign trip, each fruitless appointment and each forgettable function, so as to be able to report about it later to the press on behalf of a president who did not particularly enjoy media attention.

I had tremendous respect for his ideas, his sincerity, his unflappable kindness, his authenticity and his courage. Even so, that did not always lead me to agree with him, both about the practical decisions he had to make as president and the philosophy underlying them. Part of my job was to play the *advocatus diaboli*, and to make the case for doing things differently or for doing different things or, indeed, for not doing some things at all. Occasionally – though not very often – I prevailed. That in turn led to my appointment to a parallel role as political coordinator of the president's office, a problematic elevation, as it came with no specific powers, and its authority was largely unenforceable in a team of friends.

Over time our differences increased, not in terms of our goals, our view of the world or our role in it, but in terms of the practical conduct of the presidency. Rightly or wrongly, I felt that he would find it more and more difficult to have a real impact on the political and social developments of the country unless he organized the large numbers of his supporters and admirers into an effective political force, or let them organize themselves. He respected the argument and largely shared the analysis, but in the end he would rather live with the handicap of not having a political machine than enter the arena of factional politics. This was something that I had to respect for my part. Nevertheless, it was a major reason for my departure from the president's office at the end of Havel's second term, even though I was invited to stay on. Over a couple of drinks in the spring of 1992, Havel graciously accepted my reasons for leaving and threw his full weight behind my next career move, the ambassadorial appointment to Washington. He never ceased to be supportive of me, and continued to be generous with his time and friendship, across three continents, and whenever the occasion arose.

My own relationship to Havel can best be described by a word that I use with the utmost reluctance. But if love means not just liking another person and enjoying his company, but caring for him, worrying about him, dwelling in one's thoughts with him over considerable distances and periods of time, and being keen on his approval and reciprocation, then love it was. I suspect I was not the only person in Havel's inner circle who would define his or her relationship to him in this way. It was this bond that kept us together, and kept us going during the crazy early days of Czechoslovakia's democratic transformation.

Being in love with the subject of one's biography is not necessarily the best qualification for writing it, for it brings with it the risks of hagiography, lack of perspective and distortion of facts. While I am not sure I can successfully navigate my way around these perils, largely hidden underwater, I could do worse than to fall back on my original profession as a clinical psychologist. One less enjoyable but essential aspect of that and other medical professions is the ability to assume a 'clinical posture', i.e. the skill to watch other human beings, including people closest to you, struggle, triumph, decline, suffer and die, all the while taking dispassionate notes of the experience. The result is for the reader to judge.

18 December 2011, a Dark Cold Day

He disappeared in the dead of winter:
The brooks were frozen, the airports almost deserted,
And snow disfigured the public statues;
The mercury sank in the mouth of the dying day.
What instruments we have agree
The day of his death was a dark cold day . . .

        – W. H. Auden, 'In memory of W. B. Yeats'

IT WAS A WINTRY SUNDAY MORNING in Prague on the last weekend before the Christmas holidays. Most people's thoughts revolved around wrapping up their Christmas presents and perhaps getting some rest. It had not been a particularly happy year. Although the country was faring better than most in the midst of a European debt crisis, the economy was slowing down, and the austerity measures were beginning to bite.

The news, when it came, first on the social networks, and soon through the general media channels, came as a shock, although it ought not to have. The whole nation had known that the ex-president was ailing. Since the spring, his friends had been aware how serious his condition was. This was not the result of any acute ailment, but rather a progressive general exhaustion combined with a sudden loss of the will and the fighting spirit that had characterized him for most of his life.

If there was no sustained public interest in Václav Havel's condition, no media deathwatch outside his house, it was simply because the ex-president appeared to be old news, no longer relevant to current events and issues. He was still a subject of moderate interest to cultural and literary editors because of his recent creative exploits, and his name sometimes appeared next to his wife's in the celebrity pages. The house at Hrádeček, where he had been spending his last months, was a hundred miles away from Prague on a bad country road, with few hotels or restaurants nearby. To the media hounds, it was hardly worth the trouble.

Prime Minister Petr Nečas, appearing on a Sunday television talk show at the moment the news broke, was the first to respond publicly. 'His death is a great loss,' he said respectfully. Still nothing suggested more than a few days of polite mourning for a figure from the past.

Shortly after noon, people started to bring flowers and candles to the Castle and to lay them at the perimeter fence. Flowers and candles also appeared around the house at Hrádeček. Some good soul left two bottles of beer from the brewery in Trutnov, which had inspired Havel to write *Audience.*

At 2 p.m., Havel's successor as president chimed in. 'Václav Havel has become the symbol of our modern Czech state,'[1] said Václav Klaus. No one expected him to be ungenerous at that moment, and yet there was something remarkable in this sweeping eulogy by a man who disagreed with Havel on so many day-to-day issues of Czech politics.

A crowd began to gather spontaneously on the square under the statue of St Wenceslas, where the demonstrations had begun in 1989. People stood and rattled their keys, just as they had in November 1989. A group marched to the river, taking the same route as the student demonstration on 17 November, which set off the Velvet avalanche, but in the opposite direction. The marchers paused at the plaque honouring that seminal moment in Czech history. Some left packs of cigarettes.

There were few overt expressions of grief, no rending of garments, no hysterics. When, ten weeks later,[2] Sir Tom Stoppard paid Havel the tribute of quoting John Motley's eulogy of William of Orange, 'As long as he lived he was the guiding star of a whole brave nation, and when he died the little

---

1 Statement by the President of the Czech Republic Reflecting the Death of Former Czech President Václav Havel, 18 December 2011, http://www.klaus.cz/clanky/3002.
2 Remembering Václav Havel, RIBA, London, 1 March 2012.

children cried in the street,[3] he himself admitted to 'sentimental hyperbole'.[4] The feeling was that of a communal memory, of remembrance and, yes, of celebration. There were gatherings in other towns and cities throughout the Czech Republic as well.

One could not help ponder the contrast with another kind of mourning half a world away. Kim Jong Il, the Dear Leader of North Korea, died just the day before. There, W. H. Auden's paraphrase of Motley's words was irrefutably apt: 'When he laughed, respectable senators burst with laughter. And when he cried, the little children died in the streets.'[5] The Korean state news agency aired footage of huge columns of people wailing in unison. No doubt, many of the 200,000 political prisoners in the country were crying as well, though theirs were tears of joy.

Condolences started to come in from abroad, some official, from heads of states and governments, others from friends, former dissidents and writers. Russian state TV contributed a eulogy of its own: 'Václav Havel was the main driving force of democratization in Czechoslovakia, and the grave-digger of the advanced Czech arms industry, whose demise was one of the causes of the break-up of Czechoslovakia.' A balanced assessment, straight from *The Garden Party*.

The spokesman for the Association of Czech Travel Agencies managed to see the bright side. 'For a long time the Czech Republic had not been as visible as this,' said Tomio Okamura, who would announce his own candidacy for president just a few weeks later. 'In winter people are deciding about where they will go for their summer vacations, and although Havel's demise is a sad thing, it is a very good advertisement for the country.'[6]

On Monday, in what was still a family affair, Havel's remains were brought to Prague in a simple casket, and laid in state at the Prague Crossroads, the Gothic church that he and his wife Dagmar had restored and turned into a cultural shrine and meeting place. For the next two days and throughout the night, people lined up to pay their respects. The government declared a state of mourning. The government of Slovakia, a country that at one time seemed to have repudiated Havel, did the same.

---

3 John L Motley, *The Rise of the Dutch Republic* (EBook #4811 Project Gutenberg, 2012).
4 Remembering Václav Havel, RIBA, London, 1 March 2012.
5 'Epitaph on a Tyrant' (1940).
6 'Václav Havel died December 18, 2011', www.lidovky.cz, 19 December 2011.

On Wednesday, the state took over. The casket made its journey across the river and up the hill to the Castle, followed by thousands of people. In the Castle Guard Barracks it was loaded on the same gun carriage that had been used for the funeral of the first Czechoslovak president, Tomáš Garrigue Masaryk, and carried to the Vladislav Hall in the Prague Castle, the fifteenth-century seat of coronation ceremonies, and the venue of Havel's first election to the presidency. Once again Klaus was up to the task: 'Our Velvet Revolution and the era of restoration of freedom and democracy will always remain associated with his name. More than anyone else, he deserves the credit for the international standing of the Czech Republic, its prestige and its authority . . . As a writer and playwright he believed in the power of the word to change the world.'[7]

Friday, 23 December, the day of the funeral, was also the last day before the traditional start of the Czech holiday season on Christmas Eve. Despite the inconvenient timing, government planes started landing in quick succession at Prague's Ruzyně Airport, soon to bear the deceased's name. In what seemed an unending procession of black limousines, their passengers, eighteen heads of state and government and other dignitaries, including President Sarkozy and Prime Minister Cameron, Hillary and Bill Clinton, Madeleine Albright, Lech Wałęsa, John Major and Prince Hassan of Jordan, proceeded to the St Vitus Cathedral at the Prague Castle, where they joined around two thousand Czech government officials, friends and family.

In a familiar dilemma, I found myself torn between the need to mourn freely for a friend and the duties of the ambassador to the Court of St James's, which included being on the tarmac to greet the current and former British Prime Ministers. I knew I could never make it to the cathedral in time for the ceremony, for the prime ministers were late, and their motorcade was leaving airside straight from the tarmac, while my driver was waiting kerbside half a mile away. Without a police escort, which only the motorcade had, I would never make it through the security checks in time for the ceremony. The secret servicewoman in charge coldly vetoed my plea to piggyback on the motorcade. Trying to think what Havel would do, I jumped into the already moving limousine of Sean McLeod, the empathetic British ambassador to Prague, before the secret

---

7 Speech by the President of the Czech Republic at the solemn gathering to honour the late President Václav Havel, 21 December 2011, http://www.klaus.cz/clanky/3005.

servicewoman could speak a word into her jacket sleeve. I slipped into my seat at the cathedral with the first notes of music.

Just as Havel, a non-denominational believer, was honoured at his election by the *Te Deum* mass, he was now treated to a Catholic mass, accompanied by Antonín Dvořák's *Requiem*. Josef Abrhám, who played Chancellor Rieger in the film version of *Leaving*, read *Dies Irae*, words that uncannily reflected Havel's own thinking:

> Great trembling there will be
>> when the Judge descends from heaven
>> to examine all things closely.
> The trumpet will send its wondrous sound
>> throughout earth's sepulchres
>> and gather all before the throne.
> Death and nature will be astounded,
>> when all creation rises again,
>> to answer the judgement.
> A book will be brought forth,
>> in which all will be written,
>> by which the world will be judged.

Havel did not die a Roman Catholic, and during his last days he never asked for the last rites, but his sense of theatre and ritual would have been gratified by the liturgy, celebrated by his fellow prisoner Cardinal Duka, and by the procession that preceded it. He would have enjoyed, albeit with some embarrassment, hearing the praise from friends, Madeleine Albright, his fellow Velvet revolutionary, Bishop Václav Malý, and Karel Schwarzenberg.

For the third time, the president spoke, this time on Havel's spiritual legacy, embodied in the ideas that 'freedom is a value worth sacrificing for', that 'it is easy to lose freedom, if we care little about it and do not protect it', that 'human existence extends into the transcendental realm, of which we should be aware', that 'freedom is a universal principle', that there is 'tremendous power in a word; it can kill and it can heal, it can hurt and it can help', that 'it is able to change the world', that 'the truth should be said, even if it is uncomfortable' and that 'minority opinion is not necessarily wrong'.[8] There were many words of praise that day, but these may have weighed more than most, simply because of the man who uttered them.

While the heads of states and foreign dignitaries attended a reception given by the president, family and friends, myself among them, were making their way across town to the funeral hall of the crematorium in Strašnice for a last goodbye. Unlike in the cathedral, the speeches here were numerous, improvised and mostly heartfelt, though forgettable. Some of the closest friends chose not to speak at all. It was as much a chance to say hello to the others present as to say goodbye to the one who was gone. Then the curtain fell.

There was still a third act to follow, an evening of music, performance and entertainment, to honour Havel the bohemian intellectual, the rock 'n' roll aficionado and the chief of an Indian nation, a title awarded to him by an open-air rock festival in Trutnov. It took place in the Lucerna Hall, the house that Havel's grandfather built. The last number on the bill belonged to the Plastic People of the Universe, a band that had played an influential role both in Havel's life and in Czech history.

It was an amazing week, a week of mourning a loss, and a celebration of a great find, or perhaps a rediscovery. People emerged from 'the cells of themselves',[9] and at least for a while forgot about the coming winter, the thousand necessities of a family Christmas and the uncertain perspectives ahead. They joined in a rite of mourning and respect, were nice to their fellow men and spoke kindly of their enemies. In this strange mixture of sadness and joy, the latter seemed to have prevailed, joy at being confronted with greatness. Havel would have disliked that word. He would have been a little embarrassed by it all, and his comments would reflect a combination of modest pleasure with subtle irony, and a sense of wonder about a nation that he sometimes said was capable of the most amazing feats of dignity, solidarity and courage, if only for a couple of weeks once every twenty years.

---

8   Speech by the President of the Czech Republic at the Funeral Service in St Vitus Cathedral, 23 December 2011, http://www.klaus.cz/clanky/3007.
9   W. H. Auden, 'In Memory of W. B. Yeats'.

Born with a Silver Spoon

MYTHOLOGIES MATTER. In retrospect, it seems hardly accidental that the first-born son of a prosperous Prague family, which epitomized in miniature the achievements of a newly independent nation with an ancient history, received his name after the patron saint of Bohemia. Nor does it seem accidental that by virtue of his birth and name he became heir to a dynasty. Just as St Wenceslas,[1] the tenth-century Premyslid duke, came to be followed by three kings of the same name, the founder of the Havel dynasty, an entrepreneurial miller's son and part-time spiritualist, Vácslav Havel, gave his name to his son Václav Maria, who in turn did the same, on 5 October 1936, for his own son, the future president. The mythology does not end there, for the legendary treatment of the historical St Wenceslas constitutes a direct equivalent to the Arthurian tale, possibly with the same antecedents. Not far from Prague there is a hill called Blaník, conceivably a sister knoll of Planig in the Rhineland, Blagny near Dijon and Bligny near Paris, all of them with Celtic roots, inside which an army of knights is said to be sleeping and waiting for the moment when things could not be worse for the Czech nation, at which point, under the command of St Wenceslas himself, they will come to its rescue. Anybody using the name for the third time in as many generations must have aimed high.

There were good reasons for such ambitions. Starting from scratch with a small town sewerage project, the eldest Havel had built a construction and

---

1 Václav in Czech.

property empire, which included the proud townhouse on the banks of the Vltava River where the family lived; nevertheless, his crowning achievement was the big commercial and entertainment complex called Lucerna on the conveniently named Wenceslas Square, at once the Piccadilly and the Champs Elyseés of the bustling town. The first edifice built of reinforced concrete in the city, it was dubbed 'Palace' at the time, but with its dance hall, shops, bars, a cinema, a music club and numerous offices it might today be called a mall. Prague is not a city the size of New York or London, but neither is it a small town, and so the regularity with which the above places and symbols crop up time and again in the story of Václav Havel's life is quite remarkable.

Vácslav's two sons were no slouches, either. Václav Maria followed in his father's footsteps and expanded the construction and property business, although he was hard hit by the Great Depression in the early 1930s. Inspired as a young man by his trip to California, he conceived of an exclusive property development on the Barrandov Hills above the Vltava River, hired the foremost modern architects to build the first flat-roof, functionalist villas there, so unlike the typical Prague gable-roofed houses, and added an American-style bar and restaurant with spectacular views of the river and the city, loosely modelled after San Francisco's Cliff House.[2]

The other son, Miloš, was also inspired by California, though more by its dream entrepreneurs than by its developers. On the vacant land next to his brother's property development, he built one of the largest film studios on the continent, becoming one of the founders of the Czech film industry. The semblance to the Hollywood Hills was so striking that one half-expected there to be a big sign perched up on the hill for everybody to see from near and far. And indeed, there has been a five-metre-long steel memorial plaque with the name 'Barrande', the French palaeontologist after whom the rock is named, visible from across the river since 1884, preceding the Hollywood sign by forty years and raising questions about the original inspiration.

The brothers were close, but markedly different. Václav Maria was a serious, no-nonsense, solid family man, a paragon of bourgeois virtues,

---

2 In April 1969, Václav's brother Ivan, then on a doctoral fellowship at Berkeley, sent his father a postcard of Cliff House and the surrounding Seal Rocks. 'The sea lions are real. I saw them, barking.' In the margin, he adds: 'Inside it resembles Barrandov even more.' Ivan M. Havel's archive, Václav Havel Library (hereafter VHL) ID18301.

including a mistress or two kept discreetly out of sight. In his business dealings he was motivated not so much by the 'capitalist longing for profit . . . but enterprise, pure and simple – the will to create something'.[3] He was a pillar of society, a Rotarian, Freemason and member of assorted other clubs and associations, an enlightened patriot, who brought up his sons in 'the intellectual atmosphere of Masarykian humanism',[4] politically connected though not politically active, a cultured man, friend to important Czech writers and journalists, with a sizeable library of his own, a good husband to his wife and a 'wonderful, kind'[5] father to his two sons. He was also a genuinely decent and modest man, as is evident from the way he treated his subordinates, and even more from the quiet and dignified manner in which he coped with adversity and social exclusion during the last thirty years of his life.

Miloš the movie mogul was the bohemian in the family, a gay man of lavish lifestyle and popular parties, who preferred the company of film stars and musicians to that of bankers and politicians. He and his circle amounted to what counted for glamour in Czechoslovakia in the 1930s. By most accounts he was fiercely devoted to his studios and loyal to his stars, which led to his involvement in some questionable projects and some even more questionable concessions and compromises following the Nazi occupation of Czechoslovakia in 1939, when the studios were turned into part of their war propaganda machine.

Václav's mother Božena was no mere footnote to this family of strong individuals, but very much a personality in her own right, an archetypal Prague matron, just as her husband was the archetypal gentleman and her brother-in-law the archetypal *bon vivant*. She organized family life, saw, with the help of several nannies, to her sons' upbringing and education, remained in charge of the social diary, and dabbled in music, the arts and science. Her father, Hugo Vavrečka, another remarkable product of the national renaissance, was a Silesian engineer, journalist, author and diplomat, an early visionary of Central European integration and, briefly, a minister in the Czechoslovak government.

---

3 *Disturbing the Peace* (1990), 4.
4 Ibid. 7.
5 Ibid. 5.

Though she was by all accounts a good and conscientious mother, and though she encouraged all kinds of intellectual interests in her sons, from chemistry and science in general to literary pursuits and home puppet theatre shows, Božena was apparently not much of an emotionally nourishing parent, especially with respect to her first-born. She doted on the younger son, Ivan, born two years after Václav, made Václav responsible for his well-being and blamed him for things gone wrong – not an unusual ordeal for an older sibling.[6]

On the whole, though, it was a privileged, comfortable and happy childhood, and Václav was a privileged, comfortable and happy child. The only problem, for a child born in 1936, was that it would not last for long.

His mother, a keen documentarian, provided perhaps the best illustration of the contradictions that were to shape Havel's life. The Family Album of 1938, which she lovingly collected and illustrated with her own drawings, starts with a panoramic photograph of the Barrandov Terraces headlined 'Venóškovo' (Little Václav's),[7] with the clear, though mistaken, implication that these would one day be his.

In scores of photographs, many with his mother, father, family, their friends and brother Ivan, against the backdrop of toys, villas and luxury cars, Havel is the very model of a child who wants for nothing. He stands smiling self-confidently, dressed and nourished like a prince. His shyness and insecurity must have developed somewhat later. One of the earliest photographs of the younger brother, a few days after his birth, shows Václav prodding Ivan's nose with his finger, 'to verify that I really existed'.[8] At the age of four, he was not a little opinionated. Of a bald-headed friend of the family, one Dr Wahl, he enquired why he had no hair. When the man, in an attempt to humour the child, answered that this was because his hair grew outside in, the boy remarked helpfully: 'And do you know, uncle, that it's already growing out of your nose?'[9]

And yet there is a darker note, which Božena did not fail to document in the album. Several of its pages are devoted to disasters, billed without

---

6 Conversation with Ivan M. Havel, Košík Farm, 20 August 2012.
7 Like many frequently used names, 'Václav' in Czech lends itself to a dozen colloquial and diminutive forms, signalling various degrees of familiarity and affection, like 'Véna, Venca, Venda, Venoušek, Vašek, Vašík, Vašíček', etc., most of them applied to Havel by other people during his life. Interestingly, by dropping the 'u' in 'Venóškovo' Božena signals here her Silesian extraction.
8 Conversation with Ivan Havel, 20 August 2012.
9 Family album 1938, VHL ID1788. In reality, the album covers a period of two years, 1938–1940.

differentiation as 'Scarlatina', 'Mobilization' and 'War'. A week before Václav's second birthday, Czechoslovakia mobilized its army to defend itself against Hitler's threats, only to capitulate before the 'peace-saving' agreement negotiated by Hitler, Mussolini, Daladier and Chamberlain in Munich. Under the agreement, Czechoslovakia lost the Sudetenland with its largely German population, in exchange for guarantees of the territorial integrity of the rest of the country. Five months later, the *Wehrmacht* occupied Prague, and Hitler imposed a 'protectorate' on Bohemia and Moravia, while Slovakia declared an independent state closely affiliated with Nazi Germany. Eleven months later, World War II started, bringing about a tsunami that destroyed large parts of Europe, changed its political map beyond recognition and shattered the well-being and the certainties of millions of families, including Havel's own.

In the Havels' case the impending implosion came with a delayed fuse. In 1942, while Uncle Miloš footed a fine line with the Germans in an effort to save his beloved studios, his brother, never a flamboyant type, withdrew from public and social life and moved his family to the relative safety and comfort of Havlov, the family retreat in the rolling hills of the Bohemian-Moravian Highlands. There, the boys, catered to by a cook, a maid and a nanny, under the watchful eye of Božena, continued to have an idyllic childhood, not unlike Proust's Combray, surrounded by whispering pines, the calls of a cuckoo and the smells of Božena's tempera paints. Even the water from the well smelled sweet.[10] Indeed, from the family letters and the children's drawings, it is hard to discern that a war was on. The major events reported by Božena and the boys during the war and the early post-war period consist of skiing at Barrandov in the winter of 1941, little Václav coming down with scarlatina while visiting his Vavrečka grandparents in Zlín, being chased by geese in the village next to Havlov, or being felled by a 'cold as big as an elephant', together with an appropriate drawing of the event, elephant and all.[11] Some of the incidents described in Václav's correspondence to his grandma and grandpa were serious only from the perspective of a ten-year-old: 'In the afternoon I had to write my penalty homework because we had behaved indecently on an outing. We went to the woods to collect branches and went every which way so that the teacher

---

10 Conversation with Ivan M. Havel, 20 August 2012.
11 *A Cold as Big as an Elephant*, drawing, winter 1946, VHL ID1389.

could not find us.'[12] Even at this age Havel went in for dramatic effect: 'We went to the movies today. The film was called *Taboo*. It was quite nice, but one old man spoiled it all. He was quite old, ugly and liked young girls.'[13] A major event, referred to no fewer than three times in as many letters, was Rezi (the cook), Mařenka (the maid) and Miss (the nanny) going to a ball. Havel notes that they must have enjoyed the dance, as they came back at four in the morning. Mother Božena did not sleep all night.[14]

The confident Václav and the sweet curly-haired Ivan, addressed by his mother endearingly as Ivánek or even – in her own coinage – as Iveček, continued to stay unaffected by the turmoil around them. In the summer the family is seen dining *al fresco* at Havlov. When the boys returned with an empty basket from a mushroom-picking expedition, mummy came to their rescue by painting a small pile of appetizing ceps into the photograph. In Zlín, Václav spent a lot of time playing with the family dog, marking the start of a lifelong affection for canines. In the summer the boys swam in the lake nearby, and in winter, when it froze over, they skated there. Apparently, Václav felt physically superior to his little brother: 'After half an hour I skated like a devil. Ivan kept falling a lot.'[15]

Encouraged by his talented mother, Václav spent a lot of time on drawings and paintings. His choice of topics could be thought of as symptomatic, even though hardly atypical for a boy of his age. He drew a lot of kings and queens, castles and crowns; he even painted 'the order of St Wenceslas',[16] apparently blissfully unaware that at the time a distinction of that name was being awarded to Nazi collaborators. He enjoyed drawing soldiers in historic costumes, most of them with Havel-like moustaches or other facial hair. His drawings of birds and mushrooms are colourful and stylized, not unlike what Audubon would have drawn at the age of ten. Ivan, on the other hand, had shown a closer touch with reality, attempting to draw the likeness of Adolf Hitler.

Both boys were fascinated with instruments, complex machinery and factories. 'Grandpa, could you draw for me how the vacuum cleaner is made up so that electricity goes inside and so that it sucks the dust and rubbish?

12 Letter to Hugo and Josefina Vavrečka, 11 January 1946, VHL ID1472.
13 Ibid.
14 Letter to Hugo and Josefina Vavrečka, 2 February 1946, VHL ID1473.
15 Letter to Hugo and Josefina Vavrečka, 9 January 1946, VHL ID1472.
16 VHL ID1390.

I can't wait.'[17] Grandpa Vavrečka readily obliged. But intellectual curiosity apparently blended in young Václav with a good deal of empathy and social conscience as well. When asked the temperature one day, he replied puzzlingly: 'Sixteen on the Réaumur scale,' and then added: 'I felt sorry for the poor man. Everybody prefers Celsius, so I took pity on Réaumur.'[18]

In Havlov during the war, the two boys started attending the village school. Though nothing is known about its standards, on at least two occasions Václav boasted to his grandparents of having straight As on his report card, not failing to add that Ivan got a B in his singing and handwriting.[19]

The picture we get is of a bright, talented, self-confident and more than a little sapient child. When his grandma was coming for a visit from Zlín, his mother wrote to the older woman: 'I am sure he will want to read political editorials to you, no doubt adding his own commentary.'[20] Havel was a *zoon politikon* from the start.

For all the enviable aspects of his situation, Havel himself did not remember his childhood as particularly happy. He attributed it to the 'social barriers' he experienced as a privileged child growing up in a rural – and largely peasant and proletarian – environment. He perceived this as an 'invisible wall', behind which he, rather than his neighbours, felt 'alone, inferior, lost, ridiculed' and 'humbled by my "higher" status'.[21]

This feeling of being outcast and isolated, and at the same time unfairly privileged, remained with Havel throughout his life. In his own thinking it endowed him with a lifelong perspective from 'below' or from the 'outside'.[22] He attributed his problems, which he could not then have diagnosed as existential, to his parents' 'unwittingly handicapping care'.[23]

Unlike Franz Kafka, one of his great models, Havel never felt himself to be a victim of crushing, impersonal forces beyond his control. Maybe it was his inner stubbornness and courage that made him, time and again, challenge and struggle with such forces as an equal, and occasionally as a

17 Letter to Hugo Vavrečka, 25 January 1947, VHL ID1480.
18 Božena Havlová to Josefina Vavrečková, 22 January 1947, VHL ID1456.
19 Letters to Hugo and Josefina Vavrečka, 18 February 1946, VHL ID1474; 7 February 1947, VHL ID1481.
20 Božena Havlová to Josefina Vavrečková, 22 January 1947, VHL ID1456.
21 *Disturbing the Peace*, 5.
22 Ibid.
23 Ibid. 6.

victor and conqueror, despite, or perhaps because of, the awareness of his own frailty as an individual. It was this rebellious spirit that predestined him for the role of an outcast rather than a victim. His perspective had always been from the 'outside' rather than from 'below'.

Even so, Havel may have been overestimating the uniqueness of his own feelings. It is natural for most adolescent children to experience a sense of isolation from their peers, their families and their social situation. He himself cites the fact of being a 'well-fed piglet' as one of the circumstances that added to his sense of being outcast, not quite a unique predicament at that age.

But that is hardly the whole picture. In all of Havel's reminiscences, testimonies and interviews about his childhood, there is a gaping hole. One does not have to be a psychologist to notice that Havel's mother, unlike his father, uncle, brother and grandfathers, is rarely mentioned. This is even stranger for the fact that, taking after her father, she was of a more artistic and intellectual bent than her husband, spoke several languages and tried her hand at painting. She also believed in a hands-on approach in raising her children. Although there was a *gouvernante* in the family, Božena Havlová took it on herself to teach her sons the alphabet, and even designed the big characters that she pinned on the wall.[24] She encouraged Václav's artistic talent as well as his interest in science. Yet Havel rarely mentions her, and most of what we know about her comes from his brother Ivan.

The contrast between Havel's relationships to his mother and father is well illustrated by two later items of correspondence, both sent from Václav's boarding school in 1948, as the Communists were taking over the country. To his mother, on 31 May: 'Did not I forget my fountain pen? What were the election results in Prague and in the country? Otherwise, everything is fine. Respectfully, V Havel.'[25] To his father, around 28 September, the St Wenceslas Day: 'Dear Daddy, let me wish you on your name-day all the best that the heart can wish and words cannot express, mainly that your future name-days occur under better circumstances. Your son Václav Havel.'[26]

It is one thing to establish that Havel's relationship to his mother was not particularly close, it is quite another to guess at the reasons why.

24 Božena Havlová (2003).
25 Ivan M. Havel's archive, recent discovery.
26 Ibid.

At first sight there seems to be nothing amiss. Božena was rather typical of well-to-do Prague ladies of her time. She was the czar in her own household, she supervised the education of her children, she entertained and was entertained in turn along with her husband, and she tolerated her husband's infidelities. Theirs was a good, stable marriage, although it was Václav's second, and she was sixteen years his junior. She seemed to be both protective and supportive of her sons, and keen on their success.

But somewhere along the way, she apparently contributed to the deep ambivalence towards the opposite sex that characterized her older son throughout his life. There was the deep-seated need for female company and its tenderness and comfort, but also for the guidance and order it could provide. For all his life, Havel instinctively sought the company of strong, dominant, directive women who could assuage his sense of helplessness and insecurity. At the risk of using a tired psychoanalytical cliché, they all, in one way or another, resembled his mother.

At the same time, Havel often disrespected and persisted in running away from the very authority and order that the women in his life provided. Though thinking about the intricacies of the relationship between a man and a woman occupied a lot of his time and informed much of his writing, he spent most of his time in the company of men, where he was more often than not the dominant figure. Although he attached much importance to the sharper instincts of women and their better ability to communicate with the deeper mysteries of life, he had little respect – with a few notable exceptions – for their intellectual abilities. In *Letters to Olga*, he would exhibit a somewhat patronizing attitude to his wife's writing and thinking.

This conflicting attitude towards women is also clearly reflected in Havel's presidency. On the one hand, he kept surrounding himself with women, and at one time had even risked comparisons with Muammar Gaddafi by having two female bodyguards in his close security detail. At the same time, he would not often entrust a woman with a position of high responsibility. From among more than a hundred ministers he appointed to the government during his time as president, fewer than five were women. The two women in the erstwhile inner circle of the presidency, Eda Kriseová, an old friend and a fine short-story writer, and Věra Čáslavská, the seven-time gold medal-winning Olympic gymnast, were assigned to deal with the letters to the president and to advise on social and welfare policies, respectively. In the subsequent period of his Czech presidency, Havel relegated women to the roles of assistants and secretaries. The only professional women of importance on his team were then his legal counsels, both private and official, and Anna Freimanová, in charge of his literary rights. Ultimately, perhaps, he preferred to rely on women to protect his personal well-being and interests.

Anyone with an ambition to provide a nuanced picture of Havel's personality will thus have to deal with the deep duality traceable all the way back to his early years and not limited to his relationships with women. Combined with the awkwardness of a chubby self-conscious child, there emerged from the earliest age the assured self-confidence of a precocious boy with unending curiosity and intellectual interests well beyond his age. Through all the ups and downs of the roller-coaster life that lay ahead of him, both sides of his character remained clearly in evidence. If anything, his self-confidence increased in direct proportion to the adversity and difficulties he faced, and his doubts came to be inseparable from the moments of his greatest achievements. Such a mental disposition does not inevitably make for an easy life, but it can make its bearer well equipped for dealing with its complexities.

Portrait of the Artist as a Very Young Man

He was alone and young and wilful and wildhearted...
    – James Joyce, *A Portrait of the Artist as a Young Man*

HAVEL WAS NOT YET NINE when the war ended, but since his ear was never far from his parents' conversations he must have had an inkling that the world had changed in a profound way. The murderous yoke of the Nazi occupation was replaced by two armies of a more benign persuasion. One, coming from the East and occupying the larger part of the country, together with its capital, had not been seen in these parts since it was defeated along with the Austrians by Napoleon at Austerlitz, a Moravian town known to the natives as Slavkov. Now it came under the red flag with a star, a hammer and a sickle. The nearest the other army – under a flag with many stars and stripes – had come was France, at the end of the war to end all wars, at the behest of a president who was instrumental in the establishment of the post-war order in general, and of Czechoslovakia in particular. The language of the first of these two countries was similar to Czech, and its nineteenth-century literature, itself influenced by the French, had a massive readership among the Czech intelligentsia, but its people were very different. The second country, far away across the Atlantic, had been largely unknown to the locals until the twentieth century except as a destination of many of its tired, poor, hungry, disenfranchised and adventurous, most of whom did not return. The founder of Czechoslovakia, Tomáš Garrigue Masaryk, who had spent the last year of the war in the United States and whose wife was an American, identified with the latter country to the extent that he adopted his wife's name as his middle one, and declared Czechoslovakia's independence in Washington; at the same time, despite his sympathy for Russia as a fellow Slavic nation, he deeply distrusted both its Czarist-theocratic guise and its anti-democratic Bolshevik revolution. His successor, Edvard Beneš, a diplomat by profession as well as by heart, played the Great Game with considerable skill but little muscle, and by the end of the next war was so much under the Soviet shadow that, although he and his government had spent most of it in London, the new post-war administration was formed in Moscow.

In 1945, however, it still looked as though Czechoslovakia could choose between the two options, or at least attempt to juggle both influences more or less equitably. Democratic institutions were restored, albeit with serious limitations, and so was the intellectual debate, albeit increasingly acrimonious, between the growing number of converts to the communist creed and the defenders of the liberal humanistic traditions of the state that Masaryk had founded.

The first post-war years also witnessed a wave of righteous retribution, often conducted by the wrong people, against the German Nazi activists and sympathizers and their Czech collaborators. In fact, the retribution extended to Germans in general, three million of whom were summarily expelled from Czechoslovakia, and thousands, maybe tens of thousands, murdered by the 'revolutionary guards' and the mob. In the rising wave of hostility towards anyone who had survived the war more or less unscathed as well as prosperous, both Havel brothers found themselves under a cloud. In an effort to protect themselves, they managed to obtain an extremely qualified clean bill of health, signed by a member of an 'auxiliary committee' of the local municipality: 'We thereby confirm that so far nothing has been revealed nor do we have as yet any incriminating material against brothers Havel.'[1] Václav Maria Havel's Lucerna and property holdings remained unaffected, though not for long. Miloš Havel, on the other hand, was subsequently investigated for his contacts with the Nazis and his work with the German film industry, and, although he was acquitted of wrongdoing,

---

1 Certificate of integrity of the Havel brothers, 18 June 1945, Ivan M. Havel's archive, VHL ID18241.

he was barred from working in the film industry as morally unfit, possibly as much for his homosexuality as for his wartime activities, with his wealth deemed an aggravating circumstance. His AB studios were swallowed up in the wave of nationalization of big industries and enterprises. After a failed attempt to escape to the West in 1949, he spent two years in jail. In 1952 he finally managed to escape, and settled in Munich.

Apart from a few drawings, there is one documented project that illustrates Václav Havel's thinking and goals at around this time. *Goodyworks* (Dobrovka) is undated, but Václav's handwriting, spelling and context place it near the end of the war, possibly around the New Year of 1946.[2] Ivan was an enthusiastic collaborator on the project. Havel's self-described main goal in the document, to become a famous Scholar and Professor, corresponds with his scientific interests at the time. To become a millionaire was also important, but only as a means for the implementation of his grand project, Goodyworks, a factory employing 90,000 people, with branches in every town where a branch of Bata, prior to the war the largest shoe-making and shoe-selling enterprise in the world, already existed. This, together with calculations on the last page drafted by an older hand – possibly that of grandfather Vavrečka – suggests that the document may have been partly written in Zlín, the headquarters of the Bata empire. There is no indication as to what the factory was supposed to produce, but presumably it was to manufacture good or goodness.[3] It was also designed to make its founder extremely popular, as shown by the drawing of 'Venda, as we called him' seated on a 'Golden chair' and applauded by an enthusiastic crowd. This innocent childish dream marked the high point of a childhood whose subject was clearly destined, even in his own mind, to do great things. He would soon have to learn to lower his sights.

In the summer of 1947, just as the future fate of the country was being sealed with its Soviet-forced rejection of the Marshall Plan,[4] the time came

---

2 *Továrna dobra* (*Goodyworks*), VHL ID16271. The library catalogues the document as coming from the 1950s, but that seems unlikely.

3 In Ivan's recollection, the name was a play on words of the name of the Czech engineering giant Škoda, which, meaning 'pity' or 'waste', implies the opposite. Even more pertinently, the name Zlín is derived from 'zlo', meaning 'evil', a direct antonym. Conversation with Ivan M. Havel, 20 August 2012.

4 Cf. Vít Smetana, 'Pod hvězdy a pruhy? Pod křídla Sovětů?' ('Under Stars and Stripes? Under the Wings of the Soviets?'), in Smetana (2013), 81–123.

for Václav to receive some formal education. Wanting the best for their children, his parents sent first him, and two years later his brother Ivan, to a unique boys' boarding school in the castle of the spa town of Poděbrady, fifty kilometres east of Prague. The College of King George of Poděbrady, as if to embody the parents' dilemma, was both exclusive and state-run, both elitist and charitable, both Eton-style conservative and liberal-progressive. The students were of different backgrounds; some were children of country physicians, colleagues of the heart specialist who co-founded the school, some came from prominent Prague families, others, in a country that was quickly learning to suspect its envoys, its wartime soldiers and everyone who was connected to the world at large, were 'hostage' sons of diplomats posted abroad, and several were war orphans. The students had to pass an entrance exam to be accepted. By any standard, the school drew together a group of exceptionally talented individuals. Václav's class included the future president of the Czech Olympic Committee, physician Milan Jirásek, the future general secretary of the Communist-tolerated Socialist Party Jan Škoda and the son of a martyred legend of armed anti-Nazi Resistance, the future anti-Communist fighter Josef Mašín, a hero for some, for others a murderer.[5] The captain of Václav's bedroom was an older boy named Miloš Forman, the future director of *One Flew Over the Cuckoo's Nest* and *Amadeus*. Ivan Passer, another future Hollywood film-maker was also there.

The school accommodation, situated in a castle dating back to the thirteenth century, was impressive though not necessarily comfortable. The high-ceilinged rooms with only stoves for heating were freezing in winter, and the boys kept up a permanent relay to bring coal from the basement to the fourth-floor bedroom, where Havel's class resided. At night he read in bed. Mostly he kept to himself. His closest friend was a Lojza (Alois) Strnad.[6] Because of the proximity of the school to Prague, Václav was allowed to go home every other weekend, and sometimes invited another, less fortunate boy to go with him.

---

5 Josef and his older brother Ctirad, also a pupil at the school, were among the few Czechs who started an armed guerrilla uprising against the Communist regime and eventually fought their way to the American Zone in West Berlin. During their campaign they killed an unarmed civilian, along with several policemen. After the collapse of Communism, Havel as president rejected calls to honour the brothers publicly.
6 Skype conversation with Alois Strnad, 25 November 2012.

The school operated under a rather strict regimen. The boys were required to keep their rooms and belongings in perfect order, and were rewarded or penalized under a feared points system. Though naturally tidy, Havel was not remembered as particularly dexterous and did not score very highly. Jirásek, who sometimes accompanied Havel to Prague, remembers the ever-demanding mother Božena reproaching Václav: 'Why could you not be as good as Jirásek and Černošek?'[7]

Sixty years later, the memories of those still living are fragmentary, but no one could remember Václav as a particularly outstanding student. As with its British models, the school emphasized sportsmanship and leadership qualities. Young Havel seemed to lack both. He also could not sing. Forman remembers him as 'a little kid with intelligent eyes who was kind and decent to a fault'.[8] Only some hidden strength saved him from becoming a 'slave' to his peers, and earned him the 'friendly respect' of the younger boys.[9] When the boys were testing a donated bicycle by riding one after another out of the schoolyard, rounding the statue of King George in the town square and coming back, Havel, after mounting the machine with some difficulty, failed to make the turnaround and disappeared in the distance. 'Havel is fleeing!' cried the boys. After the teacher, Master Hofhanz, who gave chase on a motorcycle, caught up with him halfway to the next town, it turned out that Havel knew neither how to make a turn nor how to stop, his legs being too short to reach the ground.[10]

In his classes he was no troublemaker, but was rather shy and reclusive. His sense of isolation due to his privileged upbringing seems to have intensified. When a professor Bouček asked the class to talk about their parents and what they did, Havel kept silent until the end, and then only reluctantly volunteered that his father ran a bar, actually a couple of bars. 'Bars? What kind of bars?' asked the teacher. 'Well, Barrandov and Lucerna,' whispered Havel.[11]

In February 1948, the Communists took over in a putsch that was non-violent but a putsch just the same. Foreign Minister Jan Masaryk, the son

---

7 Conversation with Milan Jirásek, London, 8 August 2012.
8 Forman and Novák (1994). Quoted from the Czech translation *Co já vím?* (Brno: Atlantis, 1994), 47.
9 Ibid.
10 Ibid. And Conversation with Miloš Forman, Warren, Ct., 13 April 2013. The story, though without the embellishments, is also remembered by Jirásek, 8 August 2012.
11 Conversation with Milan Jirásek, London, 9 August 2012.

of the founding president, was found dead in the courtyard of the ministry, having fallen from the fourth-floor bathroom window of his ministerial flat under circumstances strongly suggesting foul play.[12] Justice Minister Prokop Drtina, a family friend, attempted suicide by jumping from his own window, but survived the fall with injuries, only to be sentenced to fifteen years in prison. The other top-level politician close to the family, Hubert Ripka, escaped a similar fate by fleeing abroad. Václav Maria Havel would later spend three months in custody in 1949 on suspicion of aiding and abetting a human-trafficking gang.

In the summer of 1948, despite the vortex that would soon devour it, the school somehow still managed to adhere to its elevated ethos and curriculum. The annual scouts camp took place in July at Lake Kačležský in the lovely wooded countryside of southeastern Bohemia. The group was designated as 'water scouts', and had to transport their tents and belongings by boat to the campsite with some inevitable mishaps.

Havel, whose nickname – which he did not much appreciate – was Dung-Beetle (Chrobák),[13] had already made a name for himself at school as an accomplished stylist, 'a couple of years above his grade',[14] and was appointed the camp chronicler. In his precociously mature, rounded script he recorded all the important events of the next four weeks. Unfortunately, the main event proved to be the rainiest July in years, and so much of his reporting is devoted to complaints about the weather and waiting for the sun to appear, with reports on games, guard duties, tying knots and ritual oaths taking second place. Just the same, the chronicle includes a formal word of thanks from the camp leader to Dung-Beetle for his exemplary maintenance of the chronicle. Most of Havel's daily entries started with a motto for the day, often in stark contradiction to the orthodoxy of the times. He thus notes early on that 'Even a word is an action.' In the context of the times, his Masaryk quote: 'Jesus, not Caesar', sounds like a daring anachronism.[15]

By 1950, the school, which had been in existence for only four years, became an anachronism, too. In the spring, Václav, his brother Ivan, who

---

12 See e.g. Albright (2012), 385–94.
13 Apparently given to him by Forman, although he is shy about the authorship, Conversation with Miloš Forman, 13 April 2013; Conversation with Milan Jirásek, 9 August 2012.
14 Conversation with Milan Jirásek, 8 August 2012.
15 'The scout camp chronicle', 29 June–25 July 1948, Ivan M. Havel's archive, VHL ID1654.

had arrived just six months earlier, and many other students were sent home. The rest of the students were transferred to a regular school in Poděbrady. Headmaster Jahoda ended up working in the mines.

THE SILVER WIND

Oh, silver wind, blessed's the place
Where first you caused our flag to wave
When flags go limp, and cease their waves
We'll thank you still for the breeze you gave

                 – Fráňa Šrámek, *Písecká*

ON HIS RETURN TO PRAGUE, it looked as though Havel would be deprived not only of a shot at an elite education, but of any formal education at all. By 1950, when he turned fourteen, he was branded a 'bourgeois element', unworthy even of a high school diploma. The Communists may have been atheists, but they seem to have believed in a jealous God, visiting the iniquity of the fathers upon the children unto the third and fourth generation. The only way for the sons to redeem themselves was by purification through the salutary effects of manual labour and total immersion in the lifestyle and values of the working class. Whether the job of a chemical lab assistant at the Prague School of Chemical Technology fitted that description or not, this was where Václav, with the help of his parents, found a refuge. He also discovered an opportunity to continue his secondary education; not at a day school, where he might contaminate the pure consciousness of the children of the working class, but in evening classes after work. There, at the High School for the Working People in Štěpánská Street, a stone's throw from Lucerna, he found himself in the company of similarly dubious social misfits, who shared not only some of the same problems, but also some of the same interests. In Ivan Hartmann, Radim Kopecký and Standa Macháček, Havel found mates with whom he could argue, debate and philosophize without fear of being branded a renegade. Indeed, they all bore the brand already.[1] Thus emerged the informal debating society, to which Radim Kopecký gave the name 'Thirty-Sixers', after their common year of birth.[2] Its original objective was self-improvement through debates about politics, economics and philosophy. Given the fact, however, that the chances of these Thirty-Sixers embarking upon a career in any of the above disciplines were close to nil, it is perhaps not surprising that they ventured instead into areas not as readily vulnerable to social orthodoxy, such as dance, music, photography or poetry. In its brief two-year life, the group self-published five issues of a periodical called *Dialogues 36*, and two 'almanachs' called *The Silver Wind* after a popular novel celebrating youth by the poet Fráňa Šrámek.

Kopecký and Havel soon emerged as the *spiriti agens* of the group. This was partly thanks to their networking skills and independent, oppositionist thinking; in Havel's case it was also thanks to having a meeting place to offer. The Havels' flat, where the family lived after the end of the war, was spacious, comfortable and centrally located, and Václav's parents were accomplished and generous hosts.

Although this was the time when Havel started to dabble in poetry, he saw himself primarily as a thinker. It is tempting to look for the beginnings of his later philosophical thinking in this period, but to do so would be a largely futile endeavour. Havel himself admits to having blushed when confronted more than fifty years later with his 'infantile attempts to give some positive content and meaning to everything'.[3]

Initially, the young Havel advocated a form of socialist humanism, reflecting the prevailing credo of his family and the legacy of Masaryk's own idealistic philosophy. He called this first attempt at a universal philosophical doctrine 'humanistic optimalism'. At its core was the idea of a 'standard universal optimum of needs' of every individual, achieved

---

1 Kopecký was the son of a high pre-war diplomat, Macháček's family came from the Prague *haute-bourgeoisie*.
2 Much of the information on the 'Thirty-Sixers' in this chapter is taken from an excellent in-depth study of the group *Ústně více* (*More in Person*) by Pavel Kosatík (2006).
3 Havel's foreword to *More in Person*.

through social regulation. This idea was not radically different from the idea of a 'social welfare state' practised in recent times by a number of Western societies. It was quite compatible with Masaryk's humanism and with the idea of a future pan-European entity, subscribed to by Grandfather Vavrečka. Havel himself was an early, even somewhat prophetic believer in the European integration. 'Look,' he writes in a letter to Radim Kopecký on 2 March, 1953, 'the united Europe is already being born . . .'[4] Few people at that time attached that much significance to the signing of treaties on the European Coal Community on 10 February and the European Steel Community on 1 March, 1953, especially if they lived behind the Iron Curtain. Rejecting Kopecký's advocacy of 'national socialism' (not to be confused with the Nazi perversion of the idea), Havel is prescient in detecting, and identifying with, the trend for supranational integration to which he himself would contribute in later decades.

On the other hand, Havel at sixteen, perhaps more than some of his teenage friends, was susceptible to the delusions and the tortured sophisms of the prevailing orthodoxy. In the letter to Kopecký he pays more than lip-service to the Marxist understanding of dialectics, refutes Radim's view that the policies practised by the Communists prove their ideology is in decline, acknowledges the dependence of the social 'superstructure' on 'production' – something he would famously repudiate two score years later when speaking to the US Congress – and generally endorses the socialist world-view. But it is a grudging, schizophrenic nod. 'What I wrote in brackets [], was I-Marxist speaking rather than I-I.'[5]

Humanistic optimalism was, perhaps fortuitously, not to be the final station in Havel's philosophical development. Even at this early stage, Havel was keenly aware of the coercive character of social regulation, especially as practised in Communist countries; he leaned towards free expression for the individual, if only his selfish instincts could be controlled. Seeing himself as a dialectician, he found the solution in an improbable fusion of 'monopolistic capitalism and Marxist Communism'. Even more improbably, he concluded that 'such a world order is slowly being born in the United States . . . It is neither the state nor the individual who own

---

4 Letter to Radim Kopecký, Radim Kopecký Archive, VHL ID1782. This quote can also be found in Kosatík (2006), 30.
5 Ibid.

the means of production, but the people who work with them.'[6] Perhaps it was his reading of American classic authors, from Walt Whitman to John Steinbeck, that led him to this conclusion, for he could hardly have found any evidence for it from reading the newspapers available to him at the end of 1952.

It is easy to ridicule the philosophizing of a sixteen-year-old, and to see the above lines as evidence that this was the thinking, then and later, of a closet statist. But in the context of the time he was hardly a radical. Even Radim Kopecký, a social Darwinist and a moral nihilist, acknowledged the necessity of the nationalization of large industries and some degree of social planning. In their increasingly heated exchanges, however, Havel insisted on the centrality of moral values, a belief that became a permanent component of his philosophy.

It is a rather touching picture one gets of this teenager academy, outcasts all, distinctive for the ardour and intensity of its interactions rather than for the quality of its output. While other such groups find their outlet in juvenile delinquency or substance abuse, this one got high on Aquinas, Kant and Hegel; and yet, the underlying dynamic was not so very different. The impression we get of Havel in those days is that of an intense, garrulous, slightly awkward young man, trying to mask his insecurity by wearing a bow tie and smoking a cutty pipe. His correspondence with Jiří Paukert, a member of the group from Brno, and with Kopecký reveals him as slightly overbearing, keen to prove his point and, by his own admission, somewhat dogmatic.

The above 'sins', so common to most intellectual-minded adolescents, had an upside in stimulating Havel's appetite for debate, making him a tireless correspondent, a pest to his opponents and a joy to his biographers for the rest of his life. Almost two thousand of his letters preserved in the Václav Havel Library, along with hundreds, perhaps thousands of other letters elsewhere, document both the constants as well as the developments in his thinking and style, from the cocky *besserwisser* dialectician of his teenage years to the ever-doubting moral thinker of his maturity.

---

6 Letter to Radim Kopecký, 17 December 1952. Radim Kopecký Archive, VHL ID1779. For the striking contrast with Havel's later thinking, this passage is also quoted by Kosatík (2006), and in Kaiser (2009).

The 'expansive sensitivity'[7] of an adolescent accounted also for a change in Havel's aspirations. Whereas previously he had thought of himself as a future scientist and scholar, now it was poetry that became his muse. Its coded format enabled him to vent feelings that were too strong or too dangerous to express in prose. Poetry was also more in vogue with the bohemian demi-monde to which he was increasingly attracted.

There was quite a lot in modern Czech poetry to inspire him. The twenties and the thirties brought an unprecedented poetic flowering in Czechoslovakia, partly inspired by modernist influences of Dadaism and Surrealism and other international movements, partly drawing on the work of nineteenth- and early twentieth-century Czech poets. Many, though not all, of these modern poets were active in the pre-war political Left. Dozens of poets and writers, both Jewish and Gentile, were murdered by the Nazis during the war; some had left the country before or after the fighting. Two major poets, František Halas and Konstantin Biebl, died soon after the Communist takeover, sick to death of the monster they had helped bring to life. But many were still around, trying as best they could to cope with the real-life shape of the society they had wished into being.

Those who had only known Havel as the cerebral, ironic and emotionally sparse playwright, essayist and individual would be surprised to learn that in his teenage years he had leaned towards a rich, exuberant poetry bordering on pathos and bombast. Perhaps under the influence of poets like Vítězslav Nezval, who had left their better work behind to write sycophantic verse praising the Stalinist era, the prematurely deceased Jiří Wolker, Vladimir Mayakovski, 'the soldier of the verse',[8] or Walt Whitman, whose ecstatic humanism he admired, Havel, writing at the time of 'becoming one with the land, hotly fused into the chain of hands',[9] came as close as he ever would to waxing enthusiastic about the collective utopia. 'A poem must thunder with the rhythmical march of a band of peer soldiers, who march to die for one another.'[10] It was, however, more the urge to belong, to be a part of something larger than himself rather than any rational acceptance of Marxist doctrine, that led him to write

---

7   Letter to Jiří Paukert, undated 1953, VHL ID1514.
8   Letter to Jiří Paukert, 4 October 1953, VHL ID1517.
9   Letter to Jiří Paukert, undated August 1953, VHL ID 1658, 7.
10 Ibid. 8.

lines that would make an even less sensitive reader blush. 'Exacerbated individualism, wallowing in the "night" too much subjectivism and preoccupation with one's own internal issues, constitute a sickness of art, because only a sick man feels his insides'.[11] These lines, written by Havel in 1953, could well have been used by the Communist propaganda machine thirty years later to attack the author of *Letters to Olga*.

His insistence, however, that to be a true poet one had to stay true to himself, 'to open the eyes to one's own heart',[12] stayed with Havel all his life and enabled him, even at a young age, to draw the line between art and propaganda. It was also a reliable compass in looking for models. Helped yet again by his family contacts, he overcame his shyness in order to request, and to obtain, audiences with some of the Greats. The very first visit he paid was to Jaroslav Seifert, a lyrical poet of misleading transparency and gentle imagery, long since cured of his early infatuation with Communism in the 1920s. A poet by temperament as well as profession, he rarely took the lead in making a stand against injustice, persecution and cultural barbarism, but he never refused his support for such a stand when asked. He later repaid Havel's youthful admiration by becoming an unimpeachable supporter and moral witness to his struggle. When he was eventually awarded the Nobel Prize for Literature for his lifelong work in 1984 – the very first Czech or Slovak writer to be so honoured – the official political and literary establishment would treat it as a non-event on account of his signature under Charter 77. Even his funeral two years later was boorishly interfered with and obstructed by the secret police.

Havel came to be even more impressed by a visit, the first of several, to the great magus of Czech poetry Vladimír Holan. A poet combining prophetic powers with surrealistic imagery, but also author of a celebratory ode to the Red Army soldiers who came to liberate Prague in May 1945, he now spent his time darkly brooding in his Lesser Town studio, writing mystical poetry and receiving few visitors. The encounter gave Havel his first intimation that a life in art, or, for that matter, life as such, may not be a question of choice but of destiny – what he would later describe, under the influence of Heidegger, as 'thrownness'.

---

11 Letter to Jiří Paukert, 24 October 1953, VHL ID1520, also quoted in Kosatík (2006), 46.
12 Ibid.

Still too young to legally order a beer, and eager to talk in a relatively quiet place, the Thirty-Sixers discovered, not far down the river from Havel's apartment, Café Slavia, a great pre-war establishment comparable in all respects to its counterparts in Vienna and Budapest, and one of the centres of Prague intellectual life. There they encountered, at first at a respectful distance, another group of older intellectuals and poets, who were debating and arguing just as heatedly as the Thirty-Sixers, but whose work never appeared in print, partly by official fiat and partly by choice of the writers themselves. Although still quite young, they were survivors of a pre-war circle of fledgling poets mentored by Halas (whose arguably most talented member Jiří Orten had been killed in an accident by a German ambulance before he could be transferred to Terezín or murdered in the death camps further east), as well as of the wartime Group 42, which continued to work and publish in the underground or under pseudonyms. The godfather of the Slavia table was Václav Černý, a brilliant but prickly scholar of comparative literature, and a fiery critic, ostracized by the Communists for his non-conformist, if socialist, views.[13] In time, the leading role passed on to Jiří Kolář, a poet of proletarian origin and sensitivity, who gradually came to distrust the ambiguity and abuse of words so much that he stopped writing verbal poetry altogether and preferred to express himself in collages and artifacts, embarking on a new wave of creativity and fame in the sixties, and later in his Parisian exile. Another member of the group, Zdeněk Urbánek, a translator into Czech of Shakespeare and Joyce, though older by nineteen years, became perhaps Havel's closest lifelong friend and mentor. This group represented the alternative Parnassus to the official literary establishment in the Writers' Union headquarters three doors down the street. After the premature demise of the Thirty-Sixers movement, Havel gravitated to the elders' table. 'Slavia was my literary kindergarten.'[14]

Equally importantly, at Slavia Havel met and liked a young aspiring actress from the other side of the tracks, named Olga Šplíchalová. She was three years older, and rebuffed the seventeen-year-old's awkward approaches, but this would not be her final answer.

---

13 Zdeněk Urbánek testifies to Černý's founding role, often credited to Kolář. Letter to Václav Havel, 3 October 1997, VHL ID6905.
14 'A letter from the novel of Karel Trinkewitz *1472 Steps*' in *Works 4*, 605.

The wide-ranging network of the Havels' connections also brought young Václav into contact with his first reviewer, and two important domestic philosophers. Liberal journalist and writer Eduard Valenta read Václav's first poetic attempts, encouraged him to continue and let him have the run of his own extensive library. Philosopher J. L. Fischer was an occasional visitor to the Havels' house and a popular centre-left humanistic scholar who, in spite of his ardent efforts to embrace the new conditions, was not deemed far left enough by the Party ideologues and rapidly lost his position and influence. The second thinker, Josef Šafařík, who came to the Havels' orbit through the Vavrečka part of the family, was in many ways Fischer's opposite. A self-made moral philosopher who shunned the limelight, he spent most of his life in obscurity in a deliberate effort not to let the reality of the day influence his thought – so much so, indeed, that he later deplored Havel's leadership of Charter 77 as a false escape from the first duties of a thinker. Of the two men, he was the one who influenced Havel more deeply.

In the summer of 1954, the dozen or so Thirty-Sixers were all invited by Havel's parents to spend a week at Havlov. Amid the games and pastimes of summer, one of their number, the deeply religious Jiří Paukert, who had been gradually discovering his gay identity, developed a crush on young Ivan. The event led to a lasting friendship between the poet and Mother Božena, who clearly felt the need to shelter the young man, but also to a gradual loosening of ties amid the group. There was no condemnation of Paukert, but the episode may have helped them realize that with such strongly pronounced and diverse personalities they were bound to go their own way. The 'unconditional'[15] friendship and loyalty they felt for each other, however, lasted them a lifetime. Havel kept in touch and corresponded with Paukert,[16] whom he considered his closest 'literary comrade',[17] Kopecký and Viola Fischerová, and forged a close friendship with Josef Topol, a later addition to the group and a future fellow playwright. As president, he would bestow some of the highest distinctions on the members of the group as a belated acknowledgement by the nation of their work.

In 1956, inspired by the remarks of Jaroslav Seifert at that year's Congress

---

15 Věra Linhartová, another member of the group, in an interview with Martin C. Putna, 29 March 2010, VHL archive.

16 Paukert later adopted the name Kuběna after his partner, and appears in bibliographies under that name. Havel's letters are, however, addressed to 'Jiří Paukert'.

17 Letter to František Press, 1 September 1957, unsent, VHL ID17628.

of the Czechoslovak Writers' Union, the twenty-year-old undertook his first foray into the world of official literature, in the form of an iconoclastic article 'Doubts about the Programme'[18] in the literary magazine *Květen*, and then at a seminar for young writers at the Writers' Union castle in Dobříš, an epitome of establishment luxury. In both instances he pleaded, as Seifert did before him, for the reintegration of ostracized writers, many of whom sat at the Slavia table, in Czechoslovak literature. His plea fell on deaf ears.

Not all his pursuits in the mid-fifties were of an intellectual nature, however. Much to the displeasure of his mother, he developed a taste for nightlife and started frequenting bars and wine-rooms with similarly minded friends, such as the dandy Thirty-Sixer Vladimír Víšek, a shady character later known as writer Theodore Wilden.[19] Apparently he aspired to a similar role himself and sported a mohawk or 'cockerel' as it was then known, a wide-knotted motley tie, shoes with a raised pointed tip called 'Hungarians', striped socks, trousers with tapered legs, a little short to reveal the socks, and a low-cut jacket.[20] A zoot, in the parlance of the times. He attended dancing lessons, an indispensable part of middle-class upbringing, and tried to befriend members of the opposite sex there, initially with little success.

Havel's subsequent work was also radically different from his early efforts as a member of the Thirty-Sixers. After having been confronted with the superior talents of some of his peers, he gradually gave up the ambition of becoming a poet, and discarded his early attempts at philosophical thought as largely misguided. His path to higher education in the arts or philosophy was barred because of his family background, but thanks to the Thirty-Sixers and his own pursuits, Havel was now an established member of the Prague intellectual class, and in particular of its shadow, non-conformist, bohemian underworld. Whatever he would do in future, his loyalties would always remain there.

---

18 'Pochyby o programu' ('Doubts about the Programme') in *Works 3*, 54–9.
19 Conversation with Theodore Wilden, London, 18 June 2012.
20 Conversation with Ivan M. Havel, 20 August 2012.

Good Soldier Havel

We will win this war for sure, I am telling you
one more time, gentlemen!

— Jaroslav Hašek, *Good Soldier Švejk*

IN THE AUTUMN OF 1957, twenty-one-year-old Havel wrote a remarkable
seven-page letter document with the alarming title 'Instructions for the
bereaved'.[1] Its contents, conspicuously devoid of drama, show Havel as an
extremely well-organized and responsible, if somewhat pedantic young
man, qualities that would last him a lifetime. The instructions are basically
a list of outstanding book loans, and to any Havel scholar they serve as a
good introduction to both Havel's reading habits and his social circle. The
authors, meticulously underlined with a wavy pattern, include poets Ivan
Blatný, Vladimír Holan, Comte de Lautréamont, Anna Akhmatova, Edgar
Allan Poe, Charles Baudelaire, Richard Weiner and Jiří Orten, and novelists
Louis-Ferdinand Céline, Sinclair Lewis, Leo Tolstoy and Egon Hostovský.
Among the debtors are Thirty-Sixers Viola Fischerová, Vladimír Víšek,
Jiří Paukert and Ivan Hartmann, writers Jan Zábrana, Jiří Kolář and Jan
Grossman, Poděbrady schoolmate Miloš Forman, Olga Šplíchalová, whom
he had ultimately won over to be his girlfriend, and someone called Karel
Marx. With equal care, Havel lists his own obligations towards friends and
libraries. The modestly titled third section, 'My Works', contains instructions

---

1 *'Pokyny pro pozůstalé'*, VHL ID17725.

on the distribution of the so far still manageable body of Havel's poetry and essays in manuscript. In the fourth section Uncle Miloš is requested to send from his Munich exile 1) a knee-length overcoat, 2) a pair of blue jeans (or 'Texas pants' in Czech) and 3) a Swiss atlas of film stars and directors. The fifth section instructs the bereaved, apparently the family and, in particular, Mother Božena, who devotedly attended to most of the instructions as seen from her handwritten notes on the margin, either to sell his moccasin shoes or have them repaired.

It is these last two parts that provide the clues that Havel was neither gravely ill nor contemplating suicide. The last section instructing the family to keep the 'den as I have left it to a two-year slumber' gives the game away. A high-school graduate now, Havel made several attempts to enrol at a university in arts or humanities, but because of his 'bourgeois' origin he failed each and every time. The prestigious film school of the Prague Academy of Performing Arts, where his older schoolmates from Poděbrady, Ivan Passer and Miloš Forman, were already students, was his preferred choice, but remained out of reach to him, despite the advice and support provided by a young professor of screenwriting at the school named Milan Kundera.[2]

Not exactly thrilled by the looming perspective of a two-year national military service, Havel applied, 'out of desperation',[3] to read the economics of transportation at the Prague School of Economics, where they 'were admitting anyone',[4] and where the young intellectual with no interest in either economics or transportation was indeed duly accepted. But he was bored to death by subjects like 'Gravel Sand 101',[5] and when his subsequent attempt to transfer from gravel sand to the film academy predictably failed, he quit the school, and ended up in the military anyway.

He did not go without a fight. When his application for the film school, and with it his deferment, was rejected, he pleaded 'depressive psychopathy' in front of the conscription board. The board was not impressed by what would have otherwise been guaranteed grounds for ineligibility. An army

---

2 In *Disturbing the Peace*, 28–9, Havel specifically mentions Kundera's contribution in order to dispel the 'nonsense' about the permanent enmity between the two men due to their spat about the 'Czech destiny' in 1970. For all that, the relationship between the two internationally best-known Czech writers remained charged, for reasons that are not entirely clear.
3 Ibid. 29.
4 Ibid.
5 Ibid.

political commissar allegedly declared that Havel would go to serve even with a leg missing.[6] A month later he did.

One morning at the end of October 1957, a big young man named Andrej Krob also set out to join the service from the main Prague railway station. 'On the train, I stood by one window, Václav, whom I did not know then, stood by another, but underneath his, there was this strikingly beautiful girl . . . so I looked up again and there stood this chubby teddy bear, and I told myself that the world was not fair . . .'[7]

Although Krob and Havel, in spite of serving with the 15th Engineering Battalion at the same base, did not grow close until after returning from the service, soldier Havel was impossible for Krob to overlook, because of 'his immaculately regulation apparel'.[8] They, and Olga (who was the girl), were to become fast friends, neighbours and collaborators.

While Krob was more or less resigned to what awaited him, Havel was miserable. More than most a creature of habit, he mourned the sudden loss of his friends, his books and his café-going lifestyle. 'I am sad and unhappy,' he wrote to Paukert on his induction.[9] Worse than that, he considered himself a failure. This is only understandable in the context of an 'atmosphere of permanent reproofs' at home for being a 'washout'.[10] Havel did not state where the reproofs were coming from, but it is safe to assume they did not come from his father. Nonetheless, he also showed the signs of rebelliousness, optimism and resilience in the face of adversity, which would stand him in good stead during the many trials he was to endure. 'Admittedly I have somehow failed at a certain stage of my life, but first of all there is no need to throw it in my face thirty times a day, and second, I do not accept that I have lost my life. This is ridiculous.'[11]

Military service in the 1950s was not an easy time for anybody, least of all the son of a 'class enemy'. Still, Havel was relatively lucky. Even three years before, he would have ended up in the 'Auxiliary Technical Battalions' (PTP), specially set up for the descendants of the capitalist riff-raff and other undesirables, including priests and gypsies, made to serve without

---

6   Letter to Jiří Paukert, 18 September 1957, VHL ID1610.
7   Conversation with Andrej Krob and Anna Freimanová, Prague, 21 October 2012.
8   Ibid.
9   Postcard to Jiří Paukert, 1 November 1957, VHL ID1614.
10 Letter to Jiří Paukert, 25 September 1957, VHL ID1611.
11 Ibid.

arms, and subjected to every possible humiliation. In 1957, when he was inducted, he came out a notch better, in an engineering battalion, which had been nevertheless equally destined to perish among the first in the expected nuclear Armageddon. The other stroke of luck was meeting there a kindred spirit in a young man called Karel Brynda, with whom he started a regimental amateur theatre troupe.

All lives make more sense in retrospect than in forward projection. Some of Havel's biographers treat his theatre-making in the military as an organic part of the process of refining his creative ambitions. But Havel himself denied this and maintained that his reasons for taking up theatre in the army were much more prosaic. He hated the drudgery and the mindlessness of the drills, and in particular he hated lugging a heavy bazooka around. Naturally he was aware that the army-sponsored cultural activities were supposed to elevate the ideological consciousness of the conscripts and steel them for the upcoming battle, something he would not feel comfortable aiding. Yet he would go to considerable lengths to escape boredom.

And so he resorted to a classical Czech ruse, immortalized in *The Good Soldier Švejk*, the iconic satirical novel of World War I by the Czech humourist Jaroslav Hašek. In the book, Švejk defeats the entire machinery of the Habsburg army and escapes frontline duty by attending to every absurd order and chore with such enthusiasm and devotion that he is finally declared mentally unfit by the army.

Havel and Brynda applied themselves with the same enthusiasm and devotion to staging a play called *September Nights* by the prominent young Communist author Pavel Kohout. The plot of the play resembles an instalment of a soap opera. A well-respected young officer commits an understandable yet unpardonable sin by going AWOL to visit his pregnant wife in hospital, gets reported and indicted by an ambitious, uncompromising political officer, but is in the end spared harsh punishment due to the timely intervention of a fatherly commander. It is a telling sign of the spoof that director Havel cast himself as the unthinking, overambitious zealot. Apparently, he played the unsympathetic role so convincingly that his real-life commanding officer, unable to distinguish between *Dichtung* and *Wahrheit*, punished him by stripping him of the 'honour' of carrying a bazooka – an unexpected boon.

The dubious success of the play (and ploy) emboldened the two fledgling artists to set about writing a piece of their own. Although Havel never says so explicitly, the underlying sentiment seems to have been that, if a recognized artist can write a piece of s— like this, they could do the same. When they completed *The Life Ahead*,[12] Good Soldier Švejk met with Monty Python. In what pretends to be a deadly serious plot, a young soldier falls asleep on guard duty, while another soldier accidentally uses his weapon to shoot an intruder. The sleeping soldier is then celebrated and rewarded as a hero. He faces a bright future, but in the end cannot bear the thought of acting dishonourably for his own benefit and owns up to his lapse.

There are some who see in this inane construction an early theatrical expression of the principle of 'living in truth'.[13] If true, it would be the only such straightforward application in the whole of Havel's work as a playwright; 'truth' for him always comes with twists, making it something vastly more complex and ambiguous. It is, however, much more likely that the whole thing was a 'ridiculous little . . . piece of cunning'.[14] Havel himself called it 'half-collaborationist'.[15] To compare it with *The Garden Party* and *The Memorandum*, and even to look for common threads and a 'struggle for identity',[16] is a little over the top.

The Švejkian episode could not but have had a farcical ending. The play, based on 'authentic' soldier life and written by 'authentic' soldiers, was a modest hit in the annual 'Army Youth Creativity Competition', and made it all the way to the national finals in Mariánské Lázně before anyone noticed the flawed backgrounds of the two authors and suspected a prank.

The plot of the play then repeated itself in the disciplinary proceedings that followed. The army could not simply denounce a play about falling asleep on guard duty as a travesty written by two malicious and hostile good-for-nothings, since to do so would have been to convict itself of falling asleep on duty. In the end, face was saved by focusing on the lack of verisimilitude – it was simply unthinkable that a good socialist soldier such as the main hero of the play would fall asleep on guard duty. The play was condemned as 'anti-army', but no harsher punishment followed. Havel and

---

12 *Život před sebou*, 1959, VHL ID7110. A loose adaptation under the title *Mlýny* (*Mills*) was staged by Theatre Sklep (Basement), the closest Czech equivalent of Monty Python, in 1994.
13 See e.g. Rocamora (2004), 23.
14 Karel Brynda as quoted in Keane (1999), 145. The translation of *vychcanost* as *piss-take* is, however, somewhat misleading.
15 Letter to Jiří Paukert, dated by VHL ID1619 as 17 March 1958. From the context of the letter ('219 days remaining'), the year must have been 1959.
16 Keane (2004), 147–8.

Brynda had much enjoyed spending a week in the fashionable spa resort of Mariánské Lázně ogling girls.

Few people have noticed, then or since, the hint of irony in the title of the play. The intruder, the *deus ex machina* who inadvertently sets the whole debacle in motion, lies dead on the ground. There is no life ahead for him.

As his 'instructions for the bereaved' imply, Havel's goal and dream at the time was still to follow in his uncle's footsteps and make a name in the film business. Possibly to pad his portfolio before the next round of examinations for the Film Academy, he wrote, again in collaboration with Brynda, a script for what would be a feature film by the standards of the American Film Academy, although it would be too short by the standards of the Screen Actors' Guild. Unlike *The Life Ahead, Oh, the Army*[17] is no spoof, but a fairly conventional boy-meets-girl story about a conscript who, unaware that his girlfriend back home is being pursued by a former beau, starts his own little fling with a naïve young student in the garrison town. The moral, if any, of the story is that what is good for Dick is good for Jane, although Dick, who is subjected to the hardships of military service, is judged by perceptibly laxer standards, signalling his author's somewhat skewed attitude to gender equality.

The script speaks to Havel's growing attachment to Olga, and also to the insecurity he felt about their two-year separation. No letters that he wrote to her or she to him during that time are available, but neither then nor later was she much of a correspondent. Václav's mother, who scrupulously archived all his correspondence, but did not much care for his girlfriend, would not necessarily show the same piety for anything written by 'that girl'. Havel, who spent as much time as he could with Olga during his annual leaves of absence from the army, wrote of the 'waves of resentment' this produced at home.[18] The two women's attachment to the young soldier was nevertheless touchingly demonstrated by their willingness to make a temporary truce and travel to see him together on Sundays.

His fascination with film notwithstanding, Havel also started reading plays in the service. Edgar Lee Masters, Edgar Allan Poe and Comte de Lautréamont moved over to make room for Arthur Miller, Eugène Ionesco and Samuel Beckett. Aware that the Communists considered the film

---

17 *Ta vojna*, a screenplay, 1958, VHL ID17627.
18 Letter to Jiří Paukert, 21 December 1958, VHL ID1623.

business, just like the post office, energy grid and railway network, strategic assets because of its large audiences, and despairing of his chances of being accepted at the Film Academy, he next tried his luck at the Faculty of Theatre. He conceived his attack on this fortress of the muses with all the ingenuity and attention to detail of a military strategist. He appeared in front of the examination board in full military regalia, only to be asked by a professor why he did not sport the badge of an exemplary soldier. He next tried to impress the commission by venturing to demonstrate the four laws of Marxist dialectics in a play by the surely unsuspecting Turkish writer Nâzim Hikmet, and was delighted that the prank seemed to have worked on some of the most proven comrades on the panel. But in spite of doing well in the exams, for which he had been coached by Jan Grossman, a pupil of Václav Černý and a respected literary and drama critic, and by Milan Kundera, and despite the frantic efforts of his parents, who even petitioned the office of the nation's president on his behalf, he failed to get in again.[19] He went out of the service as he went in, a washout without education and with no prospects except for the waves of resentment awaiting him at home. Olga, who had fulfilled none of the dark forebodings of *Oh, the Army*, and had stayed loyal throughout to wait for him when he came back, was the only light in the darkness.

---

19 When already a successful playwright, Havel was finally accepted by the school as an external student and graduated in 1966, with indifferent feelings.

OLGA

Time has transfigured them into
Untruth. The stone fidelity
They hardly meant has come to be
Their final blazon, and to prove
Our almost-instinct almost true:
What will survive of us is love.
　　　　　　　– Philip Larkin, 'An Arundel Tomb'

VÁCLAV HAVEL WAS NOT YET SEVENTEEN when he met the woman of his life. He would later fall in love with Dagmar Veškrnová and marry her after Olga's death, he would be enamoured at least twice in the time between, he would pursue rather indiscriminately, and be pursued by, other women, but she was his 'one certainty',[1] his companion, his conscience, his first reader, his staunchest defender and his fiercest critic for fifty years. Their relationship, which survived his mother's resentment, hardships, crises, infidelities, persecution and prison, eventually came to defy standard categories and become a category of its own. The influence Olga had on Havel (and he on her) was so pervasive that it is plausible to speculate that he would have hardly become what he became without her. But then the single-mindedness with which the young poet pursued her, despite their difference in ages (she was three years his senior), contrasting social backgrounds (she

---

1　*Disturbing the Peace*, 155.

came from Žižkov, the East End of Prague, a place not so much of destitution as of a strong and proud proletarian character), and extended periods of separation, suggests that deep down he probably knew how indispensable she would turn out to be.

The place of their first meeting was Café Slavia. The circumstances were prosaic. At his workplace, Havel became friendly with a fellow lab assistant, Zdena Tichá, and developed a kind of half-hearted crush on her, as evident from the poems inspired by her at the time. Zdena was apparently similarly ambivalent about Havel and, although she did not become his girlfriend, she introduced him in Slavia to two of her friends from the acting courses she attended. One of them was Olga Šplíchalová.[2]

Olga immediately caught Havel's fancy, but in the beginning was not equally attracted to him. He was immature, insecure and somewhat plump, she had a boyfriend, a serious adept of the acting profession and a student at the Prague Academy of Performing Arts. Havel persevered, and three years later, they were an item. Apparently, he never had a woman before then. When they did become a couple, she told him, 'You will not find the going with me easy,' but soon discovered the going with him was even more difficult.[3]

What did he see in her? She was not his intellectual equal; whatever erudition she acquired came mostly through him. She was not well connected and could not introduce him to many interesting people or famous artists. She had a beautiful, expressive face, a nice smile and a dense, somewhat spiky head of dark hair, but she would not have been considered sexy by the standards of the time. She had lost a couple of fingers on her right hand due to a workplace injury, and often wore gloves to hide this. She neither flirted nor schmoozed, nor did she go to the trouble of pretence for the sake of social decorum.

She was, however, straight as a ruler, giving people her unvarnished opinion when they asked for it and often when they did not. People who met her for the first time were sometimes taken aback by her in-your-face manner. Those who came back for more soon realized that there was no aggression, no effort to elevate herself or humiliate others, just an uncanny matter-of-factness

---

2 Anna Freimanová, 'An Interview with Zdena Pospíchalová,' in *Síla věcnosti Olgy Havlové* (*The Power of Matter-of-Factness of Olga Havel*), VHL (2013), 60.'

3 Žádná harlekýnka' ('Not a Harlequin Romance'), an interview with Olga Havel, in Wilson (2011), 143.

rarely seen with such consistency and intensity. Even more remarkable, her judgements and her instincts, mostly about other people, were more often right than wrong. It must have been this serious honesty and disregard for conventions that attracted Havel to her. Well on his way to becoming a rebel, he needed a streetwise moll rather than a debutante.

What did she see in him? Given his age, his unimposing physique and his rolling 'r's, he did not display the conventional characteristics of a desirable boyfriend. While many people found her striking, few would use the same description for Václav. His intellectual hunger and knowledge must have impressed her considerably, but they were not the qualities that would necessarily recommend him as a reliable partner on the mean streets of Žižkov. There was, however, a similarity in that there was nothing flighty or superficial about either of them. Just like Olga, though in a completely different, milder and more polite manner, Havel had the gravitas of really believing in what he was saying, even at the age of nineteen. And then there was its complement, the unwavering idealistic hope, a kind of simplicity bordering on naïvety, something almost childish and immensely vulnerable, such as the belief that good can be produced in a factory. Olga could relate to that; from an early age it was her task to take care of younger children in her extended family, and she took to it with the natural caring instinct of a loving, if matter-of-fact, mother. She was quick to see the insecure, helpless side of this young man and his voracious craving to be loved. If he took her up as his intellectual pupil, she took him up as her ward. The frequent observation by friends that she 'stood by him, more like a mother than a wife'[4] could all too easily lend itself to cheap psychobabble interpretation, but Havel was definitely not looking to replicate his relationship with his mother. It is true that, as someone who 'grew up in the loving and firm embrace of a dominant mother', he 'needed an energetic woman beside me to turn to for advice and yet still be someone I could be in awe of'.[5] At the same time though, he was looking for the kind of undivided attention and unquestioning loyalty that Božena, who doted on Ivan, could not give him. In a way, he was looking for the mother he never had.

Finally, too, they were both outcasts, she more by choice than he. There was hardly anything in the social reality around them that they would find

4 Conversation with Andrej Krob, 21 October 2012.
5 *Disturbing the Peace*, 156.

either appealing or worthy of appeal. 'The fundamental experience of my generation is . . . thoroughly living through the Communist idea of socialism in its implementation and . . . formulating a view of it, unfortunately largely negative.'[6] Their highly developed sense of truth and honesty must have recoiled from the cruelty, the pretensions and the hypocrisy of the prevailing orthodoxy. Although Olga, by virtue of her proletarian background, would not encounter the same obstacles on her way to higher education as Václav, she chose not to take that direction: she realized that it would have been totally incompatible with the kind of education she was receiving around the table in Slavia. In their defiance they learned to cling to each other, trust each other and depend on each other completely, without any reservations.

Havel's expanding circle of friends from among the Thirty-Sixers and the table at Slavia learned to accept Olga and to like her. Although she did not contribute much in the way of intellectual brilliance, she was so down-to-earth and so firmly rooted that, rather than feel superior to her, they were somewhat in awe of her, as well as in constant fear of being brought down to measure or, even worse, exposed by her as frauds.

Olga also received a relatively kind reception from Václav's father. He was an uncomplicated man, somewhat embarrassed by his once-prominent social status, even if not outright ashamed of it like his son, and he rather liked the young woman, or at any rate he respected his son's choice. Božena, on the other hand, was not nearly so thrilled. As a country girl in the great capital of Prague, she may have felt a stronger need to cling to her status as a form of security. Or maybe she was just a little snobbish. She objected to Olga's simplicity, her unaffected manner, her family, her working-class accent and her lack of education. She definitely had in mind a girl from 'the good society' for her son, someone like the nice Jana, daughter of the philosopher Jan Patočka, a well-respected occasional visitor to the Havel household.[7] Some of Václav's indirect references, however, point to Božena's deeper suspicion of the younger woman as a scheming adventurer, out to benefit from her drifter of a son after having deliberately groomed him into a successful man, hardly a reason for condemnation, even if true.[8]

---

6 Letter to Jiří Paukert, stamped 28 August 1958, VHL ID1622.
7 Conversation with Ivan Havel, 20 August 2012.
8 Letter to Václav Maria Havel, 14 July 1964, in *The Power of Matter-of-Factness of Olga Havel*, 12.

She certainly wanted her son to be happy, and she may have been even a little worried about the absence of a regular girlfriend, especially after Jiří Paukert fell head-over-heels in love with Ivan, even if the infatuation was purely one-sided. The spectre of Uncle Miloš must have hovered. If Olga could have fawned, even a little, over this formidable matron, and sought her favour and advice, all might have been well. But this would have been expecting the impossible from Olga, though she did go out of her way not to provoke the older woman. This was not altogether easy: by now the couple were spending much of their time in Václav's 'den' in the family apartment. It was the classic situation of a fight between two strong women, one a mother, the other a lover, over their man.

But from early on it was no contest. Havel respected and more than a little feared his mother, but at the same time he exhibited a strong independent streak that led him to rebel against her authority. Olga embodied the ultimate rebellion. And, while he feared disappointing his mother, he soon came to fear disappointing Olga even more. Most of all, he feared disappointing himself. In his mind, marrying Olga was a matter of 'fundamental human dignity and self-confidence, which in fact I never had'.[9] When, at his initiative, they got married, in a civil ceremony, on 9 July 1964, Havel chose not to tell his parents. He only announced the news in a letter to his father sent from the safe distance of his and Olga's honeymoon retreat in a small hotel near Karlovy Vary five days later. Apparently he left it up to his father and Ivan to break the news to his mother.

In the letter to his father, strikingly different from Kafka's famous missive in its complete absence of bitterness and acrimony, Havel summarizes – one feels more for the benefit of himself and his mother than for the addressee – his motives for the marriage and his feelings about Olga after eight years of being together. Rather than a passionate defence of a loved one, it reads like a sober cost-benefit analysis, yet it is also a testimony to a serious and responsible commitment. The bottom line is a simple statement of fact – 'we understand and feel good about each other'.[10] Instead of elaborating, Havel goes on to confess fleeting infatuations and infidelities, which 'rather than leading me away from Olga, always bring me back to her, making me realize again and again, how meaningless and trifling are all those "bedroom"

---

9 Ibid.
10 Ibid.

matters compared to a real and lasting understanding . . .'[11] Olga, he admits, 'is not and will never be a professor at Harward (sic) University.'[12] What she brought into the relationship was 'an element of healthy, unmediated and pure feeling for life and creative values; an element of primal and almost uncomfortably open natural intelligence in assessing all the proportions of the world that surrounds us.'[13]

Here and elsewhere in matters pertaining to the other sex, one can be forgiven for failing to be persuaded by the intellectual packaging of Havel's attitudes. He strikes one as a male of his generation and geography, setting out the terms of a relationship without taking into account the views and feelings of the other side. There is little doubt that Olga, although she had accepted the terms of their relationship, would have preferred a deeper and more exclusive emotional commitment on Havel's part. Still, to condemn Havel as just another male chauvinist would smack of cheap moralizing. The proof, after all, is in the pudding, and this particular pudding still tasted good after fifty years, a claim not too many people can make.

Happy couples are all alike; indeed being a pair is their defining characteristic. Two people can passionately love one another, each in his or her own way, without ever becoming a pair, often with catastrophic results. The Havels were definitely a pair, idiosyncratic and deficient in some aspects as it might have been. Their 'pairness', characterized more often than not by an ongoing argument in front of other people, acquired an air of silent shared contentedness when they were alone, each reading a different book or doing a different chore, seemingly unaware of the other's presence. The silence would be shattered the moment an external stimulus disturbed the balance. 'Olga,' Havel would implore whenever some task turned out to be beyond the limits of his dexterity, or another thing he was looking for had lost him. 'Vašku,' echoed Olga, whenever she came across another outrage in the Communist newspaper, or noticed another would-be James Bond snooping around. She was his Cerberus whenever he retired to his garden-view study at Hrádeček to write, chasing away all intruders, and she was his first reader the next morning, as he would nervously smoke one cigarette after another awaiting her approval. Many couples are broken by adversity,

---

11 Ibid.
12 Ibid.
13 Ibid. 13.

others by success; in the Havels' case, both were simply a reason to circle the wagons and show an impenetrable front. At the same time, the strength of their bond notwithstanding, she was as fiercely independent as he, more so in fact. When he was in prison, Olga would become his loyal eyes and ears, his manager and his procurer, but she would not play the grieving widow, and found things of her own to do and people of her own to see. Similarly, she dutifully appeared with Havel at state functions, receptions and visits abroad when he became president, but refused to become a full-time First Lady who spends her days performing social niceties, something as appealing to her as a cage is to a wolf. And when she fell ill, she would not parade her pain and suffering in front of the nation, but suffered and died in proud privacy, just as she had lived, paradoxically bringing about the most massive outpouring of public grief since the student Jan Palach immolated himself in protest against the Soviet occupation of Czechoslovakia in 1969. Olga was a rock, and Havel must have known it when he wrote to his father.

The Apprentice

Look on every exit as being an entrance somewhere else.
    – Tom Stoppard, *Rosencrantz and Guildenstern are Dead*

IN THE AUTUMN OF 1959, when Havel returned from the army, his marriage to Olga was still five years ahead, but life felt good. Despite having no foreseeable future, he was in some respects still better off than many of his contemporaries. He had a goal in life, a loyal girlfriend, a place to live, and a reliable source of support in his family, which, though no longer rich, was still able to draw on reserves. What he needed was a job. As there was no place for him in the film industry, theatre looked like the next best option. With the help of his father, he secured a stagehand's job in the ABC, an established repertory theatre whose respectable ensemble was dwarfed by the larger-than-life figure of Jan Werich, one of the pre-war greats of the Czech cultural scene.

It was a logical place for Havel to land, for Werich epitomized everything the Havel family stood for, an enlightened, centre-left world outlook radically opposed to the xenophobic and authoritarian tendencies that had been holding sway around Europe before the war, as well as an openness to the outside influences of the modern avant-garde, in particular German political cabaret, Parisian musical revue and the world of jazz and swing music from across the ocean. In 1925, Werich, along with his partner, the comedian Jiří (later George) Voskovec, and the composer Jaroslav Ježek, created the Liberated Theatre, a musical cabaret of the first order, with some of the best actors, singers, musicians and dancers of the era. After a wartime exile in the USA, where they continued to exert a spell over Czech audiences as the voice of free Czechoslovakia on *Voice of America*, they came back, only to find that room for political satire was rapidly shrinking. In 1948, Voskovec left again, this time for good, to start a distinguished new career in American film and theatre,[1] while his partner stayed behind. When Havel joined the theatre, Werich, though still loved by his audiences, was slowly dwindling into a shadow of his former glory.

Work with Werich enabled the young artist to imbibe the traditions of the pre-war avant-garde Czech theatre, but collaboration on a production in another of the Prague municipal theatres gave him a taste of the great classical theatre that drew on the best traditions of European drama. Alfréd Radok, at the height of his powers when Havel met him in 1960, was the director of Lillian Hellman's *Autumn Garden*, Gogol's *Marriage* and Rolland's *The Game of Love and Death*. Havel became his assistant for the adaptation of the Chekhov story *The Swedish Match*, thereby forging a lifelong bond with the director, while simultaneously developing a deep empathy with Chekhov.

As Havel repeatedly notes in his analysis of the director's work,[2] Radok was the closest Czech equivalent to Constantin Stanislavski and the Method, developing his productions in a permanent and often tense dialogue with the actors in an effort to break through their professional mannerisms and liberate their inner, natural selves. Although Havel's own absurdist brand of theatre inevitably led him in a different stylistic direction, he held fast to the idea of theatre as an irreducible form of life itself, rather than simply its imitation or reflection. He also retained a deep affection for Radok, the closest to a father figure he found in the world of literature and theatre. Their friendship is recorded in their correspondence in the 1970s, after Radok, whose career in Communist Czechoslovakia was a constant series of triumphs followed by banishments followed by reinstatements, emigrated with his family to Sweden.

Werich and Radok may have guided Havel in his first steps in the theatre, but Havel's ambitions quickly soared higher than merely working

---

1   He was Number 11, the memorable immigrant juror in Sidney Lumet's *Twelve Angry Men*.
2   'Some notes on *The Swedish Match*' (1962), reworked as 'Radok's work with actors' (1963), both in *Works 3*, 416–61, and 571–88 respectively.

as an assistant to the two directors. The functioning of an established theatre operating on the stardom principle did not offer much room for advancement. Still, ABC and the work with Radok represented a turning point for Havel in that he got the theatre bug, and in a big way. There he came to understand that 'theatre does not have to be just a factory for the production of plays or, if you like, a mechanical sum of its plays, directors, actors, ticket sellers, auditoriums, and audiences; it must be something more: a living spiritual and intellectual focus, a place for social self-awareness, a vanishing point where all the lines of force of the age meet, a seismograph of the times, a space, an area of freedom, an instrument of human liberation.'[3] When, at the end of Havel's first season, Werich retired, the theatre big band played, in his and his former partner's honour, a song entitled 'Werich is an asshole and Voskovec an old fool'.[4] An era had come to an end, and it was time for Havel to look elsewhere for work in the theatre.

Fortunately for him, a new era was being born a few blocks away. It was the first of a number of occasions in Havel's life when inspiration came, not from theatre or literature, but from music, or more precisely, from rock 'n' roll. With its subversive backbeat, its double-entendre lyrics, its outrageous dance moves and its slick fashion, it could hardly anticipate a warm welcome when it came, somewhat belatedly, to Czechoslovakia. It was not only anti-establishment – that was bad enough – but it was also American. (That its anti-establishment character could somewhat mitigate its American origin was too subtle a consideration for the cultural commissars.)

Sensing difficulties, a fledgling rock 'n' roll band, the Akord Club, based in a downtown music club called Reduta (where more than thirty years later Havel would play, after a fashion, percussion to Bill Clinton's saxophone), chose to wrap the musical contraband in simple skits and monologues, and present it as musical theatre. The ruse worked, helped by two remarkably talented men, Ivan Vyskočil, a clinical psychologist who wrote, or rather improvised, most of the theatrical intermezzos, and a graphic artist, Jiří Suchý, who wrote original, funny and poetic Czech lyrics to many of the American tunes. Driven by unprecedented, euphoric popularity, this small kernel exploded into a wave of dozens of 'small' theatres that, together with a

---

3 *Disturbing the Peace*, 40.
4 Richard Erml and Jan Kerbr, 'A Wonderful Time of My Life', an interview with Václav Havel, *Divadelní noviny*, No. 1–2, 2004.

similar flowering in literature, art and film, would totally change the cultural landscape of Czechoslovakia in the sixties.

As with all big bangs, the lifespan of the newborn constellations was extremely short; they kept morphing, mutating and multiplying. Reduta produced two major offspring, which in turn gave birth to many other acts. Jiří Suchý eventually stuck to music and poetry and with his new partner, the lawyer-composer-painter Jiří Šlitr, created the next legendary double act at the SEMAFOR Theatre, which became the craze of every Czech young man and woman in those days. Along the way, however, he was briefly present at the launch of yet another theatrical project.

One hundred metres inland from the busy Smetana Embankment, there is a tiny irregularly shaped enclave of tranquillity called Anenské Square, after the cloister of St Anne that had once occupied the church complex on its eastern side. It was there in 1958, while Václav Havel was still languishing in the engineering battalion, that a group of entertainers, led by Suchý and Vyskočil, managed to cram a tiny theatre into a house on the western side of the square, and called it Theatre on the Balustrade. After Suchý left shortly thereafter to start SEMAFOR and attain popular appeal and stardom, the Balustrade, led by Vyskočil, went in for intellectual experimentation. The dividing lines, at least in the beginning, were nonetheless fuzzy, and there was a considerable amount of cross-pollination.

Havel the stagehand, struck by the lightning of theatrical miracle at ABC, was fascinated by this invasion of the barbarians. Seeing as yet no way to make such theatre himself, he started, 'with all the arrogance of youth',[5] to write about theatre, contributing several essays on Werich and Horníček, the phenomenon of 'small' theatres, and other subjects, to cultural and trade magazines, and making something of a name as a perceptive and sympathetic reviewer. He also embarked on a career as a playwright, starting with the 'Ionescan one-acter' *An Evening with the Family* (1960), a black comedy about a senile solitaire-playing grandmother, a vacuous husband and wife exchanging non sequiturs, a materialistic couple of daughter and son-in-law, and a canary that is dead throughout the entire play, but which nobody bothers to bury or throw out. Havel's emerging theme of depersonalized characters is highlighted at the end of the play when the stagehands, the

---

5   Ibid.

only constructive figures in the performance, come to empty the stage of the props – the sleeping family, the dead canary and everything else – and proceed to take a bow.[6] He continued with the first draft of *The Memorandum*, a play of the absurd about the artificial language *Ptydepe*, the idea of which came from Havel's brother Ivan, a future student of cybernetics at the Prague Institute of Technology. In fact, trying to escape the drudgery of his own military service in faraway Eastern Slovakia, Ivan had written a whole play in Ptydepe, from which Václav borrowed some of the terminology and some of the names of the characters for the first drafts of his own play.[7] When one of the magazines to which Havel contributed invited him to a symposium along with the representatives of the small theatres, Vyskočil took a liking to the enthusiastic young supporter and, after Havel lent him the manuscript of *An Evening with the Family*, he offered him a job at the Balustrade. Though the otherwise unemployable bourgeois intellectual nominally still held the menial job of stagehand, this time Havel was offered a chance to collaborate on the theatre's profile and repertoire. He may have entered the world of theatre through the backstage door, but he was now part of a revolution.

---

6   The play, largely of historic interest, was published in *Works 2* (1999), 7–35, and only produced in 2000 at the Na Vinohradech Theatre.
7   Ivan modestly declines any credit for *Memorandum* except for the original inspiration. Initially, he was not even aware that Václav was developing the theme. Conversation with Ivan Havel, 20 August 2012.

The Garden Party

If he was merely an intellectual, well, all right. Intellectuals are sort of tolerated these days. But he keeps insisting on being a bourgeois intellectual as well!

– The Garden Party

HAVEL WOULD ALWAYS RECALL THE BALUSTRADE as a 'wonderful time of my life'.[1] Probably for the first time, he was not made to feel like an outsider; the word had no meaning in the workshop atmosphere of the place, which itself seemed to be morphing into something else every month. People were coming and going, and there were ten great ideas that never materialized for every one that did. The young stagehand did everything; he moved and assembled props, doubled as a lighting man, wrote skits, interfered as a literary adviser and even tried his hand at directing. For Vyskočil's semi-improvised revue *Autostop* (1961) he wrote *Ela, Hela and Stop*,[2] a manic skit about two ageing lady hitchhikers, who vent their frustrations and spite while waiting on the side of the road for the cars they make no attempt to flag down. Another of his skits for the production, a Kafkaesque spoof about a meeting of the Club of the Enemies of Cars, during which the main speaker as well as the audience *motomorphose* into cars, introduced the character of the inaugurator, a demented MC of sorts,

---

1 An interview with Václav Havel, *Divadelní noviny*, No. 1–2, 2004.
2 Manuscript, VHL ID16266.

who would be instrumental in his first produced feature play.[3] Although Havel was credited as co-author of *Autostop*, Vyskočil, who built and changed his performances at will as he went along, did not include *Ela* in the final production, transposed *Motomorphosis* into a one-man show, and later claimed that all the ideas came from him, anyway.[4] Another of Havel's authorial and, in part, directorial efforts was a musical vehicle for the comeback of one of the singer stars of the Liberated Theatre, *The Best Rocks of Madam Hermannová* (1962).[5] Again, Havel was credited as author together with the composer Miloš Macourek, but this time it was he who did not deem the work important enough to include in his bibliography or his collected works. He took a similarly distant attitude to the poetic 'grenoble'[6] *Demented Dove* (1963), to which he contributed three short 'inaugural' lectures.

Perhaps more importantly, this was the first production that listed Jan Grossman as co-director. The 1962–1963 season marked a changing of the guards at the Balustrade. The irascible and unpredictable leadership of Vyskočil ended up in an open revolt by the ensemble, and the great theatrical visionary left to launch a series of equally original projects, including, characteristically *The Non-Theatre*. Havel regretted the loss of the inspiration that Vyskočil had provided – if not his managerial style – and was by his own account 'one of the last people to have supported him'.[7] In reality, as much as he admired Vyskočil, his own artistic temperament, contemplative, methodical and perfectionist, was the total opposite of the older man's, for whom the process of creating a performance was always more important than its outcome. Havel may have regretted Vyskočil's departure, but he had already found in Grossman – a sophisticated literary critic, translator, director and dramaturge – another guru, one that he himself was instrumental in promoting. He was undoubtedly aware that with Grossman, a regular guest and acquaintance from the Slavia table, he was adding an element of political protest into the spontaneous combustion of creativity at the theatre.

At the Balustrade, Havel started writing a play about the adventures of

---

3 *Motomorfóza (Motomorphosis)*, manuscript, VHL ID17615.
4 Vladimír Hulec, 'An Interview with Ivan Vyskočil', in Tichý, Zdeněk A., Ježek, Vlastimil (eds.): *Šest z šedesátých, (Six from the Sixties)* (Radioservis, Praha 2003) 61.
5 In Czech, the title has a second meaning, *The Best Years of Madam Hermannová*.
6 Why the type of the production was characterized by the name of a city in southeastern France is a mystery to the author, and perhaps not just to him.
7 'A Wonderful Time of My Life' (2004).

a young man who makes it big in the world. The idea, 'about networking, connections, patronage, career or something,'[8] came from Ivan Vyskočil, as one of many in the long post-performance conversations over a glass of wine. By his own admission, however, Vyskočil 'much preferred storytelling to writing,'[9] and invited Havel to work on the idea. It was this play, still considered his best by many, that made Havel's name as an artist.

In a way, and Havel acknowledged this, the story resembles the quint-essential Czech fairy tale: the simple peasant Honza reluctantly leaves his home village and, after surviving numerous adventures and challenges, inherits the kingdom thanks to his down-to-earth charm and cunning. It is a story known to every Czech child.

The first of several drafts of the play, originally called *His Day* (Jeho den),[10] is a rather conventional, crazy comedy about a family pinning its hopes for the future of their promising son (the other, unpromising, is a 'bourgeois intellectual') on a mysterious benefactor in a high position. Like *An Evening with the Family*, *His Day* is also clearly the work of a rebellious writer; and yet, the rebellion is aimed as much against the family as against society. It is not difficult to detect common features between Petr, the no-good bourgeois intellectual, who is being asked to hide in the attic each time the family expects their important visitor, and the author; while the analytical Hugo is, somewhat unfairly, reminiscent of Ivan, his 'good' brother (the artificial language Ptydepe, Ivan's invention, which was to play a central role in *The Memorandum*, is briefly invoked by Hugo in *His Day*).

If *His Day* had been produced as it was, it would have probably provoked interest as another musical comedy (the draft included a number of song lyrics). The plot was threadbare, as in all such comedies, but more importantly the play lacked structure and rhythm. Its most interesting part was the intermezzo, in which Havel experimented with a building cacophony of increasingly improbable dialogues that became a trademark of his later plays. It was here that he put to use, with striking effect, his talent for geometrical abstraction combined with an ear for musical variation. In the later drafts, he expanded the structural principles of the intermezzo to the

---

8 *Disturbing the Peace*, 61. The text is here quoted from the original Czech version, which is closer to the character of the play.
9 'An Interview with Ivan Vyskočil' (2003).
10 A comedy of three acts and an intermezzo, manuscript, 1961, VHL ID17614.

whole play. He stripped the characters of psychological traits, suppressed the real-life aspects of the story and reduced it to a series of largely meaningless, mechanically recurring patterns, reproduced interchangeably by the actors. The waiting for the important benefactor now acquired the abstract nature of the waiting for Godot, and the farcical confusion of the main character of Hugo with other characters in the play now took on the existential meaning of the loss of identity as a personal tragedy. What had started as a musical comedy was now a fully fledged play of the absurd.

He did not get to this point unaided. In a recurring pattern, Havel did some of his best work by recruiting a colleague and/or a friend to act as a sounding board, opponent or devil's advocate. *The Garden Party* is dedicated to Jan Grossman, who more than being merely the first reader of its successive drafts, practically nursed the young playwright throughout the process. If the original impulse had come from Vyskočil, the final shape of the play may owe more to Grossman, who believed it was the Havel play in which he had the biggest 'authorial' share.[11] At Easter 1963, thanks to Havel Sr's employment by the national sports authority (a rather absurd variation on the theme of nepotism in the play), the two men spent two weeks in adjoining rooms in a mountain resort for top athletes in Harrachov, with Havel writing and rewriting through the night and sliding the pages under Grossman's door for him to read in the morning. (In between, he found time to develop a crush on a young chambermaid and tried to impress her by lending her Grossman's copy of Kafka's *The Trial*. He succeeded beyond expectations; the chambermaid did not understand much of the book, but told him he did a wonderful job writing it just the same.[12]) What emerged was a text that resembled a geometrical figure or a musical composition as much as a play. This was not coincidental; in a letter to his wife, Grossman mentions that he made Havel 'listen to Bach's *Goldberg Variations*, all kinds of fugues, and the *Crab Canon*. He enjoyed it very much and found in it an inspiration for his own composition.'[13] In the final result Grossman was credited as the dramaturge of the play, but his influence went beyond this role, indispensable in European theatres but

---

11 Kriseová (1991), 41.
12 A letter to Václav Havel by Marie Málková, 5 October 1996, Marie Málková's archive, VHL ID6786.
13 Ibid.

largely unknown or, in the guise of 'literary adviser', marginal in America. In an effort to give the play the best possible staging, and perhaps an appearance of unimpeachable respectability, the pair recruited Otomar Krejča, a leading National Theatre director, along with his colleague Jiří Svoboda, the award-winning set designer for Laterna Magika, an early multimedia performance project, which stunned the audiences at the World Expo 1958 in Brussels and brought fame, or the first taste of it, to two of Havel's intimates, Alfréd Radok and Miloš Forman. The two 'indigenous' artists of the Balustrade, however, would not give up their control of the play just for the sake of respectability. After Krejča left the rehearsals each day to attend to other projects, they tinkered with the direction. Even worse, under cover of darkness they anonymously vandalized parts of Svoboda's set that they disliked, but did not dare oppose publicly.[14] The dedication to Grossman was well deserved.

The text of the play was published beforehand by a trade magazine in a pre-emptive ruse to pacify the watchful censors.[15] It created a stir, but no one could be prepared for its reception by live audiences. People laughed uncontrollably, roared in ecstasy, applauded in the middle of the play, went through several rounds of applause at the interval and rewarded the actors with a dozen or more rounds at the end, despite the fact that the last line of the play instructed them directly: 'And now, please all disperse without unnecessary discussions!'[16] It was not unheard of for a young man or woman to have seen the play ten times during its run.[17] The Hugo parents' non sequiturs masquerading as folk wisdom ('Not even a hag carries hemp seed to the attic alone' or 'He who fusses over a mosquito net can never hope to dance with a goat') were memorized verbatim and became part of the vocabulary of a generation.

All of this came about despite the fact that the play did not make much sense or, even more likely, just because of that. Sent by the family to seek out

---

14 Related by Zdeněk Urbánek in Kriseová (1991). Other versions of the story exist, some by Havel himself, including the one in Kaiser (2009). According to Krob (conversation 11 October 2014), Krejča was a willing participant in the plot.

15 The censors, who used the Orwellian name the Central Administration of Print Supervision (HSTD), operated in a preventive manner. Once a publication of a play was cleared by HSTD it could be reasonably assumed its later incarnations were safe.

16 Quoted from the Czech original in *Works 2* (Torst, 1999), 99. The English translation, 'And now without sort of much ado – go home,' in *Selected Plays, 1963–83* (1992), 51, misses out on the association of a policeman quashing a public disturbance.

17 The author admits to seven or eight.

his benefactor, Hugo comes to a garden party of the Liquidation Bureau and, by clever verbal manipulation, insinuates the notion into the minds of the attending representatives of the Inauguration Service that it is on the verge of liquidation. He then visits the offices of the Inauguration Service and once again manages to create the impression that the Liquidation Bureau is to be liquidated. But therein lies the problem: there will have to be someone to inaugurate the liquidation.

> HUGO Who? Well – surely – the responsible inaugurator.
> DIRECTOR The responsible inaugurator? But the inaugurators
>   cannot inaugurate when they are being liquidated, can they?
> HUGO Right. That's why it ought to be inaugurated by the
>   responsible liquidation officer!
> DIRECTOR The responsible liquidation officer? But the job of a
>   liquidation officer is to liquidate, not to inaugurate![18]

In the end, Hugo Pludek, the character who has neither the expertise nor an interest in either liquidating or inaugurating, is made the head of a new institution called the Central Commission for Inauguration and Liquidation.

Clearly, the audiences recognized a pastiche of the endless struggles and transformations of the institutions of the Communist regime, its purges and condemnations, followed by rehabilitations and restorations. They laughed at the absurdity of spontaneous human impulses, like courage, change or creativity being ordered from above. 'The colleagues in the Department of Culture surely know very well why they're planning to publish a decree about artistic courage! It will take effect already in the second quarter.'[19] Without a doubt they doubled up at the laboured efforts of the characters to find the justification for the latest liquidation or inauguration, and then use the same language to argue exactly the opposite. They rejoiced in the debunking of this 'metaphysical dialectics'[20] as the official scientific and philosophical method of fostering a 'proper' ideology, by means of which it was possible

---

18 *The Garden Party* in *Selected Plays, 1963–83*, 35.
19 Ibid. 21.
20 Havel used the term in his iconoclastic remarks to the conference of the Writers' Union, 8 June 1965.

to affirm or reject absolutely everything as need be, and often to affirm and reject something simultaneously. And surely they would chuckle at – but also somewhat empathize with – the quandary of ordinary people like the Pludeks on how best to protect their families and navigate the current of permanent, sudden and irrational reversals.

> PLUDEK Hugo shouldn't have accepted that liquidation!
>
> PLUDKOVÁ If he hadn't accepted it, the Liquidation Office wouldn't have been liquidated and the liquidation would go on. And why then should Hugo be the only one who isn't liquidating? It's good he didn't turn it down.
>
> PLUDEK Because he didn't, the Liquidation Office will be liquidated, liquidation will stop, and it will be only Hugo who will keep on liquidating. It's bound to get him into trouble sooner or later—
>
> PLUDKOVÁ He should have turned it down—
>
> PLUDEK On the contrary, he should have not accepted it!
>
> PLUDKOVÁ On the contrary, he should have not turned it down—
>
> PLUDEK Shouldn't he have at the same time accepted it and not turned it down?
>
> PLUDKOVÁ Rather, turned it down and not accepted it!
>
> PLUDEK In that case, rather not accepted it, not turned it down, accepted it and turned it down!
>
> PLUDKOVÁ And what if he'd at the same time turned it down, not accepted it, not turned it down and accepted it?
>
> PLUDEK Hard to say. What do you think?
>
> HUGO Me? Well, I'd say he should have not accepted it, not turned it down, accepted it and turned it down. Or the other way round.[21]

Havel, nonetheless, clearly aims beyond a simple caricature of the Communist system. Hugo's ultimate loss of identity occurs through his confrontation with a depersonalized and dehumanized system, which is only capable of expressing itself in meaningless and contradictory phrases. It could be, and for Czech audiences it clearly was, the totalitarian system, but it could equally be any comprehensive bureaucracy, like the anonymous law

---

21 Ibid. 46.

enforcement in Kafka's *The Trial*, or the military machine in Heller's *Catch-22*. (Indeed Kafka's ghost looms large over the play, though his name or work is never invoked.) There is no other way to account for the popularity of the play, which has been produced in dozens of languages in scores of countries.

The total deconstruction of the main character in *The Garden Party* marks the condemnation by the young writer of both the social milieu from which he stemmed, and the political circumstances in which he was obliged to live. Both seemed to favour faceless, grey, obedient creatures like Hugo Pludek over talented, unconventional and courageous individuals. In the play, Hugo's father praises his son, who plays chess with himself by playing both sides of the board: 'You see? Instead of a total victory one time or a total defeat another, he prefers to win a little and lose a little each time.' 'Such a player will always stay in the game,' echoes Hugo's mother.[22]

There is, though, Havel's own dialectical twist to the play. For all his greyness, Hugo, the man without qualities, the anti-hero and antithesis of Havel's own view of life, is ultimately the one who beats the system, albeit at the price of his identity. His somewhat ominous closing variation on Hamlet's soliloquy would still send shivers down the spine of any modern audience:

> We all are a little bit what we were yesterday and a little bit what we are today and also a little bit we're not these things. Anyway, we all are a little bit all the time and all the time we are not a little bit, some of us are more and some of us are more not; some only are, some are only, and some only are not; so that none of us entirely is and at the same time each one of us is not entirely, and the point is just when it is better to be more, and to not be less, and when – on the contrary – it is better less to be and more not to be; besides, he who is too much may soon not be at all, and he who – in a certain situation – is able to a certain extent not to be, may in another situation be all the better for that. I don't know whether you want more to be or not to be, and when you want to be or not to be; but I know I want to be all the time and that's why all the time I must a little bit not be.

---

22 Ibid. 7.

You see, man when he is from time to time a little bit not is not
diminished thereby! And if at the moment I am – relatively
speaking – rather not, I assure you that soon I might be much
more than I've ever been – and then we can discuss this again,
but on an entirely different platform![23]

Eventually, the play, which largely consists of permutations of lines that
make less and less sense as it progresses, works a little like an ink-blot test
for the audiences. Almost anyone could project his own experience with
the debilitating influence of a bureaucracy into the lines. The laughter that
accompanied this recognition had a momentary liberating function. As
the spectators were leaving the theatre, the scathing analysis contained in
Havel's text did not provoke frustration or anger, but happiness.

In fact, they did not want to leave. The small bar in the anteroom of the
theatre was just as much a part of the show as the stage. There people could
share the pleasure, re-experience the laughs and discover kindred spirits.
The isolation imposed by the rigid rules, constraints and constant threats,
both implicit and explicit, of the regime was broken by the communal
experience. Later in the evening some of the actors joined the audience to
further obliterate the line between the auditorium and the stage. Frequently
the *auteur* came as well, charming and befriending strangers, flirting with
girls (carefully, when Olga was around), and modestly basking in the joy
of others. The result was a kernel of a community with shared sensitivities,
shared views and increasingly also shared goals. When this kernel merged
with others of a similar bent, they produced an avalanche.

By 1963, when *The Garden Party* opened, tickets for the 140-seat
auditorium (plus thirty or so standing room only) at the Balustrade were
as hard to come by as a permission to travel to the West. On the twenty-
third of every month, when tickets for the next month started selling at the
minuscule box office occasionally manned by Olga, there was a long line of
tired young people who had spent the night waiting their turn. The lucky
few who managed to get tickets in the years 1963–1965, when the theatre
spearheaded the cultural revolution with productions of Havel's works
and with memorable productions of plays by Eugène Ionesco (*The Bald*

---

23 Ibid. 51.

Soprano), Samuel Beckett (*Waiting for Godot*) and Alfred Jarry (*Ubu Roi*), were also treated to an exhibition of graphics in the foyer and the bar, made up entirely of characters typed on a manual typewriter. These were Václav Havel's *Anticodes*,[24] a hybrid of poetry and art, also known as *typograms*. The inspiration came from Jiří Kolář, who experimented with collages of typed text and other ways of trying to give poetic text a graphic form, and to whom the collection is dedicated. Havel composed his typograms over several years, often as a distraction from his efforts to work on a play or a longer text. Throughout his life, Havel continuously made doodles and drawings and drew diagrams better to visualize the structure of his thought, whether it be a play or a text, or, much later, a problem he faced as president.

Yet from the way the audiences were chuckling, laughing and marvelling at these simple graphics, one could tell this was not a mere attempt at abstraction, but on the contrary, an art with a message. The hidden meaning was 'encoded' in the very title 'Anticodes', which could be read alternately as acting against codes, i.e. decoding a hidden meaning, or as enciphering a coded protest against something. In the event, it was both.

The *Anticodes* were divided into several sections of typographical subjects. One dealt with various -isms, depicting i.a.

```
INDIVIDUALIsM,
dua lism,
IDEA lism,
materia LISM, and
E?X?I?S?T?E?N?T?I?A?L?I?S?M?
```

The Slogan section contained exhortations such as:

---

24 *Antikódy* (Praha: Odeon, 1964).

AID THE BACKWORD COUNTREES

and

**WE SHALL KICK THE WARMONGERS'
  ASSES
TILL THEY DRIP BLOOD**

And the 'Words Words Words' section offered a practical

**TEMPLATE
In the last few years we have
achieved in**

. . . .

**many outstanding successes.
However, we should not deny
that even in this area we still
experience some minor problems.
Especially in** . . . .
. . . .
. . . .
. . . .
. . . .
we still have a lot to do.

To the average visitor it must have seemed as if the artist was asking for trouble. If that were the case, he would soon get his wish.

The Sixties

Then all at once the quarrel sank:
Everyone felt the same,
And every life became
A brilliant breaking of the bank,
A quite unlosable game.
                    – Philip Larkin, 'Annus Mirabilis'

IT WOULD BE HARD TO GRASP the evolution of the Stalinist monolith of the fifties through the Potemkin village of the seventies into the walking dead of the eighties without the seismic anomaly of the sixties. Unlike the surrounding decades, when the world of 'real socialism' mostly danced to its own insular music, the sixties was a period of global fermentation, with the two sides of the Cold War joined in an uneasy two-step, exchanging ideas, nightmares and body fluids.

In existentialist mythology, the perceived meaninglessness of human existence in the face of the imminent spectre of nuclear war gave rise to the rebelliousness and sense of abandon that characterized the sixties. It is also possible to read that history in not quite so stark a way. The 1961 crisis in Berlin and the Cuban crisis of 1962 brought the two superpowers to the brink, but also made them stop short of the abyss. For the first time it seemed possible that a world bristling with nuclear weapons might just survive. The craziness, ebullience and joy of the sixties was thus a reflection of hope rather than despair. Certainly Havel, with a keen sense of the dangers threatening civilization, never gave nuclear war much thought. The threats he was thinking about were much closer to home.

He was both a benefactor and a beneficiary of the era, having played a major role in the incredible renaissance of Czech modern culture in general, and of theatre in particular, while spending the rest of his time busily imbibing all the new tastes, flavours and smells of the era. Some of them were of domestic manufacture, although many were imports.

The new wave of Czechoslovak cinematography brought about a flourishing of films that both reflected and helped form the sensitivities of the decade. It was parallel to, but hardly independent of, the emergence of new small theatres and new ways of making theatre. It loudly announced its arrival in 1963, the same year *The Garden Party* premiered at the Balustrade, with a duo of films under the title *Audition* by a fresh graduate of the Academy of Performing Arts Film School, who had also been Havel's room captain in the King George School in Poděbrady: Miloš Forman. The revolutionary nature of the two films was immediately apparent from their lack of interest in maintaining a coherent storyline, together with the use of non-actors in most of the roles. By doing away with many cinematographic conventions, this Czech version of *cinema vérité* came across as spontaneous, uncontrived and real, in sharp contrast to the prevailing production of films about heroic workers or resistance fighters. Ivan Passer, another of the Poděbrady graduates, was credited in both films as a co-writer. The score of the first film drew heavily on the music of Jiří Šlitr, and on the rock 'n' roll beat, the first such Western invasion onto Czech screens, and a counterpoint to the traditional brass band music in the second film.

Havel and Forman, who had remained friends since school, even started to work together on a project for a film based on Franz Kafka's *The Castle*. To that end, they undertook an expedition to the village of Siřem, where the tubercular Kafka spent the 'best eight months of my life' with his sister Ottla, and whose baroque hilltop granary could have served as the model for the castle.[1] The film was to describe the plan of a tourist authority to exploit the Kafka connection with the village. The authorities disapproved of the topic, and the film never got made. Still, an obscure international scientific conference on the life and work of Franz Kafka, held in another

---

1 Kafka nevertheless started to write the novel almost five years later, and may have been more influenced by his stay in the South Bohemian town of Planá, with the Štrkov castle nearby.

Bohemian castle at Liblice in 1963, lifted the taboo imposed on the Prague native by the Communist authorities. That this event, which had passed unnoticed by all but the most intellectually curious Czechs and Slovaks, is sometimes described as the starting point in a chain of events that led to the Prague Spring of 1968 is characteristic of the strangely bookish tinge to modern Czech history.[2] It often seems that the most important battles of its last two centuries have been fought in theatres, in lecture halls and on bandstands, rather than on battlefields or in parliaments.

Forman was the first to breach the wall. When the dam broke, he was joined by an extraordinary group of talented film-makers, including Jiří Menzel (*Closely Watched Trains*, Academy Award for the best foreign language film 1967), the Czech-and-Slovak double act Kadár/Klos (*The Shop on Main Street*, Academy Award for the best foreign language film 1965), Jan Němec (*A Report on the Party and the Guests*, 1966, with Ivan Vyskočil in the main role), Věra Chytilová (*Daisies*, 1966), Pavel Juráček (*Joseph Kilian*, 1963, and *Every Young Man*, 1965, with Václav Havel in a supporting role as a conscript), Ivan Passer (*Intimate Lightning*, 1965, perhaps the most original film of the period, in which absolutely nothing happens) and a number of others. Forman himself earned his first nomination for the Academy Award for the best foreign language film for *Loves of a Blonde* (1966), and yet another one for *The Firemen's Ball* (1967).

The same sudden blooming of talent seemed to be occurring in literature (the impression was magnified by the fact that some of the older works of until then forbidden authors were allowed to be published for the first time). *The Cowards* (1950), Josef Škvorecký's anti-hero novel about the end of World War II in a small Czech town, was only allowed to come out in 1958, and caused a scandal even then. Bohumil Hrabal, easily the most popular Czech writer of his time, was first allowed to publish only at the age of fifty (*Pearls of the Deep*, 1963, *Palaverers*, 1964, *Closely Watched Trains*, 1965). The unwashed were joined by Communist writers like Pavel Kohout (*The Third Sister*, 1960) and Ludvík Vaculík (*The Axe*, 1966) who were quickly shedding their orthodox Party beginnings. *Laughable Loves* (1963) and their sequels (1965, 1969) won Milan Kundera a mass audience, and *The Joke* (1967) established him as a major writer. An impression was

---

2 Whereas scholars and writers often see Kafka as a mystical visionary, many twentieth-century Praguers had reasons to think of him as a down-to-earth realist.

also being made by experimenting writers and poets of Havel's generation, and older ones like Věra Linhartová (*A Room for Differentiation*, 1964), Josef Jedlička (*In the Midway of This Our Mortal Life*, 1966), Ivan Diviš (*Spewing Blood*, 1964) and Jiří Gruša (*The Light Deadline*, 1964).

Similar developments reinvigorated the fields of creative arts (sculptor Mikuláš Medek, the brother of a future Havel chancellor, Vlastimil Boudník, a drinking buddy of Hrabal, Libor Fára, the court designer of the Balustrade theatre, Jiří Kolář of the Slavia table, and others), journalism and music, both classical and popular. A strongly established jazz and swing tradition so brilliantly reflected in the work of Josef Škvorecký gave way to rock 'n' roll and rock music. The first Czech film musical with an impossible English title, *The Love Story in Summer Job Camp* (1964), broke the taboo of teenage sex for a whole generation of eager youth.

It was also somewhere here that East and West met. By another accident of history, Allen Ginsberg, no more popular with Communist governments than with the American establishment, who had put him on the Dangerous Security List,[3] ended up in Prague in March, and again at the end of April 1965, having been deported from Cuba for protesting against the treatment of homosexuals there. He read 'Howl' to an ecstatic audience at Charles University, got elected the 'King' of the annual student May festival and a week later was promptly deported again for alleged soliciting of underage boys.[4] He spent a couple of evenings during his short stay in Prague in the Viola Poetic Wine Bar in Národní Street, one of the favourite haunts of young poets and writers, where he also met his first Czech translator, Havel's friend Jan Zábrana.

The role that Národní Street, a kilometre-long boulevard running from the Vltava River to Wenceslas Square, played in the intellectual renaissance of the sixties can hardly be overestimated. There, those three pillars of the establishment, the National Theatre, the offices of the Writers' Union and of its publishing arm The Czechoslovak Writer, were more than counterweighed by the presence of the young film artists in the Prague Academy Film School, the table of *les poètes maudits* in the Slavia Café, the night asylums of intellectuals in Viola, and the Cloister Wine

---

3 http://www.english.illinois.edu/maps/poets/g_l/ginsberg/life.htm.
4 Allen Ginsberg, *Selected Poems 1947–1995*, 'Kral Majales' (Harper Collins Publishers, 2001), 147.

Room, the Reduta music club, the more courageous and outward-looking publishers at Odeon and the fledgling directors in the Film Club, housed in the same building as the Laterna Magika theatre at the end of the street. There were also a number of seedier bars around the area, sometimes called the Bermuda Triangle, where some of the former talents raged against the fading light and gradually disappeared in a cloud of alcohol and despair.

Drugs came late to Czechoslovakia, and for a long time were limited to home grown and not very potent marijuana. There was, however, a surrogate market in psychotropic prescription drugs like Phenmetrazine,[5] in which Havel admits to indulging freely and over an extended period of time. In one of his first allusions to the habit, he wrote to Jan Grossman from a self-imposed isolation in a writers' summer home in Budislav, where he was at work on *The Garden Party*, asking whether Grossman could obtain for him some 'vitamin F', and: 'Would it not be possible to introduce special quotas for dramaturges on a writer's leave?'.[6] Moreover, lysergic acid diethylamide, aka LSD, of which Czechoslovakia was at one time the biggest producer in the world, was not only legal, but also offered to volunteers in controlled psychological experiments. Not everybody had to get stoned, but quite a few did.

By the middle of the decade, the depressing greyness imposed by the regime on the ancient Czech capital began to lift, revealing coats of many colours. Hair grew longer, and skirts shorter. Life was good. Havel seemed to have overcome both the privileges and the handicaps of his birth and became a recognized artist. *The Garden Party* played to sold-out houses, and Havel helped create other memorable productions at the Balustrade, notably Samuel Beckett's *Waiting for Godot* and Alfred Jarry's *Ubu Roi*. After his fame passed beyond the borders of Czechoslovakia, and after the first rejection of his application for an exit visa led to a small uprising in the theatre, he was even allowed to travel and see his plays produced in Germany and Austria. He was lucky in having been discovered and promoted internationally by a capable and loyal agent in Klaus Juncker of the Rowohlt publishing house, who became his lifelong friend. Nevertheless, only someone who had not been around to see the miracle that was the first production of *The Garden*

---

5 An anorectic stimulant with effects similar to amphetamine.
6 Letter to Jan Grossman, undated, early 1960s, VHL ID6538.

Party and the popular response to it could argue that 'without the interest of three West German intellectuals (Juncker was alerted to Havel's existence by two others) in December 1963, the Czech history of the second half of the twentieth century would probably look somewhat different'[7]. The forces that drove that history were home grown.

Like many a rising star in his twenties, Havel not only worked hard but played hard as well, perhaps in part compensating for his shy and awkward youth. In the sixties, he found willing companions for pub-crawling and other mischief in several of his peers, including film directors and screenwriters Jan Němec and Pavel Juráček, and painters and graphic artists Jan Koblasa and Josef Vyleťal. Primarily, however, he forged an incongruous but lifelong friendship with a self-taught provincial actor and future playwright, Pavel Landovský. It was a match of opposites. Landovský was a Rabelaisian force of nature with gargantuan tastes. He ham-acted, hustled and brawled his way through the Byzantine maze of the Communist system that Havel was trying to out-think and outsmart. Havel's image of a coffee-house intellectual had the same irresistible appeal for Landovský as his own lowlife style of seedy night spots had for the shy young playwright. For Landovský, Havel was a link to the world of Prague and high theatre. For Havel, Landovský represented a guide and a door-opener to the universe of worldly pleasures. 'I could get into the Barbara nightclub with Havel in my footsteps by just telling the bouncer: "This guy's with me."'[8] It is easy to think of Landovský as a corrupting influence on Havel, and the aversion that Olga felt towards her husband's friend certainly stemmed from that impression. At the same time, Landovský's open defiance of authority helped Havel steel himself for the trials ahead. And there was beneath all Landovský's theatricality, hustling and bluster a genuine, loyal and brave human being who scorned hypocrisy and decorum, and stayed true to himself. He was there for Havel not only during the prowls through night-time Prague of the sixties, but during the decades-long journey into the night that followed.

For the moment, however, the future looked bright. For the first time in his life Havel was popular and successful. Even the official Communist Party newspaper *Rudé právo* sang his praises, noting quite perceptively that *The Garden Party* 'does not conceal its origin in the land of the Liberated

---

7   Kaiser (2009), 56.
8   Conversation with Pavel Landovský, 20 October 2012.

Theatre and Švejk' and commending the author's efforts to 'identify the roots of everything that is mechanical, de-humanized and non-sensical in our lives'.[9] The world outside beckoned. Few people have become very rich by writing comedies of the absurd for small independent theatres, but thanks to the vast differences between Czech and Western pay scales at the time, Havel was suddenly quite prosperous, certainly by local standards. He had a pretty wife who doted on him. He should have been counting his blessings.

Not Havel. In his miscellaneous activities of the period we get the first glimpse of a man who is working and fighting for something bigger than his own success. Alongside the plays, he wrote a number of essays and articles on a variety of subjects. In many of them he used his newfound authority to remind his peers and the public of the existence and work of the less fortunate writers and artists who had been condemned to obscurity because of their views, their pasts or simply because they did not fit. In his second confrontation with the literary establishment at a conference of the Writers' Union in June 1965, he alerted his colleagues to the long-enforced silence of modernist poets and writers Jiří Kolář, Josef Hiršal, Jan Grossman and Jan Vladislav, and the theoreticians Jindřich Chalupecký and Václav Černý; to the bans on the work of Vladimír Holan and Josef Škvorecký, and to unpaid debts to such older writers as Richard Weiner, Ladislav Klíma and Jakub Deml. And he went even further, rejecting the supervision of the official hierarchy over the work of writers, any writers. 'The name of the keynote address delivered here was "The tasks of literature and the work of the Writers' Union", which could create the impression, as if it was the job of the Writers' Union to task literature. I believe that it should be the other way round: Literature should task the Writers' Union.'[10] This was no longer criticism, but an open rebellion.

In writing about the artist and writer Josef Čapek, the brother of the more famous Karel and the creator of illustrations to many a book beloved by children and adults alike, who had been murdered by the Nazis in a concentration camp and posthumously condemned to obscurity by the Communists, Havel offered his own criterion of an artist's value, a criterion he did his best to live up to for the rest of his life. It was to live a

9 Jan Kopecký, 'Four Theatre Evenings', *Rudé právo*, 14 December 1963.
10 Address to the Conference of the Czechoslovak Writers' Union, 9 June 1965, as reprinted in *Literární Noviny*, 19 June 1965, VHL ID4574.

'spiritual story'.[11] 'We can fully understand Čapek's real significance in the history of our modern artistic and cultural life only when we transcend the lines of individual creative disciplines and their expert criteria and attempt to gauge the artist not only by what he had done but primarily by *who he had become*.'[12]

The 'spiritual story' meant obviously a quest for the meaning of life, 'for a fulfilled and righteous life, for the gratification of a craving for an existential reconciliation and atonement'.[13] This was the final horizon, to which all the others were subordinated, including the horizon of politics. However, in contrast to many artists and most politicians, Havel approached the subject in humility, even in something resembling awe: 'Is it, however, possible to find an answer to this fundamental question? So far, the quest for knowledge had always tried to provide an answer – after all man was its *object!* – but it had unavoidably denied its validity by somehow – partially – answering it. A new solution is – paradoxically – to affirm the question, by not trying to answer it, but by simply *posing* it.'[14]

What made Havel unique among so many talents flourishing at this time was his ability to weave the manifold strains of his theatrical, critical and essayistic work into something akin to a coherent philosophy. But he was also aware that a one-man rebellion is not a revolution. If he wanted to take on the official literary establishment and the power of the Communist Party and the ideology behind it, he would need to look for a platform, and he would need allies.

11 Václav Havel, 'Josef Čapek', 1963, in *Works 3*, 547.
12 Ibid. 542–3.
13 Ibid. 546.
14 'Text in the catalogue of an exhibition of Jiří Janeček', 1964, in *Works 3*, 613–4.

A Private School of Politics

This lad is going to be dangerous for us.
> – Pavel Auersperg, the chief ideologist
> of the Czechoslovak Communist Party

IN THE EVENT, the platform came looking for him. After a bumpy start in 1964, a struggling intellectual magazine of young writers called *Tvář*[1] underwent 'a revolution of sorts' and started looking for new authors and editorial board members. Havel joined the board in early 1965, but, being quite busy in the theatre and elsewhere, did not initially contribute much as an author. As an already recognized writer, he represented a useful front for the tight-knit group of insiders who controlled the magazine and its editorial policy. In turn they represented a group of people Havel 'could work with and identify with, without any inner reservations'.[2] However, and perhaps typically of Havel, he became deeply involved only when the magazine ran into trouble for, among other things, publishing the texts of 'militant advocates of contemporary clericalism'.[3] This apparently referred to several practising Christians, who sat on the board or contributed to the magazine.

In the campaign to purge the magazine that ensued, Havel took an open and uncompromising stand in defence of his colleagues, although he

---

1 The inspiration for the name came from the eponymous collection of poems (1931) by František Halas, notable for its metaphysical air. 'The night examines me/ whether I did not forget/ the days full of mystery/ when out of darkness I stepped.'
2 *Disturbing the Peace*, 77.
3 Kaplan (1997), 40, also quoted in Kaiser (2009), 57.

had little personal stake in the matter. When the presidium of the Writers' Union began considering a 'final solution' of *Tvář*, Havel spearheaded a petition drive in its defence, collecting several hundred signatures, including those of leading writers and intellectuals, such as his early idol Jaroslav Seifert. When the Union continued to insist on the replacement of editor-in-chief Jan Nedvěd and the removal from the board of Jiří Němec and Emanuel Mandler, the editorial board refused to budge and discontinued the publication of the magazine, though they continued meeting, collecting and editing texts as if the official curse did not exist. Inspiration for these tactics clearly came from the table at Slavia; the writers there had been employing them for years. It also became a kind of model for the future. The insight that in some respects the creation and preservation of a text is more important than its publication, quite foreign to most writers living in more normal circumstances, made the emergence of a samizdat culture possible and, indeed, became its very raison d'être.

There is another pattern emerging here. Again and again, Havel would rise to take a stand over a perceived injustice, at great personal risk, and regardless of whether he was directly affected. And again and again, he would make use of his almost unlimited capacity to socialize, network and befriend large numbers of people to add weight and urgency to the protests. Far from being an effete intellectual, a guise he so often donned to escape the inconvenient attentions of both oppressors and admirers, he was a natural-born leader.

But there was also another, more ambiguous aspect to the *Tvář* episode, one that made the struggle with the establishment even more difficult, and that was to have repercussions long into the future. Although Havel had been by then familiar with the issues and dangers of politics at large, in *Tvář* he first encountered the treacherous minefields of petty boardroom politics, and discovered – much to his astonishment – that they could be as vicious as any power struggles in the politburo. The four members of the 'inner sanctum', editor-in-chief Nedvěd and board members Mandler, Doležal and Lopatka, were happy to let him fight for the magazine in the long meetings of the expert committees of the Writers' Union, but they did not take kindly to his suggestions regarding the style and the content of the magazine. In the way the group forged the editorial line and manipulated board meetings, Havel detected a kind of 'sectarianism',[4] something totally foreign to him. In turn, it seems that some within saw him as overambitious and power-hungry. Unable to accept that *Tvář* had 'its trials, its heretics, its discipline, its dogmas, etc.',[5] Havel left, then came back again for the short-lived restoration of the magazine during the Prague Spring, when it acquired new contributors, including a promising economist named Václav Klaus, but ultimately 'slammed the door'[6] on it when he was called to task for deviating from the editorial line in his speech to the Constitutional Congress of the Czech Writers' Union in 1969.

In retrospect, it is difficult to understand what exactly was the cause of the rift in such a small group of like-minded intellectuals struggling against both the monolith of Communist orthodoxy and its 'anti-dogmatic' offshoots; and yet, its echoes could be discerned even half a century later. In *Disturbing the Peace*, Havel devotes fifteen out of two hundred pages to what, at least to the uninitiated, remains an obscure episode. Other members of the original board attached even greater importance to it. Although many became involved in dissident activities, some seemed to have spent almost as much time fighting Havel and Charter 77 as fighting the regime.[7] After the fall of Communism, Mandler and Doležal transformed their pre-November Democratic Initiative into a political party, the Liberal Democrats, and entered parliament, largely to condemn the misdeeds, real or alleged, of Havel and his circle of 'love and truth'. When their political careers collapsed, they continued in much the same vein as critics and writers. As for Havel, he carried away from the episode a lasting distaste for any form of politics by committee and the backroom games that are the staple of parliament corridors, Party secretariats and . . . editorial boards. On the other hand, he may have never sufficiently realized that so much of politics consists of demolishing, often inadvertently, other little boys' mud pies, and of the retaliations that follow.

Havel himself acknowledged that the *Tvář* episode was instrumental in transforming him from a theatrical 'working stiff'[8] into a political activist. By spending a considerable amount of time arguing and debating

---

4   *Disturbing the Peace*, 87.
5   Ibid. 86–7.
6   Ibid. 87.
7   See e.g. Conversation with Petr Pithart, 28 August 2012.
8   *Disturbing the Peace*, 77.

with Communist apparatchiks, officials of the Writers' Union and fellow writers on both sides of a particular issue, he was honing not only his writing, something he was naturally good at, but also elements of political tactics and strategy. Early on he recognized as self-delusionary the politics of incremental concessions, based on the principle of sacrificing lesser values and less important people in the name of a larger 'good', calling it the politics of 'self-destruction'. Although his artistic sensitivities and instinctive inclusiveness militated almost from the beginning against the somewhat sectarian tendencies of the editors of *Tvář*, and although he was repeatedly warned, pressured and cajoled to give up on them in exchange for the preservation of the magazine, he knew that it would be the surest way to condemn the whole enterprise to extinction.

The other thing that distinguished him and *Tvář* from their ever louder reformist, or (as they preferred to be called) 'anti-dogmatic', colleagues, who were changing from the early cohorts and pillars of the Stalinist era into vocal critics of the illiberal behaviour of the system, was a somewhat paradoxical unwillingness to engage in head-on confrontation over the character of the society and the true nature of its governing ideology. In part, they knew they could not prevail in such a confrontation and, indeed, it would only make it easier for the powers-that-be to bring down their wrath upon them. But equally importantly, they were not truly interested in the debate. Unlike their reformist colleagues, they had no allegiance, no loyalty and no stake in trying to reform Marxist socialism, being convinced that it was a large part of the problem, not the answer. To say this aloud constituted a crime of 'subverting the socialist system', punishable by long prison sentences. And so they developed 'skirmish' tactics, fighting – and sometimes winning – small battles for small victories, such as the admission of a hitherto proscribed author to the Writers' Union, or winning a larger quota of printing paper,[9] or defending an issue of a magazine against censors. It was, for Havel, 'a private school of politics'.[10]

Once he made the first step, it was hard for him not to become further involved. He was originally invited to join the editorial board of *Tvář* on the explicit condition that he would become a member of the Writers' Union,

---

9 Printing paper, together with printing in general, was considered a strategic asset by the regime, and allocated in quotas for a particular purpose.
10 *Disturbing the Peace*, 77.

since his chances as a successful playwright were considered better than those of his lesser-known colleagues. Once in the Union, he was struck by the schizophrenic behaviour of many of the members, who were openly disparaging and neglectful of the positions of influence they had strived so keenly to attain. Havel, on the other hand, 'stuck my nose into everything. I came to meetings prepared, I discussed every aspect of every question, I was always criticizing abuses and making proposals.'[11] He discovered that this led to an even larger agenda and new tasks for him. As the non-communist elements of the society resurfaced in public, he became the chairman of the 'Young Authors' Caucus, a slightly wild institution,'[12] and later also of the 'Circle of Independent Writers'.

The episode with *Tvář*, together with his activities as a *fonctionnaire*, earned Havel more prestige and respect in intellectual circles, especially among the younger generation, but it also alerted the powers-that-be and caught the attention of the hidden power behind and within the state, the feared State Security (StB), fashioned, as all such predecessors of the *Mukhabarat* system, after the Soviet KGB. An anti-government leaflet sent to the theatre, likely intended as a provocation (and reported by Havel as such to the authorities), led to a Kafkaesque visit by a Captain Odvárka and a fellow secret policeman to Havel's apartment, and the subsequent listing of Havel as a 'candidate of secret collaboration'; this was a category in the StB files, which produced both future 'secret collaborators' and 'enemies of the state', depending on how the person in question was willing or able to withstand further pressure, and sometimes, at different times, it produced both in one person. The two policemen did not gather much useful information from their conversation with Havel that day, but they were neither the first nor the last to be impressed by his extraordinary politeness and courtesy. Even so, they should have known better than to take Havel's parting remark about the meeting being an 'inspiration for my future literary activities'[13] as a promising sign. This was Good Soldier Havel at work again.

---

11 Ibid. 89.
12 Ibid. 91.
13 TOMIS III, Security Services Archive, Prague, No. 597862, 23.

The Memorandum

Gross *The circumstance I've allowed myself to point out is simply a fact.*
Ballas *So what? Are we to kowtow to facts?*

– The Memorandum[1]

NOTHING SUCCEEDS LIKE SUCCESS. Suddenly, Havel was a recognized and celebrated author, whose work was applauded unanimously and, somewhat unusually, in both the domestic and Western media and performed not just on Czech and Slovak stages outside the Balustrade, but eventually in dozens of theatres in Germany, Austria, Hungary, Poland, Yugoslavia, Sweden, France, Britain and other countries. There were all kinds of offers and possibilities, but his attention immediately turned to his first love, the cinema. In February 1964, with his old schoolmates from Poděbrady, Miloš Forman and Ivan Passer, and another screenwriter Ivan Papoušek, they sold to the Barrandov studios a synopsis for a film called 'The Reconstruction'.[2] Havel's portion of the fee was 500 crowns – about twenty dollars at the time. In the same month, but with a different group of collaborators, Havel sold a synopsis for a film, possibly animated, called 'The Visit'.[3] Havel and Forman developed the idea of 'The Reconstruction'

---

1 In *Selected Plays, 1963–1983*, 95. For some reason, the second line of the dialogue, p. 153 in *Works 2*, is missing from the English translation.
2 An agreement between Barrandov Film Studios and Václav Havel, 3 February 1964, VHL ID17759.
3 An agreement between Barrandov Film Studios and Václav Havel, 14 February 1964, VHL ID17757.

into a treatment[4] for which they were paid 8,000 crowns each, nice money by the standards of the day. Even before the first night of *The Garden Party*, Havel sold the synopsis for an eponymous film to Barrandov.[5] In May 1964, he signed a contract for a literary treatment[6] and, in June,[7] for an already completed screenplay.[8]

The film has never been made – fortunately, Havel said. His literary and theatrical enterprise was still very much a cottage industry, dependent in part on the collaboration and talents of a closely knit group of friends.[9]

In *The Memorandum* (1965), Havel's second play at the Balustrade, but in fact his first 'serious' play, he returned to the idea of a comedy about an artificial language, invented to make communication between people easier, but instead making it more complicated. Havel wrote a draft of the play while still at ABC, but put the idea aside when Vyskočil thought it too risky, and he only started working on it again after the huge success of *The Garden Party*. Having in Jan Grossman a friend, a collaborator, a critic and this time also a director all in one person again played an important role. Like *The Garden Party*, *The Memorandum* takes place in a bureaucratic institution where the managing director, Gross, suddenly comes across office memoranda written in a language completely incomprehensible to him. Havel dedicated the play to the ensemble, and named some of the characters after its actors, including Grossman's partner Marie Málková; it is thus unlikely that the name for the main character was chosen by accident. As in *The Garden Party*, the language experiment, initiated from somewhere 'above', becomes the device for an intrigue by Gross's deputy and his cohorts. Having failed to see the danger in time, and defenceless against memoranda he can neither understand nor have translated without a proper authorization, which ultimately requires the knowledge of Ptydepe ('The only way to know what is in one's memo is to know it already'),[10] Gross is deposed by his deputy and his circle of

4 An agreement between Barrandov Film Studios and Václav Havel, 18 March 1964, VHL ID17756.
5 An agreement between Barrandov Film Studios and Václav Havel, 25 November 1963, VHL ID17760.
6 An agreement between Barrandov Film Studios and Václav Havel, 4 May 1964, VHL ID17755.
7 An agreement between Barrandov Film Studios and Václav Havel, 1 June 1964, VHL ID17753.
8 *Zahradní slavnost*. Screenplay, VHL ID16222.
9 Letter to Jiří Kolář, 29 November 1964, Museum of Czech Literature, VHL ID13795.
10 *The Memorandum*, in *Selected Plays, 1963–83*, 94.

advocates of artificial communication. Predictably enough, the experiment ends up badly: few people are able to learn the new language, and to make matters worse, Ptydepe itself becomes contaminated by poisonous elements of natural language. Gross is vindicated, rehabilitated and reinstated, only to find that he is now to preside over the introduction of another new artificial language – *chorukor* – built upon opposite assumptions but with the same goal, namely, to eradicate the messiness, ambiguity and the stain of humanity in the natural language.

There were similarities with *The Garden Party*. This time Havel and Grossman gave a public reading of the play in the Municipal Library to test the resolve of the censors ahead of the premiere on 26 July 1965. Both the reading and the premiere led to standing ovations. Again, the establishment media sang praises of the now internationally renowned author, even if on this occasion *Rudé právo* waited with its endorsement for more than two months.[11] Most of the critics read the play as a satire of the bureaucratic system, comparable to its predecessor. That would make it one of a number, perhaps one of exceptional quality, but still the kind of satire that by the mid-sixties was being tolerated and even encouraged as part of a necessary social hygiene. Few were able or willing to acknowledge the significant differences between the two plays and the radical intent of the author, and yet, some did. 'The mechanism of cowardice, power and indifference – all this is far from a mere product of the absurdist fantasy of the playwright, absurd as it undeniably is.'[12]

The Memorandum has a darker, a more subversive, subtext than *The Garden Party*. Manager Gross is a different kind of character to the opportunist Hugo. He is the 'decent', 'well-meaning' fellow who, whether because of courage or carelessness, sticks his neck out and gets punished for it, but who in the end 'confesses' and adapts enough to preserve his job and – as he likes to think – his ability to prevent things from getting even worse. By staying 'within' the system, and rejecting Marie's offer to 'get a job in theatre', he becomes an accessory to the evil he himself had been the first to identify and warn against.

In *The Memorandum*, Havel for the first time posed the question of a passive participation in evil that he would return to again and again in

---

11 Jaroslav Opavský, 'A Memorandum in the Ptydepe language', *Rudé právo*, 29 September 1965.
12 Jindřich Černý, *Lidová demokracie*, 1965.

the decades to come. In doing so, he shattered the moral complacency of many of his contemporaries, who were content to engage in criticism and reformist rhetoric only within carefully observed limits. In 1965, a time of seemingly ever-greater tolerance, liberalization and permissiveness, the stark warning of the play seemed to be addressed largely to the past and to target the willing victims of Communist purges, reform campaigns and reforms of reforms. Neither Havel nor his audience could have known that it would become just as relevant in the near future.

The problem of moral ambiguity is clearly reflected in the way the lines of positive and negative characters are mutually interchangeable. The same arguments used 'in earnest' by Gross will be used with the utmost cynicism by his nemesis Ballas. The audience does not know, nor is it perhaps supposed to know, whether a line of the dialogue is meant seriously or as travesty. Again, this device will be used by Havel repeatedly in future plays, and will be contemplated in his essays, with the clear implication: Words do not mean anything in and of themselves. Not even opinions that words stand for, heartfelt and genuine as they may be, mean much without the corresponding willingness to act on them. In the end there is not much difference between a cynical operator and a well-meaning weakling. In fact, it could be preferable to deal with the operator: with him one runs no risk of disappointment. Gross, who at critical moments indulges in bouts of self-pity, is reminded of this by the coldly nihilistic Ballas:

> GROSS Why can't I be a little boy again? I'd do everything differently
>   from the beginning.
> BALLAS You might begin differently, but you'd end up exactly the
>   same – so relax![13]

It is clear from this play, and many of his other texts during this period, that Havel was influenced by existentialist philosophy and its concepts of inauthenticity, alienation, the absurd, social isolation and depersonalization. Still, while the endpoint seems similar to that found in the works of Camus or Beckett, the trajectory by which this point is reached is quite different. Whereas existentialist heroes lose their bearings through the loss

---

13 *The Memorandum*, in *Selected Plays, 1963–83*, 123.

of a metaphysical horizon, or due to the intrinsic absurdity of the human condition, in Havel's world it is the society, or rather the totalitarian control of the society, that drives them to isolation, and makes them fear, suspect and avoid others. This dual perspective also points at potentially different outcomes of the existential situation. Whereas, for Beckett and others, existential loneliness is an immutable objective fact that can be transcended only by acceptance, in Havel's works it is a consequence of the desocializing properties of the governing system. Thus it is the work of humans and, as such, can conceivably be overcome. Even Ptydepe is ultimately contaminated and destroyed by the unyielding presence of the human stain. Although in the play it seems to be the system that prevails, there are signals in it that point at a more optimistic outcome:

> BALLAS What about the results [with the use of Ptydepe] in other organizations?
>
> SAVANT[14] They are all right I suppose. Except wherever Ptydepe has started to be used more widely, it has automatically begun to assume some of the characteristics of a natural language: various emotional overtones, imprecisions,[15] ambiguities. Correct, Nellie?
>
> HELENA Correct. And you know what? They say that the more one uses Ptydepe, the more it gets soiled by these characteristics.[16]

The underlying message of *The Memorandum* reflects both the spirit of the times and Havel's personal politics. On the one hand, the system has been shown to be not only corrupt in its effects but also intrinsically corrupting in its very nature as well. The problem was not with its individual actions or with its actions to correct its previous actions or with its further corrections of its previous corrections, but with the system as such. Not only did it not work; it could not work. In the mid-sixties, this was still a minority conclusion; even within this minority it was more surmised than explicitly formulated.

---

14 Why the translator, Vera Blackwell, chose loaded names like SAVANT and LEAR for the featureless Czech KUNZ and PERINA is a mystery.

15 The published English text has 'impressions' instead of 'imprecisions', obviously a typographic error.

16 Ibid. 107–8.

On the other hand, if so many deformations, absurdities and abominations stemmed directly from the nature of the system rather than from its individual actions, all of them could be challenged simultaneously. Rather than waste time by hopelessly tinkering with the system in the effort of making it livable and sustainable, it was necessary to replace it as a whole.

THE GATHERING STORM

UNTIL 1967, THE CZECH 'UR-PERESTROIKA' seemed to be progressing smoothly. Room for artistic and individual self-expression expanded in an unprecedented, if haphazard way. Small theatres, clubs and cafés were thriving. The Sexual Revolution may have come to Prague a year or two later than with '*Lady Chatterley's Lover* and the Beatles' first LP', but come it did. Dozens of rock groups with names like The Primitives or The Lost Cause sprang up. The Beat poets Lawrence Ferlinghetti, Allen Ginsberg, Jack Kerouac and Gregory Corso were published, analysed and discussed in books and magazines; Harold Pinter, Samuel Beckett, Edward Albee, Eugène Ionesco and Václav Havel dominated the stage.

Even the economy started showings signs of life. In January 1965, the Central Committee of the Communist Party tasked an academic economist named Ota Šik with drafting a programme of reforms to halt the stagnation of the command economy system, which in a mere twenty years had made a virtual basket case out of one of the ten largest world economies before World War II. As with all reforms in the sixties, this was no blank cheque. The ideological bases of the system, namely, the leading role of the Communist Party and the collective ownership of the economy, were not to be tampered with. The reformists were thus left to tinkering at the margins. Šik and his team came up with a loosening of the planning system to alleviate its inevitable price distortions and to allocate resources more effectively. It was by no means a transition to a market economy, but merely a borrowing of some market indicators to pre-empt larger problems. Similarly, the recommendation of the reformists to allow for some incentives in rewarding workers was not a move towards an open labour market. Šik's recommendations never really had the time to be tested in practice, but became nonetheless one of the items in the long list of heresies that the Prague Spring would be charged with by its domestic and foreign detractors.

Again, it was the debates of poets and novelists rather than politicians and economists that brought matters to a head. The 4th Congress of the Union of the Czechoslovak Writers heard things that could have earned a man on the street ten years in a uranium mine were it not for the fact that they were voiced by some of the country's most prominent writers and Party members. Milan Kundera spoke about the culture and tradition of the country being hijacked away from Europe by a foreign and intolerant force. Pavel Kohout read aloud a letter to the Congress of the Union of Writers of the Soviet Union written by Alexander Solzhenitsyn, which the Czechoslovak Union's leadership tried to keep secret from the membership. Most memorably, Ludvík Vaculík, a Party member with unassailable proletarian credentials, delivered a fiery, defiant speech raising high the flag of rebellion, and quoted some rarely remembered passages in the Czechoslovak constitution to claim civil rights, including full freedom of expression, assembly and association for every citizen. Even when Jiří Hendrych, the secretary of the Central Committee in charge of ideology, angrily left the Congress with the words 'You have gambled away everything,'[1] the invectives continued. Some of them were not limited to the borders of Czechoslovakia. Two weeks before, in the wake of the defeat of the Arab countries by Israel in the Six Day War, Czechoslovakia, along with the Soviet Union and other Communist countries, broke off diplomatic relations with the Jewish state. Several writers, Jews and non-Jews alike, protested this move from the tribune of the Congress.

The regime tried to hit back against what it considered a rebellion by confiscating the Union's journal, *Literární noviny*, and expelling the leading rebels from the Party. In response, many of the best-known Czech and Slovak writers publicly repudiated their allegiance to the ruling power.

Surprisingly in the eyes of some, Václav Havel, for a long time one

---

1 Kaplan (1997).

of the most rebellious of the lot, played a relatively minor role in the proceedings, and avoided making a grand statement. In his remarks to the Congress, he stayed true to the tactics of fighting small, winnable but nonetheless important battles. He called for *Tvář* to be reinstated, and for re-admission to the Union of the black sheep among writers – his non-Communist colleagues and friends – but that was as far as he went.

In fact, Havel, apparently taken aback by the radicalism of some of the previous speeches, sounded an almost disapproving, warning note:

> If it is a part of the writer's profession that he more than anyone else questions and casts doubt, again and again, upon the world, it is only logical that it is he who must, again and again – more laboriously than anyone else – win the confidence of this world. And if this world measures us by harsher standards than many others – which is an honour of sorts – we will not placate it or confuse it by citing a psychosis or a mood – in the end it will always ask each one of us with cold cruelty, what did we say and what we then did, whether what we did was true to what we said, or whether we had the right to say something we would not do. The question is simply whether we are all capable to ultimately bear the responsibility for our words, whether we are really and unreservedly able to vouch for ourselves, guarantee our proclamations by our acts and their continuity, and never be – led by the best of intentions as it may be – trapped at a certain moment by ourselves, whether because of our vanity or because of our fear. This is not a call for calculation but for *authenticity*.[2]

The concept of authentic responsibility, or, in other words, of living in truth, far from being a product of the later undeniable influence of Jan Patočka or of the dissident years, is there in its entirety, having been rehearsed around the table in Slavia and honed on the treacherous paths of institutional politics of literature.

The punishment of leading writers met with controversy and disapproval even among the members of the Communist elite. More

---

2   Address to the 4th Congress, in *The 4th Congress of the Union of Czechoslovak Writers*, (Prague: Československý spisovatel, 1968); italics author's.

importantly, the public show of disobedience at the Congress encouraged others to do the same. The October 1967 meeting of the Party's Central Committee witnessed the breach of another inviolable taboo – open criticism of the Top Brother, the leader of the Party and president of the state, a mediocrity named Antonín Novotný. Suddenly, everything was open to criticism – his mismanagement of the economy, his heavy-handed treatment of the Slovak branch of the Party and the concentration of power in the hands of one man.

At the December meeting of the Central Committee, the rebellion broke out in full, and Novotný was faced with calls for his resignation. He managed to postpone the inevitable by famously adjourning the meeting on 23 December with the argument that 'the lady comrades will need to go Christmas shopping', but on 5 January 1968 he was replaced as General Secretary of the Party by a little-known but well-liked lifelong apparatchik and secretary of the Slovak Party branch, Alexander Dubček. The 1968 Prague Spring was about to begin.

The Prague Spring and its abrupt ending has become one of the iconic stories of twentieth-century history, and for good reason: both the dynamics of the reform movement and the manner of its suppression constituted a fatal blow to Marxist ideology. Although Stalinism, the trials, the suppressions of uprisings in Berlin and in Budapest, had led many of the original believers to re-examine and renounce their faith, to be a Marxist–Leninist in the early sixties was still something not quite disreputable, if not exactly respectable. After 1968, it became a synonym for opportunism, thick-headedness or worse.

The momentous significance of the event was somewhat dispro-portionate to the extent of real change on the ground during the following seven months. Institutionally, the reforms were quite modest, with the notable exception of the abolishment of censorship at the end of June, which was not much more than a legal endorsement of the status quo, already in effect for several months. Other measures were retroactive, moral gestures, such as the legal rehabilitation of the victims of Communist terror in the years after 1948. All the rest was just talk.

Oh, but what talk it was! For the first time in twenty years, and for the first time ever for those born in the Communist period, everything, just everything was up for debate, questioning and criticism, be it private ownership, the leading role of the Party, freedom of religion, free travel, Soviet Gulags, flower power or gender equality. All this was debated, formally and informally, at hundreds of organized and improvised meetings, in lecture halls, meeting rooms, cafés and bars, in bed and in the street. New associations and clubs were springing up right and left, with or without official sanction. *Literární noviny*, reinstated as *Literární listy*, was becoming more radical by the day, but still seemed quite conservative in comparison with new sheets like *The Reporter* or *The Student*.

This discrepancy between formal and informal processes, and between nominal and real change, has led to two alternative readings of the history of the Prague Spring. On the one hand, there was the largely mythological story of 'socialism with a human face'; a movement aimed at the reinvention of the socialist ideal, led by the enlightened reformists, overwhelmingly supported by the population and violently suppressed by the Soviet-led invasion in August under the pretext of an impending 'counter-revolution'. On the other hand, there is the widely documented chain of events on the ground, which strongly suggests that, far from leading the movement, the reformists had lost control early in the process, and were being forced to adapt to ever-new demands by the emboldened population. In this reading, paradoxically, the Soviets were right to suspect a reversal, albeit a non-violent one, and of course criminally wrong to violate the sovereignty of a country to prevent it.

This does not necessarily mean that the two readings are incompatible in every aspect. The sincerity and human appeal of Alexander Dubček had won him genuine popularity. The relaxation of controls on the freedom of expression, assembly and association met with an almost universal support. The partial opening of the economy and of the market was warmly welcomed by a population starved for a broader range of consumer goods. The Soviet intervention in August gave rise to a massive and unified front of support for Dubček and his leadership.

None of this, however, can be taken to suggest that the goals of the Communist leadership and of the population at large were identical or even close. True, most people welcomed the new liberties, but fully expected to make use of them above and beyond the limits of Communist imagination. Even in the first few months of the process, the country saw the re-emergence of traditional social and political movements, such as the Boy and Girl Scouts, the national sports and gymnastics movement

Sokol and the until then underground Social Democrats. It also saw the emergence of new organizations like K-231 (a club of former political prisoners), KAN (a club of non-Communist activists) and Circle of Independent Writers, which first met in Havel's apartment and elected him as its president on 6 June.

But should anyone accustomed to his activism expect to see Havel play a prominent role in these events, he would be disappointed. Havel took a back seat to more outspoken reformist intellectuals. He attended the very first in a series of town meetings at which ever more radical ideas were voiced, but he was saddened by 'the spectacle of people who were bound by the ruling ideology clarifying for themselves, after twenty years of rule, things that had been clear to everyone else through those twenty years', and he was alienated by the 'vaudevillian' rhetoric with which they tried to outdo each other.[3] From this feeling of 'exaggerated sobriety' he moved to the other extreme at a reception on 11 July, which Prime Minister Černík hosted as an opportunity for leading writers to meet leading reformers, Havel's single close encounter with the protagonists of the Prague Spring. His own account of the meeting may not be entirely reliable, since, to overcome his shyness, he fortified himself with several glasses of brandy and proceeded to lecture Dubček about the reform process, 'making a fool out of myself'.[4] He was not persuaded by Dubček's analysis of the situation, but he was impressed by his willingness to listen to a half-drunk playwright. He maintained this ambivalent attitude ever after; although he never admired Dubček as a politician, he was sincerely fond of him as a person.

His only significant contribution to the public debate raging all around him was a measured, almost detached essay, 'On the Question of Opposition',[5] a remarkable piece of writing, which managed to sound rather conservative while espousing an idea beyond the imagination of even the most radical reformists. The old Zenonian paradox about the barber who shaves all the men in the village who do not shave themselves came in for renewed re-examination, as journalists and thinkers emboldened by the sudden absence of censorship posed the obvious dilemma as to

---

3 *Disturbing the Peace*, 97.
4 The version recounted by Josef Škvorecký in *The Miracle Game*, 149–56, and adopted by Keane (1999), 197, is a legitimate novelist's licence, but considerably less probable. It was not in Havel's character to taunt people, even when drunk.
5 *Literární listy*, 4 April 1968.

whether democratic socialism and free debate were compatible with a one-party political system. In his piece, Havel methodically examines the possibility of letting public opinion play the role of the opposition to the Communist monopoly on power, or using the puppet rumps of sometime democratic political parties within the National Front system dominated by the Communists to nurture an authentic political opposition. He comes to the unassailable conclusion that, without complete independence from the ruling party, any opposition would be inherently unstable and easy to undermine; indeed, total independence necessitates the existence of another political party capable of playing the role of the institutional opposition. Implicit in his analysis was another inescapable conclusion, namely, that any party capable of playing the role of a genuine opposition to the ruling party was also capable of replacing the ruling party and becoming the government itself. The implication did not go unnoticed in the Kremlin, which later used it as a prime piece of evidence to demonstrate the presence of a 'counter-revolution' in Czechoslovakia.[6] Like any piece of original thinking, the article found its critics, then and later. It is slightly more unusual that their number includes Havel himself. More than a decade later, he expressed a series of reservations about the piece, his scepticism about the very principle of mass membership political parties and, above all, his conviction that 'the idea of forming a new political party ought to be proposed by someone who is determined to form such a party – and I was not that person'.[7]

He remembered presenting his 'sober and reflective position' on several occasions in large auditoriums, and making a 'pitiful showing'.[8] He did sign several of the petitions and open letters, which appeared almost every day. But mostly he concentrated on smaller, practical projects, the main one of which was the founding of the Circle of Independent Writers as an openly oppositionist platform within the Writers' Union.

He still saw his role primarily as that of a writer, artist and what would today be called a 'public intellectual'. In the midst of the Prague Spring, his third full-length play, *The Increased Difficulty of Concentration*,[9] dedicated to his philosophical guru Josef Šafařík, opened at the Balustrade. The reception

---

6 Havel's article was first attacked in the *Literaturnaya Gazeta* in May 1968.
7 *Disturbing the Peace*, 98–9.
8 Ibid. 97–8.
9 With knowledge of the syntax and music of the Czech language, it is hard not to think of the title as one, perhaps subconscious, inspiration for Kundera's later *The Unbearable Lightness of Being*.

was once again favourable, yet, unlike its two predecessors, the play did not become a major public event.

In part, the diminished impact was Havel's own doing. The play lacks the clarity of purpose of *The Garden Party* and *The Memorandum*. The story of a philandering social scientist, Huml, and of his encounter with a computerized analytical robot called *puzuk*[10] is partly a farce about a man trying to juggle the demands and expectations of his wife, his mistress and his other potential sexual partners, and partly a critique of the scientific attempts to understand and analyse objectively the myriad, often conflicting and inconsistent motives and impulses that determine human behaviour. It is something of Havel's personal reflection on his newfound fame, the multiple demands on his time and attention, as well as the sexual opportunities it offered and the moral quandaries this entailed.

The other reason for the subdued response was the less than fortuitous timing of the play. Whatever it was about, it did not seem to be even remotely relevant to, or nearly as exciting as, the momentous events unfolding outside the theatre. The problem of the day was how to deal with Communism, freedom and democracy, not how to deal with one's wife and mistress.

Yet for Havel himself, the play may have been just as important as its two predecessors, and perhaps even more so. The most personal of the three, it constitutes a continuation of an inner dialogue between Havel the bohemian artist and Havel the philosophizing moralist, and it reflects the tensions growing between the two. In the concluding monologue of the play Huml says:

> The key to a real knowledge of the human individual does not
> lie in some greater or lesser understanding of the complexity of
> man as an object of scientific knowledge. The only key lies in
> man's complexity as a subject of human togetherness, because
> the limitlessness of our own human nature is so far the only
> thing approaching – however imperfectly – the limitlessness
> of others . . . By any other means we may perhaps be able more
> or less to explain man but we shall never understand him – not
> even a little – and therefore we shall never arrive at a basic

---

10 One does not have to be a psychoanalyst to wonder why the name of the machine was the same as the family nickname for Havel's brother Ivan.

knowledge of him. Hence, the fundamental key to man does not lie in his brain, but in his heart.[11]

The otherwise laudatory *New York Times* reviewer of the Lincoln Repertory production misread the last sentence as a 'platitudinous conclusion that softens much of the irony that has gone before'.[12] It is, however, not a conciliatory credo, but a parody, an irony compounded. 'Some things are most easily talked about by those who in reality abide the least by them.'[13]

The play utilizes a method Havel the playwright would return to repeatedly. Whereas in *Letters to Olga* and other essays he would formulate his moral and philosophical views and do so methodically, painstakingly and with utter seriousness, sometimes amounting to pedantry, in his plays he uses the very same views for irony and laughs, sometimes with the same words in the mouths of weak, flawed and fallible characters. And one suspects it is not only to illustrate the chasm between how his characters would like to behave and how they really act. The point of reference is clearly the author himself, as if he were trying his convictions for size in quasi-real-life situations, or even more personally, as if he were trying to reconcile his public persona with his inner self. The results of this experiment, if experiment it was, were not encouraging. Havel's characters, generally cut-outs rather than real people, are all moral failures, each and every one of them, and, in being so, they indicate something of the author's own view of himself.

By most accounts of his contemporaries, Havel was at this time behaving like many talented and successful artists at the top of their form, be they musicians, actors or playwrights. He slept long, did some writing during the day, and in the evening he enjoyed nightlife and the thrills that it offered. He still spent a lot of time at the Balustrade and frequented Behind the Gate and the Actors' Studio theatres, centres of competition featuring as their leading stars Havel's close friends Jan Tříska and Pavel Landovský, respectively. By his own account, he actively shunned politics, direct involvement in which was incommensurate with the writer's

---

11 *The Increased Difficulty of Concentration*, in *Selected Plays 1963–1983*, 179–80.
12 Mel Gussow, 'Theater: Ironic Computer', *The New York Times*, 5 December 1969.
13 Letter to Josef Šafařík, 1 February 1968, VHL ID13801.

primary responsibility of 'serving the truth'.[14] His late-night prowls in the company of Landovský, much detested by Olga, invariably started with an after-performance drink in the Mozart wine bar or in one of the joints close to the theatre, and sometimes progressed to establishments of even more dubious repute. He sought out the company of similarly talented contemporaries with similar lifestyles, apart from Landovský and Tříska, which included film directors Miloš Forman, Jan Němec and Pavel Juráček. In addition to many fascinating discussions of art and politics and contemporary issues, there was quite a lot of alcohol. And there were women.

Havel must have realized that not living by the high moral standards that he himself espoused in public life smacked of hypocrisy, but he was no run-of-the-mill hypocrite. He seems to have believed that the charge of hypocrisy would lose its sting if he were the first to acknowledge his moral failures. This may have been at the root of his lifelong habit of disclosing his own infidelities to his wife Olga, and even of seeking her understanding and advice, just as Huml does in the *Difficulty*. He must have reached the conclusion that moral perfection was beyond his capabilities, and that the next best thing was to present himself truthfully, warts and all. *The Increased Difficulty of Concentration*, to which we find no reference in the play itself, is at some level also a description of Havel's inner state of mind and his struggle with celebrity. It might also account, at least partially, for the somewhat detached attitude he took to the momentous events unfolding around him. At a time when most people were preoccupied with the human face of socialism, he was grappling with his own inner demons.

Perhaps to atone for this, he produced two shorter pieces at this time, one for the radio and one for television. The radio piece, a hybrid between Kafka and a gothic horror, is called *The Guardian Angel*,[15] the TV one-acter, *The Butterfly on the Antenna*.[16] In the former, a perfectly friendly stranger insinuates himself into playwright Vavák's home, asks innocuous questions, comments on Vavák's lifestyle and ultimately, citing a regrettable deviation from norm, cuts off Vavák's ears. An omnipresent and omnipotent bureaucracy, based on the enforcement of complex, detailed and seemingly

---

14 Interview with Jan Procházka, *Divadelní noviny*, 14 February 1968.
15 *Works 2*, 197–218.
16 Ibid. 219–56.

rational rules to govern the lives of its subjects, inevitably results in outbursts of irrational, arbitrary and absurd violence.

The TV play *The Butterfly on the Antenna*, which was never aired during the brief opening of the Prague Spring, is somewhat less abstract, and attests to Havel's bleaker reading of the events that were creating so much euphoria at home and abroad. A quintessential Czech family, symbolized by the names of its main characters, Jeník and Mařenka (the heroes both of the classical fairy tale about two eponymous children and the evil witch in a gingerbread cottage, and of Bedřich Smetana's 'national' opera *The Bartered Bride*), sit at home having a pointless conversation, while water, heard dripping behind the scene throughout the play, is rising all around them until the grandmother, the only remotely sane character in the piece, turns off the tap. This variation on *An Evening With The Family* speaks of the frustration and concerns of the author about the floods of inconsequential verbiage in the heady months of inebriation by freedom, while dark clouds were gathering over the country. *The Butterfly* is a play about dancing on the Titanic.

The playwright's detachment, conflicting priorities and increased difficulty of concentration continued well into the late spring and summer of 1968. Just as events took a dramatic turn in May and June, with the veiled threats coming from Moscow intensifying and with the Warsaw Pact holding military manoeuvres on Czechoslovak territory, Havel took extended trips abroad, first to the USA to see *The Memorandum* produced in New York, and then, after a short stop in Prague, to Britain.

He could not have chosen a more interesting time. The year was rife with events, ideas, unrest and rebellion. In the United States, a heated presidential campaign between Richard Nixon and Hubert Humphrey was going on against the background of assassinations, anti-war protests, flower power and acid trips. In France, the students were manning barricades, many of them to promote an even more militant brand of Communism exemplified by the names of Mao Zedong and Che Guevara.

Havel's sense of drama and his anti-establishment instincts were certainly in tune with the anarchic energy of the protest movement. The rejection of middle-class values that was underlying the upheavals both in the United States and in France resonated with his own misgivings about his privileged origins, and reinforced his suspicions that there were things wrong not just with the Communist experiment but also with the Western society and civilization that first gave rise to it.

Yet to present him somehow, as some people have, as a fellow traveller of the anti-capitalist protests in the West, and to use this as proof of his lifelong leftist orientation, is to miss the point. Havel surely empathized with the enormous release of youthful energy that 1968 represented, he may have admired the 'inner ethos – powerful but in no way fanatical' of the anti-war demonstrations,[17] and he carried away a permanent fascination with rock 'n' roll music and rock musicians. There is, however, no evidence that he advocated, then or later, attaining freedom through violence, hallucinatory visions or free sex that drove so many young Americans and Europeans to extremes. He was as supportive of their right to demonstrate and protest as he was repelled by their mindless violence, wanton destruction and fuddled brains. He would also be astonished that people could dream of introducing voluntarily the same kind of doctrinaire, tyrannical system he and his countrymen were busy trying to dismantle at that very moment.

In fact, Havel was a poor candidate for a revolutionary, which may have had some bearing on the velvet character of the one revolution in which he came to be directly and famously involved. The thing he had in common with revolutionaries was the inner drive that gives one the energy to do extraordinary things. At the same time, however, his strong sense of order and harmony was totally incompatible with the revolutionary penchant for wreaking havoc, his very high ceiling of tolerance made him an improbable recruit for a blood-thirsty phalanx, and his remarkable politeness and courtesy disqualified him from showing the vengeful face of the revolution to its enemies. 'I am too polite to be a good dissident,' he would admit years later.[18] His equally strong sense of introspection and self-reflection made him always doubt himself and his own motives, and safely prevented him from attaining the steeliness needed to conduct a violent revolution. Underneath it all, there was an even deeper flaw for a revolutionary. Havel neither had nor would he ever develop a concept of the Enemy. His decades-long critique of the Communist regime always strove towards the form of a dialogue, in which he went out of his way to try to understand rather than to demonize the motives of the other side and, if at all possible, always to

17 *To The Castle and Back*, 7.
18 'A report on my participation at the Railwaymen Ball', in *Works 4*, 199.

extend to them the benefit of the doubt. This approach became somewhat controversial later, when he was confronted first as the leader of the Velvet Revolution, and later as president, with the asymmetrical nature of political relationships. The fact that he did not acknowledge enemies did not mean that he and the revolution did not have any. His stance led to accusations that he was soft on the exponents of the previous regime, or even that there was possibly some secret collusion between them. On the other hand, his lack of zeal for revolutionary justice certainly helped Czechs and Slovaks to avoid bloodshed, public humiliations and bizarre kangaroo courts, such as the one that condemned the Ceauşescus to die in front of a firing squad in Romania. It also enabled him to focus on the problems of the present and the future, while many of his long-obedient countrymen clamoured for revenge to assuage their previous humiliations.

The six-week-long trip to the USA in the spring of 1968 became well entrenched in both the young writer's memory and that of the people he met along the way. There is, however, not quite surprisingly – given the event overload of that particular year – a degree of disagreement about the exact sequencing and details, largely unimportant in and of themselves, but lending themselves to misleading grand hypotheses about Havel's ideological roots and leanings.

Much of the responsibility for the confusion rests with John Keane and his *Tragedy in Six Acts*. His five-page-long reconstruction of the trip, brimming with details, is largely based on an interview conducted with Pavel Tigrid in 1996. Tigrid was almost eighty by that time, and known for rather selective and at times creative memory. Neither was he a complete stranger to playing slightly malicious pranks on starry-eyed interlocutors, particularly if they were in the habit of signing their journalistic pieces as 'Erica Blair'. In the event, Keane places Havel with Olga in Paris on their way to the USA in the dramatic context of the beginning of the French general strike on 13 May, when Havel had already been in New York for three weeks.[19] The wonderful story about the barriers between the East and West at the Charles de Gaulle airport suddenly dissolving as the border guards and the custom officers joined the strike seems to be a case of *ben trovato*. As for Olga, she never left home at all, infuriating her husband

---

19 The first US preview of *The Memorandum* took place on 23 April 1968. The Broadway
   premiere of *Hair* that Havel recalls seeing in *To The Castle and Back*, 7, took place on 29 April.

with the sketchiness of her letters on the current events in Prague. As for Tigrid, Havel did meet with him in Paris on his way back from the USA to Prague, as related by Havel himself.[20] By then, of course, the Paris revolution was winding down. To make matters worse, Keane has Havel coming back to Prague 'in time for the address to the Fourth Czechoslovak Writers' Congress'.[21] Even with the best of wills, this was hardly possible. The Congress took place a year earlier. Keane, finally, puts Havel in the May Day parade on Wenceslas Square in Prague, both an unlikely date and an unlikely place for Havel to be on that occasion.[22]

There is hardly a question that the trip saw several long-delayed encounters with people who were important to Havel's life and thought. In New York, he stayed at 63 W 69th Street, in the home of George Voskovec, part of the pre-war iconic duo of comedians, whose other half, Jan Werich, helped launch Havel's career in the theatre. He reunited with his former schoolmate Miloš Forman, who was in the process of relocating from Czechoslovakia to America. He visited and recorded an interview, later lost, with Ferdinand Peroutka, the grand old man of Czech liberal journalism. He spoke to other exiled writers, such as the novelist Egon Hostovský, and he spent a lot of time with Joseph Papp, the founder of the Public Theater in New York, who had invited Havel to come over for the first night of *The Memorandum* as a part of the Shakespeare festival in the Florence Anspacher Theater on 425 Lafayette Street.

All these meetings were significant not just for the individual pleasure and intellectual nourishment Havel, who was still only thirty-one, derived from them, but also because they give a fair approximation of his intellectual and political mindset at the time. None of the friends he met and made could remotely be described as radical. Some, like Peroutka, had a distinctly jaundiced view of flower power and youth revolt.[23] They all exemplified the open-minded, critical and questioning tradition of liberal thought ultimately based on values such as rationality, social conscience and a shared moral code, somewhat at odds with the irrational, hedonistic and morally agnostic spirit of the times.

---

20 Video interview with Petr Jančárek, 17 August 2008, www.iHned.cz.
21 Keane (1999) 186.
22 Ibid. 194.
23 Video interview with Petr Jančárek, 17 August 2008, www.iHned.cz.

Equally important for the understanding of this crucial moment in the consciousness of a generation and in Havel's mental and moral universe are the meetings and encounters that apparently *did not* take place during the trip. The postcards he sent Josef Šafařík and Jindřich Chalupecký from New York were not from Fillmore East or The Factory, but rather from the Russian Tea Room and MOMA, respectively, not exactly the centres of a world revolution, then or now. For all Havel's later admiration for, and friendship with, Lou Reed, there seems to be no record of their having met, although Havel did bring back an album of the Velvet Underground[24] from the trip. Neither did Havel meet with Andy Warhol, a patron to the group, and, under his native name, Andrej Varchola, a first-generation American of Czechoslovak descent. His musical tastes at the time were somewhat simpler. He related keenly to the songs of Simon & Garfunkel, but seems to have been untouched by the phenomenon of Bob Dylan. In the generational split between the Beatles and the Rolling Stones fans, so unimportant today, he was a Beatles man. The song he played over and over to his friends that summer before the tanks rolled in was not the Velvet Underground's 'Waiting for My Man', but the Bee Gees' 'Massachusetts', an unlikely battle hymn for a global rebellion.

Like any young person living at that time, Havel would have had to be autistic not to have been influenced by the events unfolding around him. At the same time, he identified neither with the reform process of the Prague Spring back home, nor with the radical rejection of social norms that he witnessed in the West. He sympathized with the efforts to give socialism a human face, and to transcend the consumerist society through heightened awareness of human emotionality, but they were not his battles. His artistic sensitivity responded to the psychedelic kaleidoscope of music, costumes and ideas that defined 1968, but his gentle and orderly nature revolted against the chaos and the violence that accompanied it. Politically and philosophically, Havel was made *in* the sixties more than *by* the sixties. His principal themes of identity, truth and responsibility had already been formed.

Back home, things were approaching a climax. The bold changes of a couple of months before now looked like timid compromises. The 'Action

---

24 *The Velvet Underground & Nico*, 1967.

Platform', which the Communist Party published in April, was rapidly becoming obsolete. The process of reform was quickly becoming a process of transformation. On 27 June, *Literární listy* published a manifesto called '2000 Words', initiated by a group of academicians and social scientists, but penned by Ludvík Vaculík. While it was loyalist in supporting the intentions and the reform programme of the Party, it also called on the citizens to establish civic committees and initiatives to spearhead reform at the local level. Even more brazenly, it called for the public denunciation of the secret police spies, and for the support of the government's mandate given to it by the citizens 'with arms, if need be'.[25] The statement concluded with the prophetic, though at the time little noticed words: 'This spring has just ended and will never come back. We will know everything by winter'.[26] In the eyes of the apparatchiks in Prague and in the Kremlin, this was a call for counter-revolution.

From its own perspective, the Kremlin was right. The logic of the events demanded that either the process be suppressed and the monopoly of power of the Communist Party reaffirmed, or that the system be opened up and that it acquiesce to its own demise. Twenty years later this scenario played out in full force and with unambiguous results all over the Eastern bloc and in the Soviet Union itself. Twenty years earlier it accounted for Havel's reticence and for the detachment of a large part of the Czechoslovak population, for whom the whole reform process was either a parlour game played among the comrades for their own benefit or, at best, a prelude to the real thing.

The real thing never came, but the Soviet tanks did. Only at that moment did the nation unite and stand up as one man in defence of Alexander Dubček's leadership. In doing so, however, people were not standing up for the reform process or for 'socialism with a human face', as their leaders believed, in a justifiable act of self-delusion, but for the sovereign right of a nation to do as it pleased, even if it meant to carry the reform process to its logical conclusion.

In the historical moments that burnt themselves in the memories of a generation as a series of emblems, the emotional announcement of the invasion on the radio, the crowds surrounding the Soviet tanks and

---

25 *Literární listy*, No. 18/1968.
26 Ibid.

armoured carriers, and trying to argue with young, innocent-looking, uncomprehending soldiers in the turrets, the crackle of machine-gun fire, the flattened vehicles and the bloodied bodies, the pledges of loyalty, the acts of mad bravery and the teary admissions of defeat, Havel played a minor but typically courageous and responsible role. His part in the drama, however, started only after the tanks rolled in.

While his activist colleagues were discussing the upcoming autumn Congress of the Communist Party, which was supposed to institutionalize the reforms, while the threats from the Soviet Union were becoming less veiled, while the whole nation followed in a state of animated suspense the meetings between the Czechoslovak and the Soviet Party leadership held in a railway carriage at the border depot in Čierná nad Tisou,[27] and the subsequent summit of Warsaw Pact states in Bratislava, which seemingly helped to alleviate the tensions just as the invading armies were already being deployed at set off points, Havel was enjoying the summer. A year earlier he had bought a house at a hamlet called Hrádeček in northeastern Bohemia for himself and Olga, with 14,000 crowns (some 500 dollars) of his own royalties, and the help of his friend from the Balustrade, Andrej Krob, and now he was busy trying to turn it into a comfortable home, working in the large garden and entertaining scores of friends he had missed while travelling abroad. On the night of 20 August he was drinking wine with friends he was visiting in the north Bohemian town of Liberec in the company of Olga and Jan Tříska. And then the sky fell.

---

27 Apparently Brezhnev believed his own propaganda to the extent that he feared for his safety if he crossed the border into the lawless country. His Czechoslovak comrades had reciprocal concerns, based on sounder historical precedent.

Scoundrel Times

The Ogre does what ogres can,
Deeds quite impossible for Man,
But one prize is beyond his reach,
The Ogre cannot master Speech.
About a subjugated plain,
Among its desperate and slain,
The Ogre walks with hands on hips
While drivel gushes from his lips.
                    – W. H. Auden, 'August 1968'

THE TWENTY-FIRST OF AUGUST 1968 has twofold significance in modern Czech history. On the one hand, it marks the suppression and eventual defeat of the reformist efforts of the Prague Spring by one of the most massive overnight military invasions in European history, with twenty oppressive years of 'normalization' to follow. On the other hand, it represents the culmination of the popular resistance to the governing ideology to date, and the end of any pretensions to its legitimacy. Only when everything appeared to be lost did the people truly unite and let their genuine feelings be known. For the next week it did not matter whether one was a Communist reformer, a principled opponent of Communism or an aggrieved patriot. One recognizes when one is being raped, regardless of one's political persuasion.

It was this feeling that roused Havel from his state of summer idleness and catapulted him into a whirlwind of feverish public activity. It is symptomatic of Havel that he could feign being uninvolved and disinterested while the going was good, but his hypertrophied sense of responsibility immediately kicked in when a disaster struck.

By sheer accident, Havel and Tříska, whose shock on the morning of the invasion had been compounded by a hangover from the night before, constituted a powerful combination of a sharp pen and a familiar voice, ideal for the occasion. They volunteered for resistance service in the Liberec branch of the Czechoslovak radio and also contributed to television broadcasts. For the next week, the airwaves, impervious to attacks by tanks, represented the front line of defence in Liberec and throughout the country. Radio and TV studios were moved to unmarked locations, and the broadcasts used back-up frequencies to make interference more difficult. Whenever a studio or a broadcasting antenna was located and secured by the occupation forces, a new improvised operation sprang into action within hours. For days, the Soviets seemed to be completely baffled. They were prepared for pitched battles and terrorist attacks, but not for this kind of resistance.

Havel, who was later somewhat reluctant to share in the popular mythologizing of that week in August, admitted to being particularly impressed by the 'community of solidarity', as evident in the small and large acts of kindness, protection and creativity he witnessed.

In the first of his broadcasts from Liberec during the first hours of the invasion, Havel appealed to the outside world for help. Typically for him, and also quite realistically, he did not call for the intervention of NATO or of the American troops deployed a few hundred kilometres to the west, but summoned his colleagues and friends, writers and critics, Günter Grass, Hans Magnus Enzensberger, Helmut Heißenbüttel, Kenneth Tynan, Kingsley Amis, John Osborne, Arnold Wesker, Friedrich Dürrenmatt, Max Frisch, Jean-Paul Sartre, Louis Aragon, Michel Butor, Arthur Miller, Samuel Beckett, Eugène Ionesco and Yevgeny Yevtushenko to protest the abomination. It was a strange phalanx to mobilize in the face of an armoured military operation, but Havel had his reasons, citing the role played by writers and intellectuals during the Prague Spring. 'They were among the first who roused the nation to political activity. Undoubtedly, they will be also among the first to be persecuted and jailed by the occupiers.'[1] In this he was not mistaken. It is also true that most of the writers he appealed to did raise their voices to protest the invasion.

For once in his life Havel became the spokesman for the Communist Party. On 26 August, there appeared in Liberec a detailed manual on how to behave towards the occupation and the occupiers. It may have been jointly signed by the regional government and the regional committee of the Communist Party in North Bohemia, but its language was unmistakably Havel's: 'Approach the presence of the foreign troops as you would approach, for example, a natural disaster: do not negotiate with them – just as you would not negotiate with torrential rain – but deal with them and escape them just as you would escape rain: use your wits, your intelligence and your fantasy. It seems that the enemy is just as powerless against these weapons, as the rain is powerless against an umbrella. Use against the enemy every method that he does not expect: do not show him any understanding, ridicule him, and reveal to him the absurdity of his situation . . . If at a certain moment you decide that it is more appropriate to behave like Hus,[2] behave like Hus, if you, on the other hand, decide it is more effective to behave like Švejk, behave like Švejk.'[3]

The miracle of the 'community in solidarity' lasted for not much longer than a week. When Dubček and other members of the Communist leadership came back from Moscow on 29 August, with tears in their eyes and a signed document of capitulation, a new era started. It was not apparent immediately, for the resistance, protests and solidarity lasted intermittently for the best part of another year. But it was a year of rearguard action, of an endless series of concessions and retreats that sapped the morale of the nation and presaged its eventual resignation. 'The ship was slowly going under, but the passengers were allowed to shout that this was happening.'[4]

A month later the disillusionment was setting in. It is evident from the bitter mood of the second series of Havel's typograms, dating from the 'sad days'[5] of September 1968. The slogans on every wall of the Prague Spring degenerated into incomprehensible gibberish. 'HUMANISM, FREEDOM,

---

1 'Five radio speeches', 21 August 1968, *Works 3*, 848.
2 Jan Hus, Czech religious reformer, burnt at the stake as a heretic in 1415.
3 'To All Citizens', 26 August 1968, *Works 3*, 857–8.
4 *Disturbing the Peace*, 110.
5 Letter to Alfréd Radok, 14 March 1969.

DEMOCRACY, PATRIOTISM, LOYALTY and UNITY' ended up as . . . 'cookies for Dubček'.[6] In another one he resignedly recapitulates his commandments:

> I shall not take the name of the Lord in vain,
> I shall not covet my neighbour's wife,
> I shall not kill,
> I shall not steal,
> and in the national interest
> I shall not engage in political journalism.[7]

One by one, the united national front or non-violent resistance started to crumble. Of the leading reformists, who were summarily hauled off to Moscow and, after four days of 'negotiations', forced to capitulate, only one, František Kriegel, a pre-war Communist veteran of the Spanish Civil War, refused to sign the memorandum about the 'temporary' deployment of Soviet troops in Czechoslovakia. Only four of the deputies in the Czechoslovak Parliament declined to raise their hands in favour of a treaty between the two countries that legalized the occupation *ex post facto*. Slowly, the population woke up to the fact that they were now on their own. And yet, the resistance continued. In November, students in universities and colleges went on strike to protest the occupation and demand the continuation of the reforms. In January 1969, Jan Palach, a philosophy undergraduate, immolated himself in Wenceslas Square, sparking nationwide demonstrations. Like others, Havel took to television to express his feelings. Unlike others, though, he did not succumb to the emotional maelstrom of the moment to show tears, desperation or helpless rage; instead, he spoke like a politician. He called Palach's suicide 'a deliberate political act . . . an appeal warning us against indifference, scepticism, hopelessness'.[8] He saw it as 'an opportunity given to us living'.[9] He called neither for mourning nor for empty gestures of defiance, but rather for continuing, permanent resistance: 'There is just one road open

---

6 *Anticodes II* in *Works 1*, 335.
7 Ibid. 338.
8 Appearance on Czech TV, video archive, January 1969, VHL ID6492/6495.
9 Ibid.

to us: to wage our political battle until the end . . . I understand the death of Jan Palach as a warning against the moral suicide of all of us.'[10]

In the rising tide of despair, his was one of the few clear-headed, deliberate recipes for action. The question of tactics and strategy saturated the debates in lecture halls, the media and bars alike. The options discussed ranged from the ride-out-the-storm attitude through various forms of passive resistance, to embryonic attempts of a small group of radical left activists at organizing underground cells of direct action. Inevitably, the debate also consumed two of the leading intellectuals, the novelist Milan Kundera and his sometime protégé Václav Havel. In the Christmas 1968 issue of *Listy*, Kundera published an essay, 'The Czech Destiny', offering the nation a Christmas present in the form of a soothing balm on its fresh wounds and encouragement for the times ahead. Kundera claimed that the 'significance of the Czechoslovak autumn perhaps even surpasses that of the Czechoslovak spring'.[11] In Kundera's thinking, the Prague Spring would be of lasting significance, and 'placed Czechs and Slovaks in the centre of world history'.[12] Most controversially, Kundera insisted that the politics of the Prague Spring 'withstood the terrible conflict to which it has been exposed',[13] that it 'retreated but did not dissipate and did not collapse'.[14] He deplored defeatism masking itself as criticism, and called for the continuation of the national unity in defending the project of 'socialism with a human face'. After all, 'the degree of relative security for everyone,' he wrote, 'depends on how many people will have the courage to stand his or her ground in times of insecurity.'[15]

Havel's reply a month later stunned many people by the openly adversarial, almost hostile tone with which he attacked Kundera's argument. 'Whenever the Czech patriot lacks the courage to face a cruel, but open-ended present, to admit all its aspects and to draw, mercilessly, the necessary conclusions, even should they be aimed into our own ranks, he will turn to a better, but already definitive past when we were all united . . .'[16] For Havel, Kundera's alleged national unity under the 'socialism with a human face' flag

---

10 Ibid.
11 Milan Kundera, 'Český úděl', *Listy*, 1968, No. 7–8.
12 Ibid.
13 Ibid.
14 Ibid.
15 Ibid.
16 'Český úděl?' ('Czech Destiny?'), *Tvář*, No. 2, 1969, 30–3.

was illusory, and standing ground was meaningless without the ability to 'express one's position even by a specific and dangerous activity'.[17] Havel did not subscribe to the myth of 'Czech destiny', and emphasized the element of choice. 'Our destiny depends on us. The world does not consist . . . of dumb superpowers that can do anything and clever small nations that can do nothing.'[18]

Finally, and most importantly, he questioned the lasting value of the Prague Spring itself. It was in his thinking a pompous illusion to suggest that an attempt to introduce rights such as freedom of speech, 'something self-evident in most of the civilized world',[19] should place the nation in the centre of history. Whereas Kundera saw in the Prague Spring an attempt to create something radically new, something that had never existed before, Havel saw it simply as an attempt to return to normalcy. Warning against 'nationalistic self-delusions', he insisted on being measured by the same standards as 'the rest of the civilized world'.[20]

The conflict between the two interpretations of what really happened in 1968, one as a noble effort to repair the flaws of Communism and introduce a brand-new kind of socialism, the other as an embryonic attempt at a wholesale dismantling of a dysfunctional system, one seeking refuge in a 'better but definitive past', the other confronting a 'cruel but open-ended present', was to last for the next two decades, and was finally resolved in Havel's favour only by the Velvet Revolution. By then, Kundera had withdrawn from the debate more than a decade earlier.

However important, the differences of view between two people who were quite close intellectually and for a time socially cannot fully account for the rancour of the exchange, particularly from someone as courteous and mild mannered as Havel. There must have been something more in it, whether it was Havel's moral indignation in the aftermath of Palach's pyre, his lingering doubts about the older man's courage after Kundera failed to sign the petition in defence of *Tvář* or questions about his determination and staying power. When Kundera refused to sign the petition for the release of political prisoners, for which Havel canvassed signatures

---

17 Ibid.
18 Ibid.
19 Ibid.
20 T. G. Masaryk, *Česká otázka (The Czech Question)*, in T. G. Masaryk, *Works*, Vol. 6 (Prague: Institute of T. G. Masaryk, 2000).

among colleagues,[21] and when he ultimately left the country in 1975 to focus on his writing career and deplore the demise of Central European culture,[22] Havel could have been forgiven for thinking his suspicions well founded. 'I am irritated by his repeated pronouncements about the cultural graveyard here; whatever we are we do not think of ourselves as corpses.'[23] The exchange caused a rift between the two men, still evident twenty years later. Characteristically, while the bitterness seems to have lingered more permanently in Kundera, Havel had long since stopped dwelling on the episode and made several half-successful overtures to restore the relationship and, perhaps more importantly, to help the now world-famous author re-establish bonds with his native country after 1989. When Kundera found himself at the centre of a public row over his alleged denunciation to the police fifty-five years earlier of an émigré who had returned illegally to Czechoslovakia as an American agent,[24] Havel lost no time in coming to his defence.

In early 1969, Havel had other problems to attend to. On 21 January, he reported to the police the 'accidental' discovery of a listening device in the ceiling of his apartment, serviced and monitored from the attic above. Unsurprisingly, the police investigation led nowhere. In an effort to create as much public outrage as possible, Havel got the Writers' Union and members of the parliament, both of them still showing some signs of independence, to protest these illegal practices in a statement to the prosecutor general, and to extract a convoluted admission of the bugging from the Minister of the Interior. He also wrote his own account of the affair.[25] While the bugging device was real enough, he could not very well acknowledge, however, that he had staged the whole shocking discovery, having been alerted to its existence by a sympathizing secret policeman via a friend.[26]

---

21 Kaiser (2009), 85.
22 Milan Kundera, 'The Tragedy of Central Europe' (translated by Edmund White), *The New York Review of Books*, Volume 31, Number 7, 26 April 1984 (the article is not available in the archives of *TNYRB*, at Kundera's request).
23 Letter to Jan Vladislav, 30 June 1984, National Museum, Czechoslovak Documentation Centre, VHL ID13966.
24 Adam Hradilek, Petr Třešňák, 'Udání Milana Kundery' ('Milan Kundera's Denunciation'), Respekt 42/2008, English text at http://respekt.ihned.cz/english/c1-36380440-milan-kundera-s-denunciation.
25 'A strange episode' ('Zvláštní příhoda'), *Listy*, 1969, No. 4, 5, in *Works 3*, 880–5.
26 The episode is described in detail in Kaiser (2009), 81–2.

Shortly afterwards, Havel retreated to Hrádeček, which was rapidly becoming his favourite place for both work and relaxation. He was missing many of his friends. Radok took up a directing job in Goteborg, originally for one season, and eventually for the rest of his life. Miloš Forman was trying his luck as a film director in America. Even brother Ivan was leaving to work for a PhD at Berkeley. In January 1969, Václav, too, was planning to make use of a Ford Foundation scholarship to spend half a year in the USA with Olga, but because of a 'silly feeling' that he would miss something, he postponed his plans until September. By then his passport had been confiscated. He was also without a job, having left the Balustrade before he could be fired.

As the first anniversary of another date that would live in infamy drew near, Havel wrote a letter to Alexander Dubček, who was by then no longer the leader of the Communist Party, but a figurehead of the puppet parliament, the Federal Assembly. Rightly fearing that the day was fast approaching when the Party would endorse the Soviet interpretation of the Prague Spring as a counter-revolution justifying military intervention, he pleaded with the former leader not to lend his personal seal of approval to this shameful act. Havel was under no illusions that Dubček's refusal could prevent such an act from happening, but he insisted that refusal to sign was the only way to preserve not just Dubček's own self-respect but that of the whole nation. For the first time, though not for the last, he invoked the infamy of the Munich treaty and the ensuing capitulation of President Beneš and his government. Unlike many of the reformists, who justified their retreat and ever-greater concessions as an effort to preserve some modicum of the reforms, Havel stated unequivocally: 'The Czechoslovak attempt at a reform was defeated. Even less should we admit the defeat of the truth of this attempt.'[27]

Havel's belief in the purifying and energizing role of an individual, purely moral stand may sound a little naïve. It was, however, the same conviction that later inspired Havel and others to launch Charter 77, as he himself realized when he came across the letter by accident seventeen years later. 'I had written that even a purely moral act that has no hope of any immediate and visible political effect can gradually and indirectly, over time, gain in political significance.'[28] The truth is that whether or not

---

27 Letter to Alexander Dubček, 8 August 1969, in *Works 3*, 911–29.
28 *Disturbing the Peace*, 114–15.

Dubček read the letter from a playwright he met only once in his life, and a drunk playwright at that, he found in himself the strength never to admit to heresy, and to defend the policies of the Prague Spring as an honest and well-intentioned effort to give socialism a human face. He was duly expelled from the Party and, after a short bizarre episode as an ambassador to Turkey, where the 'normalizers' dispatched him in the apparent hope that he would defect to the West and thus confirm his guilt, he spent the best part of the next twenty years in total obscurity and under constant police surveillance.

On the anniversary of the invasion, Havel joined another protest, this time not of his own making. A petition, entitled 'Ten Points', was initiated by Luděk Pachman, a brilliant if somewhat eccentric chess grandmaster and recognized theoretician, now on his way to converting from being a radical Communist to a devoted Catholic. It was given its final form, in spite of his 'horrific aversion'[29] to getting involved, by Ludvík Vaculík, a proven rabble-rouser on the record of his speech to the Writers' Congress and the 2000 Words. The petition condemned the invasion as a violation of international law, and demanded the withdrawal of occupation troops. It deplored the ongoing purges in the Party and the civil service. It voiced contempt for the reintroduction of censorship. Perhaps most importantly, it rejected the automatic leading role of the Communist Party, and claimed the right of dissent as an 'ancient natural right of Man'. Havel, already believing that 'sober perseverance is more effective than enthusiastic emotions',[30] was somewhat put off by the tone of the document, simultaneously radical and careless, and 'did not feel like signing it but signed it anyway',[31] along with ten others, including a member of the Czech Parliament, Rudolf Battěk, and the legendary Olympic long-distance runner Emil Zátopek.[32] The signatories based their action on 'the right to petition' guaranteed by the Czechoslovak constitution. Someone must have given the plot away, for Pachman's flat was placed under observation for several days before the petition was delivered on 21 August, and on the next day he was detained. A few weeks later Havel and the others were charged with sedition.

The police investigation lasted a year. Pachman, and two other

---

29 Ludvík Vaculík in a letter to the Institute for Contemporary History, 8 August 1990, Institute for Contemporary History, Prague.
30 *Disturbing the Peace*, 111.
31 Letter to Jiří Paukert, 22 April 1970, VHL ID1645.
32 Zátopek's name is, however, missing from the copy of the document in the VHL.

signatories, Battěk and Jan Tesař, a historian, spent most of that time in custody. The charge was ultimately 'conspiracy to subvert' the country's political regime, punishable by up to ten years in prison. It was, however, a cloud with no rain. The Municipal Court in Prague returned the matter to the prosecutor because of insufficient evidence and went ahead with the proceedings only when overruled by the Supreme Court.[33] A day before the trial was to start, Havel and the others received a terse notice that it was being postponed, without a new date or an explanation. The note was signed by the presiding judge, Antonín Kašpar.[34] The case of the 'Ten Points' never came to trial and was finally closed in 1980, when Havel was already serving a four-and-a-half-year sentence for his involvement with the Committee for the Defence of the Unjustly Persecuted. The sentencing judge in that case was none other than Antonín Kašpar. He would get his man yet.

The whole undertaking was in the words of one of its signatories, Jan Tesař, 'a kamikaze operation'. There was, however, nothing remotely kamikaze-like about Havel; he disdained both the pose of the hero as well as that of the martyr. He was also affected by the 'general mental fatigue . . . a feeling that everything has already been said, written, produced, filmed and exhibited'.[35] When the resistance died down and the purges started in earnest he changed his lifestyle completely. After Ivan came back from Berkeley and moved into the family apartment with his wife Květa, Havel vacated the 'strange provisional arrangement' and moved with Olga into a co-op flat in a newly built house in the Dejvice district, only now 'starting a household'. For the most part, however, finding himself the object of increasing pressure and ostracism, he withdrew with Olga into an 'internal exile'[36] at Hrádeček to 'write, read, go for walks and on occasion cook'.[37] The family was shrinking, too. Božena Havlová, the family matriarch, died of oesophagal cancer on 11 December 1970. In Havel's preserved letters from the time, there is only one reference to her demise, when he thanked the devoted Jiří Kuběna for speaking at her funeral.[38] Božena's death seemed to

---

33 Municipal Court, Prague, 6 July 1970, VHL ID17779; Supreme Court, 26 August 1970, VHL ID17780; Municipal Court, Prague, 4 September 1970, VHL ID17718.
34 Note to Václav Havel, 14 October 1970, VHL ID17638.
35 Letter to Alfréd Radok, 9 January 1971, VHL ID10862.
36 Disturbing the Peace, 120.
37 Letter to Alfréd Radok, 25 December 1969, VHL ID10861.
38 26 December 1970, VHL ID1647. Havel also corresponded with his brother about their mother's death. (Conversation with Ivan M. Havel, 14 May 2014)

weigh much more heavily on her husband, who on the advice of his doctors spent the rest of the year in a hospital before Václav and Olga transported him to Hrádeček and provided him with physical and emotional care and support, referring to him endearingly as 'tatuška' (Pops, Daddy-o).

Havel's physique, too, underwent a conspicuous change. Whereas a year earlier he still resembled a rather well-fed piglet in spite of the longish hair and modish attire, he was now leaner, sported a moustache and radiated something of a devil-may-care attitude. A dude. For better or worse, and in more senses than one, he was now a dude striking out on his own.

Mountain Hotel

Everyone must follow hotel rules.

IN APRIL 1969, HARBOURING NO ILLUSIONS about what the near future held in store, Havel made an observation that was to foreshadow his lifestyle for the next five years: 'Whenever we feel that the certainties we used to rely on have fallen apart and that we are losing the opportunity to influence the circumstances surrounding us and assert ourselves socially, we suddenly turn to friends more than ever before. The narrow "space" delineated by friendship still enables us to express ourselves freely, to freely share in our thoughts and the results of our endeavours, to preserve something of our lifestyle, our way of thinking, our language, our humour – simply to be ourselves.'[1]

A year later, the country was drifting into a long valley of nothingness and depression. Few people who did not experience the first half of the seventies in Czechoslovakia can imagine the twilight mood, the torpor, which resembled a state of semi-anaesthesia. The suppression of the Prague Spring took neither the form of full-scale terror as in the first days after the Soviet re-conquest of Budapest in 1956, nor that of a slow-burn liberalization as in Hungary in the subsequent years. It was something in between.

In fact, the scope of the oppression was massive, even if its intensity was, for the most part, not directly life-threatening. Dozens of people were

---

1 *Listář I*, April 1999, in *Works 3*, 898.

jailed. Tens of thousands left the country to start a new life elsewhere, often never to return. More than 300,000 people were expelled from the Communist Party, not so much for having supported the liberal reforms but rather for being unable or unwilling to repudiate their heresy and perform humiliating public acts of repentance.

The strategy of 'normalization', as it was officially euphemized and endlessly justified in the media under renewed censorship, succeeded in making life in the country appear 'normal'. People went to their jobs and watched television in the evening, children were born, and the trains ran more or less on time.

Underneath, however, all public and social life ground to a halt. In the media, the ferment of a couple of years before was replaced by endless, repetitive, soporific drivel. All independent organizations and associations were disbanded, all independent thought disowned. Textbooks were purged of anything remotely inconsistent with the official line or smacking of individual creativity and originality, which now were reckoned among the cardinal sins. Lovely ancient neighbourhoods and small town centres were razed to make room for vast housing projects, where large numbers of people could be efficiently housed, monitored and made to watch each other. Foreign travel was curtailed to a minimum afforded to the select few; a special exit permit was needed even to travel to socialist Yugoslavia.

It was understandable that people tried to make up for the social void and the public emptiness in their private lives. The flowering of the 'cottage' industry in the literal sense of the word, the imperative of having a place in the country where people could hole up in privacy with their family and friends and spend the weekends in backbreaking but, for a change, meaningful labour to render them livable as well as pretty, was but one of the symptoms. The overflowing bars, where men and women could spend evenings getting drunk on cheap but excellent beer, or cheap and terrible wine, were another. The rather relaxed sexual mores were still another sign. The various combinations of these three factors gave rise to an endless round of parties and other gatherings whose aim was to kill time as absurdly and pleasurably as possible. There were several well-known watering holes and late-night asylums, places like the Junior Club not far from Havel's house, where one could always find a drinking buddy or pick up a girl. There was a 'salon' that Havel occasionally frequented in the house of writer Jiří Mucha, the son of Alphonse, hosted by his mistress Marta Kadlečíková, about which murky stories of sexual orgies and political intrigue swirled, some of them true. There was a Society, the mission of which was to write its own chronicle in Italian, even though none of its members knew Italian, as well as to provide transportation and board at members' weekend houses around the country to female friends, collectively called the 'auxiliary and interchangeable women's corps'. There was a Club of Balloon Flight, where a few people actually flew balloons, but many more, including Havel, attended its annual balls. The oldest, best-known and most sophisticated of these associations was a club of artists, film-makers and athletes called 'The Fatherland's Palette'. Among its manifold activities, which included an annual formal ball, replete with white ties and long gowns, and an ice-hockey team, was an annual Rallye Monte Fatherland, which in 1971 counted among its drivers a Mexican-looking gentleman in a big black Mercedes car, who was none other than Václav Havel.

It was quite possible to take up this lifestyle as a permanent mode of existence, and some did, often with irreparable consequences, like Havel's friends writer and film director Pavel Juráček and painter Josef Vyleťal, neither of whom lived to see his fiftieth birthday.

For most people, though, such relief was temporary at best, and in the end it could not mitigate the hopelessness of the situation or the absence of any prospect for its improvement. It would always be like this, this author remembers thinking, going from one party to another, getting drunk with the same people and laid by complete strangers, and waking up in the morning with a feeling ranging from mild indifference through vague nausea to utter despair.

The toll this way of life exacted in terms of self-respect and respect for others, including old friends, was rather high. Towards the end of 1971, in the company of Jan Němec (with whom Havel had written a screenplay for a film called *Heartbeat*), Juráček and Vyleťal, Havel started a regular bar crawl, which he christened 'Free Tuesdays'. The enterprise came to a bad end, when Němec, somewhat deranged over the desertion of his wife, the iconic singer of the Prague Spring Marta Kubišová, teamed up with Pavel Landovský to steal – or, as they saw it, to 'borrow' – Havel's prized Mercedes car and then taunted him for days by refusing to return it, until the whole prank blew up in mutual insults and pub brawls.[2] At Mucha's house, on another occasion, Landovský, who still enjoyed opportunities and popularity as an actor, attacked Havel and Juráček, already banned, for having caused their own misfortune and for now playing the martyrs.[3] Kaiser[4] cites the somewhat more dubious source of the secret police monitor to place Juráček in the role of the attacker at a party, where he allegedly accused Havel of exhibitionism and disregard for the ill effects of his activities on his compatriots' lives.

In the first half of the seventies, Václav Havel was in an ideal position both to share in and to observe this way of life. He did partake in a considerable amount of partying, some of it in the places mentioned above, much of it at Hrádeček, but he never succumbed to the self-destructive urge to party to oblivion. Since the repression focused primarily on former Communists, and he had never been one, he was pronounced an enemy of socialism and ostracized by the regime, frequently finding himself under surveillance and subjected to 'dozens of interrogations',[5] but not jailed or directly persecuted.[6] His work was off limits for every theatre in the country and copies were removed from public libraries. His and Jan Němec's screenplay,[7] *Heartbeat*, a film noir, based on a previous, also joint treatment of a comic book,[8] about the life-saving practice of heart transplantation, which, in an amoral world, inevitably leads to murderous orgies, was written with international audiences in mind, but never produced. It was not a particularly brilliant effort; the reader discerns Havel's contributions only in occasional glimpses, overshadowed by the fumes of what seems to be a writing–drinking binge *à deux*. He was now without a regular job, but thanks to his income from the productions of his plays abroad, skilfully managed, administered and regularly transferred to him by his German agents at Rowohlt Verlag, he could live quite comfortably for the foreseeable future. By retreating to Hrádeček he was largely able to escape the unwanted attention of the police and the oppressive atmosphere of Prague. He and

---

2 Juráček (2003), 801.
3 Ibid. 802.
4 (2009), 87. Since both the previous episode and this one occurred at Mucha's, it is quite possible it was one and the same party and one of the sources had it wrong.
5 Letter to Alfréd Radok, 8 January 1972, VHL ID10860.
6 Ibid.
7 1970, VHL ID 16223.
8 1970, VHL ID 25597.

Olga refurbished the house and equipped it with comforts like hot water and central heating, built several bedrooms and a study for the playwright with a view of the little orchard in the garden, and opened the house to friends and acquaintances. Thanks too to his income from abroad he was able not only to buy himself a Mercedes, but also to purchase otherwise unavailable foods and beverages in hard-currency shops, and he plied his guests very generously with these.[9] He also used his earnings to buy himself state-of-the-art hi-fi equipment, which provided the ambience for the parties. Incidentally, his musical tastes in those days, prior to his initiation into the 'underground', ran to Johnny Cash[10] and Burt Bacharach.[11] Since he was now someone to avoid, with many of his former friends only too quick to oblige, the group that met at his house became exceptionally tight-knit and loyal through sheer self-selection. Still, the traffic sometimes grew to unmanageable proportions, especially during the summer, and Havel was forced to write notes to friends that could hardly be considered whole-hearted invitations: 'During the summer holidays, there are some of my Prague friends here all the time, most of them pissheads.'[12]

The frequent parties also gave Havel a pretext to engage in his hobby of cooking. Like everything else in his life, he approached it with the utmost dedication and seriousness, learning techniques, exchanging tips and writing to friends abroad to send him ingredients unavailable on the market.[13] On the whole, he preferred the experimental approach to following tried and tested recipes, sometimes with mixed results. Pavel Kohout, who shared the culinary bug, recalls the time when the two of them, this time at Kohout's house, undertook to replicate the opulent meal of the quadruple-stuffed roast for the Ethiopian emperor from Hrabal's novel *I Served the King of England*.[14] Unable to obtain camel or goat from the rudimentarily stocked Czech shops, they had to do with turkey stuffed with goose stuffed with duck stuffed with chicken. But they never had a chance to taste their

---

9 It speaks volumes about the achievements of Communism that the exotic luxuries he sought included ketchup and toothpaste (Letter to Václav M. Havel, 1970s, Ivan M. Havel's archive, recent discovery).

10 Letter to Alfréd Radok, undated 1972, VHL ID10849.

11 Letter to Alfréd Radok, 3 October 1972, VHL ID10859.

12 Letter to Josef Šafařík, 3 October 1972, VHL ID13811.

13 In an undated letter of 1972 (VHL ID10850) he expresses his gratitude to Alfréd Radok for the present of soy sauce, and asks for an esoteric mixture called 'salad seasoning', which he had come to enjoy in the USA, although he was not certain it would also be available in Sweden.

14 (London: Vintage Classics, 2009).

creation; exhausted by stuffing they went outside to have a smoke and let the roast cool off, only to find that their dogs had got to the dinner first.[15]

Many of the visitors at Hrádeček were Havel's literary colleagues. Some of them were the non-conformist and largely unpublished writers and poets, Havel's old friends from the late fifties and sixties, like Zdeněk Urbánek, Josef Hiršal and Jan Vladislav, forming a kind of summer relocation of the Slavia get-togethers to the countryside. Havel's friends from outside Prague, Josef Topol, Jiří Kuběna and Josef Šafařík, made an annual pilgrimage. Others were the recently purged 'antidogmatic' Communists like Pavel Kohout, Ludvík Vaculík, Alexander Kliment and Ivan Klíma.[16] Like most writers they craved an audience, and so they read their texts to one another – a small but significant consolation for having been expelled from the eyes of the public. The elaborate, funny and moving entries in the lovingly maintained guest books from Hrádeček, most of which seem to have been preserved through house searches and confiscations by the secret police, but which were then sadly lost as a result of the post-revolutionary chaos, house moves and changing partners, bore witness to the collective spirit and the concentration of talents.

Still, in a quote from John Lennon adopted by Havel, the decade was not 'worth a damn'.[17] He and many of his friends felt as if they were 'stewing in their own juices'.[18] 'For me, the first half of the decade is a single, shapeless fog. I can't say any longer how 1972, for instance, differed from 1973, and what I did in either of those years.'[19]

One thing he did, although it did not bring him much joy or satisfaction, was to continue to write. On the whole, Havel was a very productive writer, though writing never came to him easily or painlessly. He stuck to a discipline of reading and contemplating in the afternoon, and then writing late into the night, which he rarely interrupted even when Hrádeček was full of houseguests. He would then sleep late in the morning, guarded by Olga, leaving their guests to fend for themselves.

Most of his plays took weeks, others only days to finish. He usually wrote them with a specific stage, and sometimes even with specific actors, in

---

15 Conversation with Pavel Kohout, 22 October 2012.
16 A close to complete list of the visitors can be found in *Disturbing the Peace*, 120–1.
17 *Disturbing the Peace*, 109.
18 Ibid. 121.
19 Ibid. 120.

mind. Now he found he was spending years inventing, writing and revising plays with no specific audience in mind – if, indeed, any audience at all. 'A play, which is written for some kind of an abstract spectator everywhere and for "the eternity", often does not get understood anywhere, and history, in particular, ignores it.'[20] Lack of contact with a theatre and an audience must have played a big part in slowing down his creative process. Although he built his retreat so that he had everything he needed for life and work, he still found the going tough. 'I find it difficult to work, since I am simply a sociable type, not made at all to live in seclusion for years, albeit in relative luxury. It does not really affect me visibly, I do not go around the house looking sadly at the world like a beat-up dog . . . I do live quite a content, and I could say, joyful life . . .'[21] But still . . . The writing problem lay not so much in the isolation of the writer as in the comatose situation of the society, unable to recover from the shock of the invasion and decimated by what followed. 'Suddenly, instead of laughing one felt like screaming.'[22] To describe the atmosphere, Havel knew he had to take another approach. Faced with the threat of being engulfed by the situation as so many people around him were, he took the obvious step of distancing his stage away from it. Whereas *The Garden Party*, *The Memorandum* and *The Increased Difficulty of Concentration*, abstract as they are, clearly bear the marks of contemporary Czechoslovak society, his next three full-length plays, *The Conspirators*, *The Beggar's Opera* and *Mountain Hotel*, outwardly take place anywhere except Czechoslovakia.

In *The Conspirators*, started in 1970, revised in early 1971 and completed late that year, Havel's goals were ambitious: he apparently intended to construct a metaphor for the internal processes of suspicion and paranoia that first conjured up an armada of half a million troops, thousands of tanks and hundreds of aircraft to suppress what was at best a half-baked attempt at change, and then made many of the recent reformists, fighting for their political lives, help unleash purges and persecutions on their former comrades and fellow citizens. The initial inspiration for the play must have come from the revolting spectacle – then unfolding all around the country – of a political beast turning upon itself.

---

20 Letter to Alfréd Radok, 1 February 1972, VHL ID10849.
21 Letter to Alfréd Radok, undated 1972, VHL ID10850.
22 An afterword to *Plays, 1970–1976* (Toronto, 68 Publishers, 1977), in *Works 4*, 152.

In the play, a bunch of life-timers in a fragile democracy that has just rid itself of its long-time dictator share and mutually reinforce their uncertainties and fears. With the best of intentions, they debate ways to prop up the fledgling democracy and preserve its newfound freedoms. Gradually, they all entertain second thoughts about their own role in the emerging situation, as well as suspicions about the motives of the others. The more ominous the discussions about the threats and conspiracies against the democratic government become, the more conspiratorial are the discussions about their prevention. Or perhaps the more conspiratorial the discussions, the more ominous are the discussions about the threats and conspiracies. In the finale, all the conspirators, after crossing and double-crossing each other, execute the pièce de résistance, bringing in the only person who can effectively suppress all the threats, prevent chaos and restore stability: the old dictator himself.

It is symptomatic of the mood of those times that the play, though pregnant with Kafkaesque absurdity, is, unlike its predecessors, largely void of the playful Havelesque humour. Some of the devices Havel regularly used – nonsensical objects like a piece of string or an office pin as an instrument of torture – have a mechanical and contrived air. The circular structure of the play is too predictable; it signals the outcome well before the denouement.

The play did not find too many admirers or audiences and was disowned by the author himself as a 'chicken that had been in the oven for too long'.[23] The reasons for this self-perceived failure could, however, be more than simply overcooking the plot. In the play Havel targets the discrepancy between proclaimed political goals and the means used to achieve them, ultimately leading to a situation of *plus ça change . . .* The model could be partly applied to the events of 1968, but indeed generically to all attempts at engineered political change. In 1971, however, when the play was finished, change was not the word that first sprang to mind. Czechoslovakia had entered a long period of paralysis, euphemistically camouflaged as 'normalization'. Change, even the most apolitical and innocuous, was perceived as subversion. In fact, all Havel's major plays to date had been about failed revolts, reforms and changes. Now Havel would have to learn to write about changelessness.

---

23 Letter to Tom Stoppard, 28 January 1984, VHL ID22548; also *Disturbing the Peace*, 120.

As always, Havel was equally perceptive about what he wanted to achieve in the play and how he was failing to achieve it. He struggled for months to reconcile the two. The outward expression of this struggle is a forty-page-long commentary to the play, written in September 1972 at a request from abroad[24] to assist its future producers of the play ('they are generally somewhat confused about the play, they don't know what to think about it and they don't seem to particularly like it'[25]) but clearly it also served as a stratagem to help the writer himself make sense of what he was actually trying to do. This may be the lone exception to Havel's dictum that a work should always be somehow 'cleverer'[26] than its author. In the end, it is the commentary rather than the play, which illuminates in sharp profile Havel's evolution as a political thinker and explains his permanent distrust of politics, that was to accompany him even in political office. It is as much a commentary on a play as a declaration of the principles of anti-politics.

While clearly taking his original inspiration from the events of the Prague Spring and its aftermath, Havel's tendency towards abstract thought led him to generalize his conclusions as applying to all politics, including the politics of democracy. The play (and the commentary) is ultimately not about what 'was happening to his country, with Dubček's demise and Husák's rise to power under the programme of normalization'[27] but about what was happening to modern man, East and West, threatened with a loss of identity. It is about the 'process of evil manifesting itself'[28], through the dialogues of the characters of the play. 'Whatever our heroes are saying, whether they are right or wrong, whether they believe what they are saying or not, their utterances have one thing in common: They are not existentially guaranteed in full; they feel somewhat hollow, empty, too abstract, posing again and again – persuasive and logical as they might be – the question of their truthfulness, their authenticity, their binding nature.'[29]

The general character of Havel's observations, together with the absence of any discernible 'mapping' between real-life events in Czechoslovakia and the plot of the play, signals the playwright's more

24 *Works 3*. The original can be found in the archive of Havel's translator and correspondent Vera Blackwell, The Columbia University Rare Book and Manuscript Library, New York.
25 Letter to Josef Šafařík, 3 October 1972, Masaryk University archive, Brno, VHL ID13811.
26 *Letters to Olga*, No. 71, 171. The term is misquoted as 'clearer' in Rocamora (2004), 114.
27 Ibid. 112.
28 'Notes on *The Conspirators*', September 1972, in *Works 3*, 11.
29 Ibid. 12.

ambitious goal, namely, to diagnose a crisis of identity as the fundamental 'metaphysical illness'[30] of modern man, and to do so through the deconstruction of political discourse.

The play Havel wrote may be forgettable and, to the best of this author's knowledge, it has never been produced to anything more than mild applause. His accompanying political perceptions as reflected in the notes to the play, however, formed the bedrock of the evolution of Havel as a politician. At its core is a certain distrust of politics and politicians, all politicians, himself included, as is evident from some of his presidential texts.[31]

The relative lack of impact of the play, and Havel's own dissatisfaction with it, were by his own account caused at least in part by the fact that for the first time in his creative life he had no way to confront and develop his ideas in contact with his audiences. This helps to illumine how much his life and creative method depended on the dialogical principle, whether employed in his plays, in his books that often take the form of a dialogue (*Disturbing the Peace, To the Castle and Back*) or originated as dialogues (*Summer Meditations*), or in his massive correspondence, often in difficult circumstances (*Letters to Olga*, and from Olga, Havel–Paukert–Kuběna, Havel–Radok, Havel–Janouch, Havel–Prečan). It also helps explain why his confidence and creativity were somewhat impaired when he was largely denied this contact (as in the first part of the seventies) or let the trappings of political office come between himself and his friends and audiences.

With grim determination, Havel next addressed the task of writing a play in which nothing happens. *The Mountain Hotel*, 'an existential dada',[32] only completed in 1976, took five years to write, having been put aside, rewritten, put aside again and revised again, only to wait yet another five years for its premiere in the Burgtheater in Vienna, while its author was serving time in prison, and still another decade for its first Czech production, after the Velvet Revolution. A dozen characters in the garden of a vaguely genteel mountain hotel go through five acts of the play talking at cross-purposes, recalling non-existent encounters and

---

30 Ibid. 17.
31 E.g. The Sonning Prize speech, Copenhagen, 28 May 1991, reprinted in *The Art of the Impossible*, 69–74.
32 Letter to Alfréd Radok, 27 December 1973, David Radok's Archive, VHL ID10851.

events, stealing one another's lines, changing loyalties, struggling with and analysing relationships that are not going anywhere, and reproaching each other for past, largely unspecified sins. They all live under the oppressive supervision of an ill-defined power. 'Everyone must follow hotel rules,'[33] declares Drašar, the hotel director, in his introductory speech, except there is no evidence of any rules to follow or to violate. We cannot even be sure the introductory speech is introductory. We have no idea how long the hotel's guests have lived there or how long they are going to stay. Several mention their plans to depart soon, but in the next act they are still there. The play is set 'in the present', but in the absence of any external context there is no way to measure time or its speed. In each of the five acts, reference is made to the celebration of the director's birthday the day before or the next day, but we don't know whether the acts are set a year apart. It hardly makes a difference: there is no gradation, no plot, no catharsis, no denouement. Everybody is 'stewing in their own juices'.[34] The political reality remains outside the frame, but continues to exist as the omnipresent, threatening and deadening *deus ex machina*.

> ORLOV Can I ask you something?
> PECHAR Sure—
> ORLOV Aren't you sometimes afraid?
> PECHAR Me? Afraid of what?
> ORLOV Well, nothing in particular—[35]

This is how it felt. The final result is a remarkable document of the mood of the times, a true picture of the 'shapeless fog' rather than a compelling piece of theatre. When Havel later described the play to a fellow prisoner and asked him what he would think if he had to see it, the man told him, 'he'd think I was a fake who was trying to make a fool out of him'.[36] If it was also, as Havel himself later wrote, an attempt to free himself from 'one whole area of my obsessions . . . to summarize the volume of tried methods and explore the limits of their possibilities',[37] it

---

33 *The Mountain Hotel*, in *Works 2*, 615.
34 *Disturbing the Peace*, 121.
35 *The Mountain Hotel*, 595.
36 *Letters to Olga*, No. 71, 172.
37 An afterword to *Plays 1970–1976*, in *Works 4*, 157.

is not an overly successful attempt. In one sense, however, he succeeded. He had explored the limits of nothingness, meaninglessness and inertia, and realized that he could not go on in the same way. If the shapeless fog were to be restructured into something meaningful and comprehensible, someone would have to start restructuring it.

Roll Out the Barrels

Roll out the barrel,
We'll have a barrel of fun.
Roll out the barrel,
We've got the blues on the run.
                    – Václav Zeman, 'Beer Barrel Polka'

IT IS A MATTER OF RECORD that, in February 1974, Václav Havel took a menial job in the brewery in Trutnov, a town some ten kilometres from Hrádeček. It is far from clear, though, what made him do it. At the end of December 1973, he wrote to Alfréd Radok that he 'ran out of money'.[1] He mournfully ruminated about his cash flow to other friends as well. In *Disturbing the Peace*[2] he recalls telling Jiří Lederer in 1975 that he went to the brewery for 'financial reasons', but speculates that the need to break out of the 'suffocating inactivity' was the more compelling. Certainly, the salary of 1,700 crowns a month, the equivalent of some fifty-five dollars at the time, for physically exhausting work, which took place in freezing cold in winter and in scorching heat in the summer, was a meagre reward, considering that he had to spend a third of it on petrol to drive his big black Mercedes car from Hrádeček to the brewery every morning. True, Havel's income from the productions of his plays abroad had fallen off significantly, but when he left the brewery of his own volition, nine

---

1   27 December 1973, VHL ID10851.
2   P. 122.

months later, the situation had hardly changed. The same holds for the other reason sometimes given, that he wished to avoid the risk of being prosecuted as a 'parasite' under the often abused Communist law aimed at punishing people who had no proof of gainful employment.[3] His true motives may be best divined from the fact that he had tried to obtain a job at a printer's a month earlier only to be told by the manager on arrival there that the higher powers had vetoed the idea,[4] and that he had been offered but declined a job in a museum of antiquity not far away from Hrádeček.[5] Rather than needing money, he seems to have resented the role of prominent outcast assigned to him by the government, and the isolation that went with it. He associated the isolation and his inability to see his plays performed with his sense of dissatisfaction with his own work and, increasingly, with his struggle to do any sustained writing at all. A cosy attendant's job in a museum would neither resolve his financial situation, nor help him find new stimuli for his work. His perpetual sense of guilt at his privileged background may have also played a role in the equation. In the end, he opted for work in the quintessentially plebeian milieu of Czech society, rolling barrels in a brewery (he actually did every kind of odd job there, but it was rolling the barrels that lingered in retrospect). There certainly also seems to have been a dramatist's eye at play in his choice of jobs, limited as it was. As in *The Garden Party*, his real-life Honza was now going out to confront the real world with Švejk's glass of beer in his hand.

The world did not disappoint. Havel was assigned to work in the cold basement of the brewery with a team of local Romas (who in those days were still called gypsies). There, once again, he exhibited his ability to get along, thanks to his quiet courtesy and an absolute absence of swagger or pomposity, with people from the most varied social backgrounds. The Romas, to this day a somewhat underprivileged group in Czech society, instinctively accepted him, in the way outcasts will accept one another.

There seems to be no reliable account of why Havel left the brewery, but the timing at the end of the year offers a few clues. It is quite likely he did not fancy the prospect of another winter in the freezing basement. 'This winter,

---

3   He would later write an essay on the subject, '§ 203', 1 April 1978, in *Works 4*, 206–14.
4   Letter to Alfréd Radok, 18 February 1973, VHL ID10852.
5   Kaiser (2009), 94.

I want to stay home and write,' he wrote to Radok,[6] mentioning that he had enough to live on for the moment and would seek employment only when absolutely necessary. The prying eyes and the long arm of the secret police extended even to the brewery, and created tensions around him he would have liked to avoid. The absurd elements of the life of a banned intellectual in an establishment producing 'the liquid bread', the mild alcoholic sedative with which a large portion of the nation suppressed their sense of the existential void, may have already made his creative juices flow again.

But it may have also been a sense on Havel's part that the job was done. The isolation was broken. 'I have proved to myself that I am not yet completely lazy and that I can without much difficulty do any work at hand and make a living – this realization has a very calming effect on me, because it makes away with any nervous concerns about the future; I see that I do not have to worry much about it.'[7] He had demonstrated to himself that he was able to withstand discomfort and hardship. Since he had drafted the first version of his letter to Gustáv Husák already in 1974, the year spent in the brewery, he seems to have had a clear idea of what he was about to do, and he knew he had to do it alone.

In the end, he benefitted from his reunion with the working class both psychologically and financially. In his one-act play *Audience*, based on his barrel-rolling experience and written as a sort of afterthought to amuse his writer friends in early 1975, he returns to his natural milieu as a satirist. Gone is the dark existential brooding of *Conspirators* and *The Mountain Hotel*. Gone is the exotic, abstract location. *Audience* takes place in the here and now of the brewery. At one level, it represents the attempt of the perpetually drunk Brewmaster and the mild-mannered intellectual Vaněk, the new and future alter ego of the playwright, to find a *modus vivendi* between the constraints of the workplace and the ominous interest of the secret police in Vaněk. Equally, however, it is a play with an absurd twist, since the less than articulate Brewmaster asks Vaněk the intellectual to help him formulate the reports on Vaněk's conduct that the secret police demand of him. When Vaněk refuses, on the grounds of principle, to do what amounts to reporting on himself, the negotiation breaks down, with the Brewmaster accusing Vaněk of elitist superiority,

---

6   2 December 1974, VHL ID10854.
7   Ibid.

of letting simple blokes like himself be 'smeared with shit' as long as 'the VIP here stays clean'.[8]

One does not have to identify with the self-exculpatory accusation of the Brewmaster to realize that the author, far from writing a simple morality tale, is treating the situation as one of moral ambiguity. This is indeed one of the most consistent and most valuable elements in all Havel's writing. Although there is no ambiguity as to what positions and views he himself advocates and defends, he never ceases to warn against the moral superiority that often turns a struggle for principle into an ideological argument or a clash of egos. The only reason we know that Vaněk's moral posture, unlike that of his interlocutor, is genuine is because he is willing to make a sacrifice and forego the rewards being offered to him. The conclusion that the truth has to be personally guaranteed to be really true is one that Havel is going to make again and again.

There is, however, a third and less obvious level at which the play operates. For all the striking contrast between the uncouth Brewmaster, at turns bullying, cajoling and pleading, and the courteous Vaněk, who is consistent in his quiet dignity, it is the latter who is trying to break through the wall of social isolation and ostracism and establish some human contact with his boss. His world of theatre stars and parties, to which the Brewmaster enviously alludes, distant in both space and time, feels somewhat unreal. The Brewmaster's world of drinking mates, gypsies, police informers and innumerable glasses of beer is here and now, as real as the nauseating stink of stale spilt beer, which is almost perceptible between the lines of the play. And so, in the very last line, it is the wine-drinking Vaněk who makes the move, and crosses the divide between the two by, at least for the moment, borrowing the other man's language, his choice of drink and his view of the world: 'Everything's all fucked up.'[9]

The play was a hit with Havel's friends when he read it to them at the end of June 1975 in his living room at Hrádeček. It was not so much that they lavishly praised it, but that they could not stop laughing. It evoked the same response when performed by Andrej Krob as the Brewmaster and Havel as Vaněk in Krob's barn as a part of the annual 'garden party' in the summer of 1976, in dozens of productions around the world before 1989 and

---

8 *Audience*, in *Three Vaněk Plays*, 24.
9 Ibid. 26.

in Czechoslovakia after the Velvet Revolution. But its iconic production did not even involve a theatre or a stage. It took the form of an audio recording directed by Luboš Pistorius and recorded in the makeshift studio of the protest singer Vladimír Merta in the spring of 1977, with Havel's drinking buddy Pavel Landovský embodying the definitive Brewmaster, and with Havel lending his voice, speech impediment and all, to Vaněk. By this time Havel was under heavy police surveillance, and the small production team had to work clandestinely, a difficult thing to do in the picturesque Prague cottage neighbourhood of Kocourky, perhaps best translated as Boondocks, where Merta lived at the time. They also had to overcome numerous indispositions of Landovský, caused by drinking too much beer too early in the session, the reluctance of the playwright to speak into a microphone and his congenital inability to utter the obscenity in the last line of the dialogue quoted above, as well as the lack of equipment for sound effects (Pistorius's wife Jitka simulated the Brewmaster's loud bathroom breaks with the help of a teapot and a wash basin).[10] In subsequent years, the tape, smuggled to Sweden by two Swedish junior hockey players, was copied and copied again, and the status of its ownership became comparable to owning the original master of Dylan's *Basement Tapes*. Havel himself recalled stopping, as was his wont, for a half-frozen hitch-hiker, who after a few minutes said: 'You don't look like a swine, stopping for me in weather like this. I have got something that might amuse you,' and put a cassette with *Audience* into the car stereo.[11] It was partly thanks to this tape that Havel achieved the folk status of a national playwright, with lines from the play ('Ain't them paradoxes?', 'People are big swines, big big swines') entering everyday discourse even among people who had never heard of the play and did not know who its author was.

That year Havel wrote not one but two one-act plays. In *Vernisáž*, translated as *Unveiling* but also, and perhaps better, as *Private View*, the up-and-coming husband and wife are giving their 'best friend' Bedřich, a problem-haunted writer and intellectual, a private view of their new house,[12] their sophisticated way of life, their sexual mores and their total, absolute

---

10 Vladimír Merta, 'The recording of *Audience*', 17 October 2012, author's archive.
11 'The recording of *Audience*', cf. also *Disturbing the Peace*, 123.
12 Since Bedřich is clearly another alter ego of the author, in English translations and productions of the play he is given the name of his homologue in *Audience*, Vaněk. The two plays are often staged together, sometimes along with a third Vaněk one-acter, *Protest*.

happiness. At the same time they gently prod him to change his ways, to put his life in order and to return happiness to his own marriage. After all, he is a decent, bright fellow and there is nothing to prevent him from having the same kind of life they have.

The play, like all Havel plays, is an exercise in ambiguity and ambivalence. On the one hand, Vaněk admires, willingly enough, the cosy nest and the good life of Michal and Věra. On the other, he shows no willingness to follow suit. When he tries to take his leave, polite and considerate as ever, they take umbrage at his insensitivity, his lack of empathy and his callousness.

In its simplest form, the play shows up the vacuity of life based on material comforts and the total absence of values. The reason Vaněk has been invited in the first place is to do the single thing that Věra and Michal cannot do for themselves, i.e. to validate their own lives. But he cannot do this, any more than they can bestow their shallow happiness on him.

Just as in *Audience*, in the final confrontation on the stage it is not the husband and wife, but Vaněk who blinks first, and meekly consents to another round of the same private view. Here too, it is the sign of his existential need to break the barriers, to maintain contact with his fellow human beings regardless of their mutual incomprehension. In this and similar moments, we get a glimpse of Havel's deep, genuine humility, which makes him simultaneously more and less than a man of principle. In his writing and in life, he would continue to insist, mildly and courteously, on his duty to remain himself, to preserve his identity. At the same time, he would remain aware that, without staying embedded in the incoherent, maddening and intrinsically ambiguous network of human relationships, identity counts for little. When the two plays were produced together in the Burgtheater in Vienna (along with *The Police* by the Polish playwright and satirist Slawomir Mrożek) in the autumn of 1976, they provoked a sensation and a scandal. The Austrian and German press unanimously lauded Havel's 'diversions' as a brilliant and profound metaphorical portrait of the 'worker's paradise', and they universally condemned the Prague government's refusal to grant him permission to travel to Vienna for the opening night. The authorities in Prague compounded the scandal by accusing Austria of 'interference with its internal affairs' and of trying to stage a 'provocation' by providing a stage for a 'millionaire's son' who had nothing in common with

Czechoslovak culture.[13] Havel was becoming a cause célebre. 'His freedom is our freedom', read the headline of *Die Presse*.[14] To Havel, the triumphant return to the global stage in one of the leading European theatres brought satisfaction mixed with sadness. Alfréd Radok, who had been Havel's chosen director for the production, died in Vienna in April of that year, hours after proudly writing to Havel that he had successfully negotiated the terms with the Burgtheater.[15] The plays were eventually directed by another star of the Czech New Wave, Vojtěch Jasný.

---

13 'Prague radio criticizes Vienna over Havel', Radio Free Europe, 19 October 1976.
14 '*Seine Freiheit, unsere Freiheit*', 11 October 1976, 5.
15 Letter to Pavel Kohout, April 1976, Moravian Land Museum, VHL ID32921.

The Beggar's Opera

Life is a jest, and all things show it,
I thought so once, and now I know it.
                    – John Gay, 'My Own Epitaph'

PERHAPS MORE THAN WITH OTHER PEOPLE, the life of Václav Havel can be read as a compact, logically coherent, purposeful story, but that does not necessarily mean that he saw it in that way as he was living it. Like many things in life, Havel's re-engagement with the world at large after five years of semi-seclusion was half-intentional and half-accidental. What began as a purely theatrical endeavour and a purely political stance came to merge into a full-scale comedy of errors thanks both to the creativity and savvy of Havel and his friends, and to the troglodytic, heavy-handed actions of the powers-that-be.

As with all his writing in the early seventies, this latest effort did not come easily to him. In his letters from mid-1972, he mentioned he was working 'on something else, an adaptation of an older play'.[1] He avoided mentioning either the play or its author, as if he were concerned about getting them into trouble. For once, he need not have worried.

Havel's *Beggar's Opera* is no more a purely original play than is Brecht and Weill's *Threepenny Opera*, both drawing on and closely adhering to the storyline of John Gay's 1728 ballad opera of the same name. The idea

---

1   Letter to Alfréd Radok, summer 1972, David Radok's archive, VHL ID10850.

147

to write the adaptation was initially not even Havel's, but came from his theatrical colleagues and former competitors in the equally popular Actors' Studio, Jaroslav Vostrý and Jan Kačer. They wanted to help their ostracized colleague but, after entertaining bizarre schemes, such as exporting the play to Switzerland and then re-importing it as an anti-establishment Swiss work without mentioning the author of the adaptation, they found themselves compelled to withdraw the invitation by the time the author had finished his work.[2] They feared that they would be endangering their own careers and those of their fellow actors. This tragicomic mixture of altruistic intentions and theatrical *realpolitik* in the face of official opprobrium was an apt prelude to what followed.

Havel was immediately attracted by the political satire of Gay's piece, written as it was to lampoon the mores of the politicians of the day, specifically Sir Robert Walpole, the British Prime Minister *avant la lettre*. Havel took the theme of endemic corruption and moral decay further. Rather than simply lampoon the rich and powerful, as Brecht had done with his adaptation, he depicted a society in which truth and justice are subordinated to expediency, and its inhabitants, regardless of their positions, which are impermanent and interchangeable, are condemned to lives of treachery, double-crossing and informing on each other. With the exception of the 'honest' and doomed thief Filch, there is no moral distinction between the characters, be they criminals like Peachum and Macheath, or instruments of justice like the police chief Lockit. Not only are those who serve justice as corrupt as, or more so than, those who serve crime, but also no one can be quite certain which of the two he or she is serving at a given moment. In Gay's story, Havel found a perfect parable for a corrupt society in which none is innocent and all are, willingly or not, implicated in the crime.

Another convention that Havel, unlike Brecht, had borrowed from Gay is the use of 'high' language for conversations among the lowest of criminals. As summed up by the Beggar in Gay's original version, 'Through the whole Piece you may observe such a Similitude of Manners in high and low Life, that it is difficult to determine whether (in the fashionable Vices) the fine Gentlemen imitate the Gentlemen of the Road, or the Gentlemen of the Road the fine Gentlemen.'[3]

---

2   An interview with Jan Kačer, in Rocamora (2004), 126.
3   John Gay, *The Beggar's Opera* (London: William Heinemann, 1921), 91.

Unlike with *Conspirators*, Havel enjoyed working on *The Beggar's Opera*, although he realized quite early on that the project was probably doomed. Without contact with a theatre and a composer, he also could not develop the operatic aspect of the story, as both Gay and Brecht and Weill had done; he decided instead to transpose the musical element into the extremely sophisticated and involved structure of the piece, which, though spoken, contains carefully crafted arias, duets, variations, recitatives and codas. He also deliberately suppressed the emotional overtones of the story, giving it a matter-of-fact, almost cynical character, in order to avoid what he saw as Brecht's heavy-handed, Germanic sentimentality. 'Maybe I'm prejudiced and I don't express myself exactly but what drives me crazy is the German professorial sentimentality, something that feels to me like a bureaucratic idea of humour, adventure and poetry.'[4] The absence of music, and the lasting popularity of both Gay's original and the *Threepenny Opera* (both of which have run into tens of thousands of performances), may explain why Havel's minimalist version, albeit effective and compact as a dark comedy, has hardly ever been produced abroad with any success. Or perhaps it was the sheer inability of Western audiences to envisage a society in which 'they serve best who know not that they serve'.[5] Though Havel had high hopes for the play, and appealed repeatedly to Klaus Juncker and other friends to help find a stage for it, none of the major theatres was interested. It saw its first night abroad in Teatro Stabile in Trieste in March 1976.

The play, apparently destined to remain a footnote in the annals of theatre, took its revenge by making political history. In a symptomatically absurdist fashion, this came about as a product not of design but of coincidences, miscalculations, naïvete and cunning. As so often in Czech history, it all started with a letter.

In March 1975, after a previous, discarded attempt, Havel sat down to write a letter to the Czechoslovak leader Gustáv Husák, the politician who shrewdly and opportunistically manipulated the crisis of the Soviet invasion and its aftermath to emerge on top. Husák had the distinction of being despised and distrusted by his enemies and his allies, as well as by the population at large. As a former political prisoner during the Stalinist era for the sin of 'Slovak bourgeois nationalism', his Communist

---

4 Letter to Alfréd Radok, 3 July 1975, VHL ID10855.
5 *Works 2*, 517. The English translation is Paul Wilson's, translator's archive.

credentials were suspect in the eyes of the ruling post-Stalinists in the Kremlin. As an opportunist who turned against Dubček and his leadership after having sworn loyalty to the reforms, he was branded a traitor by many of his countrymen.

The immediate rationale for writing the letter was no particular event, or even the anniversary of an event, but rather a stand-off. It is not quite true to say that Havel spent the previous years in passive inactivity – far from it. He was signing petitions for the release of political prisoners, supporting fellow banned writers, holding a literary salon and working on five plays, which in one way or another attacked the status quo. At the same time by moving to Hrádeček, he vacated the Prague frontline, tirelessly monitored and continuously harassed by the secret police. Unlike many fellow intellectuals, he certainly did not seek or expect any favours from the regime. But he also realized that, unless he made a move first, the authorities were not going to move against him. The stalemate could last for a long time, and it suited the regime, which would be content to let him rot at Hrádeček for the rest of his life. They had no intention of making a martyr out of him or anyone else. They wanted him out of the way, powerless and forgotten. These architects of normalization elevated oblivion to a method. For an active artist it was death by other means. And so Havel knew he had to act.

The letter was clearly not created on the spur of the moment. When one reads its reasoned, unemotional text, it becomes clear that this was not an expression of despair, nor simply a cry of protest, but rather a formal declaration of war. Its intent is obvious from the form of address. In addressing Husák as 'Dear Doctor' rather than 'General Secretary', Havel was implicitly denying the legitimacy of the leading role of the Communist Party, enshrined in the country's constitution, and of the man at its head.

In its form, the letter is a pure expression of the constitutional right to petition the government. It offers the Doctor, who was not without intelligence, nor, at least at one time, intellectual curiosity, a meticulous analysis of the real 'state of the union', rather than the façade provided every day by hacks and sycophants.

It defines the basic psychological state of Czechoslovak society as a state of fear, fear for 'livelihood, positions or prospects', although it is not recognized as having precise, definite roots. The source of the anxiety is a loose 'system of existential pressure' personified by the secret police, 'the hideous spider whose invisible web runs through the whole of society'.[6] The immobilizing impact of chronic fear gives rise to indifference, apathy and conformity. Man is reduced to a 'creature whose only aim is self-preservation'. And all this is done in the name of a 'revolutionary ideology in which the ideal of man's total liberation has a central place'.[7] The situation can only lead towards 'the gradual erosion of all moral standards, the breakdown of all criteria of decency and the widespread destruction of confidence in the meaning of values such as truth, adherence to principles, sincerity, altruism, dignity, and honour'.[8]

Havel knew only too well that the Dear Doctor did not give a hoot about what was happening to man or society, and so he upped the ante. The systematic stifling of all that is spontaneous, original and individual in a country could not lead anywhere but to a state of paralysis that affected equally the victims and the oppressors. There was order in the country, but no life. The apparent calm was 'the calm of the morgue or the grave'.

Just as any movement was expunged from society, so too, the category of time became superfluous as well. In his letter, perhaps for the first time, Havel broaches the theme of timelessness, a theme to which he was often to return. Timelessness creates a vacuum that demands to be filled. 'So the disorder of real history is replaced by the orderliness of pseudo-history, whose author is not the life of society, but an official planner. Instead of events we are offered non-events; we live from anniversary to anniversary, from celebration to celebration, from parade to parade, from a unanimous congress to unanimous elections and back again; from the Press Day to the Artillery Day, and vice versa.'[9]

Havel cites the entropic principle of the Second Law of Thermodynamics as the metaphor for the social decay under the Doctor's leadership, but at the same time he points to the inherent propensity of all life to fight back against entropy. And although he gives no time frame, he is confident which of the two forces will eventually prevail. 'In trying to paralyze life, then, the authorities paralyze themselves and, in the long run, make themselves incapable of paralyzing life.'[10] Eventually life would reassert itself with a

---

6 'Dear Dr Husák', in *Open Letters*, 54.
7 Ibid. 60.
8 Ibid. 62.
9 Ibid. 74.
10 Ibid. 75.

vengeance. And Havel goes on to add: 'If life cannot be destroyed for good, then neither can history be brought entirely to halt.'[11]

In retrospect, the audacity of the claim and its validity as a prognosis are simply astonishing. This is Czechoslovakia in 1975. The rebellion has been suppressed, the reforms of 1968 ground to dust. There are precious few voices of dissent to be heard throughout the Communist monolith. The Americans are evacuating Saigon amidst chaos and despair. The Helsinki Accords, about to be signed, represent the new form of the Westphalian peace. They give legitimacy to the Soviets and to their supremacy over their vassals, they provide guarantees for the borders of their empire, and they seemingly perpetuate the division of Europe into East and West. Such pursuit of stability can easily be mistaken for an illusion of permanence. In fact, the whole post-war arrangement would collapse within fourteen years.

Havel's initiative was not entirely unique. He may have been actually inspired by a similar letter written by Alexander Dubček (by then also in internal exile, isolated from society and watched over around the clock by the secret police) to the Czechoslovak puppet parliament on 28 October 1974, the anniversary of independence in 1918. In fact, the two letters have quite a few things in common. Both protest endemic violations of human rights, condemn the omnipresent spectre of the secret police in the authors' personal lives and in the life of Czechoslovak society, and deplore the widening atmosphere of indifference, informing, suspicion and fear.[12]

When Dubček's letter went unanswered, he followed up with another one on 2 February 1975,[13] revisiting some of the same arguments and adding new evidence on illicit monitoring and harassment by the secret police. Perhaps it was his awareness of this second letter that persuaded Havel to return to his writing table and add his voice to the protest.

The differences between the letters of the two men are just as important as their similarities. Whereas Dubček spends a large amount of space by defending the policies of the Prague Spring and trying to persuade his tormenters to return to them, Havel's horizon is in the future, when life reasserts itself against its paralysed rulers. Whereas Dubček strives for rehabilitation and acceptance, Havel declares irreconcilable opposition.

---

11 Ibid.
12 See Shawcross (1990), 211, and Benčík (2012), 101–3.
13 Benčík (2012), 104.

And while Dubček spends pages bemoaning his personal ordeal, Havel is primarily concerned with the ordeal of society at large.

Something seemed to be in the air, for the spring of 1975 in Czecho-slovakia witnessed several public expressions of protest and dissent, including a letter from philosopher Karel Kosík to Jean-Paul Sartre, protesting a catastrophic search of his house, during which a number of documents, including the single manuscript of his latest philosophical work numbering 1,500 pages, were confiscated and irretrievably lost.[14] There was also a letter to the UN Secretary, General Kurt Waldheim, in which Ludvík Vaculík, the wild man of Czech literature, described and condemned another such violation against himself,[15] and a more impersonal criticism in the polemics of Zdeněk Mlynář, a close collaborator of Dubček in 1968, addressed to the Central Committee of the Communist Party on 14 April.[16]

What apparently stimulated this sudden outpouring of protest were the ongoing negotiations among diplomats in Helsinki, which finally culminated in the signing of the Final Document of the Conference on Security and Cooperation in Europe on 1 August 1975. Although the Accords were seen, rightly, as an attempt to de-escalate the Cold War by buttressing a sense of security on both sides, in their 'third basket', the Western negotiators insisted – and the Soviet bloc grudgingly accepted – that an adherence to the standards of human rights among the signatories was a legitimate concern for all, regardless of borders. There is no doubt that the Communist governments thought of this addition as a rhetorical nod to a principle in exchange for some very material concessions by the other side. In fact, they were giving their opponents a lethal weapon that would eventually be instrumental in bringing them down.

The regime responded to the wave of letters with a series of repressive measures, interrogations and house searches primarily among Communist reformers and close collaborators of Dubček in Prague, Brno and Bratislava. Havel's treatment was different. Husák's office returned the letter to him as unread with a note accusing him of trying to foster anti-communist propaganda. He was neither called in for an interrogation, nor was his house searched. In fact he was not bothered at all.

---

14 'Dear Jean Paul Sartre', *Le Monde*, 29 June 1975.
15 'An Open Letter to the Secretary General', *The New York Review of Books*, 30 October 1975.
16 23 April 1975, cf. Benčík (2012), 111.

It would, however, be mistaken to say (as some did)[17] that the secret police ignored Havel, and that it took some time before he was registered as an oppositionist. First of all, he had been registered a long time earlier, but kept on ice so long as he was content to brood, write and entertain at Hrádeček. And second, it was not in the nature of the secret police to ignore insults against the leader of the Party, and of the country, no matter how politely and logically phrased.

In reality, the Party leadership dealt with the letter as an issue of highest importance. On 18 April 1975, ten days after the letter was sent, the politburo of the Party, presided over by Husák himself, met to discuss, among other things, the 'anti-Party activities of Dubček and other persons'.[18] Resolution No. 150/75 was adopted, which, in para II/2., tasked two of its most reliable apparatchiks, Comrade Fojtík and Comrade Švestka, to present the secretariat of the Central Committee with 'a draft of measures re the letter of Havel'.[19] There is no reason to doubt that the two comrades applied themselves diligently to the task. Since little public reaction followed (Švestka was the editor-in-chief of *Rudé právo*, the Party sheet and the largest newspaper in the country), the 'measures' must have taken a different form.

As even the most moronic secret policeman would have realized that Havel was baiting them, they were not going to move directly against him. They may have even been forewarned by the Party secretariat not to do so. But there is little doubt that, throughout the summer and autumn of 1975, they were getting ready to give the playwright his comeuppance. When the moment came, the two major strands of Havel's outward expression, his theatre and his politics, merged into one.

Havel had a neighbour who was a friend, or rather the friend had Havel for a neighbour. He was Andrej Krob, the same gentle giant who first saw Olga waving goodbye to Havel at a railway station when they were both departing for military service, who reappeared as a fellow stagehand and later the technical manager at the Balustrade when Havel was its author star, and who first told Havel of the vacant farmhouse, adjacent to his own, which became Hrádeček. There, sometime in 1973 and with time to spare, Havel gave Krob the manuscript of his latest play, *The Beggar's Opera*, to read.

---

17 Kaiser (2009), 99.
18 Resolution of the Presidium of CC CPC of 18 April 1975, in Benčík (2012), 100.
19 Ibid.

Upon learning that the play did not have a home, Krob, whose own professional career in the theatre was then hanging by a thread, decided to direct it himself. Unmindful of his friend's warnings, he assembled from among other stagehands, lighting men, students and bar acquaintances an ensemble, which started to first read and then rehearse the play, all the time under the watchful eye and gentle guidance of Havel himself.[20] Havel was thrilled at seeing his play in production, even though it was only a makeshift affair, with the rehearsals taking place in Krob's barn across the garden from Havel's house in the spring and summer of 1975.

Even though the phenomenon of 'home theatre' was already flourishing at the time, The Beggar's Opera was too big to fit in a room, and it barely fitted into the barn. Krob's ambition was to stage a public performance. He cleverly drew on the nineteenth-century Enlightenment tradition of patriotic plays routinely performed by local intelligentsia in bars, inns and restaurants around the country. Posing as an amateur troupe planning to stage an unspecified adaptation of The Beggar's Opera, he secured permission from the local authorities to bring the play to an inn, U Čelikovských, in the sleepy Prague outskirts of Dolní Počernice. Ironically, the old official name of the inn was 'The Bastille'. There, on 1 November 1975, the performance finally took place in front of an audience of three hundred people, mostly relatives, friends and acquaintances of the actors, as well as Havel himself, who donned a jacket and tie for the occasion.

In the legend that grew up about the performance, everyone involved, including Havel and the actors onstage, agree that it was a once-in-a-lifetime experience. Most of the audience talked about it in superlatives as one of the greatest theatrical moments of their lives. Havel repeatedly praised it as one of his greatest achievements, greater still than all his premieres on major international stages. The only two malcontents were the emissary of the local municipality, perceptive enough to notice that 'the play had a clearly hostile context', although dumb enough to report the story as taking place in France,[21] and Krob. 'For me it was a mixture of screw-ups, curtains opening at the wrong times, mangled lines, and

---

20 On 29 September 1975, Havel wrote Krob a letter, which contains a mixture of elation over the fact that the play is being produced, with poorly concealed concern about the capabilities of the amateur director and his amateur actors. In Freimanová (2012), 500–10.
21 Citation from Andrej Krob's police file, No. 650 175, in Kaiser (2009), 100.

sweating brow. However, with the benefit of hindsight I realize that it was not so much the theatre performance itself as the fact that it took place under such unbelievable conditions.'[22]

It is difficult to gauge today whether all involved expected the reaction that would follow, although Havel himself had envisaged a smelly object hitting a fan.[23] On the one hand, they were doing nothing illegal or particularly political, and they were adhering to the terms of their licence in not selling tickets for the play and treating the whole evening as a private gathering. On the other, most of them had been aware that their *dramaturge* was not just a banned writer, but also author of the recent public letter of condemnation addressed to Dear Doctor Husák. In fact, Havel gave them a reading of the letter while they were rehearsing at Hrádeček, possibly to dispel any illusions about what they were getting into.

Given the large number of people involved in the rehearsals and the preparation of the performance, it is hard to believe that none of the numerous secret police and their agents snooping around Havel had learned about the event in advance. It is more likely that they had, but did not recognize its significance. Or they may have simply welcomed the event as a pretext finally to suppress the unruly playwright and his gang. In that case, they may have simply chosen to wait, playing their own version of *The Beggar's Opera*.

The police, perhaps for the first time, also showed some real psychological understanding of their quarry, and a shrewd, though morally debased, grasp of how best to deal with him. From the way he invited wrath on himself in openly defying the strongest man in the country, they knew that this was a man who was not afraid, or at best, who was so afraid of being afraid that he would be immune to threats, either psychological or physical, against him. But they must have also sensed that this was a man with a hypertrophied sense of responsibility, and a propensity to blame himself for the misfortunes of others. The best way to hit him was by hitting them.

This may be the only explanation as to why the response that followed was so grossly disproportionate to a single performance of an adaptation of a classical play before an elated but peaceful audience, which quietly dispersed, with the playwright and the ensemble holding an after-stage

22 Kriseová (1991), 63.
23 Letter to Zdeněk Urbánek, 15 October 1975, VHL ID5495.

party in a downtown restaurant adjacent to the headquarters of the Prague police. After spending several days analysing reports from its informers and identifying various members of the audience, the secret police first hauled off Krob for two rounds of exhausting interrogations lasting eighteen hours in total. Some of the questions were straight out of *The Beggar's Opera*, Krob recalled, giving him the opportunity to use some of the lines he had learned in his role as Lockit in his answers.[24] Then the secret police started summoning the performers and members of the audience, and the repressions started. Although even the Communist police in their paranoia were not able to construe a case to launch criminal proceedings, Krob and several others in the troupe lost their jobs. Other people lost their driving licences. A children's play was banned simply because among its audience there were several adults who had also seen the abomination in Dolní Počernice.[25] Indeed, mere presence as a spectator was considered enough of an offence to blacklist Havel's friends Jan Grossman, Pavel Landovský, Vlasta Chramostová and Jan Tříska, and condemn them to unemployment or at best marginal jobs in regional theatres. In the case of Tříska, the police harassment finally led him to leave the country and relocate with his family to Los Angeles.[26]

The whole thing did not stop there. In the following weeks, there took place a number of meetings between the authorities and theatre managers, in which the theatrical establishment was apprised of the 'provocation' and warned of dire consequences for the artistic freedom not only of the likes of Havel, but of Czech theatre in general.

It is this circumstance, more than anything else, that suggests that the whole affair actually may have been a planned operation. By blaming Havel, Krob and their associates for the tightened control over theatres, the authorities hoped to drive a wedge between the disobedient intellectuals and the rest, and isolate Havel even further. Many mediocre and even a few talented actors and playwrights blamed Havel for endangering what little creative freedom remained. Some of them thought of Havel as a reckless adventurer and poseur, while they credited themselves for humbly trying

---

24 Conversation with Anna Freimanová and Andrej Krob, 15 December 2012.
25 The facts about the performance of *The Beggar's Opera*, 25 December 1975, in *Works* 4, 114–24.
26 There he re-launched a distinguished, though modest career in American movies and theatre, e.g. *Ragtime*, *The People vs. Larry Flynt*, *Master and Margarita* at the New York Public Theater, *Largo Desolato* at Yale Repertory Theater, et al.

to preserve what could be preserved without regard for their personal dignity. Since they were mostly scared even to read Havel's plays, they could hardly have realized that they were reciting a version of Macheath's closing monologue:

> What would happen, should I refuse this offer [to save my
> life]? . . . I would be seen as a conceited exhibitionist who
> aspired to playing the conscience of the world; I would sacrifice
> myself for something nobody but me believes in . . .[27]

Judging from the similarly self-deluded reactions of some of the more established actors and directors, a few of them claiming to be Havel's friends, and from the fact that even close friends like Jan Tříska began to stay away, although they would do nothing to denounce him, the police may have succeeded in reaching their tactical objective. Nevertheless, to judge from the train of events that followed, at the strategic level they failed miserably.

---

27 *The Beggar's Opera*, in *Works 4*, 515–16. The English translation is Paul Wilson's, translator's archive.

It's Only Rock 'n' Roll

. . . but I like it.

THE INSPIRING, ENERGIZING AND MOTIVATING ROLE of the collective experience of music has been a political factor throughout history, but never has music had so direct an impact on political change as during the second half of the twentieth century. Rock 'n' roll[1] in particular played a huge role in Czechoslovakia in the sixties, just as it did in many other countries. Because of the parallel cultural revolution in the arts, film, literature and theatre, it may have played an even bigger role, comparable only to that in the United States and Britain. And it was even more despised by the authorities, and more revered by young people, because of where it was coming from. Whereas in the West the anti-establishment and rebellious nature of the music often made it a natural ally of the radical Left, in Czechoslovakia rock 'n' roll was, for the same reason, intrinsically seen as anti-Communist, most notably by the comrades themselves. And for the same reason, it ran into hard times as normalization set in. Bands were first forced to abandon their repertoire of Anglo-American standards and covers and obliged to sing in Czech, a lovely and poetic language, albeit with a pronounced shortage of one-word rhymes that does not lend itself easily to rocking rhythms. Then they were made to cut their hair, dress non-provocatively and audition in front of panels of stone-faced bureaucrats for the licence

---

1 The term is here used in its broader sense, encompassing rock music, modern blues, folk-rock and a number of hybrid and fusion genres.

159

to perform in public. Once qualified, the former rockers were subjected, often willingly, to further humiliations, such as participating in a festival of political (read: conformist) song, or singing an ode on the exploits of a courageous Communist spy who infiltrated Radio Free Europe in Munich and bungled an attempt to blow it up.

Most musicians adapted grudgingly, or at least they pretended to adapt, proving that show business under Communism was still show business. The quality of the music declined as a result, and young rock aficionados were to suffer through more than a decade of bubble-gum rock and soporific pop music.

But a few musicians persevered, using their wits and creative deception to play on, if not on TV and radio, then at least in small clubs, at outdoor festivals, and eventually at weddings and birthday parties. The early Czech pupils of Bob Dylan, led by the pioneer of the genre Karel Kryl (whose 1969 post-invasion record *Little Brother, Close the Door* provided repertoire to sing at parties and around campfires to the lost generation of the next twenty years), created a resilient school of Czech protest song that survived bans, beatings, forced exile and secret police infiltration.

The non-conformist fringe did not put much stock in trying to find ways to deceive censors in order to reach audiences. Rather, they wanted to be left alone and do their thing. They did not see music so much as a profession more as a way of life that made them feel happy and spontaneous and free. This went along with a lifestyle of sex, a limited range of drugs, mostly of domestic provenance, and large quantities of beer. There was also the Czech version of a hippie, New Age, communal spirituality. Such a lifestyle was risky, immensely difficult and impracticable in the quickly 'normalizing' Prague and most other cities. In the early seventies, the non-conformist culture thus quickly moved into the country and congregated around a number of farmhouses, where the young people could practise their music and their lifestyle relatively undisturbed. As a result, many dropped out of school and lost their jobs, or did not even start looking for one. In turn, they came to be harassed, sometimes by the local authorities, sometimes by the police, for various crimes and misdemeanours, be it for not having a paying job, playing loud music with sometimes obscene lyrics at unauthorized concerts or the possession of marijuana. After first being simply dropouts, they were gradually driven underground, which is how the whole diverse counter-culture obtained its name, courtesy of one of its ideologists, an art historian and poet in art and life, Ivan Jirous, aka Magor, a name best translated as 'Shithead', and, in this particular instance, meant as an honorific.

Magor became the manager of the leading underground group The Plastic People of the Universe, named after a song by Frank Zappa on his seminal album *Absolutely Free* whose lyrics about conformist people and boring girlfriends pretty much summed up the attitudes of the members of the group towards the establishment and the world at large. After Magor was released from prison, where he had spent a year for eating part of a page of the Communist Party newspaper *Rudé právo* in a Prague bar in front of a retired secret police major, and remarking that the same fate awaited the 'Bolsheviks' one day, he set out, together with the Plastic People and like-minded groups and musicians, to organize festivals of 'second culture'. When the police brutally dispersed a concert in South Bohemia in the spring of 1974, and at the 'first festival of second culture', held in Postupice in September of that year, the StB became alerted to the existence of an underground community of the 'hairies'.[2] Even so, it did not move to intervene until the spring of 1975, when it launched *Operation Plastic*, aimed at discouraging the younger generation from adopting a similar lifestyle.

All this was light years away from Václav Havel's lifestyle and his way of thinking. While Havel was a courteous big-city sophisticate, well used to the limelight (although he had seen little of it lately), Magor acted as a country bumpkin, deliberately as rough in his manners as he was in his language. While Havel was becoming increasingly political, Jirous and the Plastic People largely shunned anything connected to politics. While Havel's aim was to make the establishment see the error of its ways and redress the grievances, Jirous's objective was to create a parallel counter-culture that 'would not take as its aim the destruction of the establishment, because to do so would be to drive itself into its arms'.[3] While Havel, with his rather limited musicality, grooved on Johnny Cash and the Bee Gees, Jirous pursued the psychedelic variety of music to its extremes. And yet,

---

2   Pavel Ptáčník, 'První festival druhé kultury' ('The First Festival of the Second Culture'), in *Sborník Archivu bezpečnostních složek* 5/2007, 343–51.
3   Ivan Jirous, 'Zpráva o třetím českém hudebním obrození' ('A Report on the Third Czech Musical Renaissance'), in Jirous (1997), 197.

when the secret police decided to crush Magor and the underground once and for all, Havel was quick to understand the far-reaching significance of this latest attack on freedom of expression and thought, and came, at first almost single-handedly, to their rescue.

His own remembrance of how he first came to be aware of the story has the feel of a Gothic tale. 'It all began sometime in January or February 1976. I was at Hrádeček, alone, there was snow everywhere, a night blizzard was raging outside, I was writing something, and suddenly there was a pounding on the door. I opened it and there stood a friend of mine, whom I don't wish to name, half frozen and covered with snow.'[4]

The friend, art historian František Šmejkal, whom Havel only identifies as The Snowman,[5] offered to arrange a meeting with Ivan Jirous, which occurred at his place about a month later. Jirous gave Havel *The Report on the Third Czech Musical Revival* to read, 'talked and talked' while the 'long-haired people would come and go' and, most importantly, played the Plastics' music on a 'rasping old tape recorder'.[6] It was then that Havel saw the light.

A couple of weeks later, on 16 March 1976, the secret police rounded up the Plastics, their manager and a number of other musicians, nineteen people altogether. When Havel, who was at Hrádeček, learned about the arrests, he went immediately to Prague, because it was 'obvious that this was up to me'.[7] Though made in retrospect, this statement is on the face of it astonishing. There was no political, social, artistic or personal logic to it. Havel barely knew Jirous, and he did not know the others at all. Unlike his old friends among the writers, his more recent friends among the purged Communists or his theatre crowd, the 'hairies' were neither promising future political allies nor a popular cause. Indeed, after the Velvet Revolution, when Havel became president, Magor, despite seeing his books in print and receiving justified rewards and plaudits for his poetry, remained as anti-establishment as ever, attacking Havel periodically, and eventually drinking himself to death. Havel may have dreamt about a liberal democratic society, but, to the Plastics, it turned out to be as alien as the Communist system. 'I

---

4 *Disturbing the Peace*, 125–6.
5 Havel spoke and wrote quite freely about his fellow dissidents, in keeping with the spirit of openness and civic spirit of the Charter 77 community. The fact that here he declines to reveal the identity of his guest suggests that he was one of a number of close but undeclared sympathizers.
6 *Disturbing the Peace*, 126.
7 Ibid. 127.

am no less a dissident in a society of shopping, shopping and shopping than I was in a society of socialism, socialism and socialism', Vratislav Brabenec, a saxophone player with the Plastics, remarked more than thirty years later, adding a haunting parable: 'We are all like bats, flying blindly through the dark towards our creator, the God who does not exist.'[8]

The clean-cut, fastidious Havel identified more with the idea of the underground than with their lifestyle. Although he did subsequently praise their music, and host and participate in some of their concerts at Hrádeček, it was more in admiration of its rebellious, non-conformist nature, than in appreciation of the music, which had its roots in Zappa's Mothers of Invention, the Velvet Underground's John Cale and Lou Reed, Captain Beefheart, Pink Floyd and the Soft Machine. Nevertheless, he unmistakably recognized the attack against the 'hairies' as 'an attack by the totalitarian system on life itself, on the very essence of human freedom and integrity'.[9] Many people, even those who were no friends of the establishment, were revolted by the look and the sound of the Plastics, and never understood why someone as distinguished as Havel was wasting time with losers. The point Havel was making would be made – and equally misunderstood – by his Poděbrady schoolmate Miloš Forman in *The People vs. Larry Flynt* through the words of its anti-hero: 'If freedom of expression is guaranteed for me, then it will be guaranteed for everyone, for I am the worst.' The Plastics were most certainly not the worst, but they were partly by necessity, and partly by choice, the lowest. And Havel intuited that the fight must start from there, from the bottom. Early on, this distinguished him from the much admired Alexander Dubček and his fellow reformists of 1968, who were also showing signs of stirring in the mid-seventies but who – with the exception of Zdeněk Mlynář – limited their struggle to efforts to rehabilitate the Prague Spring, with themselves as its architects. While the practitioners of the classless society were defending their class, the elitist scion of a bourgeois family was fighting for the underground.

The official media of the regime had already started a concerted propaganda campaign, the standard prelude to imminent harsh punishment. On 8 April 1976, all the main Czechoslovak dailies published versions of what was in essence a single boilerplate piece written somewhere in the

---

8   Ed Vullamy, 'Children of the Revolution', *The Observer*, 6 September 2009.
9   *Disturbing the Peace*, 128.

Party secretariat. The young musicians were depicted as antisocial hooligans, alcoholics and drug addicts, motivated by their hostility towards the socialist system and its main beneficiary, the working class. 'Perhaps a musical solo on a carpenter's plane, banging on cymbals tied together with a lady's bra, beating a car exhaust or splitting wood and throwing the logs to the mostly young audience is considered art in the West . . . Here, however, we are not interested, thank you.'[10]

Knowing they had to respond, lest the caricature become established wisdom, Havel teamed up with Jiří Němec, a Catholic philosopher and psychologist, and an unanointed guru of the underground, with whom he had last quarrelled in *Tvář*. Typically for him, he meticulously planned the defence of the jailed musicians as a military campaign, complete with flowcharts. After the 'Ten Points', the writers' letters on behalf of political prisoners and the previous petition drive on behalf of *Tvář*, he was an experienced petitioner and signature-collector. Knowing that by soliciting support from fellow musicians and audiences of the Plastics he would only bring other people into trouble, he aimed for the indisputably 'serious', 'distinguished' and 'respected' members of the older generation of writers and intellectuals.

First came the Slavia table circle, Jiří Kolář, Zdeněk Urbánek and Josef Hiršal, who co-signed, together with the philosopher Jan Patočka and art theoretician Josef Chalupecký, a private appeal to President Husák.[11] This was followed by an open statement signed by Havel, the former reform Communists Pavel Kohout, Ivan Klíma and Ludvík Vaculík, but also by one of the arch enemies of the regime – professor Václav Černý. The letter contains the central argument for taking up the cause of freedom of expression in general and artistic freedom in particular, regardless of the circumstances. 'If today young people with long hair are condemned for their unconventional music as criminals without notice, it will be all that much easier tomorrow to condemn in the same way other artists for their novels, poems, essays and paintings.'[12]

All of the above, joined by the poet Jaroslav Seifert, soon to be a Nobel Prize winner for literature, signed an open letter to another Nobel Prize

---

10 'No need to worry' ('Zbytečná starost'), *Rudé právo*, 8 April 1977. Actually the above list of mortal sins was taken from Jirous's own admiring description of a performance of another band, Akord, which was not a part of the round-up at all. No matter.

11 'Letter to President Husák', 8 April 1976, VHL ID5519.

12 'A Statement', 12 June 1976, in Komeda et al. (2012), 145.

winner, the German radical writer Heinrich Böll, which was published in the *Frankfurter Allgemeine Zeitung* on 28 August, two days before the planned beginning of the trial.[13] It was an appeal to the well-known German intellectual to take a stand in the defence of non-conformist art and the freedom of artistic expression. But what made even more of an impression on Böll, as is evident from his reply on 6 September in the same paper,[14] was the understanding of the authors of the letter that the attack was levelled against them as well. 'We cannot but feel that in a way these young people are so harshly persecuted on our behalf – that is to say, exactly because they cannot rely on the solidarity of their colleagues abroad as much as we can. Although we are active in other spheres of culture, we refuse to accept the status of some kind of prominent protected species and silently accept that others, who are less protected, can be tried as criminals without the world of culture taking notice.'[15]

The trial did not take place until 21–23 September. Whether the postponement was caused by the publicity surrounding the letter to Böll or by other reasons, the preordained outcome remained the same. For aggravated hooliganism, the court sentenced Ivan Jirous to eighteen months in prison, Pavel Zajíček to a year, and Svatopluk Karásek and Vratislav Brabenec to eight months. At this stage, the regime was not yet used to the phenomenon of flagrant opposition, and this might explain why, in contrast to many of the later trials, it was conducted in public and in the presence not only of the families of the accused and their friends, but also of many of the intellectuals who took a stand in their defence. Among those present was Václav Havel, by now in his sixth year of an inner struggle between his artistic vocation, his personal concerns and his feelings of a larger responsibility to himself and others. As evidenced by his report from the trial, written two weeks later, this, more than his inner dialogues, his discussions with Olga and his writer friends, the affair of *The Beggar's Opera* or his dispassionate analysis of the pathology of time in his letter to Husák, was his moment on the road to Damascus, his epiphany, his *Aha-Erlebnis*.[16]

---

13 Reprinted in ibid. 146–7.
14 Ibid. 148.
15 Letter to Heinrich Böll, 28 August 1976, in ibid. 146–7.
16 'The Trial', 11 October 1976, in *Works 4*, 135–42.

His report, called *The Trial* in a deliberate allusion to Franz Kafka, is in contrast to many of his earlier pieces not a political polemic, but rather a part phenomenological analysis, part theatrical review and part painful introspection: 'It does not happen often and usually it happens at moments when few expect it: something somewhere snaps and an event – thanks to an unpredictable synergy of its own internal prerequisites and of more or less random external circumstances – suddenly oversteps the limits of its position in the context of habitual everydayness, breaks the crust of what it is supposed to be and what it appears to be, and suddenly discloses its innermost, hidden and in some respects, symbolic meaning.'[17]

Perhaps the reason why the experience of the trial struck Havel with such force was that he perceived it as much as a theatrical performance as a real-life trial. Havel was acutely aware that what he was witnessing was not a time-honoured process of seeking justice, but a piece of theatre, which had been scripted beforehand, with roles allotted to the judges, the accused and the audience, and with the outcome known in advance. Yet something snapped: 'The truer [the actors] were to their roles, the more clearly they uncovered its unintended meaning, gradually turning themselves into the co-creators of a completely different performance than the one they thought they were playing in, or wanted to play in.'[18]

The layout of the play was clearly a tragedy, but its tone was not. The tragic denouement contrasted with the farcical subject matter of the trial and the painstaking thoroughness with which the court laboured towards its conclusion. 'Enough of the comedy, dismiss,' Havel notes, was the only thing that should have been done, but couldn't occur under the circumstances.[19]

And yet, in this macabre spectacle, Havel found something deeply uplifting. What emerged from behind the smokescreen of arbitrary bureaucratic process was nothing less than 'a thrilling argument about the meaning of human life'.[20] He saw it in the conduct and spirit of the defendants at the bar, even now manacled as if they presented a violent threat, and in their friends and supporters who greeted each other,

---

17 Ibid. 135.
18 Ibid. 136.
19 Ibid. 139.
20 Ibid. 138.

embraced, and exchanged information in the halls and on the staircases of the courthouse, ignoring the conspicuous presence of dozens of undercover secret policemen.

> It is clear that when an event is out of joint with itself – out of joint in the deeper sense that I have in mind here – then at the same time something unavoidably goes out of joint within us: a new perspective of the world will open a new perspective of our own human possibilities, of what we are and what we could be, and so – torn out of our 'routine humanity' we stand once again face to face with the most important question of all: How to come to terms with ourselves?[21]

Rarely has a political movement been born neither of an idea of changing the world, nor of the opposition to other ideas of changing the world, but rather of an individual, internal, psychological need to find a balance in one's life. The ambition was simultaneously modest and staggering. Reaching it required nothing more and nothing less than staying true to oneself. Its corollary was ignoring or resisting the demands of the outside world to suppress, alter or mask one's own identity, demands that are present in any type of world, but which were ominously imperative and persistent in the world of post-totalitarian socialism. Reading and hearing the accounts and recollections of Václav Havel and others who were there, in the dark, unfriendly building of the Prague-West District Court in Karmelitská Street, metres away from the baroque and Gothic glory of Prague's Lesser Town, it is impossible to escape the conclusion that Charter 77, the human rights movement that all the power, might and force of the regime would be unable to suppress, was born there that day.

---

21 Ibid. 140–1.

THE CHARTER

No society, no matter how technologically advanced, can
function without a moral basis, a conviction, which is not
a matter of opportunity, circumstances or anticipated benefits.
However, morality is not here for the society to function,
but simply because it makes a human being human.
　　　　　　　　　　　– Jan Patočka, *On the duty to resist injustice*

AMONG ALL THE EASY-TO-OVERLOOK PEOPLE, one would never count Jaroslav Kořán; a boisterous, ebullient and vocal photographer and magnificent translator into Czech of Henry Miller, Ken Kesey, Kurt Vonnegut, John Kennedy Toole, Tom Stoppard and other modern Anglo-American writers. In fact, his big mouth first got him into trouble in the legendary bar incident involving Magor and the retired secret police major, and earned him a year in jail. After his release, he found work in a water purification plant whose noise, friends said, made him speak even louder in order to be heard. Yet for years he was the unnamed godfather of Charter 77. It was in his flat on one of Prague's busiest thoroughfares on 11 December 1976 that, with memories of the Plastics' trial still fresh in their minds, Havel and Němec first met with Zdeněk Mlynář, the former top-level Communist functionary of the Prague Spring, and Pavel Kohout, the early troubadour of the idealistic Communist youth, as well as an early renegade of the movement, to discuss a document that would mark the launch of a more permanent defence of human rights and civic freedoms. As befitted a former apparatchik, Mlynář was thinking in terms of a committee, whereas Havel had in mind something looser and more open, a community of like-minded people. As a compromise they agreed on a 'civic initiative'. In two subsequent meetings, attended also by Dubček's Foreign Minister Jiří Hájek, the revolutionary Marxist Petr Uhl, historians Pavel Bergmann and Vendelín Komeda, politologist Jaroslav Šabata and the writer Ludvík Vaculík, the idea crystallized into the text of a joint declaration.

Havel always sought to dismiss the debate over the authorship of the Charter 77 declaration, insisting that the text was a collective effort, emerging from a lively, often heated discussion. Kohout, on the other hand, has been unequivocal in stating that the Charter had two parents, of which he was one.[1] Unfortunately, no early draft of the document has been preserved, but even the later drafts suggest more than one or even two authors.[2] The first surviving draft, dated retrospectively 16 December,[3] already contains the crucial preamble, which anchors the initiative in the International Covenant on Civil and Political Rights (ICCPR) and the International Covenant on Economic, Social and Cultural Rights (ICESCR), both of which the participating states of the 1975 Helsinki Conference on Security and Cooperation in Europe (CSCE), including Communist Czechoslovakia, undertook to abide by and implement in their national legislations. It proceeds, like all the subsequent versions, by contrasting the specific rights contained in both documents with the actual situation in 'normalized' Czechoslovakia. Finally, it announces the formation of a 'Committee for Human Rights' to monitor and advocate respect for the rights guaranteed by the said conventions and by the domestic legislation, and lists its future tasks accordingly.

The second full draft, dated retrospectively 17 December,[4] differs from the first and from the structural outline dated 18 December, in adding the acknowledgement of its authors' 'co-responsibility' for the state of their society, and their 'faith in the meaning of civic involvement'. This may not seem a particularly revolutionary idea, but in fact it amounted to the ultimate heresy, since under the Communist orthodoxy it was the

---

1   Pavel Kohout, *And This Was My Life?*, in Kohout (2011), Vol. 2, Kindle Edition loc. 5904.
2   According to Ibid. loc. 5914, the final draft for distribution was finished on 17 December.
3   Císařovská and Prečan (2007), Vol. 3, P1/1, 4–7.
4   Ibid. P1/3, 9–12.

Party, as the 'leading force' in society, that was solely responsible for the state of society. The hysterical reaction of the authorities to a document that advocated adherence to principles they themselves had undertaken to uphold suggests that they were aware of the implication and of the threat to their monopoly that it entailed. The second draft also describes the genealogy of the initiative as a 'free, informal and open community of people of diverse views, faiths and professions'[5] emanating from the 'background of various friendly, solidarity-based and professional relationships'.[6] There is little doubt that this rootedness in responsibility as well as the inclusive and non-ideological characterization, so essential to the Charter's moral ethos and its way of operating in subsequent years, came from Havel. The title for the initiative, with its allusions to Magna Carta, and its penchant for numerals, came from Pavel Kohout. The crucial reference to the Closing Act of the Helsinki Conference on Security and Cooperation in Europe, whose binding articles were by then incorporated into the domestic law of all of the signatory countries, including Czechoslovakia, was supplied by the philosopher Ladislav Hejdánek, one of several people with whom the text was discussed. The editing, on the evidence of some of the handwritten inserts, is Havel's own.

The shorter outline of 18 December[7] preserves the preamble, but under the sub-heading 'Body' it contains, somewhat frivolously, only the words 'ha ha' (equivalent to 'blah blah blah blah'), suggesting a general consensus on what the body of the text would contain, and possibly the delegation of the responsibility for editing this part of the text to an individual, or individuals, most likely to include Havel, Kohout and Mlynář (the only lawyer among the original drafters). For the first time, the initiative is given the name 'Charter 77'.

The second draft of the text names as the sole spokesman for the group Jiří Hájek, the Czechoslovak Foreign Minister in 1968, who tried, in vain, to get the United Nations Security Council involved in the aftermath of the Soviet invasion. Petr Uhl, at the suggestion of his wife, Anna Šabatová,[8] came up with the idea of three spokesmen for the group, both to reflect its

---

5 Ibid. 11.
6 Ibid.
7 Ibid. P1/2, 8–9.
8 Kaiser (2009), 117.

diverse backgrounds and no doubt also to shield the group from instant silencing should one of its leaders be jailed – or worse. In the third draft of the document,[9] which differed only in small details from the published version, a dotted line was left to make room for the names of the additional spokesmen.

Jiří Hájek had already been agreed upon. That Havel would become one – again, the suggestion came from Anna Šabatová – seemed more self-evident to others present than to Havel himself. In a dialectical pattern that was to repeat itself thirteen years later when he was nominated for president, Havel was at first reluctant to accept a position that would cause him a whole lot of trouble, require vast amounts of his time and keep him away from his writing; at the same time he was clearly aware that he would 'feel like a clown'[10] if he rejected full involvement in an initiative he himself had done so much to organize. Moreover, Uhl took away the impression from the meeting that the suggestion was 'not expressly disagreeable' to Havel.[11]

Because the pattern repeated itself on several occasions, always with the same result, it has inevitably raised questions as to how genuine Havel's reluctance was. Since in the end he was always prepared to answer the call, there occasionally appeared snide aspersions of coyness and insincerity; and, as with all such allegations, they are hard to refute conclusively. However, Havel's misgivings and uncertainties were first and foremost directed to himself rather than to those around him. Perhaps it points to a typical intellectual tendency to explore both sides of any issue, and to dwell on finer considerations when a situation demands a radical step, a tendency of which Havel was certainly not innocent. Maybe too it was his lifelong feeling of guilt for his privileged background that made it difficult for him, then or later, to accept posts or accolades as a matter of course. But at the same time it attests to the seriousness and real sense of responsibility with which the playwright approached his decisions, always as much a matter of existential dilemmas to him as of practical consequences.

There were two candidates for the third spokesman position, philosopher Jan Patočka and literary scholar Václav Černý. Their nominations were significant. In later reincarnations of the 'spokesmen

---

9   18–19 December 1976, Císařovská and Prečan (2007), Vol. 3, P1/4, 12–15.
10 *Dálkový výslech*, 118. Translation author's.
11 Kaiser (2009) *Dissident*, 117.

team', which rotated by consensus every twelve months, one member usually represented the broad, liberal, secular opposition, in this particular case embodied by Havel, the second, the disenfranchised reform Communists of 1968, and the third, the growing number of religious-minded dissidents, both Catholic and Protestant. But Patočka was not particularly religious, at least not overtly, and Černý was avowedly secular and close to the non-Communist Left. The symbolism of their nomination stemmed from other roots. As scholars of the older generation, they both represented the bridge to the country's non-totalitarian, democratic past in the years of Masaryk's and Beneš's First Republic before World War II. Of the two, Černý had been by far the more openly political and the more directly polemical than the more reclusive and academic Patočka. These same qualities, together with his legendary abrasive temper, made Černý the riskier candidate of the two. For this explicit reason and perhaps for others as well, Havel sided from the start with Patočka's nomination, and paid him several visits to persuade him. Like Havel, Patočka was at first reluctant, but like Havel, he also saw the incontrovertible logic in the direction his lifelong work and his thinking were leading him. Nevertheless, always gentlemanly and scrupulously fair, he insisted that Černý be given the first right of refusal, a task that fell to Havel and that he quickly accomplished to everyone's satisfaction, although the lingering bitterness stayed with Černý until his death.[12] In all likelihood, Patočka's acceptance of the role cost him his life. At the same time, Havel was probably right when he wrote: 'I do not know what would have become of the Charter if in its beginnings Patočka had not illuminated its path with the light of his great personality.'[13]

When all three spokesmen were in place, the third draft of the document was submitted to the group of initiators on 20 December. Six collectors of signatures were nominated, among them Anna Marvanová, Rudolf Slánský, Jiří Dienstbier and Otta Bednářová,[14] and also Havel, who was to seek signatures among artists.[15]

---

12 Vladislav (2012), 641.
13 *Disturbing the Peace*, 136.
14 Uhl (2013), 165.
15 Kaiser (2009), 119, Suk (2013), 51. In *Disturbing the Peace* Havel himself speaks about 'around ten' collectors, but the vagueness in a book published before 1989 may have been deliberate, to mislead the secret police.

The founding document may have had more than one father, but the time-consuming and risky management of the initiative was overwhelmingly Havel's. He wrote and personally delivered instructions for the collectors, containing a different list of the people to be approached for each one, a description of the procedure for signing, information about the deadline and, for the inner group, the date of the next meeting, as well as a warning against any premature distribution or disclosure.

On 29 December, a final meeting took place in Havel's flat in Dejvice.[16] The 241 signatures collected[17] were a better result than expected, largely thanks to the more than a hundred delivered by Zdeněk Mlynář, whose task was to canvass among the ex-Communists. Apparently, there was something to be said for Party discipline even among those expelled from it. The work done, Havel produced a bottle of champagne and the group toasted the accomplishment.

On this occasion, Havel recollected both his apprehension that the police had got wind of the operation, and his amazement that it should have been otherwise. Yet nothing happened on that day, or at the next, larger meeting on 3 January 1977, convened to discuss the future plans for the initiative.

The inaction of the police invites speculation. Statistically, it defies belief that none of the quarter of a thousand signatories, let alone the scores of people who declined to sign, talked about it to their friends and family, or that one or two of this larger number did not inform the authorities. It is equally improbable that the police would not have registered the frantic activities among several of its high-priority objects of attention, and there are indications that it had.[18] The mystery is compounded by the claim of the then Czechoslovak minister of the interior, Jaromír Obzina, who stated that the secret police had known about the preparations for a document of this kind since September, i.e. at the time of the Plastics' trial.[19] One likely explanation has to do with the deliberate timing of the final preparations by Havel and the others for the Christmas and New Year period. During the holidays things slow down in most Western countries,

---

16 Keane (1999) erroneously places the meeting at the Havels' flat on the river, where Havel and Olga had not lived for years.

17 The number of signatures under the founding statement is variously given as 243, 242 and 241. The last number, based on the painstakingly thorough research work done by Prečan et al. (see Císařovská and Prečan, 2007) is the most authoritative.

18 E.g. Kaiser (2009), 118.

19 Císařovská and Prečan (2007), Vol. 3, P7/11, 169.

but in normalized Czechoslovakia, where there was little else to celebrate, the maintenance of peace and quiet combined with a lot of feasting, and, on New Year's Eve, also drinking, was a ritual respected by all. Even the secret police and their agents had families and were not going to spend the holidays watching Havel's flat. The other, somewhat more sinister explanation, is that the police more or less knew what was about to happen and decided to let it go ahead[20] so that they could round up all involved and convict them of anti-state activities afterwards. As in the fifties, even though in less dramatic fashion, the system still fed off both perceived and demonstrable threats to its stability. To confiscate a bunch of papers and a few signatures in a private home was a routine operation. To be able to parade an organized group caught peddling its wares abroad was a scoop. In either case, the secret police would not have left behind any documents that would expose it to charges of deliberate inaction.

On 3 January, Havel once again prepared an agenda for the meeting. The first part of the meeting was to cover organizational matters, such as information about the signature drive, distribution of the document, discussion of joint tactics for assumed interrogations, dealing with the media, and maintaining contact among the signatories. This was to be followed in the second half by the consideration of strategy for the future.

By the evening of 5 January, when Havel recruited his close friend Zdeněk Urbánek, who had attended some of the earlier meetings and lived a few blocks away, as a secretary to help him address, fill and seal 250 envelopes with the founding document and the list of signatories, the police had awoken from its New Year's slumber.[21] Possibly acting on information gained by bugging Kohout's flat,[22] or on signals from abroad that a number of leading papers were getting ready to publish the document,[23] they went on alert and launched an emergency operation involving hundreds of uniformed and undercover officers. Their first intervention, during the night, was an act of sabotage. Someone cut through the hydraulic lines of the clutch on Havel's Mercedes car, until then one of the principal vehicles

---

20 cf. Uhl (2013), 165.
21 According to the Czech historian Petr Blažek who had access to the police archives, one of the three spokesmen, philosopher Jan Patočka, was summoned for questioning already on 5 January (*Historical Magazine*, Czech TV, 6 July 2007).
22 Kaiser (2009), 121.
23 It is also possible that the police had a human source. In such cases they were nevertheless likely to refer to information gained through electronic surveillance to protect their 'humint'.

of collection and distribution. Havel had to walk up the hill to Urbánek's flat, where he met with Pavel Landovský, whose task had been to pick up the original signed documents from Kohout's flat in the Salmovský Palace opposite Prague Castle. Landovský noticed that the house was under surveillance. Kohout, who had also suspected that he was being bugged, treated his visitor to a show of pantomime until the actor understood that the conspiracy-minded author had hidden the precious petitions with signatures in a toolbox on the communal staircase outside the apartment,[24] and transferred them first under his coat and then into his own ageing Saab.[25] Contrary to the plan, Landovský had also brought Ludvík Vaculík, a fellow writer and a fresh signatory. In Urbánek's flat, observed from the bed by the host's twenty-six-year-old poetess-mistress, the men put the final touches on their deliveries. For reasons none of them entirely understood, they all later remembered bursting into repeated fits of laughter while going about their tasks. Finally, they put the envelopes into Landovský's car with Havel riding shotgun, and set out to drop them in a number of separate postboxes so as to diminish the risk of their confiscation in one fell swoop.

There are several accounts of what happened next.[26] The most dramatic, if not necessarily most accurate, comes from Pavel Landovský,[27] the driver of the get-away Saab, which did not quite get away, for it was immediately followed by a fleet of unmarked, though souped-up Škodas. In their desperation to be the first to get to the perps, two of the police cars collided. The chase proceeded at a breakneck pace, only interrupted by Landovský screeching to a halt in front of a postbox and Havel stuffing in a couple of dozen envelopes. Finally, as in 'a gangster movie',[28] the Saab became surrounded and was forced to stop. Landovský locked the car from the inside and let the raving cops scream and bang on the car's door and bonnet. The notoriously temperamental actor reacted in kind. According to later police records, he screamed: 'Let me out at those bolshies and I'll stomp

---

24 Conversation with Pavel Kohout, 22 October 2012.
25 Conversation with Pavel Landovský, 22 October 2012.
26 In fact, Havel wrote a hundred-page report on the launch of the Charter and its aftermath, which he had hidden so well he was never able to find it (*Disturbing the Peace*, 123).
27 As quoted in Kriseová (1991), 76–7. There are other, almost identical versions, in Landovský (2010), 227–30, and in Conversation with Pavel Landovský, 22 October 2012. The following account draws on all three.
28 Conversation with Pavel Landovský, 20 October 2012.

them into the ground.'[29] The playwright, sitting next to him, just remarked drily: 'This looks like a nice beginning to the struggle for human rights.'[30]

When Havel observed that 'the gentlemen might really be the police'[31] Landovský unlocked the door but held on to the steering wheel, screaming at the top of his lungs. The next thing he saw were the soles of Havel's shoes. 'They sucked him out like a rolled-up carpet.'[32] Vaculík met with a similar fate.[33]

As the whole thing was being recorded on a video camera by a plain-clothes officer, passers-by, recognizing a popular actor, started crowding around the car under the impression that they were watching a movie shoot.

When the police realized they would have to break Landovský's hands to pry him out, they put a young policeman in the Saab and ordered the actor to follow a police car. The young man, who explained apologetically that he was actually from the narcotics squad, told Landovský that they had been on a full alert since two in the morning. 'You fucked up, man . . . They will shoot you to pieces.'[34] The car started going down the hill from the Prague Castle, and Landovský replied: 'Look, either you're going to bring me a toothbrush and a carton of cigarettes to my cell or I'll slam this car at full speed into that wall over there. We will both be dead, but you first, since the wall is on your side.'[35] The man later brought Landovský half a carton of his favourite cigarettes, apologizing for not being able to get more because, as with many other things, they were in short supply.

More than twelve hours of interrogation in separate rooms followed. At midnight, the police let the three men plus Zdeněk Urbánek, who had been detained at home, go. In the morning all three were hauled in again and the interrogation went on. The routine continued through the next week.

Remembering the scene of the chase later for Eda Kriseová, Landovský made an important observation: 'People said about Vašek that he was such a decent, gentle fellow. But he is a tough bloke, a stand-up guy, and he had been preparing for what happened then all his life.'[36]

---

29 Special information no. 7, 13 January 1977, Archives of the Ministry of Interior V-33766HV. Císařovská and Prečan (2007), Vol. 3, p913, 212
30 Kriseová (1991), 76.
31 Ibid.
32 Ibid.
33 Ibid.
34 Ibid.
35 Ibid.
36 Ibid. 78.

The next day the story was out in the main papers in Germany, France, Britain, Italy, the United States and other countries, courtesy of an unorthodox press attaché in the West German Embassy, Wolfgang Runge, who sent it to the radio journalist Hans-Peter Riese, for a long time a thorn in the side of the Czechoslovak Communist authorities, who in turn distributed the document further and negotiated its simultaneous publication. There may have been an earlier and more romantic attempt to smuggle the text out of the country through a glamorous Czech émigré named Ilona Drumm, who allegedly memorized it by heart while drinking champagne with Pavel Kohout, but that has an apocryphal feel to it.[37] Even though the police managed to confiscate a large part of the original batch of the Charter mailings, they did not recover all of them. Surprisingly enough, the envelopes that had already found their way into the postbox before the three men were apprehended reached their addressees.

The politburo of the Central Committee met on Friday, 7 January, twenty-four hours after the confiscation of the document, and resolved that:

1. Charter 77 is an anti-state, counter-revolutionary document; a platform for the creation of a bourgeois party
2. The signatories of the Charter are adversaries of socialism . . . ranging from representatives of bourgeoisie to renegades of the workers' movement
3. The Charter was prepared in collusion with [people] abroad where it was also made public

and it decided:

— to start criminal proceeding under §112 and §98 of the criminal code
— to utilize all measures of administrative nature against the signatories[38]

---

37 Kohout (2011), location 5924–5932, also conversation with Pavel Kohout, 22 October 2012.
38 Resolution of the Politburo of the Central Committee of CPC on the Declaration of Charter 77 with instructions for the judiciary and the prosecutor's office of ČSSR No. VIII FG a 0022/77. In Císařovská and Prečan (2007), Vol. 3, P7/3, 143, facsimile 408.

1. Božena Havlová and her sons, 1938.

2. Good soldiers Havel, 1959.

3. Silver wind: Jan Zábrana, Václav Havel and Jiří Paukert, 1957.

4. The young artist in his den.

5. With Olga at Café Slavia, Prague, 1959.

6. Private view in the basement of Kohout's country house: Václav Havel, Pavel Kohout, Ludvík Vaculík, Ivan Klíma et al.

7. 'The Last Supper', 28 May 1979:
Jiří Dienstbier, Václav Havel, Jitka
Vodňanská, Karel Trinkewitz
et al.

8. The mysterious dude,
Fatherland Rally, 1971.

9. The Plastic People of the
Universe: Vratislav Brabenec,
Jiří Kabeš, Martin 'Magor' Jirous,
Václav Havel. Hrádeček, 1978.

10. The Founding Father, Hrádeček, 1980s.

12. Václav and Olga, 1970s.

11. The spokespersons of Charter 77 – Václav Havel, Jiří Hájek, Jiří Dienstbier, Ladislav Hejdánek, Václav Benda, Zdena Tominová. Prague, 1979.

13. Comrade Havel, 1970s.

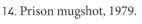

14. Prison mugshot, 1979.

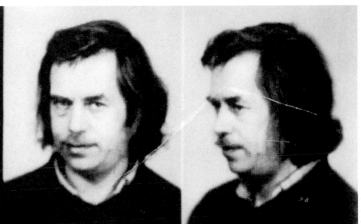

15. Hrádeček (right) and
Lunokhod (left), 1978.

16. The brewery worker, Trutnov, 1974.

17. The spokesmen of Charter 77, Jiří Hájek, Ladislav Hejdánek, Václav Havel. Prague, 1979.

18. Free at last. In the Pod Petřínem hospital with Jiří an Jan Ruml, Ivan and Olga, February 198

19. International Human Rights Day rally at Škroupovo Square, 10 December 1988. Ladislav Lis, Václav Malý, Václav Havel, Rudolf Battěk.

20. The birth of the Civic Forum, Actors' Studio, 19 November 1989.

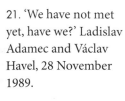

21. 'We have not met yet, have we?' Ladislav Adamec and Václav Havel, 28 November 1989.

22. 'Truth and love must prevail over lies and hatred!'
Wenceslas Square, December 10, 1989.

23. United we stand. Alexandr Dubček and
Václav Havel, Wenceslas Square, 24 November 1989.

24. Re-elected.
President Havel
and the First Lady,
July 5, 1990.

The Party propaganda mill was ready to grind. On 7 January, the first unsigned editorial with the name 'In whose interest?' made the second page of the Party newspaper *Rudé právo*. Only a vague reference was made to the unspecified antisocialist attacks and activities of a group of frustrated enemies of the regime, who, having lost their battle in 1968, had come back for another round. 'But can anyone who lies down on the railroad tracks to stop history blame the train for cutting his legs off?' asked the unknown author – an original, if rather bloodthirsty question.[39] From among the domestic 'so-called' defenders of human rights behind these activities, the paper did the honour of naming 'Mr Havel who grew up a son of millionaires and never forgave the working class for putting a stop to the various "entrepreneurial activities" of his family clan',[40] and 'Ludvík Vaculík, the author of the counter-revolutionary pamphlet "2000 Words"'.[41] The piece ends in an unmistakable threat: 'Whoever would want to stand in the way of our people and violate the laws of our socialist state must count with consequences.'[42]

A much bigger article followed, published on 12 January under the lovable title 'The Washouts and the Self-Appointees'.[43] It expanded on the previous piece by adding an ugly anti-Semitic line in crediting the 'Anti-communist Zionist centres' with this latest provocation, and by speaking of the signatory František Kriegel, the only member of the Communist leadership in 1968 who refused to sign the humiliating Moscow protocols, as a 'cosmopolitan adventurer', the Party euphemism for a wandering Jew. Havel is called a 'bitter antisocialist', Kohout a 'devout lackey of imperialism', Hájek a 'political washout' and Patočka 'a reactionary professor'. Other Chartists earned similar epithets.

The article started an orchestrated avalanche of condemnations and attacks bordering on hysteria. When the unceasing series of interrogations and house searches among the signatories failed to persuade them, apart from a single exception,[44] to retract their act of defiance, the government tried to make sure others would not follow them. In offices, schools and

39 *Rudé právo*, 7 January 1977, 2.
40 Ibid.
41 Ibid.
42 Ibid.
43 'Ztroskotanci a samozvanci', *Rudé právo*, 12 January 1977.
44 Jiří Záruba withdrew his signature on 26 January 1977 (Císařovská and Prečan, 2007, Vol. 3, 377).

businesses, employees attended mandatory meetings where their task was to outdo one another in condemning the Charter and expressing their moral disgust with its signatories. On 26 January 1977, in one of the saddest televised spectacles in the history of Czech culture, hundreds of prominent actors, directors, musicians and artists were herded into the National Theatre, the shrine of the Czech national revival and identity, made to listen to servile speeches in front of a gallery of Party bosses and then given a declaration to sign, which consisted of two pages of platitudes and chest-beating, before the operative clause: 'We have nothing but contempt for those anywhere in the world who in their uncontrollable pride, their vainglorious superiority, their selfish interest or even for base financial rewards – and a group of such renegades and traitors emerged even in our own country – have separated and isolated themselves from their own people, their lives and real interests and with an inexorable logic became a tool of the anti-humanistic forces of imperialism and heralds of disruption and discord among nations.'[45]

There were no names named; not even the Charter was identified by name. The concession required of the artists was thus seemingly small – to condemn some unspecified group of 'renegades and traitors' in exchange for continued job security and perks, which stemmed from remaining in good graces of the system. In the end, thousands signed this and similar declarations at a number of public meetings convened in theatres, publishing houses, universities, scientific institutes and other places suspected of harbouring intellectuals. Decades later some of those who signed offer lame excuses, but most still remember it as one of the most humiliating experiences of their lives.

While the obedient artists were treated to a red carpet reception in the National Theatre, the signatories of the Charter were being summarily fired from their jobs, had their tenures terminated and their contracts cancelled. These were the 'administrative measures' mentioned in the Politburo's resolution. In the effort to maintain a semblance of legality, someone in the secretariat of the Central Committee commissioned an internal study on the possibility of legal workplace sanctions against the signatories of Charter 77. Not surprisingly, the anonymous author or authors came to the conclusion that the participation of an employee in the Charter can be

---

45 'For new creative exploits in the name of socialism and peace', *Rudé právo*, 29 January 1977, 1.

qualified as 'a threat to the security of the state' and is therefore grounds for instant dismissal.[46]

Anyone who lived through those days will remember the intimidation and the pressure to join in this public ritual of self-humiliation. To swim against the tide that was sweeping along friends, colleagues and families was not easy. It is hard not to feel for people who twenty or more years later talk about this moment of shame and regret their weakness at the time. But it is definitely not true, as some would have it, that this was an empty, universal concession that everybody made or did not make at his or her own peril. There were dozens, maybe hundreds of names missing on the lists of actors, artists, musicians, scientists and writers that had been force-fed to the population every day by the Communist press. In just one Prague theatre, a pillar of the establishment, eight actors refused to sign.[47] On consideration, the risks associated with not signing were real but manageable. The punishments, such as they were, consisted at the worst in losing access to big contracts and popular TV productions, promotions or scientific degrees. Painful, yes, but hardly requiring the moral fibre of a hero.

The unceasing interrogation and public attacks created a pogrom mood that had to find its outlet. Havel, tired of the 'unnerving uncertainty', felt a sense of relief, when late in the evening of 14 January, he was told at the end of another interrogation, during which he was screamed at and threatened by a group of high-ranking StB officers, that he was under arrest and indicted for 'subversion of the state'. With the typical StB disregard for legal niceties, he was not even allowed to phone his wife to tell her that he was being detained. When Olga enquired at the Ministry of the Interior the next day, she was informed that her husband 'gave himself up to the police'.[48]

Apparently the StB felt that by decapitating the Charter and depriving it of its most agile co-founder it could paralyse the whole group. They were wrong. In a touching example of the meaning of quiet heroism, the seventy-year-old philosopher Jan Patočka, an academic through and through who did not feel entirely comfortable when he was first approached about becoming one of the spokesmen for the Charter, assumed responsibility in Havel's absence. Although he was not able to match him as an organizer, and

---

46 In Císařovská and Prečan (2007), Vol. 3, P9/5, 216.
47 Vladimír Merta, 'On the recording of *Audience*', author's archive.
48 Vladislav (2012), 21.

he did not drive a car, he was more than competent in wielding a pen. Even before the original detainment of Havel, Vaculík and Landovský, he started writing an explanatory text about the meaning of the Charter.

The essay, entitled 'What Charter 77 is and what it is not',[49] is unmistakably written by a philosopher rather than a politician or a social activist. For Patočka, the document is not so much about criticism of the existing situation in Czechoslovakia, nor even about the defence of human rights, but about the moral underpinnings of all human conduct, and the precarious inability of the current civilization, not simply just the Communist part of it, to pay them sufficient attention. 'For humankind to develop in harmony with the possibilities of technical, instrumental reason, for the progress of knowledge and skills to be possible, mankind must be convinced of the unconditional nature of principles, which are so to speak "sacred" . . . Rescue in these matters will not come from the state . . .'[50]

There is no overestimating the influence this concept of moral philosophy and the practical moral conduct of its author had on Václav Havel. He had known about Patočka and his work on Husserl and phenomenology since his youth; by his own account he had read *The Natural World as a Philosophical Problem* at the age of sixteen,[51] and he had met the philosopher on many occasions. But philosophically, Havel had been more influenced by the work of French existentialists, Martin Heidegger and his philosophical guru and family friend Josef Šafařík. Still, after Patočka died he blamed his 'foolish inhibitions' on not seeking out the philosopher more often. The truth remains that he had not written much on Patočka, and, although he enjoyed discussions with him at the Balustrade, he had not regularly visited his popular seminars, first held at the Philosophical Faculty and, after the philosopher's dismissal, in private homes. Now, when Havel was himself confronted with the 'unconditional nature' of 'sacred' principles, he found he was compelled to act accordingly.

Patočka's heroic stand was to end tragically. From 10 January 1977 onwards, he was called in almost daily for interrogation. He admitted to being familiar with the text of the Charter, and to being its signatory and

---

49 'Čím je a čím není Charta 77', in Císařovská and Prečan (2007), P3/4, 36–8.
50 Ibid. 36.
51 'The Last Conversation' ('Poslední rozhovor'), written in the Ruzyně prison, 1 May 1977, in *Works 4*, 171–6.

spokesman. Apart from that he refused to answer questions repeatedly put to him. Many of the interrogations lasted all day. Havel last saw him on 14 January in the Ruzyně prison where they were both waiting for their next interrogation. The old man, unperturbed, talked about immortality.[52]

After Havel was jailed several hours later, Patočka continued to raise his voice in protest against the unprecedented campaign to defame and silence the initiative. 'An injustice, a violation of human rights, does not cease to exist when people do not or cannot complain,' he wrote.[53]

At the end of the month Patočka was called in again and informed that the Chief Prosecutor's Office had judged the declaration of Charter 77 illegal. Again, he sat down and refuted the thinking behind this verdict in his mild-mannered, but relentlessly consistent style of a philosopher.[54]

On 1 March, the Dutch foreign minister and labour politician Max van der Stoel came to Prague on an official visit. This was far from a routine occurrence; most Western politicians in those days shunned Czechoslovakia. For the Dutch, the visit was a good-will gesture in the spirit of the recently concluded Helsinki Accords. For the government in Prague, it was an opportunity to break out of isolation.

The scenario unravelled when van der Stoel, on the first day of the visit, unexpectedly received Patočka in his Prague hotel. Typically for the period of supposed *détente*, no one, not the minister and not the Dutch journalists who first approached the philosopher, would claim responsibility for the meeting – with the exception of Patočka himself. In what was a rather brief encounter, Patočka summarized the character and the motives of the Charter, while the minister stressed both the principle of non-interference in the affairs of another country, and his concern for the observation of human rights everywhere in keeping with the Final Act of the Helsinki Conference.

For Patočka, the brief encounter with the Dutch minister proved tantamount to a death warrant. The day after van der Stoel left the country, on 3 March, he was summoned for another interrogation. The next morning, following an eleven-hour-long ordeal, he complained to his family about

---

52 Ibid. 174.
53 Císařovská and Prečan (2007), Vol. 3, P3/7, 54.
54 Ibid. P3/8, 55–7.

chest pains and was taken to a hospital where he died of heart failure on the morning of 13 March.

The vengefulness went beyond the grave. The secret police, with the cooperation of the officiating priest, who was its agent, manipulated and changed the timing and the order of the funeral. A police helicopter circled over the heads of the several hundred mourners, and police motorcyclists were revving their engines at a nearby flat track stadium to drown out the eulogies.[55]

With one spokesman in jail, and another dead, it looked as if the authorities would succeed in suffocating the protest at an early stage. Yet the Charter survived. In fact, its popularity and lasting appeal were considerably helped by the overreaction of the government. By November 1989, the document had 1,889 signatories.

---

[55] In a bizarre, scarcely believable twist, the secret police agent who had spied on the professor for a quarter of the century allegedly offered to deliver a eulogy of his own, since, after all, he had known his subject better than anyone. See Kriseová (1991), 85.

THE MISTAKE

Fistula   *Dear friend—Foustka I am not your friend!*
Fistula   *My dear, truth is not just what we think, but also why,*
           to whom and under what circumstances we say it!
                                                    – *Temptation*

HAVEL WAS CRESTFALLEN when he learned of Patočka's death, and blamed himself for having persuaded the philosopher to become a spokesman. He wasn't coping too well with the prison environment. As with many a first-time prisoner, the Stockholm Syndrome led him to become somewhat dependent on his interrogator, an avuncular StB major named Miroslav Svoboda.

The police chose a two-pronged attack against the playwright. On the one hand, he was told that the initiative had collapsed and that dozens of signatories had retracted their signatures. On the other hand, in view of the directive from the Communist leadership not to impose criminal sanctions for the mere signing of the Charter – this, in order to avoid international opprobrium[1] – the police indicted Havel for conspiring with two other men, Ota Ornest, a theatre director, and Jiří Lederer, a journalist, to smuggle abroad, with the help of foreign diplomats, documents to Pavel Tigrid, a

---

1   The plan of the interrogation in the *Investigation and Indictment File against the Accused Václav Havel* (*Vyšetřovací a trestní spis proti obviněnému Václavu Havlovi*), Security Services archive, Prague, V32021MV/7, 217–19, VHL ID3015, suggests, however, that the police were also considering indicting him for his 1975 letter to Dr Husák under §103 of the penal code.

leading exponent of 'imperialist centres' and an alleged agent of the CIA. Although the main contraband that Havel had handled was the memoirs of Prokop Drtina, a close associate of President Beneš, a minister of justice in the 1948 government overthrown by the Communist putsch, and a political prisoner during the fifties – hardly a seditious document – the clandestine manner of the operation, the involvement of Western diplomats and the nature of the addressee provided sufficient evidence of a felony by the low standards of Communist justice. The fact that Lederer and Ornest, as well as Tigrid, though a convert to Catholicism, were all of Jewish extraction gave it the features of a 'cosmopolitan conspiracy', one of the favourite scenarios of Communist prosecutors.

Havel knew he was facing jail and feared it may have all been for a cause that was lost. In true Kafkaesque fashion, as his statements to the interrogators show, he was kept in the dark as to whether he was being accused of the smuggling, the letter to Husák or his role in the launch of Charter 77. With any perspective of early freedom receding with the repeated extensions of his pre-trial custody, he became, perhaps unwittingly at first, involved in what amounted to a negotiation with his jailers about the terms for his release. On 6 April, in a moment of weakness, he addressed to his prosecutor a petition for release, in which he admitted that his 'well-intentioned initiative' might have been deliberately distorted by foreign media, and pledged, in exchange for his release, 'to refrain from public political activities' and to concentrate solely on 'my artistic activities'.[2]

The StB pocketed the concession and held out for more, at the same time letting their prisoner know that his application was being 'seriously considered' and might be made use of for 'political purposes'.[3] On 22 April, Havel, by then in a desperate state, reiterated his pledges and added a promise in writing to refrain from 'inspiring or organizing collective initiatives or public statements or to act on behalf of other persons (e.g. as a spokesman of Charter 77)'.[4]

He was not immediately released, but sent back to his cell for another extension of his pre-trial detention to dwell on what was to come. By then

---

2 Ibid. 32.
3 *Letters to Olga*, No. 138, 348.
4 *Investigation and Indictment File against the Accused Václav Havel*, 162.

he knew he was going to be released (his concessions would have little value to the police if he were not) but he also knew that he would pay a high price in humiliation after they were made public (his release would make no sense if they were not).

His premonitions came true the day after he was released from custody on 20 May. The task fell to the official news agency ČTK and to *Rudé právo*, which concocted a compilation of the small concessions he had made on three separate occasions and called them 'Havel's letter to the office of the general prosecutor'.[5]

Of all the people who found Havel's failure to defend his integrity when face to face with his interrogators inexplicable, he was the most unforgiving. When he wrote the letter to Husák and when he helped organize and launch Charter 77, he knew what he was getting himself into and he expected to spend time in jail. These were not spur-of-the-moment activities born of frustration or heroic pretensions. At the same time, no one could accuse him of a lack of courage after having persevered under the cloud of surveillance, threats and defamation for years on end.

Yet fail he did, and he could not quite understand why. In *Disturbing the Peace* and in *Letters to Olga*, he describes his obsessive attempts to understand what caused the 'failure', and offers complex psychological interpretations of it, such as a 'perverse delight' in his own 'honourable cleverness'.[6]

The truth may be much simpler. Havel, as he also vaguely sensed, likely fell victim to the shock of deprivation experienced by many first-time prisoners in combination with the 'relatively skilful'[7] strategy of his interrogator, who, rather than trying to pressure and intimidate, sensed the insecurity of his ward and gave it time and room to blossom fully. In some twenty interrogation sessions between January and May of 1979, Svoboda applied the well-tested inquisition ritual of having the prisoner go through countless reiterations of his *curriculum vitae* and descriptions of his alleged 'crimes' to probe for minor gaps and inconsistencies, hinting at associations between seemingly unrelated elements in order to provoke feelings of insincerity and guilt in the prisoner.

---

5   *Rudé právo*, 21 May 1977, 2.
6   *Letters to Olga*, No. 138, 347.
7   Ibid.

By April, this tactic had taken an enormous toll on Havel. He had trouble sleeping, lost all appetite and started losing weight. A psychiatrist would probably diagnose the symptoms as the onset of an acute depression, especially after reading the plaintive end paragraph of Havel's petition to the prosecutor requesting his release: 'In case you decide that I should continue . . . to remain in custody . . . I hereby request at least one thing . . . that my wife can send me foreign language handbooks, dictionaries, and some foreign language books. I am used to working intellectually and the inactivity to which I am condemned in custody causes me *serious mental depressions* . . . It would give my life in the prison a creative fulfilment, which would help me to cope with *states of depression and feelings of hopelessness and aimlessness, to which I have succumbed and which, to my shame, I am unable to cope with other than with the help of medication.*'[8] Havel could not understand, then or later, that what he had suffered was as much a nervous breakdown as a failure of courage or a moral lapse.

The letter to the prosecutor, written out of despair and apparently without much hope of success, only increased the weight of depression when Havel realized what he had done. With an almost superhuman effort, given his state of mind, he tried to qualify the commitments he had made and reserve for himself, in additional notes to the prosecutor, his right to express his critical opinion of the current reality, to stand up in the defence of the wrongly persecuted, to reaffirm his 'moral pledge' that had led him to initiate and sign Charter 77, and to maintain contacts with his friends or, indeed, with anybody else. His sole concession – that he felt himself to be a writer who might have views at variance with those held officially, but that he did not consider himself 'a professional enemy of the regime' – would hardly have been found reassuring by the powers-that-be.[9]

But he could not withdraw what he had already offered. Major Svoboda's crowning achievement lay in Havel's stated willingness to resign as one of the spokesmen of the Charter. When asked by Svoboda during the interview on 22 April to clarify this commitment, Havel reiterated it, while insisting that he would present it to his friends and colleagues as his own decision rather than as a promise made to the investigators, 'because

---

8 Letter to the prosecutor, 6 April 1977, *Investigation and indictment file against the accused Václav Havel*, 26–7. Italics author's.
9 Ibid. undated, 28, 28a, 29.

I was not even asked' to make such a promise.[10] Nevertheless, a promise it was.

Lack of information about what was happening outside only contributed to the prisoner's confusion and disorientation. Apparently Havel was persuaded not only by his interrogators but also by his defence attorney, a Mr Lukavec, that he was fighting for a lost cause, long since deserted or even repudiated by his colleagues. This impression seems to be corroborated by his first words to Pavel Landovský, after his release in May, 'So you have retracted everything!'[11]

The best proof, however, that Havel's lapse of will was a result of induced depression rather than a moral failure can be found in his activities following his release from prison. Like many a patient whose cloud of depression is lifted through medication, withdrawal of the pathogenic stimuli, the cycle of the disease or a spontaneous recovery, he almost immediately switched into a hypo-manic state. Although he was still under indictment pending a trial that could earn him several years in prison, he immediately resumed his opposition activities with scant regard for any commitments he might have made. He continued to blame himself for his concessions, but he realized that they had been made under duress and so were legally and morally invalid.

In the preserved police files on the case, the motivation of the StB is acknowledged explicitly as to 'maximally suppress Havel's activities after a possible release from pre-trial detention', and to conduct the interrogations of other signatories 'with the aim to discredit Václav Havel by creating an impression that the information obtained so far is based on Havel's testimony'.[12] Apparently, the StB was not quite successful in this. Over the previous five months, so many Charter signatories had been exposed to the practices, threats and insinuations of the secret state that they were well equipped to put Havel's concessions in context. Faced with the choice of whether to believe Havel or the StB, they chose Havel.

On 26 May, Charter 77, represented by its sole remaining spokesman Jiří Hájek, released a statement in which they expressed an unconditional

---

10 Ibid. 165.
11 Landovský (2010), 226. Kaiser (2009), 139, offers another, slightly different version of the story.
12 Archives of the Ministry of Interior No. VV33766, Vol.10, 161–4, quoted in Císařovská and Prečan (2007), Vol. I, D15, 44.

understanding of Havel's decision to resign as a spokesman, and poured scorn on 'an attempt to discredit the reputation of an honest man' in the media.[13] The campaign thus brought only limited results: those who saw Havel's resignation as the act of a prisoner extracted under duress were not persuaded, while those who thought of Havel as a devil incarnate did not need persuading.

It seems that the only person who was genuinely confused and ambivalent about what had happened was Havel himself. He became engaged in frantic public attempts to minimize the damage, all the while violating the very pledge to refrain from public activities that had facilitated his release from prison. The day after he was 'disgraced in public', he issued a statement trying to clarify that he only pledged to refrain from 'activities that could be considered as criminal',[14] while Charter 77, to which he continued his allegiance, was never meant as a platform for political opposition (and by implication could not be considered as criminal). On 1 June, he sued Tomáš Řezáč, a journalistic hack, for spreading false information about him on the radio programme 'Who is Václav Havel?'[15] He continued to give interviews about Charter 77, the persecution of independent intellectuals and his upcoming trial. He was also immensely gratified not only to find the Charter alive and kicking, but also by the spirit of solidarity and trust that helped him, at least in part, to assuage his feelings of guilt.

And yet, those feelings lingered, turning the sequence of petty concessions, release and subsequent self-recrimination into one of the central events in Havel's memory, 'some of the worst moments of my life'.[16] His reaction to his concessions became an experiment in moral philosophy that found numerous expressions in Havel's essays, his plays and private conversations, and it hugely informed his future conduct. First, it enabled Havel, never a conformist, to distinguish clearly between the true moral valency of an act and its external valuation, even by people whose opinion he respected. Although there was a lively discussion inside the Charter of Havel's behaviour in prison and its consequences, it was extremely

---

13 Statement on the resignation of Vaclav Havel as spokesman of the Charter, Císařovská and Prečan (2007), Vol. 1, D15.1, 43.
14 Statement of Václav Havel, 21 May 1977, Císařovská and Prečan (2007), Vol. 1, D15.1, 43–4.
15 Czechoslovak Radio, 9 March 1977.
16 Debate with Timothy Garton Ash and the students of Oxford University, 22 October 1998, VHL ID17274.

understanding and forgiving, with a few critical exceptions.[17] It also made him realize that there was not necessarily a connection between the moral significance of an act and its practical consequences, an observation he would utilize to brilliant effect a year later in *Protest*. All observers, then and later, agreed that Havel had done nothing that would cause harm to other people or to the Charter itself; he had not retracted his views or his signature, nor had he volunteered information that the secret police would not already have had. That this took Havel longer to come to terms with is suggested by the fact that in certain of his statements at the time he appears to make a Sisyphean effort to prove his innocence of charges of which no one had even accused him.

It must have been during this moment of crisis that Havel, in keeping with Patočka, came to the conclusion that his moral compass was in-built, independent of the opinion of others and independent of practical consequences; indeed, that it was a matter of his own inner identity, of being true to oneself, of living in truth. His actual crime therefore lay in pledging something he had never intended to fulfil. And whereas it would seem absurd to feel any pangs of conscience over misleading his enemies, and whereas he could feel safe in the knowledge that his conduct was understood and accepted by his friends, he was still unable to make it acceptable to his innermost self.

During the years of self-reflection that followed, he made a crucial discovery: he was not entirely alone with his anguish. The strange autonomy of a moral act, its independence of the eye of the beholder – indeed the fact it did not even require an observer, as well as the fact that it resisted all his attempts to rationalize or explain it away – implied that there was actually someone or something beyond our everyday horizon that observed and took account of our actions. Somehow, at this time, there ignited in this man of highly sceptical mind and a keen sense of absurdity a spark of spirituality, a notion of transcendence.

Another realization Havel made, first perhaps only implicitly, but with increasing clarity as time went on, was that the only way to atone for his moral lapse was to reaffirm his identity and to renew his sense of living in harmony with his own views and his own values. Corollary to this was his

---

17 Kaiser (2009), 138.

awareness that he would 'probably try to erase it [his 'disgrace'] with several years in prison'.[18] There is a fine metaphysical distinction here as to whether he saw his return to jail as a proper punishment for his 'sin', or just as a logical consequence of the renewal of his identity; and yet, he knew without question where all this was headed. Moreover, he knew that 'not even that would rid me entirely of the stigma'.[19]

Finally, and this is something all too often missing from tales of heroism, here was also the recognition of its limits. Havel left prison not only humiliated, but also, and perhaps more importantly, humbled. He realized that, for all his determination to resist evil, he was no superhero, but only a frail human being facing forces that might be beyond his power to withstand. From then on, he would try to be as realistic as he could about the challenges ahead and his capacity to surmount them. It came to the fore a couple of years later when a prison term, this time considerably longer than his first incarceration, loomed large. His oft-cited remark, 'I will give them five years of my life but not a day more', does not need to be taken literally: there is little doubt that he could, and would, have coped with six. Rather, it is an admission that his capacity for sacrifice was not limitless. He would continue to resist to the full, but he would not consider becoming a martyr – arguably a sign of maturity. The humbling experience also affected his demeanour; it made him into the person all those who knew him want to remember. Previously, he had been polite and civil to most people, but not entirely free of moments of cockiness, even arrogance. Now he exhibited an almost tender respect, along with the seemingly infinite tolerance of someone who is keenly aware of other people's fragility, as well as his own.

Although he did not resume the spokesman's role for the Charter until November of the following year, and then only as a surrogate, he did resume his involvement in its manifold activities. If anything, he acted as a dissident on steroids. 'I may have gone somewhat overboard; I was too uptight, if not hysterical, driven by the longing to "rehabilitate myself".'[20]

On 18 October 1977, Havel was given a suspended sentence of fourteen months of prison for his role in the smuggling of Drtina's memoirs abroad.

---

18 *Letters to Olga*, No. 138, 348.
19 Ibid.
20 *Disturbing the Peace*, 143.

Privately, he was not overly displeased by 'not too harsh a sentence' as it might 'improve my reputation a little'.[21]

It was not quite that simple. Although Havel was spared a jail term, his co-defendants Ota Ornest and Jiří Lederer were sentenced to three and a half years and three years in prison, respectively, despite Havel's selfless efforts to solicit some support for Lederer from notables like Jan Werich. It would be too much to expect the justice administered by the Communist court to be that discriminating in weighing the respective proportions of 'guilt' of the three men. Moreover, unlike Ornest and Lederer, Havel also had been indicted for having published abroad his letter to President Husák, not to mention his authorship of Charter 77, the skeleton in the cupboard, which was not a part of the prosecution. It is therefore not unlikely that, by giving Havel a relatively lenient sentence, the authorities intended to foment further discord among the opposition, to discredit the playwright and portray him as compromised by his April concessions and by his testimony. Of the four defendants, only Jiří Lederer served the full sentence. The sixty-seven-year-old Ota Ornest, who had been suffering from ill health, made a painful-to-watch *auto-da-fé* on prime-time television in exchange for the promise of a pardon, which he received six months later. For full rehabilitation, in his own eyes more than in the eyes of others, Havel had to wait a while longer.

---

21 A letter to Jan Werich, 24 July 1977, National Archives, VHL ID20754, quoted by Kaiser (2009), 141.

THE GREENGROCER REVOLT

A spectre is haunting Eastern Europe.
                    – 'The Power of the Powerless'

IF HAVEL ESCAPED JAIL for the time being, it was not for lack of trying. One Sunday at midnight, shortly before Christmas 1977, Havel, Landovský and another friend, on their periodical 'free day' pub crawl, attempted to gain entry to a wine bar, which was supposedly closing at 1 a.m. After knocking and ringing the bell in vain, Havel became uncharacteristically aggressive and tried to kick the door in, whereupon he was seized by the burly head waiter and his colleague, dragged inside, unceremoniously beaten and then thrown back outside onto the pavement. Pondering the event later, he realized that if he had fought back he would probably have ended up in jail, charged with 'hooliganism'. This could have had very unpleasant consequences, since he had already been under a suspended sentence for the smuggling affair.

This minor incident, which had not been, as Havel himself realized, much to his credit, led him to write an essay in exorcism. In a place as frustrating as Czechoslovakia was in the mid-1970s, it was inevitable that people would vent outrage over their humiliations in similar irrational outbursts. For such people, the plastic paragraph no. 202 of the penal code on hooliganism represented a suitable and expedient punishment. It also helped to lock them into a vicious circle: as punishment for venting off over their humiliations, they were likely to be subjected to even greater humiliation, which might lead them to misbehave even more seriously, etc . . . Havel concludes his short essay with a strangely prophetic line: 'At the end of 1977 I got away – by a hair's breadth and at a painful price – with trying to kick down a door. Would I get away with something like that this year?'[1]

He would know the answer in two weeks, even though the next incident was entirely decorous and innocent, at least on the part of Havel and his fellow Chartists. After a year of interrogations (every signatory was interviewed at least once), house searches, job dismissals and media attacks, the Chartists could be forgiven for feeling slightly isolated and socially deprived. Winter started, the New Year came, and with it the beginning of Prague's ball season, a staple occurrence on the social calendar of the city for centuries, even if somewhat less glamorous under the 'people's democracy'. Many balls were public events, with tickets sold in advance in the same way as tickets were sold for theatre performances or football matches. And it was to one such event, the Ball of the Railwaymen, that the Chartists bought over a hundred tickets. The idea came from some of the ladies in the group, ostensibly as a pretext to buy new dresses. Rudolf Battěk, the endlessly kind Social Democrat of the Fabian variety, who had spent a year without trial in jail for the 'Ten Points', and then another three and a half years for distributing opposition leaflets before an election, had undertaken to secure the tickets. It sounded like an innocent prank, and perhaps also an evening of fun; there was patently nothing illegal or antisocialist about it. Havel, who would never miss an opportunity for fun, arrived for the occasion from Hrádeček; he had donned cufflinks and a black tie, combed his longish hair and was out to have a ball. Pavel Kohout, smelling trouble, wanted to stick to his blue jeans, and in the end compromised on a suit.[2]

The railwaymen probably did not care one way or another; the police, however, apparently alerted to the plan by an informer, possibly one of the hairdressers the ladies felt it incumbent upon them to visit before the ball,[3] did. When the Chartists arrived at the ball and presented their tickets, they were informed by the organizers – backed up by a group of burly

---

1 § 202, 17 January 1978, in Works 4, 182–90.
2 Kohout (2011), loc.16920.
3 Ibid.

characters – that their presence at the ball was 'undesirable'.[4] Their tickets were confiscated, although, whether to the credit of the railwaymen or the secret police, they were at least given the price of the tickets back.[5]

But the evening was not over yet. As the now ticketless Chartists stood in the vestibule of the hall and out on the pavement discussing what to do with the evening after putting on their Sunday best and going to so much trouble, the burly characters started, roughly, to push them back, thus provoking the very public disturbance that they and their uniformed colleagues were now all too pleased to quash, using batons and fists. As a result, several of the Chartists, including women, ended up with injuries, Pavel Kohout with an ugly lump on the back of his head, and Havel, who tried to intervene on Pavel Landovský's behalf as the latter was being led away, ended up in custody as well, later complaining of being tickled when the police performed a body search.[6] The charges this time were disturbing the peace and attacking a public official, but even the Communist jurists found them frivolous, and no one went to jail, even if Havel, Landovský and Jaroslav Kukal of the underground rock band DG 307 spent six weeks in pre-trial detention.[7]

If the incident was meant as a final warning, it fell on deaf ears. On the contrary, it provided an inspiration of sorts for the next initiative, which, in the eyes of the authorities, put Havel and his closest colleagues definitely beyond the pale. As he and others were awaiting trial in jail, a group of Chartists organized a committee dedicated to their defence. This was not an original idea; the Polish Workers' Defence Committee (KOR), launched by the activist Jacek Kuroň and others, had already been operating for two years; moreover, the formation of a committee to defend victims of Communist persecution had been discussed in the early stages of the preparation of the Charter by Němec and Kohout.[8] After the release of the 'hooligans', the committee morphed into The Committee for the Defence of

---

4 'A report on my participation at the Railwaymen's Ball', in *Works 4*, 193.
5 'A statement on the police operation and the imprisonment of three signatories of Charter 77 in connection with the events at the Railwaymen's Ball in Prague, 28 January', 1978, in Císařovská and Prečan (2007), Vol. I, D43, 119.
6 'A report on my participation at the Railwaymen's Ball', 199. The whole episode was dramatic enough even without the sensationalist and wildly inaccurate rendering by Keane, 256–7, who has Havel 'stunned and bleeding' on the ground, while being tickled is the most Havel himself complained about.
7 According to Kaiser (2009), 142, Havel and others were acquitted by the court partly thanks to an 'unusually objective [lady] public prosecutor'. According to Keane, a trial never took place and he seems to be right on this point. The case was finally dropped in April 1979, Suk (2013), 113.
8 Kaiser (2009), 114.

the Unjustly Persecuted (VONS). Although Havel had been originally the beneficiary rather than the initiator of this idea, or perhaps because of it, he joined sixteen other Chartists on the Committee, which announced its existence on 27 April 1978.

It may not seem immediately evident why this next step irritated the authorities so much. It was after all a natural extension of the activities of Charter 77. But there was a difference. The regime could conceivably live with general pronouncements on human rights and general criticism of the social atmosphere, and retaliate for it by not much more than persistent harassment. To be accused of perpetuating injustice in specific cases, however, involved a direct questioning of the Communist monopoly on the administration of justice. Moreover, as with its counterpart in Poland, there was in the Committee an explicit element of self-defence on behalf of a group of citizens, something tantamount to sedition in the Communist book.

Aware of their shared philosophy and goals, the Charter and VONS found it natural to establish and maintain contact with Adam Michnik, Jacek Kuroń and other Polish colleagues in the KOR. So too did the police in trying to prevent them from meeting. Deprived of passports and opportunities to travel, they still succeeded in holding two meetings at the public path on the crest of the Krkonoše mountains, which forms the border between the two countries. The secret policemen of the two countries saw no alternative but to join forces as well, and they managed to prevent the third meeting on 1 October 1978, arresting and harassing a number of dissidents. Only Havel and Pavel Landovský, who approached the meeting place more strenuously but less conspicuously by way of the woods and a cable-car track, escaped the raid. 'If it were not for this struggle for human rights,' quipped Havel, 'one would not get any fresh air exercise at all.'[9]

Police harassment intensified almost at once. For several years now, Havel had spent most of his time in Hrádeček, but the police followed him even there and sought to discourage others from visiting him by keeping an ostentatious if irregular presence around his house.

Still, he fared better than others at this time, possibly because of his voluntary seclusion. Other Charter and VONS activists were subjected to

---

9 Pavel Landovský in *Talks in Lány* (*Hovory v Lánech*), 30 December 1990 (Prague: VHL, 2013), 360.

harassment, bullying, beatings, blackmail intended to make them leave the country,[10] kidnappings, illegal house raids and searches, along with other forms of abuse.[11]

There were fewer visitors than usual at Hrádeček in the summer of 1978. The playwright was busy working, but this time the result was not a play. At 24,000 words, it was the longest piece of prose he had written until then; it proved to be one of his most admired works even if it has been somewhat misclassified. 'The Power of the Powerless' is invariably called an essay, but, brilliant a piece of writing as it is, it pursues perhaps too many objectives to be deemed an outstanding essay. This was, however, not the author's fault. As its first words clearly indicate, it was written and intended as a political manifesto. Havel was too conscious a writer to be unaware that, in beginning his piece with the words 'A spectre is haunting Eastern Europe', he was paraphrasing, no doubt ironically, the *Communist Manifesto* of Karl Marx and Friedrich Engels of 1848 – which is, for that matter, not much of an essay either.

In 'The Power of the Powerless', Havel set out to define the phenomenon of 'dissent', its 'ideology' or lack thereof, but first he felt he had to define and analyse the 'post-totalitarian' system, which formed the background, the raison d'être, of the dissidents' activities and at the same time their principal challenge. Through the example of a greengrocer who in his shop window exhibits the Communist slogan 'Workers of the world, unite!' without believing in it – and more interestingly, without the authorities expecting him to believe in it – he demonstrates that the totalitarian system operates by pressuring people to 'divest themselves of their innermost identity' through such rituals.

Havel's distinction between the totalitarian system, as practised by Stalin or Hitler at the height of their power, and the post-totalitarian system, as practised by Husák's 'normalizers' in the mid-seventies, does not lie merely in the considerably smaller amount of violence and brute force exerted by the latter. By soliciting empty expressions of popular support, the system obviates the sharp distinction between the 'tyrants' and the 'victims',

---

10 A secret police operation to that purpose with the ominous name 'Slum Clearance' was in effect since January 1978 and would become responsible for the forced emigration of dozens of Charter 77 activists, as well as for the title of a future Havel play.
11 See e.g. Suk (2013), 117–20.

which is characteristic of pure dictatorships. 'Individuals . . . need not accept the lie. It is enough for them to have accepted their life with it and in it. For by this very fact, individuals confirm the system, fulfil the system, make the system, *are* the system.'[12]

Once Havel considered the mechanism through which the system exercises its power, it was not difficult for him to realize that it hinges only on the greengrocer's willingness not to withhold his ritual approval. 'Individuals can be alienated from themselves only because there is something in them to alienate. The terrain of this violation is their authentic existence. Living the truth is thus woven directly into the texture of living a lie. It is the repressed alternative, the authentic aim to which living a lie is an inauthentic response.'[13]

The human capacity to 'live in truth', to reaffirm man's 'authentic identity', is the nuclear weapon that gives power to the powerless. As soon as the system is no longer able to extract the ritual endorsement from its subjects, its ideological pretensions collapse as the lies they are.

In the second half of his manifesto, Havel examines in detail various aspects of the power of the powerless, and he proposes a methodology for wielding that power. In keeping with the concept of Charter 77, he refrains from advocating its use for attaining specific political goals; instead, he stresses its defensive character in safeguarding a space for living in truth and for the independent life of society. Specifically, this means defending the fundamental human rights that make such life possible.

Havel's political programme is purely subject-oriented. Rather than spend time plotting how to overthrow the Communist system (and risk a massive retaliation), he tries to find ways to secure some room within the system for the individual to remain independent. What his enemies and even some of his friends may not have realized was that the two were in fact one and the same. Given that the system derived its legitimacy from the willingness of its subjects to pay it symbolic tributes, it could not for long survive the re-emergence of independent individuals, those very 'dissidents' within it. Far from an 'intellectually radical narrow-mindedness', one of the ugliest phrases ever coined by the otherwise

---

12 'The Power of the Powerless', in *Open Letters*, 136.
13 Ibid. 148.

elegant Petr Pithart, a sharp critic of the piece,[14] Havel's programme opens the way for the 'parallel polis' to become the polis.

Havel pays special attention to the concept of legality, rather than civil disobedience or outright confrontation, as a method for attaining the goals of his strategy. Against the background of persecutions, jailings and gross violations of human rights in the guise of administering 'socialist justice', his insistence on legality must have been seen by many of his friends and enemies as not much more than a tactical device. But Havel genuinely felt that it was much more than a form of 'Švejkian obstructionism'.[15] Not only was the insistence on legality less risky and open to fewer retaliatory measures, but it was also the system's Achilles heel, for in trying to avoid the use of force while extracting ritual approval from its subjects, it had no choice but to mask itself under a veil of legal niceties and empty guarantees. In true jiu-jitsu fashion Havel proposes to exploit these weak points and turn them to the advantage of the human rights defenders, while simultaneously revealing the ideological bankruptcy of the system. All this time he remains aware that the proper exercise of legal standards is but a means to an end, the end being the internal liberation of the individual, a mandate to live 'within the truth'.[16]

Hand in hand with the concept of legality goes the concept of non-violence. Again, his anthropological perspective comes into play. Violence can liberate the system, but it imprisons the individual, making it just as impossible for him to live in truth as in the previous system. This line of thinking led many people to think that like Gandhi before him, he had absolutely sworn off the use of violence, and they would be disappointed later when Havel, by then president, turned out not to be a pacifist after all. But it only shows they did not read 'The Power of the Powerless' thoroughly enough; there Havel goes on to write: 'Generally, the "dissident" attitude can only accept violence as a necessary evil in extreme situations, when direct violence can only be met by violence and where remaining passive would in effect mean supporting violence: let us recall, for example, that the blindness of European pacifism was one of the factors that prepared the ground for

---

14 *Dizi-rizika (Dissi-risks)*, in *O svobodě a moci* (*On Freedom and Power*), (Index: Köln, 1980), 281.
15 'The Power of the Powerless', 185.
16 Ibid. 190.

the Second World War.'[17] Sometimes one could only live within the truth by taking up arms.

If some of these goals could be considered as largely defensive safeguards for protecting the space of 'living in truth', the creation of 'parallel structures', a term coming from Havel's fellow Chartist, the Catholic philosopher Václav Benda, as well as that of a 'second culture', a term coined by 'Magor' Jirous, had a more combative significance.[18] It made 'living in truth' concrete by freely engaging in various unsanctioned social activities in whose 'permitted' variants one could only engage by 'living a lie'. The concept was at the root of many dissident activities, before and after the Charter, starting with 'parallel' publishing, exemplified by Vaculík's samizdat edition *Petlice* ('Hasp') and Havel's later *Expedice* ('Expedition'), both running into hundreds of titles, the 'parallel' underground music of the Plastics, the DG307, Svatopluk Karásek et al., and branching into parallel education and academy (Home University,[19] Kampademie[20]), parallel theatre (Chramostová's and Kohout's Home Theatre), parallel art (the 'backyard' exhibitions in Prague, the Reduced Price Drugstore Gallery in Brno, the Minisalon of Joska Skalník) – and even a sort of parallel foreign policy through establishing independent contacts with decision-makers and opinion-makers in the West, and with like-minded opposition groups within the Soviet bloc.[21] Havel resolutely conceived of these small parallel structures not as a 'retreat into a ghetto',[22] but as open, living organisms that would radiate energy and attract new adherents to their activities. In the thinking of a group of non-conformist Slovak sociologists in the eighties, these structures represented 'islands of positive deviation',[23] which, given enough time, would eventually merge in Benda's 'parallel polis'. As subsequent developments would show, this was not some intellectual fancy, but rather a realistic way to conduct politics under the most difficult conditions.

---

17 Ibid. 184.
18 Ibid. 193.
19 Day (1999), Scruton (2014).
20 Kroupa (2011).
21 The second meeting of Charter 77, represented by Havel, Benda, Dienstbier et al., with the Polish KOR, represented by Kuroň, Michnik, Lipinski and Romaszewski et al., took place at the end of September 1978, and resolved to establish joint working groups and invite human rights defenders throughout the Soviet bloc to join in the collaboration (Communiqué Czechoslovak–Polish Meeting, September 1978 VHL ID3030).
22 'The Power of the Powerless', 194.
23 Martin Bútora, 'Vyvzdorúvanie alebo každodennosť pozitívnych deviantov' ('Habitual Defiance or Everyday Life of Positive Deviants'), in Ač, Michal (ed.), *Lesk a bieda každodennosti* (*The Glamour and the Misery of Everyday Life*) (Bratislava: Smena, 1990).

In the last, and perhaps the most controversial section of his manifesto, Havel attempted to extrapolate his analysis and his conclusions, rooted as they were in the conditions of post-totalitarian Communist society, to modern Western society. Although he had always seen 'the West' as a branch of the emancipated, secular modern society spawned by the Enlightenment, which also gave rise to both the socialist and the Communist ideologies, in 'The Power of the Powerless' he followed this logic to its conclusion. He postulated the need for a similar change of Western consciousness aimed at living in truth, if man was to overcome the alienation and the 'automatism' of modern technological society. He suggested that because of the radical experience of the dissidents, involuntary as it was, the parallel structures might even serve as a kind of blueprint, namely, that 'these informed, non-bureaucratic, dynamic, and open communities that comprise the "parallel polis" [may represent] a kind of rudimentary prefiguration, a symbolic model, of those more meaningful "post-democratic" political structures that might become the foundation of a better society.'[24]

Admittedly, this is a somewhat lofty claim, made by a writer who had for the past ten years often found it difficult to venture outside his own house, let alone his country. After the Velvet Revolution, this became the prime piece of evidence for those who wished to see Havel as a militant closet-leftist, a utopian thinker or even as a dangerous radical trying to undermine the foundations of liberal democracy in the West just as he had undermined 'real' socialism in the East. Václav Klaus, his successor as president, may have praised him as a 'principled proponent and advocate of the values of humanity, democracy and human rights' over his coffin. but a year later he was less than complimentary when he said: 'Instead of democracy he advocated elitist post-democracy, instead of . . . traditional values he advocated a modernistic destruction of the existing human order. It was more an echo of the French Jacobinism than of British . . . classical liberalism.'[25]

On the face of it, the criticism is not without merit even if the charge of Jacobinism misses the mark by a wide margin. Havel was deeply convinced, then and later, that our contemporary civilization, with its spiritual

---

24 'The Power of the Powerless', 213.
25 In *Do Rzeczy*, February 2012. When queried about the contrast by the author, Klaus said he saw no contradiction at all. Conversation with Václav Klaus, 30 August 2013.

emptiness and its total reliance on technological solutions, was in the long run unsustainable. That, however, made him neither a left-wing radical, nor necessarily a utopian. While it is true, as some writers pointed out,[26] that there has not occurred, even in Czechoslovakia after 1989, the existential revolution Havel had called for, it does not follow that such a revolution is neither possible nor desirable. Had it occurred, it would have had little in common with the radical concepts of revolution, entertained by Jacobites, radical Marxists, Maoists or theologians of liberation, who invariably rely on organized political action, and not infrequently on violence, in pursuit of their political aims. Havel's revolution, as he makes repeatedly clear, takes place on the inside, and for the most part disavows political action. His observation that 'we look on helplessly as that coldly functioning machine we have created inevitably engulfs us, tearing us away from our natural affiliations (for instance, from our habitat in the widest sense of that word, including our habitat in the biosphere),'[27] is hardly a radical statement.

It is undeniable that Havel, often considered a prophet of non-partisan politics, had a somewhat jaundiced view of political parties, both as a dissident theoretician and as a practising politician. Through daily confrontation with the world of practical politics, he came grudgingly to acknowledge, and even to respect, the role of political organizations as agents of change and condensers of political energy to that purpose. At the same time, his complaint that 'this static complex of rigid, conceptually sloppy, and politically pragmatic mass political parties run by professional apparatuses and releasing the citizen from all forms of concrete and personal responsibility . . . can only with great difficulty be imagined as the source of humanity's rediscovery of itself'[28] rings perhaps more true today than it did thirty-five years ago. His call for 'the rehabilitation of values like trust, openness, responsibility, solidarity, love'[29] as the prime movers of political action may sound a little naïve, however desirable in our age of distrust, insecurity, irresponsibility, hostility and frustration. His rather commonsensical argument that 'the leaders' authority ought to derive from their personalities and be personally tested in their particular surroundings,

---

26 E.g. Kaiser (2009), 157.
27 'The Power of the Powerless', 206.
28 Ibid. 208.
29 Ibid. 210.

and not from their position in any *nomenklatura*'[30] can hardly be translated into a call for 'charismatic and powerful leaders'.[31]

Whether there can or should exist the kind of 'post-democratic system' envisaged by Havel, and whether the dissident community born out of despair and surviving on trust, love, solidarity and responsibility can serve as a model for it is a question that should be approached with a critical mind and perhaps with even some scepticism. That modern democracy is undergoing a crisis is on the other hand more apparent now than it was at a time when it was held together by the powerful bond of solidarity necessitated by facing the mortal totalitarian enemy. 'Only a God can save us now' is Heidegger's phrase that Havel quotes in 'The Power of the Powerless'.[32] He spent the rest of his life in the pursuit of this notion.

---

30 Ibid.
31 Kaiser (2009), 159.
32 Ibid. 206.

The Empire Strikes Back

Václav is not a coward. Which is more than being brave.

— Pavel Landovský

ALL THE TIME AS HAVEL WROTE 'The Power of the Powerless', he was acutely aware that he had company he neither asked for nor enjoyed. Since 5 August 1978 there had been a police car parked on the road past his house at Hrádeček, although the road itself became impenetrable as a result of a pile of gravel on the one end, and a 'No entry' sign on the other. The police stopped all visitors, warning them they could only enter 'at their own risk', and harassed them by imposing arbitrary fines or confiscating their driving licences. Havel's driving licence was also fair game, and he spent more time having to walk without it than driving with it. Two policemen accompanied the playwright wherever he went, shopping in town or walking his dog.[1]

In November, Havel visited Prague and, ignoring his previous pledges, reassumed the post of spokesman for the Charter. The next day he came under close surveillance by a squad of plain-clothes policemen, who accompanied him everywhere, even to the sauna. On one of these trips, an embarrassed elderly policeman with a pacemaker asked him to wait until his sauna-fit replacement arrived. A month later, when the Havels again visited Prague, they found that they became prisoners in their own home. A permanent patrol of two radio-equipped policemen was now camped on

---

1 *První zpráva o mém domácím vězení* (*The First Report on My House Arrest*), 6 January 1979, in *Works 4*, 335–6.

207

the staircase landing in front of their door and would not let anyone in or out. Only when the police apparently realized that they were condemning their prisoners to a slow death by starvation did they allow Olga to go out shopping. After three days, Václav and Olga retreated to Hrádeček. There, other surprises awaited them. During Christmas, in the field across the road from their house, the police constructed a small watchtower on stilts, resembling the Soviet moon walker device, the Lunokhod, which is what Havel called it. There the police worked irregular shifts, keeping an eye on the dangerous rebel.[2] Characteristically, Havel bore no grudge against his watchers, most of them local policemen and some of them clearly not happy about their monotonous and conspicuously absurd assignment. Prague, like any large city, provided a degree of anonymity to everyone, even the police. In a small place like Vlčice, the nearest village to Hrádeček, people were aware of all that was going on and mostly did not even pretend to be amused. Often, Havel would empathize with the policemen's ordeal and go out of his way to make them feel at ease by engaging them in small talk. Trying to remain civil even in the face of this nuisance, he sometimes offered them coffee or tea, much to the disapproval of Olga, who famously declared she would not give the police the name of their dog.[3]

Other surprises were more bothersome. Although the authorities apparently much preferred Havel at his country place, where he could be more easily watched and isolated, they also tried to make his life there impossible by sabotaging the central heating, water pipes and plumbing. In the end, there was little rationality in their behaviour. On the one hand, they made a legal (and eventually unsuccessful) attempt to confiscate the Havels' apartment in Prague, in order to force the playwright and his wife to live permanently at Hrádeček, and on the other hand, they tried to make it impossible for them to live there too.

Despite all the discomfort, Havel felt more at peace at Hrádeček, his 'existential home'. By doing chores around the house, where something always required his attention, tending the garden, cooking dinners and then retiring to his study to write, he maintained some kind of control over his life. There were not nearly as many distractions in his country house as there

---

2 *První zpráva o mém domácím vězení* (*The First Report on My House Arrest*), in *Works 4*, 335–44;
    Druhá zpráva o mém domácím vězení (*The Second Report on My House Arrest*), in *Works 4*, 363–74.
3 E.g. Kriseová (1991), 85.

were in Prague. In those days he had no telephone at Hrádeček. Unlike in Prague, the police were not situated right in front of his door, but in their 'Lunokhod' across the road, where they apparently made their duty less monotonous by bringing along drinks and girls. And at Hrádeček he was at much less risk of suddenly being hauled off for interrogation and having his daily schedule disrupted.

There was another piece of writing he completed at Hrádeček in 1978, a one-act play called *Protest*, featuring his alter ego Vaněk as one of the two main characters. The play became a natural part of the Vaněk trilogy, along with *Audience* and *Private View*.[4] It is similarly inspired by Havel's personal experience, this time with trying to solicit signatures for various petitions and protests in the normalized Czechoslovakia. Vaněk's counterpart Staněk is another writer and intellectual, one still working within the confines of the system, but nevertheless sympathetic to the opposition and its causes. It is actually Staněk who initiates the meeting to alert Vaněk to the case of a young musician (incidentally a boyfriend of his daughter) who is being unjustly persecuted by the authorities. Staněk expresses a more general empathy with the dissident struggle and even offers some money to help the families of political prisoners. When it turns out that Vaněk did not need persuading and had already organized a petition drive on the young musician's behalf and brought it for Staněk himself to sign, the man engages in a quintessentially Havelesque monologue, brilliantly explaining why his signature would be counterproductive. As Vaněk, clearly embarrassed, prepares to leave, there comes another twist. It turns out that Staněk may have been right – the young musician had just been released from prison. If Vaněk had launched the petition a few days earlier, the authorities, feeling cornered, might have preferred to keep him there.

Although Havel counted *Protest* along with his other one-act plays as a minor work, sort of a Greenesque 'entertainment', it shows how keenly he was aware not just of the moral importance of what he and his friends were doing, but also of the inherent ambiguity arising from the absence

---

4 The Vaněk series became so popular that other authors borrowed the figure for their own plays, to show their solidarity as much as artistic affinity, e.g. Pavel Kohout (*Attest*, 1978, *Marasm*, 1981, and *Safari*, 1985), Pavel Landovský (*Arrest*, 1983), Jiří Dienstbier (*Kontest*, 1978) and, *mutatis mutandi*, Tom Stoppard (*Rock 'n' Roll*, 2006). At the time of writing they number eleven works of theatre, and thousands of performances, in scores of productions home and abroad.

of a direct causal relationship between a moral action and its outcome. In the real world, the effect of a moral action could be negative, just as the effect of inaction might bring positive results. Things were never simple. This insight protected Havel and many (though not all) other Chartists against the danger of self-righteousness, so commonplace in so many revolutionary movements.

It is the same insight that informed the polemics between two close allies, friends and fellow writers, Ludvík Vaculík[5] and Václav Havel,[6] provoked at the time by Vaculík's contemplating the question 'Am I mature enough for prison?'. He answered himself that either one should conduct himself so that there is no need to even ponder the question or decide beforehand whether one's conduct is worth such a risk – clearly a dilemma that must have occurred to both men and their colleagues time and again. In his reply, just as in *Protest*, Havel argues that, in a world of arbitrary justice, the question is nonsensical because it is impossible to tell beforehand what will land a man in jail, just as it is impossible to gauge what will keep him out.

Despite all the constraints on his freedom of movement, Havel still found time for some private mischief. After *The Beggar's Opera*, he grew close to Jana Tůmová, a bookshop assistant during the day, a music-club *garderobière* in the evening and an amateur thespian on weekends. Jana, who played Elisabeth Peachum in the *Opera*, was an uncomplicated girl who supplied Havel with hard-to-obtain books, and Olga seems to have tolerated the fling as unthreatening. The situation may have become the model for the comical Pechar–Pecharová–Milena triangle in *The Mountain Hotel*.[7] More seriously, for quite some time, Havel was conducting a passionate affair with Anna Kohoutová, the beautiful, Yugoslav-born brunette ex-wife of Pavel Kohout. The two men were now sharing dissident adventures, innumerable bottles of wine, elaborate home-made gourmand meals for families and friends, theatrical characters, houses and ultimately beds.

---

5   'Meze statečnosti' ('The Limits of Courage'), in Václav Havel, *O lidskou identitu* (*On Human Identity*) (Prague: Rozmluvy 1990), 201.

6   '*Milý pane Ludvíku*' (*Dear Mr Ludvík*), in *Works 4*, 345–9. It is symptomatic of the respect in which the two men held each other that they invariably addressed the other with studied formality as 'Mr Ludvík' and 'Mr Václav'.

7   Conversation with Anna Freimanová and Andrej Krob, 15 December 2012.

Such emotional permutations were a recurring phenomenon in the dissident community; if it resembled a libertine wife-swapping community, this was dictated by sheer necessity, the result of severely limited contact with the outside world and its sexual opportunities. Havel's girlfriend was Kohout's ex-wife, just as Ivan Havel's wife Květa was the future wife of Jiří Dienstbier, and Věra Jirousová, the ex-wife of Magor, became a girlfriend to Jiří Němec, whose own soon-to-be ex-wife Dana would be grateful to Olga Havel for occasional help tending to one of her seven children. The amount of liberty and tolerance involved in these exchanges can be admired or condemned in hindsight, but it is remarkable how well the interpersonal relationships among the dissidents survived turnarounds that would spell the doom of many conventional friendships.

It was not that Olga was indifferent to what was going on. She loved her man, and occasionally displayed a bitter jealousy. But at the same time she would rather fall back on her 'maternal' side and maintain a measure of control, rather than risk the collapse of the marriage. She also seemed to have been genuinely fond of Anna, and not infrequently the two women spent time together at Hrádeček, when Havel was otherwise occupied. Even though Olga realized that her husband and Anna were deeply in love with each other, and that the exclusive character of her own relationship to Václav was now under threat, she never blamed her rival, and treated her with genuine, if somewhat tense, respect. Neither did Anna use her momentary superiority to attempt to tear Václav away from his wife. As Olga lay dying, almost twenty years later, Anna sent Václav a note: 'I am so happy that Olga is back home with you and Ďula. I love you both. I am thinking of Olga and praying for her. Yours Andula. P.S. I feel so terribly, terribly sad!'[8]

The night of 28 May 1979 found all the three protagonists in different places. Olga was alone at Hrádeček, Anna was at home and Havel was at a party, whose guests included, among others, a popular Dadaist poet–singer Jan Vodňanský and his wife Jitka, a curvaceous psychotherapist who immediately became the object of Havel's glances. Glances often led to attentions, but on that evening Havel was blissfully unaware that this was to be his last close contact with the opposite sex for almost four years. The next afternoon, after breaking down the door of his empty flat in the

---

8   Anna Kohoutová to Václav Havel, undated, VHL ID4210.

belief that he was hiding inside, and then spending several hours looking for him,[9] the police finally arrested him at Anna's flat. When he came out of jail in February 1983, he rushed back into the arms of the woman whom he had last seen on the night before his arrest – except it was not Anna but Jitka Vodňanská.

---

9 In the *Tragedy in Six Acts*, Keane mysteriously claims that the police roused Havel from sleep early in the morning, and embellishes the incident with other counter-factual details. If Havel slept, it would have had to have been an after-lunch nap.

THE TRIAL

From a certain point onward there is no longer any turning back.
That is the point that must be reached.

— Franz Kafka

THE TWENTY-NINTH OF MAY 1979 was a Tuesday, and Havel had not been home since the previous evening. The arrest came suddenly, but was not unexpected, judging by the blue bag he had on him, containing four shirts, underwear, toiletries, a sweater, pyjamas, slippers and a copy of the Czech translation by Jaroslav Kořán of Ken Kesey's *One Flew Over the Cuckoo's Nest*. Its 1975 cinematic version, directed by Havel's Poděbrady buddy Miloš Forman, became the first film in forty-one years to sweep all the major Oscar categories.

Unbeknownst to Havel, the police also raided Hrádeček and did a house search there, but found only Olga. Sixteen other members of the VONS were arrested on Tuesday morning. Ten were remanded in custody and indicted for subversion. This time the authorities were not fooling. Immediately after Havel's arrest, a motorized crane came to Hrádeček and transferred the Lunokhod to the back of a truck, a clear signal Havel would not need close surveillance for some time to come.

It was the logical conclusion to Havel's activities over the previous two years, and he knew it. In some way, as he had himself acknowledged, it was the result of his effort to 'rehabilitate' himself, of the feverish activity that, he knew, he would 'most probably end up in prison again'.[1] It was also the only practical way to disprove a myth shared even by some in the dissident community that there were among the Chartists people so well known, respected and well connected, both home and abroad, that they stood above the risks of punishment imposed on lesser troublemakers. While Kohout rather enjoyed this feeling of invincibility, took extraordinary risks with it and on occasion flaunted it before his interrogators, Havel resented it, taking it as another instance of his undeserved privilege. In fact, the guilty awareness that completely unknown, innocent and apolitical young people had been brutally persecuted as the proverbial unwashed, while he was allowed to live off his hard-currency royalties, drive a Mercedes and cook lavish dinners had been one of the impulses that had made him approach Kohout and others with the idea that germinated in Charter 77.

And as he was now to demonstrate at a considerable cost to himself, the myth had never been more than just that. By the late 1970s, largely for reasons of self-preservation, the regime had learned to think in terms of cost-benefit and trade-offs. Every individual's destiny and well-being could be thus reduced to a function, taking into account his willingness to conform, his propensity for making trouble and the amount of respect he or she enjoyed, both at home and abroad. To some extent it depended on the person in question whether they would respect the limits of their particular function or choose to overstep them, as Havel consciously did. But there was also, as Havel argued in 'The Limits of Courage' exchange, an arbitrary element in the authorities' behaviour. While Havel had been under house arrest, Pavel Kohout was allowed to leave the country for a one-year stay at the Burgtheater in Vienna, and a little later, so was Pavel Landovský. The secret police excelled at driving home the meaning of loneliness.

It was one of the hottest summers in years. The prison cell housing Havel and several others was unbearably hot and stifling. He went on a hunger strike[2] to protest his detention, but soon realized it had no effect.

There was still a chance at freedom for the playwright. The authorities, aware of the international opprobrium that would follow the trial and punishment of human rights activists, offered Havel, just as it had Kohout,

---

1 *Disturbing the Peace*, 144.
2 Prison record, 1 June 1979, VHL ID18121.

an easy way out in the form of a year-long 'theatrical fellowship' in New York. To give the offer a semblance of respectability it was presented to Havel in person by the head of the North American section at the Foreign Ministry. The offer was real enough and had actually been the subject of a communication between the US State Department and the Foreign Ministry in Prague.[3] The lifeline, initiated by Forman, was thrown by Joe Papp, the founder of the Public Theater, which first staged *The Memorandum* in 1968. After mulling over the offer and consulting with Olga during her visit on 5 September, Havel turned it down.

Memory is a great leveller. In *Disturbing the Peace*, Havel says that he never regretted refusing the chance to travel to the USA.[4] To an interviewer twenty years later[5] he recounted Olga's visit to jail and their conversation about the offer as something of a laughing matter, at least on her part. According to Kosatík,[6] aware as she was of the difference in their respective situations, Olga deferred the decision to her husband, but she was clearly negative about it when talking to some of her friends. To others, however, she said she would not mind getting out for a while.[7] In fact, it was an agonizing call. Havel's lawyer Josef Lžičař who, unbeknownst to Havel, suffered from a case of dual loyalties, reported to his StB control that if Havel faced six or seven years in prison, which was a perfectly realistic expectation, he would choose emigration over jail.[8] To Havel's circle, Olga related what Václav told her during one of the prison visits: 'I'll give them five years of my life but not a day more.'[9] Understandably, some biographers[10] have raised the question of why the sentence, which had been a matter of political fiat, rather than judicial deliberation, was not sufficiently high to force the playwright to leave. An element of the Prisoner Dilemma game, in which two prisoners plan an escape together but can only guess about each other's real intentions, was apparently at play here. The authorities could not very well let Havel know the length of his sentence in advance so as to enable him to make an informed decision.

---

3 Rocamora (2004), 175.
4 *Disturbing the Peace*, 155.
5 Kaiser (2009), 167.
6 Kosatík (2008), 147.
7 Vladislav (2012), 595.
8 Kaiser (2009), 167.
9 Anna Freimanová in ibid. 167.
10 Ibid. 167.

At the same time, they could not very well let him go and enjoy the thrills of theatrical life in New York after giving him a harsh sentence.

The most authentic record of Havel's thinking at the time, his own letters to Olga from prison, offer a somewhat more complicated picture of the 'fellowship' offer. In letter No. 10, written on 22 September,[11] Havel deplored his 'excessive caution' regarding the proposal, and speculates 'had I reacted somewhat differently . . .'[12] things might have been better for me today'. Since Olga's letters to Havel have never been found, we can only guess at what her answer was, but from Havel's letter No. 13 of 3 November, in which he referred to her 'sermon', we can deduce that she was none too pleased at his becoming tangled up 'again' in 'some inappropriate speculations'.[13] The 'again' can only mean that Havel had been giving the matter serious thought. Nonetheless, in the above-mentioned letter he not only attributed Olga's reprimands to a 'misunderstanding' due to his 'obfuscatory language', but also attempted to turn the tables on her by recalling that, during her visit the day before, it was she who had suggested that the offer might be 'in fact worth considering'.[14]

In remembering the episode later, Havel may have become something of a victim of his own heroic myth. From the context it is apparent not only that he seriously thought about going to America, but also that for a time he thought of little else. In a postscript to his letter of 1 December, he writes: 'I often dream about Honza Tříska, Miloš Forman and Pavel K.[ohout]. All of them foreigners.'[15]

Faced with many years in jail, only a moron would not have considered a more palatable alternative. The puzzling thing, on the contrary, is why Havel, so brutally honest with himself on most occasions, would dissimulate somewhat in this particular case. The obvious explanation is his fear akin to a panic that he would be once again caught in a moment of weakness like the one in April 1977. He could not have realized that the full truth was even more heroic than the simplified version. He arrived at the decision to serve out his sentence not as some kind of dissident superman, but as a deeply torn individual in full awareness of the options and their consequences, dreaming

---

11 Letter to Olga, No. 10, facsimile, Museum of Czech Literature, VHL ID2833.
12 The line that follows was crossed out by Havel, but likely reads: 'e.g. if I had waited for some time', ibid.
13 *Letters to Olga*, No. 13, 42.
14 Ibid.
15 Ibid. No. 15, 56.

of doing the easy thing, but choosing the hard one. 'Can I endure this for five years? Hopefully. I don't have a choice, anyway. Or perhaps I do – but I don't know what would have to happen to make me choose it. I have made up my mind on this. I am a Czech bumpkin and I will stay one.'[16] Olga's thinking process, on the other hand, seems to have been more straightforward. She found it easier to steel herself against hardship, although her own did not compare to his, and in any case, there was not much for her on the other side of the ocean. The man had many facets; the woman was of one piece.

The depressing thing about the trial itself, which started on 22 October and ended the next day, was that it was so anticlimactic. The whole thing, presided over by the same judicial miscreant with the symbolic name Kašpar (Clown), who had already briefly appeared during Havel's previous indictment and who was eventually rewarded for his troubles by being made the Minister of Justice, had the scripted feeling of a Stalinist trial. Of the eighteen places in the small courtroom, five were left reserved for nondescript individuals coming and going, and the sixth was occupied by a reporter from *Rudé právo*. The twelve remaining chairs were not nearly enough for the families of the six accused, Václav Havel, Jiří Dienstbier, Petr Uhl, Václav Benda, Otta Bednářová and Dana Němcová, a mother of seven.

The police harassed and threatened the small crowd of relatives and friends who could not get in. Several people were beaten. Others were searched. In the courtroom, Kašpar did his best to intimidate the accused, the witnesses and the public. He had notes taken by the relatives confiscated, and Anna Šabatová, the wife of Petr Uhl, was forcibly expelled from the courtroom.

The conduct of the prisoners, all of whom were aware of the trial's foregone conclusion, showed their different political philosophies and temperaments. Whereas Havel tried to reason with the judges, and argued that no criminal offence had been committed, even within the extremely narrow Communist concept of legality, the radical socialist Petr Uhl followed in the footsteps of his revolutionary predecessors, from Georgii Dimitrov to Fidel Castro, and rejected the legitimacy of the tribunal altogether.

It hardly mattered. After a mere two days, the court found all the defendants guilty of subversion and sentenced Petr Uhl to five years, Václav

---

16 *Dopisy Olze No. 18*, in *Works 5*, 94.

Benda to four, Jiří Dienstbier to three, Václav Havel to four and a half and Otta Bednářová to three years in prison. Only Dana Němcová escaped with a suspended sentence of two years – her estranged ex-husband Jiří Nemec, also a member of VONS, was himself incarcerated at the time, and the court was apparently wary of the expense of taking on their seven children as wards of the state. After an equally futile appeal, Havel, Dienstbier and Benda were shipped on a prison bus to the Heřmanice prison in Ostrava on 7 January 1980. Exactly three years from the publication of Charter 77, the regime had its revenge.

DEAR OLGA

I never saw a man who looked
With such a wistful eye
Upon that little tent of blue
Which prisoners call the sky
                    – Oscar Wilde, 'The Ballad of Reading Gaol'

WHAT WE KNOW OF HAVEL'S YEARS IN PRISON, first in pre-trial custody, which lasted five months, and then serving his sentence, comes from his court and prison files, the fragmentary memories of some of his fellow prisoners, and from his often elliptical and considerably abstract letters from prison, most of which found their way to the collection known as *Letters to Olga*. When directly approached on the subject, e.g. by Hvížďala in *Disturbing the Peace*, Havel sounds rather evasive, blaming his lack of 'narrative' talent,[1] and his inability to tell stories that do justice to the real experience. Under pressure from the interviewer, he disclosed that in Heřmanice, he worked as a spot welder but was hard put to meet the assigned quotas. After several months of hardships and humiliation, he was reassigned to work with an oxy-acetylene welder, working alternate shifts with his fellow Chartist and prisoner Jiří Dienstbier, the former journalist and future foreign minister. In his next prison, Bory, on the outskirts of Pilsen, he worked in the laundry room ('a very exclusive workplace') and ended up stripping insulation off

---

1   P. 145.

cables. The rest was lost 'behind a strange haze'.[2] At times Havel reluctantly remembered specific punishments and humiliations, such as solitary confinement for not meeting the quotas, withdrawal of correspondence, packages and visiting privileges, and other forms of being reminded – this, in a country that denied the existence of political prisoners – that he was something considerably worse than an ordinary criminal. He was more forthcoming about the mostly respectful behaviour of his fellow prisoners (he was much in demand for helping with their letters and petitions to the authorities) and even the occasional kindness of some of his jailers. In late-night conversations with friends, he occasionally contributed an anecdote about the inner workings of the prisoner hierarchy, the sexual abuse of some prisoners and the operation of the inmates' black market.

Havel's reluctance to remember even made some people think that there must have been episodes during his time in prison that he would much rather not recall. While memory generally works to suppress uncomfortable experience, and while it is mostly impossible to prove that something did not happen, there is nothing to suggest that Havel would later deliberately conceal or misrepresent anything during his four years in jail.

In reality, Havel dwelt on immediate experience throughout his life, and when something interesting happened, he would recount and rehash the story for hours or days and tell it with elan to anyone interested to hear. But soon the process of distillation began in his long-term memory, fitting the experience into an already existing abstract framework, or provoking the elaboration of a new one. 'Rather than miss the meaning of that experience it's better not to deal with it at all,'[3] he said; it was the meaning, not the experience that he was after.

Although the paucity of stories from Havel's prison period, at least as told by himself, has led one biographer[4] to suggest, rather darkly, that this was the period of his life about which the least is known, the contrary is probably true. Apart from the fact that serving time in prison is rarely an eventful period, Havel's letters to Olga, written regularly every week or two and using up all the four handwritten pages allowed by the prison regulations, provide a unique document of his moods, his concerns and

2 Ibid. 146.
3 Ibid. 147.
4 Kaiser (2009), 161.

his thinking, of a life turned inside out and taking place for the most part in the prisoner's mind. Whereas the record for the rest of his life until then is at best patchy, consisting of various versions of well-known events and anecdotes, with long intervals about which much less is known, in his letters to Olga, the only record in Havel's life akin to a diary, we have a regular time sequence, enriched further by partial knowledge of the intellectual input that came to Havel in the 'letters from Olga'[5] (in fact from his brother Ivan and his friends; Olga's own and much shorter letters have not been found).

The case actually needs to be put more strongly; there is no other period in Havel's life about which we know so much as about his life in prison. Obviously, we miss the detailed record of his welding work and its output, his learning to use the oxy-acetylene torch, the rather monotonous menu at the prison cafeteria and other minutiae of prison life. It is, however, unlikely that they would add much to our understanding of him. As for his inner life, by contrast, rarely has anyone engaged in introspection as thorough and as eloquently recorded as Havel did in his letters to Olga. For a student of the soul, they provide an embarrassment of riches. Havel came to the task equipped with a writer's lexicon, with self-discipline and with the analytical tools of a student of phenomenology and existentialist thought.

One sometimes hears that the *Letters to Olga* are an epistolary novel or a philosophical treatise conceived and executed in the sole form of writing in which the prisoner was allowed to engage. This is simply not the case. Neither are they a form of love correspondence, as the romantically minded would have it. They are a vehicle of survival, pure and simple, for Havel as a physical being, as a writer and as the possessor of a soul. They have equally become a priceless source of information about Havel's internal universe for his readers and jailers alike. 'It is necessary to pay attention to his correspondence,' writes his chief prison 're-educator'. 'Some of it is objectionable.'[6]

The first fifty letters or so deal mostly with the many practical matters that a man snatched away without warning in the middle of the afternoon must deal with: the personal effects he would need in prison, issues of his

---

5 Collected as Ivan M. Havel et al., *Dopisy od Olgy* (*Letters from Olga*), Václav Havel Library, Prague 2010.

6 'Evaluation of the conduct of prisoner Václav Havel during his stay in the correctional facility Ostrava-Heřmanice', document of Prison Service, 17 July 1981, National Archives, VHL ID18061.

legal defence, and domestic matters of unpaid bills, a car in need of a repair and the means of disposal of the furniture he so hated in their Prague flat. A lot of ink is spent on Hrádeček, what needs to be done there and how, and how to deal with the latest attempt of the authorities to make life impossible there, or to deprive the Havels of their 'existential home' altogether. Beyond all this, there is a subtle but unmistakably urgent, almost desperate tone in Havel's letters during the first six months. Again and again he assures Olga (and, one suspects, also himself) that he is ready for his ordeal, that he accepts it with 'a calm mind', that he does not regret a thing, and yet his assurances are so numerous that one gets a faint whiff of second thoughts, of a lingering sense of doubt, as in his obvious flirtation with the idea of emigration. There seems to be a clash here between the calm resignation, almost satisfaction, at unwaveringly following the course he had set out for himself, with his so keenly desired 'rehabilitation' into the bargain, and the gloomy contemplation of the sentence as 'a large bucket of bitterness'[7] and even perhaps 'God's punishment for my pride'.[8]

Yet there were probably other elements to Havel's conflicted feelings than the fact of the imprisonment itself. That was something he had seen coming, and to which he had reconciled himself long before. What he did not count on, but which can quite reliably be reconstituted from his letters and the testimony of his friends, was that instead of coming to prison in a stoical mood, psychologically equipped to cope with everything the regime could throw at him, he found himself to be a mental wreck.

The years of clandestine activity, of stress and suspense, of interrogations and surveillance, combined with Havel's work-hard-party-hard lifestyle must have taken their toll. But what must have been much harder for him to take was the awareness that his marriage to Olga was on the rocks at exactly the moment when he was least able to do anything about it. He could not have yet realized that, in reality, prison may have been what saved the marriage; a year before, he and Olga were on the verge of going their separate ways.

It was not that their marriage was dead. On the contrary, surrounded by hostile reality they had come to depend on each other even more than before. Olga was a model of loyalty, and she was deadly serious when she

---

7 *Letters to Olga*, No. 13, 46.
8 Ibid. No. 12, 41.

said she would follow Václav everywhere, even to jail.[9] But she was no longer certain about whether she could expect the same loyalty from him. It was not the fact that he had a lover – in fact, at least two lovers. There had been infidelities before, many of which he felt strangely obliged to report to her; somehow she had been able to live with those. She must have attributed them to his artistic temperament, to his bohemian lifestyle, to the unhealthy influence of friends like Pavel Landovský and to the generally relaxed sexual mores of the generation of the sixties. Olga could live with Václav's paramours in the sure knowledge that ultimately he belonged to her.

This time, however, it was different. Havel fell deeply in love with Anna Kohoutová, and Olga felt she could no longer claim a monopoly on his loyalties. Typically, it was she rather than he who apparently gave some thought to leaving. He, on his part, saw nothing strange or impossible in maintaining a double or even triple set of loyalties, all genuine, and each based on different emotions and considerations.

Things were coming to a head, with Olga in a self-imposed exile at Hrádeček, and Václav in Anna's flat, when the *deus ex machina* materialized in the form of an StB arrest squad. It is possible that only when the iron door of the prison cell closed behind him did he realize that his marriage was in danger.

The rest can be found, if one looks for the clues, in the *Letters to Olga*. Havel's constant complaint that Olga was not writing to him and that, when she did, her letters were gruff and matter-of-fact cannot simply be attributed to the fact that Olga was not a 'letter person'. It is likely that, for the first few weeks at least, she did not feel much like writing. After all, what graver proof of disloyalty is there than your husband getting arrested in another woman's flat, and for that matter, not even for adultery?

Ten years on, in February 1990, the president's staff stood at attention when Jane Fonda paid a visit to one of the most talked-about men of the day. After both sides exchanged every compliment imaginable, Fonda came to the point. She thought it would be wonderful to make a film about Václav and Olga, actually a film called *Václav and Olga*, and she would undertake (no one questioned her ability to get the funding) to produce the film, possibly with herself playing Olga. Havel did not reject the idea out of hand, but it

---

9 Ibid. No. 9, 35.

was apparent that it made him rather uncomfortable. Standing alongside Havel as his press secretary, I did my best to hide my amusement, imagining this modern-day *Eugene Onegin*. With all due respect to the famous actress, I did not think it was such a great idea, or that she would be up to the task. In fact, I could not think of anyone who would be able to do justice to this most unusual and complex relationship.

Most durable marriages are either partnerships of equals or a pairing of complementary roles in which one party is dominant and the other submissive. But since human relationships are consummated at various levels, it is possible to think of a relationship in which both sides are dominant and both submissive at various times and in various situations. This was the case with the Havels. Much has been written about the maternal aspect of Havel's women, and to a degree Olga certainly fitted the stereotype of a fussy, protective mother, just as Václav fitted the stereotype of a precocious, gifted, spoiled and sometimes petulant child. In *Letters to Olga*, his reproaches about her letter writing, his detailed instructions as to how she should go about her everyday life, how she should dress and do her hair, his criticism of her prose and other shortcomings, his demands that she should study his letters, attend to his requests, think of him always, and at specific times,[10] and love him without asking to be loved back, make him look almost like a self-centred little tyrant. Verging on the incomprehensible, he even required her to pass tender messages, pieces of verse[11] and little presents to not just one but two other women. He could be just as demanding in their domestic life with his meticulous habits and insistence on order, which constantly clashed with the unregulated stream of visitors of all kinds and with spur-of-the-moment parties, trips and happenings. When he was upset about something, rather than calling her 'Olgo' in the vocative, he would call her 'Olga' in the nominative, just as ladies of a big house would call their domestic staff. She would be required to be an ever-ready hostess and companion one moment, and a fierce guardian of his time the next, when he retired to write through the night. The next morning Olga would hush dogs, houseguests and children so that Václav could get some sleep. All this would appear to add up to a rather unappetizing picture of a domestic deity, as self-centred and egotistical as many great men are, attended to by a subservient

---

10 'On my birthday, at exactly 7.00 p.m., think of me. I'll think of you too.' *Letters to Olga*, No. 10, 39.
11 Letter No. 15, 1 December 1979, facsimile, Museum of Czech Literature, VHL ID2838.

housewife.

That however, would not remotely describe the true quality of their relationship, for Olga gave as good as she got. Not simply an extremely demanding child, Václav was at the same time totally dependent on Olga's approval and emotional support. Apart from his constant pleas in the letters to be paid attention to, listened to and loved, outside the prison it was also Olga he ran to with every bit of news, every new piece of work and every problem he encountered. In the hectic revolutionary days of 1989 and the equally busy first weeks of the presidency in early 1990, his 'Where is Olga?' became almost a tic and a symptom of his need to be witnessed and approved of by the person who knew him best.

And although Olga was totally devoted to her husband, she was unsentimental about their relationship and its limitations. Yes, she would follow Václav even to jail. But should he not return, one could imagine her giving the same answer Dorothy Parker allegedly gave to a nosy neighbour who enquired what she could do to help when her husband committed suicide: 'Get me a new husband.'

In the end, their complex relationship, which was asymmetrical on so many planes, evened out into a marriage of equals. In Olga's words, 'Most of the time we both do as we please. Sometimes I listen to him, at other moments I have it my way.'[12] Although they often focused on addressing the practical issues of their lives, it was not a pragmatic relationship, either. After more than twenty years, they still deeply cared about each other and enjoyed spending time together. When they sat down with their coffee and cigarettes in the kitchen or on the porch in Hrádeček, silently cherishing the moment of peace, one had a sense of the deep satisfaction they drew from their closeness. It was also clear, however, that what held them together was not sexual in nature, not by the mid-seventies anyway. In his need to be cuddled, Havel was attracted to well-rounded, soft-featured women. Olga was somewhat bony and angular, except for a beautiful and expressive face, which could assume any range of emotions, from pensive tenderness to cold rage. She was wise enough to see that their relationship and the pleasure they both derived from it went far beyond sex. The recurring scenes in Havel's plays such as *Mountain Hotel*, *The*

---

12 'Not a Harlequin Romance', an interview with Olga Havlová, in Wilson (2012), 142.

Beggar's Opera and *Largo Desolato*, in which the wife advises her husband on how best to conduct his extramarital affairs, were apparently inspired by real-life situations. Here too, though, Olga was no long-suffering timid housewife to her worldly husband but an equal partner. What was good for the gander was good for the goose. Free of her husband's insecurity, she did not have the same neurotic need constantly to prove her worth by new conquests, but when she felt really attracted to someone she apparently followed her own desires even before Havel's long stint in jail. This led to another asymmetry. Like many a philandering man, Havel could be absurdly jealous where his own wife was concerned.

This informal arrangement (there is nothing to suggest it was an explicit one) worked well enough as long as both sides felt secure in the centrality of their own relationship. Olga felt she was losing this security when Havel became enamoured of Andula Kohoutová and even played family with her and her daughters, albeit in a distinctly unorthodox way.[13]

There is only indirect evidence in the *Letters to Olga* of the deep hurt she must have felt, but it is ample. In letter No. 13 Václav comments on a number of aspects of his situation, reiterates several requests, requests vitamins that 'can be obtained from A's [Andula's] doctor friend' and finishes with a series of commands in CAPITAL LETTERS, the last of which, after 'STUDY MY LETTERS CAREFULLY AND TRY TO CARRY OUT THE TASKS I SET YOU', is 'LOVE ME' (his own love he apparently took so much for granted that he saw no need to mention it). And then there follows a postscript about a late-night upset, with Havel writing: 'So there it is: water doesn't flow through my veins *either*.'[14] We do not know exactly what Olga had written, but the message is loud and clear.

The very first letter from the pre-trial detention, dated 4 June, shows that the prisoner harboured no illusions about the situation he found himself in or the length of time he was going to spend in jail. After his previous incarcerations he was well prepared for the ordeal. What he once found disturbing 'no longer surprises me or upsets me', although he admitted that prison is 'a terrible bore' and complained about the stifling heat. The letter also shows what was foremost on his mind during the first week. He thought

---

13 Boučková (1991) contains a novelistic, not necessarily accurate rendering by the daughter of Pavel and Anna Kohout of her mother's affair with Havel during her own teenage years.
14 *Letters to Olga*, No. 13, 48. Italics author's.

of the comforts he knew would make the imprisonment less intolerable, and asked Olga to get him 'the usual: powdered juice, lemons, cheese slices, cigars, a little instant cocoa and so on'. He asked Olga to write him 'a lot' about every 'scrap of information', including 'news how our lawn copes with the dry spell', the last possibly a coded question about the situation in the Charter community. And he also asked his wife to give many greetings to 'Andulka' and give her the letter to read. Of course, Andulka was Anna Kohoutová. (In subsequent letters written while serving his sentence, Havel refers to his lover as 'Květa', his sister-in-law and one of the people he was technically allowed to communicate with.) Finally, he asked Olga to give his best regards to several friends, including Jana Tůmová of the *Beggar's Opera* troupe, his other *petite amie*.

Rain came the next day and suddenly the air in prison was breathable and the prisoner in high spirits, pledging only to compose letters in this kind of mood from now on. He reported that he had worked out his next play on a Faustian theme and that it was 'almost half written', although he was still not happy with it. Again, it is a conspicuous reference in a letter that, as Havel knew, would be closely examined by his jailers. Olga was usually very much up to date about the state of his writing. The unexpected disclosure could either suggest that at the time of Havel's arrest their communication had broken down, that he worried about the manuscript and wanted her to hide it away or, finally, that it was intended for someone else. There is also the mysterious reference to some 'out of character' remarks Havel apparently made as he was being arrested, which the police took as an attempt to 'impress a young woman who was listening', most likely Anna's older daughter Kateřina.[15]

In the second letter, only a part of which has been published, Havel compared his current feelings with the first two imprisonments, finding himself more fatalistic as 'the inevitable has finally happened'. He suggested that waiting for this moment accounted for his recent nervousness, and expressed hope that, when this ordeal was over, he might finally be 'more at ease with myself', which might have a 'calming effect on things around me as well'. Also some of the 'intimate reasons' that were preoccupying him for the last two years might pass. This amounts to an admission that things had

---

15 Ibid. No. 1, 23–5.

not been going well lately.[16]

The third letter attests to the fact that, even with several years in prison looming on the horizon, Havel remained as organized as ever, instructing Olga to requisition books he had out on loan according to a list he kept, to buy heating fuel for the winter and to record for him any interesting concert or show she would attend. At the end, though, the letter becomes somewhat personal. 'When I come back I will be more special to you, which cannot hurt after so many years of daily coexistence. And needless to say, you will be more special to me.' He signed the letter 'Cheers, (you) Grumbler'.[17]

The fourth letter, dated 8 July, saw Havel missing an opportunity to wish Olga his best for her upcoming birthday on 11 July, even while asking her to convey his 'special greetings' to 'my girlfriend' Andulka. He also notes that, because of the prison censor, he is compelled to write legibly, 'somewhat like a child', and confesses to feeling nostalgic and sentimental, as illustrated by a little drawing he enclosed.

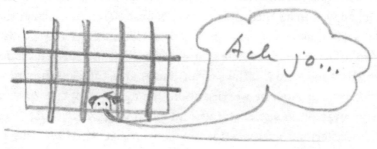

(Oy vey . . .)[18]

He apologizes for the omission to wish Olga Happy Birthday in the fifth letter on 21 July, and promises a present after he gets out. (In 1977, while in prison, he made a necklace for Olga out of bread, which she apparently did not take a fancy to.) In a truly characteristic note, Havel rejoiced about Olga having written to him and how it made him eager to start writing again (she mentioned a group that had read his plays) and simultaneously complained about her not sending him a kiss and suggesting he knew why. 'I don't know why!' he protests. If he was sincere, as he almost always was,

---

16 Letter to Olga No. 2, facsimile, Museum of Czech Literature, VHL ID2825.
17 Letter to Olga No. 3, facsimile, Museum of Czech Literature, VHL ID2826.
18 Letter to Olga No. 4, facsimile, Museum of Czech Literature, VHL ID2827.

the passage reveals a slightly alarming regression to childish behaviour, as there are ample reasons in the first four letters for even a very tolerant wife like Olga to deny him a gesture of endearment.

In the same letter Havel also sends love to his father, who had been recovering from a respiratory disease in hospital, with the hope that he was already back home and restored to full health. This was not to be. As he was writing, his father, his *taťuška*, suddenly died. Ivan on whose shoulders it fell to arrange the funeral, just as it had fallen on Václav's shoulders when their mother died while Ivan was in Berkeley, remarked, 'It is probably fated that only one of us arranges for the funeral of one of our parents.'[19] The prosecutor kindly agreed that his prisoner, in civilian clothes, could attend the funeral. Immediately afterwards, Havel was escorted back. In his sixth letter, three days later, he reflected on the sad event he had been dreading for a long time and the surprising calm with which he took the news. There immediately followed perhaps the longest list yet of most detailed instructions regarding things to be sent to him in prison and things to be done at home. He even instructed Olga to retype them into a checklist and mark them off as they were being completed. A little ironically, on the most important issue, namely whether to sell the apartment in Dejvice and move to his father's apartment, now available, he left the decision to Olga and Ivan. The letter ends with two pieces of endearment: 'Grumbler, don't forget to pay the rent!' and 'Don't send almonds – they make me crave wine.'[20]

After his sentencing, most of Havel's anxieties seem to have receded. His poorly hidden concern for the state of his and Olga's relationship also subsided. He still betrayed some uncertainty as the trial started ('The first day of the trial you smiled at me oddly as though you were making a face at me'[21]), but he could not have any doubts when she was allowed to say a few words in his defence, in spite of her concern that he would faint whenever she said something in public.[22] He was now reasonably assured both that it would be years before he'd get out, and that she would be waiting for him when he did. 'We've survived a lot already and we'll survive this too.'[23]

Methodical as ever, Havel made a to-do list before starting to serve his

---

19 Letter to Václav Havel, 3 August 1979, in Ivan M. Havel et al. (2010).
20 Letter to Olga No. 6, Museum of Czech Literature, VHL ID2829.
21 *Letters to Olga*, No. 12, 41.
22 Wilson (2012), 155.
23 *Letters to Olga*, No. 13, 46.

sentence. It read:

> Plans for prison:
> 1. to remain at least as healthy as I am now
>   (and perhaps cure my haemorrhoids);
> 2. generally reconstitute myself psychologically;
> 3. write at least two plays;
> 4. improve my English;
> 5. learn German at least as well as I know English;
> 6. study the entire Bible thoroughly.[24]

On the whole the exercise proved a failure, although Havel was not entirely to blame. He was eventually let out of prison an ill man; the authorities let him go because they feared he might die on their hands. His breathing problems due to the pneumonia in prison persisted and worsened for the rest of his life (his haemorrhoids, to which he periodically refers in his letters, continued to bother him for years, even after surgery in the prison hospital in September 1980). He did not write a play, although he thought through several versions of the Faustian theme, which became *The Temptation*. His English had not improved perceptibly.[25] Learning German was apparently a non-starter, and Havel did not return to that ambition again. As for the Bible, he read two books of the Pentateuch in pre-trial custody before being transferred to Heřmanice, where the good book was apparently taken away from him, and his knowledge remained patchy. Conceivably he progressed the furthest in his effort to 'reconstitute himself'. Outwardly, he came out of the prison much the same man he went in, perhaps with a sense of more detachment gained through long bouts of solitary meditation. But in a deeper sense, as clearly evidenced in the letters to Olga, he had undergone a metaphysical revolution. Whereas previously he worked with the theme of identity and with the theme of moral responsibility in his plays and writings and in his civic activities, by posing the question of the ultimate meaning of life, of its 'vanishing

---

24 Ibid. No. 14, 51.
25 Listening to the BBC interview with Joan Bakewell, the 'thinking man's crumpet' and a later *paramour* of Havel's colleague and admirer Harold Pinter, from the end of June 1968, one feels that this English was as good as Havel ever spoke.

point' and of the 'mystery of existence', he now put them at the core of his being. It is not by accident that revelations of this kind regularly occur to people in situations of harsh monotony and reduced sensory input, such as deserts, mountains . . . or prisons. Perhaps only there and then, without the interference of the myriad of objects, people and concerns that make up everyday life, is there a chance to glimpse the vanishing point of the 'metaphysical horizon'. It is also a fact of life that this kind of psychological transformation, long lasting as it may be, is not necessarily permanent. As with every human transformation – even though one can only admire Havel's disciplined and deliberate approach – it is subject to erosion and decay when the original conditions that gave rise to it pass.

Be that as it may, the experience made Havel uniquely well prepared for the single-minded focus towards the tasks ahead, culminating with his leadership of the Velvet Revolution. Although he did not come out of the prison an ascetic, but continued to enjoy life and even remained entangled in some of its foibles, he exhibited, after the initial shock of freedom passed, a clear sense of priorities, which could be called a sense of mission. People who knew Havel only from things written about him in the Communist press or at best from his plays could be forgiven for wondering what gave him the sense that he was equipped to lead a revolution or become a president. Those who knew him well wondered only why anyone should ask such questions.

The prison psychologist, Lt Čapčová, assessed him as a 'highly intelligent extroverted personality, self-reliant, with an imaginative inner life, ambitious, perhaps insecure . . . anxious . . . sensitive to the approval and disapproval of others . . . emotionally somewhat detached but dependent . . .'[26] All in all, not a wildly inaccurate profile. He generally got along well with the other inmates, most of them ordinary criminals. Like any new arrival to prison he was subjected to a series of tests, humiliations and hazing incidents. There is evidence that he acquitted himself well in these and came to be respected for his unfailing civility and courtesy as well as for his writing and paralegal skills, which were much in demand. The fact of being a 'political', though it came with no formal status, put him fairly high in the inmates' hierarchy of respectability, with accomplished burglars and bank robbers near the top, and child sex offenders at the bottom. Most of the

---

26 'The pedagogical and psychological characteristics of prisoner Václav Havel', 22 January 1980, VHL ID18114.

prisoners had no reason to sympathize with the regime. Havel remembered how they told him and his 'political' colleagues that they would one day be presidents, ministers and cardinals. 'And indeed, there had been in our ward a future foreign minister, a senator, a Primate of the Czech Catholic Church, and a president.'[27]

The letters and the testimonies also offer glimpses of Havel's treatment by the prison authorities. The head warden in Heřmanice, a petty lieutenant-colonel sadist named Košulič, wrote of his own volition to ask the court what would happen to the fourteen months of suspended sentence Havel received in 1979; he must have been bitterly disappointed when the court failed to oblige him.[28] A telegram authorizing Olga's visit to the prison, two hundred miles away, for 24 February 1980 at 9 a.m., was delivered to her on . . . 24 February.[29] In several of the letters, Havel explains the pause in his writing as a minor 'unpleasantness', hinting at a period spent in solitary confinement. In more than a dozen recorded transgressions, he was disciplined for smoking in an unauthorized place and for not fulfilling quotas by having his money allowance decreased and by being forbidden to watch films and television for one month. More painfully, he had his package privileges taken from him, once for lying down during the day and most deplorably for 'lending a German handbook to a fellow convict who was not authorized to study languages'.[30] Originally assigned to a 'geography study group', he was not allowed to join, apparently for fear of his involvement in such an explosive subject. He was barred from joining the prisoners' governing body right from the start. He was also at least once punished for the contents of a letter, which shows the severity of the constraints to which he was subjected.

In mid-1981, as he was approaching the midpoint of his sentence, he seems to have undergone a minor crisis, ending up in solitary for fifteen days, for 'disobeying an order', falling ill as a consequence and ending up in the Prague prison hospital. Whether Košulič decided to wash his hands of him, or his superiors started to fear the effects of his 'care' on the prisoner,

27 A joint interrogation of Václav Havel and Dominik Duka, 11 November 2011, Czech Television, http://www.ceskatelevize.cz/porady/10389664200-Václav-havel-a-dominik-duka-spolecny-vyslech/31129838012/.
28 'Inquiry regarding the manner of the sentence of Václav Havel' ('Urgence ohledně způsobu trestu Václava Havla'), 24 February 1981, ÚSNV-9658-Z/41-81, VHL ID18064; Municipal Court in Prague, 1 T 11/77, 5 March 1981, VHL ID18090.
29 Zdeněk Urbánek's archive, recent discovery.
30 Prison card of Václav Havel, VHL ID18040.

Havel was transferred straight from the hospital to the Bory prison on the outskirts of Pilsen. Although he had remembered the prison as a dark, scary place from visiting his uncle Miloš there as a child, now he was elated to be away from Heřmanice. For a time, he was sent to work in the prison laundry, a cosy job for an inmate, which also gave him more time for writing his letters. 'In Bory . . . I hid my rough drafts in a mountain of dirty sheets stained by millions of unborn children,' he later remarked poetically.[31] Both at Bory and in Heřmanice, he was considered a mediocre, though unproblematic prisoner. When one half of his sentence was up, he was duly not recommended for parole.[32]

On the whole, however, Havel did not appear to waste much precious energy on either his jailers or on his fellow prisoners, but spent it in the single-minded effort to survive the experience physically and mentally intact, and to achieve the psychological reconstitution he dreamt of. Never a man for pointless physical exertions, now was the first and perhaps only time in his life when he maintained something like a physical regimen. He did yoga exercises, and prided himself on attaining a full headstand, a skill that he apparently made no effort to maintain after his release.

The occasional parcel he was entitled to was the only thing that brightened the monotony of his prison diet, and he was quite fussy and exacting about the specifics of his requirements. Tobacco products, be it cigarettes, small cigars or rolling tobacco, were at the top of the list. Powdered orange juice and fruit parcels were something he also craved, to avoid the adverse effects of a largely vitamin-free diet. Formerly a typical intellectual coffee-drinker, he largely switched to tea in prison, after finding out there was no way to make a decent coffee there, with Earl Grey, the afternoon drink in England 'of little old ladies',[33] becoming his favourite blend. What is not immediately apparent to a non-Czech reader or a Czech reader of a later generation is that most of these products were unavailable not only in prison but also on the general market as well. Here Havel's foreign currency earnings that, converted to 'Tuzex vouchers', could be used in special hard-currency shops came in handy. Any surpluses of these doubly exotic items could be readily exchanged for goods and favours in

---

31 *Disturbing the Peace*, 151.
32 Prison record ÚSNV – 018829 – Z/409,921-81, 14 September 1981, VHL ID18063.
33 *Letters to Olga*, No. 25, 8 March 1980, 76.

the inmates' informal economy.

Prison food left a lot to be desired in terms of sophistication and variety, but it must have been relatively plentiful and edible, for Havel repeatedly complained about 'getting fat' in spite of the gruelling manual work. However, several respiratory ailments culminating in life-threatening pneumonia meant that his eating habits underwent a radical change during his time in jail. Prior to his arrest he had considered himself something of a gourmand, liked to cook sumptuous dinners and eat out in a couple of favourite restaurants in the vicinity of the National Theatre – the Cloister Wine Room or the Rotisserie in a nearby side street, with his favourite *escalope parmesan*, of which he dreamt and wrote longingly from jail.[34] After his release, however, his menu increasingly came to resemble that of a sick man. He could not eat large quantities of food, and he lost both the appetite and the stomach for spicy meals. To banish the memories of a prison diet of thick soups containing a variety of unidentifiable ingredients, he came to prefer clear consommés, which, along with a glass of white wine, comprised his whole lunch, often to the disappointment of his table companions, who felt compelled to follow suit. He often did not finish the meals he ordered at dinner, and increasingly relied on liquid nutrition, with alcoholic beverages comprising a significant part. He never regained much weight, and in the last two years of his life he gradually dematerialized before the eyes of his helpless friends. Only at breakfast, with a newspaper to read and a cigarette to smoke with his coffee, did he seem to enjoy his food. Whoever has said he did not pay a price by going to prison is lying.

Of the few available pastimes in jail, his favourite was watching television, which gave him the opportunity to comment on the quality of its dramatic production, usually soap operas about the flies in the ointment of an otherwise perfect life of the socialist worker. He also took up chess, and even presided over the inmates' chess group, but was, surprisingly, only a middling player. He had the wrong temperament for the game, approaching it as a creative artist with a preconceived plan, but without fully taking into account his opponents' moves. He later exhibited a similar tendency in politics, much to his own disadvantage. At any rate the chess group was in fact a front for a clandestine mass, conducted by a fellow prisoner and

---

34 Ibid. No. 60, 21 December 1980, 138.

Dominican priest, Jaroslav Dominik Duka, today a Roman cardinal and Primate of the Czech Catholic Church.[35] It was a transgression punishable by several weeks in solitary for the prisoners, and additional years in prison for the priest. This may have been the closest Havel came to being part of a religious congregation. As he later remembered, he drew much consolation and spiritual strength from the service, and the observation of such rituals as fasting on Good Friday.[36] However, the conclusion of some of Havel's friends[37] that this experience amounted to a conversion or at least a confirmation of Havel's nominal Catholicism seems to be unwarranted; it has been disputed, not least by Monsignor Duka and by Havel himself, as well as by other scholars.[38] In one of his last letters from prison on 18 December 1982, Havel admitted to a deeper understanding of Christianity, thanks no doubt to the long-distance exchanges, through Ivan's letters, with the Christian philosopher Zdeněk Neubauer, and most certainly thanks to the unmentionable experience of the Eucharist in jail. 'However, I am not a practising Catholic and will hardly ever become one,' he informed his wife.[39] It is another key moment where Havel is forced to draw the line between his deep spirituality and organized religion. His approach is no different from his approach to politics; he will be involved, he will deal in the language of religion or politics, but he will not subscribe to a dogma. Havel's concept of living in truth is incompatible with the concept of revealed truth: whereas the latter is a fixed point, the former is always a moving target.

As time went by, prison life wore Havel down physically, with recurring respiratory problems and the scourge of his haemorrhoids tormenting him, subsiding for a while and then recurring. His spirit, on the other hand, soared. At the end of 1980, when he again fell ill and spent several weeks in the infirmary 'getting fat', he seems to have thought through the dilemma that had been a constant hindrance in his correspondence. On the one hand, he longed to write about things other than himself, his physical needs and physical ailments; on the other, he was constantly reminded of the rules by his prison 'educator', and had his letters confiscated whenever he overstepped

---

35 In his reminiscence of their time together at Bory, Duka remains silent about this aspect of the Shabbat afternoon, 'the happiest day', possibly because of the 'crypto-Zionist prison administration'. In Ivan M. Havel et al. (2010), 466–8.
36 *Letters to Olga*, No. 123, 306.
37 Zdeněk Neubauer in Ivan M. Havel et al. (2010), 418–19.
38 An in-depth sensitive analysis of the issue can be found in Putna (2011), 215–21.
39 Letter to Olga, No. 159, unpublished, VHL ID2978.

the line. It must have been then, during this ongoing battle of wits with an unseen opponent, that he developed a dislike of editors, or of anyone else interfering with his texts. For some time, and with considerable patience, he had been trying to educate the educator, by linking subjects of general interest to writing about himself, testing the boundaries. In early 1981,[40] he decided to take an observer's perspective to write 'about myself . . . as I appear to myself at this point of time, during my imprisonment'.[41] In effect, by ostensibly giving up on philosophy and switching to psychology, he was smuggling in the deeply psychological philosophy of existentialism and the ostensibly anti-psychological phenomonology through the back door. It seems to have worked. Maybe the educator got tired of reading about his prisoner's internal states, maybe he was just fatigued by reading such complicated syntax and by having to consult his dictionary on whether a particular word was outlawed as foreign or not. The transfer to Bory that summer may also have helped. In any case, Havel's hints at confiscated letters gradually ceased, and over the next two years he developed and recorded the body of thought that makes the reading of *Letters to Olga* so fascinating.

This systematic effort at introspection, embarked upon in 1981, culminated in a series of essayistic pieces in 1982, already with a view to their eventual publication. The changes not only document the maturity of Havel's thinking and his growing self-confidence, but also demonstrate his amazing success in conducting what amounted to a fully fledged philosophical symposium under the very eyes of the prison censors.

The credit for much of this, though it is not immediately apparent from the early editions of *Letters to Olga*, belongs to his brother Ivan. Even Václav, who often took the support given him by his immediate family almost for granted, felt compelled to write: 'Thank Puzuk very much . . . for the conscientious way he has led our clan and for overseeing my affairs.'[42] Much has been written about Olga's loyalty to her husband, but Ivan's exemplary devotion to his brother matched hers in every possible way. His conduct was even more admirable in that he shared many of the drawbacks of his elder brother's fame, sacrificing a chance at a career and promotion, suffering through house searches and detentions, and

---

40 *Letters to Olga*, No. 68, 161.
41 Ibid.
42 Ibid. No. 13, 46–7.

repeatedly losing jobs, but without sharing in the limelight. He helped with the legal defence, kept the papers in order and was there for Václav whenever a chance for a visit came up. Together with Olga, he took over the demanding task of collecting, editing and distributing the manuscripts of *Expedice*. In due course, both he and Olga attracted the attention of the state security as well. Following an interception by the police of a French van packed with banned periodicals and other political literature at the end of April 1981, an event that had led to considerable stretches of time in jail for several courageous dissidents and twenty years of accusations and counter-accusations about the sources of the leak that had led to the bust, they were both detained and interrogated for four days on account of their activities, with Ivan indicted for subversion.

Above and beyond all these expressions of brotherly affection, however, stood Ivan's role as the part-source and part-mediator of intellectual nutrition, without which he knew Václav would find prison hard to bear. The more than ninety numbered letters to his imprisoned brother between June 1979 and January 1983[43] (there had been apparently several other incidental or technical messages) were written with the explicit aim, 'so that you don't atrophy mentally.'[44] This purpose Ivan accomplished not just through being a diligent correspondent, but also through acting as a tutor, mentor, spiritual guide and a medium for the thoughts of others. Altogether this comprised a full-time job rather than a weekend spell of letter writing.

First of all, Ivan, who was more familiar than most people with his brother's insatiable intellectual curiosity, took it upon himself to be his *Time Out* and *The New York Review of Books* in one, and reported to Václav on every new film premiere, publication, article or exhibition, as well as on the premieres of his plays abroad and their reception. The scope and the general orientation of his reading list suggests how much Václav's intellectual armoury owed to that of his brother. It contains Carlos Castaneda's *The Teachings of Don Juan*, Wittgenstein's *Philosophical Investigations*, Tolkien's *Hobbit* and *The Lord of the Rings*, Proust's *In Search of Lost Time*, Robert Pirsig's *Zen and the Art of Motorcycle Maintenance*, Hofstadter's *Gödel, Escher, Bach*, Kerouac's *On the Road*, Bulgakov's *The Master and Margarita*,

---

43 Ivan M. Havel et al. (2010). Ivan's unworldly modesty is best illustrated by the title of the volume. None of the letters had Olga as its signatory.
44 Ibid., No. 1, 15 June 1979, 28.

Kesey's *One Flew over the Cuckoo's Nest*, Kurt Vonnegut's *Slapstick*, Musil's *The Man without Qualities*, Conrad's *Heart of Darkness*, and many others. He reports on what's new in the movies, and comments on films like Robert Altman's *The Wedding*, Jiří Menzel's *Cutting it Short* and Robert Redford's *Ordinary People*. He keeps Václav up to date about the latest exhibitions of his friends, the artist Libor Fára and the photographer Bohdan Holomíček. He even reviews soap operas and TV documentaries, some of which his brother would be allowed, with a bit of luck, to watch in prison.

Drawing on his own studies, he interprets for Václav the foundations of quantum mechanics, the new works on the anthropic principle, Ilya Prigogine's dissipative structures and other phenomena on the borderline of science and philosophy. As he delves deeper into philosophical subjects, in particular the works of Emmanuel Levinas and Martin Heidegger, he includes other guests from his regular Monday evening home seminars, primarily the biologist Zdeněk Neubauer and the Christian logician Petr Hájek, in the communication, lets them read his brother's letters and transcribes their own *responsa* and commentaries in his letters to Václav.

The exchanges both helped to develop and clarify the prisoner's thinking and made him realize that he was now writing for a broader audience. The idea to transform the letters into a publishable work of literature came naturally. Originally it revolved around the 'Sixteen letters' of the summer of 1982 (edited letters to Olga Nos. 129–144), published, with Neubauer's introductory essay *Consolatio philosophiae hodierna*, by Ivan in the *Expedice* edition in a print of eleven copies. These comprise prolegomena to Havel's metaphysics and ontology, apparently motivated by the author's need to enlighten himself as much as others. Starting with the 'thrownness' of the modern individual, the I, 'longing for the lost fullness of Being',[45] they develop the concepts of responsibility, transcendence and meaning, and the universal memory of Being. The key to the meaning of life is to reach for its 'mysterious order', its 'absolute horizon' and thus reaffirm one's identity. In this endeavour lies, for Havel, the 'existential revolution' carried by a specific form of 'communality' of 'love, charity, sympathy, tolerance, understanding, self-control, solidarity, friendship . . .'[46]

In an important personal victory, he also finally came to terms with his

---

45 *Letters to Olga*, No. 135, 337.
46 Ibid. No. 143, 371.

'sin' of offering concessions to his interrogators five years before. In three of his *Letters to Olga*, Nos. 137–139, among the most moving in the collection and perhaps in the history of epistolary literature, he first examined the transcendental horizon of moral responsibility, using a parable of a man who pays his fare in a deserted streetcar. In the second letter, he used this perspective to re-examine his moral lapse of five years earlier. Once again he revisited the 'darkest period of my life . . . weeks, months, years, in fact, of silent desperation, self-castigation, shame, inner humiliation, reproach and uncomprehending questioning'.[47] Once again he engaged in bouts of painful introspection, questioning some of his own qualities, which were to haunt him on other occasions as well – 'my tendency to trust where inappropriate, my politeness, my silly faith in signs of good intentions on the part of my antagonists, my constant self-doubt, my effort to get along with everyone, my constant need to defend and explain myself'[48] – all hardly mortal sins, but undoubtedly chinks in Havel's armour that many of his adversaries learned to identify and exploit.

The conclusion he came to after five years of soul-searching, at once unbelievably simple and exceedingly difficult, finally enabled him to put his mistake, his torment and his disgrace to rest. Instead of continuing to search for in-depth psychological explanations and splitting hairs as to what he had really said and written or had not said and written, what had been and what had not been permissible to say and write under the circumstances, and which of his character traits had led him down the garden path, he ultimately claimed his mistake as his own, lock, stock and barrel, and in doing so he was reconciled to it: 'It is not hard to stand behind one's successes. But to accept responsibility for one's failures, to accept them unreservedly as failures that are truly one's own, that cannot be shifted anywhere else, and actively to accept . . . the price that has to be paid for it: that is devilishly hard! But only thence does the road lead . . . to a renewal of sovereignty over my own affairs, to a radically new insight into the mysterious gravity of my existence as an uncertain enterprise and to its transcendental meaning. And only this kind of inner understanding can ultimately lead to what might be called true "peace of mind", to that highest delight, to genuine meaningfulness, to that endless "joy of Being".

---

47 Ibid. No. 138, 348.
48 Ibid. 349.

If one manages to achieve that, then all one's worldly privations cease to be privations, and become what Christians call grace.'[49]

It was around this point that Havel, who had all the time in the world, apparently came to the conclusion that he had gone as far as he could under the circumstances. There is no grand revelation, no true path to follow. On the contrary, Havel warns that 'every meaningful community must constantly confront its actions with its intended aims, reassess itself to make certain that it is not terrorizing or fanaticizing itself and the world with its reified "truth"'[50] and he concludes on a stoical note: '[these meditations of mine] are a defeat because in them I have neither discovered nor expressed anything that hasn't already been discovered long before and expressed a hundred times better – and yet they are, at the same time, a victory: if nothing else, I have at least managed . . . to pull myself together to the point where I now feel better than when I began them. It's strange, but I may be happier than at any time in recent years.'[51] In the next letter, he largely reverts to the discussion of vitamins, his own depressions, Norman Mailer's *Of a Fire on the Moon* and his expectations of Olga's upcoming visit.[52]

Whatever difficulties the censors may have had with understanding Havel's letters, they could see that it was not the writing of a beaten man. They, or rather their superiors, must have also registered that Havel's reputation and his international renown were growing all the time while he was behind bars. Even the income from his writings, which hit a low point in the mid-seventies, had recovered nicely. With one year or less left in his sentence (he applied for a temporary suspension to have his elbows operated upon) he began to see the light at the end of the tunnel. He drafted an elaborate script for the first few days after his return from jail, starting with an intimate dinner at home with Olga, which would consist of crab cocktails, pork chops with chips and sauce tartare, a walnut tart for dessert, an aperitif, wine, a brandy as a digestif and a cigar. 'Afterwards (although I will eat and drink very little) I am probably going to puke,' he added sombrely.[53] The next day he was visited by a Major Říha, whom he had encountered previously,

---

49 Ibid. 351–2.
50 Ibid. No. 143, 371–2.
51 Ibid. No. 144, 375–6.
52 Letter to Olga, No. 145, 11 September 1982, unpublished, Museum of Czech Literature, VHL ID2966.
53 Letter to Olga, No. 153, 6 November 1982, unpublished part, Museum of Czech Literature, VHL ID2973.

and another secret policeman, who spent three hours trying to convince him to apply for a presidential pardon with the implication that it would be granted.[54] He turned them down, but it must have given him a tremendous boost, for he now knew he was winning his fight.

He would just have to wait, noting that for the first time no day in a year he would spend in jail would repeat itself. The hopes for an early release were nevertheless fading. The supervising physician decided that the painful growths on his elbows were not large enough to warrant an operation, and Major Říha had not been heard from again. Havel spent the Christmas holiday period in gloomy thoughts.

On 23 January 1983 he came down with a high fever, spending two nights in agony, with his bed shaking and his whole body aching. He contemplated death, and wanted to write a last letter to Olga, except he was not strong enough to do so. Antibiotics for a chest infection had been administered too late, and the prisoner had to be transferred to the Prague prison hospital. There the doctors spoke of pneumonia, exudates and possible nephritis.[55]

After he described his symptoms in a letter of 30 January without any regard for the niceties of censorship, Olga and Ivan sprang into action, pestering the doctors and the prison administration, and sending messages abroad. With his usual resourcefulness, Pavel Kohout initiated an emergency international drive to petition the Czechoslovak government for Havel's release to save his life.

Havel was transferred in a hurry from Bory to the infirmary in the Pankrác prison in Prague, with the express stipulation: 'Return after the completion of treatment' on the escort order, as if he were a package in the post.[56] But this was only the wishful thinking of his jailers. The spectre of having their most famous prisoner dying on their hands must have alarmed the authorities so much that they gave up, even after Havel's life was no longer in danger. Thanks to a powerful cocktail of antibiotics, he stopped 'walking like a rectangular grandma'[57] and started recovering, so much so that in his very last letter from prison he recounted his latest

54 Letter to Olga, No. 154, 13 November 1982, unpublished, Museum of Czech Literature, VHL ID2974.
55 Letter to Olga, No. 164, 30 January 1983, unpublished, Museum of Czech Literature, VHL ID2984.
56 Escort order, 28 January 1983, National Archives, VHL ID18125.
57 Letter to Olga, No. 165, 5 February 1983, unpublished, Museum of Czech Literature, VHL ID2985.

dream about the unbelievably sexy Anna, which must have pleased Olga no end. By the night of 7 February, when a large group of doctors, nurses, prison guards and officials burst into his room to inform him that his sentence was being temporarily suspended, he felt so comfortable in his cosy prison hospital room that he asked to be allowed to stay another night. As with all his previous appeals, this one was turned down as well, and he was unceremoniously shipped off to a civilian hospital. After 1,351 days in custody Havel was free.

Free at Last

JETTISONED FROM PRISON, the inmate turned patient luxuriated in Pod Petřínem, one of the smallest Prague hospitals, across a little valley from the Prague Castle, and about one hundred metres up the hill from the German Embassy, which was soon to make history as well. On 4 March 1983, he was finally evicted from the cocoon of the hospital into the dangerous world outside. He had meticulously planned the course of his re-adaptation to civilian life, but soon he had to acknowledge that he could not cope with the 'information explosion, blackouts, the overpowering surfeit of love . . .'[1] along with many other problems. Instead of the quiet time with Olga, the intimate dinner and bottle of wine that he had dreamt about in prison, one hundred and sixty people came to his homecoming party, bearing gifts of wine and spirits, together with the accumulated output of all the samizdat editions of the previous four years. It was more than he could bear. He was as scared to walk the street alone as he was to stay alone at home even for a short while. He felt totally uprooted and unable to exert control over his life – something perhaps more torturous to him than it would have been to anyone else.

He still maintained some sense of priority. First there were debts to pay. In his first interview with Antoine Spire in Le Monde he stage-managed some of the questions so as to be able to express his thanks for the untiring support of a large number of organizations, such as Amnesty International or the French A.I.D.A., and a list of individuals, including Samuel Beckett, Kurt Vonnegut, Yves Montand, Arthur Miller, Friedrich Dürrenmatt,

---

1 Letter to Pavel Kohout, 20 March 1983, National Museum, Czechoslovak Documentation Centre, VHL ID13981.

Tom Stoppard, Siegfried Lenz, Harold Pinter, Simone Signoret, Günther Grass, Joseph Papp, Bernt Engelmann, Saul Bellow, Heinrich Böll and Leonard Bernstein – something of a *Who's Who* in the world of theatre and literature. For lack of space he was not able to name all his supporters, but he highlighted the solidarity, by then much more than just a word, of the Polish KOR, themselves persecuted, interned and hunted in Poland after the Jaruzelski putsch. He wrote an individual letter to Samuel Beckett, calling him 'a deity in the heavens of spirit',[2] and thanking him for the dedication of his play *Catastrophe*, which was staged, or, in Beckett's view, massacred, at an evening in Havel's honour at the 1982 Avignon Theatre Festival.

He was impatient to get back to writing, but he had difficulties finding the right subject; he did speak of having a general theme, most likely the Faustian motif that had been germinating for a long time. To find the time and concentration for writing he contemplated gradually curtailing his work for the Charter.[3] Naturally it did not quite work out that way.

He did write a short sketch at the invitation of František Janouch, an exiled nuclear physicist and his Swedish correspondent, who wanted a piece of Havel's writing for an evening in Sweden in the autumn, in support of jailed dissidents; perhaps Janouch sensed the inner turmoil that threatened to engulf the freshly released inmate. *The Mistake*,[4] written 'in two hours' some time at the end of April or the beginning of May 1983, shows Havel's considerable talent for miniature, depicting a murderous attack by convicts on a new cell-mate who responds neither to invitations nor to threats aimed at making him accept their code. By the time his fellow prisoners realize that he does not conform simply because he does not understand their language, it is already too late. The existential anecdote about 'otherness' bears a resemblance to Havel's short story *Azimuth*[5] some twenty years earlier; it seems to be a form of exorcizing some of his nightmares at the time.

Havel had the schizophrenic feeling of having a dual personality. There was the old physical Havel, struggling with his writing, health,

---

2 Letter to Samuel Beckett, 17 April 1983, František Janouch's archive, VHL ID5852.
3 Letter to Pavel Kohout, 27 June 1983, National Museum, Czechoslovak Documentation Centre, VHL ID13979.
4 *Works 2*, 675–84.
5 *Plamen*, No. 6, 1964, 115–16, VHL ID608. The style of this earlier piece is, however, strangely uncharacteristic of Havel. In fact, it seems to have been written by his brother Ivan.

persecution and numerous personal dilemmas, and then there was suddenly 'the levitating legendary me burdened with countless Goals, Missions and Expectations'.[6]

His feeling of having lost control in the world of endless possibilities, so unlike the regimented environment of the jail, did not limit itself to the choice of clothing for the day. Having resumed his affair with Anna Kohoutová, he started another one with Jitka Vodňanská, the psychotherapist he met on the night before his arrest. A strong personality, and like every therapist something of a manipulator, it took Jitka little time to wrest emotional control from her rival. Though a more conventional girlfriend, she could satisfy Havel's strong need for self-examination and maternal guidance better than Anna. On his part, he fell in love with her as deeply as ever, albeit not unreservedly. Even with the women he felt closest to, Havel would protect his identity as fiercely as he did against the hostile secret police, the wardens in jail, or the masses of his admirers as president.

To his astonishment, he was not the only one who found a new and deeply satisfying partner. During his time in jail, Olga did too, in Jan Kašpar, a single, handsome stagehand and one of the actors in the historic production of *The Beggar's Opera*, who was twenty-two years her junior. When she told her husband and declared their life as sexual partners over, although she did not propose a split, Havel took it badly. All of a sudden, his so far undisputed claim on Olga's affections and loyalty was imperilled. His conception of the world, unlike Olga's, did not allow for the possibility of desertion by those closest to him, and he went into a deep blue funk. To be claimed by no fewer than three women simultaneously but not exclusively (Jitka had a small son, Anna two adolescent daughters, and Olga had Jan), while becoming a national institution, was simply too much for him. By several accounts, he was not only confused, but also became deeply depressed.[7]

This complex entanglement of personal loyalties, sexual passions and moral dilemmas dragged on for years. In 1984, Jitka became pregnant. She wrote a letter to Olga to apprise her of the situation and to explain how much she was in love with her husband. Havel came back with a message from Olga that she refused to divorce, but proposed a *ménage à trois* instead.

---

6 Letter to Pavel Kohout, 27 June 1983.
7 E.g. Letter of Vera Blackwell to Tom Stoppard, 28 September 1983, Václav Havel Archive, National Archives, VHL ID26497.

Václav and Olga never had children, and they were both reticent about the reasons. Many people surmised, based on Havel's occasional offhand remarks, that he was infertile. Directing the blame to himself was typical of him, but seems to contradict the facts, and not only in this particular situation. Quite likely it was something that gnawed at him in private. In one of the letters to Olga from prison he describes a dream about her giving birth to twins, after a sixteen-month pregnancy. The father was 'some American professor. The professor didn't bother me at all. I only regretted that the twins weren't mine . . .'[8] He would not take an opportunity to be a father lightly.

For his part, Havel was considering a divorce, but couldn't make himself go through with it. He persuaded Olga to part with Jan, but he could not do the same with Jitka; she was terrified of bringing up a child alone, and had an abortion. She then wrote to him, reproaching him for being too weak to make a decision. Olga reproached him for not keeping up his part of the bargain. The whole thing looked like a scene from one of his comedies of the absurd, except that it made life impossible for the protagonists. As always when he felt he had a problem, Havel turned to writing to sort it out.

There is more than one candidate for Havel's most depressive play. If the oppressive air of *The Mountain Hotel* emanates from an existential void, in *Largo Desolato* (1984), 'a musical meditation' on the weight of human existence, dedicated to Tom Stoppard, it comes from an existential anguish. Leopold Kopřiva appears to be a thinly disguised alter ego of Václav Havel, a non-conformist intellectual under imminent threat of going to jail for an essay he wrote. As he wanders through his apartment, looking apprehensively through a keyhole all the time, he is confronted first by two admiring strangers exhorting him to follow through on his writings by taking decisive action, then by a close friend who conveys the concerns of an unidentified circle of friends that he is no longer a central figure, but a spent force, and still later by his mistress Lucy who excoriates him for being unable to show emotion. The most benign figure is Leopold's wife, or, in the play, his permanent companion, who only comes home to bring him dinner, before leaving to spend the evening with another male friend.

---

8 *Letters to Olga*, No. 40, 99.

When two 'fellas' finally ring the doorbell, Leopold is resigned to the inevitable, perhaps even seeing it as a solution to his dilemmas, only to discover that they have come to offer him a deal. If he denies that he is Leopold Kopřiva, the author of the incriminating essay, then the felony will be blamed on an unknown perpetrator. He is tempted, but sufficiently aware of the dubious nature of the bargain to ask for time to consider the proposition.

In the second part of the play, which mirrors the first, the two admirers make another appearance, encouraging Leopold to act, the wife brings home yet another dinner before going to a ball with her male friend, and Lucy is replaced by Markéta, a younger version of herself who promises to cure Leopold's misery with her pure, idealistic love. When the 'fellas' reappear, Leopold has had enough. He grabs his personal effects and confronts his visitors, refusing to sign anything even at the price of his freedom, only to learn, astonished, that they are in no hurry to take him away. The verdict is being postponed for the time being, the authorities still not able to identify the perpetrator. The only remaining path for Leopold to assert his identity, i.e. by going to jail, is being denied him. He is condemned to carry on wandering around his apartment and looking through the keyhole.

Perhaps because the pain is so much closer to the surface, and because, in contrast to Havel's other plays, the characters resemble real-life figures – himself, Olga, Andula and Jitka – the play does not work as well as it should. Havel, so brilliant in making his amoeban characters go through their paces, seems at a loss when tempted to create a character with a psychology. Ultimately, as he acknowledges in the production notes for the play, all the characters speak like himself. In fact, they all are himself. The play, in Havel's view, 'only wants to disturb the spectator's soul – just like it is disturbed by a modern sculpture or musical composition,'[9] but it is so obviously the soul of the author that is disturbed.

If Havel was half hoping that the police would drag him back to jail and solve his problems for him, he was hoping in vain. They kept him under constant surveillance, documenting his dates, his sleepovers and his stays at Hrádeček with one or the other woman, sometimes two at a time. Olga, although she did not particularly like Jitka, kept inviting her and her son

---

9   *Notes on Largo Desolato, Works 4,* 502.

Tomáš to stay, possibly out of charity, since the divorced young therapist was as poor as a church mouse. This presented the dramaturge with a number of interesting problems such as the seating order at dinner. When Olga was away, Jitka presided over the table that regularly hosted quite a few hyper-cerebral men, such as the participants in one of the regular summer sessions of the Kampademia; this was a group of philosophers whose meetings at Hrádeček were initiated by brother Ivan during Václav's stint in jail and included Radim Palouš, his son Martin, nuclear physicist Pavel Bratinka, biologist Zdeněk Neubauer and Daniel Kroupa, with Václav as an honorary member. For the occasion, the playwright had Jitka dress in a long white gown and descend the stairs to the accompaniment of the seven philosophers' singing 'Heigh-ho, heigh-ho, it's home from work we go . . ' The menu for the dinner was titled 'Snow White and The Seven Dwarfs'. In fact they were somewhat more like hobbits (Tolkien's tetralogy was actually one of their cult works).

Sometime in 1986 Havel invited all three women to the Cloister Wine Room in another futile attempt to sort out his allegiances; by then Anna, the most submissive of the three strong women, was already fading from the picture. Olga remained, but the nature of their relationship had irrevocably changed. In the Wine Room, Jitka could not help noticing the contrast between the two grey-haired, though still beautiful ladies and herself, a blonde, buxom *seductrice*. She could not have known that she was initiating a pattern. Nothing was resolved at the meeting.[10]

The affair with Jitka led to another bizarre comedy of errors when, in August 1985, Havel decided to 'out her' and introduce her to some of his friends around the country. Typically for him, he planned every detail of the trip beforehand, and corresponded extensively with his would-be hosts at every way station, all the while perfectly aware that there might be more than one pair of eyes reading his correspondence. He was followed from the moment he left Prague with Jitka in his new silver VW Golf, which he drove with reckless abandon. On their first stop to visit Ladislav Lis, a left-wing dissident activist, at his goat farm in Northern Bohemia, he was detained and driven to Prague, to cool off for the forty-eight hours allowed

---

10 The preceding and following paragraphs are largely based on several conversations with Jitka Vodňanská in the summer of 2012. Naturally, Olga, who has passed away, and Anna, who was not well at the time of writing of this book, might have had a different perspective.

by the law before charges had to be brought. Released, he returned to the Lis house and continued the journey with Jitka, repeatedly engaging his pursuers in discussions about the purpose of the exercise, trying to explain that if their orders were to harass him he would rather go home and spare everybody the trouble, and being in turn assured that there were in principle no objections against his taking a summer trip with his girlfriend. Under the watchful eyes of squads of police, who were passing their wards on to the next detachment in a well-organized relay, the lovers managed to visit the actress Vlasta Chramostová and her cameraman husband Stanislav Milota in Northeastern Bohemia, the Catholic activist Augustin Navrátil in Olomouc and the renowned explorer Miroslav Zikmund in Zlín. On their last stopover in Bratislava, to visit the ex-Marxist philosopher Miroslav Kusý, one of only six signatories of Charter 77 in Slovakia, they were detained as they were dressing for dinner, and the house was searched. After another forty or so hours in jail, Havel was released and told not to come to Bratislava again for the next twenty years. Jitka Vodňanská, in an evening dress and with her personal effects locked away in the silver VW, was escorted by a policeman on a train to Prague, where she spent the next morning borrowing clothes from friends. In the end it was a memorable trip, though for reasons other than those they had in mind. Havel estimated that altogether they had wasted the time of about three hundred policemen involved in the operation.[11]

When they took another trip together the next summer, Havel took care not to advertise it beforehand or plan any visits to friends, and they managed to spend the week undisturbed in the wooded wilderness of Malý Rozsutec in the Slovak Fatra mountains.

Although it could seem that Havel spent the first few years after his release entirely absorbed in solving the complexities of, or indeed further complicating, his love life, nothing could be further from the truth. After he recovered from the shock of freedom, he resumed his public activities, driven both by a sense of responsibility and by his new stature as the uncrowned leader of the opposition. His role changed somewhat, however, with his position. Whereas prior to jail he often stressed the collective nature of the Charter and its consensual character, he now felt emboldened and encouraged by the requests for interviews, and the various honours

---

11 Letter to the prosecutor general, 25 August 1985, National Museum, Czechoslovak Documentation Centre, VHL ID10955.

accorded to him, to speak on his own behalf as well, playing the role of 'a focus point and a shop window' for the whole dissident movement.[12] Naturally, not everybody in the extremely diverse community, which had brought together Trotskyite revolutionaries, Prague Spring reformists, liberal thinkers and Catholic philosophers, agreed with everything he said. But it would be sadly mistaken to suggest that after his release he no longer 'had much time for involvement in dissent',[13] or that he was 'saving himself for the important things and so attempted to put himself above the everyday activities of the dissidents'.[14]

True, Havel did become somewhat less conspicuous, no longer spending much time in Prague after the first frantic months. It is also true that prison had taught him some elements of self-preservation and discretion that he had previously lacked. But, if anything, he exhibited even more energy and discipline than before, most of it spent on the dissident cause, and a large part directed outside the country. Keenly aware of how much the protests in the West had contributed to his largely indifferent, if not kind, treatment in prison, and eventually to his release, and having learned how close the Charter came to extinction during his absence,[15] he realized that there was not much future to the fight unless he made it global.

He had some help from several quarters. Thanks to the remarkable diplomacy of William Luers, who had been the American ambassador to Prague from 1983 till 1986, his wife Wendy and a few of his fellow diplomats, Charter 77 and the whole Czechoslovak intellectual opposition had never been entirely cut off from the world of ideas and politics across the ocean. One of the things that made life in 'normalized' Czechoslovakia more bearable, if not more trouble-free, was going to the ambassador's grand residence in Prague, and meeting there with Kurt Vonnegut, Bill and Rose Styron, Edward Albee, John Updike,[16] Philip Roth[17] and many others.[18] This called for an elaborate choreography, since the government

---

12 Conversation with Roger Scruton, 24 January 2013.
13 Kaiser (2009), 184.
14 Ibid.
15 Ibid. 176–80.
16 Described in *Bech in Czech* (1985) and published as part of *Bech at Bay* (1988).
17 Roth's visit to Prague was immortalized in *The Prague Orgy* (1985), the epilogue to the Zuckermann trilogy.
18 Among them, earlier on, Arthur Miller, whose play *The Archbishop's Ceiling* (1977) is based on his encounters with Havel, Pavel Kohout and a few others of the beautiful unwashed.

bureaucrats that the ambassador also had to entertain would not be caught in the same room with the washouts and self-appointees. They would not even be caught with them in the garden. On his arrival at the 1985 US Independence Day Celebration in Prague, a brilliant summer's day, the deputy Czechoslovak Foreign Minister Jaromír Johanes, representing the Communist government, took about a minute before he identified Havel among the guests milling about the lawn, said, 'He is here,' spun around and walked out with all the other officials from the Foreign Ministry.[19]

Havel's authorial persona was well taken care of, courtesy of his friend Klaus Juncker at Rowohlt Verlag. Thanks to his affiliation with the prestigious Burgtheater in Vienna and its artistic director Achim Benning, personified by the presence there of his friends Kohout and Landovský, he had a reliable outlet for his dramatic work. Both provided him with a solid source of income. That, however, was not the situation of most of the other Chartists, who eked out a meagre living in menial jobs and often had to take care of much larger families. Furthermore, it was becoming clear that the outreach capacity of the opposition, mostly in the form of typewritten and carbon-copied samizdat, would remain very limited without some source of funding and office technology.

Havel was still under surveillance, and could rightly presume that both his post and his telephone conversations were monitored. To be able to communicate he had to find one or more reliable and secure channels to the West. The need for secrecy was paramount. Being caught sending one's own views or manuscripts abroad could lead to unpleasantness, a slap on the wrist, or a couple of years in jail at worst. Smuggling money and technology was something else; it could easily be billed as espionage and earn the culprit, particularly someone like Havel (who would now be treated as a habitual offender), a decade or more in prison.

The effort to solve this problem became yet another story of courage, ingenuity, trust and strong human relationships, and it predated Havel's return from jail by years. It revolved around a small, mercurial woman, sociologist Jiřina Šiklová, a former Communist and present Chartist, who, like Havel, had spent time in prison at the beginning of the eighties for smuggling dissident manuscripts. After her stint in jail, Šiklová, who had

---

19 Conversation with William and Wendy Luers, Washington Depot, 13 April 2013, and
correspondence with William Luers, 19 and 22 April 2013.

previously been using Western tourists as couriers, got wiser and befriended several Western diplomats who, with or without the knowledge of their governments, used their status to smuggle letters and books back and forth. By the time Havel opened his personal underground railroad, the traffic was being carried first by the Swedish cultural attaché Peter Tejler (code-named Vasco de Gama),[20] by the German diplomat Wolfgang Scheuer and, after he left Prague in 1986, by his colleagues Peter Metzger and Joachim Bruss, as well as Canadian Peter Bakewell.[21] Šiklová was usually given Havel's mail by Dagmar Havlová Lá-Ilkovičová Havlová, the new wife of brother Ivan, and in the riskiest part of the operation, she handed it over to the diplomats, along with messages from other dissidents.

Two men in particular became Havel's regular correspondents after his release. One, František Janouch in Sweden, was a nuclear physicist, the other, historian Vilém Prečan, lived in Germany. Both were former Communists turned dissenters, and both were forced into exile. Both deserve enormous credit for helping to preserve the Charter and dissident literature as an organized force and a living word, and for enabling it to be heard. Janouch founded the Charter 77 Foundation, which gradually became the main fundraiser for dissident activities back home, and Prečan, along with other writers and intellectuals, collected, archived, distributed and promoted samizdat works. The informal undertaking, first known as *Home Enterprise*, eventually morphed into the Czechoslovak Documentation Centre for Independent Literature, with a statute, board, non-profit status and as complete a library and archive of the dissident works as was possible under the circumstances, all partly funded and from 1986 housed by an exiled Czech aristocrat, Prince Karel Schwarzenberg, at his castle in Bavarian Scheinfeld.

Over the next five years, in the least talked about and the most discreet part of his dissident career, Havel exchanged some five hundred letters and scores of telephone conversations with the two men. Some pertained to his rapidly growing international agenda, and dealt with award ceremonies in his honour – which he could only attend by proxy for fear he would

---

20 Roman Tureček, *Neoficiální informační kanály mezi Československem a Západem v období 1969–1989 se zaměřením na tzv. kurýrní cestu* (*Unofficial Information Channels Between Czechoslovakia and the West in the Period 1969–1989 with Special Focus on the So-called Courier Channel*), magisterial thesis (Masaryk University, Brno 2010) 72.
21 Havel and Prečan (2011), XIX–XX.

not be let back into the country even if he were allowed to travel – with translations, interviews and publications. But, in addition to this, Havel was operating as de facto treasurer of, and procurer for, the opposition. At the other end of the line stood the eminently practical Janouch, who already in December 1978 registered the Swedish Foundation of Charter 77 as a vehicle to receive and forward financial support for the dissidents. The first contribution of 15,000 Swedish crowns (SEK)[22] came from the Swedish cultural award Monismanien.[23] Over the years, the annual amount distributed by the foundation in Czechoslovakia grew from approximately 100,000 SEK in 1979 to more than half a million in 1989.[24] The foundation opened branches in Norway and in the United States. The money came from a number of cultural and charitable institutions and individuals in Europe and the United States, including major donors like the Ford Foundation or the Open Society Fund of George Soros, the largest single contributor.

The problem then was not so much the money itself as how to get it to the recipients. In the Communist system, hard currency was the object of the most stringent regulation, and its unauthorized possession could lead to criminal penalties. To send large amounts of money to the country by clandestine means was therefore exceedingly risky, and practised only in emergency situations. It was, however, legal to send money as a personal gift or a fee through the state banks, provided it was then converted into Tuzex vouchers.

The spirit of solidarity and mutual aid among the Chartists made it a relatively straightforward affair to identify the most needy individuals who could then be sent the money. It was, however, much more difficult to send money to meet the operational needs of the opposition, i.e. the cost of samizdat publishing and distribution, documentation and research, and some of its cultural enterprises. Obviously, the sums collected abroad could not cover the entire cost of the opposition enterprise, but it was a significant and welcome help.[25] It could not, however, be earmarked from abroad for individual projects, because, for one, they had no institutional

---

22 Around $3,000 at the time.
23 Jiří Suk, 'Podrobná zpráva o paralelní polis' ('A Detailed Report on the Parallel Polis'), in Havel and Janouch (2007), 9–29.
24 Ibid. 14.
25 The Janouch channel was certainly not the only one in this shadowy funding and distribution network, which involved a large number of brave and generous individuals and groups, but it was the most important and most pertinent to the story of Václav Havel.

front office that could receive them, and for another, they would be instantly criminalized if they had. And so the money could again only go to individuals as a personal donation, and had to be redistributed once again within the country.

Although Havel did not look and behave like a managerial type, he dedicated a considerable portion of his time and ingenuity to the problem. Thanks to the Swedish channel there emerged inside Czechoslovakia two clearing 'accounts', the Fund of Civil Assistance and the Operative Fund. The task of the first, which was started by VONS in 1979 as a mechanism to support families of political prisoners, but which had temporarily fallen into desuetude after the arrest and imprisonment of several of its members, was to identify the most pressing cases for humanitarian assistance and propose the allocation of concrete sums to individuals. The Operative Fund, on the other hand, collected money from surrogate, bogus recipients of humanitarian help and divided it into support for individual projects. Havel played a key part in designing and gradually streamlining the system, and even summarized it in a hand-drawn flowchart.[26]

In dozens of his letters Havel then micromanaged the issue, asking for a bigger contribution to one recipient or another, updating the list of bogus recipients, and informing Janouch about new editions and projects worthy of support. The standing orders for 1986 contained more than 160 names.[27] He helped organize steering boards for the two funds, recusing himself from both (as far as one can see, he was never a personal recipient of the funds), while still remaining Janouch's principal interlocutor.

As if money was not enough of a headache, Havel became deeply involved in technical matters, well above his level of expertise. It started with simple devices like dictaphones and tape recorders, but progressed to more sophisticated gadgets like cameras and video recorders for the underground newsreel *Original Videojournal*, code-named Čeněk and sponsored by Olga, and ultimately to printers and computers. Janouch, a nuclear physicist, was computer-literate by the standards of the day but Havel's dabbling in high-tech reached farcical proportions when the two men corresponded about the rather complex issue of how to programme or alternately hard-wire the Czech character set on the early PCs: 'If you

---

26 Havel to Janouch, No. 170, 1 August 1988, Havel and Janouch (2007), 395.
27 *Seznam trvalých příkazů* (*Standing Orders for 1986*), VHL ID5444.

were to send a computer, the experts close to me would like to ask you that the localization for the Czech alphabet be solved through software means rather than through interfering with the EPROM[28] . . . Mr B tried to modify the EPROM in the previous machine and was very proud of it, but I understand that by doing so he ruined the computer, or rather stripped it of most of its capabilities . . . I am just conveying what I was told without having the faintest idea what it means.'[29]

The correspondence with Prečan was less preoccupied with money and hardware matters, but was just as important for getting the message of the Charter across. Prečan, a conscientious, modest and disciplined historian, clearly more at home in an archive or a library than in a television studio, introduced a semblance of order into the rather chaotic dissident production, catalogued and archived its documents, and forwarded them to opposition outlets abroad, whether Pavel Tigrid's *Svědectví* in Paris, Jiří Pelikán's *Listy* in Rome, Zbyněk Benýšek's *Paternoster* in Vienna or Josef Škvorecký's 68 Publishers in Toronto. He and Janouch also communicated with the slightly more controversial Palach Press of Jan Kavan, an activist of the left wing of the British Labour Party and of the European Nuclear Disarmament (END), in London, which contributed its share to the dissemination of information about the dissidents, but might have been involved in several leaks and indiscretions.[30]

Prečan who first lived in Hanover but later moved with the documentation centre to Scheinfeld, much closer to the Czechoslovak border, served also as Havel's confidant, first foreign reader and postman. Apart from the more than 200 letters the two men exchanged, Havel sent through him texts of his essays and Charter documents he wanted to be made public, his lectures, plays and the recorded tapes of his answers to questions posed by the journalist Karel Hvížďala – later to become the book *Disturbing the Peace*. He also sent him his personal letters to forward to dozens of friends and acquaintances abroad and his replies to a growing number of interlocutors from the West.

---

28 Erasable Programmable Read-Only Memory.
29 Havel and Janouch (2007), No. 130, 2 November 1986, 289. The 'experts close to me' were naturally brother Ivan and his wife Dagmar, mathematicians and computer scientists both. The unfortunate Mr B was Havel's fellow prisoner, philosopher Václav Benda.
30 After November 1989, Jan Kavan returned to Prague, got elected to the parliament, was shown to be listed as an agent of the secret police, but was later exonerated in court, and, in a domestic career as controversial as was his career in exile, eventually became the Czech foreign minister.

Havel's correspondence with the two men is the record of an inspired clandestine enterprise. While his personal needs were largely limited to seeing his writing reach as wide an audience as possible, and to spur-of-the-moment requests for spices or music recordings, the letters contain innumerable pleas for help to other dissidents and their families, emergency requests and invocations of special circumstances, sometimes on behalf of people he could not call his admirers. Prečan and Janouch, however, turned out to be more than just archivists, quartermasters, fundraisers and relay stations. Being on the outside, they were in a better position to provide Havel with some feedback and occasional criticism. The feedback was badly needed. Over the previous seven or eight years, Havel and most of the other dissidents had seen a lot of each other, but had few contacts outside their circle. Moreover, Havel had not been out of the country for seventeen years. Even his ravenous appetite for books and other sources of information, the constant stream of visitors to Hrádeček and the daily ritual of listening to Voice of America and Radio Free Europe through the static of the jamming antennas could not make up for first-hand experience. When Janouch pointed out that some of Havel's statements and essays were simply too long to be reproduced in full even by the most sympathetic media,[31] Havel, who had never heard of a soundbite or a datapoint, raved at the superficiality of the Western media and refused to make changes. 'I am telling myself, what business of mine is their business? What business of mine is their laziness to read more than ten pages? What business of mine is the bloody Western crisis of thought, concentration, time, explosion of information, and all that? After all, the only thing I have won by deciding to put up with jail, surveillance, permanent harassment, total legal insecurity and inability to travel, is some sort of freedom. I am in a situation when I can actually write what I want. And now I should curtail that freedom?'[32] When the media abridged his essays to conform to their format, as happened in the case of Roger Scruton's *Salisbury Review* with Havel's 'Politics and Conscience',[33] – written as an acceptance speech of an honorary doctorate at the University of Toulouse, where it was delivered on the absent Havel's behalf by Tom Stoppard – Havel protested at being censored and swore never again to give

---

31 Janouch to Havel, 23 April 1985, Havel and Janouch (2007), 167.
32 Ibid. Havel to Janouch, 14 May 1985, 174.
33 Conversation with Roger Scruton, 24 January 2013.

Scruton a text to publish.[34] A few weeks later, he grudgingly admitted that Scruton may have had a point.[35]

To self-define themselves politically in the international context was a more serious problem for Havel and the ideologically diverse Charter, and it wasn't helped by the tug-of-war for its soul among the equally diverse exile groups, from the anti-Communist Atlanticists around Pavel Tigrid in Paris and the Munich-based radios, through the Nachtasyl underground in Vienna and Jiří Pelikán's Eurocommunist group in Rome, to the radical comrades in London. One of the most serious internal disputes started when the Charter applied to participate in the Congress for Peace and Life,[36] a showcase peace extravaganza held in Prague at the end of June 1983. The processing of the application resembled a slapstick comedy: the organizing committee officials actually ran away from the two Charter spokesmen who came to enquire, and locked themselves inside their offices.[37] Not surprisingly, instead of an invitation to the conference there came the summons from the secret police to investigate the brazenness of the dissidents. Nonetheless, several Chartists, including Havel, not yet three months after his release, managed to meet on 23 June 1983 with several delegates and observers to the Congress in a wooded preserve on the Western outskirts of Prague. True to the occasion of a peace conference, they were accosted by scores of secret and uniformed policemen, pushing and shoving, confiscating cameras and documents, and making threats against both Czech and foreign participants, who included assorted Social Democrats, French peaceniks, German Greens and two CND activists from Britain. Havel was rather pleased by the incident, which made nice publicity for Charter 77 and bad publicity for the regime, but he was less pleased by the Western media coverage, which highlighted the participation of the Greens, at the time still considered a radical group with possible links to terrorist organizations.

The incident, combined with subsequent Charter statements and Havel's personal replies to invitations by various peace organizations, led to an acrimonious debate within the Charter. Marxist reformists like Jaroslav Šabata were delighted; they saw in the Western European peace

---

34 Havel to Janouch, 3 August 1986, Havel and Janouch (2007), 268.
35 Ibid. Havel to Janouch, 6 September 1986, 281.
36 30 May 1983, in Císařovská and Prečan (2007), Vol. I, D243, 519.
37 Ibid. 12 June 1983, D244, 520.

movements their natural, if ostensibly, non-Communist partners. The conservatives, led by Václav Benda, were incensed. To affiliate themselves with people they considered the Soviets' 'useful idiots' in the West was anathema to them.

The debate went on for several years. Havel often found it difficult to hold the middle ground, voicing understanding and sympathy for the activists' general goal of peace, not a difficult thing to do, while refraining from endorsing their specific positions on controversial subjects. He initiated a comprehensive Charter document on peace, only to see it vetoed by Benda, one of the spokesmen at the time. Finally, prodded in part by Prečan, he decided to elaborate his own thinking on the subject in a piece called 'The Anatomy of a Reticence'.[38]

In the essay, which is basically an attempt at drawing boundaries, Havel explains why a Czech dissident, let alone an ordinary citizen, could never identify with the goals and proclamations of the Western peace movement. The asymmetric character of the situation in which the young peace activist in the West was free to criticize nuclear weapons or missiles on NATO territory while a peace-loving person in a socialist country would be praised for doing the same, but threatened with jail for criticizing missiles at home, signalled the deeper underlying issue: people on the Eastern side of the Iron Curtain feared their own governments more than they feared any alleged threat from the West.

Unlike Benda, Havel was not turned off but rather intrigued by the anti-establishment lifestyle and rhetoric of many of the Greens and other participants, which was in keeping with his thesis about the general crisis of Western civilization. On the other hand, he was able to see quite clearly that, perhaps unwittingly, in this particular struggle they were not serving freedom and democracy, but something more sinister, in particular those who advocated unilateral nuclear disarmament – in his eyes a particularly disingenuous way of committing suicide. He also detested the hypocrisy with which the followers of the Western peace movements vented their outrage about the Vietnam-era misdeeds of the United States without even mentioning that at that very moment the Soviet Union was engaged in a bloody occupation of neutral Afganistan.[39]

---

38 *Works 4*, 523–61.
39 Ibid. 547–8.

At the same time, Havel admired and sympathized with the young people who 'place a concern for the destiny of the world ahead of concern for their own personal well-being',[40] even when he did not approve of their positions. In the end, as he makes clear in the essay, 'war is caused not by weapons as such but by political realities'[41] and the only way to achieve peace is by 'a fundamental restructuring of the political realities that lie at the roots of the current crisis'.[42] In his view, in contrast to that of the Western peace movements, the true threat lay not in the disruption of the uneasy status quo of the Cold War, but, on the contrary, in its preservation. For, 'without free, self-respecting, and autonomous citizens, there can be no free and independent nations. Without internal peace, that is, peace among citizens and between the citizens and the state, there can be no guarantee of external peace: a state that ignores the will and the rights of its citizens can offer no guarantee that it will respect the will and the rights of other peoples, nations, and states.'[43]

Politics is a game of strange bedfellows. In its history the world has seen the most bizarre coalitions, the most cynical marriages of convenience and the saddest cases of the blind leading the blind. Here was a dissident, not even a politician, who was willing to sacrifice the short-term advantage of a tactical partnership for a fundamental transformation of the logic of the situation.

Prečan's gentle feedback served to alert Havel to the possible inconsistencies or redundancies in his and other Chartists' positions. Occasionally, by his own admission, Prečan ventured into the mine-strewn territory where the public and private personae of the dissidents met and sometimes clashed. In one letter[44] he obliquely addresses the issues of 'marital-sexual promiscuity of the Prague dissent', and quotes letters criticizing Jiří Němec for 'leaving seven children and two wives', and Jiří Dienstbier for finding solace in the arms of 'perhaps already the fifth woman in a row'. Prečan does not mention Havel explicitly, but his concern is clear. He is aware of the contrast between the experience of the dissidents, for whom intimate relationships could represent 'the only

---

40 Ibid. 549.
41 Ibid. 549–50.
42 Ibid. 550.
43 Ibid. 551.
44 13 August 1984, Havel and Prečan (2011), 216–17.

sphere of freedom, the only opportunity to freely decide about one's own life' as compared to that of couples in exile, who experienced for the most part 'the strengthening of relationships'; and for whom the 'adultery of one of the partners . . . is a disaster for the other partner'. His main concern was at the obvious potential for the various affairs to be used against the dissent by its enemies. Many dissidents had been reminded during interrogations of their infidelities or sexual mores, sometimes documented by pictorial, audio or even video evidence, and blackmailed to make them cooperate. In the most famous incident, during a house search the police confiscated erotic photographs of Ludvík Vaculík with his mistress at, of all places, a cemetery and threatened to publish them unless he cooperated. Vaculík, like Havel on several occasions, resolved the dilemma in the spirit of living in truth by making a full disclosure to his wife, and publishing the story – photographs, blackmail and all – in samizdat. The secret police delivered on their threat regardless and the pictures were published in the staid women's magazine *Květy*.

Hard as it may have been to square their publicly espoused moral positions with their private love lives, for Havel, Vaculík and others it was only part of a bigger dilemma. Not only had they no ambitions to be moral icons in the more puritan sense, but also they had second thoughts about being beacons of resistance in general. In the aforementioned book, Vaculík recalls dreaming about being alerted by Ivan Klima that everything has changed, freedom has triumphed, Kohout is flying back from Vienna, Havel has been released from jail and Vaculík should report immediately to the editorial offices of *Literární noviny* to resume its publication. This offer Vaculík declines with some relief: 'It's great that everything has changed. At least it's no longer any business of mine.'[45] Havel, too, repeatedly expressed a longing to step out of the limelight, cut down on his public activities and devote his time to writing, which he considered his true vocation. 'Paradoxically, my primary wish is to retire to Hrádeček, write a play, and take a little rest from my dissidence, but the permanent harassment prevents me from implementing this plan, however welcome from the police's point of view. I should now write a foreword to Vaculík's *Czech Dream Book* for its publication abroad, and when I was thinking about the

---

45   Vaculik (1990), 325.

book I realized one thing, among many others: it is quite endearing and touching, how throughout the book Vaculík is determined to shirk the role of the dissident and how he is hopelessly failing at the same time: he keeps collecting signatures and doing things he is in fact determined not to do. It appears that man does not really quite choose his own role, but that the role chooses him, or that rather than choosing a role, man falls into it. It is a general theme.'[46]

Havel elaborated on this theme in the foreword to Vaculík's book, probably the best novel from within the dissident environment; among other things, it is about the 'unsuccessful rebellion of a man against his own role, his struggle with it, motivated by the effort to preserve in spite of it some sort of independence and privacy'.[47] He could hardly have been unaware that his essay was self-referential. But unlike Vaculík, who, true to his dream, shunned all public roles after the Velvet Revolution, and continued to write novels and feuilletons, by turns profound, hilarious, touching, infuriating and sometimes plain silly, Havel was to be imprisoned in his role not only for the rest of the Communist period, but well beyond it.

46 Letter to Josef Škvorecký, 1 September 1983, Hoover Institution Archives, VHL ID33246.
47 'Odpovědnost jako osud' ('Responsibility as Destiny'), in *Works 4*, 407.

THE PRAISE OF FOLLY

He who despairs of the human condition is a coward,
but he who has hope for it is a fool.

– Albert Camus

WITH THE MOST BUFFETING turbulence behind him for the moment, Havel attempted to settle into a routine of sorts. Before Christmas 1985 he was able finally to receive his doctoral ermine and diploma from Toulouse, courtesy of the French Embassy – 'an unbelievable story. The main problem was in the ambassador, who is more afraid of the government here than of his own government back home (maybe he should be the next Czechoslovak ambassador in Paris).'[1] The move back in February to his native house on the embankment of the river was surely of more significance to him. The launch of Charter 77 in the flat in Dejvice was perhaps the most important moment of his life, but he had never thought of it as a home. Plagued as so often at this season of the year with respiratory problems, he spent the winter of 1985 in Prague and much of the rest of the year, with short interruptions, at Hrádeček, where he divided his time between writing, opposition agenda, his dual marital life, various household chores and entertaining friends on most weekends. 'Since June my main profession has been that of a host and hotelier.'[2]

Despite the distractions, the idea of writing another play stayed at the back of his mind. In October 1985, he suddenly sat down to write. He

---

1 Havel to Janouch, No. 95, 8 December 1985, Havel and Janouch (2007).
2 Havel to Prečan, No. 121, 14 September 1985, Havel and Prečan (2011).

later described the experience of writing a play in ten days as 'going into a trance'.[3] The creative rush came at a price. 'After finishing the play I sort of collapsed, both mentally and physically and spent several terrifying weeks at Hrádeček. The demons took their revenge on me for messing up with them.'[4]

If *Largo Desolato*, in both content and structure, reflects the chaos and confusion experienced by Havel after his release from jail, *Temptation* (1985) laid bare a deeper contemplation. While *Largo* depicted the post-penitentiary depression that awaited an unprepared Havel in 1983, the Faustian idea of *Temptation* dated back to his previous incarceration and the 'failure' of will for which he had been blaming himself. Havel remembered wild dreams and 'unexpected things' happening to him around the time of his release in May 1979, accompanying his struggle with the moral dilemma of winning his freedom at the price of a humiliating if largely meaningless concession.

The story of a little Czech sorcerer's apprentice, a knowledge-craving scientist named Foustka, is a metaphysical rather than magical treatment of the subject. Although Foustka encounters a character called Fistula, who exhibits some outward Mephistophelian qualities, nothing supernatural occurs. Foustka is tempted to go beyond the boundaries of established research into more esoteric areas; he discovers that this makes him a more interesting person, and one of considerably more sex appeal. As he nears his inevitable exposure and ruin, for Fistula is in fact a spy for the supervisors of scientific orthodoxy, Foustka tries to cover his 'sin' by inventing ever more ingenious explanations and interpretations of his behaviour, ensnaring himself deeper and deeper in contradictions and inconsistencies. When finally exposed, he must pay the price not for something he has done, but for pretending to subscribe to beliefs he did not hold. Nevertheless, in a final double twist echoing the ending of *The Memorandum*, it is not he who pays the price, but a completely innocent girl whose only mistake was to have believed in Foustka. Havel's two main themes of truth and responsibility combine here to powerful effect.

Although he usually sat and brooded on everything he wrote for some time, he dispatched the new play on its way instantly as if he were

---

3 Letter to Pavel Landovský, 16 March 1986, VHL ID16216.
4 Ibid.

afraid that the 'demons' of this or the other world might play another trick on him. In spite of the usual panicked bouts of insecurity he was clearly pleased with it, so much so that he took the unusual step of voice-recording the text for distribution among friends as well as for 'security' reasons. The writing of the play apparently served him as the last stage of a drastic auto-therapy involving four years in jail, the reassessment of his priorities and a crisis in the family. It seems to have worked. There is no mistaking the new confidence in Havel's artistic and physical voice as he constructed the play and read it for the audience that mattered most to him. His delivery was steady, almost monotonous, but the author's quiet satisfaction with his work was as recognizable as his rolling 'r's. The play opened in the Burgtheater in Vienna in May 1986, and then in other theatres across Europe and North America; the universal acclaim it garnered, with the *Daily Telegraph* calling the author 'the first playwright in Europe', stood in contrast to the somewhat muted reception of *Largo Desolato*. Andrej Krob and friends made an underground video of the play, filmed in his barn at Hrádeček, with the playwright's brother Ivan in the role of Foustka.

The play – not unlike the Vaněk one-acters – also served as stimulus for further intellectual endeavours. In the first half of 1986, its metaphysical vistas were a fertile ground for some profound deliberations of the Kampademia group on the Faustian archetype and the limits of freedom and morality.[5] Others added their reflections as well.[6] When new contributions kept appearing (many of which were assembled in a volume for Havel's fiftieth birthday that October) Olga got the idea of launching a periodical dedicated solely to the theatre. It was an immensely time-consuming and technically sophisticated project by the standards of the opposition, with a number of contributing editors: Anna Freimanová and Anna Lorencová as editorial staff, Karel Kraus as editor-in-chief and Olga as a managing editor. Over the next two years, they together produced and distributed five issues of *On Theatre* (*O divadle*), each containing several hundred pages, in several hundred copies, which were then copied and distributed further by the first users. In an emerging trend, the contributions to the journal were both by prohibited dissidents and

---

5 Bratinka et al. (2010).
6 E.g. Ivan Martin Jirous, 'Havlovy hlubiny' ('Havel's Depths') in Vokno 11/1986, VHL ID4302.

by 'legit' writers and theatre scholars, writing first under pseudonyms, but gradually shedding even that degree of deception.[7]

The efforts of Havel, Charter 77 and its supporters in exile were bearing fruit. Not only were his plays produced abroad and accolades offered him with 'The Power of the Powerless' and other essays printed, reprinted and discussed in many countries, but the case of human rights behind the Iron Curtain was increasingly taken up by groups and organizations in the West. The International Helsinki Federation (IHF), with a secretariat in Vienna and national branches in the capitals of a number of Western countries, the London-based Index on Censorship, the US Helsinki Watch, Amnesty International, International PEN club and others, along with many important writers and intellectuals, were regularly raising their voices in protest against the jailing of dissidents and human rights violations.

In this respect, the civil society was far ahead of their governments. Only Ronald Reagan and Margaret Thatcher confronted the Soviets directly and consistently over human rights abuses. Most Western governments, while disapproving of the heavy-handed policies of the Soviet bloc, had until quite late in the day preferred to reap the fruits of *détente* and avoid direct confrontation.

Recognition was therefore of the essence. Soon after Havel's release from jail, Janouch launched a campaign to have Václav Havel awarded the Nobel Peace Prize. In the dying days of *détente* he did not get very far, although he did manage to secure the support of a number of European intellectuals. Ever a practical man, he went for the next best thing. In 1986, the Rotterdam Erasmus Foundation decided to give Václav Havel the Erasmus Prize, awarded annually to individuals or institutions that had made notable contributions to European culture, society or social science. It brought with it a purse of 200,000 Dutch guilders, and the high visibility of a laureate speech in the presence of the Dutch Royal Family in Rotterdam Cathedral.

Havel was pleased by the news, but it soon turned out that it was much easier to win the prize than to receive it.[8] First of all, it was highly doubtful that he would be allowed to travel to the Netherlands for the occasion.

---

7 On more *On Theater* see Kriseová (1991), 133–5, also Havel's letter to Janouch, 7 July 1986, in Havel and Janouch (2007), 263.
8 Statement on the awarding of the Erasmus Prize, 22 January 1986, in *Works 4*, 612.

Second, he was somewhat embarrassed by being singled out for the honour[9] and agreed with Janouch that it should be awarded to Charter 77, or at least jointly to the Charter and himself. Janouch, acting as Havel's representative in the matter, soon discovered that the idea was a non-starter. Not only would an award to the Charter be seen as inappropriately political, but Havel was being discouraged from even mentioning its name in the acceptance speech. For a long time, it was not quite certain whether the queen would be allowed to attend the ceremony by the government, which, under the Dutch constitution, is responsible for the monarch's conduct.

If the Dutch constitution was a headache, the Czechoslovak laws were another. If Havel accepted the money that went with the award and that he felt rightfully belonged not to him but to the Charter, it would be subject to strict hard-currency regulations; furthermore, the government would confiscate a considerable portion of it as a transaction fee and then go on to monitor how the rest was spent. If, on the other hand, Havel were to donate the money to an offshore trust fund he would be depriving the Communist state of its share – for a 'classless society,' it had always been quite money-conscious – and could end up with a stiff jail sentence. So he could do neither. Strictly speaking, he could not even decline to accept the money, for to dispose of it he first had to become its legal owner and thus fall liable under the law. The only feasible way, which Janouch eventually negotiated, was to accept the prize on condition that it would not be accompanied by any financial reward and then leave it to the Erasmus Foundation to dispose of the money as it decided.[10] In the event, the Foundation saw fit to donate the sum to Janouch's Charter 77 Foundation in Stockholm; he would then see to it that it found its way to the bogus recipients who would pass it on to the proper recipients. It was a somewhat convoluted but acceptable way of doing business.

The third issue was the Chartists themselves. Clashes of ego, vanities and petty jealousies were perhaps less of a problem in the Charter than in other groups of its size, but they existed nonetheless. Since it was obvious that Havel would not be able to travel to Rotterdam, the question arose as to who would accept the award on his behalf and who would read the acceptance

---

9 'I have more publicity and honours than I deserve.' Havel to Janouch, 25 January 1985, in Havel and Janouch (2007), 155.
10 The assessment of legal risks of accepting the financial award of the Erasmus Prize, 1986, VHL ID5456.

speech. Janouch tried to form a triumvirate made up of himself, Pavel Kohout and Zdeněk Mlynář to handle the protocol of the ceremony, but this was not wholly accepted by the other exiles, even more because, leaving aside all their honourable efforts over the past two decades, the three were all former Communists. In the end, Havel had to make the call. He wisely decided to spread the risk; he authorized Janouch to accept the diploma, while he entrusted his old friend now living in California, the actor Jan Tříska, himself not a Charter signatory, to read the speech. Janouch then had to scramble to find travel money and housing for the exiles whom Havel had invited as his personal guests; few of them, after all, were people of independent means. The Erasmus Foundation paid for six people, other charities provided for maybe a dozen more. Some bitterness still lingered. Havel drily commented on the problem: 'East is East and West is West . . . I cannot imagine, if I were receiving an honorary doctorate from the university in Olomouc and invited one hundred friends from Prague that it would occur to a single one to ask me or the university or Janouch to pay for their trip. The idea would be totally absurd. Some people would hitchhike, someone would borrow the money from someone in a pub, another from a rich friend, for whom he would perhaps carry twenty sacks of cement up to the fourth floor in return.'[11]

A month before the ceremony on 13 November, the finer points of political sensitivities remained unresolved. A spokesman for the Dutch government mentioned misgivings about the 'political' character of the speech, and said it should only be delivered after the end of the official ceremony.[12] In turn, some of the invited exiles took offence and pledged to boycott the ceremony if this happened.

In the end everything worked out well. Most of Havel's guests made it to the ceremony, the queen came, Janouch accepted the diploma on Havel's behalf and Tříska read the address. In his speech, Havel identified with the great Dutch humanist Erasmus's *Praise of Folly*: 'The first thing I am recommending here is the courage to be a fool, fool in the most wonderful sense of the word. Let us try to be fools and to demand in all seriousness that the allegedly immutable changes!'[13] The link to, and mention of, Charter

---

11 Havel to Janouch, 6 September 1986, in Havel and Janouch (2007), 281.
12 'The Unwelcome Speech' ('Rede unerwünscht'), *Frankfurter Allgemeine Zeitung*, 20 October 1986.
13 The Erasmus Prize acceptance speech, in *Works 4*, 616.

77 was retained, although in the official English text the formulation 'the honour that is accorded through me to the Charter 77, albeit indirectly'[14] is replaced by 'the honour which is being shown to me'. In accepting the award for his struggle for human rights Havel was censored after all.

Times were a-changing, and not just to the west of the small farm in northeast Bohemia. In March 1985, succeeding the rather farcical trio of the living dead, Leonid Brezhnev, Yuri Andropov and Konstantin Chernenko, at the summit of the Soviet pyramid of power, a fifty-four-year-old provincial apparatchik named Mikhail Gorbachev took over the reins of the ailing superpower and soon showed signs of a pragmatism, openness and common sense unseen in his predecessors. After a false start with an anti-alcohol campaign (a non-starter in Russia of all places) he unveiled the notion of comprehensive economic and political reforms – the so-called perestroika – at the Party Congress in February 1986.

For a long time, however, it seemed as if perestroika were taking place everywhere but in Czechoslovakia. In the Soviet Union glasnost was on the rise; in Poland, Solidarność was re-emerging from the underground; in East Germany, ferment was spreading around the previously tame Protestant church. In Hungary, a relatively open intellectual debate was taking place in various publications, seminars and conferences. In Czechoslovakia . . . nothing. True, Gorbachev visited Prague in April 1987 amidst high expectations. But in the end he came and went without saying much of note, other than expressing his full support for the increasingly senile and isolated Communist leadership.

And yet, during his visit there occurred a memorable encounter of which he was almost certainly unaware. That evening, Václav Havel took his dog out for a walk from his flat by the river. As he was nearing the National Theatre, he saw massive numbers of police. Driven by curiosity ('I am by nature a bystander') he made his way, helped by the dog, to the front row of the cheering crowd, in time to see the Soviet leader emerge from the theatre. At that moment, Havel experienced four unexpected sensations. The first was sadness at the incorrigible nature of his cheering fellow citizens: 'How many times have they pinned their hopes on some external power, which they expect to solve all their problems for them, how many times have they

---

14 Ibid. 613.

been bitterly disappointed and forced to admit that no one would help them unless they helped themselves – and now again the same mistake!' Second, Havel was surprised by feeling sorry for the predicament of the man in power, little knowing that soon he would be in the same unenviable position: 'The whole day he sees the unappealing faces of his bodyguards, his schedule is busy with endless briefings, meetings and appearances, he must speak to a vast number of people, remember them all and not confuse them one with another, he must keep saying things that are witty but correct, things that the world, which is ever hungry for sensation, cannot snatch and use against him, he must keep smiling and attend even such performances as the one tonight while he would certainly rather rest – and he can't even have a drink after a day like this!'

While Havel chided himself for feeling sorry for the man, who probably had what he wanted, and for being like 'the Western idiots who melt like a snowman in the oven whenever some oriental ruler gives them a charming smile', Gorbachev went past him, waving and smiling in a friendly way – 'and I suddenly realize he is waving and smiling directly at me'.

Hence came the third surprise: 'I realize that my sense of courtesy, which commands me to respond, is quicker than my political considerations; I raise my hand, shyly, and wave back.'

On the way back home with the dog there came the last surprise: 'I do not blame myself at all for waving back. Indeed, I really have no reasons not to return a greeting by an enlightened czar! That is to say, one thing is to respond to a greeting and quite another is to betray one's own responsibility by transferring it to him.'[15]

The process of perestroika unfolding in the Soviet Union was apparently an inspiration for Havel's next play, *The Slum Clearance*.[16] In what was emerging as his modus operandi, motivated as much by the fear of a writing block as by the need to finish the manuscript quickly and hide it away before the next house search, its first draft was written, this time in Prague, in five days, and then revised, fine-tuned, retyped and read to tape by the author at Hrádeček in another five days in October 1987.

---

15 *Encountering Gorbachev* (*Setkání s Gorbačovem*), July 1987 in *Works 4*, 960–3.
16 In some English translations also called *Redevelopment*, though this does not quite do justice to the original *Asanace*, synonymous with the secret police operation designed to drive the Chartists out of the country.

The play, like many of its predecessors, is, among other things, about failed attempts at the reform of an unreformable system. A group of architects and officials tasked with the redevelopment of a traditional small-town community first experiences moral qualms when several of the local citizens come to protest against being moved out of their obsolete but cosy homes into a modern but unappealing housing project. As they struggle with the moral dilemma, and some even show signs of sympathizing with the protesters and are about to be punished, there is a sudden change of policy at the top. Tradition and diversity are embraced, and redevelopments are frowned upon. The group sets about enthusiastically redrawing their plans, only to halt in their tracks when their joy proves to be premature and the system goes for a hard-line restoration. The play ends in a tragedy when one of the team succumbs to despair and jumps to his death from the ramparts. In yet another Havelesque double-twist he is neither a disillusioned stalwart nor a frustrated reformist, but the hardnosed realist Kuzma Plechanov[17] who had harboured no illusions all along. The only character in the play whose interactions with the rest bear a semblance of authenticity, he can be said to live in truth, however unpalatable, and is thus the only one 'who earns the right to die'. In Havel's epigrammatic formulation, the message of the play is a question: 'If we have to die, why cannot we at least first live?'[18] The play, with its setting in a castle and its employment of urban planners, a slightly more activist form of surveyors, is Havel's perhaps unconscious homage to Franz Kafka: 'There is a goal but there is no way. What we call a way is only wavering.'[19]

It might seem that, between the Kafkaesque brooding of *The Slum Clearance* and the looming onus of officialdom, Havel's signature humour was becoming an endangered species, but instead his elevated status seems to have fed his tendency to find absurdity, laughs and irreverence everywhere around him. His *Prase, or Václav Havel's Hunt for a Pig* (1987), grew out of his real-life attempt to please Olga by celebrating her birthday to which she invited her Self-Help Library Society The Tomb, with a traditional Czech

---

17 Here as in other pieces, Havel borrowed names of friends and acquaintances for his characters. In real life, Plechanov is a Czech Russian-born systems engineer, one of the Hornosín crowd, who was later tasked with building the first computer network and document-handling system in the presidential office.

18 'On Slum Clearance' ('O Asanaci'), in Freimanová (2012), 589.

19 Franz Kafka, 'Reflections on Sin, Pain, Hope, and the True Way', *The Great Wall of China: Stories and Reflections*, trans. Willa and Edwin Muir (New York: Schocken, 1946), 283.

hog-killing followed by a weekend of gluttony and toasts. Havel's effort to secure a suitable animal in the nearby village of Vlčice, not an easy feat in Communist Czechoslovakia, led to a town-wide conspiracy in which the whole village was leading the gullible and increasingly despairing writer down the garden path in order to drive up the price of the pig. Havel, well used by that time to making weighty pronouncements on all kinds of issues to the world media, wrote up the whole story in the form of a fictitious interview with the reporter of a major international news agency, patiently responding to deadly serious and simultaneously trivial questions about the details of the pig-procuring operation, the exact time of the crucial developments and the reactions of the main players, in a way befitting an account of the latest confrontation with the regime. Only when the reporter finally asks: 'What do you think of Mr Gorbachev?' does the leader of the Czechoslovak democratic opposition reply: 'Fuck you!'[20]

Eventually perestroika made a tentative entrance even in Czechoslovakia. In December 1987 the Party leadership finally summoned the courage to replace President Husák, the symbol of normalization and stagnation, as the General Secretary of the Party, with Miloš Jakeš. This was hardly an improvement. Jakeš was the most colourless and probably the least intelligent of the top Czechoslovak apparatchiks, notwithstanding rather tough competition. He earned his spurs as the chairman of the Party's auditing commission and as the supervisor of the post-1968 purges. Nothing about Jakeš suggests that he went about his job with burning faith or any ideological zeal, but there is also nothing to suggest that he had any moral qualms about doing it. This made him almost scary. One could imagine him compiling the lists of people for the camps. And one would not be far off the mark. After the Velvet Revolution, the archives of the secret police revealed the existence of 'Operation Norbert', a blueprint for rounding up thousands of 'hostile elements' for internment and perhaps worse in the event of an 'emergency'. Václav Havel was high on the list.

He had no way of knowing about it, but even if he had, it would hardly have stopped him. All around him things were stirring. General passivity was giving way to something more appealing. The 'islands of positive deviation' grew bigger and more numerous. They kept adding new and more audacious

---

20 *Prase, or Václav Havel's Hunt for a Pig* (Prague: Gallery 2010) 11.

forms, from 'matchbox art' through 'hiking groups' (a front for the scouting movement), unashamedly independent theatre culture in regional centres like Brno or Ústí nad Labem (though not so much in Prague), open-air music festivals, or the interdisciplinary seminars on the borderline areas of mathematics, philosophy and life sciences, frequented, among others, by Havel's philosopher and biologist friend Zdeněk Neubauer and his younger brother, artificial intelligence researcher and mathematician Ivan.

The more strenuously the authorities strived to deprive the independent-minded groups of public space, the more resourceful they became in creating parallel space of their own. Each July since the early eighties, there congregated at the shores of a lake in the middle of a deep forest in South Bohemia near the hamlet of Hornosín, an inconspicuous community of young and middle-aged couples with children, dogs and cats. They built a camp of tents and two wooden sheds for cooking and storage, which they time-shared with a Young Pioneer squad from a nearby town, a perfect front. There were enough psychologists and psychiatrists there to staff a big-town mental hospital; in fact the original idea, before the families and friends took over, had been to start a training therapeutic community. In a few years, the group, numbering well over a hundred souls on the weekends, became a clearing house for samizdat literature, an incubator for petitions and protests big and small, and a stage for subversive seminars during the day and even more subversive music-making around the campfire at night. At roughly the same time, there emerged on the deserted pastures of Brízgalky on the plateau of the Kysúce mountains in Western Slovakia a very similar community of Slovak intellectuals, musicians and artists, joyfully thriving in even more primitive conditions (one of the upsides was that, with no electricity and telephone, the risk of electronic eavesdropping was not much of an issue). In time, the two groups interconnected and became a federal network, with strong bonds of friendship lasting to this day. The intellectual clout of this network was remarkable. Apart from several leading mental health professionals, it boasted among its members singers and composers, playwrights, writers, philosophers, translators and, after the Velvet Revolution, several ministers, party leaders, members of parliament and an ambassador or two.[21]

---

21 Including myself – I had been going to the camp since its inception.

It was here to Hornosín Jitka Vodňanská brought her notorious boyfriend one summer in the second half of the eighties. That afternoon, in a big military tent, with torrential rain beating on the roof, Havel treated the congregation to a political lecture on the natural alliance between the dissidents of the Eastern bloc and the anti-establishment political groups in western Europe, such as the German Greens. Although the group included several environmental activists, on the whole they found the idea ridiculous and did not lose any time letting the playwright know. Havel, who by then had become accustomed to a more reverential reception of his ideas at home and abroad, knew a good intellectual discussion when he saw one, and after that first day, kept coming back for more. In 1990, already president, he came accompanied by two carloads of bodyguards, suffered the elevation of the presidential standard on his tent, and proceeded to discuss the finer points of the new constitution he was proposing. The reception was just as boisterous as the first time.[22]

Then too the opposition movement itself, with Charter 77 at its core if not its centre – for there was no centre – was growing bigger and stronger. Two journalists from the group applied for a licence to publish the *Popular Daily/Lidové noviny*, an heir to the liberal newspaper of record in prewar Czechoslovakia, and, when their application was predictably turned down, proceeded to publish anyway. A group of younger – and more radical – oppositionists published the underground *Revolver Revue* – a modernist stream of art, poetry and commentary. Lay activists in the Catholic Church such as Augustin Navrátil (locked up for his efforts in a psychiatric hospital in one of the few demonstrable abuses of the mental health care system during the normalization period) demanded autonomy and separation of the church from the state in a petition signed by more than 600,000 believers.[23] Even the official church establishment, led by the primate of the Czech Catholic Church, Cardinal Tomášek, stiffened its spine.

Václav Havel did not and could not play a central role in each and every one of these events. With the benefit of hindsight, however, it is astounding to realize with how many of these endeavours he was directly or indirectly

---

22 A group conversation at Hornosín, 23 July 2012.
23 Petr Pospíchal, 'Obituary of Augustin Navrátil', in http://www.totalita.cz/vysvetlivky/o_navratila.php.

linked as an instigator, an inspiration, a spectator or as a friend. It almost appears as if he were a spider at the centre of a web, spinning and waiting.

More and more often, he also ventured outside the ghetto, often in my company as we grew closer, to attend theatre performances, concerts and exhibition openings, more out of irrepressible curiosity than a conscious attempt to test the authorities. Wherever he went, he was met with conspiratorial smiles and autograph seekers. The musical club Na chmelnici, with largely alternative programmes and audiences, was among his favourite haunts. He even ventured to attend open-air performances in the largest Prague park, Stromovka. On such occasions, he would sometimes ask me: 'Will you be my bodyguarrrd tonight?' What he meant, knowing how ill-equipped I was for the job, was that someone must let Olga, and the world, know should anything happen.

His new status was now also evident in the respect accorded to him from some of the most unlikely quarters. In a phone call with Karel Schwarzenberg in Vienna one day late in 1988, he described what happened when relatives from Slovakia came to visit him and Olga. 'There was nothing to drink in the apartment, and so I took a jug and went to get some beer from the Rybárna pub around the corner. But the cop who was on duty that night guarding our apartment stopped me and said, "Mr Havel, I know that you have visitors and that this is just family, and no politics. Why don't you go back to keep them company and I'll go and get the beer for you myself."' It was at that moment, Schwarzenberg recalls, that he realized the regime was doomed.[24]

Around this time Havel must have realized himself that he was on a transitional trajectory from being an artist and dissident to becoming a politician. Two years later he might still feel uncomfortable about becoming the head of state, but he could hardly claim that he was completely unprepared for a political role.

In the summer of 1988, while at Hrádeček, Havel felt a typical need to take an inventory, and wrote, mostly for himself, 'A Description of My Desk'. It contained, in the furthermost left corner, two manuscripts by other writers he had promised to read, a stack of blank paper with a list of short texts he had promised to write before returning to Prague, a few office

---

24 Conversation with Karel Schwarzenberg, 2 March 2012.

utensils, some correspondence he planned to answer, including a letter from Tom Stoppard, and the last issue of the samizdat *Lidové noviny*. 'That's all. If anyone, after reading this description, feels I am more of an official than a writer, then his feeling is entirely correct. A stack of notes for my next play is absent here, which bothers me more than anything else.'[25]

---

25 'Popis mého psacího stolu' ('A Description of My Desk'), Hrádeček, 1988, in *Works 4*, 1068–70.

THE BATTLE FOR WENCESLAS SQUARE

We live in Prague –
this is where
the revelation of the Spirit
will once occur . . .
> – Egon Bondy

IT HAS BEEN SOMETIMES NOTED that Czech history has a mysterious tendency to produce pivotal events in twenty-year periods, often in a year ending with the digit 8. In the twentieth century, the country's independence and sovereignty came about in 1918, and was brought to an end by the Munich Agreement in 1938. The Communist takeover marking the end of democracy took place in 1948 (slight discontinuity here, perhaps explainable by the acceleration of history during a global conflagration), and the failed effort to give Communism a human face ended with the Soviet-led invasion in August 1968. True, the Velvet Revolution in November 1989 ran a year late, but its first stirrings were on time.

On 21 August 1988, the twentieth anniversary of the occupation, ten thousand people marched through Wenceslas Square singing the Czechoslovak national anthem and calling for the reinstatement of freedom and sovereignty. The authorities were so taken by surprise that the protesters were not attacked by the police until they had marched the whole 700-metre length of the square, and then without much brutality.

Havel, who had been spending the summer at Hrádeček, re-emerged in an unexpected place on the first weekend of September. Lipnice nad Sázavou is a small town in eastern Bohemia, whose main claim to fame is a ruin of a sizeable Gothic castle and a pub with a symbolic name, The Crown of Bohemia; there, between 1921 and 1923, Jaroslav Hašek wrote *The Good Soldier Švejk* while drinking himself to death. On 3 September 1988, during the popular local open-air music festival, Jan Rejžek, a fiery-tempered and fiery-haired music critic, persuaded Havel to talk to the audience during a break between two sets. The enemy of the people was greeted as a rock star and pursued backstage by young women for autographs.

The twenty-eighth of October 1988 marked the seventieth anniversary of the independence of Czechoslovakia. For the first time in two decades the government acknowledged the date by holding official festivities the day before in a vain attempt to steal the thunder from the opposition. Yet on the 28th, 10,000 people marched down Wenceslas Square and continued to the Old Town Square with its statue of the martyr Jan Hus, one of the sacred grounds of the national struggle for freedom and independence.

This time the police were ready, using not only riot shields, long batons and water cannons, but also dogs. For most of the people the first confrontation with the growling Alsatians straining at the leashes was a rather terrifying sight, but they soon discovered that there was more bark than bite in the canine show of force, as long as they limited themselves to verbal rather than physical expressions of protest. In later demonstrations the police stopped using the dogs altogether. Although Charter 77 and five other opposition groups convened the rally, Havel was absent. The previous day he, and at least a dozen prominent dissidents, had been detained and their homes searched.[1]

The cat and mouse game continued before an elite global audience in November, when Havel announced to the authorities an international symposium to be named *Czechoslovakia 88*, drawing on the symbolism of the multiple anniversaries that year. The symposium was to take place on 11 November[2] in the Paris Hotel, a neglected art nouveau gem of Prague architecture. Instead of risking international opprobrium by harassing

---

1 'Police round up dissidents to block protest', by Michael Wise, Reuters News, 27 October 1988.
2 Kriseová (1991), 139, gives the date as 10 November.

the foreign participants, who included the publisher of *Die Zeit* Marion Gräfin Dönhoff, historian and journalist Timothy Garton Ash, the dean of Copenhagen University Ove Nathan and politologists Pierre Hassner and Alexander Smolar, the government let them roam freely, snatching away the Czech dissidents with whom they were to meet. Havel made it to the meeting literally two steps ahead of the law, and managed to declare the symposium open. His next sentence was: 'Well in this moment I am arrested', as three plain-clothes men descended on him. As Hassner observed, Havel as convener never had a chance to close the symposium (and so presumably it continues to this day).[3] At least forty dissidents and historians were detained, with half of them held over the weekend until the foreign participants started leaving.[4]

Havel was by now well used to the tedious ritual of spending four days (two times forty-eight hours, the legal limit of detention without charge) in the familiar environment of the Ruzyně prison. He was far more upset that the police had confiscated his cherished PC during the house search, and he wrote a furious protest to Prime Minister Adamec. With his keen sense of the absurd, he could not omit the detail that 'the police thought the computer was the keyboard, calling the computer itself an amplifier and leaving without the screen which it deemed to be a TV'.[5]

On 10 December 1988, the first visible crack in the impermeable wall of the system appeared. The day, which is celebrated as Human Rights Day in memory of the signing of the UN Universal Declaration of Human Rights in 1948, was chosen for a public rally by five opposition groups. Their application to hold it at the central Wenceslas Square was duly denied, and so they applied for permission to hold the rally at a little-known place in the third borough of Prague. To everybody's amazement permission was granted. The fact that the French president, François Mitterrand, had just left Prague after hosting Havel and seven other dissidents for breakfast at the French Embassy the previous day may have helped.

As historical gatherings go, this one was quite modest. There were maybe a thousand people, with more in the adjoining streets. The

---

3 The quote and other details are taken from 'The Prague Advertisement', by Timothy Garton Ash, *The New York Review of Books*, 22 December 1988.
4 'Police roundup to block Prague seminar nets over 40 dissidents', Reuters News, 13 November 1988.
5 Letter to Prime Minister Ladislav Adamec, 14 November 1988, Národní Museum, Czechoslovak Documentation Centre, VI-19, VHL ID10954

organizers were so unprepared for holding an officially sanctioned event that the best they could produce in the way of a PA system was a hand-held, battery-driven megaphone. People in the back could not quite hear as Havel called for the release of political prisoners; others went as far as to demand the end of the Communist Party monopoly on power. But those who stood closer to the podium passed Havel's central message back into the crowd: 'Our country is beginning to recover from its long slumber.'[6] The plain-clothes police who were out in large numbers all around the perimeter fared even worse, leaving future historians no decent recording of what transpired in the ninety minutes that the peaceful demonstration lasted. But the very fact that it had taken place at all and was not dispersed by force like so many before was more important than what was said.

The authorities apparently assumed that, having paid lip service to the Helsinki Accords and human rights standards, they could afford to tighten their grip again at least until the following December or the next presidential visit. The opposition meanwhile felt that the tolerance shown towards the demonstration signified a possible change of attitude towards reform on the part of the government, or a weakness, or both. The stage was thus set for an unexpectedly violent confrontation.

The sixteenth of January 1989 marked the twentieth anniversary of one of the most heroic and desperate acts in modern Czech history, the self-immolation of Jan Palach under the monument of the Czech patron St Wenceslas on top of the eponymous square. A week before the anniversary, Havel reported to the police that he had received an anonymous letter allegedly written by a student who planned to honour Palach by repeating his fiery sacrifice. He wanted to appear on Czech TV to dissuade the would-be self-immolator, but in the end had to broadcast his message through the BBC, Radio Free Europe and Voice of America. An enemy of the people could not be allowed to be heard in the Communist-controlled media, even to save a life.

The lines were drawn early. The opposition, led by Charter 77, made no secret of the fact that it wanted to commemorate Palach, and applied for permission to hold a peaceful rally. The government made it clear it would not allow any public commemoration. Driven crazy by the

---

6   'Thousands cheer dissidents at authorized rally', by Michael Wise, Reuters News, 10 December 1988.

symbolism of the date, the secret police even confiscated Palach's death mask from the studio of the sculptor Olbram Zoubek. They detained and interrogated Havel twice during the week, and warned him and the leading Chartists of dire consequences if they attempted a demonstration. When Sunday came, the streets around Wenceslas Square were cordoned off by the police, with armoured cars, water cannons and Alsatian dogs. Yet almost 5,000 made it into the square, shouting 'Freedom, freedom'. Several people were arrested, and dozens beaten up including a West German TV cameraman.[7] People chanted, 'Long live Havel', but only his brother Ivan made it to the square. Havel and a group of leading dissidents had been blocked off by the cordons. When he realized he could not get through, he retreated to the nearby apartment of Vlasta Chramostová, and wrote a brief eyewitness report of what he saw.

On Monday morning, the whole thing looked like little more than a skirmish, to the vast relief of the authorities. In fact it was the beginning of the Battle for Wenceslas Square that would last for almost a year, and result in a total defeat for the government. At 3 p.m. that day a small group of dissidents approached the monument of St Wenceslas to lay flowers and light candles. The whole thing was over in a jiffy. Charter spokesmen Dana Němcová, Saša Vondra and twelve others were detained the moment they emerged from the northern approach to the square. Hundreds of onlookers, more numerous than on a normal day, were dispersed by riot police wielding batons and firing tear gas[8] to the shouts of 'Gestapo'. The square was cleared within an hour.

Knowing he was the primary target, Havel prowled around the perimeter of the demonstration, beating a tactical retreat as the police clampdown intensified. Just as he was leaving the square, Havel was arrested, booked and transferred to pre-trial detention. The charge was 'incitement' (trying to dissuade would-be suicides from self-immolating) and 'obstruction of the implementation of the competencies of a public official' (not leaving the square quickly enough).

But if the government believed that this would be the end of the

---

7 'Prague police attack thousands chanting demands for freedom', by Michael Wise, Reuters News, 15 January 1989.
8 'Police attack demonstrators in Prague for second day', by Michael Wise, Reuters News, 16 January 1989.

matter, as they apparently did, this time they were badly wrong. Twenty-four hours later, twice as many people came to the square. Unlike the previous demonstrations, they did not all belong to the traditional (semi-) organized opposition, and many were simply incensed by the reports of police brutality. Many of them were students, clean-cut middle-class young people, until then mostly concerned with partying, romantic engagements and dreams of a career. Some were people simply walking home from work who joined the rally first out of curiosity and then out of solidarity.

This time the police did not hold back. When riot shields and batons did not do the job, water cannons entered the square from the adjoining streets.[9] People were not just dispersed, but chased as they were trying to escape, and mercilessly beaten. Dozens of young people were arrested, herded into vans and brought to the police station in Školská Street where they were again beaten, humiliated and threatened. Some were driven out of the city in police cruisers and left stranded on freezing country roads in the dark. When the square was finally cleared early in the evening, water from the cannons was still running along the pavements. A few shoes lost in the stampede were left lying in the street, like foundered toy boats.

Reasonable people would have stayed away from the monument until things quietened down. But 'fools in the wonderful sense' kept coming back for more. By Wednesday it looked as if the government might be giving up. People came and called for the release of political prisoners, for the end of occupation and for political change. Afterwards they went home, watched and sometimes harassed by the hundreds of riot policemen on the perimeter, but not beaten up or arrested.[10]

When two thousand people came again on Thursday, the police, assisted by the universally hated People's Militias, the 'ironclad fist of the working class' in the days of Communist ascendancy but after forty years more like a bunch of old geezers playing soldiers, went berserk, hosing, beating and arresting.[11] The shouts of 'Gestapo' rose again from the crowd.

Friday marked the end of what became known as the 'Palach week'. The number of people who came to protest was smaller, and they soon

---

9 'Police use truncheons and water cannon to disperse crowds', by Michael Wise, Reuters News, 17 January 1989.
10 'Prague police let thousands demonstrate after US protest', by Michael Wise, Reuters News, 18 January 1989.
11 'Truncheon-wielding police crush Prague protest', by Michael Wise, Reuters News, 19 January 1989.

retreated before the advance of the riot shields. Both sides had made their points. But there was still one point to be made. In 1973, the authorities removed Jan Palach's remains from Prague and had them quietly reinterred at the cemetery in his home town of Všetaty. When the protests flared up, the authorities rightly guessed at the possibility of another place of confrontation, and started to plan the defence of the walled cemetery as though it were Stalingrad. They locked all the side gates, closed down the place for 'repairs' and stood a cistern truck in the main entrance. On Saturday, 21 January, when a procession to lay flowers at the grave was expected, the police besieged the small municipal railway station, identified and detained scores of young people (a bouquet of flowers constituted the evidence of a crime) and put many on the train back to Prague.[12] Only a few people, including the utterly fearless Moravian activist Stanislav Deváty,[13] who crawled with his bouquet through the frozen fields and climbed the cemetery wall like a latter-day partisan, breached the defences.

The Palach week, with Havel's arrest as one of its central events, marked a watershed. The protests, which had been sporadic until then, became a permanent feature of the public mood. The dividing line between the dissident ghetto and the much larger number of discontented citizens became blurred. Havel, who had been merely a recognized authority among the dissidents, and the best known of the Czechoslovak oppositionists abroad, became a national figure, and as he was being sentenced for another nine months of prison, with a month later taken off on appeal, he became the focus of another protest, a petition for his release. Hundreds of activists collected signatures for the petition in schools, theatres, cafés and work places. A gallant mother carried the signature sheets around in a pram underneath her baby. More than three thousand people from all walks of life, some of them recognized figures with careers at stake, signed, and still others kept signing.

The psychology of civil protest revolves around the phenomena of habituation, shared awareness and critical mass. At first, the balance of forces in a confrontation is so skewed that one has to be slightly crazy

---

12 '800 detentions in biggest wave of protests in 20 years', by Michael Wise, Reuters News, 22 January 1989.
13 After November 1989, in a twist of historical irony, Deváty became the head of the Czech Security Information Service (BIS), the reluctant heir to the StB.

in order to undertake it at all. When you are faced, for the first time, with a solid line of space-helmeted grim-faced young men with their metre-long batons and Star-Wars shields, with the bare-toothed snarling attack dogs straining at their leads, or with the business end of a water cannon, you wish with all your might to be somewhere else. When it happens for the fifth time, and you are still around, and still the same person, give or take a couple of bruises, it starts to feel like something you can take. There might even be a bit of a sense of thrill, unwise as this appears. When your instinct is telling you to run for your life, but people next to you, some of them perhaps your friends, don't, your legs do not move either. Increasingly, you draw resolve and encouragement from the shared chanting of slogans, from exchanged looks, from the brush of your shoulder with the one next to you. There is always someone ahead of you who takes even greater risks and who is braver and crazier than you are. And so you stay. In Czechoslovakia during 1988–1989, the number of protesters who risked being hit over their heads or splashed down the pavement by water cannons remained more or less stable at between five and ten thousand people. Throughout the year various Western journalists developed rather sophisticated methods of head-counting in the uniform rectangle of Wenceslas Square, itself some 700 by 60 metres. When they compared notes over drinks in the evening, the numbers did not seem to change much. But beneath the stasis, the accumulated frustration, anger and desire for change kept constantly growing. It was now a question of time.

Then the government blinked again. The weight of the thousands of signatures on the petition (there were actually two), combined with international protests, forced it to reconsider the incarceration of its most famous prisoner. On 17 May, four months after his arrest, Havel was brought in front of a parole board in the Pankrác prison; the warden recommended his early release on the grounds of 'good behaviour', 'tidiness in making his bunk and tending to his personal effects' and 'social integration', exemplified by Havel's eagerness to watch the daily prime-time TV news. Havel's natural politeness, his compulsive orderliness and his interest in public affairs had rarely served him so well. An hour later he was a free man, escorted home by Olga, Ivan and a small group of friends. He looked healthy and rested. He commented on his incarceration by saying that during his previous four-and-a-half-year-long sentence he had been treated as 'an outcast among outcasts, a pariah among pariahs . . . whereas this year I was a privileged inmate with conditions other prisoners can only dream about'.[14] His personal effects were tidily packed inside a string bag and proudly carried by the present writer, at the time the Prague correspondent of Reuters.

14 'Czech dissident Havel freed after serving half jail term', by Michael Wise, Reuters News, 17 May 1989.

That Velvet Thing

Every revolution was first a thought in one man's mind.

– Ralph Waldo Emerson

THOUSANDS OF PAGES have been written about whether the 1989 November events, which brought the Communist era to a close, were a revolution, an implosion, a negotiated transition, a secret coup or something else. To anyone who was around at the time, the answer could only be that except for the secret coup it was all of the above. It was something quite unique, impossibly velvet and probably never to be repeated. To say this is not to ignore its radical character, especially in retrospect. It was certainly a revolution, in the sense that it radically and abruptly altered the individual and social consciousness of all involved. What had been unimaginable one day was popular wisdom the next. What had seemed immutable and eternal ('With the Soviet Union forever') turned out to be a fleeting episode. Overnight people shed their fears, their protective camouflage and their restraints. The only thing they could not shed was their past. Twenty-five years on, in its geographical, geopolitical, economic, cultural or psychological aspect, the face of Central and Eastern Europe has changed beyond recognition.

Another reason to grant the label of revolution to the events of 1989 is that to attach too much importance to the stereotypes about political revolutions as violent upheavals would make them hostage to those who seek to prevent them. The strategy of the opposition movements everywhere in the region was similar, based on civic-minded, non-violent, popular protests. Whether blood would be spilled depended almost exclusively on the powers-that-be and their willingness to use the vast security apparatus at their disposal. If the Communists in Czechoslovakia had decided to use force against the demonstrations on 24 November 1989 as they did in Romania later that year, there would have been bloodshed and martyrs, and the events could be more readily classified as a revolution, but it is doubtful whether the outcome would be more revolutionary.

One thing that continues to amaze, for all the sense of inevitability afterwards, is that nobody saw it coming, not the Kremlinologists, who had built an industry out of reading the tea leaves of sitting arrangements at the First May parades in Red Square, nor the intelligence agencies, who spent fortunes recruiting assets, stealing secrets and sifting through the verbiage of the censored media, nor the Western media, who sent some of their brightest young people to interview the extremely reticent 'reformers' in the *nomenklatura* as the apparent decision-makers of tomorrow, nor the Western diplomats. According to a cable from the US Embassy in Prague sent a week before the revolution, 'widespread popular pressure for it [real political reform] remains muted'.[1] Ambassador Shirley Temple Black attributed this to the 'deeply risk-averse psychology of the Czech people'.[2] Thus 'the average man, distinct from dissident and intellectual circles, has become more, not less, cautious about change in the face of the GDR developments'.[3] But it would be unfair to single out American diplomats for this ignorance. The Communist government, on the one hand, with its monopoly on taking the temperature of the people through its secret police spies, its mandatory trade union chapters and monitored bar conversations, and the dissidents, on the other, were just as surprised and unprepared as those watching on in the West. Interviewed in a Prague fish restaurant in September 1989, Václav Havel expressed his hope that change was coming, but suggested that 'we might not live to see the day',[4] which at that very moment was some six weeks around the corner. It was not so much an expression of pessimism as to the possibility of things

---

1 Telegram from the Embassy in Czechoslovakia to the Department of State, No. 07892, 9 November 1989, in Prečan (2004), 45.
2 Ibid. 47. Ambassador Black's spelling is actually 'risk-adverse'.
3 Ibid.
4 Michael Žantovský, 'Resumption: The Gears of 1989', *World Affairs Journal*, January/February 2010.

changing, for Havel was always something of an optimist – and at any rate, he was at that very moment busy trying to bring the change about – but rather his sure sense of the unpredictability of history and of the silliness of historical fortune-telling. 'I find people who are completely prepared for history rather suspect,' he wrote years later.[5]

On the night of Havel's release, 17 May, there was an improvised party in his flat, attended, apart from the usual suspects, by Alexander Dubček and the then *Time* magazine writer Walter Isaacson. Perhaps for the first time in the role I would later assume as Havel's press secretary, I was serving as phone operator and connecting Havel to friends and media abroad. There was no post-prison depression on this occasion. Neither was there a return to the loyal but small ghetto of Charter 77. Those two petitions demanding his release, which had gathered thousands of signatures within days, persuaded him to 'shift up a gear'.[6] The next day he met, in his favourite local restaurant Rybárna (The Fishery), with Saša Vondra, the youngest spokesman of Charter 77 in its twelve-year history, and Jiří Křižan, an organizer of the petition for his release, whose father had been judicially murdered by the Communists. More meetings of the group followed, with a final strategy session at Hrádeček.[7] On 29 June, not yet six weeks after his release from jail – and since he had been released on probation, it was more than enough to put him back in jail – they launched, together with Stanislav Devátý, the radical activist who crawled through the fields to the cemetery in Všetaty, another petition document called 'A few sentences'.[8] In retrospect, it was a moderate set of demands, far less challenging than some of the slogans chanted during the January 1989 demonstrations. It called for the immediate release of political prisoners, an unconstrained freedom of assembly, opening the room for independent initiatives, end of censorship, freedom of religion, independent environmental impact assessment of all new major industrial and construction projects and, last but not least, for the opening of a debate about Czechoslovak history, including the Stalinist period, the Prague Spring and the invasion of the five armies of the Warsaw

---

5   *To the Castle and Back*, 58.
6   Alexandr Vondra, in art.ihned.cz/c1-37533960-autori-nekolika-vet-prepnuli-jsme-na-vyssi-rychlostni-stupen, 22 June 2009.
7   Conversation with Alexandr Vondra, 9 August 2012.
8   The title, fashioned after the famous '2000 words' document of the Prague Spring 1968, came from Křižan, who apparently felt that a few sentences would suffice. In fact there were just 458 words.

Pact in 1968. The petition, open to any citizen to join, gathered forty thousand signatures in the first three months. This was no longer a dissident cry in the wilderness, but a citizens' movement on the rise. The names of the signatories were read every night on the Voice of America by its Viennese correspondent, musicologist Ivan Medek, one of President Havel's future chancellors.

The regime, fearing a new wave of even larger demonstrations, chose not to go for arrests, purges or large-scale interrogations (although dozens of signatories were called in to provide an 'explanation'). Indeed, the Communist leadership refused to heed calls from the secret police to prosecute the four initiators.[9] Nor, however, did it opt for opening a dialogue with the civil society. *Rudé právo* condemned the petition as an antisocialist pamphlet calling for confrontation in an editorial called 'Inherit the wind'[10], no doubt unaware of the biblical allusion. At one of the hastily convened 'ideological seminars' of top Party officials on 17 July, the General Secretary of the Communist Party, Miloš Jakeš, aimed to provide guidance for dealing with the crisis. Instead, Jakeš's keynote speech was the stuff of slapstick comedy. In an effort to show off his perestroika credentials, he made a spectacular concession to private enterprise by saying 'why not let them run a pub in the middle of nowhere that the government is losing money on anyway', accused the ecological activists of idle talk and called on them to 'clean that stream themselves', and mournfully summed up the plight of the Communist Party: 'And we are alone like a fence post.'[11] A recording of the meeting was leaked within days and made Jakeš and the whole Party the butt of ribald jokes throughout the summer, boosting the courage of every malcontent in the country.

When the anniversary of the 21 August invasion came, Havel, himself under a house arrest,[12] called on the restive citizens to stay at home this time, as he feared for their safety. Yet thousands made it again to Wenceslas Square, to face off against police batons and the People's Militias in battle

---

9 Jiří Urban, '*Několik vět*' (A few sentences), *Paměť a dějiny*, 2010/1, 39–41.
10 *Rudé právo*, 30 June 1989, 2.
11 This hilarious entertainment can be seen for free at www.youtube.com/watch?v=4KPzOT9qKVw.
12 Milan Bárta, *K zajištění klidu a veřejného pořádku* . . . (To ensure peace and public order . . .), *Paměť a dějiny*, 2009/4, 8.

fatigues.[13] Several people were arrested, including two young Hungarians who came to express their solidarity. One of them was Tamás Deutsch, a future minister for FIDESZ in the Hungarian government, today an MEP.[14]

For Havel personally, the series of increasingly dramatic anniversaries pointing inevitably to an impending catharsis almost ended up in a putrid epitaph. At the end of August, deprived of privacy in Prague and in Hrádeček by mounting interest in him from his fellow citizens, the police and the media, he embarked on a tour of the country to visit various 'understanding lady friends' who were concerned about his health and well-being. At Hrádeček he left a sealed letter of instructions and his itinerary in the event something happened, like 'Gorbachev needed to talk to me urgently'.[15] On the night of 2 September, following a local concert of one of the proscribed rock groups, which called itself The Sure Thing (*Jasná páka*),[16] Havel attended an after-show party in a mill-farm owned by the frontman of the group Michal Ambrož, in Okrouhlice, a small village in southeastern Bohemia.[17] Wandering with a painter friend around the dark grounds, he fell into a disused millrace filled with refuse and overgrown with rotting weeds. Unable to climb or be pulled up the slimy concrete walls of the tank, he imbibed several mouthfuls of the foul stuff and thought himself a goner, imagining gleeful headlines in the Communist press, 'He ended up the way he lived', and the like,[18] before the musicians managed to bring a ladder and pull him up. In retrospect, he ascribed a mystical significance to the event: if he could survive such shit, he was obviously chosen for higher things.[19]

In the meantime, things were happening elsewhere on a larger scale. Already in the spring, the Polish government opened round-table talks with Solidarność, and agreed on a power-sharing scheme, which resulted

13 'Prague riot police charge protesters on invasion anniversary', by Michael Wise, Reuters News, 21 August 1989.
14 'Two Hungarians involved in Prague protests to be tried', Reuters News, 26 August 1989.
15 Audio record No. 6, Gerová (2009).
16 The pettiness of the authorities went so far that they banned even the name of the group, forcing it to adopt an outrageously bland name *Music Prague* (*Hudba Praha*).
17 In Keane (1999), 363, the farming village is called 'a picturesque countryside retreat in north Bohemia', thus needlessly confusing the would-be pilgrims.
18 Audio record No. 6, Gerová (2009).
19 Conversation with Eda Kriseová, who was present at the party, although she did not witness Havel's near-drowning, 23 March 2013. Havel described himself on the occasion as 'completely sober' only getting drunk after his rescue. For the mystical significance of the event he refers to Eda Kriseová in Letter to Jiří Gruša, 28 September 1989, VHL ID18167.

in the triumph of the independent trade union in the June elections.[20] Protests were spreading around cities and towns in East Germany. Since mid-August many of its citizens headed for the West, first by successfully crossing the once impenetrable border between Hungary and Austria and then by camping in and around the Bundesrepublik Embassy in Prague and demanding free access to the western part of their divided country. By 27 September, there were 1,400 people in the grounds of the embassy, creating a small humanitarian crisis.[21] After several days of negotiations, in which the Czechoslovak government was the least willing party, 6,300 happy East Germans departed Prague on five trains, leaving behind hundreds of the inexpensive Trabant and Wartburg two-stroke engine cars, which were cannibalized within twenty-four hours for spare parts by Czech drivers of the same models. Almost ten thousand more East Germans followed in the next five days. For anyone who cared to watch, the event and its denouement provided a graphic demonstration that the Iron Curtain was crumbling.

Havel, back in Prague on the night the East Germans left, was walking home through the Malá Strana district. He saw the contrasting pictures of people giving a euphoric sendoff to the buses taking the East Germans on their way to freedom, and of thousands of riot police with trucks, armoured carriers and water cannons sealing off the whole district, in order to conceal from the rest of the world the humiliation of the regime.[22] The fear was palpable, yet it was no longer the citizens but the regime that was afraid.

The next day was Havel's birthday, but also the day when the Nobel Peace Prize Committee in Oslo announced its awardee for the year. Havel had been nominated by several Western human rights organizations. In a precautionary measure, fearing that he would be immediately cut off and isolated by the authorities, he had recorded a fall-back interview with Janouch to be released if he were awarded the prize. It is memorable mainly for the fact that for the first time he publicly, albeit grudgingly, admitted the possibility of assuming 'some sort of office' in 'an emergency situation'.[23] The interview, only published eighteen years later, would never be needed. Half an hour before the

20 A delegation of Solidarnosc led by Adam Michnik came to see Havel at Hrádeček in July 1989 in an obvious gesture of 'combat' solidarity.

21 Oldřich Tůma, 'Exodus východních Němců přes Prahu v září' 1989 (Exodus of East Germans via Prague in September 1989), in Soudobé dějiny, 1999, No. 2–3, 147–64.

22 A telephone conversation with František Janouch, 4 October 1989, in Havel and Janouch (2007), appendix XVIII, 529.

23 Havel and Janouch (2007), appendix XIX, 5 October 1989, 531–4.

official announcement, Reuters broke the news around the world. The prize went to Tenzin Gyatso, the 14th Dalai Lama of Tibet. Havel had no way of knowing that the man who beat him for the award would become perhaps his closest conduit to the spiritual world, but he was pleased just the same. As he repeatedly explained in those days to anyone who cared to listen, he thought it important to dispel the illusions of many of his co-citizens that change would be brought about through the benevolent intervention of an external factor, be it Gorbachev and his perestroika, Western pressure or the deliberations of the Nobel Peace Prize Committee. The job had to be done at home.

There was another birthday gift, however, that pleased Havel greatly. On 7 October, *Rudé právo* printed in its classifieds section a birthday greeting to 'Ferdinand Vaněk of Little Castle', Vaněk being the name of Havel's alter ego in his one-act plays, and Little Castle in Czech the synonym of Hrádeček. There was even a photograph. The bastion was no longer impenetrable.

Music continued to play a role. On 10 June, at the Bratislavská lyra music festival, until then the epitome of schmaltzy pop-music entertainment, Havel, three weeks out of prison and followed by the StB all the way from Prague, still made it to the hotel room of the festival's celebrity guest, the folk singer Joan Baez, where some 'mischief'[24] was planned, and he later carried Joan's guitar case to the concert hall, moonlighting in his old job of stagehand. There he appeared in a cameo role, when Joan dedicated in Slovak one of her songs, 'Swing Low, Sweet Chariot', to Charter 77 and another dissident group. Using her musical ear to repeat phonetically the introduction Havel had previously dictated into her tape recorder, she alerted the audience and the beams of the house spotlights to the presence of the playwright, before the live TV feed was cut and the mikes and the lights were turned off at the behest of the secret police.

Suddenly the limits were being tested in all kinds of ways. On 1 August, a group of writers and translators, both dissident and 'official', met to re-launch the Czech chapter of PEN, banned during the Communist era. Apparently, though, someone had reported the meeting to the authorities, and Havel was detained to prevent him from attending. It appears that some of the same people were doing the re-launching and the reporting. With a group of his writer colleagues, all prominent dissidents, Havel

---

24 Conversation with Joan Baez, Prague, 20 October 2012.

applied for the licence to start a co-op publishing house, which would presumably bring their rich literary output, in its quality vastly surpassing anything produced by the dozen or so existing publishers, above ground. The licence was not forthcoming by the time things came to a head, but the mere fact that it was not rejected out of hand and became a matter of polite, if fruitless correspondence with the authorities signalled a loss of confidence by the government, directly proportional to the growth in confidence among the opposition.

Another honour came to Havel on 15 October, when he was awarded the prestigious annual Peace Award of German Booksellers in a formal ceremony in Frankfurt. The laureate was absent, as the Communist government would not let him travel; he would not have gone even if he had been allowed, for fear of not being able to return. A modest but agile manager of the Karel Čapek Bookshop, Petr Koháček, soon to become a member of the parliament, organized a surrogate ceremony in his Prague shop. In the absence of Chancellor Kohl, it was considerably more relaxed than the real event, but in his improvised remarks Havel noted that this was 'the first time in twenty years that I have been invited by an official manager of an official bookshop'.[25]

Havel's acceptance speech 'The Word about Words', read in Frankfurt by the actor Maximilian Schell, was dedicated to the 'power of words to change history'. It started by comparing the explosive power of words in a tyranny such as the Communist regime to their relative insignificance in the unconstrained universe of a liberal democracy such as West Germany. After citing some famous examples of epoch-making and liberating words at home and abroad, he went on to illustrate the power of the same words to cause unspeakable harm and evil, whether in Nazi Germany or in Khomeini's Iran. Having made the point that it is humans who have the capacity to use words for good or evil purposes, he gets to the real message, which sounds somewhat counterintuitive coming from a man for whom words are his stock in trade: 'It always pays to be suspicious of words and to be wary of them, and we can never be too careful in this respect . . . The same word can be humble at one moment and arrogant the next. And a humble word can be transformed easily and imperceptibly into an arrogant one, whereas it is

25 Gerová (2009), 106.

a difficult and protracted process to transform an arrogant word into one that is humble . . . '[26]

In the end, however, he went a step further, well beyond warning against the corruptibility of words by power, something already brilliantly done by George Orwell and others. The responsibility, which he had in mind, was not simply a social, political or civic responsibility, although it could be all of those as well. It was a metaphysical duty: 'As such, however, it is situated beyond the horizon of the visible world, in that realm wherein dwells the Word that was in the beginning and is not the word of man.'[27]

For Independence Day on 28 October, the government resorted to tested tactics. The night before, the police came to detain Havel, who had been unwell for most of the previous week and was in bed in his Prague flat. Olga was on guard as always, and categorically refused to open the door unless the police produced a warrant. The two young uniformed policemen on the other side of the door were at a loss as to what to do. 'Oh let them in, Olga,' they suddenly heard the voice of Havel, who climbed out of bed in his pyjamas. 'You could get them fired.'[28] Since he was not particularly keen to re-experience the familiar comforts of state hospitality, he sought, with the grudging consent of the police, refuge in a hospital in central Prague.[29] It was a compromise that suited both sides, and especially the patient, who was rumoured to have befriended one of the nurses there. But now everything was a good pretext to vent the rebellious mood. A small crowd of well-wishers gathered in front of the hospital, chanting 'Long live Havel'. That same night, Realistické, a large professional theatre, ran a scenic montage to celebrate the anniversary of the Independence, which for the first time since 1969 included excerpts from a Havel play, *The Garden Party*. The rally of over 10,000 people the next day was broken up by the police, who waded in with truncheons, but refrained from causing serious injuries – thanks perhaps to the foreign media observing the event.[30]

The air of suspense was becoming intolerable, as everybody, the opposition, the citizens, the media and even the police, was waiting for the

26 'The Word about Words', translated by A. G. Brain, *The New York Review of Books*, 18 January 1990.
27 Ibid.
28 Conversation with Daniel Kroupa, 1 March 2013.
29 'Czech dissidents detained ahead of pro-democracy demonstration', by Michael Wise, Reuters News, 27 October 1989.
30 'Police break up rally of over 10,000 in Prague', by Michael Wise, Reuters News, 28 October 1989.

other shoe to drop. Then, on 9 November, the Berlin Wall fell. Prague was by then full of foreign journalists, busy filing marginal reports and drinking through their per diems, much to the impatience of their editors. Everybody seemed to know it was coming, but nobody had any idea when it would happen. The best bet was the International Day of Human Rights, the first anniversary of the first legal human rights demonstration in Prague, still a month away on 10 December. In fact, Havel and his associates were already planning for a major rally that day on Palacký Square, two hundred metres up the river from his house. But time, which had stood still for so long, was now accelerating exponentially. Nobody could wait that long, and certainly not the students. The seventeenth of November was the fiftieth anniversary of the day when the Nazis arrested more than a thousand Czech students, executed nine leaders of student organizations, and shut down universities and colleges for the duration of the war. The anniversary of this tragic event had been misappropriated by the Communist-run International Student Union and declared 'International Students Day'. The student rally was convened by the official Youth Union, but open to the participation of all students, including many of the protesters from the Palach week.

The ambiguity revolving around the event made it a poor candidate for a final showdown. The dissidents had heard about it, but had neither much to do with its organization nor any idea that it could become a trigger for the revolution.[31] It did not particularly appeal to Havel, who was spending the week at Hrádeček. According to some accounts, including his own, he left Prague because he did not want to become the catalyst for a violent suppression of the rally. According to others, he wanted some quality time with Jitka to celebrate her birthday.[32] At any rate, based on an interview given at Hrádeček two days before the fatal date,[33] it is clear that he was pinning his hopes on the Human Rights Day rally at Palacký Square, and had already set the time (2 to 4 p.m.) for the demonstration.

The leader of the revolution was thus some hundred and fifty kilometres away when the student march of between ten and twenty thousand people[34] deviated from its officially approved course, turned into an anti-government

---

31 Conversation with Alexandr Vondra, 9 August 2012.
32 Conversation with Jitka Vodňanská, Hornosín, 12 July 2012.
33 Gerová (2009), 130.
34 Müllerová et al. (2009), 31–5. The organizers gave higher estimates, upward of 30,000 people, but these are hard to square with the physical realities of the later phases of the march.

demonstration with chants of 'Long Live Havel' among others, and was first surrounded and then brutally attacked by the more than usually frenzied riot police. Hundreds were beaten, scores injured, including elderly passers-by and foreign journalists.[35] A student was reported dead, wrongly as it turned out, by human rights activists,[36] and the news, broadcast back to the country by radio, created shock.

There hardly exists a better proof of the central role Havel played in the opposition to the Communist regime and its overthrow than what transpired in the next seventy-two hours. Although he was a non-participant in the triggering event of the Revolution, he was firmly in the lead, if not in charge, when Monday came.

On Saturday, amid the confusion following the crackdown of the night before, he rushed to Prague. The grapevine and the international media were alight with the buzz of the student killed by the police during the demonstration.[37] In the afternoon, about a thousand people marched in protest through the largest Prague square, with police nowhere in sight. In the evening, Havel and many of the opposition activists met in the Realisticke Theatre. The students were going on strike. The theatres were about to follow. And Havel was pondering integration. On Sunday morning, the meeting continued in his house, partly a debating forum, partly a steering committee. People kept coming and going. Havel suggested the 'Civic' label. Jan Urban, a teacher of history, added 'Forum' inspired either by antiquity or by the already rampaging 'Neues Forum' in neighbouring Germany.

In the end, it was not Havel's home stage at Balustrade that became the birthplace of the Civic Forum, but its foremost competitor, the Actors' Studio, made available thanks to the efforts of the actor Vladimír Kratina, a friend of Křižan,[38] and his colleague Petr Čepek.[39] Havel came in early on

---

35 Paula Butturini, reporting for *Chicago Tribune*, ended up in hospital with a broken head. She still fared somewhat better than her husband, John Tagliabue of the *New York Times*, who got shot and almost killed in Romanian Temesoara a month later.
36 'Czechoslovak student beaten to death in protest, activist says', by Michael Žantovský, Reuters News, 18 November 1989.
37 The erroneous rumour was based on alleged eyewitness reports conveyed to journalists through leading dissidents Petr Uhl and Václav Benda. The two independent sources, on which some journalists, including this author, wrote their copy in the end turned out to be the same witness, certifiably unreliable and possibly an actor. Havel had no part in, and initially no knowledge of, the story.
38 The story of the Velvet Revolution is at the same time the story of the Prague theatrical avant-garde dating back to the 1960s. See e.g. Romacora (2004), 282.
39 Conversation with Alexandr Vondra, 9 August 2012.

Sunday afternoon, to avoid detention. As many of the participants observed in retrospect, if the government decided to decapitate the opposition that evening, they would have found it very easy. To all the uninitiated, including the dozens of undercover agents and unmarked police cars patrolling nervously around Wenceslas Square and the adjoining streets, it must have looked as if people, alone, in pairs or in small groups, were walking to catch a show. But there was no show, at least not the kind rehearsed for weeks and advertised in newspapers. On the small stage, with another hundred people in the audience, sat or stood a rather incongruous group of actors. There were Jiří Křižan and Saša Vondra, the co-organizers of 'A few sentences', there was Jan Škoda, Havel's mate from boarding school and a high official of the fellow-travelling Socialist Party, there was Jiří Svoboda, representing the younger generation in the Communist Party, and, as it later turned out, a sincere though ineffective reformist. There was Milan Hruška, a fiery miner from the North Bohemian coal mines. There was Radim Palouš, the sonorous philosophical godfather of Kampademia. There was Petr Miller, a forgeman from the Prague ČKD plant. And there was Havel. After about two hours of passionate, though unstructured debate, in which he played but a minor part, the meeting adopted the Declaration of the Civic Forum, written by Havel earlier in the day.[40]

The tone of the declaration is radically different from 'A few sentences'. It reflects both the anger provoked by the senseless violence two days earlier, and the growing confidence of the opposition. The declaration demanded the immediate resignation of five leading Communist officials who were directly linked to the plan for the invasion of the five Warsaw Pact countries in August 1968, of President Gustáv Husák, and of the Communist officials responsible for the violence against peaceful demonstrators, an independent investigation of these events and the immediate release of all prisoners of conscience, including those detained during the demonstrations. In support of these demands the Civic Forum called for a general strike on 27 November, which had been already proposed by the students.

There were a number of people who could have convened a forum of Charter 77, or meetings with other, smaller opposition groups. There were

---

40 Müllerová and Hanzel (2009), 25.

likewise people who could have mobilized actors, students, reform-minded Communists and even trade unionists. But only Havel could have pulled off a full-length theatre performance of disparate individuals, conflicting ideologies and disjointed narratives with the awareness that it was, at one and the same time, both essential and absurd. Havel, as philosopher Ladislav Hejdánek described him, was the 'carbon',[41] a chemical element capable of linking with many others to create a compound of irresistible strength, filled with contradictions yet stable enough to set in motion the momentous transformation that lay ahead.

The students and the actors had already declared a strike. The declaration adopted by the meeting was a bold step, but it did not a revolution make. Late in the evening, a small group of the participants in the meeting at the Actors' Studio retired to Havel's favourite local restaurant Rybárna, to plan the next moves. This was the seed of the 'Action Group', never numbering more than twelve people, who became the *spiriti agens* of the events of the following weeks and months.[42]

On Monday the dam broke. The international media had been waiting on Wenceslas Square since early afternoon. When the headcount, instead of the usual five, ten and sometimes (hotly contested by the government) twenty thousand, reached a total of 150,000[43] and kept rising, all that remained was to write the headline: It was all over.

---

41 Hejdánek, Ladislav, *Havel Is Carbon* (*Havel je uhlík*), Sešity VHL 3/2009.
42 Conversation with Ladislav Kantor, Roztoky, 27 February 2013.
43 Telegram from the Embassy in Czechoslovakia to the Department of State, Prague, 21 November 1989, in Prečan (2004), 106. Other sources, e.g. Suk (2013), 330, give the number as 200,000, probably too high. The 300,000 asserted for the rallies in the following days in ibid. is highly unlikely, suggesting a density of eight people per square metre.

THE FOG OF REVOLUTION

I saw a great tumult, but I knew not what it was.

– 2 Samuel 18:29

ON MONDAY, THE UNELECTED but widely recognized leadership of the Civic Forum scrambled to stay abreast of events as they unfolded. In the absence of the Forum representatives, who were busy hunting for office space and organizing committees, the demonstrators in the square were exposed to the rhetorical skills of a most unexpected and unwanted speaker, the burly chairman of the Socialist Youth Union, Vasil Mohorita – one of the gang that had roughed up the would-be Chartist ball-goers. He failed to sway the crowd by promising reforms and his own resignation should violence be used again. 'We have had enough!' answered the crowd.

The crowd did not want Mohorita. They wanted an authentic leader. Many people called for Alexander Dubček, the recently re-surfaced hero of the Prague Spring. Others called for Havel. At the early-evening meeting of the Civic Forum leadership in the Realisticke Theatre, Havel and others realized that there might be as many or more people at Wenceslas Square the next day and that they neither could nor should stay away. Křižan, Ladislav Kantor, an independent rock and folk musician and impresario, and the fiery activist John Bok were imploring Havel to take to the streets lest 'they drown us here like rabbits'.[1] The problem was: where in the streets? Mohorita spoke

---

1   Conversation with Ladislav Kantor, Prague, 27 February 2013.

from under the statue of St Wenceslas, the patron saint of Bohemia, at the top of the square, but that place was in the middle of the crowd, vulnerable to provocation, entrapment or worse. Moreover, anyone speaking there could not be seen or heard by more than the few hundred people around him. What was needed was an elevated stage, somewhere near the middle of the square: the revolution was about to become a performance.

The problems with finding the stage looked insurmountable. There was a building with a suitable balcony at the right spot, but it belonged to the Socialist Party of Czechoslovakia, one of the four parties comprising the National Front, which, faithful to its name, *fronted* for the power monopoly of the Communist Party. Its executive secretary, however, was Havel's school buddy Jan Škoda, scout name Nosák, who could be persuaded to let the rebels in. The balcony itself, however, was in the offices of the publishers of the Czechoslovak–Soviet Friendship Union, an unlikely place to launch a protest against decades of arbitrary and foreign-imposed rule.[2] That obstacle, too, was overcome with the help of Petr Kučera, a journalist employed by the socialist paper *Svobodné slovo*.[3] Still, Havel needed to make himself heard. The hand-held loudspeaker of the year before would not do. As if out of nowhere there appeared at Kantor's and Hanzel's behest stagehands, sound technicians and stage managers of various rock 'n' roll bands. Havel's loyalty to the genre had paid off. He could now speak to the crowd, but he was well aware that a monologue does not a show make. The preparations for the big December rally that never was now came in good stead. Another friend, Petr Oslzlý, the artistic leader of the Theatre on the String in Brno lent a hand with the programming. When Tuesday afternoon came, there were a number of opposition speakers led by Havel, alternating with students, workers, actors, musicians and singers, most of them legends, many even more so for the fact of having been banned and ostracized for years. Marta Kubišová, the first dame of the Prague Spring who had sacrificed a stellar career in pop music rather than make compromises, sang the national anthem, followed by the underground protest singer Vladimír Merta, the Dadaist poet-singer Jiří Dědeček and others. Kantor was put in charge of the running order. The dean of Czech protest singers Karel Kryl, who had spent the previous years

---

2 A popular joke in the form of a quiz question went Q: Are the Soviets our friends or brothers?
   A: Brothers, because friends you can choose.
3 Conversation with Ladislav Kantor, 27 February 2013.

broadcasting from Radio Free Europe in Munich, suddenly materialized on the balcony. Three days later the folk singer Jaroslav Hutka, exiled by the regime to Sweden, landed at Prague airport and demanded entry. A couple of friends on the other side of the border partly cajoled and partly blackmailed the frightened border policemen into opening the gate. The next day he sang for the largest audience he had ever seen. Nobody has ever claimed credit for having invited Karel Gott, the 'Golden Nightingale of Prague' and a pillar of the establishment. Kantor thinks the idea was so absurd it must have come from Havel.[4]

The velvet character of the week during which 'history came back to our country after twenty years of timelessness' was no foregone conclusion. True, the rallies were largely good-natured and peppered with large doses of irreverent but harmless Czech humour. Just the same, the dynamics of mass psychology is notoriously unpredictable; there was an unmistakable darker edge in slogans such as 'We have had enough'. Havel played a crucial role in stressing the non-violent character of the revolution, both in his own remarks and in helping to choose speakers who would appeal to the crowd in a similar way. Václav Malý, a signatory of Charter 77 and a banned Catholic priest, was the shining star of the rallies, effectively demonstrating the Christian virtues of forgiveness and humility in practice. And Havel found the language that reflected both the frustration and anger accumulated over decades and the need to refrain from striking out now that the opportunity had arisen: 'Those who have for many years engaged in a violent and bloody vengefulness against their opponents are now afraid of us. They should rest easy. We are not like them . . .'[5]

This was, however, no classic performance but a piece of modern theatre in which the audience was not a passive observer but part of the show. They applauded and cheered, sang with the performers, clinked their keys and chanted mockingly: 'Miloš, it's over.' Miloš was Milouš Jakeš, the Secretary General of the Communist Party, who, a few months earlier, had discovered that he was alone as a fencepost. Now they were rubbing it in. They cheered the speakers whose credentials included months or years spent in jail, and they jeered everybody they suspected of opportunistically hitching his wagon to the revolutionary train. When

---

4 Conversation with Ladislav Kantor, 27 February 2013.
5 A speech to the demonstrators in Wenceslas Square, 22 November 1989. In *Works 4*, 1161.

a million people came to the Letná plain the following Sunday (such numbers simply would not fit into Wenceslas Square) they applauded the two editors of the underground *Lidové noviny* (Popular News) who had been released from jail just a few hours earlier. 'We still had breakfast in jail,' said one of them into the microphone as a way of explanation. 'How was it?' asked the multitudes in one voice. 'Lousy,' said the editor. 'Shame, shame,' cried the million people. For most, it was the best show they had ever seen in spite of the freezing cold.

The revolution now had a stage and was building a backstage. After the first chaotic press conference in the art gallery U Řečických', in which, torn between my role as a journalist and a member of the Civic Forum, I doubled as translator into English for the foreign media, the Forum moved to bigger premises at the Laterna Magika theatre in the basement of the Adria Palace on Národní. There, press conferences were held against the background of the stage of a production called *The Minotaurus*, giving them a somewhat eerie feeling. But Havel felt at home in a place whose beginnings were associated with Alfréd Radok and Miloš Forman.

On 24 November, Miloš Jakeš and the entire Party leadership resigned. The Central Committee proceeded to elect as their leader a nondescript railway man named Karel Urbánek, possibly the only man dumb enough to accept the job. When a member of the government called on him to ask for instructions, he offered him a piece of salami and a sausage and said: 'There has been the past, there will be a future.'[6] When the crowd in Wenceslas Square heard the news, they went wild with joy. Until then, nobody could be quite confident there would not be a setback of the murderous kind that the rejoicing masses had experienced in Budapest in 1956 and in Prague in 1968, or the clampdown that the victorious Solidarność was subjected to in Poland in 1981. The crowd would have been even more concerned had they known that until that day Jakeš and his comrades were trying to summon the courage to unleash the tanks, armoured carriers and rapid deployment units that had been standing at the ready several kilometres outside Prague. The despised People's Militias, 85,000-strong, were put on alert on 19 November. The situation 'could still be resolved by the use of force.'[7] But in the end the

---

6   Interview with Marián Čalfa, Institute for Contemporary History, Prague, 1994. The translation does not quite do justice to the Czech '*nějak bylo, nějak bude*'.
7   Ibid. 34.

comrades went down with hardly a whimper. Some people would give them credit for common sense and even a bit of decency; however, they acted not out of common sense, nor decency, but rather ordinary fear. If they had felt the slightest possibility that they could rely on shelter and support from their Soviet protectors, the tanks would probably have rolled in.

The occasion called for another piece of theatre. Late in the afternoon that day there appeared with Havel on stage the man who had for most people symbolized the potent aura of hope twenty-one years earlier, as well as the abject despair of later seeing that hope crushed, Alexander Dubček. He was still a well-liked but somewhat controversial figure. People did not question his motives and mostly did not blame him for the defeat of the Prague Spring. Quite a few, however, could not forgive him for signing the capitulation in Moscow (admittedly he would have been risking his life had he not), for signing the draconian anti-protest laws of 1969 and for staying silent for most of the intervening twenty years. For the moment none of that mattered. The crowd needed its heroes.

There were quite a few who now belatedly auditioned for the role. Far fewer were those who had been heroes for a long time, but were now content to shun the limelight. One of them was Ludvík Vaculík, the writer, feuilletonist and underground publisher, who now fulfilled the threat from his *Czech Dream Book* to mind his own business when things finally changed for the better.[8] He now wrote Havel a note explaining his reluctance to appear alongside him on stage before an ecstatic audience of last-minute revolutionaries. He concluded with an epitaph: 'After you extricate yourself from your unique and brave role, there might be the time to discuss it in the Paroplavba bar confidentially, perhaps under the cover of a communiqué about broads. I wish you everything that can be wished "for the cause" and even more so to stay "above the cause".'[9]

Now the times they were a-changing. A two-man mediating mission of the rock composer and singer Michael Kocáb and lyricist Michal Horáček had been conducting informal talks with the officials of the government since before 17 November. Prime Minister Adamec was willing to meet with representatives of the opposition, but at first drew the line at Havel, whom he had publicly called a 'nobody' only a couple of months earlier.

After huge pro-democracy rallies and a symbolic two-hour general strike on 27 November, he finally bowed to the inevitable and agreed to meet with a delegation of the Civic Forum led by Havel the next day. For the government this was not a negotiation from a position of strength as was made crystal clear when, after a civil enough handshake between the two men, Adamec opened the conversation by saying: 'We have not met yet, have we?'[10] A compromise was reached for a caretaker government under Adamec's premiership. But as often happens in revolutionary situations, the man in the street was already way ahead of the leaders. The new government, in which three quarters of the ministers still represented the Communist Party, was made public on 3 December, but there was no applause. The revolution had won; no one wished to look at the familiar grey faces even for another day. When Adamec's last-ditch trip to Moscow in an effort to win Gorbachev's support failed, the game was up. The next day, on 5 December, when confronted with demands by the Civic Forum for more far-reaching changes in the government, the prime minister suddenly lost interest in standing at its head. There was a hidden hitch, however. Although Adamec no longer wished to be prime minister, he was not averse to the idea of stepping up to the presidency. Pushed by popular impatience, the Forum's position hardened overnight.[11]

The record of the three meetings between Adamec and his people and the delegation of the Forum led by Havel reads like the transcript of a chess game between a veteran grandmaster and a line-up of enthusiastic amateurs. The professional keeps confusing his opponents by feigning and disguising his true intentions and sacrificing pawns to bolster his position. The amateurs do not see beyond the next move and are condemned to watch their attacks being parried and frustrated. It would have been no contest were it not for the fact that the professional had lost his queen early in the game. And Havel, ever polite, was still able to see through the duplicity of his opponent and stood ready to call his bluff at a critical moment: 'Let's go to the Castle [meaning to the president] and propose someone who will be more understanding . . .'[12] He may have lacked the subtlety and the

---

10 Hanzel (2006), 44.
11 In contrast to a previous interview (Institute for Contemporary History, 1994, 29) Adamec's successor Čalfa believes this was Adamec's plan all along, although he never gave it a chance of succeeding. (Conversation with Marián Čalfa, 29 August 2013).
12 Hanzel (2006), 179.

negotiating skills of his opponent, but in the end, with some help from his colleagues, he prevailed.

There was, however, a problem that Havel and his associates thought better not to advertise. In a group composed of dissidents and oppositionists, most of whom had spent the last twenty years as window-cleaners, stokers or at best archive assistants, and of writers, musicians, actors and psychologists, there was hardly anyone with the experience to manage a town hall let alone the government of a country.[13] There was enough intelligence, erudition and expertise around to draft policies and legislation in general terms. But to manage the paper flow, the secretarial and clerical work needed to turn policy into a workable directive or a bill, was another thing altogether.

And so the attention came to focus on Marián Čalfa, a youngish Slovak lawyer who, while not occupying a prominent position in the Communist Party hierarchy, had managed and coordinated the legislative work for the government, and was effective in arranging and managing the agenda of the meetings between the government and the Forum. He seemed to be the right choice for a caretaker prime minister until the new non-Communist ministers learned the ropes.

Čalfa was willing but he was also shrewd. Well aware of how quickly sands might shift, he knew that his job security would be extremely low. Unlike the Civic Forum, which only thought it possible to announce Havel's candidacy on 10 December, the day the new prime minister and his government were installed and President Husák resigned, Čalfa took his cue from the slogans of the crowds in the street a week earlier. Realizing that the Civic Forum had no clue as to how to elect Havel president, he offered to facilitate the process in an implicit exchange for something more than just an emergency premiership. 'They knew who, and I knew how,'[14] was a perfect summation by the bargain-wise lawyer. The one-to-one meeting in the cabinet office on 15 December almost failed to materialize: Havel feared that he would be walking into a trap and only relented after a personal intervention by Pithart,[15] while Čalfa had to find a room in his own office that was not bugged, a difficult task by the standards of the Communist

---

13 This led to instances of gallows humour: 'Budaj is a stoker, isn't he? Maybe he should be the Minister of Fuels and Energy' (Recording of a meeting of the Civic Forum, tape 6, Vladimír Hanzel archive).

14 Conversation with Marián Čalfa, Prague, 29 August 2013.

15 Conversation with Petr Pithart, 28 August 2012.

government. In the end he simply took Havel to the empty office of the most insignificant official he could think of.[16] There, as Čalfa put it, 'two people met who . . . made it clear to each other that they are responsible people who can cooperate.'[17] Twenty-four years later Čalfa discounts any calculating motive on his part, pointing out, rightly, that once Havel became president he could always fire him the next day.

The meeting became key to every subsequent conspiracy theory that the Velvet Revolution was a complot between professional dissidents supported and funded by the West and the ruling elements of the Communist Party; or collusion between a Free Mason–Jewish cabal and the Gorbachevite renegades in the Party; or even orchestrated by the KGB and StB through its agent operatives, of whom Havel, of course, was key.

It seems inevitable that every great historic event from the Kennedy assassination to the first moon landing, or, indeed, to the election of the first African-American president, will provide fertile ground for crackpots, loonies and paranoiacs to come up with conspiracy stories. The conspiracy theories of the Velvet Revolution draw on three scenarios. The first is that the student demonstration on 17 November and the police crackdown were in fact a piece of political theatre masterminded by high KGB officials whose presence in Prague on the eve of the march has been documented, and that they were enacted (down to an StB agent in the role of the dead student) to create a confrontation that would facilitate the replacement of the tired and discredited leadership with fresh faces who were nevertheless trusted collaborators. In the second scenario, there existed a deal between the Communists and the Civic Forum with express promises of immunity from prosecution for the Communists in exchange for ceding the government to the Forum. According to the third, there was a personal deal between Havel and Čalfa on 15 December, under which Čalfa would arrange for a problem-free election of Havel as president and would in turn enjoy Havel's support and unfettered rule as prime minister.

There is a dearth of evidence to support the first assumption, but much to disprove it. For most practical purposes a direct role of the KGB can be

---

16 Conversation with Marián Čalfa, Prague, 29 August 2013. The Bondesque version with mysterious 'Danish professionals' sweeping the room for bugs in Suk (2013), 393, apparently originating from Pithart, seems to be pure conjecture.
17 Ibid.

discounted. The geo-strategic game was over by the night of 17 November, with Poland, Hungary and East Germany all irretrievably lost. Neither did the StB function as a coherent force any more. As subsequent investigations have shown, there were no clear orders from above, and certainly none to use force against the demonstrators.[18] The political instruction was to use 'political means' to resolve the crisis. The coordination of StB activities was so weak that Ludvík Zifčák, its undercover officer on the scene, got roughed up so badly by his fellow comrades that he would have been within his rights to sue his employers.[19] And no one could have controlled what happened afterwards, with hundreds of thousands in the streets, certainly not the Civic Forum, or the Public Against Violence, its counterpart in Slovakia. The best proof of the innocence of the Forum from the charge of conspiracy was the somewhat chaotic way in which it operated. Far from controlling the galloping events, all its leadership could do was to hold tight to stay on horseback.

The second hypothesis relies on the empirical fact that in spite of all the crimes, depravities and injustices of the Communist era, some of which were punishable even under its own laws, the Party and the culprits got off lightly. Hardly anyone went to jail, with the exception of a few people, such as Prague Party secretary Miroslav Štěpán, who made the mistake of authorizing police brutality against peaceful demonstrators from the roof of one of the buildings on Wenceslas Square during Palach week in January 1989. Even he was out of jail on parole in a year.

It is one question whether there was an under-the-table deal between the Forum and the Communists; it is another whether the Forum was politically responsible for being soft on the Communists; and it is still another whether it was right in taking this approach. But on the first count, the answer is a resounding no. Twenty-five years of historical and investigative research have found no evidence that any such deal had even been contemplated. The most compelling reason for its absence is that it would not have been worth the paper it was written on. In a rapidly changing situation, with the Communists quickly losing instruments of power, there were no internal or external safeguards either side could rely on, no arbitrators and no trust.

---

18 The only significant order, which came from deputy Interior Minister Alojz Lorenc, who had been in charge of the StB, was to shred the 'live' files, making it harder for the new government and later historians to identify the agents of the old regime.

19 Müllerová and Hanzel (2009), 37.

The idea that the prisoners and dissidents of yesterday would conclude a gentleman's agreement with their jailers and oppressors, and that either side would expect the other to honour such an agreement is risible.

The answer to the same question looks rather different, however, if one replaces the word 'agreement' with the word 'understanding'. From the perspective of the regime, that must have been the real purpose of the negotiations. The government was giving up power, unconditionally, and the rebels were taking over, also unconditionally, albeit reluctantly. And so the negotiations served primarily to sound out the intentions and test the determination and the will of the opponent. After several rounds of talks, it must have been clear – and a huge relief to the departing government – that Havel & Co were not coming in with an iron fist. The whole train of events until then corroborated this. The non-violent, velvet character of the revolution was absolutely spontaneous. The multitudes on Wenceslas Square did not need to read 'The Power of the Powerless' to choose 'We are not like them' as their rallying cry. And it was just as clear to them as it was to Havel and his colleagues that the Communists were not getting ready for a last stand, that they had no will left, no stamina and nothing to keep them going. Havel did not have to make deals.

Similar thinking applies to the question of a possible personal deal between Havel and Marián Čalfa. Here it seems to have been a little more than an understanding and a little less than an agreement. Čalfa certainly kept his part of the unspoken bargain, and Havel stayed true to his for the next two years. The difference was that, while he may have had no need for the Communists, he did sense a need for Čalfa, not just as a capable administrator, which he proved to be, but also as a sign of a national consensus, a palliative of sorts, whose everyday visibility and respectability may have kept his former comrades from trying something desperate. And lastly, there was the unwritten consensus that, if the president were a Czech, the prime minister had to be a Slovak; the last thing Havel or the country needed was a Slovak rival. Čalfa would be pliable.

Conspiracy there was not, but the cultivation of Čalfa makes the way Havel became president look easy in retrospect. It was anything but. First and most importantly, Havel had to make up his mind whether he wanted to be president. The discrepancy between Havel's stated misgivings about the role allotted to him by the Forum and his apparent readiness to play it gave rise to later charges of hypocrisy, the stock in trade of many politicians, but a damaging accusation to one professing to live in truth. The charge cannot be totally dismissed, but is much less serious to anyone familiar with the dynamics of the political process and the personality of the candidate.

The assumption that Havel actually wanted to be the top man, or at least knew he could not escape being the top man, is reasonable enough. That, in the beginning, did not readily translate into being president, because there was a considerable amount of uncertainty as to how long the transition would take, how much resistance the Communist parliament would offer and what would be the new constitutional arrangements. But in fact, it would have been very strange if Havel had contemplated anything other than the top leadership role. He did not have to insinuate himself or scheme to position himself because he had occupied that role all along, as the voice of the non-Communist opposition in 1968, through his early initiatives in the aftermath of the Soviet invasion and his undisputed domination of Charter 77, to his authorship of 'A Few Sentences' and the founding declaration of the Forum. The support for this role among the members of the Forum and even among the Chartists was never unanimous, but whenever an alternative was raised, the thinking reverted quickly to Havel. In short, Havel did not win the right to be the candidate of the revolution in the first ten days of December 1989 but in the twenty years preceding it. 'Deep inside, he was ready.'[20]

Because of his credentials, he did not even have to put his name forward. Others would do that for him. His reservations and objections never took the form of a refusal of the nomination or of a serious quest for an alternative, but rather represented a sort of negotiation between Havel . . . and Havel. He was clear-minded enough about politics to realize what the job would entail in terms of the loss of privacy (for that he needed to get Olga's acquiescence, which could not be taken for granted, and which she eventually gave with grave misgivings). He was conscious enough of the obstacles that would have to be overcome not to fully embrace the nomination until he could be reasonably sure of winning. He was respectful enough of the other candidates not to dismiss their claims out of hand. And he was prescient enough to realize that for any president there would be rough sailing ahead, that he would first become an object of almost ecstatic

---

20 Conversation with Alexandr Vondra, 9 August 2012.

expectations and then of equally unrestrained frustrations when those expectations could not be realized.

His hesitancy at accepting the nomination, clearly expressed in the recordings of the Forum's discussions as late as 7 December,[21] can thus best be explained as a series of tactical moves, part positioning, part timing and part insurance against a rainy day. At the same time, it was also an expression of his genuine modesty and discomfort at the thought of aggrandizing himself. The sense of guilt, which seized him with every victory, every reward and every honour accorded to him, could not have left him when he was offered the biggest prize of all. But this was an internal, psychological process, which translated into words and pained expressions rather than actions.

There is some competition for the honour of having nominated Havel for president. Olga, who knew him best, had suspected him of presidential ambitions for decades. Pavel Tigrid, the influential exile publisher, prophesized his presidency in print almost a year before it came true.[22] Pavel Kohout saw it coming,[23] and Daniel Kroupa was sure of it.[24] I was laughed at by some of my fellow foreign correspondents in Prague in the summer of 1989 when I predicted it would happen. Michael Kocáb raised the question of Havel's nomination in the meeting of the steering committee of the Forum on 5 December, setting off an inconclusive debate. A meeting of Havel's close circle convened in the pause of the larger meeting endorsed the idea and produced a semi-willing candidate. A rushed 'primaries' within the steering group on 8 December ended with an overwhelming support for Havel save for six abstentions. Three out of the six, all close to Havel during the dissident period, were former Communists. Two of the other three apparently had personal reasons.[25] The sixth, according to handwritten minutes of the meeting,[26] was a 'grey zone' economist brought in by Havel's friend Rita Klímová. His name was Václav Klaus, although Havel introduced him in their first meeting with Prime Minister Adamec as Dr Volf.[27]

---

21 'I have accepted [the presidency]? Just a moment, I haven't accepted anything.' Suk (1998).
22 Pavel Tigrid and Jan Otava, 'A Report on the Situation in Central Europe', Svědectví No. 87/1989, 525.
23 Conversation with Pavel Kohout, Prague, 22 October 2012.
24 Conversation with Daniel Kroupa, Prague, 1 March 2013.
25 Petr Pithart says he simply could not believe Havel really wanted to be president. Conversation with Petr Pithart, 28 August 2012.
26 The wider Crisis Group, 8 December, Ladislav Kantor archive, quoted in Kaiser (2009), 223.
27 Václav Klaus admits the idea of Havel for President made him 'raise his eyebrows' but does not recall taking a position on the subject in a vote. Conversation with Václav Klaus, 30 August 2013.

THE ROAD TO THE CASTLE

The Castle gentlemen are so sensitive that I'm convinced they couldn't bear the sight of a stranger, at least unless they were prepared for it.
                                        – Franz Kafka, *The Castle*

ON 10 DECEMBER, the day President Husák appointed the new government and promptly resigned, a popular actor named Jiří Bartoška was chosen to announce Havel's nomination to a cheering crowd in Wenceslas Square. In retrospect he admitted to some stage fright, but was encouraged when Havel told him: 'Just go out there, you will have a bigger audience than Elvis Presley.'[1] The move was certainly appropriate to the occasion, but it may have also been an effective way to quash any presidential ambitions the departing Prime Minister Adamec may have entertained. Havel's meeting with Čalfa on 15 December took care of the parliamentary niceties of the election. To anyone wondering how the vote of a parliament of two chambers and 350 deputies could be settled beforehand in the meeting of two men, neither of whom was even an MP, suffice it to say that this was a parliament so used to taking orders it would have elected Dracula if told to do so by the government. With the spectre of hundreds of thousands of people marching at its gates, there was never a risk of its mustering a mind of its own.

There were nonetheless a few other candidates and one serious contender. All of them were former or current Communists, and in more

---

1   Conversation with Jiří Bartoška, Prague, 1 March 2013.

than one way throwbacks to the previous era. During the Prague Spring of 1968, Čestmír Císař was a students' candidate for the presidency, Valtr Komárek was an economic adviser to Fidel Castro, and Zdeněk Mlynář was one of the top reformists in the Communist Party. The only serious contender was Alexander Dubček, the symbol, the hero and the vanquished of that brief period of hope. The campaigns of the first three either never took off, or self-destructed shortly afterwards. Dubček was something else, however. He was immensely popular at home, mainly for being nice; he was easily the best-known Czech or Slovak abroad, and he was a Slovak, which spoke in his favour as long as Adamec, a Czech, was the prime minister. On the less engaging side, he had a sense of bitter entitlement after twenty years in political limbo ('That they should have done this to *me*' was his pitiful line on learning the news of the Soviet invasion in the early morning of 21 August 1968) and with age he had become increasingly prone to tearful self-pity and irrational stubbornness. He staked his claim early and was not about to abandon it without a fight.

Circumstances that went far beyond the personalities and merits of both candidates made the situation awkward. On the one hand, this was clearly a contest between the past and the future. As much as people liked Dubček, they could not easily forget that 1968 was an experiment that had failed, with catastrophic consequences for a whole generation. When Gorbachev said 'Twenty years' in response to a question about the difference between perestroika and the Prague Spring, he apparently thought he was being complimentary about the Czechoslovak experiment, but it was hardly a compliment to many people in Czechoslovakia, especially the young. If all the revolution promised was a return to the endless theological debates about reconciling the democratic process with the doctrine of the leading role of the Communist Party, about combining the impersonal state ownership of the economy with private initiative, then many would consider it a waste of time. On the other hand, there was the national element. The Prague Spring and its denouement may have been an unmitigated disaster for the Czechs, but it did represent some lasting, though modest, achievements for the Slovaks, in the federalization of the country, theoretical as it was under the monolithic rule of the Party, and in its having a Slovak politician at the top of the political pyramid for the next twenty years. If the Dubček candidacy was not handled in a sensitive way there was a danger of alienating both large numbers of former Communists and large numbers of Dubcek's Slovak compatriots. On 9 December, the Public Against Violence qualified its support for Havel's presidency by limiting it to the transitory period before free elections could be held.

It fell to Havel to handle the Dubček problem personally. In no fewer than five separate meetings over two weeks, he reasoned, argued and pleaded with the older man. After their first meeting, which took place in a dressing room in the Laterna Magika, Havel thought they had reached an understanding that Dubček would stand aside, only to receive a call that evening to the effect that he had changed his mind. In the second meeting, held in Havel's temporary asylum of Joska Skalník's studio, the original understanding was reaffirmed: Havel would be the president and Dubček the speaker of the parliament, the second post after the president. But the two men also seem to have reached an understanding about the next step: after the initial period of Havel's presidency there would be the first free elections, following which Havel would make way for Dubček to replace him. Apparently even this was not enough to reassure Dubček, who suggested going the other way around. His argument was based mainly on the emotional satisfaction it would give him after twenty years in political purgatory. Havel, on the other hand, argued the centrality of his role in leading the Civic Forum and in the negotiations with the Communist government on a peaceful transition of power, a far weightier set of reasons. Dubček seemingly bowed to the inevitable, only to succumb to misgivings again.

There is little doubt, and Havel himself never said anything to the contrary, that Dubček was given grounds to believe that in a few months his turn would come to stand at the summit. In the twenty years since those meetings, when Havel's critics sought to impugn his character, the violation of 'the promise' to Dubček was often cited as prime evidence of Havel's sanctimoniousness and double-dealing. Havel was never enough of a *realpolitiker* to use the Levi Eshkol defence: 'Yes, I promised but I never promised to keep the promise', but he never felt particularly guilty about not holding up his end of the bargain, either. Whether he knew it or not at the time, he had no way of delivering on it. In the six months between December 1989 and June 1990, when his first term ended, Czechoslovakia had travelled sixty years on in its history. Instead of the Communist parliament, so terrified of the spectre of popular vengeance that they would have elected Al Capone tax collector, there was now a body of freshly elected dissidents, anti-Communists, activists and nascent party hacks, brimming with ideas, pride and confidence. They would take orders from no one, Havel included. Unlike in December, the chances of their electing a symbol of past failures, no matter how respectable, instead of the icon of recent triumphs, were nil. Did Havel's sharply honed sense of where the situation in the first act of a play would take his characters in the next act mean he knew it already six months earlier? Hard to tell. But it says something about the changed circumstances that Dubček, so insistent and obdurate in December, would not even remind Havel of his promise, privately or publicly, in June. For the next thirty months he presided as speaker over the Federal Assembly, only to die in November 1992 of injuries suffered in a horrendous car accident two months earlier. Unlike Havel, he did not live to see the end of the country to which, for all his shortcomings, he was unquestionably loyal.

Throughout the second part of November and the whole of December, Havel behaved like a true revolutionary leader, doing what he thought was necessary rather than what was simply right. It is definitely not true, however, that he somehow discovered this quality in himself on the morning of 18 November. What had always distinguished Havel from many of his fellow dissidents was his sense of the possible, and of the practical steps needed for attaining the possible, although often disguised as the musings of an intellectual. This, as much as his personal characteristics of shyness and humility, accounts for the rather mild and unconfrontational tone of his letter to President Husák, the original Charter 77 document, or the 'Few Sentences' petition. While many of the dissidents, and in particular the disenfranchised reformist Communists of 1968, saw the Charter activities as primarily a protest against social and personal injustices, a gesture through which they were able to retain a measure of personal dignity, Havel always believed not just in their moral justification but also in their power to effect change. It is fair to point out that, when the struggle for power came out in the open, Havel and the Civic Forum took steps to win it in the shortest time, with the least disruption, and at the smallest risk of a violent confrontation. It is simply wrong to suggest the existence of a gentleman's agreement with the comrades. Let this also be a final note on Havel's 'reluctance' to be president. Havel probably never dreamt about being president, nor did he particularly wish to assume the office. Throughout his life he thought of himself primarily as a writer; what people thought about his writing affected him much more personally than what they thought about him as a politician. Nonetheless, in the reality play of his life, through his writings, his courageous resistance to the Communist regime and his sacrifice in spending five of his best years in jail, he set the stage in such a way that, when the final act arrived, the logic of the piece inexorably led him to assume the leading position. He finally 'fell' into his role.

This is perhaps also the moment to consider Havel's and the Forum's conduct during the first month of the Velvet Revolution. In particular, criticism has been levelled at the late-night session of the Forum on 5 December, which missed the opportunity to get rid of Adamec and constitute a non-Communist government led by Ján Čarnogurský.[2] Perhaps. But the problem was not to get rid of Adamec; at that particular moment the Forum was strong enough to get rid of any establishment official; the problem was how to get a new government appointed by the president, how to force the president to resign and how to get a new president elected. Perhaps instinctively, the Forum felt that for the time being they would be better off with an apparatchik.

This cautious strategy chosen by Havel and his associates can hardly be faulted, even on theoretical grounds. Unlike historians, the direct participants had to consider their moves in almost complete ignorance of their opponents' intentions, resources and will. This held true much more for the opposition, which had no way to gather reliable intelligence from the government and the Party, than for the other side, which had been accumulating intelligence about the opposition for years, and had several of its agents within the headquarters of the Forum at that very moment. 'We had our own information channels,' confesses Čalfa.[3] Havel therefore chose to allow Adamec to become a partner in the transition, although, as his private comments showed, he had precious little respect for him. 'It was like chatting in a bar . . . We parted with him saying that he was going to retire and let us have it all,' Havel reported on one of his one-to-one

---

2 Suk (2003), 142.
3 Conversation with Marián Čalfa, 29 August 2013.

conversations with Adamec to his colleagues in the Forum.[4] By eschewing the early offers of power sharing, for which the Forum was not yet ready, he avoided the danger of being co-opted into a position of weakness. Adamec pursued a similar strategy: rather cleverly he worked to keep himself and, by implication, the Party in the game, thus blunting somewhat the energy of the protests, with a clear intention of eventually coming out on top. What he failed to see was that, by agreeing to talk to him but refusing to talk at first to the Communist Party, thus forcing him to dissociate himself from his power base, by going ahead with the general strike in spite of his appeals, by letting him form the first government at his will and responsibility and then rejecting it, by dictating the terms of the second government, and by effectively undercutting his last desperate attempt to catapult himself to the presidency, the Forum could now afford to discard him as an empty shell. All that time, Havel was clearly aware of the danger of being used by Adamec, but in the end it was the latter who was used.

Could things have evolved otherwise, if the Forum had been better prepared, its negotiators more skilled and its political resolve stronger? Certainly, for history is the garden of forking paths, most of which are overgrown by grass. But the Forum did the right thing in minimizing the risk of violence, and not just for humanitarian reasons. In a violent confrontation one group of people with guns might prevail over another group of people with guns and proclaim democracy, as they did in Romania. But it would not be the democrats; they had no guns. It is hard to think of a better outcome to the one attained by the Forum, partly by improvisation, partly by luck, partly thanks to a feeble opposition, but largely thanks to the caution and modesty exercised by Havel and his group. One of the valid criticisms of the conduct of the reformists in 1968 was that they had overplayed their hand and underestimated clear and present risks. Havel was not going to make the same mistake.

Moving carefully, almost by stealth, he was now the uncontested candidate for the presidency. In more ways than one it was probably too much of a good thing. Havel had already been busy planning his election campaign, which appealed to his sense of theatre. Now that there was no one running against him, and both the government and the opposition

4   Suk (1998), 62–3.

agreed that the president would be elected under the current constitution by the partly reconstituted parliament (in one of the thousands of small ironies of the time it was the Communists who all of a sudden toyed with the idea of a popular election), the idea of a campaign was scrapped. Havel still felt the need at least to introduce himself to his future constituents, and he addressed the nation on prime-time state television; four days later he almost sparked another revolt when he suggested that the time may have come to extend an apology for the expulsion of three million Sudeten Germans from Czechoslovakia after the end of World War II. Even the hint of such an idea ran counter to the forty years of Communist indoctrination, the timbre of Marxist historiography, and the deep-seated suspicion and distrust of Germans accumulated during a millennium of common, though not always harmonious, history. The Civic Forum spent much of the next day trying to explain that Havel did not mean what he said, without trying to deny he said it or make him look unqualified to be the president. But he meant what he said, fully expecting to create a stir,[5] although he may not have calibrated his words precisely enough. More than seven years later the Czech government and Parliament came to a similar conclusion.

Christmas time, the first in decades when people did not have to worry about rejoicing at the birth of Christ in public or going to church, helped to calm things down. There may not have been many presents because so many people had been otherwise preoccupied for weeks, but there was enough good will to last a century, or so it seemed.

The carnival atmosphere would not let up. Many friends from abroad, both Czechs and foreigners, used the holiday season to be at what felt like the beating heart of freedom. Two days before the inauguration, William and Wendy Luers invited Havel, Dienstbier and other undesirables in the process of becoming ministers, ambassadors and high officials to the Seven Angels restaurant in the Old Town. They had been meeting there annually for the last five years, and this would be the first (and also the last) time without police assistance. During an evening of many silly toasts, Ambassador Luers compared the atmosphere to 'a religious mystical experience' or 'the pleasurable human experience that had sustained the

---

5 Conversation with Alexandr Vondra, 10 August 2012.

Czechs through the long hard times of Communism – the orgasm'.[6] As for the Czech participants, many, myself included, were too exhausted after six weeks of revolutionary turmoil to think about either.

On 29 December, Havel was proposed as president to the Federal Assembly by Alexander Dubček, and duly elected. The occasion was made even more solemn by the *Te Deum* mass celebrated afterwards in St Vitus Cathedral. People hugged, smiled and celebrated. There were only a couple of visible flies in the ointment. First of all, the good bureaucrat Čalfa performed his task to secure votes for Havel's election a little too thoroughly. The election was unanimous, which may have been immaterial to its outcome and a nice perversion of the Communist fetish for unanimity, but also an aesthetic flaw of major proportions. No one had considered the implications. Most likely no one expected it to happen. Even among the Communists one would have expected a somewhat stiffer spine. The other visible flaw concerned Havel's grey suit, described as second-hand by one biographer,[7] and as immaculate by another.[8] The suit was indeed expensive, tailor-made for the occasion. Nonetheless, the trousers were an inch or two short, giving the new president a slightly Chaplinesque air.

---

6 William Luers, 'Remarks at the Lion and the Eagle Symposium', NYU, New York, 8 May 2012.
7 Keane (1999), 382.
8 Simmons (1991), 196.

The Bag of Fleas

There should be two presidents. One will spend the whole day receiving
ambassadors, shaking hands and giving interviews, and the other one
will govern. Because I'm only governing when I have a free second.
                                        – Václav Havel, 21 May 1990

IT WAS ALL VERY WELL to be elected president, to contemplate the
sacred along with the profane during the *Te Deum* mass, and to bask for a
day in the adulation and rejoicing, but with the pulse of the times at a life-
threatening pace, tomorrow had to be just another working day. Except
the working conditions would be less than ideal. For one thing, the next
day would be a Saturday. For another, it would be a Saturday preceding a
Sunday, and not just an ordinary Sunday, but a New Year's Eve, which was
in turn preceding the New Year's Day, another holiday. Third, a head of
state is dependent for his work on a large number of supporting characters
who staff his office, handle the phones, write his diary and run errands.
When Havel arrived in his office on Saturday morning, not only was there
no staff, but also the place was locked and it took some time to secure
the keys. All that was awaiting him was a delegation of presidential office
staffers eager to offer a welcome, report on the establishment of the 'Prague
Castle Civic Forum' and assure Havel of their loyalty and revolutionary
zeal. They did so with all the warmth, spontaneity and perspiring brows of
al-Qaeda's hostages. Most of the other employees either did not arrive at all
or hid themselves so well in the endless labyrinth of the Castle's corridors,
nooks and crannies that it took weeks before they were discovered.

This was not entirely unexpected to Havel. He knew he would not find many people in his new job with whom he would or could find a working relationship. It was not simply a matter of differing political loyalties, for in many cases the bureaucrats would adjust quickly enough, all too quickly in the eyes of Havel's people. For this very reason, Havel had laid down as one of his conditions for accepting the nomination that he would be joined in the Castle by a group of people that he could trust, and that he would personally select from among his friends. This was the 'Advisory Team', later the 'Collegium', or more informally 'the bag of fleas'. Actually it was the bag of fleas No. 2, because Havel had previously used the same designation for the steering committee of the Civic Forum. More importantly, he was soon to discover that the whole nation at whose head he was now standing was itself one big bag of fleas. This particular bag, whose roots had been in the Action Group of the Forum, was much smaller, but it was also closer; it would provide Havel with unflinching support and sustenance as well as some headaches[1] for the next two and a half years.

The motley crew that followed Havel to the Castle was to become an object of fascination, gossip, criticism and derision, but it was far from a random collection of individuals. Although they all had played a role during the Velvet Revolution, they were not all, or even most of them, Chartists or prominent dissidents, but rather a group resulting from Havel's efforts to build bridges over the years. During the last decade of the normalization era they all in their various capacities provided Havel with contacts, information, secure channels, intellectual nourishment, aesthetic fulfilment and occasional good times, as he did them. Most of them walked the fine line between open dissent and conformity. They were all friends, and all very much personalities in their own right. In the beginning, there were ten:

Jiří Křižan, Havel's adviser on domestic and security affairs, nicknamed 'Hippo', was a hunk of a man from the Wallachia hills of northern Moravia, country of a legendary folk of unclear ethnic origins, tales of outlaws, haunting folk music harmonies and moonshine of unparalleled quality. His father, a big local farmer and forester, had been executed by the Communists, and Jiří was brought up by his Calvinist grandfather. He became a well-

---

1 'You swarm around me like chicks around a hen, so that I have a headache and am completely exhausted by the time I get to my office.' Minutes of the Collegium, 21 May 1990, Bára Štěpánová's archive.

known screenwriter of films dealing with moral dilemmas and issues of character, courage and betrayal.[2] In his new capacity, he was to bear the brunt of all the domestic scandals, affairs and intrigues that Havel had to deal with during his first two presidencies. The sheer volume of human tragedy, ambition, pettiness and depravity he had to cope with in his job ruined first his marriage and then his health. After Havel's resignation in 1992, he briefly became a deputy minister of the interior, but his heart was not in it. When the forests and fields that his father had owned were returned to his family, he went back to Wallachia and tended the woods, brewed moonshine and wrote more screenplays for morally challenging films.[3] When he died of a stroke in 2010, the whole team, including Havel, attended his funeral in Wallachia.

Alexandr 'Saša' Vondra was by far the youngest of the advisers, a mere twenty-six at the time of the revolution, but he was certainly neither the least active nor the least known. The only Chartist in the group, one of the Charter's former spokesmen and one of those arrested during the Palach week, he became the president's adviser on foreign affairs. He summed up the reasons: 'I read geography at the university and bought myself newspapers.'[4] His natural self-confidence and sharp mind helped him overcome the handicap of his youth, and he quickly learned to be at home in the world of high international politics and diplomacy. After serving as ambassador to Washington at the end of the century, he became the foreign minister, minister for European affairs and, later, the defence minister in the Czech government.

Ladislav Kantor was perhaps the most abused member of the team. A folk-rock musician and concert organizer who helped to stage-manage the massive rallies during the Velvet Revolution, he became the head of the private office. This may not have been the most fortunate choice, because of Láďa's prickly and fiery temperament, but then there was no one in the group remotely qualified for this particular job. Kantor prided himself on a fierce, Doberman-like loyalty to his leader, defending him against every unwelcome (and sometimes welcome) intrusion, and making himself a long list of enemies in the process, with Olga not the least important of

---

2 E.g. *Signum Laudis* (1980).
3 E.g. the award-winning 'Eastern' *Je třeba zabít Sekala* (*Sekal Must Die*, 1998).
4 Conversation with Alexandr Vondra, 9 August 2012.

them. After Havel's resignation he became the general manager of the Czech Philharmonic Orchestra, and dabbled in local politics.

Miroslav Masák had been a leading Czech architect, one of the co-founders of the SIAL studio, which aimed to follow up on the best traditions of the influential Czech Modernist architectural school before World War II. For his pro-democracy activities during the Prague Spring he was ostracized after 1968; though he continued to teach and work, he was not allowed to participate in significant projects. Of the group, he had known Havel the longest. His main job at the Castle was the Castle itself. He was the crucial influence in helping Havel implement his vision of the de-Communization of the Castle premises,[5] including the vast surrounding gardens, making them attractive and accessible to the general public, and enlivening the thousand-year-old hallowed grounds with pieces of modern art. This transformation and his larger plans for the city and the country were subject to his regular one-on-one meetings with the president, code-named 'Clearance of the Slum Clearance' (*Asanace v asanaci*) in his diary.

If Masák's task was to change the outward face of the Castle, Petr Oslzlý's job was to do the same for the style of the presidency. A handsome man with long and wavy greying hair, he was an accomplished actor, dramatist and moving spirit in the Brno Theatre on the String, the Mecca of Czech independent and alternative theatre in the eighties.[6] An initiator of the *Open Dialogue* group, along with Jaroslav Kořán, that aimed to bridge the gap between the underground opposition and 'legally' working artists (and to which both Masák and I also belonged), he took the considerable risk of bringing Havel's work back on stage in *Res Publica I* and *Res Publica II*; he was Havel's and the Forum's principal image maker in the improvised variety shows on Wenceslas Square and Letná during the revolution, helping Havel implement his ideas of politics as theatre. A gentle intellectual, he found his new task, namely, to overhaul the practices of state sponsorship of the arts, much less rewarding.

---

5 Havel's zeal in trying to eradicate every piece of furniture, painting or decoration that smacked of the Communist era betrayed one of the idiosyncrasies for which he was often, and sometimes rightly, criticized. Even some of his collaborators in the office felt that he spent too much time trying to do away with the aesthetics of Communism and too little time trying to bring its criminals to justice.

6 The real name of the theatre was HuSa na provázku (The Goose on the String), in which HuSa stood for Humour [and] Satire rather than for the bird. Unfortunately, the close affinity of the word Husa with the name of the country's normalizing President Gustav Husák (meaning 'a gander') made the name of the theatre unacceptable to the powers-that-be, and so Husa's neck was cut.

Eda Kriseová's main role was to be the good fairy to the president. Although her relationship with Havel was not of a romantic nature, she exemplified the deep need Havel had, in the absence of Olga, who mostly stayed away from the Castle, for a caring, motherly female to assist him, to soothe him and to correct him if and when he became confused. Not that Eda, a brilliant writer of short stories in her own right, was your typical stay-at-home mother; nevertheless, she certainly did help Havel to feel calmer and more confident. In time, she took her task of tending to Havel's inner peace a little too far, and clashed with the more sceptical male part of the team when she hired an unknown and thoroughly unvetted alternative healer, whose sole task was 'scrubbing the president's karma'. After a semblance of order was introduced in the office, Eda took up the momentous task of unofficial ombudswoman, answering the thousands of complaints, requests and letters addressed to the most popular person in the country. Nobody envied her the job.

Věra Čáslavská was the one person on the team as famous as Havel. Actually, as a seven-time Olympic gold medallist in gymnastics, the still most decorated Olympic female athlete of all time, she had been for a long time incomparably more famous than Havel. Like him, she possessed a strong character and a sense of independence that prompted her to boycott the Soviet medal celebrations at the Olympic Games in Mexico in 1968, a month after the invasion of Czechoslovakia. The consequence was that she spent the next twenty years as a non-person. She was appointed as the president's adviser for social policy, but she also provided the female side to her boss's glamour; and in the same way that she went about winning at the Olympics – with all the strength, heart and emotion she had available.

Joska Skalník was a painter and graphic designer who specialized in Magrittesque blue skies with white clouds. In 1986 he ended up in custody before the trial of the independent music association Jazz Section, whose main crime was to distribute a newsletter and brochures with articles and works about Frank Zappa, Miles Davis and poems by independent Czech writers. Joska's studio played an important role during the Velvet Revolution as a place where presidential nominee Havel could go into seclusion to prepare for his new role. Unfortunately, it came out that during his time in prison Joska had apparently made a Faustian bargain with the secret police, and, under the code name 'Gogh' (the StB had a rather cheap sense of humour), became one of its sources of information.[7] He left the president's office involuntarily before the first election in June 1990, but kept popping up in Havel's vicinity. For his part, Havel never repudiated the friendship.

Stanislav Milota, a cameraman, the husband of Vlasta Chramostová, and an old friend, had stuck close by Havel's side throughout the revolution. It was natural that he would follow him into the Castle, though he was obviously not born to be a bureaucrat. A direct man of gruff manners and volatile temperament, he served in many capacities at once, and none in particular, dabbling in protocol, office management, security supervision and playing the *advocatus diaboli*. Gradually he became critical of Havel's governing style and of the workings of the office – and the office of him – and he left before the parliamentary elections; however, his departure was neither as dramatic nor as one-sided as described in some accounts.[8]

I was the last addition to the team, having to extricate myself first from my obligations as the Prague correspondent for Reuters (a predetermined conclusion after the beginning of the Velvet Revolution, which presented me with an insoluble dilemma of covering a story in which I was also involved), and also from my short-lived tenure as spokesman for the Civic Forum. My journalistic experience, albeit rather limited, earned me the role of the spokesman and press secretary to the president. There had been no such person speaking for the previous president or his predecessors, and the procedures, rules and the whole press department had to be designed and built from scratch. To do the job in the frantic atmosphere of the times, when a single day brought enough events for a decade, I remained in the closest proximity to Havel for the next two and a half years, leading both Olga and my first wife to complain on occasion about being married to someone who was married to someone else, although technically it could hardly constitute bigamy.

The obvious flaw of the team, apart from the fact that it was better qualified to run a theatre than a presidential office, was that it contained only Czechs (counting the proud Wallachian Křižan and the proud Moravian Oslzlý). Havel lost no time in inviting Milan Kňažko, maybe the most popular Slovakian actor of his generation, and the tribune of the people in

---

7   http://www.lidovky.cz/havluv-pritel-joska-skalnik-donasel-na-americany-f6x-/zpravy-domov.
aspx?c=a091201_213155_ln_domov_ani.
8   E.g. Keane (1999), 410–12.

the Tender Revolution (as it was called in Slovakia) to join. The bag of fleas did not find it hard to accommodate a Slovak Bohemian, although they soon noticed with some amusement that Kňažko was invariably the flea to follow immediately after Havel whenever the team accompanied the president. They understood the need to present both faces of the Czechoslovak identity. After some time Havel, too, noticed the now regular order of protocol, and made a fatal mistake of jokingly calling Kňažko 'my vice president'.[9] The joke came back to haunt him when Kňažko left the office in a huff at the end of Havel's first presidency and soon became the voice of Slovak nationalism and one of the president's harshest critics.

There was yet another person who eventually became a part of the core team. His full name was several lines long, but within the office he was known as 'the Prince'. Karel Schwarzenberg, aka Karl Johannes Nepomuk Joseph Norbert Friedrich Antonius Wratislaw Menas, 12th Prince of Schwarzenberg, Count of Sulz, Princely Landgrave in Klettgau, and Duke of Krumlov, is the scion of one of the oldest Czech and Central European noble families, whose history largely overlaps that of the Austro-Hungarian Empire itself. According to the royal protocol he should be addressed as His Serene Highness, but since noble titles were outlawed by the parliament of newly independent republican Czechoslovakia in 1919, his friends limited themselves to occasionally calling him 'Serenity'. Born at the ancestral Orlík Castle, his staunchly Czech and democratic loyalist family was first deprived of its seat and its property by the Nazis, and then hounded out of the country by the Communists. Though Karel left the country at the age of eleven and could not go back for forty years, he still spoke idiomatic if idiosyncratic Czech. Although he could not join the anti-Communist opposition inside the country, he provided it for years with financial support, a home for the archive of the samizdat literature at Scheinfeld, one of his castles in Germany, and support through his work as a human rights campaigner and president of the International Helsinki Human Rights Federation. After the regime relaxed its grip, Karel was allowed back into the country and started to appear at informal gatherings and also as an

---

9 *To the Castle and Back*, 100. In retrospect, it would not have been such a bad idea and might have even helped in the controversies that followed. The author remembers discussing it with Havel and other members of the team but cannot recall the reasons why they all agreed it would be impractical. Havel's recollection that the post may have been included in the draft constitution he presented to the parliament does not correspond to mine.

observer at trials of dissidents, including the trial in Jihlava of Ivan 'Magor' Jirous, guru of the Plastic People of the Universe, where we first met. After the Velvet Revolution, he became a part of the close circle around Havel, but because of his credentials it was not easy to find a place for him in the emerging quasi-bureaucratic structure. His age, status and international experience made him a natural candidate for the office of the president's chief of staff, the chancellor in traditional parlance. But that job was already occupied by Josef Lžičař, the lawyer who had defended Havel during his trials in the Communist period. Only when the archives compelled him to take an early leave was he replaced by the Prince, who turned out to compensate amply in terms of loyalty, friendship, generosity, good humour and charm for what he may have been lacking in terms of managerial skills. Equally important, he became Havel's calling card at a number of European royal courts, most of them related to him by blood, and to a number of European politicians he had befriended over the years.[10]

This then was the core of the office, which expanded in the following weeks to accommodate the packed diary and manifold responsibilities of the president. When a person was needed to deal with sensitive intelligence information, Křižan thought of a film translator who was a big fan of John le Carré. Indeed, Oldřich Černý eventually became the first director of the foreign intelligence service in the democratic Czech Republic. When the private office came under a siege of thousands of invitations and requests for appointments, Helena Kašperová was brought in to provide a calming balance to Kantor. When I felt a pressing need for an internal office communication and data management system, the office hired Anatolij Plechanov, a systems analyst and database specialist friend, after whom Havel had named the tragic hero of the *Slum Clearance*. Since the early days of the revolution, Havel's personal needs were attended to by a duo of personal assistants, close as Siamese twins and as unlike each other as complete strangers. Saša Neumann was a gentle Buddhist with a taste for esoteric world music, while Miroslav Kvašňák was an athletic playboy with a limitless talent for mischief. Some people dropped in for a visit and never left. Bára Štěpánová, the actress and 'prankstress', who had become notorious as the leading light of the Society for a Merrier Present, came to

---

10 Karel Schwarzenberg went on to become the minister of foreign affairs of the Czech Republic. His bid to follow in Havel's footsteps as president narrowly failed in January 2013.

provide Havel with a scooter after she had heard him complain on the radio about the endless corridors in the Castle; she stayed on as a secretary. As there was no office left in the vicinity of the boss, she was allotted a bathroom with a desk laid over the bathtub, from where she radiated a rather sensuous but effective secretarial presence. Other friends came, recruited from bars, theatres and obscure academic establishments; even an economist and a lawyer were eventually found.

Aside from the Castle, or 'upper' office, there emerged also the 'lower' office, situated in an empty ground floor flat of Havel's apartment building, which dealt with the president's private and literary matters. Vladimír Hanzel, his secretary from before the revolution and an eyewitness and diligent documentarist of its most dramatic moments, was in charge. Anna Freimanová, the wife of Havel's stagehand colleague and Hrádeček neighbour Andrej Krob, dealt with the vastly increased demand for his plays and writings from all over the world. Iva Taťounová, a niece of one of the friends at Hrádeček, became Olga's personal assistant. Still a high-school student, she came to boast a unique handwritten letter to excuse her absence from school: 'Please excuse Iva Taťounová from her classes the week of the twentieth of February due to her participation in the state visit to the United States, [signed] Havel.' Antonín Maněna, another Hrádeček friend, eventually became the chief of the Castle police and security detachment.

On New Year's Eve 1989, the freshly elected president gladly fulfilled the traditional duty of every Czech to get drunk in the evening, made even more obligatory by the fact that there was finally something to get drunk about. In this instance the rather wild party, complete with a number of foreign dignitaries, returning exiles and newfound best friends, dancing on the tables and discreet puffs of marijuana joints in the corridors,[11] took place in the former National Hall in Smíchov (renamed the House of the Workers in the Metal Industry by the Communists), the fall-back destination of dance-craving Chartists eleven years earlier.

---

11 Although Havel himself was never a fan of the weed, marijuana formed an inseparable part of the underground and opposition milieux. It was almost exclusively homegrown, quite mild in its effects as a consequence and shared for free.

The President of Rock 'n' Roll

*He's a kind person, so it's something of a miracle that he became a
president of anything.*

– Tom Stoppard

MONDAY, THE NEW YEAR 1990, brought Havel's first serious official act in
the form of the traditional presidential speech to the nation.[1] It was as
revolutionary as the events that had preceded it. From the first sentence on,
Havel went straight to the point: 'For forty years you heard from my predecessors
on this day different variations on the same theme: how our country was
flourishing, how many million tons of steel we produced, how happy we all
were, how we trusted our government, and what bright perspectives were
unfolding in front of us. I assume you did not propose me for this office
so that I, too, would lie to you. Our country is not flourishing.'[2] And Havel
proceeded to give the nation an unvarnished picture of the catastrophic state of
the country's economy, infrastructure, environment and moral fibre after forty
years of Communist rule, and of the enormous challenges that lay ahead. Most
of his listeners, instead of being horrified or discouraged, had a vast sense of
relief at hearing something that corresponded with the world as they knew it.

Already in preceding days Havel had keenly sensed that the level of
euphoria that had taken hold of the nation was not only unsustainable but
also outright dangerous. 'We are coming in as heroes,' he told his team, 'but

---

1 Havel wisely wrote and recorded the speech the previous day before the party.
2 *New Year's Address to the Nation*, 1 January 1990. In *The Art of the Impossible*, 3.

in the end, when they realize what a mess we're in and how little we can do about it, they will railroad us, tarred and feathered, out of town.' Some of his associates thought he was joking. The impossible had been achieved in a mere six weeks, so what could now go wrong?

Havel also realized that the velvet was wearing thin, and that the hunt for villains, scapegoats and culprits would start soon. Personally, he felt no such need. Unlike many people who had not really suffered, and unlike some of his dissident friends who underwent even harsher treatment, alone and out of the limelight of the international media, he was not in the least embittered by the ugly experience of the previous twenty years. A few weeks after he became president, he made one of his many 'glorious raids' to the prison in Bory on the outskirts of Pilsen where he had spent almost two years of his life. The prison guards at first refused to open the gates for the president, and relented only at the sight of his security men who clearly meant business. Havel asked to see his former cell and to shake hands with one of the wardens who had been kind to him. He also enquired about another warden who had given him a hard time, but surprisingly, that man was nowhere to be found.[3]

Havel's theatre persona may have helped him in coping with the past, enabling him to take a spectator's attitude to his own persecution and to find solace in the many absurdities that went with it. It also spoke of his deep personal stability and self-confidence that his diffident manners could not quite mask. He strongly disagreed with the concept of collective guilt, an argument he had already thought through and tested in the debate about the expulsion of the Sudeten Germans, and which he now reapplied to the Communists. He also perceived the need to reiterate the idea of personal responsibility, the essential prerequisite for the transformation of society that was to be his next task. And so in his New Year's speech he said, 'We had all become used to the totalitarian system and accepted it as an unchangeable fact and thus helped to perpetuate it. In other words, we are all – though naturally to differing extents – responsible for the operation of the totalitarian machinery. None of us is just its victim . . . It would be very unreasonable to understand the sad legacy of the last forty years as something alien, which some distant relative bequeathed to us. On the contrary, we must accept this

---

3 Conversation with Pavel and Petr Král, Prague, 22 February 2013.

legacy as a sin we committed against ourselves. If we accept it as such, we will understand that it is up to us all, and up to us alone, to do something about it.'[4] To the millions of his listeners that noon, the words rang painfully true. But whether they wanted to hear them was another matter.

The speech-making that he had been involved in since the start of the revolution presented Havel with an opportunity to make use of his talents as a writer in the new job, but it also brought with it difficult challenges. Almost immediately, it became clear that while he was a gifted speech-writer he was not a great orator. His natural delivery was in a low voice, and at a low pitch, somewhat hesitant and instantly recognizable by his rolling 'r's. This served him in good stead as a personal signature and, thanks to the similar speech impediments of some of his colleagues, like the new foreign minister Jiri Dienstbier, or his future chancellor Karel Schwarzenberg, the imperfect 'r's practically became the trademark of the revolution. The non-verbal side of his speech-making was a bit more of a problem, especially in the days of television. In his revolutionary speeches, he mostly spoke off the cuff, with few notes to help him, and then the demonstrators only saw him from a distance. Now he had to read his speeches from a text (neither Czechoslovak television nor the president's office had ever heard of a prompter, and Havel rejected the device as an inauthentic trick). For this he needed glasses, which immediately made him look somewhat formal and inaccessible. It also made it more difficult for him to establish eye contact with his listeners, something he was not particularly given to doing anyway. The second problem arose from the unavoidable redundancy and repetitiveness of political speech, which must reiterate platforms, priorities and positions, and which often uses uniform language to do so, lest the audience, the media and the pundits get the impression that something has changed. But everything in Havel the writer rebelled against the stylistic drudgery of repeating himself. In speeches and in interviews he again and again struggled in vain with the dilemma, either by more or less sticking to the script and being frustrated and disappointed with himself, or by following his artistic instincts and confusing the audience – and often doing both at the same time. Already, in August 1990 he complained, 'Apparently I have been president for too long, and for too long I have been forced to write speeches on the same subject. Indeed, my inability to repeat

---

4 *New Year's Address to the Nation*, in *The Art of the Impossible*, 4–5.

myself and keep writing speeches about the same thing has reached the top and I have spent my time at Hrádeček in a single bout of anguish resulting from the fact that, of the two speeches I undertook to write here, I have not completed a single line.'[5]

Havel experimented, more successfully, with the choice of a suitable tone for his speeches. His natural authorial voice was somewhat dry, ironic, erring on the side of understatement. But in late November and early December he knew his role was to unite and motivate, to channel the energies of millions, and so he spoke louder, used grander metaphors and did not shy away from strong words. The iconic slogan of the revolution 'Love and truth must prevail over lies and hatred', which originated as an improvisation during one of the big rallies,[6] was a case in point. But now, with the acute phase of the revolution over, he felt the need to tone down the volume. In the wings of his New Year's performance this dilemma was already felt. 'How should I finish the speech?' he asks his team off camera. 'Should I say something like "Truth prevails", or should I simply say "Goodbye"?'[7] In the event, he ended up with one of the most elevated phrases in the Czech national mythology, ascribed to the great seventeenth-century Czech educator Jan Amos Komenský (Comenius): 'People, your government has returned to you!' Goodbye would just not do.

The other momentous decision Havel took on the first day of the new era was to declare a general amnesty. This prerogative of the president, a vestige of the monarchic era, had been utilized by his predecessors, too, often marking their coming and leaving, but never with such sweeping scope. Under the terms of the amnesty, 23,000 people out of a total of 31,000 – that is, everybody except for the most serious criminals – were released from prison onto unsuspecting families and social services, though many had no place to go. Suddenly a wave of criticism descended on the new president, with his detractors (many of whom, not surprisingly, belonged to the vanquished *nomenklatura*) painting gleeful populist pictures of an orderly society suddenly invaded by crime, chaos and mayhem. The threat was grossly exaggerated; only nine per cent of all criminal offences would

---

5   Instructions to the Castle, author's archive.
6   Speech to the demonstrators at Wenceslas Square, 10 December 1989, http://www.89.usd.cas.cz/en/documents.html.
7   *Václav Havel, Praha-Hrad*, a documentary film by Martin Vidlák and Petr Jančárek, Czech TV, 2000.

be committed by the amnestees in 1990; but there was no way of knowing that at the time. Still, even many of Havel's admirers could not understand why he should be pardoning large numbers of ordinary criminals along with the few hundreds unjustly persecuted for political reasons. Havel, while completely aware that he was doing himself no favours, never had any second thoughts about the decision. As a former dissident and jailbird, he understood better than most of his fellow citizens how the injustice of the previous regime had affected common and political prisoners alike. He felt that, to dispense justice, a government first had to conform to the rule of law and observe due process, something of which the Communists were patently innocent. Directed by the compass of shared responsibility for the past, he felt that this magnificent chance at a new beginning could not be denied to those who were behind bars.[8]

The next day, accompanied by an entourage of friends, he boarded a government plane and took his first foreign trip. This description of what is a routine task for any head of state hides several firsts, as well as a series of absurdities and one serious controversy. For Havel it was the first time in twenty years that he was free to cross the border of his own country, something as unimaginable then to most people living in the non-Communist part of Europe as it is today to any young Czech.[9] The president and his entourage did not so much resemble a statesman and a group of polished diplomats as a singer and an accompanying rock group, complete with stagehands, groupies and hangers-on. There were no selection criteria. Whoever wanted to get on the plane did. The crew of the plane itself, a big, sturdy and loud Soviet affair, were no ordinary pilots and stewardesses, but belonged to the squadron of the ministry of the interior, and were in fact employees of the state security, the same branch of government whose task it had been to make Havel's life as difficult as possible. The destinations on the trip were two cities whose very names made many Czechs feel uneasy. The first was Munich, where Adolf Hitler had begun his infamous political career and

---

8 He was also familiar with the harsh and humiliating conditions in the overcrowded penal establishments, and instinctively felt the need to let off steam. Indeed, two months into his presidency, the government was confronted with the largest prison uprising in Czechoslovak history in its infamous maximum security prison in Leopoldov, where Petr Uhl once did time. Miraculously, no one was killed in the ensuing suppression of the revolt.

9 Ironically, following his request to be allowed to go to Sweden to receive the Olaf Palme Prize, his passport was returned to him a week into the Velvet Revolution, when going to Sweden was the last thing on his mind. The prize was presented to him at home by the Swedish ambassador.

where the Munich Agreement, stripping Czechoslovakia of its border regions – inhabited mostly but not solely by ethnic Germans – was signed by the leaders of Nazi Germany, fascist Italy and democratic France and Britain, with the Czechoslovak representative not even allowed into the room. The second was Berlin, where the occupation of the rest of Czechoslovakia was simply notified to the Czechoslovak ambassador six months later, and where the war ended after six years, with sixty million dead and more than ten million ethnic Germans, including three million from Czechoslovakia, expelled from their homes in Central and Eastern Europe in the aftermath. The ensuing recriminations and resentments in Germany, dreams of return by the Sudeten Germans and the spectre of German irredentism, exaggerated by Communist propaganda to justify the militarization of the Soviet bloc, made the two countries, the closest and most interrelated of neighbours for a thousand years, complete strangers, distrustful and suspicious of each other. This was the legacy Havel felt he needed to confront, to open the way for the reintegration of Czechoslovakia into its natural European home.

He should have realized how far ahead he was of the popular mood at home, and to a degree in Germany as well. The reaction to his pre-presidential statement on the expulsion of Sudeten Germans from Czechoslovakia should have given him enough of a warning. Going to Munich and Berlin first was, therefore, risky.

But then where should Havel have gone first to start promoting the new democratic Czechoslovakia abroad? A first trip to Moscow would have been a must for any of his predecessors, which was exactly the reason why he could not go there. A trip to Washington, not so easy to organize in a few days, would have suggested to many that Prague was just switching allegiances from one superpower to the other, without claiming an independent mind of its own. A trip to Paris or London would also still bring back reminiscences of the Munich Agreement, the prime trauma of modern Czechoslovak history. If he had pursued this avenue of thought, Havel would in the end have had to stay home for another twenty years.

There were some who thought they had the answer and they never forgave Havel for not heeding their advice, even if it remains uncertain whether they made it known at the time. In their view, he should have gone to Bratislava. Slovakia may not have been abroad, but it was a sufficiently distinct part of the country that, by not paying it the first visit,

Havel showed some insensitivity to, and even ignorance of, the feelings of his Slovak compatriots.[10] In this he may have sown the seed of the future differences, which finally led to the dissolution of Czechoslovakia three years later. True, Havel had visited Slovakia a week earlier, but that was before he was the president, and so it did not really count, went the argument. It remains true, however, that at the beginning of January 1990 he saw the repair of the relationship with Germany[11] as a higher priority than attending to national differences at home. The visit itself came too early to bring any specific results, but signalled that both countries were determined to put their relationship on a new footing.

The scramble to establish priorities was hopeless. Havel's working day, far from being governed by the orderly protocol and measured pace befitting the office of the head of state, continued to be an endless series of crisis meetings. Not surprisingly, many of them revolved around security issues. The army stayed in the barracks, but it remained under the control of Soviet-trained generals, and there were no guarantees it would not change its mind. Fortunately, the one thing it was superbly trained to do was to eschew initiative and obey orders. For the next twelve months Havel left in place as secretary of defence the army's former chief of staff, General Vacek. It later turned out that the same general was involved in laying down the plans to crush the November demonstrations by using armoured columns,[12] which led to his rapid exit. In the meantime, however, he proved as reliable in obeying Havel's orders to maintain peace as he would have been if given the orders to shoot only months before. But with the army's air of secrecy, protected by draconian laws still in place, no one could be quite sure. For quite some time Havel started his daily briefings with a half-serious question: 'Was there a coup overnight?'

And yet, compared to the world of secret police and intelligence services, the army was a model of transparency. Here the new government entered a maze of mirrors and boxes within boxes that took several months to neutralize, the best part of a year to dismantle, and most of the next two

---

10 Pithart (2009), 248.
11 It takes an effort to remember, but there had been actually two Germanies. Havel met with the leaders of the Bundesrepublik in Munich, and with those of the GDR in Berlin.
12 Operation ZÁSAH (INTERVENTION) envisaged the deployment of 7,632 officers, 476 trucks, 92 armoured carriers and 155 tanks. The Closing Report of the Commission for the Investigation of the Events of 17 November 1989, Federal Assembly of the Czech and Slovak Federative Republic, http://www.psp.cz/eknih/1990fs/tisky/t1236_01.htm.

decades to map out and analyse. In some respects the work is still going on. The obstacles were insurmountable, starting with finding out who the secret police really were: the dual identities, the duplicitous assignments and the coded references to an army of agents and collaborators were entangled with a deplorably low level of computerization (for which, until then, the opposition could have been grateful). The problem was compounded by the fact that the man in charge of all these shady structures, first Deputy Minister of Interior General Lorenc, gave orders to destroy most of the 'live' files of the secret police when it became clear that power was changing hands. Although much of the evidence was later reconstructed due to the redundancies built into the system, which kept separate but cross-referenced files on operations, targets and agents, there was little to go on in the beginning. A new interior minister, Richard Sacher, one of the men on the stage at the Actors' Studio on 19 November, immediately decreed the disbanding of the StB; however, since many of its components and its individual members remained anonymous, this did not quite entail cutting off the head of the snake. Indeed, the snake, it seemed, had many heads. Some of them may have been rather innocuous, but they had to come under formal scrutiny. In the first few months of Havel's presidency it turned out that not only his flying detail, but also the Prague Castle fire brigade, the ceremonial marching band greeting visiting dignitaries and the waiters serving them drinks were listed as parts of the secret police. Vetting commissions, comprised of members of the Forum, were created, to screen former secret service employees, and to determine who could be relied upon to continue serving the state and who should be asked to leave. It was an imperfect process at best, even more so for the fact that, unknown to the others, some secret police agents and collaborators ended up sitting on the commissions. But then, as the coded file and name indexes were gradually located and deciphered, the revelations started to leak out. Names of high-ranking people in the Forum, recently appointed officials in the government or newly established media executives appeared on the list. It took another eighteen months to establish a legal process dealing with such cases, but initially there were no legal sanctions, no recourse to courts, no authority in charge of the process; as a result, most of the high-profile cases ended up on Havel's desk. Some of them were intensely painful because they involved friends or close associates. Havel did not quite shy away from dealing with the problem, but he much preferred a discreet way of resolving the issue; a voluntary departure by the person in question in order to spare them public humiliation, or worse, in the charged atmosphere of those days. The result was a series of quiet one-on-one or two-on-one (with Jiří Křižan present) conversations, which Havel intensely dreaded. They were usually followed by a departure or resignation for health or personal reasons. Some of the people went quietly, some professed their innocence, some pleaded and cried, and some reneged on the verbal agreements reached and later accused the president of a plot and conspiracy for political reasons.[13] By the time the first democratic elections were held in early June 1990, the whole of the president's office and most of the top tiers of the government had been screened and vetted as thoroughly as the fragmentary evidence allowed. It was not the end of the story by far.

Trying to coordinate the political process of the election from the top of the pyramid proved equally difficult. When Havel was first nominated president, he gave up his leadership of the Forum, along with the less than impressive title of its 'representative', and together with a group of close associates in the 'Action Group', most of whom later joined him in the Castle, sequestered himself, much to the displeasure of some of his long-time colleagues.[14] It is not entirely clear what led him to make such a clean separation of his new office from the political force that had elevated him to it. It is telling that, along with the Action Group, Havel helped create various other groups in the Forum, 'where we placed people who would hinder action from taking place'.[15] Havel was once again following his inclusive instinct. Just as he transcended the confines of the dissident ghetto to form a larger informal structure, which eventually became the founding pool of the Civic Forum, he now saw his role and his loyalty as primarily civic and national. His ambition was to be the president of all Czechs and Slovaks rather than the president of the Civic Forum. He did not quite realize that in doing so he was also cutting himself off from a source of popular support and authority that the Forum (and Public Against Violence, its Slovak counterpart), though diverse and rather ineffectual, had provided him with.

---

13 One such theory drew on a silly, though innocent whispered remark at a press conference by this writer, transmitted by a live microphone. When Deputy Minister of Interior Jan Ruml, a friend of mine, was reluctant to disclose the financial details of one such case to journalists, I whispered to him, 'Well, cough up something.' (*Tak tam něco prskni.*)
14 Conversation with Petr Pithart, 29 August 2012.
15 Conversation with Alexandr Vondra, 8 August 2012.

The foundations of the new political system had to be laid down. In this process Havel did not play as central a role as might befit the leader of the revolution, and he lost quite a few of the battles in which he became involved. The first concerned the electoral system. Havel and his close circle supported a majority vote system, which would have led to the emergence of fewer political parties and rather strong governments that could rely on sizeable majorities in the parliament. This was, however, not Havel's central consideration. In keeping with his political philosophy he thought that a member of the parliament elected by a majority vote system in a constituency would have a direct relationship with his voters, which would give him a genuine responsibility for a specific part of the country and would enable his voters to hold him responsible in turn. Conversely, a proportional representation system, even with a threshold needed to enter the parliament, would lead to a number of parties being represented, which would have to enter into coalitions to form weak and inherently unstable governments. It would also enhance the power of party secretariats rather than empower individual deputies. Havel was defeated by a determined opposition of former reform Communists, who hoped to make a political comeback in a group called 'Renaissance', and were joined by some former fellow dissidents, most of them too with Communist pasts. The Communists' motives were easy to understand. They feared that they would be wiped out in any majority election. The fear was well founded; for the next twenty years the electoral results of the Communist Party stayed largely constant between ten and fourteen per cent, enough to pass the five per cent threshold, but not enough to win seats on a majority basis. When the Czech Senate, which would be elected by a majority vote, came into being seven years later, the Communists won three out of eighty-one seats. The motives of some of Havel's associates were less comprehensible, perhaps even to themselves. Some of them, notably Petr Pithart,[16] actually feared winning too large a majority, which would inevitably turn into a plebiscite on the past and the future. One would have thought that, after forty years of totalitarian rule imposed by force, people were perhaps entitled to a plebiscite. But fears of

---

16 In retrospect, Pithart (2009) argues that in the first democratic elections a majority system would have led to a parliament with two parties, the Forum and the Communists in the Czech Republic, and VPN and the Communists in Slovakia. This is mistaken. Based on the actual figures, with the Forum winning over half of the votes, in a majority system the Communists probably would not have won a single seat in the Czech Republic. In Slovakia they were not even the second strongest party.

Jacobinism, of which Havel was admittedly a most outspoken opponent, prevailed. One only needed to think with some regret of the first semi-free election in Poland a year before. It was a plebiscite, and it gave the Solidarność a strong mandate to shape the future.

This debate had a side effect of profound consequence. At a meeting in Havel's private office around 10 January, Zdeněk Jičínský, the foremost advocate of proportional representation, tried to placate Havel by saying that the system would be in effect for only two years and could then be changed if it did not work.[17] Havel took this as a general justification for curtailing the first mandate of freely elected representatives, including the president, to two years, which suited his still profound ambivalence about the job he was assuming. However, this decision would have adverse effects on the constitutional stability two years later, with the national issue at its most controversial, facilitating the train of events that led to the dissolution of Czechoslovakia.

The other battle, with equally serious consequences, almost passed Havel by. In January, the parliament passed an essential law on political parties, based on the principle of the unencumbered right of association. For some reason, though, the law ignored the existence of the country as a sovereign entity. It made it possible for Czech political parties to register and establish themselves in the Czech Republic, and for Slovak political parties in Slovakia. It did not, however, provide for the existence of federal, Czechoslovak political parties. Nor could Czech political parties be active in Slovakia, and vice versa.[18] The implications for the cohesion of the Czechoslovak political system were far-reaching, though they went largely unnoticed at the time.

Then there was the office of the president itself, as well as the vastness of the Castle that housed it. After weaning himself from the political movement that had helped him get there, Havel could no longer rely on working through the Forum, or its deputies in the parliament (the government was another matter because he appointed its ministers), and he knew he would need a strong and efficient office. The organization that he and his ten original advisers entered was far from answering such a description. There were no files, no procedures and no guidelines. There

---

17 Conversation with Petr Pithart, 28 August 2012.
18 To do that, they had to create a separate party in the other republic, albeit with the same name.

was no car pool and no computers, not even electric typewriters, just a few antiquated manual machines. No staff, no secretaries, no protocol officers, no communications, no analysis and no planning. Yet the whole thing had to be set up and running in a matter of days. Friends were called and then friends of friends and friends of their friends. Mário Soares, the President of Portugal, donated the first presidential limousine. A few weeks later the US Ambassador Shirley Temple Black brought the news that the US government had donated the first armoured Chevrolet limousine; unfortunately, when its suspension encountered the cobblestoned streets of Prague it made Havel carsick and so was rarely used.[19] Given the deplorable state of Castle security, at least from Havel's point of view, the US government also supplied a shielded safe room, nicknamed 'the fridge', for secure communications.[20] As for secretaries, Havel's people drew from a number of sources, including the pool of young Castle guides, who could at least be expected to communicate in other languages. Wire services were installed, and some time later one of the first office networks in the country, a relatively sophisticated system, whose ethernet spine was installed through the attics of baroque and Renaissance roofs (over the loud protests of Castle conservationists). A media operation with a press centre and regular weekly briefings was set up. A small analytical team came in to read the polls and analyse trends. Protocol officers with backgrounds in engineering and nuclear physics were learning the rules of the etiquette.

Some jobs required a professional background. The head of the military office of the president and commander-in-chief had to be a general, but again there were no such officers, other than those who had risen through the stages of Communist training and indoctrination. How to choose a loyal and relatively open-minded professional from among such people? Havel appointed a recruiting commission made up of me, perhaps because I had been a psychologist in my earlier life, his screenwriter adviser on domestic

---

19 Shirley Temple Black, who died this year, was generous, though not very lucky with her gifts for the president. The preserved piranha fish with the dedication 'To Václav Havel from STB', evoking the memories of the Communist secret police rather than the lovely ambassador, ended up in my office. Another time she brought him a plastic flower in a pot, which gyrated to pop music when a button was pressed. It was rarely to be seen in action. At her farewell audience she offered to leave him her dog, which she did not want to put through the ordeal of travelling all the way to California. 'But I already have a dog,' protested Havel mildly.

20 It was a counter-surveillance rather than a surveillance device, as misclassified in Keane (1999), 401.

and security policy Jiří Křižan, his actor adviser on style and image Petr Oslzlý, and Eda Kriseová, who was known to be in communication with the higher spheres of the universe, to address the task. There were four candidates waiting in the corridor with perspiring brows, looking as if they were as scared of winning as of losing the job. Questions about their military record and background elicited monosyllabic answers, which were identical in their lack of information. Finally, it occurred to me to ask the candidates about their bedtime reading. One apparently only read the statutes and the order of battle manuals, the second read all the Marxist classics in Russian, and the third, slightly more enlightened, enjoyed reading histories of battles and campaigns from Hannibal to von Clausewitz. The fourth, an anti-aircraft missile brigade commander, hesitated for a long time, after which he stuttered: '*Catch 22*'. It was no contest. General Tomeček stayed for most of Havel's time in the Castle.

The physical appearance of the president's office took as much of his time and attention as hiring the right personnel. Admittedly, the place gave any normal person the shivers. It was vast but almost empty. A good number of the gates and doors were locked, with keys nowhere to be found. Some of the early discoveries included a room full of people with headsets in front of consoles eavesdropping on telephone calls – yes, all calls, even the president's calls – in the interests of 'security'; a tiny locked chamber with a telephone that offered a direct link with the Kremlin;[21] and an underground maze of tunnels, which were apparently designed to provide shelter for the top Communist leadership in the event of nuclear war.

The offices themselves were obviously designed to scare off visitors rather than provide any semblance of hospitality. The heavy furniture looked as though it was made on a butcher's block, the pictures on the walls documented not so much the bad taste of the previous occupants as the complete lack thereof. The presidential suite and the adjoining rooms were equipped with a plethora of bathrooms, which would lead any psychoanalyst to speculations about a Pontius Pilate complex.

True, except for the stunning views of the city from the windows, it was a disconcerting, irritating and not a little depressing environment to

---

21 The incorrigibly curious Havel decided to test the apparatus on the spot, managed to reach a Russian-speaking lady and demanded to be connected to President Gorbachev. The lady asked him to hold, after which the line went dead, permanently.

work in; but so are many other work places. Havel found it unbearable, and immediately addressed the problem, bringing in pieces of modern art from his own collection, sending to the Castle storage for whatever usable furniture could be found, commissioning his painter friend Aleš Lamr to enliven the walls with some colourful graffiti, and in the meantime, spending as much time as possible with his advisers in the Castle restaurant Vikárka and in the Gothic-style castle dungeon that the conservationists had somehow prevented the Communist rulers from refurbishing. His dream was to convert the dungeon into a presidential ops centre complete with maps, wall displays and consoles. The conservationists were against that, too.

Within several weeks the look of the place changed. The heavy curtains were taken down and light was let in. By the time black mahogany furniture arrived, courtesy of German President von Weizsäcker, Havel had an office with a view over the ancient city to kill for. Nonetheless, he was still not happy. He ventured further and further afield within the Castle walls, all the time discovering new aesthetic atrocities, neglect and abuse. As he tried to apply his perfectionist criteria to a building four storeys high, a kilometre in length, and a hundred and fifty metres wide, with a multitude of satellite buildings, gardens, courtyards, cellars and dozens of miles of corridors, tunnels and hallways, it became evident that he was fighting a losing battle. He would not give up, strongly supported by his advisers on culture, architecture and theatre, and equally strongly opposed by his advisers on domestic and foreign policy, media and economy. He ran around the rooms and corridors, personally straightening paintings, which were not hanging at the right angle, poring over blueprints, sketches and designs. In contrast with his usual demeanour he mercilessly overruled the objections of the bureaucrats and conservationists. 'For those who would rather not touch anything because everything is a monument: if our ancestors thought like this, we would have no Castle at all – just some sort of a pagan hearth and a hole in the ground.'[22] Feeling that, in spite of all the changes he had made, the spirit of Gustáv Husák would not quit his office, he vacated it to me, and moved to the next room, starting a long migration westward that ended up with him finding shelter in the anteroom of the old Tomáš G. Masaryk apartment.

The theatrics continued with the Castle Guard and the military

---

22 Instructions to the Castle, 1 January 2002, Jaroslava Dutková's archive, VHL ID5657.

marching band. The drab olive garb and the Soviet-style goose-step offended Havel's image of a decent, democratic country. It appeared relatively easy to make the soldiers stop exerting themselves and to lower their step. When, before the election of the president, Jiří Křižan instructed General Vacek to effect this change in time for the new president's first review of the guard of honour, he earned himself lasting enmity of the foot soldiers, who, it turned out, had to practise the new marching step at night.[23] For the new uniforms, Havel recruited his friend from the Fatherland's Palette, Theodor 'Doda' Pištěk, the Oscar-winning costume designer for Miloš Forman's *Amadeus*. The new sky-blue uniforms with white and red trimmings conformed to Havel's instructions to offer a friendly, non-threatening face of the Castle to the outside world, but they also looked a little like costumes from a Franz Lehár operetta. The reviews ran from awkward to openly critical, but soon the public and the tourists got used to the new style, as any visitor to Prague can attest. For the new marching music to replace the heavy-beat assault marches, Havel consulted with the rock musician Michael Kocáb, who had the perfect idea to use the allegretto of Leoš Janáček's *Sinfonietta*, undoubtedly equally aware that it had been first dedicated to the Czechoslovak armed forces, and adapted by the avant-garde rock band Emerson, Lake & Palmer. The positive aesthetic effect of the change was undeniable. The only problem was the high *b* in the fanfare, always a touch-and-go issue for the military players, not all of them philharmonic material. Unlike the uniforms, the fanfare did not survive Havel's presidency, falling victim to an act of petty cultural barbarism in the Klaus era.

Sometimes the concern for style was carried a little too far. Like all great costume designers, Pištěk was not content with designing a single uniform. Instead, he designed a whole line, including a presidential uniform in two colours, complete with golden epaulettes. Although it made Havel look like a character in Woody Allen's *Bananas*, it did not take much persuading to make him put it on. After all, he spent most of his childhood drawing soldiers and uniforms and dreaming about becoming a general.[24] Worse, other friends learned about it. When Vojtěch Jasný, the director of 1960s Czech film classics like *When The Cat Comes* (1963) and *All My Compatriots* (1969), accompanied

---

23 Interview with Jiří Křižan, 19 August 2006, Prague, Institute for Contemporary History.
24 Interview of Václav Havel by Mikuláš Kroupa, 17 March 2010, http://www.pametnaroda.cz/witness/clip/id/1627/clip/7118/#cs_7118.

by Miloš Forman, came to Lány Castle to shoot a presidential documentary *Why Havel?*, they immediately saw the film potential of shooting him in the uniform. The resulting footage was slightly *risqué*, but tolerably so until the president, exhilarated by the company of friends and a free morning, burst into the Castle kitchen with a drawn sword, which he had received as a present from the Castle Guard, and, to the horror of the local village lady cooks, started to use the ceremonial weapon to chop onions that were being readied for the goulash at lunch. I had been prescient enough to reserve the right of the final cut on the documentary in my role as press secretary, and invoked it on this occasion. I was made to feel like a censor for weeks afterwards, and Jasný would not speak to me for the next two years. It was no wonder then that the president's preoccupation with style and aesthetics drove some of his people insane. Not that they did not see a lot of sense in what he was trying to do, or that they were blind to the changes he gradually brought to the Castle, making the place once again a symbol rich in history, culture and humanity. But time was at a premium, and there were countless issues affecting not just the Castle compound but the country at large that needed the president's focus.

The situation might well be called *The Increased Difficulty of Concentration*. The momentous transformation that the country and the region were undergoing not only posed enormous demands on the president's time, but also made him a global celebrity and an obvious object of attention for sympathizing politicians, fellow celebrities, intellectual visionaries, opportunistic schemers and headline-seeking journalists. The team did its best to screen him from all but the most worthy visitors, but they were no match for the drive and ingenuity of people who were set on seeing the man of the moment. Most of them meant well, and many had helpful things to say or do. In the first two months of his presidency Havel met in the Castle with scores, maybe hundreds, of foreigners, who sometimes resembled a constant procession of visitors lined up to see the *Mona Lisa* in the Louvre.

Some of the visits left an indelible memory, for various reasons. It was moving to see Havel reunited with old friends returning from exile, such as Ivan Medek, Karel Schwarzenberg, Pavel Tigrid, Vilém Prečan and Pavel Kohout.[25] It was fascinating to listen to the conversation of Havel with Harold

---

25 The last remembers the experience as having been first embraced, and then offered an important office by Havel, only to be ejected following interventions of some of Havel's associates because of his Communist part. He is partly right, though Havel was well aware of what was going on.

Pinter and his wife Antonia Fraser at a dinner, with Havel as interested in the latest developments in English theatre as Pinter was in the question of how a playwright becomes a president. Not all the meetings were as enjoyable. Barbara Walters, who interviewed Havel for ABC's *20/20* news magazine, was positively underwhelmed and underwhelming. She complained about his not maintaining eye contact with her (from his perspective she was just another kind of interrogator) and for not showing any emotion, which she singularly failed to provoke in him. On the other hand, he hit it off immediately with Katharine Graham and Meg Greenfield, the two grand ladies of the *Washington Post*. Frank Zappa, 'one of the gods of the Czech underground'[26] and a spiritual godfather of the Plastic People of the Universe, summed up the global significance of his host with the words: 'You are sending a message to people in America: You smoke!'[27] Havel reciprocated by remembering Zappa's album *Bongo Fury* with Captain Beefheart. As a result of his reception by Havel, Zappa's status reached cosmic proportions in the country at that time. Ever a rock 'n' roller, he was able to solicit a letter from the deputy prime minister appointing him the roving Czechoslovak envoy plenipotentiary in matters cultural and commercial. The appointment had to be withdrawn shortly thereafter.[28] Nonetheless, as far as anyone knows, Zappa did no harm, which is more than could be said about some of the other largely self-appointed advisers, consultants and envoys who made the popular pilgrimage to Prague at that time. Lou Reed, now firmly part of Havel's musical Olympus, came to the Castle on behalf of *Rolling Stone* to conduct what must be one of the most interesting unpublished interviews of all times. It turned out that Lou, the epitome of cool, was so stressed out by the responsibility of interviewing a statesman that he failed to turn on the tape recorder. He may have lost the interview, but in the first of many meetings with Havel he found a good friend. Eight years later, when Havel came to the United States to provide moral support for another friend, Bill Clinton, in the midst of the Monica Lewinsky scandal, Lou Reed, the Velvet Underground rebel, along with Mejla Hlavsa, the frontman of the Plastic People of the Universe, got to play in the White House at Havel's request, albeit on condition that 'Walk on the Wild

---

26 Václav Havel, 'Revolutionary', *The New Yorker*, 20 December 1993.
27 Reception of Frank Zappa at the Prague Castle, 22 January 1990, VHL ID17191.
28 Secretary of State James Baker, visiting Prague on 5 February 1990, allegedly declared: 'You can do business with the United States or you can do business with Frank Zappa.' The author, who was at the meetings, has no recollection of this.

Side' would not be on the playlist.[29] This minor accomplishment pleased Havel immensely. Clinton, for his part, acknowledges that Havel's 'raising his flag for me', along with King Hussein of Jordan, the president of South Korea Kim Dae-jung, king of Saudi Arabia Abdullah and Prime Minister Tony Blair, meant a lot to him at this most difficult time of his political career.[30]

Typically for Havel, the event that had the most far-reaching implications during his first month in office was not any personnel or administrative decision, but another speech. On 23 January 1990, he revealed to the assembled deputies of both houses of the Czechoslovak Federal Assembly that in his offices in the Prague Castle he 'did not find a single clock. There is something symbolic in this: for many years there had been no need for a clock there because time stood still. History stopped, not just in the Prague Castle but in the whole country. Today when we finally freed ourselves from the straitjacket of the totalitarian system, history hurtles forward all the more quickly, as if trying to make up for the time lost. We all, you and I, are just doing our best to keep up.'[31]

The speech started with Havel's depiction of plans for his own office, the Prague Castle and the institution of the presidency as such. The president spent more than ten minutes outlining the composition of his team, the travel itinerary for the next few months, his plans for a brand-new image for the Castle interior, including details about furniture and bathrooms, the new costumes for the Castle Guard and the transformation of the Prague Castle into an 'attractive European cultural and spiritual centre'.

It was original, refreshing, endearing and not a little naïve. Havel's principal mitigating circumstance, and that of his team, was that none of them had ever had to deal with a parliament. The deputies, even the glum majority inherited from the previous regime and accustomed to playing the role of furniture that could be shunted around at will, waited to be humoured, cajoled, pleaded with and kowtowed to. Instead they were being told about someone else's plans for a big spring clean-up. They remained distinctly unimpressed.

And then Havel, after some mild prodding of the parliament to adopt an electoral law that would emphasize the role of decent and capable individuals

---

29 For the story of Havel's 1998 visit and the White House dinner, see Vondra's account in Matějková (2012), 242–3.
30 Conversation with Bill Clinton, 11 November 2013.
31 *Works* 6, 25.

and de-emphasize that of political parties, dropped a bombshell. Citing his prerogative of proposing legislation to the parliament, he submitted a bill aiming to change the name of the country from Czechoslovak Socialist Republic to simply Czechoslovak Republic, the name given to it by Masaryk in 1918, and to change the heraldic symbols of the state accordingly.

The deputies sat up. For the previous month they had been immersed in the ultimately hopeless effort to graft some democratic norms onto what was a rather vague, but unmistakably totalitarian, constitution and body of laws. There had been few lawyers and even fewer brilliant minds in the old parliament. Now there was finally something they could grasp, they could understand and they could do something about. And so they set to work.

The episode that followed, tragic and farcical at the same time, came to be known in Czech history as the 'hyphen war'. Havel's proposal may have been reasonable and natural, its essence being simply to remove the word 'socialist', which qualified and predetermined the nature of a society that was now free to decide for itself what kind of a country it wanted to be, but it had not been previously discussed and negotiated with the parliament. Under the standing rules it could not be voted upon without the positions of the government and of the parliamentary committees first taken into account. In the past few weeks, the parliament had often happily ignored procedural niceties to stay abreast of events, but not this time. The rebellion in an impeccably legal disguise was spearheaded by deputy Zdenek Jičínský, a constitutional lawyer, co-architect of the Constitution of the Czechoslovak Socialist Republic of 1960, purged reformist of 1968, one of the original signatories of the Charter, and one of the few opponents of Havel's presidential nomination within the Forum. In the following weeks, months and years he worked diligently to assure the continuity of the emerging legal framework with the previous Communist code, to thwart radical attempts at de-Communization and to maximize the authority of the parliament at the expense of that of the president, the senate or anyone else.

The parliament thus had its first debate – and what a debate it was! Few if any of the deputies advocated retaining the word 'socialist'. The bone of contention became instead the word Czechoslovakia or Czechoslovak. In the eyes of many Slovaks it was not respectful enough of their nation and should read Czecho-Slovakia and Czecho-Slovak. In the minds of many Czechs this evoked unhappy memories of the agony of Czecho-Slovakia, as it was then called, between the Munich Agreement and March 1939, when Bohemia and Moravia were swallowed up by Nazi Germany, and Slovakia became an independent state allied with the Nazis. When the parliament finally adopted a compromise proposal, under which the name of the country would read 'Czechoslovak Federative Republic' in Czech and 'Czecho-slovak Federative Republic' in Slovak, a storm of protests broke out in Slovakia against the lower case 's' in 'slovak', which the Czechs had foolishly insisted was the grammatically correct spelling. The parliament thus had to revoke the law again and finally agreed on the name 'Czech and Slovak Federative Republic', which violated every norm of grammar and aesthetic sense, but finally made the storm subside, at least for a time.

The symbols of the state were an even tougher nut to crack. The original Czechoslovak symbol was in the form of the two-tailed Czech lion with a crown with the Slovak St Stephen's cross in a shield on its chest. The Communists did away with the cross, stole the crown and saddled the poor lion with a five-pointed red star on his head. Now Havel wanted to remove the star and restore the crown and the cross. In deference to Slovak national feelings he proposed that the lion and the cross now be co-equal and each form two of the four quadrants in a diagonal.[32] But he could not help thinking of an embellishment, and so added a small emblem of Moravia, a red and white chequered eagle in the centre of the four quadrants. This was immediately read in Slovakia as implying a federation of three rather than two entities and vetoed accordingly.

It is probably wrong to suggest that the ill-considered initiative led to the resurgence of nationalistic passions in Slovakia. Rather, the Slovak reaction to Havel's proposals indicated the discontent that was already there. It also showed to the parliament, docile until then, that the president, for all his popularity, did not command an automatic majority and could be thwarted and frustrated. On Havel's part it created a deep-seated distrust of the parliament, which perhaps could have been avoided.

The fiasco also pointed at some limitations of politics based on symbols, which Havel had been practising. Symbols in politics can be

---

32 The new coat of arms was created by one of Havel's advisers, the graphic designer Joska Skalník.

very powerful simplifiers, amplifiers and energizers, offering shortcuts through otherwise complex and intractable problems, provided that they are universally understood. Without this understanding, the amplifying capacity of symbols works in exactly the opposite way.

Equally, the controversy spoke to the limitations of the phenomenological approach, emphasizing direct, personal experience in dealing with matters of state. Of course Havel dwelt on the transformation of his office and details of his diary to highlight the pressing need for a revolution of hearts and minds in the country at large. But the problems of the tastelessness of the lavishly furnished rooms at the Castle and in the president's summer residence at Lány were not at the top of most people's lists; they, after all, were just embarking on a road strewn with obstacles and uncertainties regarding their own personal well-being and that of their families.

In a way, though without realizing it, Havel was adopting a strategy common to most politicians. He was focusing on problems that were relatively easy to solve, while deferring solutions to essential issues to which there was no simple solution. In doing so, he was caught slightly out of kilter in the rising storm of demands for economic prosperity, social security and historical justice that was raging all around him.

For the moment, however, the whole episode looked like a minor setback, soon to be forgotten. The president was basking in glory, at home and abroad, enjoying receptions normally accorded to rock stars. The spectre of a coup receded. New political parties, newspapers and businesses cropped up right and left. The debate about the future was just as clamorous and heated as any democrat could wish. The elections were on their way. And the rock stars, too, kept coming. On the eve of the first free democratic election 'my friend, Paul Simon', as Havel introduced him proudly, entertained a happy crowd in Old Town Square with the 'Sounds of Silence'. In its aftermath, the Rolling Stones played in the largest stadium in Europe, previously used for the giant Communist gymnastics festivals, in front of over 100,000 people. Before the concert they were received with full honours by Havel in the Prague Castle, and duly engaged in a conversation about democratic transformation and human rights – all, that is, except for the slightly indisposed and conversationally challenged Keith Richards. The group was then offered the ultimate accolade of appearing alongside the president at the balcony in the third courtyard of the Castle and greeting the crowds. The snag, as Mick Jagger later remembered,[33] was that for ten awkward minutes nobody could find the key to the balcony.

The election itself, closely watched over by international observers from many countries of Europe and North America, including a delegation of the NDI headed by Madeleine Albright, went off without a hitch and resulted in a predictable triumph for the Civic Forum in the Czech lands and the Public Against Violence in Slovakia. The presidential elections[34] were to follow within weeks, but they now looked like a mere formality. At home and abroad, there was now one man who symbolized the new Czechoslovakia, a man quickly growing into the Camelot myth of a philosopher king surrounded by the Knights of the Round Table, and governing a country of brave and intelligent people with wisdom, humanity, glamour and wit. If lightning had struck Havel then and there, that is indeed how he would have been remembered, for ever.

---

33 Letter to Václav Havel, 24 August 1990, VHL ID 4775.
34 Havel, the Forum and the Public had insisted on an abridged six-month term instead of the full five years on the grounds that only a fully democratically elected parliament could give the head of state full legitimacy.

First we Take Manhattan

'VÁCLAV, YOU NEED TO GO TO AMERICA,' Havel was told by Madeleine Albright over a soup at the Vikárka restaurant in the third courtyard of the Prague Castle, which doubled as Havel's lunchtime office. 'You need to make the case for the new Czechoslovakia there.'

'Vašek, you need to go to America,' he was told by Rita Klímová, the Czechoslovak ambassador designate to the United States, a fellow Chartist, and a regular translator of Havel's press conferences at Laterna Magika. 'You need to have the administration and the Congress in your corner.'

'Mr President, you need to go to America,' he was told by Shirley Temple Black. 'You will be a star.'

When Bob Hutchings, the National Security Council's director for European affairs in the White House of George H. W. Bush, conveyed the president's invitation to Havel's foreign policy adviser Saša Vondra, pandemonium broke out. First of all, Havel and his team had precious little idea what such a trip would entail. So far, Havel had only travelled in his presidential capacity to Munich and Berlin, Warsaw and Budapest, all of them an hour's flight away, and to Bratislava, which hardly qualified as a foreign country, not at that time anyway. There was little knowledge about the protocol, the etiquette, or the politics of DC.[1] Nobody in the office had seen the real America for twenty years.

---

1 The desperate need for enlightenment is best illustrated by the fact that much of what little was known in the president's office about American politics came from me, and that was a result of reading and translating rather than any direct experience.

If Havel felt overwhelmed by the task ahead he never let on. From the first moment he treated the trip as another of his 'little projects' or 'little ideas', as he used to call them. He started to consult on the priorities he should discuss with President Bush. From the start, his agenda was continent-wide and global rather than simply national or regional. He wanted to discuss the Soviet Union and the looming reunification of Germany and its implications for the region, and he wanted to map the road 'back to Europe'. A small delegation, a nice chat with the president, an hour to make his points, and then quickly go back and continue trying to turn the fish soup back into a fish.

Then things started to snowball. Next to the invitation from President Bush for talks in the Oval Office, Havel received an invitation from speaker Foley to address a joint session of the US Congress, a rare honour. The New York intellectual crowd demanded a bash, the exile organizations a hearing. And everybody back home wanted to come along with an ironclad justification: the ministers to meet their counterparts, the students to study, the advisers to advise, the bodyguards to guard and the hangers-around to hang around. One of Havel's endearing traits as a person and one of his more problematic qualities as president was a total disregard of hierarchies.

In the end, the number of seats, around one hundred, on the Soviet IL-62M four-engine government jet dictated the size of the delegation.[2] That was obviously too many to fit inside the Oval Office. It was also too many to get the president to Washington on a direct flight, and so two other state visits, one to Reykjavik, the other to Ottawa, were scheduled as stopovers. In Reykjavik, Havel was treated to a fish dinner by the president of Iceland, Vigdís Finnbogadóttir, and to a performance of his play *Slum Clearance* at the city's National Theatre of Iceland. In Canada, the president met not only with Prime Minister Brian Mulroney, but also with Czech and Slovak expatriates, many of them refugees who had been able to settle in the country thanks to the generous support of the Canadian government after the Soviet Spring. Perhaps for the first time, he encountered a rather cold if not hostile reception on the part of some of the Slovak émigrés. On the other hand, he enjoyed reuniting with one Czech in particular, old friend and fellow writer Josef Škvorecký, who, along with his wife Zdena, became a hero

---

2 There was yet another planeload on a slightly different itinerary, with those who could not fit in the first plane.

25. Without the goose step. Reviewing the honour guard after the election, 29 December 1989.

26. The president and his spokesman, 29 January 1990.

27. At breakfast, April 1990.

28. Speaking to the joint session of the US Congress, 21 February 1990. Vice-president Dan Quayle and Speaker Tom Foley at the top. Author bottom left.

29. Goodbye to red ties. With Mikhail Gorbachev in the Kremlin, 26 February 1990.

30. The Stones in the Castle, 18 August 1990.

31. Communist leader Antonín Zápotocký makes room for Winston Churchill. With Margaret Thatcher, Prague, 18 September 1990.

32. The federal conundrum, Vikárka restaurant, 4 March 1991. Right to left: Václav Havel, Alexander Dubček, Karel Schwarzenberg, Vladimír Mečiar and Dagmar Burešová.

33. The abdication, Lány, 20 July 1992.

34. With Tom Stoppard at the Czech premiere of *Travesties*, 1992.

35. 'Welcome, Your Holiness, among us sinners.' With Pope John Paul II, Prague, 20 May 1995.

36. 'Ma'm, let me present Gyula.' With the Queen, Prague Castle, 27 March 1996.

37. Dancing with Hillary, White House, 1998.

38. With Bob Dylan and Dáša, Prague, 2000.

To Michael Zantovsky
With best wishes,

39. The presidents and the first ladies, Madeleine Albright and author, White House, 2002.

40. 'The man of my life.' With Dagmar Havlová, 4 May 2006.

41. With the Dalai Lama, Prague, 1 December 2008.

42. The premiere of *Leaving*, Prague, 22 March 2011.

43. The Mourning. Wenceslas Square, 23 December 2011.

44. A step too far. Cabo da Roca, Portugal, December 1990.

to thousands of Czechs, and an anathema to the Communist government, by running for years the best-known Czech exile publishing house on a shoestring from his Toronto apartment under the name 68 Publishers.[3]

There are all kinds of ways to enter a foreign city. Most of them involve negotiating the maze of an airport and an endless ride from the middle of nowhere. When a US Marine helicopter en route from Andrews Air Force Base dropped off Havel into a waiting limousine at the Reflecting Pool, he should have known he had arrived. The next three days went by in a kind of haze. First the meeting in the Oval Office with the president, who went out of his way to make his new colleague feel comfortable and among friends, although he could not help noticing the small contrast in appearance between Brent Scowcroft and Marlin Fitzwater, and Havel's long-haired entourage. Havel did his part. On the advice of his team, who had been tactfully encouraged by the NSC and the deputy chief of Mission of the US Embassy in Prague Ted Russell, he dropped his open-ended musings about the phasing out of the structures of the Cold War, including the Warsaw Pact and NATO. He did not ask for financial aid, but he did ask for political support for the economic transformation ahead. He was forthcoming about the reunification of Germany, a controversial issue on which the US president had shown a considerable amount of vision and courage. He asked Bush to support the democratic transition in Russia. And he offered friendship in the simplest and most personal terms that the Oval Office was likely to have witnessed for a long time.

In the evening it was time for Havel to be mobbed at a reception given by Rita the ambassador in the Czechoslovak Embassy at Linnean Avenue in the Rock Creek Park.[4] As absurd scenes go, this one came directly from Havel's imagination. The post-Stalinist building of the embassy (if there was such a thing as Brezhnevite architecture, this would be it) was packed with ageing Czechoslovak exiles, some of whom still remembered Masaryk, as well as administration officials, academicians, Cold War warriors, artists and Americans of all kinds. They all wanted a piece of Havel, including a delegation of a Native American tribe whose chief presented Havel with

---

3 Škvorecký survived Havel by two weeks.
4 At the initiative of the wife of a neighbouring Central European ambassador, part of the street was subsequently renamed the somewhat corny Spring of Freedom Street in honour of the revolutions of 1989, much to the displeasure of DC taxi drivers whose life was made difficult for years afterwards.

a beautiful hand-carved ceremonial pipe. Like the proverbial rifle on the wall in the first act of a Chekhov play, this prop was yet to play a historic role. The poor Czechoslovak diplomats on duty, most of them thoroughly vetted Communist cadres (there had been no time to replace the staff in the embassies, and no reserve team of diplomats on stand-by to replace them with anyway), tried their best to maintain some kind of control and prevent the president from suffocation, only to be repaid unkindly for their trouble by some of the guests, who remembered being treated as sworn class enemies until recently. For Havel's team, the whole riot came down in the end to extricating the president in one piece. The FBI detail in the adjacent nineteenth-century mill cottage[5] on the banks of Rock Creek, which for years had been there to watch over and eavesdrop on the Czechs and the Hungarians, did nothing to help.

There was still time for a walk through the night-time Mall with Senator Edward Kennedy for a guide. Kennedy too was taken with Havel, so much so that apparently a little elated, whether by the mood of the moment or something else, he stumbled and fell head-over-heels from the stairs of the Lincoln Memorial, only to be saved by a stern-faced secret-service man.

The president was more than happy about how the meeting with Bush went, but a little confused about the White House itself. From afar, the aura of the place gives it almost supernatural dimensions, but coming from the Prague Castle, according to the *Guinness Book of Records* 'the largest ancient castle in the world', it looked like, well . . . a big white house. The Blair House, which was Havel's official residence during his stay in Washington, would look very much like an ordinary house if it were not for the regal presence of Ambassador Joseph Verner Reed, President Bush's chief of protocol. Madeleine Albright was there from the first moment, to advise and help Havel negotiate the treacherous waters of Pennsylvania Avenue and the Hill. She even went as far as to bring in a speech coach, media consultant Frank Greer.[6] He asked Havel to read through the text of the speech to Congress but gave up after the second paragraph. The hesitant, halting, half-mumbled delivery, the avoidance of eye contact with the audience, the absence both of the dramatic accent and dramatic pause apparently led him to believe that Havel could not make an impression at a meeting of the local Parent

---

5 The building is now the Rock Creek Gallery.
6 See Albright (2003), 116.

Teacher Association. Havel politely thanked him for his efforts, but looked a little puzzled. After a lifetime in theatre, he seemed to have no idea of what was required of him.

Addressing the joint session of Congress on 21 February 1990 must have been one of the most memorable experiences in Havel's life until that moment, and it turned out to be equally memorable for many of the congresswomen and congressmen.[7] When the joint legislatures of the pre-eminent world power heard Havel's words: 'The salvation of this human world lies nowhere else than in the human heart, in the human power to reflect, in the human meekness and in human responsibility', one could tell that the audience, which had heard its share of speeches, was not simply impressed but moved as well. The address, which was televised live all the way to Czechoslovakia, elicited seventeen standing ovations. On the whole, it worked out better than the speech coach could have expected.

After the speech, Havel, accompanied by Speaker of the House Tom Foley and the Senate majority and minority leaders George Mitchell and Robert Dole, met with members of both houses. All of them wanted to congratulate him and shake his hand. Some, though, were more inquisitive, and asked him what he meant when he said: 'Consciousness precedes being, and not the other way around.' But Havel could not linger to explain what he meant. New York beckoned.

Driving downtown in a motorcade from La Guardia was like falling straight into the middle of the American Dream, both the standard and the Maileresque versions. Havel was confronted head-on with the fact that his authority was not automatic, that in the land of the free even a president has to win his respect the hard way. The thoroughly multicultural drivers of the zillions of battered yellow cabs on Grand Central Parkway, the Triborough Bridge and FDR Drive, most of whom probably had no idea who Havel was and would not care if they had, took no heed of the motorcade of dozens of police cruisers with sirens on and lights flashing. One die-hard gentleman

---

7   And for me also, though for different reasons. Havel did not trust his English, and I was to be his voice for the occasion, translating his words from the podium. On the inbound flight, however, I developed a painful blockage first in one ear and then the other because of the pressure changes. There was no time to see a doctor before the speech. I could hardly hear a word Havel was saying, and found my way through the speech largely by reading the president's lips, a risky undertaking during that particular administration. It was the most dreadful experience. For years, whenever Havel remembered addressing the joint session of the US Congress, I had my revenge by teasing him that in fact he had been addressing me, and I was deaf to his words.

with ancestry apparently somewhere in South Asia refused to budge even after several appeals of increasing emphasis, until a police car drew level and a cop aimed what looked like a .45 straight through the open window. This argument the man clearly understood and he moved aside, although not too hurriedly, so as to protect his dignity. This was America. Havel loved it.

He had loved it for most of his life. America was the country of freedom, Hollywood and rock 'n' roll. He had admired it from afar as an adolescent, and he had fallen in love with it during his first visit more than twenty years earlier. America was the country of the wild, long-haired, irreverent and experimenting 1960s, a period close to Havel's heart; he himself had lived its equally wild Central European equivalent before the Soviet tanks put an end to it. He loved the spirit and the idea of rock 'n' roll in its most rebellious form. Immediately upon his arrival in New York, he changed into jeans and a sweater and made for the CBGB music club at Bowery and Bleecker Street.

It was nonetheless the world of literature, theatre and ideas to which he felt closest and with which he was most familiar. All of a sudden, all his friends from the past, along with many others, were there to greet Havel out in the open, to fete him as only New Yorkers can. The only problem was how to squeeze them all into one day. One moment Havel dropped in at Mayor Dinkins at the Gracie Mansion, the next he was seen with UN Secretary General Perez de Cuellar in the East River headquarters. At a moving, though hurried, reception at the Human Rights Watch headquarters he met with Robert Bernstein, Jeri Laber and other Americans who had helped focus the attention of the Western world on human rights abuses in the Soviet bloc. In the Public Theater, Havel was reunited with Joe Papp, who had produced Havel's first play in the USA. One by one, actors and directors stopped by to say hello. The guy who looked like Paul Newman was indeed Paul Newman. Havel remarked to his entourage: 'I'm amazed to see someone who is such a legend that I didn't believe he really existed.' Newman sat down to speak to Havel about his Czech ancestry.[8] Havel was rushed away to the Cathedral of St John the Divine for an extravaganza attended by 5,000 people, to be toasted and celebrated by a galactic combination of singers, actors and authors. Paul Simon, James Taylor, Placido Domingo and Roberta Flack alternated with Gregory Peck, Paul Newman and Tom Hulce, who had

---

8 Actually his mother, Terézie Fecková, was Slovak, but this was not the time to dwell on minor details.

played Mozart in *Amadeus*, directed by Miloš Forman, also in attendance. Paul Newman summed up the overwhelming feeling of all present: 'I've been in the presence of great statesmen, and I've been in the presence of great artists, but I've never been in the presence of a great artist–statesman.' Havel looked like a little boy set free to rampage in a sweet shop. Olga did her best to look embarrassed for both of them.

The problem was that there were too many well-wishers not for one evening alone but for two or three, the show was running terribly late and there was one more item on Havel's agenda that evening, an equally important meeting with fellow writers on the stage of the Vivian Beaumont Theater at the Lincoln Center. The team had to extricate the president practically over the dead body of Caroline Stoessinger, the New York pianist and organizer, who had put an incredible effort into making the St John the Divine event happen.

By nature and upbringing, Havel was nevertheless an extremely courteous person who could not bear the thought of letting other people wait, all the more when the 'people' were the likes of Norman Mailer, Kurt Vonnegut, William and Rose Styron, Arthur Miller and Edward Albee. For the next two hours, he would greet old friends, discuss the power of the powerless and living in truth, try to outline the challenges facing Czechoslovakia and Central and Eastern Europe, and the even more difficult challenges facing the Soviet Union, happy in his true environment of a half-lit theatre stage, the dusty, mysterious darkness of the wings, and the envelope of blue smoke produced by himself and his team that seemed to move with him wherever he went.

Havel and America were a love story at first sight. America responded massively to his unquestioned bravery, to his visible modesty, and to his perceived cool. And Havel related just as strongly to the unfettered freedom and individuality of the country, to its openness and energy, to its tolerance to diversity and to its solidarity with people who were being deprived of the very same freedom and individuality elsewhere. There and then he seemed to have made the strategic determination that in his lifelong struggle for freedom and human rights, not just for himself and his countrymen but for other people as well, the United States was ultimately a more reliable and a more consistent ally than friends nearer to home. This made for a subtle but permanent tension and source of internal conflict in his decision-making, because in most other respects, such as his views on capitalism and the welfare state, the death penalty or environmental concerns, he was much closer to the concepts practised in Europe in general, and the EU in particular.

But it was the all-permeating character and the energy of politics on the other side of the Atlantic that fascinated him, although he may have wrongly identified Washington with America. Years later, during his fellowship at the Library of Congress, he wrote, 'Here people enjoy politics; in our country they merely complain about it. Here politicians, scientists and academics, journalists and other important people appear to stay fresh the whole day and perhaps they say the cleverest things in the evening. In our country, by the evening such people are either tired, or desperately trying to catch up on work, or they're drunk, or just glad to be home, watching television with no need to talk to anyone.'[9] He could stay for years. But it was time to move on. The next stop, for better or worse, was Moscow.

---

9 *To the Castle and Back*, 101.

THEN WE'LL TAKE THE KREMLIN

ON 25 FEBRUARY 1948, Klement Gottwald, the syphilitic Communist leader and Czechoslovak prime minister, declared the victory of the Communist takeover in front of a crowd of ecstatic sympathizers. A visibly elated Gottwald said he had just come back from a meeting at the Prague Castle with President Edward Beneš who had capitulated to all of his demands. On the same day forty-two years later, a visibly tired Václav Havel told an equally enthusiastic crowd at the Old Town Square that he just came back from a meeting in the White House with President George H. W. Bush, who had promised to stand firmly behind the democratic transformation of Central and Eastern Europe.

This was Havel at work as a dramatist, using historical anniversaries as counterpoints to highlight the significance and the enormity of change. There were just a few problems with the script. First, Havel was dead on his feet after a fourteen-hour flight back from the United States; second, there were still an estimated 70,000 Soviet soldiers at military bases all over the country who might have their own views on the issue of democratic transformation; and third, in another exercise of *mise en scène*, Havel was scheduled to fly to Moscow in a few hours to meet with President Gorbachev to discuss exactly this.

At least this time the government plane could make the journey in one fell swoop. But if anyone thought he could get some rest on the two-hour flight, he had another 'little idea' coming. 'How about drafting a joint declaration from the meeting, in which the Soviets and ourselves would pledge to put the past behind us and treat each other as equals, and in which the Soviets would apologize for all that they had done wrong and promise they would never do it again?' the president said as the plane started rumbling down the runway. The delegation, made up of Foreign Minister Dienstbier, foreign policy adviser Saša Vondra, yours truly and Dienstbier's spokesman Luboš Dobrovský, just stared at him and mumbled, 'Yeah, sure,' or words to that effect. But Havel was serious, and the drafting, done with a felt pen over a bottle of beer, began. In the end, the language on apologies was watered down, and the document became more future-oriented. But the basic idea that from now on relations between the two countries would be based on equality and a respect for each other's sovereignty remained. Nobody in the delegation really expected the Soviet leader to sign it. At the very best, they could expect a tedious round of negotiations with thick-skinned Soviet bureaucrats, in which the language would be diluted to the point of irrelevance. When the delegation disembarked the plane in Moscow, the paper was handed over to the new Czechoslovak ambassador in Moscow for a speedy translation. He did not think the plan would work, either.

But the very fact that there was a new ambassador in Moscow showed how quickly things were changing. He was Rudolf Slánský, a Chartist and the son of a former General Secretary of the Czechoslovak Communist Party of the same name, who was hanged by his comrades in 1952 in the largest show trial of the period, stage-managed by Soviet KGB advisers. The ambassador's sister Naděžda was kidnapped as a nine-year-old in Moscow in 1943 during Slánský's wartime exile there. The family never saw her again.

As befits a head of state, the delegation was scheduled to spend the night in a government guest house. No one had warned them, however, that the guest house was a gloomy Chekhovian villa in the middle of a vast military compound, surrounded by walls with barbed wire, and guarded by stern-faced soldiers with machine guns. The place made Havel positively depressed, and he retired for the night. The rest of the delegation, left to their own devices, managed to get hold of a sullen-faced *dezhurnaya*[1] straight from central casting, and, speaking a semblance of

---

1 Literally, the woman on duty (Russian).

Russian, persuaded her to produce a bottle of vodka and a chess set. Then we proceeded to play chess, consume the bottle and speak only Russian, or what passed for it, for the benefit of the microphones we were sure were hidden in the ceiling. It was great fun.

When we woke up to a dark cold morning, Havel was already at the breakfast table, looking bright and optimistic. The Kremlin beckoned. We came in through the side entrance, whether as a matter of standard procedure or a finer point of protocol is unclear. Before the meeting he was treated to a guided tour through the Kremlin halls, with the emphasis on their size and grandeur, one thing guaranteed to fail to make any impression on him. And then he was suddenly standing face to face with the nominal leader of the 'camp of peace and socialism' and at the same time the man who had done so much to shake it to its foundations.

For the meeting, Gorbachev put on a poker face. There was no hostility in his demeanour, but not much friendliness either, just a hint of curiosity. When Havel, to hide his nervousness, asked Gorbachev for permission to smoke, an ashtray duly arrived from the outside despite the fact that Gorbachev gave no instructions and no one left the room. When, after courtesies had been exchanged, Havel explained that he had not come to harp on the past, disagreeable as it was, and that he wanted to put relations between the two countries on a new and positive footing, the ice melted. Even more astoundingly, when Havel suggested that the time had come for Soviet troops to leave Czechoslovakia, where they had been stationed since that fateful August, and that an agreement should be signed to that effect, Gorbachev did not object.[2] He merely sought an assurance that there would be no persecution of the Communists. Havel responded by stressing the idea of drawing a line underneath the past, without retribution, repression or recrimination. Then came the dramatic point. Havel produced the hastily translated document, not yet a day old, and proposed a joint declaration on the principles of fairness, equality and sovereignty.

Gorbachev looked not so much surprised as puzzled by the hands-on approach of this newcomer to the world of international negotiations. He took the paper, inspected it without reading it and handed it over to

---

2 In fact, preliminary talks had already been going on at a diplomatic level since January.

his foreign policy adviser Georgy Shakhnazarov,[3] a cerebral-looking older man. Shakhnazarov had listened intently but silently to the conversation so far. He now took the paper, looked at it and then, whether for better comfort, concentration or simply to win some time, proceeded to take off his shoes and tuck his legs under him on the armchair. It was hard not to feel encouraged by this human gesture. The adviser read slowly and carefully. When he came to the end of the document, he went back and started again from the beginning. After a long while, he looked at Gorbachev and nodded. Gorbachev looked at Havel and nodded. Havel had his declaration, which was then carried for finishing touches to an adjoining room where Foreign Ministers Dienstbier and Shevardnadze held their own talks.

The time had now come for the pièce de résistance in Havel's script. He thanked Gorbachev profusely for his kind reception and understanding, remarked deliberately on his previous, equally warm reception in Washington, mentioned the gift of a ceremonial pipe from a chief of a Native American tribe, and then . . . produced the actual object. 'Mr President,' he said, 'it occurred to me right there and then that I should bring this pipe to Moscow and that the two of us should smoke it together as a pipe of peace.' Now Gorbachev was really astounded. He looked at the pipe as if it were a hand grenade with the fuse off, stared uncomprehendingly at his guest and stuttered: 'But I . . . I don't smoke.'[4]

Gorbachev may not be remembered for his sense of humour, but he succeeded in convincing Havel that he was serious about breaking with the past and about letting the former countries of the Soviet bloc forge their own destinies. He was equally serious about trying to transform the totalitarian Communist system into something better, more efficient and more democratic, an impossible but honourable task. Unlike his successor Yeltsin, Gorbachev did not have a 'bohemian' bone in his body, but Havel nevertheless grew to like and respect him. In 1999, on the occasion of the

---

3 Shakhnazarov, like Shevardnadze and many other Soviet reformists, was not an ethnic Russian but an Armenian (Shakhnazaryan), born in Azerbaijan. He was no stranger to Prague, having worked there in the *Marxist Review* aka *Questions of Peace and Socialism*, a Soviet-controlled propaganda outlet, which however became a breeding ground for many a future Soviet reformer, including Gennadi Gerasimov, Alexander Lukin, Yegor Yakovlev and Georgy Arbatov.

4 In his own recollection of the incident (*To the Castle and Back*, 145) Havel, typically for him, is generous to a fault. 'I don't know whether it was lack of understanding or an attempt to be witty but I prefer to believe the latter.' Vondra's version of the story, identical but in details, can be found in Matějková (2012), 111.

tenth anniversary of the Velvet Revolution, Havel awarded the highest honour in the country, the Order of the White Lion, simultaneously to six politicians who had played a crucial role in dismantling the Iron Curtain and opening the road to democracy for the formerly subjugated countries of Central and Eastern Europe: George H. W. Bush, Margaret Thatcher, Mikhail Gorbachev, Helmut Kohl, Lech Wałęsa and François Mitterrand *in memoriam*.[5] When he received the former Soviet president in his study, he pointed out to him the fresco painting on the wall with a shady character lurking surreptitiously between the books on a shelf. 'You know who this is? This is a KGB agent. You know KGB?' Gorbachev just nodded resignedly. After ten years he knew what to expect.[6]

Back in 1990, since this was Russia, the deal had to be sealed through food and drink. *Obed* actually means lunch in Russian, but in the Kremlin, apparently in recognition of the relaxed daily habits of Russian aristocracy, it was formally served in the evening, and consisted of a full meal with beverages not considered appropriate for consumption at lunch anywhere else. Dozens of Soviet officials as well as the entire Czechoslovak delegation attended. The event had a distinctly zoo-like atmosphere, though it was hard to tell whether the Soviet bureaucrats looked more exotic to their long-haired visitors, or the Czech and Slovak dissidents, artists and intellectuals to the home team.

There were also debts Havel had to pay. One of them was a visit to Vostryakovskoye Cemetery, where Andrei Sakharov is buried. Sakharov, who had publicly supported Charter 77 just as it had supported him, had died only two weeks before Havel was elected president. He would have been overjoyed, his widow Yelena Bonner told Havel. Among those present was also Larissa Bogorazova who in an act of almost insane courage had marched along with six others in a protest against the invasion of Czechoslovakia on Red Square on 25 August 1968, and spent four years in Siberia in punishment. A meeting in the embassy with the long independent fringe of Soviet culture, including Yuri Lyubimov, Yevgeny Yevtushenko, Bulat Okudzhava, Oleg Tabakov, Chingiz Aitmatov and Elem Klimov, was the cherry on the cake.

---

5 The honour would have certainly also accrued to Ronald Reagan, but he was by then too ill to receive it.
6 *Václav Havel, Praha-Hrad*, II, a documentary film by Petr Jančárek, Czech TV, 2009.

In June, Havel came to Moscow again for the summit of the heads of states of the Warsaw Pact, with the clear idea of seeing it vanish into the dustbin of history. This was not as difficult as it might seem. Gorbachev was quickly losing control, and the newly democratic governments of Central and Eastern Europe were confident enough to assert their positions. Although the dissolution itself took place at the next summit in Prague on 1 July 1991, the bell had clearly tolled.

When the time came to disband the only military alliance in history that attacked its own members, Gorbachev was preoccupied with the worsening political and economic situation in the country; the man who came to Prague was a featureless apparatchik recently elevated to the post of the Soviet vice president, Gennady Yanayev. There was, however, no question but that the present moment belonged to Havel, Wałęsa and thousands of others who had been involved in the once hopeless struggle against the suffocating Soviet embrace. In speaking to the meeting, Havel saw no reason to hide his pleasure or his intentions. 'We do not hide that our goal is the inclusion of Czechoslovakia in the West European integration,'[7] he said, while calling for the abolition of the dividing line between the East and the West. The meeting duly repudiated the Warsaw Treaty of thirty-six years earlier. Czechoslovakia as the last presiding country of the Pact inherited its insignia and operating instruments, which consisted of a pouch containing a seal and a rubber stamp. The pouch was last seen in the possession of Foreign Minister Dienstbier.

The nineteenth of August 1991 began like any other day. Havel was still sleeping when the phones in the office started ringing with the news that the 2nd Guard Tamanskaya Motor Rifle Division was occupying Moscow. Gorbachev, on holiday in Crimea, was deposed on the grounds of ill health. The nondescript Yanayev was declared president.

Fortunately, the last details of the Red Army had left Czechoslovakia three months before. But the developments were still a cause for acute concern. One of the history lessons the region had learned the hard way was that the bear is the most dangerous when thrashing in agony. And what was a cause for acute concern in the Castle was not necessarily perceived as such elsewhere: in the foreign ministry five hundred metres away, some of the diplomats of the old school started opening bottles of champagne.

---

7 The last meeting of the Political Advisory Committee of the Warsaw Pact, Prague, 1 July, 1991, VHL ID944

It was one of the crowning ironies of the era. Twenty-three years after the Soviet-led invasion of Czechoslovakia, the crumbling empire finally invaded itself. But twenty years, as Gorbachev himself said, made all the difference. Brezhnev, Kosygin and their cronies who gave the orders to suffocate the reform movement in Czechoslovakia were battle-hardened survivors of the Stalinist era and World War II. Utter ruthlessness was part of their DNA. They stood at the head of a superpower with a significant if crude industrial output, formidable armed forces and an omnipotent secret police. Many of them still had Marxist pretentions. On the other hand, The Gang of Eight[8] which masterminded the coup attempt of August 1991, were for the most part a bunch of corrupt bureaucratic lifers, a shining example of the system's propensity for negative selection. The only Marxian aspect of the event was the famous press conference, at which the trembling Yanayev's stupor was apparently the result of hefty doses of terror at what he had done mixed with alcohol in equal measure, straight out of the Marx Brothers' *Duck Soup*. No one who watched it would ever believe that the plotters could last a week. In the event, the coup lasted little more than a day. In the early hours of 21 August, twenty-three years to the hour after the forward elements of the Soviet Army started crossing the Czechoslovak border, the Tamanskaya withdrew from Moscow.

The man of the hour, the president of the Russian Federation and the future president of Russia, Boris Yeltsin, was not an unknown quantity to Havel. Earlier that year he had visited Prague in his capacity as the president of the largest republic of the Soviet Union. Because of his by then open conflict with Gorbachev, there was certain sensitivity about his being received by Havel, who sympathized with his democratic leanings but at the same time felt a sense of obligation to Gorbachev. The compromise solution was to meet outside the protocol, in the Prague pub U Kalicha, the legendary meeting place from Hašek's *The Good Soldier Švejk*, where 'we shall meet at 6 p.m. after the war is over'. Yeltsin said all the right things about democracy, disbanding the rule of the Communist Party and rejoining the West. For all that, he was a little too ebullient, too talkative and too expansive for Havel's taste, especially when compared to the more reticent Gorbachev. Havel, by then a meagre eater, ordered beer, a duck for his guest and a snack

---

8   Oleg Baklanov, Vladimir Kryuchkov, Valentin Pavlov, Boris Pugo, Vasily Starodubtsev, Alexander Tizyakov, Gennady Yanayev, Dmitriy Yazov.

for himself, and watched with awe as his visitor proceeded to consume the whole bird. 'He looked like he could have put down another one,' he remarked afterwards.

One of the main items on the agenda of the next visit to Russia in 1992 was a meeting with the idiosyncratic speaker of the Duma, Ruslan Khasbulatov. An outspoken populist of Chechen extraction, he had to wait for his moment in the limelight for two years longer than Yanayev, though with a similar outcome. He would be one of the leaders of the failed anti-Yeltsin rebellion in October 1993. The main item on Havel's agenda on this trip was the small sum of around 5 billion dollars owed to Czechoslovakia by the Soviet Union for all kinds of industrial products and goods shipped eastward during the period of fraternal love.[9] Khasbulatov listened to Havel's explanation of the problem and then flatly dismissed the claim. When Havel mildly objected that even debts amassed in the Communist period had to be repaid, Khasbulatov gave a wry laugh. 'Look,' he said, 'we were occupied by the Communists just like you were. You want the money, sue the Communists.' After all, the date was 1 April. The debt was finally settled ten years later during the premiership of the current Czech president Miloš Zeman, although to call it 'repaid' would be stretching it a little.[10]

From all these meetings Havel gained a very plastic picture of the enormity of the challenges and the complexity of the issues that the Russians faced in transforming their country. He never subscribed to the Russophobia that was prevalent in Central and Eastern Europe after 1989, but he remained alert to any sign of renewed Russian expansionism, even if it was not aimed in his direction. Though he had not much in common with the rebel government in Chechnya, the brutal war waged against the whole Chechen nation by Putin persuaded him that some of the worst Russian instincts were not yet extinct.

His relationship to the Russian leaders also changed over the years. He respected Gorbachev, although he was unable to establish the same kind of rapport with him that he enjoyed with other world leaders. He was

---

9 A truck driver once described to his friends in a Prague bar the whole range of goods he was regularly shipping to the Soviet Union. 'And what do you ship on the way back?' they asked. 'Back? Back I walk.'

10 The deal mediated by an opaque company at a sizeable discount involved a delivery of the latest model of Russian military helicopters, two heavy airlift transports and even Czech participation in the Russian manned space programme. At the time of writing, all three have yet to materialize. At the end of 2013, however, the debt has been considered settled.

intrigued and amused by Yeltsin, who was a character out of a Gogol novel, but on the whole he believed in his democratic and westernizing leanings. It was something else with Putin, and not only for Havel. While much of the Western world admired Putin's cool demeanour, his smart dress and passable German, Havel could hardly forget even for a minute the origins of that cool and that linguistic skill. Putin was a *chekhist*, a KGB cadre officer, someone that people like Havel spent years learning to recognize, watch out for and outsmart. The idea of a *chekhist* having a change of heart was akin to a bank robber changing professions: possible but unlikely.[11] For Havel, 'the Putin era has brought a new type of dictatorship, all the more dangerous for its inconspicuous mask. It is remarkable in that it weds the worst of Communism with the worst of capitalism.'[12]

But there was always the other Russia. People who suspected Havel and other former dissidents of Russophobia were confusing the country with its recent political representation. For a Central European intellectual like Havel, it was natural to imbibe the great tradition of Russian classical literature, poetry and drama, along with similar influences from the German, French or Anglo-Saxon realms. Although he based his theatrical work on the absurdity principle and loved *The Government Inspector* by Gogol, he was even more deeply touched by the human kindness and understanding of Anton Pavlovich Chekhov.

Havel showed the same admiration and fondness for some of his contemporaries in the Russian democratic opposition and human rights movement. Apart from Andrei Sakharov and the Magnificent Seven from Red Square in August 1968, he held in high esteem Anatoly, today Natan, Sharansky and the *refusenik* movement. Being familiar in detail with the Czechoslovak prison and detention system, he often marvelled at the bravery and resilience of people like Sharansky, who had gone through the incomparably harsher experience of the Gulag and come out unbeaten. He met with him repeatedly during his visits to Israel, and in 2007 they together organized a democracy conference in Prague, to which they invited human rights activists and dissidents from Iran, China, the former Soviet Union and the Middle East, and . . . President George Bush. To the surprise of everyone

---

11 The dislike must have been mutual. For Havel's funeral, Putin sent the president of the Russian Paralympic Committee, Vladimir Lukin.

12 An interview with Petra Procházková, *Lidové noviny*, 19 March 2008.

but the organizers, Bush came. After all, Havel was one of his heroes and he allegedly kept Sharansky's book *The Case for Democracy* at his bedside.

Havel was fond of Russia, but never sentimental about it like so many people in Europe and elsewhere. The idea of a 'Slavic soul' was foreign to him. Like his great predecessor Tomáš Garrigue Masaryk, he was totally immune to the idea of panslavism that infected so many Czech politicians at the end of the nineteenth and the beginning of the twentieth centuries; the concept still carried some weight with certain democratic politicians in Slovakia, such as Havel's colleague from his dissident days, former Slovak Prime Minister Ján Čarnogurský. Along with Karel Havlíček, the nineteenth-century writer and founder of Czech political realism, Havel believed that the term 'Slavic' refers to ethnography rather than to soul, and that not 'just language but also customs, religion, government, and education' determine the relations between nations.[13] He distrusted Putin and his 'managed democracy' and would have a thing or two to say about 'resets'.

---

13 K. H. Borovský, *Slovan a Čech* (*The Slav and the Czech*), *Pražské noviny*, 1846.

The Innocents Abroad

HAVEL'S CHALLENGE, AND HIS AMBITION as well, was not simply to replace servitude to one superpower with allegiance to another, but to build anew the country's ties to the rest of the world. Although it may have not appeared so at first sight, in 1989 there was barely a normal relationship between Czechoslovakia and any other country. Its ties to the Soviet Union and the rest of the Soviet bloc were based on coercion and subservience. Its thousand-year-old relationships with Europe to its west, the primary source of its historical legacy, its culture and its wealth, were abruptly severed by the descent of the Iron Curtain. Its neighbourly relations with Germany and Austria were poisoned by the past wrongs, the Cold War, and characterized by endemic suspicion and distrust. Communist Czechoslovakia prided itself on its friendship with many of the developing countries in Asia and Africa, but, as a proxy of the Soviet Union, it mostly used them in turn as proxies in the Cold War conflict with the West, and as markets for the exports of its armaments, mostly on credit, which was rarely repaid. Following the Six Days' War, Czechoslovakia severed its diplomatic ties with Israel, the home of many of the few of its Jewish citizens who had miraculously survived the Holocaust. A nominally Catholic country, albeit traditionally somewhat lukewarm in its religious zeal, it had waged for many years a silent war against the Vatican, trying to subvert and corrupt the episcopal hierarchy within the country.

This realignment was a gargantuan task, but Havel lost no time in confronting it. Having visited the two Germanies on 2 January 1990, he spoke in the Polish Sejm, and visited Hungary before the end of the month. While many people, both to the East and West of the collapsed Iron Curtain, still struggled with the dilemma of whether they liked Germany so much that they preferred two of them, Havel found a persuasive answer when he framed the question within a larger one, of vital importance to both Czechs and Poles: 'These are two sides of the same coin. It is difficult to imagine an undivided Europe with a divided Germany, just as it is difficult to imagine a united Germany in a divided Europe.'[1] In the same speech, he invited his Polish and Hungarian counterparts to come to Bratislava for talks about regional cooperation. The meeting, which took place in April, gave rise to the Visegrad Project, an agreement on regional cooperation, formally launched at the eponymous site nine months later, which has survived the division of Czechoslovakia and the entry of the Czech Republic, Hungary, Poland and Slovakia into the EU.

This concept of regional cooperation has had unanimous support since the very beginning, but has only developed in fits and starts and suffered occasional setbacks. The problem was synchronization, and sometimes also different personal chemistries. Invariably, one of the three, and later, after the split of Czechoslovakia, four, countries suffered from some kind of an internal, political or economic problem, and the others, in their rush to rejoin the West and reap the fruits of market economy, were reluctant to wait.

The problem of personal chemistry between the respective leaders led to moments of comedy. When Havel first visited Poland as president in January 1990, his colleague and ally Lech Wałęsa was still just an esteemed leader of a revolution, whereas the president of the country was Wojciech Jaruzelski, the general who declared the state of emergency against the Solidarność in 1981. On this occasion, Wałęsa found it hard to cope with a protocolar role that would be inescapably subordinate to both his Polish jailer and his Czech friend, and refused to leave Gdansk for Warsaw. A surrogate, bilateral meeting between Havel and Wałęsa was quickly organized in early spring at the mountain top in Krkonoše, where Charter 77 and Solidarność activists used to hold their clandestine meetings. But the meeting did not go too well; Wałęsa was still waiting for the presidency, and responded coolly to Havel's intellectual musings. Finally, he, too, was elected president and came to Prague for a state visit in September 1991. This time, the team had tried to

---

1   *Works 6*, 44–53.

make sure that Havel was prepared, so that the meeting would go smoothly. They did a psychological profile of Wałęsa and proposed a list of talking points heavy on hands-on management of the political problems of the day, and light on abstract concepts and elevated rhetoric. Once again, things did not go as planned. Apparently, some people in Warsaw had done their homework as well; Wałęsa wanted to talk about nothing but philosophy and metaphysical horizons. Both men had deep admiration for each other, but somehow were never able to dance to the same tune.

On 15 March, the anniversary of the day in 1939 when the German Wehrmacht occupied Prague, and Hitler triumphantly reviewed the honour guard in the courtyard of the Prague Castle, the German President Richard von Weizsäcker came at Havel's invitation, 'not with tanks but just walking'.[2] Havel praised the German president for 'having uttered, on behalf of his nation, some harsh truths about the suffering that many Germans caused us and other nations'. In the same breath he added: 'But have we on our part said everything we should have said? I am not sure.'[3] He went on once again to condemn the principle of collective guilt, which ostensibly gave justification to the expulsion of three million German men, women, and children from Czechoslovakia at the end of World War II. More than just feeling the need to express his regret for this act, he expanded on the topic of moral contamination that is omnipresent in his writings: 'And as often in history we caused harm not only to them but even more so to ourselves: we settled accounts with totalitarianism by opening our conduct and our souls to the contagion and shortly afterwards we paid dearly for this by our inability to resist a new, different totalitarianism imported from elsewhere.'[4]

Going to Great Britain was another exercise in repairing ties. Not only had the two countries been separated by the Iron Curtain, but also most Czechs held deep-rooted resentments about the role of the Chamberlain government in the Munich Treaty, which stood at the beginning of fifty years of national misfortune. Only with Margaret Thatcher did the democratic opposition in Czechoslovakia find a political advocate, fierce and unafraid of

---

2 Václav Havel, Prague Castle.
3 Speech on the occasion of the visit of President Richard von Weizsäcker, 15 March 1990. *The Art of the Impossible*, 21–8.
4 Ibid.

the Russians.[5] For all this time, however, there had been many people in the British academia, arts and civil society who did their utmost to help the Czech friends in need. The role of philosophers Roger Scruton, Barbara Day and Julius Tomin in organizing the underground university in Prague and Brno, the unwavering support of the Moravian-born playwright Tom Stoppard, both in the form of his writings and in his civil activities, the empathy of Harold Pinter and other theatre artists, the regular protests in front of the brutalist building of the Czechoslovak Embassy in London against the latest incarceration of Havel and other prisoners of conscience, the presence of the British press in Prague, the biggest contingent of all countries, and the well-informed broadcasts of the BBC World Service in Czech and English did much to sustain Havel and others during the time of timelessness.

It may be misleading to draw conclusions about individual countries and their people based on the knowledge of hotel rooms, conference halls and government officials. Still, the comparisons could be often amusing. Among other things, the president's party was discovering that each country's secret service sang to a different sheet of music. The Americans were given to vast amounts of overkill and attached an obvious importance to the deterrent factor. Most secret service agents' stern demeanours signalled not too subtly a clear message: 'Don't even think about it.' The French were efficient in their own statist way and thought nothing of closing the *peripherique* for twenty minutes just to let the president pass safely. The Italians were wonderfully operatic; they rode fast Alfa Romeos with open doors, out of which a heart-throb of a *carabiniere* was leaning a full metre with a sub-machine gun cocked at the ready. The British, on the other hand, were understated, running a relay of motorbikes, which took turns to shut down only the next crossing. When Havel stepped out of the car to take a walk down Regent Street, they melted into the crowd so that he could enjoy, if only for a few moments, the illusion that he was actually walking through a foreign city alone and unrecognized.

In the republican Paris, Havel was treated to a royal reception. During the two decades of 'normalization', it was the French intellectuals who had been perhaps the most active and the most vocal of any country

---

5 The new policy of 'engagement with the real democrats' was formulated by Foreign Secretary Howe at a meeting in Chequers convened by Thatcher already in September 1983 (private correspondence, author's archive).

in supporting Havel and the Czechoslovak opposition. Havel took the opportunity to thank François Mitterrand for the gesture of having breakfast with him and other dissidents during his official visit to Czechoslovakia in December 1988. In contrast with Margaret Thatcher, both leaders saw eye to eye on the need to reunify both Germany and Europe. Mitterrand's cerebral, dispassionate approach to the European integration as a staged process, with concentric circles and various degrees of belonging was, however, at odds with Havel's more generous and inclusive concept of Europe one and whole. Mitterrand's dapper associates also showed some signs of being not overly impressed with their shaggy visitors. At the evening banquet in the Élysée one of the top French officials imprudently asked the guests if they had ever seen such a beautiful palace. The visitors stayed silent, largely due to their elementary French as much as their good manners. There was, however, an audible snort in the back, where Karel Schwarzenberg lingered to look at some paintings. 'This is wherre one of my ancestorrrs drrrrank himself to death,' declared the Prince in his best Austrian accent. His distinguished ancestor was the Austrian minister to Paris.

There were a few errands to be made in London the day after the next. The president and most of his advisers were caught rather unprepared by history, particularly attire-wise. The luckier ones had the suits they got married in. The president had his inauguration outfit. But none of this would surely do for a lunch with the queen at the palace. Luckily, the office had a fashion guru in the person of Karel Schwarzenberg, soon to become chief of staff. Schwarzenberg did not need a new suit, but knew where to buy one. While the president was touring the Westminster Palace, a small entourage followed the Prince to Harrods where he saw to it, at his own expense, that the delegation would have some respectability when presented to the sovereign.

The queen was still very much in Havel's mind, though for different reasons, at the dinner given by Margaret Thatcher at No. 10. There were four or five courses with speeches in between, and Havel was once again dying for a cigarette. His mood clouded when he was informed that only after the Loyal Toast to the sovereign would he be allowed to indulge in his vice. He could still consider himself to be lucky; a present-day president would have to wait till hell froze over.

The dinner was preceded by talks, which were all business. Margaret Thatcher wasted no time in letting her opinions be known, on Gorbachev (positive), on the reunification of Germany (wary) and Europe (cautious), on democracy (resigned), freedom (enthusiastic) and the free market (ecstatic). She had no time for idle conversation and she was not particularly interested in theatre or philosophy. As a host she was gracious enough, but when she visited Prague a few months later she hardly put her handbag down before she gave Havel a stern lecture on everything he had done right so far and a few things he had done wrong. There was a slightly extraterrestrial air about her, but Havel admired her no less for that. Admittedly his political philosophy, his lifestyle and his image were very unlike those of the Iron Lady. A guest at the dinner at No. 10 reportedly said that 'he had never seen two people sitting next to each other with less in common,'[6] the kind of facile remark that makes the food at British official dinners more digestible, but one had to wonder. Few politicians could be as easily reduced to the least common denominator of character as those two.

In April the president visited Israel, after first having received Shimon Peres and restoring the diplomatic relations during the visit of Foreign Minister Moshe Arens in Prague. True to his message of reconciliation and new beginning he also received Yasser Arafat. He even toyed with the idea of using his considerable moral authority of the moment to mediate in the Middle East conflict, but he and his team lacked a detailed knowledge of the facts on the ground. Neither did Arafat or then Prime Minister Yitzhak Shamir show much enthusiasm for the project. The Orient House in Jerusalem, which still served as the informal Palestinian headquarters in the holy city, saw a cordial but inconclusive meeting of the president with the Palestinian CNN star of the moment Hanan Ashrawi and other Palestinian notables. For the president's party it was the first experience of the external attributes of the peace process, tense and laid-back at turns, with Israeli snipers on the roofs following Israeli government limousines in their sights. The incredibly complex topography of the Old City increased the sense of confusion. This feeling only intensified during the state dinner hosted by the Israeli president in honour of his Czech counterpart in a strange atmosphere of excitement and suspense, none of which seemed to have anything to do with Havel, the restoration of diplomatic ties or the fall of the Iron Curtain. People kept whispering in Hebrew, exchanging notes and running away

---

6   Dominic Lawson, 'Inside the castle', *The Spectator*, 15 September 1990.

from tables in the middle of a course. Only in the morning did it dawn on Havel that he had been an eyewitness to *HaTargil HaMasriah*, a failed attempt by Shimon Peres to overthrow the Shamir government in a move that went down in Israeli history as the 'stinking manoeuvre'.

The confusion was not lessened by a nearly fatal incident in the King David Hotel where Havel spent the night. In the morning, his personal secretary Miroslav Kvašňák, a hip and irreverent prankster, dressed in a *jalabiya* bought earlier in the day and a towel wrapped around his head and shouting the religious invocation of a holy warrior, used the connecting door in the presidential suite to accost the unsuspecting boss. Havel first flinched, and then, recognizing the assailant, became angry and bodily pushed the offender out of the door – only this time it was the door to the outside corridor, where it took the three men of the Shin Bet guarding the suite about a nanosecond to produce guns. Only a silly grin on his face may have saved Kvašňák that day.

Perhaps wisely, Havel reverted to familiar ground and dedicated his speech at the Hebrew University, where he was being given an honorary degree, to the probably most famous Prague Jew, his fellow writer and model. The speech is worth quoting *in extenso* for yet another reason. It may comprise Havel's most ambitious, if somewhat hyperbolic, attempt at self-analysis. It is at any rate refreshing in its openness, so unlike the constipated defensiveness of most professional politicians.

> This is by no means the first honorary degree I have received, but I accept it with the same sensation that I always do: with deep shame. Because of my rather sporadic education, I suffer from feelings of unworthiness . . . I can easily imagine a familiar-looking gentleman appearing at any moment, snatching the just-obtained diploma from my hands, taking me by the scruff of my neck and throwing me out of the hall . . . I'm sure you can see where this odd expression of my gratitude is leading: I want to use this opportunity to confess to my long and intimate affinity with one of the great sons of the Jewish nation, the Prague writer Franz Kafka.[7]

---

7 'The Hebrew University', Jerusalem, 26 April 1990. In *The Art of the Impossible*, 29.

In Kafka, Havel says, he found a direct reflection of many elements of his own experience:

A profound, banal and therefore utterly vague sensation of culpability as though my very existence were a kind of sin. Then there is a powerful feeling of general alienation, both my own and relating to everything around me . . . an experience of unbearable oppressiveness, a need constantly to explain myself to someone, to defend myself . . . As though I am constantly lagging behind powerful self-confident men whom I can never overtake, let alone emulate. I find myself essentially hateful, deserving only mockery . . .

The hidden motor driving all my dogged efforts is precisely this innermost feeling of mine of being excluded, of belonging nowhere, a state of disinheritance, as it were, of fundamental non-belonging . . . I would even venture to say that everything worthwhile I've ever accomplished, I have to conceal my almost metaphysical sense of guilt. The real reason I am always creating something, organizing something, it would seem, is to defend my permanently questionable right to exist . . .

I am the kind of person who would not be in the least surprised if, in the very middle of my presidency, I were to be summoned and led off to stand trial before some shadowy tribunal, or taken straight to a quarry . . . Nor would I be surprised if I were to suddenly hear the reveille and wake up in my prison cell, and then, with great bemusement, proceed to tell my fellow prisoners everything that had happened to me in the past six months . . . The lower I am, the more proper my place seems; and the higher I am, the stronger my suspicion that there has been some mistake.'[8]

The language is remarkable not so much because it describes the experience of a misfit among politicians, but because it reveals what many have always suspected about politicians, namely that their craving

---

8 Ibid. 30–1.

for power and honours and recognition reflects their deep-seated inner insecurity. Recognizing this as Havel does is not necessarily an antidote to all the folly political ambition may lead to, but it is the first step to controlling it.

Havel himself mentioned the possibility that the speech could be but a pose, but the tone is too authentic, too emotional, almost desperate. Moreover, its nightmarish tinge is demonstrably not just a one-off tribute to Kafka for the benefit of his fellow Jews. A month earlier in Buckingham Palace, Havel told the queen when she asked him how did it feel to change from a prisoner to president almost overnight: 'Ma'am, if that door over there opened and they came to take me away I would not be at all surprised.'

As often happens, it turned out to be most difficult to renew ties with the people closest to home. The Czechs and the Austrians shared a common history for the best part of a millennium, as kingdoms or principalities in the Holy Roman Empire and later as parts of the Habsburg Empire ruled mostly from Vienna, though occasionally from Prague. Many Austrians, Viennese in particular, show Czech ancestry in their names and family trees. On the other hand, a number of German speakers in the south of Bohemia and Moravia became somewhat reluctantly citizens of Czechoslovakia at the end of World War I and ended up being a part of the forced transfer of Germans out of Czechoslovakia at the end of World War II. Many illustrious Czech natives, like Sigmund Freud or Gustav Mahler, were more often thought of as Austrians. Many of the leading Czech noble families had dynastic ties to Austria.

All this did not make the relations between the two nations any easier. One of the founding myths of nascent Czechoslovakia, a fulfilment of the dreams of a century of Czech nationalism, was the history of the oppression of Czechs by Austrians, both real and imagined. For the Austrian part, the reluctance to acknowledge the role of Austrians in the history of Nazism and World War II did not bring the two countries much closer. Nor had the Cold War, and the Austrian anti-nuclear stance, which led to protests against the building of a nuclear power plant on the other side of the border in Southern Bohemia. Early in his presidency, Havel received an invitation to deliver a keynote speech in the presence of the presidents of Austria and Germany at the seventieth musical *Festspiele* in Salzburg, the highlight of the cultural year. To speak in the birthplace of Wolfgang Amadeus Mozart, who adopted Prague as his spiritual capital ('My Pragers understand me'), was natural for a Czech president. The only problem was that the Austrian president was Kurt Waldheim, ostracized by many governments for his undisclosed service with SS troops that had committed atrocities in the Balkans during the war. For Havel to go to Salzburg meant meeting with Waldheim, and a meeting between Havel and Waldheim meant a moral compromise for the president of Czechoslovakia, and a cleansing elixir for the president of Austria. It was perhaps the first of many such dilemmas in Havel's presidency, a confrontation of moral politics with real politics.

'There is no way you can go,' said the advisers. 'Nobody speaks to the man. He is a *persona non grata* in the United States. New, even more damaging revelations may come to light just as you will be shaking his hand. He lied about his wartime service, he lied about his affiliations, and you are the president of truth.'

Havel was not persuaded. Like many others, he suspected that the revelations about Waldheim were not exactly news for those who had used him for their own purposes as an international diplomat and secretary general of the United Nations, and so he treated the air of condemnation surrounding him as overdue at best and hypocritical at worst. 'Look, what can happen to me?' Havel wondered aloud. 'I shook hands with Yasser Arafat. I will go, but I will not be silent about history.'

That sounded like an even stronger reason not to go. The thought of a public confrontation between the two presidents on the stage of the festival was too dreadful to ponder. Havel went anyway, defying orthodoxy as always. And he spoke about history, clearly and to the point, without ever mentioning Waldheim's name. After speaking of fear, which the uncertain future evoked in many people in the newly liberated countries after decades of certain, though miserable past, he changed the subject: 'For us, fear of history is not just fear of the future but also fear of the past. I would even say that the two fears are conditional, one on the other: a person who is afraid of what is yet to come is generally also reluctant to look in the face of what has been. And a person afraid to look at his own past must fear what is to come.

'All too often in this part of the world fear of one lie gives birth to another lie, in the foolish hope that by protecting ourselves from the first lie we will be protected from lies in general. But a lie can never protect us from a lie . . .

'The idea that a person can [painlessly weasel one's way through history and]⁹ rewrite his autobiography is one of the traditional self-deceptions of Central Europe. Trying to do that means hurting oneself and one's fellow countrymen.'¹⁰

There is to this author's knowledge no record of what Waldheim said or thought of the speech. But the two men did shake hands.

Other trips abroad in the first year included a visit in May to the Council of Europe, the first European organization to which the new Czechoslovakia was applying for membership. In August, Havel attended a unique conference in Oslo on the Anatomy of Hatred. His participation at the World Summit of Children at the end of September was memorable mostly for his meeting with Woody Allen in Mia Farrow's house on Central Park West. Organized with some difficulty by me, as a devotee of both men and author of a book on Woody Allen, it proved to be a mismatch of the century. The two men, both naturally shy and reticent, had little to talk about, since Havel had never seen any of Allen's films, and Allen was clearly unfamiliar with Havel's writings.

In September, Havel visited Italy. The state visit included meetings with President Cossiga and Prime Minister Andreotti, but was a brainchild of Italian Foreign Minister Gianni de Michelis. One of its high points was a visit to Capri, where Havel received the prize named after the Italian maverick intellectual Curzio Malaparte and was treated by de Michelis to a rather wild evening at the local discotheque full of beautiful young women. When the visit progressed to Rome the next day, it turned out many of the women were still with the delegation as members of de Michelis's staff. Gianni was not your typical austere diplomat, and later ran into some difficulties on that account.

In October Havel returned to Paris, this time for the summit of the CSCE. The occasion was the signing of the Paris Charter for a New Europe, drawing a line under the Cold War and heralding 'A new era of Democracy, Peace and Unity'. A new secretariat of the Conference would be established in Prague. But the drama of the meeting was the sight of the forlorn figure of the British Prime Minister Margaret Thatcher, at her most commanding

---

9   This phrase in the Czech original of the speech in the digital archive of the Václav Havel Library, VHL ID14107, has been omitted from the English translation.
10 'The Salzburg Festival', 26 July 1990, in *The Art of the Impossible*, 53.

only a month earlier in Prague, who could not fight back tears in public on learning in the middle of the meeting that she was being deposed from her job. Although Thatcher was ideologically much closer to Václav Klaus, who would make her his model, than to Havel, he empathized with her on the occasion and retained a lasting fondness of her for the rest of his life.

Visits to Switzerland, Spain and Portugal completed Havel's itinerary for the year. In Switzerland, Havel met again with his colleague Friedrich Dürrenmatt, whom he first met in the sixties and who would die only three weeks later. Dürrenmatt's laudatory speech to Havel, in which he compared the Swiss draft resisters to the dissidents of the Communist era, and his own country to prison, might have been somewhat embarrassing to a visiting head of state if it were not for the fact that most of the audience seemed to know what to expect from their national playwright.[11] Frankly, it was not easy for the visitors to visualize Switzerland as a totalitarian dungeon. At the same time, Havel could be pleased that a fellow writer related to his sense of a deeper malaise of modern society than just Communism.

King Juan Carlos and Queen Sofia of Spain took a lasting liking to their non-aristocratic visitor. The feeling was reciprocal, and Havel would come back to one of the Spanish royal retreats to spend parts of his holidays there. Meeting with Catalan President Jordi Pujol in Barcelona, he realized that Czechoslovakia was not the only country with a problem of nationalities. He was also completely mesmerized by the beauty of the city and by the Gaudí modernist architecture in particular.

In Portugal he renewed his friendship with President Soares, the first head of state to come to Prague after the Velvet Revolution in December 1989 and meet with Havel even before his election. The other memorable event of the trip was Havel's walk on the beach at Cabo da Roca, which resulted in a famous photograph of the curious president getting his trouser legs wet.

Some of the trips could be called triumphant and all were successful, except one, which was not a state visit, although it preceded successful visits to Nicaragua and Mexico in July. Longing for some rest, Havel and Olga accepted an invitation from a well-to-do Czech widow expatriate to

---

11 Friedrich Dürrenmatt, 'Switzerland – a Prison', speech on the occasion of the Gottlieb Duttweiler Preise to Václav Havel, Zürich, 22 November 1990.

spend a couple of weeks in her villa in the Bermudas. The first couple left, accompanied only by a bodyguard.[12] The house was all right, but the lady turned out to be a demanding alcoholic. What was worse, she developed a crush on Havel. Instead of spending time at the pool or on the beach, the presidential pair locked themselves in their room and waited for a rescue. It took no lesser a figure than Madeleine Albright to fly to the Bermudas and relieve the siege by taking the president sightseeing. When they visited the NASA tracking station on the island, Havel pointed to the giant antennas and asked his guides innocently: 'Did you find any aliens up there?'[13]

The holiday from hell signalled a trend: Havel, who loved to travel and was perhaps subconsciously trying to make up for the years he had spent locked up behind the Iron Curtain or behind bars, generally did not prosper especially when travelling for pleasure. His trips coincided with a rich medical history of depression, headaches, fevers, falls, fractures and near fatalities.

For all the glamour and excitement, there was little superfluous or accidental in Havel's itinerary in the first year of his presidency. With the exception of his summer visit to Central America he confined his travels to a gradually expanding circle of past and future partners and allies. The same held for his official guest list back home. The visit of von Weizsäcker in March and the meeting with Chancellor Kohl in Bonn in May a year later were crucial to the future of the relationship with Czechoslovakia's most important neighbour.[14] The visit of President Bush in November, symbolically underlining the anniversary of the Velvet Revolution, represented a further step in building a bond with the country's most important future ally. It was also an introduction to the American way of doing things. Bush came with 700 people, the Air Force One jumbo jet and a spare, his own armoured limousine and a spare, his own armoured

---

12 They were later joined by the foreign policy adviser, Alexandr Vondra.
13 Conversation with Madeleine Albright, Washington, 9 November 2013.
14 The latter meeting spawned several rounds of backroom diplomacy aimed at a compromise solution to the issue of the Sudeten Germans, comprising the annulment of the Munich Treaty on the German side, and the opening of a way for individual Sudeten Germans to reclaim Czechoslovak citizenship. Although the two parties were reportedly close to a deal, Kohl discontinued the talks after an alleged indiscretion on the Czech side. According to others involved, the deal-breaker was Kohl's demand for the restitution of property contained in a letter to Havel, which has since disappeared. In his talks with Havel in Prague on the occasion of signing a treaty between the two countries on 27 February, 1992, only the question of a joint foundation to compensate the victims of war wrongs on both sides was discussed (Meeting notes, author's archive). The 1997 Joint Declaration adopted this very idea.

reading stand and a spare, and a hundred-people-strong advance team including dozens of secret service agents, who used every argument short of force to persuade Havel's advisers to vacate their offices for a week so that they could secure them. Every step of the president, every angle of the camera and every word of his speech were meticulously planned. It did not go quite according to the plan though. In his main appearance on Wenceslas Square on 17 November, Bush, encouraged by Havel, ventured out of the safety of the protected shelter the secret service had built for his speech in order to greet the ecstatic crowd. At the same moment an agent noticed a plastic bag on the ground a few steps away. 'Bomb! Bomb!' resonated the earpieces, and a phalanx of security men started to descend on the two presidents to hustle them away just as one of Havel's bodyguards moved to inspect the bag. 'Bomb, my eye. It's sausages.'[15] The rest of the visit went smoothly.

Two other memorable visitors to Czechoslovakia in the first year of freedom at Havel's behest were both statesmen of the spirit rather than territory. The first was a modest, smiling, humorous man named Tenzin Gyatso, better known as the 14th Dalai Lama of Tibet. In the West, this symbol of the spiritual resistance of the Tibetan nation to the Chinese Communist rule was for decades paid homage to from a distance so as not to provoke the wrath of the modern-day Middle Empire. Havel was the first head of state of a democratic country to extend the Dalai Lama an invitation to visit. The Chinese ambassador made disapproving noises, but did not leave the country when his protests were to no avail. Nevertheless, the visit was treated as private. For better or worse, it was also the seed of a doctrine. Never during the thirteen years of his presidency would Havel refuse to receive a visitor because of political expediency or the lack thereof.

The president had a different problem. He wished ardently for a meditation session in private with the Dalai Lama. In the Buddhist etiquette, however, one cannot, president or not, simply request a meditation with a master. Rather, one has to wait to be asked. It took a bit of backroom diplomacy, but the Dalai Lama evidently saw some promise in the new pupil. The meditation, on 3 February, took place seemingly incongruously in

---

15 Interview with Pavel and Petr Král, 21 February 2013.

the Roman Catholic Church of the Holiest Name of Jesus in the president's country retreat in Lány.

The Pope came next. Any pope would have been welcome given the long, though unusually complex history of Czech Catholicism, but Karol Wojtyla, Pope John Paul II, was a Pole from just across the border, a symbol, an inspiration and a catalyst of the faith and courage of the Polish nation in resisting the Communist orthodoxy, a charismatic figure and, incidentally, a poet and playwright in his youth. Havel had expressed the wish for an early papal visit already in his New Year's speech, in the clear hope of helping to inspire a spiritual reawakening in the steaming nihilist ruins of the late Communist period. The visit meant a lot to him, and he prepared his welcoming remarks at the airport and his subsequent speech at the Castle with the care reserved for the most important occasions. At the airport he chose words that were unusually emotional for him:

'I do not know if I know what is miracle. Still I dare to say that at this moment I am witnessing a miracle: a messenger of love is coming to a country devastated by the ideology of hatred; a living symbol of learning is coming to a country devastated by a government of ignorants; a messenger of peace, dialogue and mutual tolerance, respect and kind understanding, a herald of brotherly unity in diversity is coming to a country, ruined until recently by the idea of confrontation and division of the world.'[16]

The tone of the speech in the evening was less ecstatic and more thoughtful. Havel addressed a topic he grappled with for most of his life, the source of his own unmistakable spirituality in spite of the fact that not only did he not subscribe to any organized religion but also that he had no specific notion of deity. 'I strongly believe that your visit will remind us all of the genuine source of real human responsibility, the metaphysical source . . . of the absolute horizon to which we must refer, that mysterious memory of Being in which each of our acts is recorded and in which and through which they finally acquire their true value.' And he concluded on another of his recurring themes, that of his own and most other people's fallibility: 'I welcome you, Holy Father, among us sinners.'[17]

During the evening part of the visit to the Castle, Havel took the Pope aside for a tête-à-tête, not an unusual occurrence during a state visit. But

---

16 Welcome to His Holiness John Paul II at Prague Airport, 21 April 1990, VHL ID11191.
17 Welcome to His Holiness John Paul II at Prague Castle, 21 April 1990, VHL ID909.

unlike on other occasions, he never related the details of this meeting to his advisers. Although he had never been confirmed as a Catholic, he called the meeting 'my confession'.

In fact, the close relationships Havel developed with the Pope and the Dalai Lama were part of a unique spiritual triangle. The Dalai Lama had met with the Pope no fewer than eight times, more often than any other foreign dignitary. The three men shared many things together, including the direct experience of a totalitarian regime, the concern for human rights and well-being of individuals, and a universalist, non-exclusive understanding of the transcendent. Beyond and above all this, they had the same infectious smiles and the same kind humour laced with a sense of the absurd. The evening with the Pope was all smiles, and so were the many meetings with the Dalai Lama. Probably at no other time was Havel seen to smile more frequently.

Among the many paradoxes surrounding Václav Havel was the fact that, although he was not a religious man, he was a man of faith. At times he came closer to identifying that 'mysterious memory of Being', which informed his philosophical thinking and which gave a moral basis to his politics, but in the end he always shied away. His God, if God it was, was a form of being that could not be named, pictured or otherwise identified. The 'order of being', where 'all our actions are indelibly recorded and where, and only where, they will be properly judged',[18] is a concept that permeates his writings from the *Letters to Olga* to his last book of memoirs. It is different from the concept of the last judgement in that it does not necessarily assume afterlife. Our actions are judged independently of us and of the fact or form of our existence.

Havel's existential sense of personal responsibility as a prerequisite of freedom and living in truth concedes too much to free will to be compatible with the concept of an omnipotent god. Omniscient He may be, hence the dilemma of a person cheating on the fare in an empty streetcar, but omnipotent He is not. In fact He may be struggling with His own dilemmas. A passage from the Old Testament comes to mind, in which God is seen as hesitating, not quite sure what to do, until He is reminded of *His responsibility* by Abraham: 'Won't the Judge of all the earth do what is just?'[19] And so in Havel's universe; everyone is responsible.

---

18 'Address to the Joint Session of the Congress', in *The Art of the Impossible*, 19.
19 *Genesis*, 18:25.

This is not meant to suggest that Havel was closer to the God of the Old Testament than to others. All attempts to appropriate him for a particular religion are plainly silly. Equally, although Havel occasionally toyed with New Age concepts, and 'mystery' was a key word for him, there is actually little in his thinking that is mystical and practically nothing that could be called occult. When Havel, gently provoked and guided by his brother Ivan, questioned and endeavoured to transcend the positivist concept of science, he was largely reflecting modern science's greater tolerance of paradox, ambiguity and uncertainty in the wake of the quantum theory, the uncertainty principle and the relativity theory. But unlike many people who pass through life without wondering, Havel was able to see the mystery of existence in every human action, every human impulse and every human dilemma. And the core of the mystery was moral. He would not discount it as superstition, just as he would not ascribe it to Providence, the Supreme Being or the superego. As he argued a number of times, the mystery would not be less if it were given a name or an explanation. It would just move further away.

Making the Fish

Anyone can turn a fish into fish soup,
but it is much harder to turn fish soup into a fish.

IT MIGHT SEEM AS THOUGH the president spent his first term globe-trotting; in reality most of his time and energy were spent on domestic issues. Things were becoming difficult. Without the monopoly on power, the planned economy was collapsing and the nascent market economy was still too weak to replace it. It was clear that sooner rather than later the country would be in need of a stand-by facility from the IMF. There was no domestic capital, much need for investment, and foreign investors were still wary. The constant avalanche of stories about Communist agents in high places poisoned the public mood and helped obscure the fact that the former Communist bosses were quietly establishing themselves in business and industry. Havel did his utmost to stay ahead of the curve. He kept conducting his glorious raids, visiting dozens of places, sometimes unannounced, in a particular region every week, pressing flesh, making speeches. He kept on attacking 'the dark forces of the past' and their efforts to gain a stranglehold on the future. At my instigation, he started a weekly radio talk show, inspired by FDR's fireside chats, adding a dessert to hundreds of thousands of Sunday family lunches. His popularity was still enormous. His quality of life, though, had deteriorated considerably. He worked long into the night, workdays and weekends. He was exhausted and often ill, having to cancel items in his diary or even whole days. He underwent a hernia operation in the spring. He rarely saw Olga, his anchor in life, partly because of his own commitments and partly because of her involvement with the Committee of Good Will, a charity to help the sick and the handicapped, which she had set up with the total commitment that characterized her. On the plus side, from his advisers' perspective anyway, he did not have much time for girlfriends. Jitka was quickly drifting out of the picture, and, although he had started his romance with Dáša, his future wife, in the spring of 1990, it was still quite tentative.

It was also time for Havel to realize that there was no light at the end of the tunnel. As the end of his first term approached, it became clear that there was no one who could conceivably replace him, neither the ageing Dubček, nor the likeable and popular Dienstbier, nor the incredibly hard-working and combative Klaus. The parliamentary elections brought about massive majorities and a strong mandate for the two reform movements that had spearheaded the Velvet Revolution, the Civic Forum in the Czech Republic and the Public Against Violence in Slovakia. It also augured their imminent eclipse. The reasons were not entirely unexpected. While the two movements represented a popular consensus on the need to do away with the previous system and to introduce a government based on a democratic mandate, the rule of law and respect for human rights, this was as far as the consensus went. There was no such unity on what was to be done about the economy, on how to provide for the country's security, in which direction to steer its foreign policy or, indeed, how best to frame the relationship between its two constituent nations. What was left of the consensus was still strong enough to assure Havel's re-election by an overwhelming majority in the Federal Assembly at the beginning of July. But right after people returned from their holidays at the end of the summer, things started to unravel.

Already before the election there had been small but significant defections from the Forum. A group of dissidents, largely Catholic conservative politicians, some of them previously involved in the Kampademia and its annual retreats at Hrádeček, launched the Civic Democratic Alliance in December 1989. Another conservative Catholic group, centred around Václav Benda, first joined the fast-reforming People's Party, and then split off to start the Christian Democratic Party. Some Civic Forum activists like Rudolf Battěk joined the re-established Social Democrats, the oldest and arguably the most respectable of the traditional parties, had it not been for its capitulation in the face of the Communist putsch in 1948. Havel's old colleagues and enemies from *Tvář*, Emanuel Mandler and Bohumil Doležal, had long since started their Liberal Democrats. The bulk of the Forum remained, but it soon started to coalesce into two separate camps. One was a group including many of the Forum founders and former Chartists and dissidents. It would be unfair to call them 'the Charter grandees' for there was not much that had been grand in their previous lives, but they were a moral authority for many of their rank-and-file members. The other group consisted of a number of the new, largely younger activists who helped to establish the local branches of the Civic Forum during the November days. Many of them were from outside Prague. Rather than having transferred their pre-November loyalties to the movement, they saw it as an open platform full of thrilling challenges but also opportunities. They had little time for the sophisticated political and philosophical debates that were the core meaning of the Forum for many of their older colleagues. They wanted to get things done and, in doing so, they also wanted to get ahead. These two visions of the Forum became personified in the struggle for its leadership. In the end the campaign pitted Martin Palouš, the son of one of the most deliberate and the most philosophical of the grandees, a philosopher in his own right and a member in good standing of the Kampademia, against the finance minister Václav Klaus, the 'grey-zone' economist of the Chicago School persuasion, and a much more abrasive personality by nature. Klaus went around the country locals looking for grassroots support, while Palouš relied on the moral authority of the dissidents. Klaus won the election hands down and a schism ensued. The traditionalists turned to Havel for support.

But Havel was now too far removed from the Forum to be able to play an effective role. He invited all the protagonists to Lány for reconciliation talks, but to no avail, and in the end agreed, albeit reluctantly, to a negotiated division of the Forum. His relationship with Klaus, never particularly cordial, had already suffered when Havel, alerted to the finance minister's power ambitions and a total absence of team spirit (unless he stood at the team's head) tried to ease Klaus out from an executive role. Deliberating on the appointments for the new government following the elections and spurred on by some of the leaders of the Forum, he considered offering Klaus the immensely important but non-political job of governor of the

Central Bank. The attempt backfired and showed, not for the last time, that in a direct confrontation Havel could not hold his ground against an opponent not burdened by considerations of respect. It was a meeting of two worlds; in Václav Klaus, the advocate of non-political politics met a consummate political animal.

Nonetheless, the negotiated demise of the Civic Forum was to become a blueprint for a more serious event. In forcing the split and freeing his hands for making his faction of the Forum into a political party of which he would be the unchallenged leader, Klaus proved to be not only ruthless but also practical. He had no intention of getting entangled in arguments about which of the two sides would inherit the name of the Forum, who would keep its property, and who would be its legal successor. Towards all such questions he took a reasonable and often magnanimous stand, keeping his eyes on the prize, which was control not of the movement but of the government. To his opponents, he was becoming the grave-digger of the revolution. To his supporters, he was the herald of the new order.

It was this new order that was now the main task ahead of the new government. In keeping with the predictions of the political scientist Ralf Dahrendorf in the aftermath of the *annus mirabilis*,[1] the foundations of the new political system were laid down in a mere six months. It would now take the best part of the next six years to make the momentous decisions about the future shape of the country's legal system, its economy and the countless institutions that make a free society work and flourish. Nobody gave much thought yet to the third part of Dahrendorf's prophecy – that it takes something like sixty years for the mindset of people to change.

One did not have to believe – as Havel did not – in the economic determinism of Karl Marx and many of his epigones to realize that an effective economic reform was essential for the future well-being of the country. The realization in itself, however, did not amount even to the outline of a recipe. The scope of the problem was just staggering, and Havel, along with most people in the country, was ill-equipped to deal with it. For all his voracious reading and self-education, not only was he ignorant of the fundamentals of economic theory, having been instead force-fed the bizarre mixture of Marxist propaganda and dialectical sophistry called political economy, but

---

1 Dahrendorf (1990).

he was totally unfamiliar with the practical workings of a real economy. Havel was forced to rely on the advice of economists, who, to make matters more complicated, came in two varieties. One group, composed of academic economists exemplified and largely dominated by the figure of Václav Klaus, had made good use of their time spent in research institutes and academia, ostensibly trying to make planned economy adhere to a minimum of rationality, but in reality using their access to foreign literature and fellow scientists to learn as much as possible about the theoretical underpinnings of the free market. Nonetheless, they had no practical experience in running an economic enterprise, let alone a country. The economists in the other group, recruited mostly from among the purged reformist managers of the Prague Spring period, were well versed in trying to make a factory or a business work even under the dogmas of the socialist economy, but had only a vague theoretical concept of how free-market economy operated. These two groups now engaged in a battle for Havel's and the nation's soul.

In the government 'Script of Economic Reform', approved by the Federal Assembly in September of 1990, the aim of the economic transformation was described as 'transition from a centrally planned economy to a market economy'. While no one was yet ready to tackle the economy as a whole, a pilot project of sorts emerged in the form of the so-called 'small privatization', in which thousands of small enterprises, such as shops, restaurants and workshops, were auctioned off to the highest bidder. Although the method was ostensibly fair, and as transparent as the government could make it, it paid little notice to the obvious fact that there was a very uneven distribution of wealth in the country, which did not come through the natural allocation of winners and losers in a free market over decades, but as a direct or indirect consequence of arbitrary Communist rule. The vast majority of people simply had had no money and could not make any. The wage scale was skewed in favour of the manual professions. There was no means of investment – shares in businesses and companies did not exist – and only a token interest on savings. It was illegal to own more than one property for living in and a secondary residence for resting. No capital could have accumulated.

The only people with access to capital were the Communist *nomenklatura*, and black-market entrepreneurs ranging from money-changers, who bought and sold the otherwise unavailable hard currency at several times its official but purely theoretical rate, to professionals and tradesmen who were able to provide unavailable goods or services. In reality, these two groups were interlinked and interdependent parts of a single mechanism, as the *nomenklatura* depended on the black market for the monetization of its power and patronage, and the black marketeers depended on the *nomenklatura* for protection.

It was thus a foregone conclusion that the only people to benefit from the auctions would be the two groups described above. The only feasible alternative on offer was to transfer the ownership of the assets being privatized, either wholly or in part, to the people working there in the form of employee shares. Unfortunately, this was before the method became popular in the restructuring of such giants as United Airlines. It was also reminiscent of the specific road to socialism as practised in the former Yugoslavia, and was condemned as such.

Havel, ever sensitive to signs of discrimination and inequality, convened a meeting of the responsible officials to persuade them to take the employees' interests into account. Lacking the ability to speak the economists' language, he based his case on anecdotal evidence, such as the unfairness of the auction system for the manager of his favourite local restaurant, Rybárna, Ms Beranová. His arguments did not carry the day. About 23,000 small enterprises were privatized in auctions, mostly to former Communist officials and black marketeers. In fact, the two allied groups went one better. With the tacit approval of the authorities, they formed cartels to drive the auction price down and win many of the assets, which had been previously cleansed of liabilities, in the so-called Dutch auctions, with progressively decreasing asking prices, for peanuts. Ms Beranová soon lost her job.

Then there was the vast amount of private property, which the Communists had nationalized or confiscated and mostly run to ground. Some of it was individual property, houses, land, forests, factories and businesses. Some of it had belonged to groups and corporations, of which by far the largest was the Catholic Church. Some of it had been stolen from Jews by the Nazis, and its owners murdered. After the war, the government never got around to returning such property to the heirs. Generally, the original owners were long since dead, their heirs often in exile or hard to trace, and the property damaged or transformed beyond recognition.

All in all, Havel and the government were standing before a vast malodorous pile of wrongs and grievances. There was no doubt about their determination to try to repair at least some of it, but where to begin? As with the victims of the Holocaust, not all the past wrongs and controversies could be attributed to Communists. Some of them dated back to the end of the Austrian–Hungarian empire and the emergence of independent Czechoslovakia, which saw the first wave of nationalization of the property of aristocrats and great landowners. Some of them ran as far back as the sixteen twenties, when, in the aftermath of the defeat of the Protestant party at the start of the Thirty Years War, the great estates of the Protestant nobility were confiscated by the victorious Catholics. Then there was the sensitive matter of the three million German expellees at the end of World War II.

Some people thought the answer to the question was not to start at all. Some of their arguments made sense. It was not as though the property had not changed in form or value over time. Some of it was gone, some worthless, some burdened with debts. The state was simply not rich enough to pay full compensation for the value of the property at the time of the confiscation, any accrued interest notwithstanding. Any cut-off points and constraints used would inevitably be arbitrary, and would thus create further injustices. In a large number of cases, mostly concerning houses and land, the property already had new private owners. Surely, the state was not going to repair one wrong by committing another. There was also the residual distrust of large property owners in general, sown through forty years of Communist indoctrination, resentment of churches, especially the Catholic Church, and an open hostility towards exiles, who 'left the country to make good in the West while the rest of us suffered Communist rule'.

Whereas Klaus was preoccupied with the issue of privatization and took a 'reserved view' of the necessity and the scope of restitutions,[2] Havel was less ideological on the issue of forms of ownership, but he was more insistent on restitution as a matter of historical justice. Since both men concurred on the principle of inviolability of private property, both in the end agreed that the state should make an effort to repair the wrongs, and both realized that not all wrongs could be repaired in full or in part. But the left-wing opposition to the plan seized on the fact that Havel (and also his

2 Conversation with Václav Klaus, 30 August 2013.

by-then chief-of-staff Karel Schwarzenberg, the scion of one of the oldest and richest noble families) stood to benefit from restitution, since his family had owned the largest entertainment complex in Prague, the Barrandov Terraces bar and restaurant, and quite a few other things as well. Perhaps for this reason, and to avoid any semblance of a conflict of interest, Havel did not take an active part in the legislative campaign except to advise on caution lest new wrongs were committed in the process. Just the same, from about this time he was caricatured by the political left as an advocate of the interests of the rich and his own to boot.

The law, which was passed by the parliament after an extended debate, was finally titled with some realism as 'An Act on the Alleviation of the Consequences of Some Wrongs Regarding Property'.[3] The cut-off point was set at 25 February 1948, the date of the Communist takeover, and the claimants could only be Czech or Slovak individual citizens resident in Czechoslovakia.[4]

At its time, the law was perhaps the most ambitious and the most consistent attempt to repair the injustices of the past in the post-Communist world. Simultaneously, though, it opened a Pandora's box, which kept producing newer and newer controversies. There were cases of falsified title documents, a rush by descendants of some of the former owners to reclaim Czechoslovak citizenship, and an avalanche of protest by all those who had been similarly wronged in the past yet did not qualify under the terms of the law.

Havel did his best to play the role of moral arbiter he was predisposed to, both by his current status and by his proven moral integrity in the past. He left it to his brother and sister-in-law to initiate the legal process on behalf of the Havel family property, and he vowed not to seek any personal benefit from the restitution for himself, being quite content with the income from his literary works and his presidential salary, most of which he gave to charity anyway.

The next, by far the largest, wave of property transfer, starting in November 1991, was the one in which Havel was least involved. It became the linchpin of the whole reform process, but also the source of countless future controversies. The 'big privatization', as it was called to

---

3 *Zákon o zmírnění následků některých majetkových křivd*, No. 403/1990 Sb.
4 The condition of residency was later waived.

distinguish it from the small privatization of the year before, aimed to change the ownership of the bulk of the national economy. The operation posed unprecedented challenges. At its core was the problem, which the economist Jeffrey Sachs characterized as reconstructing the fish out of the fish soup. The issues were both economic and political in nature. On the economic side, it was the classic problem of letting the market allocate ownership in a quasi-rational manner, thus enabling the economy to function efficiently. But there was hardly any capital in the country to make such allocation possible. Politically, it was not feasible simply to offer property to the highest bidder, because practically all of it would end up in the hands of foreigners. An ingenious scheme emerged that overcame the problem through what was in reality so much play money. It was called voucher privatization. For a nominal sum, covering the technical costs of the process, each citizen was entitled to buy a book of vouchers, which were in turn tradable for shares in the enterprises being privatized. The scheme was invented by one of the followers of Václav Klaus, a bright theoretical economist, Dušan Tříska. Born into a prominent Communist family, he had been one of those who had educated themselves about modern economic thought while pretending to work at resolving the contradictions of the system of planned economy. In his spare time, he liked to smoke marijuana with friends while playing Monopoly. Play money and outlandish schemes came easily to him.

There was an element of genius, yet also something deceptive about the simplicity of the scheme. For about thirty dollars one received a book of vouchers with a nominal value of about one thousand dollars. One then had a choice to exchange the coupons for shares, playing the market, and hopefully watching their value grow, or one could put them in trust with one of the rapidly emerging 'investment funds' and for a small fee let them do the work. It was a win-win, especially after some of the funds offered to buy the vouchers up front for a multiple of the original investment. And six months before an election it was politically immensely rewarding especially if you were the minister of finance, and had every single voucher furnished with a facsimile of your signature.

THE END OF CZECHOSLOVAKIA

*Among the most formidable of the obstacles which the new Constitution
will have to encounter may readily be distinguished the obvious interest
of a certain class of men in every State to resist all changes which may
hazard a diminution of the power, emolument, and consequence of
the offices they hold under the State establishments; and the perverted
ambition of another class of men, who will either hope to aggrandize
themselves by the confusions of their country, or will flatter themselves
with fairer prospects of elevation from the subdivision of the empire into
several partial confederacies than from its union under one government.*
            – Alexander Hamilton, Federalist No. 1, quoted by
            Václav Havel in a speech on the first anniversary of
                the Velvet Revolution, 17 November 1990[1]

IN HIS FIRST NEW YEAR'S ADDRESS to the nation on 1 January 1990,
Havel set as his first task 'to ensure that we soon step up to the ballot boxes
in a free election'. This was widely accepted, but some would question his
sense of priorities when he proclaimed that his second task would be 'to
guarantee that we approach these elections as two self-governing nations
who respect each other's interests, national identity, religious traditions,
and symbols'. The words turned out to be prophetic, though perhaps not
sufficiently so. They showed that Havel had spent years thinking about what

---

1 *Works 6*, 299–300.

was wrong with Czechoslovakia, and not just in terms of ideology. Just as with the German issue, he was able to sense the seismic faults underneath the seemingly solid façade of the country's geography, demography and federal make-up. The new Czechoslovak state had been dreamt up during World War I by Masaryk and Czech and Slovak exiles in Paris, London and New York, agreed upon in Cleveland and Pittsburgh, declared in Washington, DC, and given international blessing at the Versailles Peace Conference in 1919. There ensued a bitter argument about the guarantees and pledges given to the smaller nation by the bigger one during the negotiations, regarding autonomy, self-governance and balanced representation. There was a lot of good will on both sides to make the marriage work, but not enough understanding, and, on the Czech part at least, not always enough sensitivity. Although Czech teachers, administrators and bankers came to run Slovak schools, offices and banks more out of necessity than out of any colonial instinct, they were still resented by the local population as foreigners and often as overlords – in fact, as not all that much different from their previous Hungarian masters. When, in the aftermath of the infamous Munich Agreement, Czechoslovakia collapsed under the Nazi onslaught, the Slovaks did not see much reason to continue being loyal to the common state and went their own way, disastrously aligning their destiny with that of Hitler's Germany. Although Czechoslovakia was reunited after the defeat of Nazism, the resentments lingered until they were, along with much else, suppressed by the brutality of totalitarian Communism, one of whose first targets was 'Slovak bourgeois nationalism'. The brief thaw of the Prague Spring provided the opening for a fresh discussion of the national issue, and paved the way for the constitutional reforms that turned Czechoslovakia into a federal state. The reform was enacted, but the dark cloud of normalization, under the leadership of one Gustáv Husák (once jailed by his fellow Communists as a Slovak bourgeois nationalist) obscured it before it could be implemented and applied to real life. And thus, days after the Velvet Revolution, Czechoslovakia found itself with some of the institutions of a fair and equal federation, but little sense of fairness and equality. Havel was one of the few people who saw this.

What took a little longer to sink in was the inescapable sense of different priorities on the two banks of the Morava river, which divided the two parts of the federation. Whereas Bohemia and Moravia, the zone of prosperity and industrial excellence before World War II, had suffered its worst decline in two centuries during the twenty years of normalization, the Slovaks could point to the federation as a significant if largely symbolic accomplishment, and to the economic benefits of industrialization driven by the defence industries newly located there. As a consequence, there were far fewer people in Slovakia willing openly to confront the Communist regime. Of the initial 241 signatories of Charter 77, only six were Slovaks, including Havel's friend Miroslav Kusj, and the bewitching storyteller Dominik Tatarka. In November 1976, Zdeněk Mlynář tried to contact Alexander Dubček to gain his support for the initiative, in vain. By 1989, around forty of the almost 2,000 Chartists were Slovak. In other words, whereas normalization had been a national disaster for the Czechs, Slovak society still saw itself, in spite of all the problems, as a 'society on the rise.'[2] The urgency to rid itself of most vestiges of the Communist era was less palpable there. Also the drive to reunite with the West, so self-evident for the Czechs, had less unanimous support in Slovakia, a more traditional society with historically stronger pan-Slavist leanings.

The exacerbation of the differences between Czechoslovak, Czech and Slovak political representations, and to a lesser extent between Czechs and Slovaks themselves, was by far the most serious of the myriad of problems and crises to be addressed during the first two and a half years of Havel's presidency. Just like the Civic Forum in Bohemia and Moravia, the Public Against Violence in Slovakia started to unravel almost immediately after the first victorious election. In another parallel, the split occurred between the original leaders of the movement with pre-revolutionary credentials, and the new breed of ambitious pragmatists parachuted into government and parliamentary positions. Whereas the first group, strong on claims to moral leadership but weak on real power, continued to cooperate with the president and the federal government, the second, led by the Slovak Prime Minister Vladimír Mečiar, sought to buttress its power and in doing so was not averse to exploiting resentments and feelings of inferiority that existed, rightly or wrongly, in Slovakia.

Once again, Havel was appealed to for advice and rescue in his role as the moral arbiter-in-chief. For more than a year, he tried in vain to

---

2   Martin Bútora, and Zora Bútorová, 'Nesnesitelná lehkost rozchodu' ('The Unbearable Lightness of Separation'), in Kipke and Vodička (1993).

bridge the differences between the 'revolutionaries', whose ranks included a number of his personal friends, and the 'opportunists', in a series of visits, often improvised, to Slovakia. Many of the meetings took place in Bórik, the former Bratislava Communist Party hotel built like a bunker above the city to oppress and intimidate both the population of the Slovak capital and its own guests. And once again, Havel found that his magic was failing when applied to politicians who were immune to moral arguments and prone to populism. He was also treading a very fine line, trying to adjudicate quarrels within one of the two national governments, and thus opening himself to the charge of interfering in affairs that were outside his constitutional brief.

Slovak Prime Minister Vladimír Mečiar was unlike any of the Czech politicians Havel had met. A former corporate lawyer and amateur boxer, fiercely proud and self-conscious simultaneously, he was prone to bouts of sentimental devotion alternating with open, irrational hostility, both harnessed to an unflinching drive for power. This cyclical aspect of his personality was so pronounced that at several critical moments he disappeared from his office for days on end and was rumoured to be wandering, in deep depression, through the vast forests in the mountains of central Slovakia. In November 1990, during one of Havel's regular stays in Bratislava, the panicking leadership of the Public Against Violence sought an urgent meeting with the president in the Borik Hotel, just as he was preparing to leave. The Slovak prime minister left his office earlier in the day, leaving a resignation letter giving as the reason, 'I was deserted along with my nation', and was nowhere to be found. Could Havel persuade him to come back? Havel could not quite understand. Were they not the same people who complained to him about Mečiar every time he came to Bratislava? Should not they be pleased that Mečiar was finally taking the burden off their shoulders? Yes, yes, but there was no one as popular in Slovakia as Mečiar, and if he left now, the government would fall, chaos would ensue and the radical nationalists would sense their opportunity with unforeseeable consequences. Havel relented, but to fulfil his task he first had to get hold of the elusive politician. When he finally succeeded in contacting Mečiar through his attractive red-haired personal assistant Anna Nagyová – nicknamed 'Anna the Divine' by the president's men – the Slovak Prime minister agreed to meet, but only one-on-one and under the condition that the incriminating abdication letter would be 'disppeared'. In a mad chase on the highway connecting Bratislava to Prague he finally caught up with Mečiar in a roadside motel, 'At The Red Rock', on the Czecho-Slovak border, while the leadership of the Public Against Violence was hiding behind the trees to avoid being seen. According to Havel and Karel Schwarzenberg, on whose presence Havel insisted, he was in bad shape, paranoiac and emotional in turns, but he finally agreed to return, pledging his eternal loyalty and friendship to the 'only politician in the country that I can trust'.

But the internal problems within the Slovak leadership did not go away. When in March 1991 Mečiar initiated his own political faction 'For a Democratic Slovakia', the leadership of the Public Against Violence finally decided to act, deposed Mečiar as prime minister, and had him replaced by Ján Čarnogurský, a respected, though not popular Slovak Catholic dissident and nationalist. They soon discovered the truth in Lyndon B. Johnson's comment about J. Edgar Hoover that it was 'probably better to have him inside the tent pissing out, than outside the tent pissing in', for from that moment on, Mečiar, who immediately launched a new party, the Movement for Democratic Slovakia (HZDS), worked unwaveringly and effectively to undermine the position of the federal government in general, and of Havel – whom he suspected of personal betrayal – in particular. This was a recurring problem, for which the expectations of people who mistook Havel's invariable civility and kindness in personal encounters for expressions of political support were more to blame than anything Havel really said or did.

Mečiar was far from being alone. There was the nationalist, often delusional fringe of Slovak politics, some of them assembled around the repository of the Slovak national heritage, Matica Slovenská (The Slovak Matrix). There were elements of the Slovak Catholic clergy, partly discredited, just like its Czech counterpart, by collaboration with the Communist regime, turning to the wartime Slovak State for a model of national autonomy. The nationalist contagion expressed itself not only in anti-federal or anti-Czech sentiments, but also in attacks against Hungarians, exemplified by repeated efforts to enact Slovak as the only national language in a country with a ten per cent Hungarian minority, against the Romas and against Jews. And there were Havel's former allies, including the two most public faces of the Tender Revolution in Slovakia, Ján Budaj and Milan Kňažko, who both felt betrayed and embittered at having been wronged or neglected.

Budaj, an environmental activist and a consummate political animal, had to leave the leadership of the VPN under a cloud because of alleged ties to the Communist secret police. He protested his innocence and appealed to Havel for moral support, but was spurned on the advice of some of Havel's closest Slovak friends. Kňažko turned against Havel following the vice-presidential gaffe. After the second presidential election, he returned to Slovakia and became the minister of international affairs in the Slovak government, and eventually, though temporarily, No. 2 in the Movement for Democratic Slovakia, which Mečiar had founded as a vehicle to regain power.

The break-up with Mečiar and Kňažko, and its not insignificant consequences, for both enjoyed considerable popularity in Slovakia, illustrate Havel's tendency, not easily explainable, to make bitter and irreconcilable enemies. Of course, politics is one area of human activity where it is much easier to make enemies than friends. Even so, of all politicians, Havel probably took the most pains to be consistently respectful, polite and cooperative with his peers. One would never catch him saying something disparaging about another public figure in public, and only rarely in private. Even then, it would come as an offhand, humorous remark rather than as a hostile condemnation.

The clue can most likely be found in the expectations that Havel unwittingly provoked in people he befriended or cooperated with at various points in his life. They were a direct complement to the unique magnetism of his personality. Whether this was his small, somewhat frail physique, his soft demeanour, his explicit acknowledgements of helplessness, ignorance, confusion, fatigue and despair, he seemed to be constantly in need of help, to radiate a permanent Mayday signal, causing a large number of people to rush to his rescue, to offer sympathy, help or tender care. It is impossible to tell whether he was aware of this, but sometimes it seemed as though he were himself the ultimate embodiment of the power of the powerless, a man who could achieve almost anything by making clear his utter inability to do it alone. Having been drawn out to extend their sympathy and devotion to Havel, often to a degree directly proportional to his perceived helplessness, some came to expect reciprocity, only to realize that it was not forthcoming, or at any rate not forthcoming to the same degree. On the one hand, this is almost a trivial fact about most exceptional people: they do not sing to the same sheet of music as the rest of us, nor do they observe the same norms.

Any personal and emotional relationship with them is thus asymmetrical by definition.

In Havel, however, there was an added complexity, in that, unlike many of the greats and giants of history, he was totally free of any egomaniacal or narcissistic preoccupation with himself and his own needs. He was the most considerate person one could find, always worrying about the welfare of others, always wary of trying to elevate himself or of exaggerating his own importance or, especially, hurting others' feelings.

Perfect, though, Havel was not. He was always there for his friends when alerted by others, never refused a plea for help, but in his preoccupation with a myriad of ideas and issues he was often slow to detect a crisis, an expectation or a hurt in a person close to him. 'I'm not really an empathetic man,' he admitted himself.[3]

After the 'hyphen' affair, there followed one crisis after another, most of them hardly epoch-making, many quite petty and some ridiculous. The first broke out after Havel publicly confirmed Foreign Minister Dienstbier's announcement that the Czech and Slovak Federative Republic, as it was now called, until recently the fourth largest arms manufacturer and exporter in the world, would henceforth discontinue its practice of supplying arms to every bloody dictator and every terrorist group around the world.[4] Havel's motives were primarily humanitarian, but they were also sound foreign policy, helping to rebrand the country quickly as a responsible and morally aware member of the international community.

Disastrously, Havel failed to take into account the fact that, because of the strategic considerations of the Warsaw Pact leaders, the bulk of the Czechoslovak armaments industry had been moved from the traditional industrial heartland of Bohemia and Moravia to rural Slovakia, away from the East–West frontline. At the time, it had brought a measure of industrialization and prosperity to the underdeveloped parts of central Slovakia. Now it was Havel's moral gesture that was seemingly to blame for ending that prosperity and for the ballooning unemployment in many of the Slovak one-industry towns. It was no use trying to explain that the prosperity was over in any case since there were suddenly few markets

---

3 Letter to Ivan Medek, 27 January 1984, VHL ID9100.
4 This included large amounts of Semtex plastic explosive sold to Colonel Gaddafi, who readily rerouted it to the IRA or Black September.

and fewer customers for Soviet-designed armoured carriers, towed guns and bazookas. In Slovakia, Havel was becoming unpopular. He realized the danger, to the country more than to himself, and worked hard to offset it. He altered his diary to spend more time in Slovakia, not just to visit, but to conduct his presidential duties there for a few days every month, receiving foreign officials and domestic politicians, and trying to see and speak to as many Slovaks as possible. The results were mixed. His meetings with workers in the rapidly rusting Slovak industrial belt did not go too well, and his determination to highlight human rights issues, such as the dreadful living conditions in the shantytowns inhabited by the Roma ethnic minority, hardly constituted a popular cause with the average Slovak.

Extending the presidential presence to Slovakia and its capital seemed like a logical move. A branch of the Office of the President, headed by the former dissident Miroslav Kusý, opened in the compound of the Bratislava Castle to represent him in his absence and to provide support when he was present. The presidential flag flew over the ancient castle, and the presidential guard in Pišték's new uniforms stood before the gates whenever the president visited. A team of smart and pretty young women handled the president's Slovak diary, his contacts with the Slovak government and parliament, and his uneasy relationship with the Slovak media.

Havel also increased the Slovak presence in the Prague Castle. Undiscouraged by the mixed experience with Milan Kňažko, he recruited Martin Bútora, a sociologist and writer, and one of the leading brains of the Public Against Violence, to join the team as an adviser on minority and human rights issues. After the first elections, he persuaded the philosopher Milan Šimečka, perhaps the most respected former dissident in Slovakia, to come to the Castle as a roving adviser. Unfortunately, Šimečka felt miserable in the office, whether because of the gathering clouds over the Federation or because of misgivings about the way Havel handled the issue; he died of a stroke only three months later.

Even though both political representations agreed on the concept of a 'fair and equitable' federation, they found it difficult to agree on what this definition meant. In December 1990, after a marathon session, the Federal Assembly finally adopted the law dividing the competencies between the federal and the two national parliaments, devolving the federation further. The breakthrough occurred after Havel personally intervened with the parliament, and proposed legislation on referendum, the constitutional court and emergency powers for the president to pre-empt a possible gridlock.

After a year, Havel also felt he needed to break out of the oppressive ghetto of the Borik Hotel, and he asked the Bratislava office to find him more hospitable accommodation for his regular visits. The good news soon arrived that the girls had discovered a brand-new privately-owned hotel in the forested hills above the capital. The president was pleased. On the next visit to Bratislava, the presidential motorcade stopped before a modern white building secluded in a garden away from the traffic. Havel liked what he saw and proposed a drink in the bar before retiring to get ready for the following day's schedule. The drinks arrived, and with them a number of rather attractive and friendly young ladies in various stages of partial attire. Havel's advisers paled. They were not about to blame the girls from the office, who were new to the job and commendably inexperienced in the ways of the world, for putting the president up in what was obviously a brothel, but they were terrified of the spectre of the next day's headlines in the Slovak nationalist newspapers. 'The president of love and truth in a whorehouse' was the mildest they could think of. Possible condemnations of the Czech sexual imperialist-in-chief coming to Slovakia to prey on innocent local girls seemed more ominous. To minimize the damage they tried to drag Havel away and lock him up in his room; instead, they ran into the incurable curiosity of the playwright, who recognized an absurd scene with a potential when he saw one. He finished his drink at leisure, shielded against temptation by a wall of his advisers' bodies.

Other incidents were not so amusing. Against the better judgement of some of his Slovak staff, Havel decided to take one of his regular trips to Bratislava on 14 March 1991, the anniversary of the declaration of the autonomous but Nazi-allied Slovak state in 1939. The nationalists were planning a demonstration in the same square where, fifteen months earlier, crowds had been glorifying Havel and the Tender Revolution. Havel felt that by not going he would be showing weakness. After a heated argument with the team he agreed to pay tribute to a new memorial to Czech and Slovak solidarity by the river and to go straight from there to his Bratislava office, avoiding a confrontation with the demonstrators. But, as he was passing by on the embankment of the Danube some five hundred metres away, and heard the shouting and the slogans, his curiosity once again took over. 'There is nothing wrong with me going to take a peek, is there?' he argued. 'There is no law to prevent the president from visiting any public space he wants to see, no?' There was no point in arguing and so the president went.

What he saw and experienced was more than he had bargained for. As soon as the crowd took note of his presence, the slogans turned personal and aggressive. 'Czechs back to Prague!' 'Shame on Havel!' were some of the more printable. Then mass instincts took over and the crowd surged to confront Havel and his party. The Slovak police cordon around Havel was soon outnumbered, and so was the presidential security detail. In the end, Havel was shielded by a couple of bodyguards and a circle of friends who locked their arms around him. The feeling was suffocating. The attackers were becoming more hostile and aggressive with every minute. A boy, not more than ten years old, kicked Jiří Křižan, a giant of a man from good Moravian Protestant stock, in his shins with the cry: 'You dirty Czech Jew!' It was a near miss. There was actually a Jewish Czech standing right next to him.

It took about ten minutes and a large number of none too gentle shoves and pushes to extricate Havel from the centre of the maelstrom and escort him out through one of the side streets. For all that time he showed no more emotion than his typical mild curiosity. 'They seemed to be rather animated,' he said. 'Why did we leave so soon?'

It took about a week for the bruises and scratches to heal. The deeper wounds in the relationship between Czechs and Slovaks, however, showed no signs of healing. Although the tone of the political debates and arguments remained largely civil and for most part respectful, the nationalist crowd of about 3,000 in Bratislava that day having been an exception to the rule, the newly liberated media, and in particular its previously non-existent tabloid wing, kept stoking up a frenzy of accusations, allegations and slander, purporting to show either Czechs as hell-bent on dominating and exploiting Slovaks or, conversely, Slovaks as conspiring with ultra-right Catholic and crypto-fascist circles abroad to reconstitute the wartime Slovak State. Some politicians, mostly on the Slovak side, quickly saw the issue as an ideal vehicle on which to hitch their wagons. Gradually, a constitutional and parliamentary gridlock emerged. Although the federal constitution was built on the assumption of the precedence of federal laws over the state (national) legislation, there was no institution to enforce the precedence. The requisite power of the Constitutional Court, requiring a constitutional majority in the parliament to come into force, was blocked by the Slovak half of the upper chamber pending the approval of the new federal constitution, for which there existed no constitutional majority, an exemplary Catch-22.

Havel and wiser heads among the politicians on both sides knew from the start that the issue would not be resolved through demonstrations or media attacks. The president took the initiative and convened the first of what would become a marathon of constitutional negotiations with the national leaders. The chances looked good. A great deal of mutual respect and even liking on both sides, as well as a genuine respect for the president, still existed. There were several moments when the participants seemed to arrive at an agreement, only for the deal to unravel at the next news conference, or upon the return of one of the two national delegations to their respective capitals.

The problems became even more intractable when the Czech prime minister, Petr Pithart, whether out of impatience, ambition or both, initiated direct bilateral talks with the Slovak political representation, eschewing the federal level altogether. In August 1990, the two national governments met publicly for the first time in Trenčianské Teplice. It is this moment that Čalfa, a Slovak but a committed federalist, saw as the fatal step on the road to perdition. As long as there existed the asymmetric triangulation in the talks between the federal and national representations, a solution might have been impossible, but so was an irreconcilable split. The introduction of symmetry opened the way to a divorce.[5]

The fact that there was not one but two kinds of national demands on the Slovak side complicated the talks still further. Ján Čarnogurský and his colleagues from the Slovak Christian-Democratic Party, supported by nationalists of the traditional variety, were more open to compromise over some of the practical issues of government, but adamant about redress of what they saw as the original sin of violating the pledges made to the Slovak representatives in the founding of Czechoslovakia in 1918. From this perspective, they saw the founding moment of the state and everything that followed as of dubious legitimacy, and insisted on a complete renewal

---

5 Conversation with Marián Čalfa, 29 August 2013.

of the Czech and Slovak bond, this time on an absolutely free and equitable basis. The Czechs had no fundamental objections to renewing the vows. But they did not feel comfortable with Čarnogurský's argument that to make such an act voluntary beyond any doubt would necessitate the disbandment of Czechoslovakia, even if only for one fraction of a second. Whether it was because of the legal implications of this approach, or because of doubts as to the real intentions of their Slovak colleagues, fuelled by Čarnogurský's stated ambition for a Slovak star in the future firmament of the EU, the idea was a non-starter for the Czechs.

The other Slovak school of thought, exemplified by Vladimír Mečiar, was not much focused on the issues of history or the niceties of the constitutional process. Their perspective was simply the division of power between the national and federal governments. They did not have too many problems in preserving what they called a 'genuine' federation, as long as the real power rested with the national governments. In reality, the devolution was proceeding quite fast as it was. The national governments already had total responsibility for areas such as education, health care and environment, and a shared responsibility for the economy, police and public order, and fiscal matters. It was not enough. Mečiar and his colleagues now argued that a genuine federation was impossible without the Slovak government also acquiring responsibility for the army on Slovak territory, for the representation of Slovakia abroad and for currency and monetary matters, including a Slovak central bank. Although minor compromises had been reached, such as the emergence of national ministries for international (but not foreign) affairs, the fundamental objection of the Czech side was that shared defence and foreign policies, and a monetary and fiscal union constitute the fundamental characteristics of a country, and without them there would not be one country but two. Mečiar was not impressed.

While all of the negotiations, which took place in various Czech and Slovak towns in the effort to find the right chemistry (Lány, Kroměříž, Slavkov, Budmerice, Biela Papirničky, Židlochovice, Karlovy Vary), were long, exhausting and inconclusive, the clearer it became that there was no consensual solution to be found for a federation of two with two equal votes, the more depressing and tiresome the talks became. In the beginning of February 1991, during one such meeting that as usual dragged on long into the night, Jiří Křižan, the president's domestic policy adviser, scribbled a note to me: 'The federation, my dear friend, is up shit creek.' 'That's what I've been telling you,' was my reply.[6]

There was also a touch of tragicomedy. As the Slovak demands grew and the Czech opposition weakened, there suddenly appeared politicians in Moravia, historically always part of the same country with the same language and much the same culture as Bohemia, who had apparently discovered their own nationalist fervour. It was hard for anyone, including its propagators, to take this idea very seriously, but still the Moravian party managed to win over ten per cent of the vote in the elections for the national parliaments, giving it a voice at the negotiating table in the talks. The catharsis came at a meeting of the president with representatives of the national parliaments in the Slovak town of Budmerice, when the leader of the Moravian party, an ageing and somewhat confused psychologist, Boleslav Bárta, engaged in a long-winded justification of Moravian claims based on data from the recent national census. When he succeeded in completely exhausting both his audience and himself, he slumped in his chair, dead. It took a while for his neighbours to notice. The Moravian idea did not survive him for long.

One could reasonably conclude that as long as the dialogue remained civil, and as long as the claims were voiced as suggestions rather than ultimata, the process could continue for any length of time without seriously threatening political or social stability. Unfortunately, this was a luxury the country could not afford. It was caught in the middle of a monumental political, social and economic transition, which would end up in failure without reform measures to be agreed upon and implemented. The external context was just as ominous. Yugoslavia, a nearby country of the same pedigree dating back to the end of World War I and with a similar, though vastly more complex ethnic make-up, was falling apart in a paroxysm of nationalistic hatred, violence and atrocities. It had been and remained unthinkable that anything like that could happen in Czechoslovakia, but the thought must have occurred to Havel and others, at least as a nightmare or a bad dream. It had certainly occurred to Michal Kováč, the future first president of Slovakia, who later praised the ultimate division of Czechoslovakia as having prevented 'a conflict in the centre of Europe'.[7]

When the intended demonstration of Czech and Slovak unity in

---

6 Handwritten notes, 3 February 1991. Author's archive.
7 Michal Kováč, Address to the Slovak nation, 31 December 1992.

Bratislava on Independence Day, 28 October 1991, attended by Havel and other leading federal politicians, both Czech and Slovak, was pelted with eggs, Havel felt that something had to be done to arrest the slide of the country into a constitutional and political stalemate. On 3 November 1991, he invited top federal and national politicians,[8] to join him at Hrádeček for a final attempt to break the impasse. He left nothing to chance, inviting the guests to stay overnight and cooking his own goulash for the dinner. As the *pièce de résistance* he produced a twenty-three-year-old bottle of slivovitz that the village locals had buried in the ground on the day of the Soviet invasion in August 1968, to be recovered in better days. The meeting produced a transcript of more than 200 pages of spirited and amiable debate, with no clear result. Participating in the meeting as an assistant cook, constitution co-drafter, psychologist on duty and communiqué wordsmith, I proposed a joint statement endorsed by the president on four separate occasions, only to see it bogged down in a metaphysical discussion about the competencies of the federation emanating from a treaty between the two constituent nations, which, however, could not be a treaty under the federal constitution, and would thus have to revert to the two hens conceiving one egg, which would have to be delivered by another chicken. Or something. The slivovitz was excellent, though.

Even if the dignitaries could somehow agree to a way forward, it might not have made much of a difference. The two most popular politicians in the country apart from Havel, Václav Klaus and Vladimír Mečiar, the leaders, respectively, of the Czech Civic Democratic Party, and of the Slovak Movement for Democratic Slovakia, were conspicuously missing. Any agreement would count for little without their support, which was, for different but compatible reasons, not forthcoming.

Untypically for him, Havel decided to 'bang the table'. In several weeks of frantic activity in the last two months of 1991, a package of draft constitutional amendments was put together in the presidential office, which did not prescribe any specific way of resolving the federation's problems, but suggested ways out of the impasse. The proposals included an immediate constitutional provision for a referendum on whether the nation should

---

8 Speaker of the Federal Assembly Alexander Dubček, Federal Prime Minister Čalfa, Slovak Prime Minister Ján Čarnogurský, Czech Prime Minister Petr Pithart, Speaker of the Slovak National Council František Mikloško, Czech Minister of Justice Dagmar Burešová, Deputy Speaker of the Czech National Council Jan Kalvoda, and federal ministers Jan Stráský and Pavel Hoffmann.

remain as one entity comprising two equal and autonomous republics, or become two separate, independent countries.

Knowing all too well that his proposals did not stand much of a chance in the gridlocked parliament, Havel decided to summon the people's power. In a scene reminiscent of the days of the Velvet Revolution, he proclaimed his proposals from the same balcony in the middle of Wenceslas Square from which he had spoken during the revolution, before proceeding to submit them formally to the parliament at the top of the square. This time, too, the people arrived and supported the president.

But the power of the powerless, as Havel repeatedly found, did not work nearly so well in a parliamentary democracy. True, the politicians were shocked and not a little shamed by the clear popular appeal to stop the obstructions and find a compromise everybody could live with. And for the first few days they made a lot of mollifying noises. Then, when the popular excitement subsided, Havel's proposals quickly got bogged down in procedural objections, amendments and committee votes. They did not even make it to a vote on the floor.

There was also the fact that there was no outpouring of public support for Havel's proposals in Slovakia. A few hundred people demonstrated publicly, and another initiative called 'The Bridge' came into being, but that was basically all. One thing that the Czech and Slovak politicians did find easy to agree upon was that this was after all a matter that could not be resolved in the streets but in the parliament. The president could not very well disagree with this, except to point out that the matter was not being resolved.

The repeated failures of the president to push his ideas through parliament led some of his advisers to argue the necessity of creating his own political machine, a president's faction, to advocate and defend them throughout the legislative process. A non-paper by the present author to that effect was circulated to the president and his advisers in early 1991.[9] I wasn't necessarily advocating a classical political party, but perhaps a cross-party coalition relying on the support of Havel's friends and allies from revolutionary days and before, who were now members of several political parties. It could even be one of the existing political parties, which would

---

9   To: Havel, Schwarzenberg, Křižan, Vondra, Kantor, Masák, 25 February 1991. Author's archive.

recognize Havel as its leader and his ideas as its platform. The orphaned Civic Forum, now calling itself the Civic Movement, could possibly fit that description. Or it could be a brand-new political movement, providing a political home for everyone who continued to support the idea of a Czech and Slovak federation as a democratic, secular, humanistic, modern and cultured country.

Havel was sceptical but willing to listen. When the situation continued to deteriorate, a war game of the 'pro-party' and 'anti-party' factions, drafted from among Havel's team, was organized over a weekend in the presidential retreat at Lány in January 1992, with a view to the next parliamentary elections coming up in June. The outcome was inconclusive. The anti-party had to concede that without a political vehicle there was little the president could do to prevent the looming split or to achieve other goals. The pro-party, to which I belonged, had to acknowledge that the move would radically alter the character of Havel's presidency and bring it closer to the daily grind and mill of faction politics, which Havel wished to transcend.

After two days it became clear that Havel was unwilling to make the compromise. In summing up the discussion, he acknowledged all the reasons that spoke in favour of the party solution. It would be the right thing to do, he said. But he could not see himself at the head of such a thing. And with whatever feelings, his advisers on both sides of the issue could not see him there, either. In all likelihood, it hardly mattered. It was too late.

When the last-ditch attempt at a treaty between the two national parliaments, negotiated by the expert groups of the two national governments at Milovy in March 1992, failed to clear the steering committee of the Slovak National Council by one vote, the writing was on the wall. Even if it succeeded, the validity of such an act by two governments that were both rapidly losing popular support would have been challenged after the election that June. In Mečiar's view, the document from Milovy could not even be considered an agreement. His Movement for Democratic Slovakia came out triumphant in the elections, surpassing the polls, the expectations of its supporters and the worst fears of its federalist opponents. The Civic Democratic Party (ODS) of Václav Klaus scored an equally big victory in the Czech Republic. The Civic Movement bombed, not making it into the parliament at all.

What followed was the last controversial fiat in the history of Czechoslovakia but arguably also one of the smoothest processes in dividing a country in the history of mankind. It was masterminded and largely controlled neither by Havel, who was faced with the impossible task of appointing a federal government made up of two parties whose leaders could not agree on almost anything except not ceding control to the president, nor by Mečiar, who apparently was not entirely sure whether he wanted to push for full independence or just maximize his gains in the new situation, but by the most decisive and clear-minded of the three, Václav Klaus.

Klaus could not envisage serving in a government headed or co-directed by Mečiar, whose economic ideas ran much closer than his to a corporativist concept of the state. The two men's personal characteristics of stubbornness and assertiveness verging on egomania portended a clash of apocalyptic proportions. Perhaps more importantly, Klaus knew that in the new parliament there was no chance of overcoming the constitutional gridlock and arriving at a workable compromise that would enable reforms to go ahead. As the cool-headed, logical chess player that he was, he must have realized that there was only one option acceptable to him: to divide a state that had come out of the ruins of World War I and barely survived World War II, after seventy-four years.

Mečiar did not take much persuading. Spokesmen for the two leaders emerged from a late-night meeting in the improbable setting of Mies van de Rohe's Villa Tugendhat in Brno to announce that by a joint agreement of the two parties Czechoslovakia would be no more before the year was out.

As the results of the election were coming in, Havel and his team assembled in the presidential office; they recognized that the bells were tolling for the federation and the presidency. For Havel this meant not just a catastrophic political defeat and a shipwreck of the state on his watch, but a blow at the very core of his philosophy of tolerance and of a civic, rather than national, ethos. It also presented him with a grave constitutional dilemma. As the head of state, who had sworn allegiance to the integrity of the federation and its constitution, should he stand up to what was after all a private deal between the leaders of two political parties, even if they were both legitimate winners of a democratic election in their respective parts of the country, or should he accept the inevitable? Again, days and nights were spent in an agonizing analysis of the options, none of which seemed to yield an honourable way out. Havel strongly felt and publicly insisted that if the federation was to be divided it should happen on the basis of a popular referendum rather than a backroom deal, even more so because neither of the two victorious parties had clearly campaigned on a platform of separation. At the same time he knew that he had no way of forcing a referendum without a constitutional majority in both sides of both houses of parliament, and this was not forthcoming. And he was realistic enough to know that even if this could somehow be achieved, and even if a majority of the voters in both the Czech lands and Slovakia came out in favour of the common state, as opinion polls still indicated they might, the parliament would still be gridlocked, the constitutional stalemate would not be overcome and the country would become dangerously dysfunctional. There loomed the spectre of a breakdown of democratic institutions; for a referendum to provide a cure it is necessary for the losing side to accept its results. There is no such certainty with large and determined minorities, and the Czechoslovak crisis did not occur in a vacuum. The ongoing and worsening bloodshed in former Yugoslavia had been preceded by a referendum in four of its six republics. As difficult as Havel found it to accept the legitimacy of the process leading to separation, he knew that throwing the full power of his office behind an attempt to stop it in its tracks would pose unacceptable risks. In fact, he had stated his position vis-à-vis a situation that he hoped would never occur, more than a year before: 'Rather than to live for years in a non-functioning federation or in some kind of a pseudo-federation, which is only a burden and a source of complications, it is better to live in two independent countries.'[10]

Knowing that it was most likely a waste of time, Havel still went through the motions dictated by the constitution, and by political decorum. He consulted with the political parties in the new parliament. He went to Slovakia for his last trip as the federal president, and visited the newly elected Slovak National Council. He invited Mečiar to a meeting at the Prague Castle and reported on its results, or the lack thereof, in a late-night press conference. Walking on hot coals all this time, he never let up, never succumbed to frustration or anger. He saw it as his residual task to do his utmost to preserve as much of the good will between the two nations as possible. He accepted the proposals of the two parties for a weak, caretaker federal government, while the two strongmen, Klaus and

---

10 An Address to the Slovak Nation, Bratislava, 14 March 1993, *Works* 6, 336.

Mečiar, stood at the head of their respective national governments, leaving no one in doubt about where things were headed. Havel may have bowed to the inevitable, but he would not preside over it. On 17 July, a few hours after the Slovak parliament adopted a declaration of sovereignty, in effect elevating the validity of the Slovak constitution and legislation above that of the federation, Havel announced his impending resignation. Three days later, in shirtsleeves, looking tired but at peace with himself, he said farewell at a press conference held in the park of the Lány retreat on a hot and humid summer afternoon.

Waiting as a State of Hope

Hope is not a conviction that something will turn out well, but a certainty that something has a meaning regardless of how it turns out.

— Václav Havel

FOR THE SECOND TIME IN HIS LIFE, Havel's exhilarating roller-coaster ride fuelled on the adrenaline of success and popular admiration, an endless chain of cigarettes, glasses of beer and wine, and a formidable combination of prescription uppers and downers, ended up by hitting a wall. As of 20 July, when his resignation came into effect, his previously overcrowded diary was suddenly empty. The process of separation, in which succession rights had to be established, assets, including military equipment and embassies abroad divided, and the parameters of the relationship between the two new countries, including the establishment of a customs and currency union, the mutual recognition of degrees and qualifications, as well as various issues regarding citizenship, took almost another six months. Havel did not play a part. He felt, in his own words, 'like a deflated balloon'. Previously, in similar situations, he had managed to reinsert himself into the equation by acts of singular courage and profound reflection. This time was different. He could not endorse the rush towards the separation, which ran against the grain of his conviction, his philosophy, his understanding of democracy and his sense of responsibility, but neither could he, in view of the risks and uncertainties this would pose for 15 million of his fellow citizens, take a heroic stand against it. He had not simply suffered a defeat, something that he had been used to and which in the past had inspired some of his best writing and some of his bravest acts of civil disobedience, but he now found himself, at least temporarily, irrelevant.

He withdrew from the Castle to the 'lower office' in his house on the embankment, which had previously served as his private bureau, handling his theatre and literary rights, private assets, Olga's diary, and the like. There he had a loyal team of friends from pre-revolutionary days, such as Anna Freimanová, Vladimír Hanzel and others, who could provide him with personal comfort and basic clerical support. If he were to continue in politics, however, he would have to look for a new political team, for his old one had totally disbanded and scattered by mutual agreement even before the end of Czechoslovakia and the federal presidency. The break-up was friendly and warm-hearted but still painful. Both the president and his team felt that things had to change. The advisers were exhausted and spent. To Havel's critics they grew to exemplify the bohemian, non-bureaucratic style of his presidency, which made them surrogate targets for attacks actually aimed at Havel himself. Both they and the president took it largely as part and parcel of the deal. Havel often referred to the fairy-tale mythology of the good king surrounded by evil counsellors, and never hesitated to speak in their defence. Nevertheless, he must have also felt exhausted and constrained by the permanent consideration he extended to them not just as his collaborators, but also as his personal friends.

There were also some differences of opinion, which naturally emerged in the course of Havel's presidency. Although Havel and his friends continued to share the moral core of his understanding of politics, with its emphasis on individual responsibility, human rights and civic involvement, some of them began to differ on questions of its conduct and strategy. They felt that Havel's ideas remained as valid as ever, but his efforts to make them widely accepted were ineffectual in the increasingly standardized environment of political parties, parliamentary committees and backroom lobbying. They also found it difficult to design and implement consistent procedures and policies in the ever-changing environment of the office, subject to the president's latest inspiration or whim. A tightly knit group of friends inevitably functioned as a club, Havel's creative whims gave it the aspects of a court, and the president needed an office.

And so the bag of fleas dispersed. The foreign adviser became deputy foreign minister, the domestic adviser deputy minister of interior, the security consultant head of the new foreign intelligence service, and I became ambassador to Washington. The cultural advisers returned to theatre, architecture or literature. The Prince finally had some time to think about some of the property that had come back to him in a rather devastated condition. In reality, though, the group never left, but rather expanded outward. Although they missed the daily contact with Havel, they all remained close, working with him on a number of projects, corresponding and exchanging ideas, offering support and advice. Havel reciprocated in kind. At more or less regular intervals the bag of fleas and the president came back together for reunions, parties and celebrations. Most of the team members were there on his last birthday party on 1 October 2011. All of them, those still alive, were at his funeral.

But the decision Havel had to make at the end of July 1992, he had to make alone. Although the process of separation still had to play out, it was quite clear that some time around the end of the year the Czech Republic would be an independent country and need a new head of state. There were too many unknowns for Havel to be sure he could, or even wanted to, play that role, nor did he ever imply otherwise. But he did make a decision not to retire and vacate the public arena altogether. As in 1989, he made it clear that he was willing to serve if needed. Unlike in 1989, however, he could not have been quite sure he would be needed. Without a political machine, even one as loosely organized as the Civic Forum, he had neither a clear way, nor the inclination to campaign for the presidency.

He did the only thing he could do under the circumstances: wait – a skill generally in short supply among politicians. But it was not an unproductive wait. He dedicated to the phenomenon his acceptance speech as a new member of the French Academy of Humanities and Political Science in Paris on 27 October 1992.

In the speech, he drew a line between two different kinds of the phenomenon of waiting. One, waiting for Godot, is provoked by hopelessness. People who feel powerless to change the conditions of their life pin their hopes on some indeterminate 'salvation from the outside . . . It is the hope of people without hope.'[1]

The other type of waiting 'was based on the knowledge that it made

---

1 'The Academy of Humanities and Political Sciences', Paris, 17 October 1992, in *The Art of the Impossible*, 104.

sense on principle to resist by speaking the truth, simply because it was the right thing to do, without speculating whether it would lead somewhere tomorrow, or the day after, or ever . . . waiting as a state of hope, not an expression of hopelessness.'[2]

Havel went on to use the distinction as a tool to analyse – and subject to harsh criticism – his own impatience over the previous three years, when nothing was ever completed on time, if at all, and then only rarely according to plan. This impatience was for Havel another instance of the 'vain belief in the primacy of reason' and the erroneous assumption that 'the world is nothing but a cross-world puzzle to be solved . . . Without even being aware of it, I, too, submitted to the perverted belief that I was a master of reality, that the only task was to improve reality according to some existing recipe that it was entirely up to me when I did it and thus that there was no reason not to do it right away.

'In short I thought time belonged to me.

'It was, of course, a big mistake.

'The world, Being and history have their own time. We can, of course, enter that time in a creative way, but none of us has it entirely in his hands . . . If I consider my own political impatience, I realize with new urgency, that a politician of the present and the future . . . must learn, in the deepest and best sense of the word, the importance of waiting . . . His actions . . . cannot be based on a sense of superiority but must spring from humility . . . Even I – the sarcastic critic of all those who vainly attempt to explain the world – had to remind myself that *the world cannot just be explained, it must be . . . understood as well*.'[3]

Anyone can deplore the arrogance of politicians. But to say that people should be electing politicians for their ability to wait is outrageously audacious. Voters, many people would say, elect politicians exactly for their ability to change things, to achieve results – not to wait. And how many, the counter-argument would go, fulfil these expectations, how many really accomplish what they promise? Does not much of the current frustration of voters with the politicians stem from their failed expectations? But even more to the point, do the voters, in electing always the same politicians, the same parties and the same promises of change, really believe that things will

---

2 Ibid.
3 Ibid., 105–7, italics author's.

change? Are they not just pretending to expect change just as the politicians are pretending to deliver it? Ultimately, aren't the voters waiting for Godot who 'will not come, because he does not exist'?[4] The speech's indirect refutation of the romantic Marxist maxim that 'philosophers have only explained the world, it is necessary to change it as well'[5] raises the question of how much of this doctrine is still preserved as the justification of politics, all politics.

But isn't this false modesty, from a man who has been credited with contributing to one of the most momentous changes in modern history? Had he not struggled and suffered for years, exactly to achieve this change? In the speech and elsewhere, Havel would dispute that this was what he had done, and even more, that this was why he had done it. He would invoke the self-justifying nature of living in truth rather than its instrumentality in achieving change. To him, his actions would have been just as meaningful if no change had been achieved during his lifetime.

Now that there was another kind of change under way, one he had neither planned nor wished for, he was able to accept it as a proof of his belief that history unveils itself in mysterious ways, and he was content to wait.

The new power group that had emerged with the victory of the ODS in the elections was entirely different from its predecessor. Ideologically cohesive, organizationally compact, they were a group of younger men forming a tight circle around their undisputed leader, Václav Klaus. They shared his distaste for intellectual dithering, his sense of pragmatism and his penchant for quick, decisive and simple solutions. Like him, they were also not a little ambitious and wanted to get ahead, both as a political force and individually. Even less than him did they have much time for opposition, minority opinions or nuanced solutions. To some, though not all, of them Havel was something of a has-been. As they now occupied crucial positions in the government and the parliament, it was far from certain that they would support him for president.

Havel was content to wait, but did not quite expect the humiliating uncertainty to which he would be subjected. While the smaller parties in the parliament, the Christian and Social Democrats, made their support

---

4 Ibid. 107.
5 Karl Marx, '11th Thesis on Feuerbach' pamphlet.

for him as president clear, the ODS didn't declare its position publicly until the day of the election by the parliament.[6] In the end, having realized that 'there was no alternative'[7] to the ex-president in terms of moral stature and international reputation, ODS supported him, though only after making Havel painfully aware that his political destiny was now at their mercy, and framing the new constitution in such a way that he could never get out of control. Or so they hoped.

---

6 In private talks the party's representatives were more forthcoming (meeting notes, 7 July 1992, author's archive).
7 Conversation with Václav Klaus, 30 August 2013.

The Bonfire of Scruples

It is a natural disadvantage of democracy that it ties the hands of those who wish it well, and opens unlimited possibilities for those who do not take it seriously.

– *The Conspirators*

VÁCLAV HAVEL'S THIRD PRESIDENTIAL TERM thus started on a very different footing from his first two. Not only was he now elected president of a different, indeed a new, country, and not only would his powers and autonomy be significantly curtailed, but the mood had changed too. Three years before there had been wild euphoria and a sense of unlimited possibilities, but the beginning of 1993 was marked by uncertainty, doubt and a sense of loss. This was a crucial element of the Velvet Divorce; while the two parties rationally agreed that it would be best if each went their own way, they could not help but reflect on what they were losing. And not surprisingly, the sense of loss was more acute in the Czech Republic than in Slovakia, which had won genuine independence for the first time in recorded history. For a long time, it took a conscious effort to realize that the country now ended at the Morava river, and the national anthem stopped in the middle. As Jacques Rupnik, Havel's friend and external adviser, put it, 'the Czech Republic was in fact founded by the Slovaks'. The sense of a phantom limb came into play when the two nations set about building their relationship anew. In spite of the initial coolness during the Mečiar era in Slovakia, the enormous amount of good will, genuine affinity, and quite possibly a sense of guilt on both sides, eventually restored the relationship to a quality it may never have possessed during the federal period. If, in retrospect, this made the separation look like the right thing to do, it also made it seem somehow pointless. 'Ain't them paradoxes!' the Brewmaster would say.

In the beginning, however, things were gloomy. Some of Havel's friends mused aloud whether it was really necessary for him to run again, all the more so because under the new constitution, now the founding document of the country, he would be, if not subordinate, then certainly second in importance to the prime minister, his occasional ally and frequent adversary, Václav Klaus. As always when fundamental political documents were conceived, Havel had been keen to play a central role in the drafting, but holding neither an office nor a mandate, he had to do it surreptitiously, meeting with members of the parliamentary commission on the new constitution in Prague, and in a number of country pubs in the vicinity of the Lány Castle, where the commission retreated to finish its job. He was more successful in shaping the preamble of the constitution than its body.[1] He would also not be the sole candidate for the country's highest office. The Communist Party of Bohemia and Moravia, the direct heir to the unfettered rulers of the country for the previous forty years, saw it as appropriate to propose a respectable, though unknown lady cancer specialist. It was clearly a PR move, not intended to win any significant support in the parliament. The other candidate, leader of the ultra-nationalist Union for the Republic, Miroslav Sládek, was a different kettle of fish. A former official in the national censor's office during Communist days, a skilled orator with innocent blue eyes in an angelic face, he based his campaign on sowing xenophobia and hatred towards the Roma, the Germans, the Jews, the Americans . . . and Václav Havel. His sidekick, MP Vik had this to say about the governing coalition candidate when proposing Sládek to the parliament:

'The damage done by Havel's "humanistic politics" is so extensive that we cannot even contemplate its consequences . . . The three years of his rule brought about a collapse of the economy, catastrophic criminality . . . and what is worst . . . he bears the cardinal blame for the demise of our beloved

---

1 Špaček (2012), 11.

country, Czechoslovakia.'[2] He was even less complimentary about the Havel team: 'The Castle is still haunted by the spectre of greasy and weird-looking advisers and their chancellor, a typical example of patriotic nobility, proudly claiming its estates and our historical monuments. It is still haunted by the figure of the ruler in a jester's hat with bells, a megalomaniac and an artist with a chip on his shoulder . . .'[3]

The election on 26 January 1993 was broadcast live from parliament, and Havel awaited the judgement at home in a state of melancholic suspense. Watching live the debate in parliament before the vote, he believed he would not be elected.[4] For the parliament was now truly the sovereign. The era of the philosopher king was over, the era of parliamentary democracy had begun.

It must have been rather painful to watch the insults, the comparisons to Nazis, the incessant innuendo against Germans, Jews and traitors to the nation, but Havel, who had lived through more than his share of abuse and defamation during the Communist era, was hardly affected by this. What troubled him much more was the underlying malaise of the society that made such language, not heard in the country since the late nineteen thirties, tolerable or even possible. If he had ever had any doubts as to whether the whole thing was worth it, this was the time. Yet he seemed to have been less willing and more hesitant to accept the office when he stood at the pinnacle of the Velvet Revolution than now, when he was being offered a diminished pulpit. Could he have become the victim of the process of being corrupted by power that he had described so well in his speech on accepting the Sonning Prize in Copenhagen eighteen months earlier? 'Do we know, and are we at all capable of recognizing, the moment when we cease to be concerned with the interests of the country for whose sake we tolerate these privileges and start to be concerned for the advantages themselves, which we excuse by appealing to the interests of the country? . . . There is something treacherous, delusive and ambiguous in the temptation of power. On the one hand, political power gives you the wonderful opportunity of confirming, all day long, that you really exist,

---

2 Digital archive of the House of Deputies of the Parliament of the Czech Republic, http://www.psp.cz/eknih/1993ps/stenprot/002schuz/s002003.htm.
3 Ibid.
4 Conversation with Ladislav Špaček, 31 May 2013.

that you have your own undeniable identity, that with every word and deed you are leaving a highly visible mark on the world. Yet within that same political power and in everything that logically belongs to it lies a terrible danger that while pretending to confirm our existence and our identity, political power will in fact rob us of them.'[5]

Possible, but unlikely. This was after all the man who had been offered the limelight, the pleasures and the luxuries of the West, but chose prison to stay true to his own identity. This was the man who only six months earlier had walked away from the presidency with no certainty that he would ever be invited back. And this was the man who said in the same speech: 'Being in power makes me permanently suspicious of myself.'[6]

Friends who spoke to Havel in those days knew that he harboured no illusions. On 28 September, his nameday, he came to say goodbye to me as I was leaving for the United States the next day to take up my post as ambassador, and hosted a farewell party in a low-life Prague pub, with classic rock 'n' roll, and dancing on the tables. 'You won't miss much here,' he said. He knew there would be times when he would hate his job. What made him do it was not a sense of opportunity, but a sense of responsibility made heavier by a sense of guilt. Without saying so, Havel blamed himself for all that was wrong with the country, for all that went wrong with Czechoslovakia and for being there at all. He knew he was in for an ordeal, but he probably felt he deserved it. If there was a self-serving consideration in his thinking at all, it stemmed from fear rather than a desire for power and the perks of office – the fear of leaving behind a spiritless, embittered country, which some would see as his legacy.

The tone of his inauguration speech, after the haters had had their say and the parliament had elected Havel president with 109 votes, a majority of merely fifty-five per cent, reflected the humility of the moment. In sharp contrast with the iconic New Year speech of 1990, when Havel shocked the nation by making clear the extent of its decline and the difficulties of the challenges ahead, he now tried to focus on what had gone right and what could still serve as a solid point of departure for the new country. He appealed to the best traditions of the nation, the spirit of decency, mutual respect and solidarity. At the same time he warned against the worst instincts

5 'The Sonning Prize', 28 May 1991. In *The Art of the Impossible*, 73.
6 Ibid. 138.

of people, against 'spineless adaptability, provincial small-mindedness, unbridled greed and cynicism passing for realism'.[7] Without question, he knew what was coming and he knew it would not be nice.

The time had now come for the largest transfer of property in the thousand-year-old history of the land. It was inevitable. Whereas at least some areas of trade, agriculture and commerce were left in private hands in the neighbouring countries of Poland and Hungary, practically everything had been confiscated, expropriated or nationalized in Czechoslovakia. To make the economy function again the process of privatization now continued through the voucher scheme and large-scale restitutions. Property worth billions of dollars was changing hands. Raw greed combined with opportunity released some unsuspected creative talents. It was amazing to watch how many people who had been until just two years before cut off from the practical workings of capitalism and the market did not miss a trick when it came to making a fast million or two. Pyramid schemes, fake collateral such as over-assessed low-grade precious stones of little value, insider dealing, incest ownership, with the daughter company secretly owning the mother company, and asset stripping abounded. Most of these activities did not yet even have a name in the penal code. Some of the liberal theoreticians of the privatization process, convinced of the need to attain a concentration of the domestic capital needed for investment by whatever means, spoke of a need to 'run away from lawyers',[8] others of the necessity to turn off the lights.[9] The prime minister himself professed his ignorance of any effective method to distinguish between clean and dirty money. Others took the hint. In less than four years many of the small banks offering above-the-market returns folded; the rest were sinking under the weight of bad loans, millions of participants in the voucher privatization scheme lost their investment, a number of brand-new millionaires made off for tax havens, and the country lost its innocence.

This was the time of the great bonfire of scruples that Havel detested, but nonetheless willy-nilly presided over. He was largely powerless to

---

7 Inauguration Speech, Prague Castle, 2 February 1993, in *Works 7*, 41.
8 The quote is ascribed to Tomáš Ježek, the minister of privatization in the Klaus government, see e.g. Petr Pithart, 'Právo a právníci v procesu privatizace' ('The Law and the Lawyers in the Process of Transformation'), 10 October 2006, www.pithart.cz.
9 See e.g. the last federal Prime Minister Jan Stráský: 'Co Klaus sám necítí, nikdy neposlechne' ('What Klaus Does Not Feel Himself, He Will Never Listen To'), 3 March 2013, www.ihned.cz.

stem the tide or even significantly to affect it, except to remind the nation time and again of the centrality of moral values for the well-being of any society. But a large part of the nation did not want to be reminded, and Havel's personal popularity plummeted. His exhortations earned him the status of a moralistic sorehead, badly out of touch and out of place. He was constantly reminded of his place by the new masters of the new country. Almost every Wednesday in the first years of his new presidency, he received the prime minister, ostensibly to be briefed on the latest meeting of the government, just like the English queen. He dreaded the experience intensely, knowing that in fact he was in for a dressing down over the tiniest phrase in a speech that did not conform to government policy. The prime minister did this effectively and mercilessly. Havel, having never had or learned the arrogance that comes with being the top dog, never found a defence.[10] He even gave up the advantage of home turf and met the prime minister in a pub over a beer to lighten the mood, for all the difference it made.

Sometimes the prime minister deemed it necessary to voice his displeasure publicly. After Havel received Salman Rushdie in September 1993, when the author was still condemned to live a clandestine existence, Klaus publicly criticized the president for endangering the interests and the security of the country. When Havel argued through his spokesman Ladislav Špaček that the minister of foreign affairs and the minister of the interior, himself a former political prisoner, had both been apprised of the visit beforehand and voiced no objections, a storm ensued, with the government insisting that Havel sacrifice his spokesman. Having to choose between a principle and a person, Havel as always chose the person, withdrawing the claim but retaining the spokesman.[11]

But if Klaus believed he could grind Havel to dust or make him do his bidding, he underestimated the capacity of the president to withstand abuse. After all, for Havel this was nothing new. He continued to be humble and polite, but he would quietly stand his ground and look for an opening. And he was also aware that, although he might be a nuisance to Klaus and others, he was also indispensable as the symbol of democratic changes at home, and an emblem and the good will of the country abroad.

---

10 cf. Špaček (2012), 17.
11 Ibid. 89. The situation will be painfully familiar to any current or former spokesman.

Under the new constitution the president 'represented the country abroad', 'concluded treaties and agreements' with other countries and appointed ambassadors. Some of these acts had to be countersigned by the prime minister, but there remained a vast grey area where the president was largely autonomous. He was now going to exploit that autonomy to the hilt.

IN SEARCH OF ALLIES

BACK HOME IN 1993, most Czechs felt that nothing much had happened. True, there was now a new country east of the Morava river where they had previously gone to hike and ski without the need of a passport. But nothing had changed within the Czech lands, Bohemia, Moravia and a stump of Silesia.[1] They were still there as they had been for a thousand years, a country of milk and honey, hard-working, peaceful people, known around the world for their skills, intelligence and culture.

From the outside, the picture was slightly different. After the break-up of Yugoslavia, the Soviet Union and Czechoslovakia, there were suddenly a dozen new countries in the eastern half of Europe, an area of tumultuous changes, ethnic strife and people killing each other in places with unpronounceable names. Czechoslovakia, yes, that rang a bell, although it was easy to confuse with Yugoslavia, no, that was Tito. Czechoslovakia was the country with great beer, a world-class ice-hockey team, the country of Alexander Dubček and Václav Havel. But this new country, one did not even know what to call it, Czechia, Czech Republic, Czechlands or simply Czech? A letter sent to me in Washington was addressed to the 'Republic of the Czech Embassy'.

There is a question of branding, not only with detergents but also with countries. It took some time and effort to put the country back on the map. In Václav Havel, the Czech Republic had perhaps its greatest asset. For proof of this, one only had to look across the border to see how much rougher the sailing was for Slovakia under Vladimír Mečiar.

---

1 The whole of Silesia used to be a part of the Crown of Bohemia before Frederick I of Prussia seized it in the War of Austrian Succession in 1742.

Even so, a fledgling country of ten million people would have hardly been a foreign policy priority at a time when the Soviet empire had disintegrated into a number of much bigger and less orderly entities, and when the fighting in former Yugoslavia brought about the worst atrocities in Europe since World War II. Havel rightly sensed, as he had three years before, that the new country could play a meaningful international role only if it engaged with the acute problems of international politics and security in the name of values larger than narrow national interest.

In his speech at the unveiling of a monument to the founder of Czechoslovakia, Tomáš Garrigue Masaryk, he quoted the first president: 'We had been buried when we ceased to live the larger life.'[2] And he left no doubt as to what was meant by these words in the present: 'It is an appeal to realize that the immeasurable suffering of our fellow human beings in Bosnia and Herzegovina is of fundamental concern to us, that we must address it unequivocally and identify the main culprit, that we must accept our own share of responsibility for peace and justice in Europe, and that, should all other solutions fail, we must, within our capabilities, support even more forceful steps of the international community. As people who once became the victims of a shameful concession to a bully in Munich, we must know even better than others that there must not be concessions made to evil, even when it is not committed directly against us. Our indifference towards others can after all result in only one thing: the indifference of others towards us.'[3]

This rather inconspicuous speech on an anniversary occasion in the ancient Moravian town of Olomouc contains perhaps the most comprehensive outline of the 'Havel doctrine' of humanitarian intervention. It is striking in its simplicity. It emphasizes the shared responsibility of people to stand up to evil wherever and whenever it is being committed, and the unacceptable nature of appeasement, inaction or indifference in the face of evil. It is the converse of the maxim attributed to Edmund Burke, 'All that is necessary for evil to triumph is for good men to do nothing.' The historic reference in Havel's case was to the Munich Agreement, as the immediate precursor to World War II. This is the doctrine that Havel

---

2   Address on the occasion of the unveiling of a monument to Tomáš Garrigue Masaryk, Olomouc, 7 March 1993, in *Works 7*, 66.
3   Ibid. 69.

invoked for Kuwait and the former Yugoslavia, and that he would invoke in the future, more controversially, for Kosovo and Iraq. Its weakness lies in the question of who determines what is evil. Not everybody could be trusted with the definition as well as Havel, who had been well aware of the dangers when he wrote: 'Defending human beings is a higher responsibility than respecting the inviolability of a state. One must, however, constantly and carefully scrutinize such humanistic arguments to determine that it is not just a pretty façade concealing far less respectable interests . . .'[4]

Czechoslovak troops had already been a part of 'Desert Storm', the international coalition that drove Saddam Hussein out of Kuwait in 1991. Now the Czech Republic offered its troops to assist in the international intervention in the former Yugoslavia, first with the UN-run UNPROFOR, and then with I-FOR and S-FOR under NATO command. On his first trip to the United States as Czech president in April 1993, Havel spent much of his precious time with President Clinton, arguing for US efforts to help stabilize the region as a whole and to open NATO's door to new members. The occasion was the opening of the National Holocaust Museum on 22 April 1993, an outdoor ceremony in freezing rain, which soon turned to snow as the guests, including several heads of state, were left waiting for almost an hour for the new president to arrive; he was still running on what was called 'Clinton time' and justifiably distracted by the fiery disaster of the Waco siege three days before. There was still more of a wait at the reception in the White House, which followed. As Havel and Lech Wałęsa, who shared the same vice, started looking for ashtrays, they were tactfully but firmly reminded that, on the orders of the First Lady, the White House was now off-limits to smokers. 'But we need to smoke. Where can we smoke?' insisted the Polish president, who was easily the more impulsive and assertive of the two. On the porch, went the answer. This was after all DC, a Southern town. 'Let's go, Vašek.' Wałęsa tugged at the sleeve of the reluctant Havel. Just as they set out to look for a porch in the White House, the president arrived. Both Wałęsa and Havel then had a brief one-on-one meeting with the president, largely about the prospects of NATO enlargement. At a private dinner at Madeleine Albright's house in Georgetown that evening, Havel went out of his way to persuade

---

4 *To the Castle and Back*, 167.

the reluctant American president that, without the US participation in a peace-keeping, or even a peace-making, international operation in former Yugoslavia, the bloodshed, atrocities and ethnic cleansing would continue without end. Clinton had been similarly warned, but in a much sterner fashion, when Elie Wiesel went off script at the museum opening earlier in the day: 'What have we learned? We have learned some lessons, minor lessons, perhaps, that we are all responsible, and indifference is a sin and a punishment.'[5] It was, however, the dinner with Havel, along with appeals by Pope John Paul II that made an indelible impression in Clinton's mind.[6]

Clinton was facing a dilemma. He had run his campaign against George H. W. Bush, the victor of the first Gulf War, largely on a domestic agenda, with the focus on 'the economy, stupid'. There was little support in Congress for US involvement on the ground in Yugoslavia, which was seen as a European backyard. In 1993, the administration found it impossible to persuade its European allies of the wisdom of the 'lift-and-strike' strategy, which would enable the Bosnian Muslims to hold their territory without the need for deployment of peace-keeping troops on the ground.

But Havel (not alone) persevered. The events, sadly, proved him right. When the Bosnian Serbs overran the UN-declared protection zone in Srebrenica and massacred its male inhabitants, and when they bombed the marketplace in Sarajevo, the USA initiated the NATO-led bombings of Serbian arms depots and other targets, in the end forcing the belligerents to come to the negotiating table at Dayton and sign an agreement under the watchful eye of the late Richard Holbrooke.

The case of former Yugoslavia illustrates well the potential and the limitations of the doctrine of humanitarian intervention. It should be primarily an instrument to stop bloodshed, encourage the parties to find compromises through negotiations, and, when atrocities have been committed, to bring the culprits to justice. But it is a blunt instrument, not best equipped to solve protracted, often centuries-old conflicts. When the ultimate goal of such an intervention is nation building, it most often fails, and will be seen by one or more parties to the conflict as biased, hostile or simply as an enemy to be confronted. Perhaps this intrinsic difficulty, rather

5 www.ushmm.org/research/library/faq/languages/en/06/01/ceremony/?content=wiesel.
6 Conversation with Bill Clinton, 11 November 2013.

than ulterior motives or criminal negligence, ought to be considered the main problem with the war in Iraq.

Havel's staunch advocacy of interventions in former Yugoslavia and Kosovo, and even more so his later open support for the effort to remove Saddam Hussein (rather than for the method of his removal), came at a price, tainting his idealized image as a saintly patron of non-violence. But it is the image rather than the man that is at issue here: Havel, like Gandhi and Mandela, was advocating non-violence not only as a matter of moral principle but as a weapon of political struggle. Havel would always give precedence to a peaceful and amicable way of conflict resolution but he believed too strongly in the inadmissibility of appeasement when facing an evil to be a pacifist. Whether his perceived combativeness in these instances actually deprived him of the chance to win the Nobel Peace Prize, for which he was nominated several times, can only be a matter of speculation, but if true, it would be more of a commentary on the Nobel Peace Prize than on Havel.

Havel's thinking on security in general went along similar lines. It is true that in the very beginning he was leaning, in keeping with the views of some of his friends, Foreign Minister Jiří Dienstbier the foremost among them, towards a universalist, collective security concept; under this approach, with the end of the Cold War, its two huge military alliances, the Warsaw Pact and NATO, would be disbanded to make room for a new pan-European security arrangement that would build on the foundations of the Conference for Security and Cooperation in Europe (CSCE). Havel had expressed hopes of 'belonging to Europe as a friendly family of independent nations and democratic states, a Europe that is stabilized, not divided into blocs and pacts, a Europe that does not need the protection of superpowers, because it is capable of defending itself and building its own security system'.[7] But the first two years of his presidency convinced him that thinking about the two camps in terms of symmetry had not only been wrong while the Cold War was still on,[8] but was also bound to be wrong for the foreseeable future. It was not only the Soviet Union but even post-Communist Russia that continued to express a different geopolitical view of the world and its current problems, as during the first war in the Gulf, or the war in former

---

7   Address to the Polish Sejm and Senate, 25 January 1990, in *Works* 6, 50–1.
8   cf. 'The Anatomy of a Reticence', in *Works* 4, 523–61.

Yugoslavia; moreover, it continued to be at the very least unhelpful when it came to problems in some of the post-Soviet states, like the Baltic countries, Moldova or the Trans-Caucasus. The OSCE, in its attempts to address the crises in former Yugoslavia, in Transnistria or in Nagorno-Karabakh, proved to be an ineffectual instrument of collective security. There was no residual common ideology, will or trust in the Warsaw Pact to make it anything but a relic of the past or a potential threat for the future. NATO was thus the only effective organization left that could offer a genuine guarantee of a country's security in a rapidly changing world. Its original, if unofficial purpose, as summed up immortally by its first Secretary General Lord Ismay, 'to keep the Russians out, the Americans in, and the Germans down', suited Czech priorities quite nicely, or at least its first two parts did. In the forty years of the Alliance's existence, Germany proved its commitment to the values of freedom and democracy and its worth as a major contributor to the security of the continent. The purpose was no longer to keep it down but to keep it an active partner at the core of the NATO mission.

The thinking of Havel's political aides was rapidly turning in this direction. They found willing if initially cautious interlocutors in some of their counterparts in the George H. W. Bush administration, notably Robert Hutchings, the NSC director for Central and Eastern Europe, Paul Wolfowitz, the undersecretary of Defense for Policy and I. Lewis 'Scooter' Libby, the deputy undersecretary, who came to Prague with the first US delegation for political consultations on defence and security matters.[9] The encouragement of Senator Lugar, a former and future Republican chairman of the Senate Committee on Foreign Relations, who visited the Castle in April 1991, strengthened their determination.

Soon after his election to the Czech presidency in January 1993, Havel started to pursue the question of the expansion of NATO. The first signs were not promising. The European member nations of NATO were busy drawing their peace dividend and could not be expected to take the lead on an issue that might aggravate the Russians. Although Clinton says he contemplated the enlargement of NATO as a way to secure the gains for

---

9 If this looks, with the benefit of hindsight, like an early version of the neo-conservative cabal, it also shows there is not that much benefit to hindsight. Whatever criticism may be levelled against Wolfowitz and Libby in their subsequent careers, they played an essential and constructive role in helping to stabilize Europe following the end of the Cold War.

freedom and democracy in Central and Eastern Europe during his election campaign in 1992,[10] the Administration was initially wary. Their main argument was that, in the absence of a clear security threat, an enlargement of NATO was not necessary, and might even be counter-productive. The State Department took the view that Russia should be an integral part of any new European security architecture. Even the faithful Madeleine Albright, now the permanent US representative to the UN, could not be initially prevailed upon to take up the cause lest she was seen as lobbying for her native region.[11] (Even this did not spare her from being the butt of Clinton's remark to Havel that the Czech Republic was the only country with two ambassadors in Washington.[12]) Partnership for Peace, a confidence-building and limited-cooperation plan, eventually adopted by NATO in October 1993, was at first as far as the Administration was willing to go. Several things changed that picture. The war in former Yugoslavia was enough to focus the attention of the Clinton Administration on the need to build viable and reliable security structures in post-Communist Europe. The wild excesses and occasional xenophobic outbursts of Yeltsin's Russia made it an unlikely candidate for a responsible role in guaranteeing European security. Some of the European members of NATO were becoming keenly aware that there would have to be a security solution for Central and Eastern Europe if destabilization and conflict were to be prevented. Manfred Wörner, the NATO secretary general, warmed to Havel already on his first visit to NATO's Brussels headquarters in March 1991, and while bound to reflect the consensus of the NATO council, made his sympathies clear. Important thinkers in the US security and foreign policy establishment, in particular a group at RAND, argued that NATO enlargement is not threat-driven but rather a part of a strategy of projecting stability and unifying Europe.[13]

Bipartisan support of the US Congress was absolutely crucial for the success of the enlargement plan. Initially there were few congressmen willing to adopt the issue as their own. None of the potential candidates had enough clout in Washington to launch a major lobbying effort on the

---

10 Conversation with Bill Clinton, 11 November 2013.
11 Albright (2003), 252 (CZ).
12 Conversation with Bill Clinton, 11 November 2013.
13 Ronald F Asmus, Richard L Kugler and F Stephen Larrabee, 'Building a New NATO', *Foreign Affairs*, September–October 1993, 28–40.

Hill or enough money to hire professionals to do it for them. It took little time for the Czech, Hungarian and Polish envoys in DC to realize that they had to join forces and lobby as a group to have any chance of success. Now the Visegrad idea conceived by Havel in Bratislava and affirmed by the leaders of the three countries at a historic Hungarian castle on the banks of the Danube – where three kings, Jan Luxembourg of Bohemia, Hungarian Karel Robert and Pole Kazimierz the Great, had met to forge an alliance in 1335 – began to pay dividends. With the help of sizeable and politically active Czech, Hungarian and the even more numerous Polish minorities in states on the Eastern seaboard and in the Midwest, along with Florida and Texas, the US legislators began to listen. Several bills, starting with the NATO Participation Act of 1994 and continuing with the NATO Enlargement Facilitation Act of 1996, were successfully enacted into law.

Although President Clinton had been originally hesitant, as a consummate politician he too saw the writing on the wall. In no small part, the impassioned appeals of Havel and Wałęsa in their meetings with him, both separately and together, in April 1993 made him 'inclined to think positively toward expansion from that day on'.[14] For Clinton, who has admitted to being influenced by Havel long before they met, the Czech president 'embodied a personal plea' on his part to get things moving.[15] The balance of the argument gradually changed, with National Security Adviser Anthony Lake, though opposed by some on his staff, becoming more forward-leaning than the State Department and the Pentagon. With increasing support for the enlargement on the Republican side, the Administration did not want to be caught on the back foot. After the arrival of Richard Holbrooke as the assistant secretary for European Affairs in September 1994, the State Department came on board, too.

There was considerable headwind as well. Many in the Administration saw the developments as an unwelcome distraction from domestic priorities, and conducted a covert but effective rearguard action against the new policy. A large part of the foreign policy establishment around the Council on Foreign Relations was worried about the impact of the enlargement on what they saw as the more important relationship with Russia. Thomas Friedman

---

14 Goldgeier (1999).
15 Conversation with Bill Clinton, 11 November 2013.

raged against the enlargement in the *New York Times*.[16] It became clear that this was going to be an uphill struggle.

But Clinton had already made up his mind. He decided to announce the change of policy in a spectacular fashion during his trip to Europe for the summit of NATO in January 1994. He sent Madeleine Albright and John Shalikashvili, the new chairman of the Joint Chiefs of Staff, ahead on a whirlwind tour of Central and Eastern European capitals, to encourage and reassure the new democracies that would, for the time being, learn to cooperate with NATO and strive for military and political interoperability within the Partnership for Peace. And with some gentle lobbying, he chose Prague, one of the most scenic backdrops in Europe, to declare that 'now the question is no longer whether NATO will take on new members but when and how.'[17]

Havel was naturally thrilled that the US president chose the Czech capital for the announcement and for a meeting with a larger group of Central and Eastern European leaders, notwithstanding the huge organizational and logistical challenges this posed for a country that was exactly one year old. While in November 1990, George H. W. Bush's party numbered seven hundred souls, the Clinton delegation, in keeping with his stated goal of 'reinventing the government', weighed in at nine hundred, not to mention the delegations of the other countries. As always, however, Havel was looking to give an informal, human and intellectual dimension to the trip. After conspiring with Madeleine Albright and me at the Prague Blue Duck restaurant over an eponymous bird, he set his ambush on the night before the announcement.

The plan almost collapsed when the ailing mother of the US president died just several days before the visit. The American advance team insisted, understandably, that all parts of the programme that could be seen as frivolous were cancelled. The playwright's scenario for the visit, assembled with the same attention to detail as any of his plays, was up in the air, literally, as the presidential plane was approaching Prague. But there was a co-conspirator on board Air Force One to take up the host's

---

16 Twenty years later he still considers it 'one of the dumbest things we've ever done' (*Why Putin Doesn't Respect Us*, 5 March 2014), ignoring the stark contrast between today's Poland, the Czech Republic or Estonia on the one hand, and Belarus or Ukraine on the other.

17 President Clinton's News Conference with Visegrad Leaders in Prague, 12 January 1994, http://www.presidency.ucsb.edu/ws/index.php?pid=49832#ixzz1tLuVTvbf.

case. As the president was descending onto the tarmac followed by his entourage, Havel's eyes were as much on Clinton as on the US permanent representative to the UN, Madeleine Albright. When she gave the thumbs-up sign, Havel smiled. Clinton had relented and out of respect for his Czech counterpart had agreed to the original schedule with only minor cuts. After the official welcome and a round of talks, Havel showed Clinton his private study at the Castle, adorned with spectacular pieces of modern art, including two nudes. 'Can you imagine what people would say if I had something like this in my office?'[18] Clinton said, somewhat wistfully. Little did he know. The schedule then took the two presidents across the Charles Bridge to the notorious Prague pub where for years the king of Czech storytellers Bohumil Hrabal and his buddies had been spinning stories while putting countless pints away. Then they crossed Národní Street to the Reduta jazz bar, whose name symbolized the great era of the small theatres in Prague in the 1960s, and among whose founders was Havel's erstwhile guru Ivan Vyskočil. A jazz group fronted by Jiří Stivín, a legendary Czech saxophonist, flautist and improviser, was playing for the presidents. When they finished a set, Havel got up and unveiled his personal present for the visiting US president, a brand-new, golden and Czech-made tenor saxophone, complete with his signature and a heart.[19] Clinton knew instantly what was expected of him. After a few trial puffs he embarked with the band on an unrehearsed but respectable rendition of 'My Funny Valentine'. Then he set his own ambush, inviting Havel to join him on percussion in 'Summertime'. The latter gave a spirited, if not nearly as accomplished effort. The evening almost ended in an incident when a car exhaust misfired loudly just as the US president was leaving the club. The secret servicemen, fearing a more serious ambush, bundled him unceremoniously into his armoured limo and were off in seconds.

The struggle itself was far from over. Clinton's declaration, vague in terms of a timeline, or the countries that would join NATO, was still only half a policy and half a rhetorical statement of intent. To make it reality, the other fifteen NATO member countries, their governments and parliaments, and last but certainly not least the US Congress, had to be persuaded. Among

---

18 See also Albright (2003).
19 Clinton still uses the instrument, along with a vintage one, made by Adolf Sax himself in 1861. Conversation with Bill Clinton, 11 November 2013.

the European member countries, there was much hesitation, and even open reluctance. The Partnership of Peace was itself a compromise, which could be construed as a first step to enlargement by those who were inclined to support it, or as a holding station of undetermined duration by those who were not. The latter group represented a numerical majority, and included important member countries like France, which had for a long time been opposed to anything that might strengthen the Alliance.

In the United States, the struggle continued unabated until shortly before the NATO summit in Madrid in July 1997, which formally agreed upon the enlargement of the Alliance by the Czech Republic, Hungary and Poland. The Administration and the aspiring countries faced a formidable coalition of 'Russia firsters' and geopolitical realists, both of whom were unwilling to trade the chance of putting the relationship between the two Cold War adversaries on a new track for a militarily insignificant, politically risky and economically costly enlargement by the impoverished and still fragile democracies of Central and Eastern Europe. The grand old man of American diplomacy George Kennan pronounced: 'Expanding NATO would be the most fateful error of American policy in the post cold-war era.'[20]

Havel took the fight to the opponents. He refused to think about NATO as guarding a piece of territory, but saw NATO primarily as a guarantor of values and principles comprising liberal democracy. Now that the countries of Central and Eastern Europe espoused the same values and principles, there was no reason why they should not be given a chance to share in the security benefits and responsibilities of the Alliance. To deny them that chance would mean to preserve a dividing line artificially that had been erased by the end of the Cold War. It would not only be illogical, but also unfair and immoral. It would grant a posthumous victory to those enemies of democracy who had started the Cold War in the first place.

The core Havel concept of responsibility, evidenced by the presence of Czechoslovak, and later Czech, troops in the liberation of Kuwait and in the peacekeeping troops in Yugoslavia, shielded the country from the allegation that all that the Czechs (and other Central and Eastern Europeans) wanted was a security umbrella for a rainy day with the Russians. Although this

---

20 'A Fateful Error', *New York Times*, 5 February 1997.

consideration – undoubtedly and not surprisingly, given the Central European experience of the last forty years – did play an important role in Czech thinking, they were able to demonstrate that they were willing to be security providers and not just consumers.

Havel and his Polish colleague and (sometimes tough) friend Wałęsa were undoubtedly key in the drive to join NATO. With unassailable moral credits and the aura of revolutionary leaders, they could not be simply dismissed as Russophobes looking for a place to hide. For all the similarities, however, there were subtle differences in their approach. While Wałęsa embodied the heroic past of the Polish nation, with its brave if sometimes futile resistance to foreign oppressors, who often turned out to be Russian, Havel exemplified the fundamental unity of Central Europe with the rest of the West in terms of culture, philosophy and political thinking. While he was well aware of past disasters and possible future threats involving the Russians, his take on Russia, starting with his speech in the Congress, was unprejudiced and forward-leaning. Bill Clinton highly valued Havel's support for Boris Yeltsin as 'Russia's best hope for a non-aggressive democratic state'.[21] Together, Havel and Wałęsa complemented each other as well as any pair since Laurel and Hardy. It is hard to imagine that the enlargement would have occurred without either of them. They gave the debate the urgency that made it possible to accomplish the task by the end of the century. If the debate had still been under way at the time of 9/11, other considerations would surely have taken over.

It is another question whether the triumph of the Havel–Wałęsa crusade represents also a lasting accomplishment for European and Atlantic security, or marks a geopolitical dead-end entered due to the residual inertia of Cold War thinking, as people who never came to terms with it would claim. To answer the question, it is useful to observe the results of one of the biggest natural experiments in the history of Europe. The countries of Central and Eastern Europe that eventually joined NATO in two waves, in 1999 and in 2004, represent today a zone of political and economic stability of 100 million people, and are increasingly indistinguishable from their neighbours in the west of Europe. The stabilizing effect of the NATO accession process and entry helped pave the way for their slower and more difficult integration

---

21 Conversation with Bill Clinton, 11 November 2013.

into the European Union. By contrast, the countries between this zone and Russia, namely Belarus, Ukraine and Moldova, still find themselves in a geopolitical void, torn between their conflicting instincts and affinities, prone to reversals, instability, and political and economic mismanagement. The same thing is true of the countries in South Eastern Europe that stayed outside of the enlargement field of gravity as well as of the Trans-Caucasus region. With resurgent Russia, and Europe weakened by the financial crisis, the window of opportunity has closed, at least for the time being.

And Russia would never have been a less complicated interlocutor, with or without the enlargement. The trauma of a collapse of the largest country in the world and the most ambitious ideological movement in Europe since early Christianity would have played out regardless. With its history of tyranny and xenophobia, and with its perpetually warring Westernizing and Slavophilic instincts, the country could only regain its footing in contrast and opposition to what it saw as a triumphalistic West. No amount of Western economic aid such as was offered, provided and wasted in the mid-nineties, no amount of security assurances, such as those masterminded by the United States and Secretary Albright in the form of NATO–Russia Council and the NATO policy of 'three nos' of 1997[22] or any number of resets would have changed that.[23]

If most of Europe today is safer than at any time in its history, it is not least thanks to the vision of statesmen like Bill Clinton, Lech Wałęsa . . . and Václav Havel.

---

22 No intention, no plan and no reason to deploy nuclear weapons on the territory of the new member states.

23 The lesson compressed in the last two paragraphs is even more persuasive against the backdrop of the Russian aggression in Ukraine, as I am revising the text of this book.

BACK TO EUROPE

THE SAME ARGUMENT underlying the efforts to join NATO, about the fundamental identity of values, societies and cultures, informed Havel's thinking about the European Union. Indeed, it followed as a matter of course. Within weeks of the revolutions in Central and Eastern Europe, the slogan 'Back to Europe' emerged, spontaneously and independently, in Czechoslovakia, Hungary and Poland. Already in January 1990, Havel spoke of the joint 'return to Europe' to the Polish Sejm and Senate. In May 1991, in Aachen, on the occasion of receiving the Charlemagne award for his contribution to the European idea, Havel spoke of the ambition to win full membership in the EU. It took another thirteen years for the Czech Republic and other countries of Central and Eastern Europe to get there.

Again, Havel became one of the focal points for the European ambitions of the Czech Republic and the region. The idea of European integration came naturally to him as a lifelong opponent of dividing lines and narrow nationalism, and an advocate of universal values and broad responsibility. For the next ten years, even after he had left the presidential office, he was a stalwart supporter of the Czech accession, and a critic of what he saw as narrow-mindedness among some of his more Eurosceptic countrymen.

Yet he was never the starry-eyed, uncritical admirer of the European Union some painted him to be. From the very beginning, he conceived of the European project not as an exclusive club, and even less so as Fortress Europe, but as an integral part of a larger whole, reflecting an 'inherent connection between the civilization of Europe and that of continental North

America.'[1] Even more courageously, he proclaimed that 'no future European order is thinkable without the European nations of the Soviet Union, which are an inseparable part of Europe'.[2] In his first speech to the European Parliament on 8 March 1994, fully aware of how long the road was that his own country still had to travel, what obstacles it had to overcome, and how much it would depend on the good will of the EU institutions including the parliament, he did not stop at expressing his genuinely felt admiration for the European project, but went on to offer some critical reflections, which in retrospect could be seen as rather far-sighted. After praising the EU as 'an admirable work of the human spirit and its rational skill',[3] and extolling its achievement in building the system of pan-European institutions, a single market and the beginnings of a common currency, he went on to say: 'This admiration, almost exaltation, has, however, been mixed with a feeling, which is less encouraging . . . What has been addressed, was my reason rather than my heart . . .'[4]

What was missing in the European project, in Havel's view, was 'a spiritual, moral or emotional dimension . . . Various great empires . . . which have brought some benefits for mankind were not only characterized by their methods of administration and of organization, but were invariably imbued with a spirit, idea, ethos, and I would not be afraid to say, charisma, that in turn gave rise to their structure. . . . They always had to offer . . . some kind of a cue to the people, as to how to emotionally identify with them, some ideal that could internally appeal to them and inspire them, some set of universally comprehensible values, which everybody could fully share and which would be valuable enough for the people to make sacrifices on behalf of the entity that embodied them, in the extreme case even of their own lives.'[5]

Although the EU is based on a grand complex of civilizational values, Havel continued, 'many people may have an understandable impression that the EU consists only in the never-ending arguments about how many carrots can be exported from one place to another, who will determine that number, who will supervise him and possibly who will impose sanctions

---

1 The International Prize of Charles the Great, Aachen, 9 May 1991, in *Toward a Civil Society*, 128.
2 Ibid.
3 In *Works 7*, 219–30.
4 Ibid.
5 Ibid.

on those who violate the rules . . . That is why it seems to me, perhaps the most important task that the EU is facing today is a new and really clear consideration of what could be called "European identity", a new and really clear articulation of the European responsibility, an enhanced interest in the very meaning of the European integration and its broader context in the contemporary world and a new creation of its ethos, or if you wish, charisma.

'Reading the Maastricht Treaty, its historic importance notwithstanding, will hardly win the European Union genuinely enthusiastic supporters, real patriots who will experience this complex organism as their real homeland, or as one of the levels of their homeland.'[6]

In subsequent years, Havel emphasized time and again the great opportunity that the process of European integration offered for 'civilizational self-reflection', and promoted the idea of 'Europe as a mission'.[7] In the first decade of the new millennium, the gruelling, infinitely complex and politically sensitive process of the integration of another twelve, and now thirteen, countries into the EU has been successfully accomplished, but Havel's voice remained that of a man crying in the wilderness. Whoever had had misgivings about the potential of the Maastricht Treaty to inspire the people of Europe only had to wait to read the Lisbon Treaty, or, at any rate, try to. In the meantime, the EU, particularly its advance guard of the Eurozone, became mired in a crisis, which laid bare the limits of the willingness of governments, and even more of the people, to identify with the 'ethos' of the Union and to make the necessary sacrifices.

In 1999, Havel elaborated his simultaneous enthusiasm for, and criticism of, the European project in a speech to the French Senate, in which he traced the concept of Europe to its roots in Antiquity, Judaism and Christianity, and identified a specific European concept of time as a dynamic, forward-driving force, that in his thinking accounted to a large degree for the European obsession with progress and modernity and for the intrinsically expansive character of European civilization. Speaking in one of the temples of European rationalism, he posed the radical proposition that Communism was but a 'smokescreen' that had been obscuring the larger danger of the

---

6   Ibid.
7   'Europe as a Mission', The International Prize of Charles the Great, Aachen, 15 May 1996, in
    Works 7, 596–608.

'self-propelling planetary civilization', which is hurtling towards a disaster. Since it was European civilization that had put the world on this trajectory, it should be Europe, or more specifically the European Union, that should take responsibility and confront this danger. 'The responsibility for the world is being born when looking into the face of the other,' Havel paraphrased the French Jewish philosopher Emmanuel Lévinas, whose ideas gave him solace and inspiration during his prison years.

A European Union that could undertake such a momentous task would be, according to Havel, radically different from the present 'immensely complex administrative enterprise that only a special class of euro-experts can understand'.[8] Rather than creating newer and newer treaties, institutions and bureaucracies, Havel envisaged an increasingly federal Europe united by a simple, comprehensible constitution, and governed by a bi-cameral parliament elected much like the US Congress rather than by unelected bureaucracies that are unaccountable to the citizens of individual countries. It is doubly striking to note both how much this proposal resembles some recent ideas offered as a way out of the current crisis by leading European politicians,[9] and how far it is from being implemented.

In April 2002, in the last year of his presidency and at a time when the wave of Euro-exceptionalism was reaching dangerous heights, Havel once again pointed to the 'immensely contagious, almost aggressive idea of continuous change, permanent progress, aggrandizement, enlargement, expansion, conquest, endless growth and endless growth of growth, as well as the idea of a perfect world, which it is necessary to build peacefully, and if it does not work, by force' as ideas that are typically European.[10] He criticized as silly the European boasts at the time about the need to 'catch up with and overtake' the United States, so reminiscent of the past that he and his compatriots had left behind, and deplored as hypocritical the 'periodical bouts of European anti-Americanism' building to a crescendo in the aftermath of 9/11. Drawing on one of the leitmotifs of his thinking and one of his deepest personal traits, he admonished his august listeners – and himself: 'The European history also includes the sceptics, the critics,

---

8 Speech to the French Senate, 3 March 1999, in *Works 7*, 826–39.
9 E.g. German Finance Minister Wolfgang Schäuble on receiving the Charlemagne Prize twenty-two years after Havel. See http://www.karlspreis.de/preistraeger/2012/rede_von_dr_wolfgang_schaeuble.html.
10 'Europe and the World', speech to the Italian Senate, 4 April 2002, in *Works 8*, 159–67.

the shy spirits who question all the realities of this world and first of all themselves, and who are even able to brilliantly articulate their doubts! Or do not such personalities as Albert Camus, Franz Kafka, Samuel Beckett, Umberto Eco and others embody the very tradition of European awe and European humility, which perhaps we should at this moment follow first and foremost?'[11]

It almost seems like one of the great Europeans of the twentieth century grew into a bane of the institution he tirelessly worked to join and promote. For all that, Havel rejoiced when, a year after he retired, the Czech Republic joined the EU, and was a supporter and defender of the European project until his death. Indeed, the debates of the new century in which he took on the ever more numerous and influential Eurosceptics among the Czech political elite, and the populace at large, represented the increasingly rare occasions when he re-entered public life.

---

11 Ibid.

The Yin and the Yang

The best idea is one that leaves room for the possibility
that everything is exactly the other way round.

– Václav Havel

ON THE DOMESTIC FRONT, PARADOXICALLY, it was far more difficult for the president to make himself heard. When on occasion he voiced an opinion, however mildly, that was at odds with that of the government, he was reminded not too subtly, both by incensed parliamentarians and by the government-friendly media, that he was serving at the pleasure of the parliament, which could easily change its mind. More painfully, he continued to be taken to task by the prime minister at their regular Wednesday meetings, which invariably opened with the prime minister's detailed and aggrieved analysis of the latest presidential misdeed. In Czech political parlance, this has been called 'the scrub' and Havel was too polite, too wary of confrontation and, in the end, too introspective not to have felt the smallest sense of guilt over the most innocent act or word. The Klaus–Havel encounters were in a sense the perfect repetition of the Sládek–Vaněk dialogues, except that Klaus, unlike Sládek, was rather disciplined in his drinking habits. Just like in *Audience*, they invariably ended with a dominant Klaus and a subdued Havel. Until the next time, that is, for the one thing that Havel was not doing was changing his ways.

In principle, Havel supported and endorsed the economic reforms that the Klaus government was rapidly introducing. He did have some partial objections, but because of the non-executive character of the presidency and his limited economic erudition he could hardly have challenged Klaus on this field. The battleground turned out to be a sphere that Havel, but not Klaus, took to be self-evident.

'The grand-scale de-etatization taking place in our economy must in my opinion rapidly find its counterpart also in the sphere of civic and public life. The faith in the individual as the real creator of economic prosperity should be deliberately and much more courageously than has been the case until now expanded into faith in the individual as citizen, someone who is capable of accepting his own share of responsibility for public matters.'[1]

Klaus begged to differ. In his conservative view of the world, the citizen had only one political responsibility, namely, to elect his representatives. The running of society and the state was thereafter a matter for the elected representation. Various civic groups and organizations were just so many self-appointed advocacy groups for partial interests, and could not and should not represent the interests of the society as a whole, and were to be tolerated at best. In time, Klaus came to identify such groups with a 'leftist' or 'human rightist' way of thinking, in spite of the fact that many would take offence at this characterization. Endowed with a considerable talent for caricature, Klaus became so adept at inventing all manners of '-isms' to be ritually exhibited and rhetorically slaughtered in front of the public that one could not help thinking that there was a genuine craving in him for some '-ism' of his own.

He would probably not deny it. Unlike Havel, with his concepts of 'non-political' and 'non-ideological' politics, Klaus believed that politics could only be conducted as a battle of ideological alternatives embodied in the political parties competing for power. In his thinking, there was basically room for just two such alternatives, the socialist way, and the 'non-socialist', conservative, liberal capitalist way. There were just two ways, the socialist and the other, the wrong and the right, them and us. As he was fond of saying, 'The Third Way is the fastest way to the Third World'.[2]

There were other differences as well. Some of them revolved around foreign policy issues. Klaus was dutifully supportive, aware of the 'giant

---

1 New Year's Address 1994, in *Works 7*, 223.
2 Václav Klaus, in *The Third Way and Its Fatal Conceits*, a speech to the Montpelerin Society, Vanvouver, 30 August 1999, www.klaus.cz.

symbolism of the step,[3] but less than enthusiastic when it came to the Czech efforts to join NATO. 'I will not spoil it for you' was the best endorsement NATO enthusiasts like me could get from him. He was even less positive about joining the EU, although, unlike some of his affiliates, he recognized that there was no other realistic path forward for the country. As an economist, he welcomed the benefits of the common market and a single economic space. But he was deeply suspicious about the growing power of European institutions with a doubtful democratic mandate and little accountability, and about its social, environmental and institutional agenda, which he saw as Leftist social engineering. Distinctly more Czecho-centric, Germano-phobic, and Russo-philic than the Western-leaning majority of Czech politicians, he continued to see the nation state as the basic unit of geopolitical organization, and distrusted supranational institutions as power-hungry intruders without real democratic credentials. He was an early critic of the project of common European currency for much the same reasons that have recently been singled out as underlying the Eurozone crisis. The differences in their understanding of European integration and of the costs and benefits of Czech participation in it, led to scores of semi-public and public skirmishes between Klaus and Havel over the ten years of Havel's Czech presidency. In contrast to purely domestic affairs, Havel, supported by the larger part of the Czech body-politic, public opinion and international support, came out of these mostly victorious, with Klaus often left sniping on the sidelines.

Another, potentially damaging area of disagreement between the two men on the conduct of foreign policy were the often conflicting approaches to the various hotbeds of tension that arose during the decade, with Havel invariably on the side of humanitarian intervention, while Klaus took the line of extreme realism, preferring to stay away from all conflicts that did not directly affect Czech interests, and even from some that did. Moreover, Klaus himself, the embodiment of a 'strong', forceful leader, although one playing by democratic rules, had a weak spot for other such leaders. Certainly, he did not particularly like the democratizing, bumbling, chaotic Boris Yeltsin, but he related much better to the methodic use of the instruments of power by Vladimir Putin. He objected to Havel's loud

---

3   Conversation with Václav Klaus, 30 August 2013.

condemnation of the Russian war against breakaway Chechnya and of the terrible human rights violations committed in the process. He accused Havel and the West of a biased attitude in their treatment of the conflict in former Yugoslavia, and disagreed with the NATO bombing of Yugoslavia to prevent ethnic cleansing in Kosovo in 1999.

But the main battle between Klaus and Havel was waged over the character of Czech society and over the values and principles it should abide by. For Klaus, these values could be reduced to individual economic and political freedom and a vague allegiance to the national community as the conduit of history, culture and traditions. For Havel, they encompassed also values such as solidarity, tolerance, human and minority rights, care for the environment and civic activism. The chasm widened over the years, leading to a caricature of Klaus as a soulless, cynical technocrat of power, and of Havel as an embodiment of 'leftism', 'environmentalism', 'human-rightism' and 'truth-and-lovism'.[4]

Yet underneath it all there was more respect between the two men than people generally, or indeed, either of them, would be willing to acknowledge openly. Klaus was not a little jealous of Havel's international stature, but he was also keenly cognizant of what this stature meant for the good will of the country. It is fair to say that Havel probably could not have become the first Czech president without Klaus's help. Klaus, on the other hand, happily acknowledged his debt to Havel for having invited him to the Civic Forum in November 1989. Klaus was also, unbeknownst to most people, a cultured man, with real appreciation for literature and music. Almost a contemporary of Havel, he must have been impressed and influenced by Havel's theatrical and essayistic talent. 'Going to the Theatre on the Balustrade to see Havel's plays was undoubtedly a part of the formation of my life outlook.'[5] And although he was ready, for political purposes, to undermine the 'elitist' image of the dissidents, deep down he admired Havel's 'brave struggle against Communist totalitarianism'[6] during the years of normalization. Unlike others, he recognized that 'the Communist prison and persecution had transformed him into a symbol

---

4   After the defeat of his former party ODS, in the parliamentary election of October 2013, Klaus blamed the result on the infiltration of the party by 'Havlism'.
5   Conversation with Václav Klaus, 30 August 2013.
6   Statement of President Václav Klaus on the demise of Václav Havel, 18 December 2011, www.klaus.cz/clanky/3000.

of resistance against totalitarianism and predestined him for his key role of the leader of the November [1989] revolution.'[7]

As for Havel, he had a genuine respect for the enormous organizational and managing role that Klaus played in the transition of the Czech Republic to a market economy, although he was critical of the gold-digging, self-enrichment and political exploitation that accompanied the process.[8] He was respectful, perhaps even slightly jealous, of Klaus's solid academic erudition. He admired his tireless energy and single-minded application. He envied his rigorous self-discipline, which enabled him to prevail in arguments at three in the morning as his opponents fell aside one by one, totally exhausted. All these were things he knew he could not match. He was too perceptive an observer not to be aware of the yin-yang quality of their relationship. For Klaus's sixtieth birthday he wrote him a private letter: 'I am discovering that you're still five years younger than me. For the future I wish you good health (not too many broken legs) and mainly peace in your heart.'[9]

If the differences, criticisms and conflicting aims between Havel and Klaus almost never grew into an open and destructive public fight, it was to the credit of the two men rather than their surroundings. There was extensive demonization of 'the other' in both the Klaus and the Havel camps, intensified by the efforts of the media, who saw advantage in playing the conflict to the hilt. Havel, though, for all his misgivings, was able also to recognize a part of himself in the other man. It is more doubtful whether the same can be said of Klaus, yet he, too, admits, 'If we had sat together more often, we would have found out that we shared views on many more things.'[10] He blames Havel's 'worlds', and the people who surrounded him, for contributing to the antagonism. There might be a point there, although even here Klaus and his 'worlds' were in some respects more similar to Havel's than he realizes.

Many were tempted to see a recounting of the struggle between Havel and Klaus in Havel's last, post-presidential play, *Leaving*. The inference is easy to make, but carries some serious risks. If Patrick Klein, the slick,

---

7 The address of President Václav Klaus at the solemn gathering to honour the memory of President Václav Havel, 21 December 2011, www.klaus.cz/clanky/3004.
8 The criticism pertaining to Klaus in this respect is that he turned a blind eye to many of the shenanigans rather than materially profiting himself.
9 June 2001, VHL ID15756.
10 Conversation with Václav Klaus, 30 August 2013.

greedy careerist, is indeed supposed to be Václav Klaus, then Havel is the equally unappetizing Chancellor Rieger, a man pathetically disloyal to his family, his friends, his ideals and himself. If we are willing to grant that Havel was not such a man, we have to give a pass to Klaus as well. By his own account Havel conceived his *Lear* play, as he called it, in 1987; it had been germinating for almost twenty years. Undoubtedly, his own experiences with the inconstancy of political loyalties, with the temptations and corruption of power, with the double-speak and newspeak of politics and the coarseness of the media, and with the price to be paid in terms of private life, are all reflected in *Leaving*. Settling scores, however, it is not, just as that forms no part of any of his essays, memoirs or interviews. Klein and Rieger are not Klaus and Havel, but the caricatures the outside world would want them to be.

Between Life and Death

In the Castle he lost his life.

– Ludvík Vaculík

THE FIRST FIVE-YEAR TERM of the Czech presidency was marked not only by Havel's struggle for the preservation of his political vision, but by serious personal upheavals. Havel seemed to spend those five years in an almost permanent sub-depression, which in turn affected his outlook and his quality of life. On a political level, he struggled with the new balance of power in the country, with the humiliations that were regularly meted out to him, and with the massive monetization of politics, human relationships and society at large. His depression was worsened by his feeling, rightly or wrongly, that he had been co-responsible for these phenomena, or at least co-responsible for not doing enough to prevent them. Havel gave what was probably his last extensive interview on 11 November 2011, a television 'interrogation' of two former fellow inmates, Havel and the new Catholic archbishop, soon to be cardinal, Dominik Duka. During the interview, Havel described as his most serious mistake that he had not more energetically promoted his vision of a humanistic and moral society during his time as president.[1] To most people, he had done little else.

Could he have been more effective in fighting the growing greed, corruption and individual selfishness he perceived in the new Czech

---

1 http://www.ceskatelevize.cz/porady/10389664200-Václav-havel-a-dominik-duka-spolecny-
   vyslech/31129838012/video/.

Republic? Possibly, but not while president, when he was constrained by the constitutional limits of his office, and by a hostile political environment. In order even to try – and therein lies the rational core of the criticism that he may have stayed too long at the Castle – he would have had to revert to the power of the powerless and conduct the struggle from outside the political system. With his unique combination of creativity, humility and stubbornness he might have eventually been heard, but that would take another twenty years, and he felt he did not have twenty years. He still would not keep silent, but his protests now had a quixotic quality.

His physical condition suffered as well. Never an athlete of robust health, he kept himself going by consuming sometimes two packs of cigarettes a day combined with a generous amount of alcohol, mostly white wine, and an increasing variety of prescription drugs, administered by his personal physician. Havel's shopping list from sometime in 1998 includes Stilnox (a hypnotic), Paralen, Alnagon or Atonalgin (all analgesics), Pineapple Power Drink (a caffeinated energy drink), Oikamid (a stimulant) and 'the white miracle pills for good mood' (?), with a note 'lots of everything'.[2] He took uppers when he felt tired, he took downers when he could not sleep, and he took more sleeping pills when he woke up in the middle of the night. After several weeks of such a regimen he regularly suffered a partial collapse, usually expressed as breathing problems, and had to retreat to Lány or Hrádeček to recuperate.[3] His writing, which he could not concentrate upon in the office amid his thousands of other duties, had to be done during those retreats, and became more and more of a struggle he dreaded. If the quality of his best speeches during the Czechoslovak period is comparable to world-class essay writing, in the new period the language becomes a little tired, the ideas a little repetitive and the architecture a little less elegant.

The rigorous mental discipline with which he had examined and dismissed various myths about the human condition and society seems to have weakened as well. In his most controversial post-modernist guise, exemplified by his 1994 Philadelphia speech,[4] in which he dwelled at length

---

2 A list of medicines, VHL ID10413.
3 The author, a former medical professional himself, observed Havel's health situation directly and discussed it in general terms with his personal physiotherapist.
4 The Philadelphia Liberty Medal, 4 July 1994. *The Art of the Impossible*, 165–72. The draft of the speech triggered a heated argument between Havel and the present author, then ambassador to Washington. Havel made a few cosmetic changes but largely stood his ground.

on the Anthropic Cosmological Principle and the Gaia Hypothesis, he reminded some otherwise sympathetic observers of a 'mad hippie or else like one of the crazed theologians who roam the novels of John Updike'.[5]

His schedule had also become somewhat more controversial. While he and the nation had benefited from the visits of the internationally famous, who underscored Havel's global acclaim during his early presidency, his invitations no longer met with universal approval. When Michael Jackson came to Prague for his first concert in the Czech capital in September 1996, some of Havel's best friends advised against the necessity of meeting with him. Havel's curiosity prevailed. He not only received Jackson, but attended his concert as well.

Another meeting a month later almost failed to materialize, when Havel's schoolmate Miloš Forman came to Prague with an early print of his latest film, *The People vs. Larry Flynt*, and its cast of stars, including Woody Harrelson, Courtney Love and Edward Norton, accompanied by the late journalist Christopher Hitchens, his wife Carol and their baby Alexandra. The entourage arrived with Flynt, on his private plane. In view of the scandalous reputation of the subject of the movie and a hysterical campaign against it in the American media, spearheaded by Gloria Steinem, almost the entire presidential office rose in revolt at the idea of the President of Truth and Love receiving the publisher of *Hustler* in the shrine of Czech nationhood. For once, Havel heeded the pressure and cancelled the invitation, which included a private viewing of the film in the presidential screening room. Havel failed to realize that he was putting Miloš Forman, the impresario of the trip, in an impossible position. Miloš could not possibly explain to his stars why the Czech president, of whom he spoke as a close friend, would not see them; nor could he explain the snub to Larry Flynt, who was, after all, his ride. More seriously, he could not accept Havel's motives, which he saw as hypocritical. His Larry Flynt was after all a noble rogue, the last in a long line of outcasts from George Berger in *Hair*, R P McMurphy in *One Flew over the Cuckoo's Nest*, and Mozart in *Amadeus*. Forman was livid, and one of Havel's oldest friendships hung in the balance.

In the end, diplomacy came to the rescue courtesy of the present writer, at the time still Czech ambassador to the USA. After a round of

---

5   Paul Berman, 'The Poet of Democracy and His Burdens', *The New York Times Magazine*, 11 May 1997, 32–59.

mediation, Havel agreed to meet with Forman, Flynt and the rest of the cast in a downtown hotel for a meal and a friendly discussion. The meeting was not a great success. Since Havel had not yet seen the film, there was little to discuss. Woody Harrelson's three-month-old baby kept rudely interrupting the president's polite remarks, and Courtney Love kept retiring to wash her hands every fifteen minutes. Norton, a Yale graduate, acted intellectually superior to everyone present, including Havel, who was unable to discuss *Primal Fear* since he had not seen it. Everybody, including Carol Blue's baby, wanted to take a picture with the Prez, making him even more embarrassed than usual. Only Larry Flynt kept his cool.

Still, the meeting saved Havel's and Forman's friendship and helped break the ice. In one of his usual bouts of guilty introspection, Havel relented. In the afternoon of the next day, there materialized a discreet screening of the film at the president's office. Flynt was there, and I moonlighted as the simultaneous translator of the dialogue. Havel liked the film. The Castle survived.

As careful as Havel was not to succumb to the perks and temptations of power, he was not an unwilling victim as far as women were concerned. Never a paragon of constancy in his marriage, he sometimes remarked with glee how much easier his conquests became with the benefit of Henry Kissinger's best aphrodisiac. There were several brief liaisons and a few more failed attempts. As far as can be ascertained, he never misused the power of his office to harass or pressure women he was interested in. Most of his flings remained at a platonic level. And even his consummated affairs more often resembled a cry for help than the conquests of a serial philanderer. His aides could not do much more than try to protect his privacy, and did their best to discourage a fair number of groupies and gold-diggers.

But, just as before, Havel needed a more stable and serious relationship. Quite early on, in the spring of 1990, he started seeing Dáša Veškrnová, a well-known theatre, film and TV comedienne. They had met six months earlier, at the thirtieth anniversary of the SEMAFOR Theatre, whose founder, Jiří Suchý, introduced them. Havel came in a parka, behaved surreptitiously and urged Dáša to keep her distance, lest she ran into trouble. Dáša, on her part, noticed that he smoked too much and had 'pretty shy blue eyes'.[6] Something was apparently stirring, but Havel's handlers successfully sabotaged any

---

6   Conversation with Dagmar Havlová, 11 July 2012.

chance at a more intimate conversation on several occasions, all of them involving theatre performances. They were, however, powerless to interfere when Havel asked Dáša for a dance at the annual Prague-Vienna ball on the night of his return from Israel. Afterwards, he invited himself for a discreet 'cup of coffee' at Dáša's flat so that 'no one would be any wiser'.[7] With his inimitable gift for conspiracy, it was perhaps unavoidable that, when she arrived home by taxi that night, there were secret service cars with flashing blue lights parked in the street, and the whole apartment block where she lived glued to their windows to see what was going on. Five days later she found an unsigned note on a letterheadless piece of paper in her mailbox: 'A mystery man will be expecting you in the Cloister Wine Room at 8 p.m. on April 30. He will have a carnation.'[8] Havel was not changing his spots and the romance took off.

It made his aides somewhat uneasy. Dáša was pretty, and a formidable actress, but not known as an intellectual, and quite certainly not a dissident; indeed, her name appears on the list of the signatories of the 1977 declaration condemning the Charter, along with most of her colleagues.[9] She must have sensed the coolness with which some people in the office of the Czech president treated her, and she never forgot it.

The loyalties of friends were also tested in the unique environment of Havel's love life. Many were fiercely devoted to Olga. Others feared for the president's reputation. To make matters more complicated, there were still other claimants to Havel's attentions. The result was a rather complex presidential diary, with bogus schedule items, stand-ins, cut-outs, security covers and a conspiracy of silence.[10] A few in the close circle made the mistake of making their misgivings about Dáša known to the president. Those who knew him better knew better. They accepted Václav's choice, safe in the knowledge that Dáša was destined for the role of a *maîtresse* as long as Olga was around.

Tragically, she would not be around for long. In the second part of 1994 she was diagnosed with cancer and died eighteen months later. A lifetime

---

7 Ibid.
8 Ibid.
9 'Anti-Charter 25 years later', *Lidové noviny*, 24 January 2002, 18. Dáša does not recall signing any such document.
10 Already in the first two Havel administrations, there was a plethora of non-existent bird-like characters, such as 'Professor Nightingale', 'Ambassador Lark' and 'Mr Sparrow' in the president's schedule.

of smoking exacted its toll. The news of her passing generated long lines of silent mourners waiting in the January cold to pay respects before her coffin. 'She will forever remain an irreplaceable and essential part of my soul,' Havel remarked a year later, on the day he remarried.[11]

There is not much direct evidence of their last years together. Shortly after his re-election, Václav and Olga decided to look for a new home and eventually bought a villa in a fashionable Prague neighbourhood. After almost sixty years, he finally moved out for good from the family apartment on the banks of the Vltava, and sold his share to his brother Ivan and his family. The reasons for the move might throw some light on Havel's existential considerations at the time. Neither Václav nor Olga got along well with Ivan's second wife Dagmar, a Slovak computer scientist with a passion for *ikebana*. After Ivan transferred to her the title to most of his property, a fight ensued between the two branches of the family for the control of Lucerna. Václav's decision to sell his half of the complex to a firm with links to the Communist past, which would later go bankrupt, sealed the rift with Ivan and Dagmar, who thought they should have had the right of first refusal. When another Dagmar entered the picture following Olga's death, the relationship deteriorated even further. Neither of the two brothers was the kind of family patriarch able to stop the feud. They stood loyally by their wives and watched their own relationship suffer. Moving apart seemed like a sensible thing to do.

It was Olga who had furnished and decorated the new house, and it was there where Havel had her transferred from the hospital for the last three days of her life so that she could die in her home. It never became a real home for him, though. Once Havel became president, he kept moving, only partly forced to do so by circumstances. First came the game of musical chairs in the Prague Castle until he settled on an office he could call his own. His living circumstances were even less stable. He spent less and less time at the apartment on the embankment, and for a time played with the idea of moving permanently to the presidential summer resort at Lány, Masaryk's favourite place to relax. He even tried horse riding in Masaryk's footsteps, but the hobby did not catch on. Then came a short-lived stay in the so-called Masaryk apartment behind the president's office, which could never

---

11 'We love each other and we want to live together', ČTK, 6 January 1996.

be turned into a cosy home because of the number of people moving around the Castle, security concerns and the constraints of the conservationists. From there Havel and Olga moved temporarily to the so-called Husák's Little House, an Imperial-style villa in the Castle gardens, almost ruined by attempts to adapt it to Communist tastes. Not only did he hate the place, but he also suffered another near-death experience there, having locked himself in the red-hot presidential sauna, unable to open the door or to alert his bodyguards who were watching television, until he discovered a superhuman strength and brought the door down. So finally he settled on a villa in Dělostřelecká, a ten-minute walk from the Castle, a rather grand but unlovely affair with its own swimming pool and a little gym. Later, already married to Dáša, he bought a house in a windy Portuguese resort with complete strangers for neighbours, and not much to do.[12]

Havel always set about furnishing and adapting every new house with much enthusiasm, but soon his energy waned, as if he had already become a little tired of the place. The end result was always a semi-finished product, with many memorabilia and the latest gadgets, but sadly lacking in warmth and even comfort. The only exceptions were Hrádeček and Havel's presidential office, his true homes for forty-five and thirteen years of his life, respectively. It was there one could witness the sense of harmony as well as his loving, almost obsessive attention to detail, whether it was a favourite drinking cup at Hrádeček, or a Tibetan *tanka*, a present from the Dalai Lama, on the wall in the office. All the other abodes stayed half finished, provisional, and served only as way stations before their owner's escape to another such place, equally unsatisfactory.

In the middle of the decade Havel struggled between the sense of duty to his lifelong and now terminally ill partner, and his increasing affection for the woman he'd fallen in love with. He knew the dilemma was insoluble, and, true to his sense of honesty in life, he therefore did nothing to solve it. But then, on 27 January 1996, Olga died.

There is no doubt that Havel's mourning for Olga was deep and genuine. But overt expressions of grief were not his style. His reaction was subdued, almost understated. What gave the game away was the sense of numbness, the sudden flatness of expression, in a man capable of the deepest

---

12 It was sold again in 2005.

introspection. His dilemma, however, had been solved for him. Not only was he now free to focus his attention on Dagmar, but also Olga, before she died, told him the obvious in her usual blunt way: he was unfit to live alone and should remarry.[13]

Before he could do that, he experienced his own brush with death. At the beginning of November 1996, his chronic breathing difficulties, which plagued him the whole summer, suddenly got worse, he started to run a temperature and became very tired. His personal doctor Michal Šerf was not overly disturbed. Over the years, bronchitis or the onset of pneumonia had been recurring crises, coming almost predictably in the spring, and again in the autumn. This time, Dagmar wanted a second opinion. A new X-ray and MRI, done in the name of the head of Havel's security to avoid publicity, showed a spot on Havel's lungs. Further examinations pointed to a cancerous growth. Professor Pafko, a leading Prague surgeon, suggested an immediate operation. Havel was just about to leave for a state visit to Ukraine and his aides urged him to go regardless, but Dáša resolutely intervened.[14]

The four-and-a-half-hour-long surgery itself on 2 December 1996 succeeded in removing the tumour, together with one half of the right lung. In retrospect, the fact that Havel did not suffer a relapse until his death in 2011 is the best indicator of its success. What followed, however, brought Havel to the brink of death, created a vast public and medical controversy, and gave birth to the most outrageous rumours, accusations of unethical behaviour of the media, and a book by a tabloid journalist,[15] which was neither as accurate as its author insisted, nor as blasphemous as the president's camp claimed.

Two days after the operation, the patient's breathing problems increased and doctors had to use suction to remove the sputum from his lungs. When the problems persisted, Pafko had no choice but to perform a tracheotomy to enable the president to breathe with the help of a ventilator. But there was no ventilator in the downtown Prague hospital, which exemplified the situation of the Czech public health system inherited from the Communist period, staffed by a large number of highly qualified doctors and nurses, but haunted by a chronic shortage

---

13 *The Talks in Lány*, 5 January 1997, VHL ID2074.
14 Conversation with Dagmar Havlová, 11 July 2012.
15 Svora (1998).

of funds for infrastructure, plant and equipment. There was no central oxygen grid in the hospital. When the pressure in the oxygen cylinder by the president's bedside decreased, it took some time to find the orderly to replace it. Because of the tube in his trachea, the president could not speak and had to communicate with the nurses and staff through notes, scrawled with much difficulty, but invariably courteous and signed with the iconic name and heart. The only thing he complained about was his inability to speak and the need to communicate through mimicry. 'People are so uncomprehending,' he scrawled with a touch of irony.[16]

Finally, Dagmar, overcome by fear for her boyfriend, decided to take matters into her own hands. Rapidly losing trust in the power of traditional medicine to help the patient, she recruited a lady homeopath who managed to infiltrate the hospital and get past the staff and security to reorient the president's bed and install several 'gammastones' with curative properties. This new therapy was discovered when the patient complained of something hard under his back. A major row between the medical staff, the homeopath, Dagmar and the president's staff ensued. Whether the therapy worked is a matter of conjecture, but by 7 December, Havel felt somewhat better. The crisis had abated.

Dagmar's fears, however, had not. She lost all confidence in the hospital, in the medical staff and in the loyalty of Havel's aides, and decided to seek help elsewhere.

When she called me in Washington to tell me that the president was dying and demanded that I arrange for the immediate help of the best medical professionals I could find, it was three in the morning in DC. I did not know any US pulmonary surgeons, but started to work the phones as early in the morning as I could be reasonably certain that the person at the other end of the line would not slam the phone down. Wendy Luers got hold of Paul A Marks, president of the Memorial Sloan Kettering Hospital Cancer Center in New York, who called me back and agreed to dispatch his top surgeon, chief of the thoracic surgical service, Dr Robert Ginsberg.

When the doctor arrived in Prague on an overnight plane the next day he found a patient who had been for the most part stabilized, and a team of fellow professionals who were naturally worried, but on top of the situation.

---

16 Notes from the hospital after surgery, mid-December 1996, VHL ID9531.

He made a few examinations of his own, spoke at a press conference, at which he identified with and praised the work of his Czech colleagues, and left the next day.[17] When I visited the patient a few days later, the president was more keen to talk, with some difficulty, about the latest crisis in the Czech government and about the appointment of Madeleine Albright as the US secretary of state than about his illness. He was let out of the hospital the day after Christmas.

The crisis reverberated for weeks, fuelled by various public claims, counterclaims, rumours and leaks. It did much to give rise to the image of Havel's girlfriend as an emotional, unpredictable and not a little vengeful fury, inordinately protective and jealous of everyone who even remotely threatened her privileged relationship to Havel. The medical profession looked askance at her amateurish and in its view dangerous attempts to take his treatment into her own hands.

Be that as it may, it is entirely possible, even likely, that it was Dagmar's tireless vigil, her pleas and exhortations, as well as her outbursts, that in the end helped overcome what was for Havel undoubtedly a life-and-death situation. At the risk of making herself unpopular, she certainly saw to it that everyone did their best and then some. We will never know, but we have it from Václav Havel himself that she was 'the woman who saved my life'.[18]

There would be a happy ending of Hollywood proportions to the story. Originally it was to follow a scenario, meticulously scripted by Havel himself after he asked Dáša to marry him and after she consented in April 1996.[19] That summer at Hrádeček he compiled a list of wedding guests, made drawings of the ideal wedding costumes and of the bride's bouquet, and, just as twenty years before with Jitka, he scheduled a list of seven public events to 'out' his new partner.[20] The wedding itself was planned for 26 April 1997 and was to take place in a country church in Madé Buky, a short ride from Hrádeček.[21] The illness, however, not only wreaked havoc with Havel's

---

17 Wendy Luers claims, based on her conversations with Paul A. Marks (Dr Ginsberg died in 2003), that Ginsberg actually performed a second operation, removing two more cancerous nodes. The author was unable to find an independent corroboration of this. Conversation with Bill and Wendy Luers, 13 April 2013.
18 *To the Castle and Back*, 329, and elsewhere.
19 Conversation with Dagmar Havlová, 11 July 2012.
20 Ibid.
21 Ibid.

schedule, but was such a strong reminder of mortality that he decided he did not want to wait.

In his New Year speech of 1997, the president spoke not only of the darkly looming clouds on the horizon of Czech politics and the economy, but also of his own brushes with death during the last twelve months, first when Olga died and then when he himself hovered for a week between life and death. He said: 'And I understood, with a new sense of urgency, that the only real source of a will to live is hope, hope as an inner certainty that even things that can appear to us as purely nonsensical can have their own deep meaning and that it is our task to look for it. And I understood, maybe somewhat better than before, why human life ceases to be a life worth living without the love of those close to you.'[22]

On 3 January 1997, he put his heart where his mouth was and married Dagmar Veškrnová in the same town hall where he had married Olga more than forty years before. Jan Tříska was once again Havel's witness. Táňa Fischerová, an ethereal actress colleague of Dagmar's, was hers. It was to be a small private civil ceremony, but due to leaks it ended up in a frenzy of television coverage and tabloid media.[23]

---

22 The New Year Address 1997, in *Works 7*, 663–5.
23 One hitherto unexplained aspect of the story of Havel's illness and his subsequent wedding is who among Havel's closest staff had been leaking deeply private information to the media throughout the whole crisis. Suspicion fell, as it always does in such cases, on the spokesman, Ladislav Špaček, who, however, professes innocence and points to the presidential security detail as likely sources of the leak (conversation with Ladislav Špaček, 31 May 2013).

THE UGLY MOOD

Apart from the usual wishes, just one more thing:
Never become a president.

– Congratulations to Harold Pinter on his
seventieth birthday, 10 October 2000

THE CHANGE IN HAVEL'S MARITAL STATUS provoked an unexpected reaction in the national immune system, which reverberated for more than a year. For reasons, which may not have been altogether rational, the media, the public and even the political class found it difficult to adjust to the president's new marriage. The gap, a little less than a year between Olga's death and the wedding, was criticized as being in poor taste. The contrast between the two women, one of whom had shunned the limelight all her life, whereas the other made her career on the stage, was highlighted to Dáša's disadvantage; the media implied that there was something of a parvenue about the new first lady, without actually saying so. The obvious albeit unfair comparison with Evita Perón had been made.

For a time it seemed as though nothing the presidential couple, and the spouse in particular, ever did was right. She was criticized as being both unprepared for the role of first lady and too keen to play it. Her wardrobe was found too pedestrian and too ostentatious at the same time. In the office of the president, she had to fight tooth and nail for access to her husband, clerical help and office support. When the president suggested publicly that perhaps the first lady should have some legal status, which would clarify her position and rights, he met with an uproar as if he were trying to orchestrate a coup. The initiative went nowhere, but Havel finally dug in his heels, writing a stern memorandum to his staff in which he made it clear that a share of blame for the unhappy situation 'belongs to the president's office, not an insignificant part of which never came to terms with my new marriage . . . Whether someone likes it or not, as of 4 January 1997, there is a married couple in the Prague Castle, a constitutional official elected by the parliament, and a woman elected by him (and hopefully he by her).'[1]

After conquering the illness and marrying Dáša, Havel hoped to reintroduce some kind of order and harmony into his life. It was hard going. A slow-burning political crisis had been brewing in the country. Havel was torn between his official duties and a natural wish to spend some quality time with his new wife. His mental composure had not been helped by the fact that he was now under strict medical orders to refrain from smoking, which he observed with considerable difficulty after more than forty years of indulging the habit.

In the spring, the first couple finally felt free to go on their first holiday together, a kind of post-honeymoon. In a pattern that would keep repeating itself, it turned out to be a game of musical chairs. Havel and Dáša were unimpressed by the elegant and no doubt romantic medieval mansion that Karel Schwarzenberg found for them in the Tyrolean Alps near Bolzano. 'He chose what had been best suited to his aristocratic taste, a house apparently haunted by the largest number of his ancestors', commented Havel drily.[2] Having found the place spooky, not to mention expensive, the couple moved to a *pension* in the beautiful wilderness of the mountains, where Havel's only dilemma was whether to work on his next speech or to relax. 'I cannot do both.'[3] He did neither. After less than a week the Havels unexpectedly descended from the mountains and rushed across half of Europe to stay in a 'luxurious and beautifully furnished bungalow'[4] in the Netherlands. 'I will ask you to stop enquiring about the reasons for this move and trust us to have had good ones,'[5] was as much of an explanation as he ever provided.

---

1 Instructions to the Castle, undated, February 1997, Ladislav Špaček's archive, VHL ID5650.
2 Notes and instructions to the Castle, 13 April 1997, Ladislav Špaček's archive, VHL ID5649.
3 Ibid.
4 Ibid.
5 Ibid.

The illness or the marriage, most likely both, seemed to have altered his understanding of his job. Although he had been complaining about work overload practically since day one in the Castle, now his complaints turned into an open rebellion. He refused to spend as much time in the office as he used to, and insisted that all but the most important meetings and events be removed from his diary. He wanted to cut down on official travel abroad and focus more on domestic issues. He dreamt up the idea of a 'prize trip', travelling with Dáša at his own expense and collecting various awards and accolades extended to him. In a rare bout of extravagance, he insisted that the US leg of the trip be done via the Concorde supersonic jet.

All this was perfectly understandable. Havel enjoyed Dagmar's company more than he enjoyed spending time in the office or with foreign statesmen. He was sixty-one years old and had achieved more than most people manage in a thousand lives. Whether he was aware of it or not, there was also no conceivable way for him to better his record. He could no longer control political developments and give them direction as he had done right after the Velvet Revolution, and he had to be content with the role of a moral authority, both at home and abroad. Democracy and capitalism had triumphed, and were now showing their everyday face, warts and all. In his criticism of the shortcomings of the process, he ran the risk of being seen as a sore winner. The Czech Republic was safely on its way into NATO and the European Union. Not only did he have no need of the job, but arguably the job no longer had need of him. Yet he persisted. On 13 July 1997, citing the joint wish of the four democratic parties in the parliament and his own sense of responsibility, he announced that he would be running again for the presidency in six months' time.[6] This time there seems to have been none of his former hesitancy. There are some indications though, such as the inordinate importance he attached to his speech in the parliament, five months ahead of the event, that he had become convinced that the country was not going in the right direction, and having had enough of being 'an inexhaustible source of hope in hopeless circumstances', he decided to step in once more to help correct its course. Once again, he would be fighting a lonely battle.

In November 1997, Havel was back in hospital with pneumonia. Again there were fears for his life, and again there was Dáša by his bedside.

---

6 Statement of the President on his nomination for the Presidency, 12 July 1997, VHL ID5561.

Politically, he could not have picked a worse time to be ill. The presidential election was two months away. What was worse, the country was sinking deeper and deeper into a political crisis, occasioned by a looming trade deficit, a failing banking system, reports of slush funds kept in banks abroad by certain political parties, and the electorate's loss of trust in politics in general and in the government in particular. The crisis had been brewing for much of the year. Havel had held discreet high-level consultations with the leaders of the three coalition parties in the government, and of the party caucuses, in order to enquire about the degree of the coalition's cohesiveness and possible alternatives to the current political set-up.[7] The political crisis came to a head at the end of November with the collapse of the governing coalition amid allegations of secret accounts stashed away in tax havens abroad by the prime minister's party. The political career of Václav Klaus and many of the politicians who had run the country for the previous five years seemed to be in tatters. It is quite possible that Havel more than silently approved of these developments. It is another thing to claim that he had been actively conspiring to bring Klaus down, a myth akin to an article of faith among some of the prime minister's supporters, but discounted by Klaus himself (though he did blame Havel for contributing to the general atmosphere of discontent).[8] A brief look at Havel's diary in 1997 shows that between illness, marriage, post-honeymoon trips and official travel he had little time to attend to domestic issues, and even less to engage in something as time-consuming as political intrigue. He may have been aware of the rebellion against the prime minister brewing inside the coalition and done nothing to stop it, but this is hardly an impeachable crime. One thing is sure: he had not been opening bank accounts abroad.

His parliamentary speech on 9 December 1997 went down in history as the 'ugly mood speech', although Havel had used the phrase months before, and turned out to be as memorable as he had wished, though not as course-changing as he had hoped. Undoubtedly, it was rather audacious. There cannot be too many instances in which a candidate for a political job spends forty minutes chiding his prospective voters. Ten days after the collapse of the government and the political hierarchy, Havel presented a

---

7 E.g. Coalition Castle Notes, 22 May 1997, Ladislav Špaček's archive, VHL ID5722. The author admits to having been the leader of one of the coalition parties.
8 Conversation with Václav Klaus, 30 August 2013.

justifiably gloomy picture of the country and its political system. 'Many people . . . are disturbed, disappointed or even disgusted by the general condition of society in our country. Many believe that – democracy or no democracy – power is again in the hands of untrustworthy figures whose primary concern is their personal advancement instead of the interests of the people. Many are convinced that honest business people fare badly while fraudulent nouveaux rich get the green light. The prevalent opinion is that in this country it pays off to lie and to steal; that many politicians and civil servants are corruptible; that political parties – though they all declare honest intentions in lofty words – are covertly manipulated by suspicious financial groupings. Many wonder why – after eight years of building a market economy – our economic performance leaves much to be desired, and even compels the government to patch together packages of austerity measures; why we choke in smog when so much money is said to be spent on environment protection; why all prices, including rents and electricity tariffs, have to go up without a corresponding increase in pensions or other social welfare benefits; why they must fear for their safety when walking in the centres of our cities at night; why almost nothing is being built except banks, hotels, and homes for the rich; etc. etc.'[9]

Havel duly attributes part of the blame to the 'post-Communist morass', an inevitable consequence of rapid change, inexperience and the absence of rules and institutions common to all post-Communist countries. The second part of the diagnosis, however, is pure Havel.

'It appears to me that our main fault was pride . . . We behaved like a spoiled only child in a family, or like the top of the class who believe they can give themselves an air of superiority and be everyone else's teacher. Oddly enough, this pride was combined with a kind of provincialism or parochialism . . . Many of us ridiculed all those who spoke about global responsibility in the interconnected civilization of today's world, and maintained that a tiny country like ours should deal only with our tiny Czech problems . . . Fascinated by our macro-economic data, we disregarded the fact that this data, sooner or later, reveals also that which lies beyond the macro-economic or technocratic perception of the world: the things that constitute the only imaginable environment for any economic advancement,

---

9   An address to the House and Senate of the Czech Parliament, 9 December 1997, in *Works 7*, 733–44.

although their weight or significance cannot be calculated by accountants – things like the rules of the game; the rule of law; the moral order behind that system of rules, which is essential for making the rules work; a climate of coexistence.'[10]

The mood at the end of the year was indeed ugly, and Havel was no longer sure that he should run again and could be elected, if he did.[11] It speaks volumes about Havel's still incontestable moral authority that the parliament, many of whose members felt humiliated and offended by Havel's speech, still elected him for the fourth term in office on 20 January 1998, albeit by a meagre majority and in the second round,[12] following a protracted debate consisting mostly of abuse by the deputies representing the Communist Party and the radically nationalist Republicans, whose leader Miroslav Sládek was currently in jail awaiting trial for promoting national hatred. Many of the endorsements of Havel by deputies of the democratic parties were somewhat qualified. Even those like me, now a senator of the Czech Parliament, whose support was unequivocal, felt compelled to place the vote in context: 'We know that we are electing neither a demi-god nor a philosopher king. We are electing one of us, someone fallible like the rest of us, nonetheless a man, who had at an enormous price sacrificed a large part of his life, including the last eight years, to serving the public and this nation . . . This country does not suffer great men gladly, but many of us as well as a large part of the world see at least one great man among us, a fallible great man admittedly, there being no others, and the man is Václav Havel.'[13]

The announcement of the vote was followed by a cry of 'Shame on you, Mr Havel', by the Republican deputy Jan Vik, answered by a shrill whistle from the gallery. The whistler was Dáša Havlová, supporting her husband. At least Havel now knew that this had been his last election; the constitution barred him from running again.

On 2 February 1998, he was once again inaugurated president of the Czech Republic. Things seemed to be looking up. He had a new presidential

---

10 Ibid.
11 Conversation with Petr Pithart, 28 August 2012.
12 Havel won by a single vote in the House ballot; he would have nonetheless won by five votes had the voting gone into the third round, where both houses of the parliament would vote together.
13 1st Joint Meeting of the Two Chambers of the Parliament of the Czech Republic to Elect the President of the Republic, 20 January 1998, www.psp.cz/eknih/1996ps/psse/stenprot/001schuz/index. htm. Ashamed as the author is of quoting himself, there were few instances of serviceable oratory that day.

term and a new wife. His latest health crisis subsided somewhat, and so did the political crisis. Klaus was gone from the prime minister's office. His place was occupied, pending an early election, by Josef Tošovský, formerly the president of the country's Central Bank, at the head of a caretaker government, which owed its authority and legitimacy in equal measures to the president and the political parties holding seats in parliament.

Instead of feeling satisfaction, however, he felt depressed. 'I spent the last weekend in one of my deepest depressions in a long time,' he wrote a month after the inauguration.[14] In response to criticism that he was becoming a 'run-of-the-mill politician' he acknowledged that his speeches were no longer 'poignant and written with pleasure'.[15] It had become an unmistakable symptom of his frustration with the way things were that he ordered yet another reorganization of the president's office. Untypically for Havel, in this period he frequently lost composure, complained to his staff about insufficient support for his work and made ill-conceived accusations, some of which he had to retract. On one occasion he complained to television cameras of the 'laziness' of his office during his absence. 'I am generally overwrought, I get upset easily and in doing so I often unintentionally wrong people,' he acknowledged to his staff in a written apology more typical of him, blaming his irritation in part on withdrawal symptoms from smoking.[16] Natural as the explanation seems, it was hardly the whole story. Not only was he dying for a smoke, but his attempts to turn the country around, back in the direction he believed it should go, were not proving successful.

Before the June 1998 parliamentary elections, Václav Klaus came back from the dead, and campaigned effectively under the banner of 'mobilization' against the allegedly looming takeover of the country by the left. 'To the left, or with Klaus' was the clear-cut choice that his party's billboards offered to the voters. When the left, headed by the leader of the Social Democrats Miloš Zeman, won anyway, followed by Klaus's ODS in second place, Klaus cut a stunning deal called 'the opposition contract' or more loftily 'agreement on political stability', in which he undertook to underwrite Zeman's minority government in an unspoken exchange

14 Instructions to the Castle, 3 March 1998, Ladislav Špaček's archive, VHL ID5651.
15 Ibid.
16 Instructions to the Castle (Dear Colleagues), 6 June 1988, Jaroslava Dutková's archive, VHL ID 5772.

for a number of posts on the boards of state-owned companies for the luminaries of ODS. The country moved to the left, with Klaus.

To make things even more difficult for the president, these events had been preceded by another brush with death. On 14 April 1998, five days into another ill-fated romantic trip to the Austrian Alps with Dáša, Havel was airlifted to a hospital in Innsbruck with acute abdominal pains. Professor Ernst Bodner, a leading Austrian surgeon, diagnosed an intestinal perforation and operated immediately. In all likelihood, Havel was a few hours away from dying of sepsis, and only the surgeon's skills, Havel's remarkable will to live and the ministrations of Dáša, who did not leave his side for a minute, saved him. He recovered and returned to Prague in mid-May.

His health problems continued for the rest of the year. In August, in hospital for another surgery to remove a fistula introduced in a previous operation, Havel's breathing problems resumed, and his heart started failing. He underwent four tracheotomies within two years.

The whole ordeal was accompanied by intrusive and incessant media attention. Apart from a genuine concern for the president's health, a lot of ink was spilled in sweeping generalizations about the comparative state of Czech and Austrian health care, and a number of snide attacks on Dáša, as if she were the cause of his health problems.

It is interesting to note that it is during this very period that Václav Havel was supposed to have transformed himself into a scheming, power-hungry Machiavellist, whose machinations were largely responsible for the temporary removal from power of Václav Klaus. Where Havel's sympathies lay is patently clear, but beside the point. The salient fact is that, of the two years during which his scheming was supposed to be at its most intensive, Havel had spent a full twelve months being acutely ill or recovering from illness. Even had he wanted to fight Klaus, an epitome of fitness, he was too busy fighting for his own life.

It is no exaggeration to say that most people in the country had not expected Havel to be around for much longer. The obituaries had been written, scenarios for a succession discussed. Even those who had known Havel well fought the temptation to resign themselves to the inevitable, but they were not about to underestimate the tenacious fighter within him.

It was not only Havel's health but also his popularity that was declining. Once an untouchable icon, now he was fair game not only for legitimate political criticism, but for the most repulsive gossip of celebrity hunters. Part of it was the adverse reaction to his second marriage and his glamorous spouse. The second part, deliberate and sometimes apparently orchestrated attacks by politically affiliated hacks, is easier to grasp, being a part of the political process everywhere, although traditionally the post of the president at the Castle had been considered somewhat above the political fray. The picture, however, would not be complete without noting the disastrous mishandling of media relations in the two-year period 1996–1998, not so much by Havel's office, but by the president himself.

Being a wordsmith himself, he had always reacted strongly to perceived inaccuracies, fallacies and unfair criticisms of his activities. His instinct was to reason with his critics and explain where they were mistaken. The instinct of those around him was to dissuade him from doing so, in the knowledge that many critics did not give a hoot about reasoning or explanations. 'You need to treat the press like rain,' used to be my resigned advice when I was Havel's spokesman. 'You may find it uncomfortable and unpleasant, but that is all you can do about it.' Fairness and openness to the media was, in my view, the most the president could do for his public image. Spin did not become Havel.

Havel listened most of the time, but not always. As he had already noted in the *Letters to Olga*, he had an irrepressible urge to explain himself when no explanations were needed. I always dreaded the moment when Havel ordered the latest public accounting of the workings of his office, and even more of his personal finances. The motivation of guilt was clear to anyone but the president, who every six months or so felt compelled to disclose how much he was earning from his presidential salary (in tens of thousands of dollars a year), his perks (a cool million crowns, or close to fifty thousand dollars, plus expenses), his literary royalties (much more than that) and the proceeds of the sale of his restituted property (in tens of millions crowns, or millions of dollars) and how much of it he gave to charities and worthy causes (everything he earned by virtue of his presidential position and much more). The result was predictable. Half of the nation was scandalized by the sums he was taking in; the other half dismissed his generosity, since apparently he could so easily afford it. It was a public relations nightmare.

But this was nothing compared to the feud Havel and his wife were now waging with the media. Havel rarely felt the need to defend himself for the stands he took, but he was fiercely protective of Dáša, and reacted to every new perceived slight of her, sometimes disproportionately. He did not have a good grasp of how the media was operating, and he engaged in impractical schemes such as planting a ready-made interview of his wife, questions and all, in the largest of the daily papers *Právo* – incidentally the successor of the Communist Party mouthpiece, which had spent years denouncing and defaming him. The interview never saw the light of day.

Havel then recruited Lída Rakušanová, a friendly journalist formerly of Radio Free Europe, to write a 'true' story of Dáša and their relationship. When the book[17] finally came out, it was largely and not entirely unfairly dismissed as hagiography, unworthy of Havel's literary and moral standards.

Such incidents abounded. Once, after he felt he had been unfairly attacked by the largest Czech commercial television station, Nova, never a great admirer of his, Havel, using the line of the Prague Castle police in desperation, called the news desk of the public-owned Czech News Agency at ten in the evening and demanded the right to dictate a correction. To make matters worse, he failed to inform his press secretary, Ladislav Špaček, about this escapade, thus causing him to deny the whole incident on record the next day. The media had a ball.

When the first lady came up with the initiative to have a dedicated tabloid journalist accompany her on state visits, the press secretary rebelled. The tabloid journalist came along anyway.

It went on and on. Blissfully unaware that he was helping to feed the frenzy, Havel bitterly blamed everybody in sight, the media, his political opponents, even his office. In the autumn of 1998 he finally arrived at a simple solution: 'I stopped reading newspapers, watching TV and following media monitors. What a beautiful life!!!'[18]

It would have been great, if it could have lasted. A month later Havel was embroiled in another media controversy, this time with moral undertones. Among the luminaries to be decorated with the highest distinctions of the state at the annual ceremony marking Independence Day on 28 October was the former mayor of Vienna, and a longtime advocate of close Czech and Austrian relations, Helmut Zilk. A few days before the ceremony, the

---

17 Rakušanová (1997).
18 Note to Ladislav Špaček, 29 September 1998. Ladislav Špaček's archive, VHL ID9483.

Süddeutsche Zeitung published the information that Zilk had been a paid agent of the Czech secret intelligence in the mid-sixties. Zilk denied the accusations. In a mad scramble amid conflicting signals, Havel withdrew the award, causing a strain on Czech-Austrian relations, already strained by disputes about the Czech nuclear power station in Temelín near the border of the country's fiercely anti-nuclear neighbour. In the aftermath of the scandal, Havel invited Zilk to a meeting in his private villa and expressed regrets for the incident, blaming media hostility and the poor job done by his office. Václav Benda, the fellow prisoner and fellow dissident from the days of old, now a conservative senator in Klaus's ODS party[19] and director of the newly formed Office for the Documentation and Investigation (UDV) of the Communist past, a homologue of the Gauck's Institute in Germany, accused Havel of having known about Zilk's unsavoury past beforehand; he had in fact obtained the information, based on the files of the StB, from Benda himself. In turn Havel accused Benda of lying; however, his chief of staff, the gentlemanly and dignified Ivan Medek, then publicly acknowledged having run the candidates through the UDV files at the behest of the president. Medek had to leave the Castle. The whole steaming mess was mercifully overshadowed by another of Havel's pulmonary events and the upcoming Christmas holidays.[20]

---

19 Benda, who died six months later, was sometimes described as the father of the 'opposition contract', with some justification.

20 The newspaper *MF DNES* reprinted a series of facsimile documents from the StB files, which showed that between 1965 and 1968 Zilk, under the name of HOLEC, was listed as a collaborator of the StB and obtained a significant amount of money for his services, along with assorted presents.

Farewell to Arms

I was truly catapulted into a fairy-tale world, only to
find myself falling back to earth for many years.
– Václav Havel, City University of New York, 20 September 2002

INEVITABLY, THE TWO YEARS OF PROBLEMS caused Havel's popularity to suffer. In a public opinion poll taken in December 1998, fifty-five per cent answered affirmatively when asked: 'Should the president consider resigning?' although the question itself was so leading it smacked of political bias.

If Havel thought about resigning he never let it be known. He was in for another difficult year, but this time he was up to the fight. On 12 March, one of his longest-held ambitions, the accession of the country into NATO, came to fruition after almost a decade of tireless advocacy. As described in a previous chapter, in January 1994 in Prague he was able to extract from Bill Clinton the pledge that the question was not if but when. Using the same approach as Lech Wałęsa, he wined and dined Boris Yeltsin in the Lesser Town Golden Thirteen Tavern until the latter couldn't tell the difference between the Warsaw Pact and NATO and did not care if he did. In 1997, he was present at the Madrid summit of the Alliance when the decision to invite the three countries of Central Europe was taken. He kept prodding and urging, both at home and abroad. Well aware of the Marxist (*sensu Groucho*) maxim about never wanting to become a member of a club that would have someone like him for a member, he sought to give assurances that the country would walk the walk as well. Three months before the date of the enlargement, he added a quasi-treasonous handwritten note to his letter of thanks to Secretary of State Madeleine Albright: 'Confidential! Secret! Be strict with us before our entry into NATO! We are a nation of talkers!'[1]

Now the Czech Republic, along with Hungary and Poland, became the first post-Communist countries to be members of the North Atlantic Alliance. The exact moment, 12 March 1999, was the depositing of the instruments of accession at a ceremony at the Harry S Truman Presidential Library and Museum in Independence, Missouri, a spot two hours away on I-70 from Fulton in Truman's home state, where Churchill had proclaimed the Iron Curtain descending over Europe 'from Stettin in the Baltic to Trieste in the Adriatic'.[2] If the dissolution of the Warsaw Pact formally marked the end of the Cold War, the enlargement of NATO put to rest the long shadows of the Yalta Conference of February 1945, an occasion that had been construed, rightly or wrongly, as the handover by the Western allies of Central and Eastern Europe to the tender mercies of Stalin. The 'ancient states of Central and Eastern Europe'[3] were now reunited with their Western neighbours.

If Havel and most of his compatriots had envisaged a solemn, ceremonial entry into NATO's zone of security and stability, they got more than they bargained for. Twelve days after the enlargement came into force NATO aircraft started bombing Yugoslavia to stop the campaign of intimidation and ethnic cleansing against the Kosovo Albanians. The new members, who could hardly contribute to the aerial campaign with their ageing Soviet-made, NATO-incompatible aircraft, were caught somewhat unprepared by the developments. The Czech government debated for hours about the wisdom of the operation, while NATO aircraft stood with their engines idling at the Aviano airbase waiting for the required unanimous consent. Havel, on the other hand, had been clear in his mind about what had to be done for some time. 'The parties to the conflict must be made aware that there is no other option but to sit down and negotiate. It must be clear that the only alternative to negotiations for Belgrade is the use of force by the Atlantic alliance.'[4] Although he did not rejoice, calling the operation an 'extreme solution', he expressed his unequivocal support for the action, which was in

---

1 Letter to Madeleine Albright, 7 December 1998, National Archives, Prague, VHL ID15910.
2 Churchill, Winston, *Sinews of Peace*, Speech at Westminster College, Fulton, Missouri, 5 March 1946.
3 Ibid.
4 Statement on the situation in Kosovo, Prague, 28 January 1999, VHL ID1106.

his view 'wholly unavoidable'.[5] As always when faced with a difficult decision, he fell back on a simple moral precept: 'Our own historical experience has taught us that evil must be confronted rather than appeased.'[6] He chose to disregard misgivings expressed by both leaders of the 'opposition contract' parties and the minister of foreign affairs, Jan Kavan; the latter, together with Giorgos Papandreou, the Greek foreign minister, would launch his own peace initiative, which subtly undermined the NATO order of battle by envisaging the cessation of the bombardment first and negotiations later. Havel was unimpressed. 'The government had two meetings about our participation in the war and none of the ministers could be bothered to pick up a phone and call the commander-in-chief. This sets me free. I don't have to feel any sentimental regard for those people.'[7]

He had been most likely unaware that he was crossing a Rubicon of sorts. Eschewing the painful deliberations of a moral philosopher, he felt he was doing his job as a statesman, and a commander-in-chief, who had to make a clear yes-or-no decision. By doing this, he also earned the lasting enmity of a coalition of domestic and foreign opponents of the NATO intervention, ranging from isolationist conservatives through advocates of hard-nosed *realpolitik*, to conspiracy theorists on the far left, who saw the whole thing as another instance of the American imperialist plan to rule the world. For Kosovo, more than Bosnia or the Gulf before it, tiny, insignificant, and without any apparent strategic or economic importance to the West, gave rise to the doctrine of humanitarian intervention, a military action whose sole purpose is to prevent the killing of innocent civilians. It was controversial then and is now, when it has been renamed 'responsibility to protect (R2P)'. Václav Havel is rightly seen as one of the ideological fathers of this doctrine, along with the similarly Czech-born and Munich-traumatized sister figure of Madeleine Albright. From the opposing perspective of post-Stalinist thinkers like Slavoj Žižek,[8] and libertarian socialists like Noam Chomsky, a sworn enemy of Havel since

---

5 Statement on the situation in Kosovo, Prague, 25 March 1999, VHL ID1113.
6 Statement of the President of the Republic Václav Havel on the NATO military intervention in Yugoslavia, Prague, 24 March 1999, VHL ID1112.
7 Instructions to the Castle, 11 April 1999, VHL ID5656.
8 'Attempts to Escape the Logic of Capitalism', *London Review of Books*, Vol. 21, No. 21, 28 October 1999, 3–6.

the latter's 1990 speech in the US Congress,[9] he is seen as a 'useful idiot' of American imperialism, a label applied on this occasion by the otherwise sympathetic late Tony Judt.[10] Unlike the moral dilemma of supporting the use of a lethal force to prevent more death, the name-calling, to the best of my knowledge, never caused Havel to lose a night's sleep.

He had become increasingly irritated, on the other hand, with the continuing infringements on his privacy and with any sort of criticism, overt or implied, regarding his personal affairs and, above all, his marriage. In the autumn of 1998, following the presidential pair's state visit to the United States, the tabloids began to speculate about possible marital problems and even infidelities.

None of these, or other similar, claims has ever been independently corroborated, and most of them can be subsumed under the pile of tabloid rubbish that gets written about any important figure in the postmodern era. It is, nevertheless, an undisputable fact that Havel went into a profound depression, for the first time entertaining the possibility of resigning the presidency.[11] He showed ever more numerous signs of frustration and disappointment, two states of mind to which he had always seemed to be immune. In one of his depressive fits, he wrote to the 'Castle': 'Dear Castle, the cup hath spilled over. There is something rotten either in me, or in the society. Whatever it is, I can't take it any longer. I work like there is no tomorrow, have a hundred things on my plate every day, not a single day of rest, and the result? I appear more and more like an asshole . . . I am in a state of revolt. I have been signalling this for a long time and it is a pity no one has noticed . . . I want peace. I want to write, read and rest. I do not deserve this everyday humiliation after everything I have done for this country. By the way, Dáša and I are buying a small house by the sea in Spain . . . and we will stay there as often as possible. Let my country flourish under Klaus.'[12]

The psychological crisis had been exacerbated by recurring respiratory

9 'On Václav Havel Speech', in Alexander Cockburn, *The Golden Age Is In Us* (Verso, 1995), 149–151.

10 'Bush's Useful Idiots', *London Review of Books*, Vol. 28, No. 18, 21 September 2006, 3–5.

11 'He is considering resignation.' Diary of Jaroslava Dutková, private secretary to Václav Havel, 9 September 1999, Jaroslava Dutková's archive, VHL ID10306.

12 Instructions to the Castle (Dear Castle), 23 September 1999, Ladislav Špaček's archive, VHL ID5713. It is perhaps symptomatic that at the moment the country was more or less flourishing under the social democratic government of Miloš Zeman, rather than under Klaus who held the ceremonial post of the Speaker of the House. Also, the house that Havel and Dáša eventually bought was in Portugal rather than Spain.

problems and bouts of illness. In a pattern that was rapidly becoming regular, Havel alternated between attending to his duties, spending time in hospital, recuperating at Lány or Hrádeček to gather strength for a foreign visit, and then falling ill again and convalescing at home or abroad. He now had to attend to his health problems for about half of the time. The will to transcend difficulties and overcome obstacles seemed to be draining away from him. 'After all those surgeries and struggles I don't feel like fighting on,' he confided to his secretary in one of his weaker moments.[13] Deep down, however, he probably knew that he had no choice but to go on. Too many people relied on him and he felt responsible to too many people. 'Please, do not give up on anything, neither the most public nor the most personal,' fellow writer and friend Jiří Stránský, the president of the Czech PEN club, wrote to him.[14]

Havel fought on, grimly but without much enthusiasm or energy, in the face of continuing attacks. In an opinion poll in April 2000, fifty-three and a half per cent of the respondents, mostly on the political left, thought Havel should resign.[15] In mid-2000, together with what remained of the parliamentary opposition, he fought to prevent the two parties of the 'opposition contract' from changing the voting system for the lower house of the parliament in a manner that would for all practical purposes wipe out the smaller parliamentary parties and lead to the establishment of a two-party system (the Czech constitution dictates that the House be elected under a system of proportional representation). The opposition lost the vote in the parliament and the House overruled the president's veto, but Havel immediately appealed to the Constitutional Court, which struck down the offending parts of the legislation.

He did not shy away from an even fiercer conflict with the government when he appointed the new governor and vice-governor of the Central Bank, contrary to the explicit wishes of the governor's predecessor and former prime minister, Josef Tošovský. Prime Minister Miloš Zeman insisted, along with the rest of the government, on his right to co-nominate the new governor, and harsh words were spoken when Havel

---

13 Diary of Jaroslava Dutková, 29 March 2000, Jaroslava Dutková's archive, VHL ID10318.
14 Letter of Jiří Stránský to Václav Havel, 27 February 2000, VHL ID6823.
15 Sofres-Factum poll, Czech News Agency, 9 May 2000.

did not budge in a face-to-face meeting.[16] Once again, the constitution was clearly on Havel's side, but he paid the price by being exposed to vitriolic attacks in the press and accused of dictatorial ambitions or even treason. Sometimes, it seemed like too much to take. 'He called that he's moving to Portugal and let the Czech nation govern itself,' noted his secretary.[17]

This particular, and not very happy, period of Havel's life can be seen either as a proof of his sheer stubbornness and determination to cling to his office at life-threatening cost, or alternatively as heroic self-sacrifice in the name of his responsibility to serve. Perhaps it was both. The cold truth is that between November 1996, when his health problems started to mount, and the end of the millennium, Havel spent no less than twenty-two months, almost one half of the total, either being ill, hospitalized, recuperating or convalescing, and much of the rest of the time feeling miserable. The truth is also that in the same period he shepherded the country more or less intact through the most serious crisis of government in its short history, helped to prevent the kidnapping of the constitution to serve the interests of the two most powerful parties, protected the independence of the Central Bank from the government, finalized the membership of the country in NATO, and made it deal honourably if not resolutely with the first military operation of its membership, put it on the irrevocable course to join the EU, and continued to be the international face of a democratic and humane Czech Republic. It might therefore be asked whether another man or woman in his position and with the same limited constitutional powers could have done as much or more.

Although the end of the nineties could hardly be called Havel's most creative period, he was not entirely idle in that department, either. He searched for and found the intellectual home for his life philosophy in the Forum 2000 conference, which he started with Elie Wiesel in 1997 under the sponsorship of Yōhei Sasakawa; this was initially intended as a one-off affair, but has now survived him and is entering its seventeenth year of two-day discussions of global political, social and spiritual issues, and

---

16 Diary of Jaroslava Dutková, 23 November 2000, Jaroslava Dutková's archive, VHL ID10324. The incident has been also confirmed by Ivo Mathé, Havel's chancellor at the time, in a conversation with the author, 31 August 2013, and Dáša Havlová, 'I had to take exception to Zeman's attack on my husband,' ČTK, 1 December 2000.
17 Diary of Jaroslava Dutková, 25 July 2000, Jaroslava Dutková's archive, VHL ID10320.

growing all the time.[18] The physical expression of the same philosophy was the restoration, through the efforts of his and Dáša's VIZE 97 Foundation, of the deconsecrated Church of St Anne, a spiritual site with more than a thousand years of history opposite the Theatre on the Balustrade, and its transformation into the Prague Crossroads, a meeting and debating space for thinkers and intellectuals from around the world. In 2004, Forum 2000 moved its opening ceremony to Prague Crossroads, symbolically merging the two initiatives. Over the last fifteen years, Prague has seen, among others, His Holiness the Dalai Lama, Bill and Hillary Clinton, Elie Wiesel, Madeleine Albright, Shimon Peres and George Soros debating the problems and the future of the planet, with Richard von Weizsäcker, Francis Fukuyama, Paul Wolfowitz, James Woolsey, Grigory Yavlinsky and Henry Kissinger. Aung San Suu Kyi, Havel's soulmate that he never met, spoke to the Forum by video from her involuntary seclusion in Burma.[19]

On a personal front, Havel gave himself a welcome present by publishing, in December 1999, 'the little green box', a seven-volume edition of his collected works.[20] In terms of time and attention lavished on it, the enterprise could have seemed a mere vanity project. But the evidently superior quality and range of the writing, as well as the author's clear desire to satisfy his own sense of order rather than any *delusion de grandeur*, obviate any such suspicion. After all, Havel was first editing his 'collected works' at the age of seventeen.

Occasionally, Havel also mused in public about his writing plans for the time after the presidency. He kept mentioning a new play, sometimes hinting at going back to the *Lear* motif he had left unfinished before the revolution, sometimes at a play about a new and surprising subject, having 'nothing to do with politics'. He made it repeatedly clear that he did not plan to write a book of presidential memoirs, although he referred to a book drawing on his presidential experience, 'something between Henry Kissinger and Charles Bukowski'.[21]

Catering to his lifelong need for intellectual stimulation, Havel also sponsored a series of informal and non-public debates involving a score

---

18 Disclosure: the author serves on the Program Board of the Forum 2000.

19 When Daw Aung San was finally able to come to the Forum in 2013, Havel was already dead.

20 Prague: Torst, 1999. An eighth volume of works written between 1999 and 2006 was released by the same publisher in 2007.

21 'Havel is planning to write a book', *Lidové noviny*, 30 August 2001.

or so participants on various topical subjects, most of them held in an elaborately carved wooden hunting lodge, 'Amálie', deep in the wooded game preserve of the Lány castle. Eighty-four such debates, ranging in theme from the war in Iraq through constitutional issues to green policies, were held between 1994 and 2010, the tradition once again surviving the presidency.

The last couple of years of the Havel presidency were marked by his effort to keep his health problems, always a contaminated breath away, at bay, and to conserve what strength he had for a small number of priorities. Few of them concerned domestic politics; after the clashes of 1999 and 2000 the struggle between the president and the political establishment reached an uneasy stalemate. Having fought off attempts to alter the constitutional balance, Havel was largely powerless to intervene in day-to-day politics, controlled by the two parties of the opposition contract. The sole exception was foreign policy, where the constitution combined with his enormous international prestige mostly gave him an upper hand in skirmishes with the tirelessly scheming Foreign Minister Kavan. Indeed, Havel was vastly relieved when the minister decided to run for the ceremonial post of president of the General Assembly of the United Nations for the period 2002–2003.[22]

It was therefore not surprising that Havel focused his energies on two major international events of his last year in office. The first was his last official visit to the United States, the country where he experienced perhaps his most glorious political moments, and which had remained for him the shining beacon of freedom and democracy. The second was the summit of the heads of member states of the Atlantic Alliance to be held in Prague in November 2002, the first such meeting in a former Communist capital, and hopefully the opening stage for the second wave of the enlargement of NATO by seven post-Communist countries, including the post-Soviet Baltic countries of Latvia, Lithuania and Estonia. The prestigious summit was awarded to Prague thanks to active and persistent lobbying by Havel himself, and his long-time loyalist, later ambassador to the United States, Saša Vondra, who would be put in charge of organizing the event. As early as eighteen months before, Havel was already laying down his plans

---

22 Instructions to the Castle, 15 May 2001, Ladislav Špaček's archive, VHL ID5664.

for the summit, conceiving of it as a poetic extravaganza as much as a formal meeting of statesmen and generals planning the defence strategy of the West.

Two events intervened to alter the character of both the trip and the summit. The first was 9/11. By the time Havel went to Washington, America was on a war footing and the countdown to the invasion of Iraq had started. Havel's invitation to a meeting in the Oval Office was not only a farewell gesture in recognition of his historical role, but also a reward for the unflinching support, both moral and material, the Czech Republic had given the United States in the aftermath of the terrorist attacks. 'You were the first to support me [after 9/11]. I have learned something from you. One must speak morally [and] clearly.'[23] Bush also told Havel: 'There is no doubt in my mind that Saddam has weapons of mass destruction and that he is going to acquire nuclear weapons. There is no doubt in my mind that he is going to continue murdering his own citizens.'[24]

Such assurances from the chief executive of the remaining superpower were enough for Havel to express his clear support for the policy of confrontation with Iraq that Bush had embarked upon: 'The evil must be resisted at the start . . . We feel a co-responsibility with the United States . . . Most countries in the Security Council will adopt a similar position if Saddam continues to violate the UN resolutions.'[25]

His general support of the American position remained consistent throughout the run-up to the war, but it was not entirely unqualified. In speaking about Iraq at an Aspen Institute conference preceding the NATO Prague summit, he was absolutely frank about the moral dilemma such support entailed: 'Personally, I am usually inclined to believe that evil should be opposed in its embryonic form before it has a chance to grow, and that human life, human freedom and human dignity are higher values than state sovereignty. Perhaps this inclination gives me the right to open this undoubtedly extremely serious and complex question.

'During my life my country had learned two lessons, both with immense, far-reaching and long-lasting consequences: the first was the Munich capitulation, when the two principal European democracies,

---

23 Notes of the meeting in the Oval Office, 15 September 2002, Ladislav Špaček's atchive, VHL ID5721.
24 Ibid.
25 Ibid.

supposedly in the interest of peace, yielded to Hitler's pressure and allowed him to dismember the then Czechoslovakia. Naturally, there was no peace. On the contrary: Hitler took their conduct in Munich as the last sign that he was free to unleash a bloody European and ultimately world war. I think that not only I but most of my fellow citizens understand the experience of Munich as an argument supporting the idea that evil must be resisted at the very beginning.

'But we also have a different experience: the occupation [of Czecho-slovakia] by the countries of the Warsaw Pact in 1968. The whole nation then repeated the word "sovereignty" and execrated the official Soviet claim that it was a "fraternal assistance" done in the name of a higher value than national sovereignty, i.e. in the name of socialism that had been allegedly imperilled in the country, which in turn allegedly threatened the very hope of the human race for a better life. Almost everyone back home knew then that what was at stake was simply Soviet hegemony and economic exploitation; nonetheless millions of people in the Soviet Union probably believed that national sovereignty was being suppressed in the name of a higher, humanistic value.

'This second experience leads me to be very cautious. And it seems to me that whenever we want to intervene against a country in the name of the protection of human life, we need to ask ourselves – if only for a second and surreptitiously – whether this was not after all some version of a "fraternal assistance".[26]

The other event that coloured the mood of this last period of Havel's presidency was of domestic origin and not man-made. In August 2002, a once-every-five-hundred-years flood devastated large parts of the Czech countryside and the riverbanks of Vltava in Prague, killing seventeen people, causing damage in the billions, and flushing a sea lion from the Prague Zoo all the way to Lutherstadt-Wittenberg in Germany, some three hundred kilometres away. When the catastrophe hit in the middle of August, Havel was resting in Portugal. Having to deal alone with incomplete and confusing information about the extent of the disaster and to improvise the logistics of his return to Prague from the remote resort with no direct flight connections, it took him a respectable forty-eight hours to arrive

---

26 Opening speech at the conference 'The Transformation of NATO', Prague, Sovovy mlýny, 20 November 2002.

back at his post. In the meantime, however, his press secretary Ladislav Špaček, suffering from the same paucity of information, said truthfully but unfortunately that he was not aware of any plans by the president to return.

It was Hurricane Katrina, three years before. Although the powers of the Czech president to deal with natural disasters on this scale are vastly smaller than those of the US chief executive, the media played up the story of the president idling on a beach while his subjects were drowning in mud. The media storm passed much more quickly than the effects of the flooding, yet Havel felt painfully humiliated, all the more so because he had acted as decisively as he could. He blamed his office for letting him down and was determined to cancel all the other planned R&R trips for the remainder of the presidency. 'The feeling of ultimate disgrace at the close of my career is more dangerous to my health than the Bohemian smog.'[27]

In the end, the country recovered from the disaster more quickly than its president. When he came to the United States in September 2002 for his last dinner in the White House as Czech president, he was still bombarded by statements of sympathy and support, but he felt no need to ask for material help.

The NATO summit itself was to be Havel's swansong and he did not intend to let it go unnoticed. By then a veteran of such occasions, he was well aware that all the speeches, statements and choreography are pre-cooked well in advance, so that on delivery they taste like an airline dinner. There would be little room for him to deviate from the script, and even less inclination on his part to try to upstage the guest heads of state by rhetorical fireworks. Yet he was determined to make his mark. The opportunity to do so was at the official dinner on the first day of the summit, which, unlike the meeting itself, was to take place in the Castle and had no formal content or prescribed format.

The preparation for the big night had demonstrated all the strengths and weaknesses of Havel's governing style. Eighteen months before the date he was choosing the theme, creating the dramaturgy and remodelling the Castle to suit the occasion. As usual, his perfectionism would not allow him to stick to the main subject, but led him to dwell on the contents of the

27 Instructions to the Castle, 26 September 2002, Ladislav Špaček's archive, VHL ID5679.

menu, the centrepieces on the tables and the colour of the lighting fixtures in the hallway. Even so, he was not about to lose sight of the bigger picture. His ambition was to turn the meeting of statesmen, bureaucrats, strategists and military brass into a spectacular celebration of freedom, not just in the political sense, but in the sense of being free to enjoy one's inner freedom. The first thing the guests saw on arrival at the dinner was a great neon heart, for a long time a part of Havel's signature, shining high above the Castle, the work of sculptor Jiří David.

The dinner, an elaborate four-course affair, with speeches and toasts by Secretary General Robertson and President Jacques Chirac, and only a short welcome by the host, did not take place, as most state dinners do, in the ornate baroque Spanish Hall or Rudolf's Gallery; rather, it was held in the medieval Vladislav Hall where coronations, royal banquets and balls had been taking place since the fifteenth century, and where Havel was elected president for the first time in 1989. But the main course came after dinner, in the shape of a 'Celebration of Freedom', a song-and-dance extravaganza featuring a modern ballet choreographed by Jiří Kylián, a native of Prague and the artistic director of the Nederlands Dans Theater, along with a strikingly postmodern medley of songs, including Lennon's 'Power to the People' and 'Imagine', Beethoven's *Ode to Joy*, the post-Civil War 'Oh, Freedom' and, for good balance, the 'Marseillaise'. The music was arranged by Michal Pavlíček, a legendary Czech rock guitarist, and performed by leading Czech rock stars. A challenge was presented by the text of the *Ode to Joy*, whose nineteenth-century English translation was deemed by Havel too archaic for the purposes of the evening, and so he approached me. I was by then the distinguished chairman of the Committee on Foreign Affairs, Defence and Security of the Czech Senate, but among my many other sins I also had been a mildly successful rock lyricist in my younger days. Now I was horrified. 'Oh, come on, Václav, you can't be serious. This is Schiller, and Beethoven, not the Mamas and Papas. No way I can do this.' 'I understand,' said the ever tolerant president, 'it is your call, but have you ever had a song of yours performed in front of fifty heads of state?' And so I wrote the lyrics, leaving out the cherub and the daughter of Elysium.

Judging by the applause, the evening was a success with most, if not all, of those present. When a guest asked Vice President Cheney how he had enjoyed the performance, Cheney said: 'Well, me, I am from

Nebraska.'[28]

There was one more extravaganza to come on 30 January 2003, this time not of Havel's making. Unbeknownst to her husband, Dáša had been putting together, scripting and producing an 'Homage to Václav Havel', in which many of the most popular actors, musicians and singers in the country would express their appreciation of the great man, along with videotaped praise from Madeleine Albright, Kofi Annan, Sean Connery, and Bush father and son. The show, for a hand-picked audience of the mighty and the glamorous, took place in the 'Golden Chapel' of Czech national and cultural life, as the Prague National Theatre is traditionally called.

For all the effort Dáša put into organizing the event and all the talent she had managed to recruit, it was not an unmitigated success. While the line-up was unmistakably an A-list of the most popular performers, many of Havel's friends felt it had little to do with his life and the kind of man he was. The programme featured some of the well-worn stars of the 'normalization' era, headed by the multiple 'Golden Nightingales', Karel Gott and Helena Vondráčková, and included even a police informer or two. On the other hand, some of Havel's inner circle, most conspicuously the Plastic People, were missing.

Many of the absentees were waiting for the president across the street in the Parnas restaurant next to the Slavia Café, to share a drink after the show and say a word of thanks. True to form of this crowd, the tributes came so disguised that an outsider would not recognize them as such.

The second of February was Havel's last day in office, and an exercise in humility. He deliberately spent the day doing what he always insisted was not the reason he wanted to be president – laying wreaths, one to T G Masaryk at his statue in front of the Castle, two to the graves of the victims of the Communist persecution, and one to the statue of St Wenceslas in the eponymous square, where Jan Palach had set fire to himself, and where the seeds of the Velvet Revolution had been sown.

In the evening he said farewell to his fellow citizens. He thanked 'all those of you who have trusted me, sympathized with me or in any way supported me', and he thanked his wife. He reassured the listeners

---

28 David Remnick, in 'Exit Havel, The King leaves the Castle', *The New Yorker*, 17 February 2003, has Cheney say, 'I didn't understand anything, I'm from Chicago,' but that must have been hearsay. Cheney is not from Chicago.

that 'I have always tried to abide by the dictates of the authority under which I took my oath of office – the dictates of the best of my awareness and conscience', all standard farewell stuff, a cynic would say. But then he added a line, which was genuinely, unmistakably and uniquely his own, worlds apart from the world of *realpolitik*: 'To all of you whom I have disappointed in any way, who have not agreed with my actions or who have simply found me hateful, I sincerely apologize and trust that you will forgive me.'[29] And then he was gone.

---

29 Farewell Address to Czech Citizens by Václav Havel, President of the Republic, Czech Television, Czech Radio, 2 February 2003. http://www.Václavhavel.cz/index.php?sec=3&id=1&setln=2.

PAROLED

How wonderful it is, by comparison, to be a writer! You write something in a couple of weeks, and it's here for the ages. What will remain when the presidents and prime ministers are gone? Some references to them in textbooks, most likely inaccurate.

– To the Castle and Back

AFTER THIRTEEN YEARS, HAVEL'S STATURE, popularity and influence were perceptibly diminished and some even thought of him as a figure from the past. Yet the impression could only be taken as a measure of the man if one ignored the remarkable balance sheet of his presidency. He had to be given credit for the peaceful transformation of the country from totalitarian rule to democracy; for building a stable system of democratic and political institutions, comparable in most respects, flaws included, to long-existing systems in the West; he had successfully brought the country back to Europe and made it an integral part of Western political and security alliances; and he remained an inspiration and indefatigable supporter in the struggle for human rights and freedoms around the world. On the debit side of the ledger, he stood at the helm when Czechoslovakia veered towards a split, but this failure was itself mitigated by the peaceful and consensual character of the divorce. He conspicuously failed at making the society at large adhere to his ideals of morality, tolerance and civic spirit, but that said more about the society than about him. Arguably, he had never expected to succeed fully.

His departure from the office and Klaus's election to the presidency clearly marked the end of an era. Gone were the improvisation and the spur-of-the-moment initiatives. Gone was also the idealism of the revolutionary days. The new era belonged to pragmatists, political managers and media experts. On the international scene, the aura of the country, perhaps never truly deserved, as a Platonic republic run by artists and philosophers in an enlightened democratic manner (although Plato himself was no democrat) faded somewhat. The new president was undoubtedly a strong figure with strong views to match, and the willingness and ability to make them known both at home and abroad, but internationally, both he and his views were definitely a minority taste. Perhaps more than the views themselves, it was his contrarian, in-your-face style that made many people wistfully remember the diffident yet cool Havel.

Havel was not going to complicate matters for Klaus. He knew that at least initially he had to make himself inconspicuous. He also needed a long rest. At the same time he did not think of retiring, playing golf or tending flowers. His diary was crowded with all the requests for visits and appointments he did not have time to grant during his presidency and so too his mind was swarming with ideas he had been nursing for years, waiting for the moment of liberation.

For the first time, the country's government and legislators were faced with the problem of what to do with a former head of state. Most of the previous presidents, from Masaryk onwards, conveniently died in office or shortly after leaving it. After a year-long deliberation, and on a second attempt, the parliament granted Havel and all his successors a modest rent, a grant for an office and staff, the use of a car, and a personal protection detail.[1]

Once again, the syndrome that Havel repeatedly described on his release from prison, and on a larger scale, following the release of the country from the prison of totalitarianism, now repeated itself on his release from the prison of the presidency. 'My ideas of how free I would become turned out to be big illusions.'[2] He felt uprooted and confused. He was also totally exhausted after thirteen years in the highest office. His health was precarious, mainly because of the loss of lung capacity. Any small respiratory infection

---

1 Act on the Providing for the Needs of the President of the Republic after the End of his Mandate of 21 January 2004, No. 48/2004.
2 Interview for *Lidové noviny*, 15 November 2003.

was potentially life-threatening. Once again he felt like 'a deflated balloon'. In a few months, he realized that the terms of his newfound freedom were even more complex and contradictory than he thought. Try as he might, he would never be entirely free again. Rather than being set free, he had been let out on parole.

In his first post-presidential year, at least, he tried to take it easy. He finally had time to spend with Dagmar and to do things he'd dreamt about for years, like being able to drive a car (an ardent advocate of environmental causes, he bought himself a huge Mercedes SUV) and cook his own meals. That summer he and Dagmar took a trip across the continent all the way to Andalusia. There the expensive tractor broke down and they had to return by rail and air. There were other trips that year, to Barbados, to the house in Portugal twice, to the Tyrolean Alps and to Gran Canaria at the end of the year. Havel also spent almost a month in Hrádeček. He took few 'official' trips, all of them short, including a three-day trip to the United States in July to receive the Presidential Medal of Freedom, the highest civilian award bestowed by the Chief Executive. Among the fellow recipients that year were Edward Teller, the creator of the H-bomb, and Charlton Heston, the Oscar winner for *Ben Hur*.

It was not like Havel, however, to be inactive for long. When the accumulated fatigue of a quarter of a century on the frontline had worn off, he once again became restless. He also became more outspoken, no longer feeling any need to safeguard the dignity of his office. He was irritated with the materialistic, insular and petty-minded mood that seemed to be prevailing in the nation. When an avant-garde 'equestrian' statue of Franz Kafka, the German-Jewish native of the city, was unveiled in front of the Prague Spanish Synagogue in December 2003, Havel contributed to the ceremony with a tongue-in-cheek speech purporting to express the vox populi: 'We live at a time when every conscientious and honestly working or enterprising Czech realizes with a new urgency the importance of the Czech national interest and of our struggle for this interest. Our national interest is in our interest and we need to be interested in how it is defended and whether everything we do is really in the interest of our interest. As an honestly working and enterprising Czech I therefore must pose a question which may be unpopular but which is in our interest: "Aren't there enough genuine, honestly working or enterprising . . . Czechs who still do not have a monument in Prague and who would deserve it more than [Franz Kafka] because of their work for our nation and their patriotism?"[3] The dissident was back at work.

So was his humour. Its disappearance, though never total, had been probably the best indication of the bleak discontent that had permeated his last years in office, and of the poor state of his health. But it seems that his health itself had suffered as a result of his unhappiness with his job. In striking contrast to the previous five years, Havel suffered not a single episode of serious illness from the day he left the office till the end of the year. He started seeing friends again, he went to the theatre, to the cinema and to the concerts of both the Rolling Stones and, in the company of his friend Mia Farrow, Bob Dylan in Prague, and he could be found from time to time in one of his beloved 'little bars' downtown. Gradually, his working energy also returned.

There were several projects nearing completion and others to attend to. The Prague Crossroads was largely finished and taking off. The Forum 2000 was humming along, growing bigger every year, under the able stewardship of Oldřich Černý, the one-time security adviser and head of the foreign intelligence service. Dagmar attended to the practical matters concerning the VIZE 97 Foundation.

There were two other things on the former president's mind. One was his legacy. By any standards of literature or politics, Havel was a hugely productive individual. Apart from a score of dramatic works and dozens of seminal essays, he was the author of hundreds of shorter texts, and hundreds of speeches and op-ed pieces, the subject of thousands of interviews, and both author and recipient of a voluminous correspondence. The secondary material, works written on and about Havel, documentation on the productions of his plays, his decisions and instructions in his capacity as president, and the paraphernalia of life in the president's office, was more extensive. And little of it would make much sense without the context of the radical historical changes in which he had played such an important role.

There was clearly a need for a dedicated institution, which would collect, sort out, analyse and make available to the public all this material. Inspired, as so often before, by the American model, Havel started to think

---

3 Speech of Václav Havel on the Occasion of Unveiling of a Monument to Franz Kafka, 4 December 2003, VHL ID3793.

in terms of a presidential library. Craig Stapleton, the US ambassador in Prague at the time, was instrumental in helping him develop the idea. In fact, the idea had already been in his mind as he was leaving office. A wealthy entrepreneur, Zdeněk Bakala, encouraged by a mutual friend, Bessel Kok, provided much of the initial and long-term funding for the project. In July 2004, the Václav Havel Library started its activities. In the years since, it has done an enormous job of collecting and digitizing all Havel's primary works and much of the secondary material.[4]

The second task that Havel was thinking about was more complicated. Throughout all his years as president he had stuck, sometimes desperately, to his core identity as an artist and playwright. In keeping with the dictum of Jan Patočka that the measure of a man is not how he copes with the goals he has set for himself but how he copes with the challenges that life puts in his way, he thought of his political career as something that was thrust upon him by the vagaries of history, as a temporary detour from his true vocation in life, important and honourable as it might be. Now it was time to go back to what he really wanted to do.

Not surprisingly, it was easier said than done. Apart from friends and fellow artists, the outside world did not remember all too well Havel's previous career, nor did it much respect a writer's need for quiet and seclusion in a former president. Its demands on Havel's time and attention did not perceptibly decrease, while Havel's capacity to accommodate them had, deprived of the support mechanisms of the president's office and state protocol. In part, it was Havel's own doing. Never very good at saying no, he had postponed many of the invitations, appearances and promises of writing until such time as he was free of the official duties of the president. Now he had to pay his dues.

But he also wanted to write. In his presidential farewell remarks to his fellow citizens he acknowledged that he owed them 'an account' of his time in the office. At the same time he warned that, to do that, he would need 'time, reflection, health and composure'.[5] Two years were hardly enough for detached consideration. His health was a borderline affair, always prone to a sudden crisis. He did not have any time for the present, and he was

---

4 Its leadership and staff have also hugely contributed, through access, cooperation, advice and
   friendship, to making the work on this book remotely manageable.
5 Farewell Address to Czech Citizens, 2 February 2003.

concerned as well that he did not have much time left. Worst of all, it was impossible for him to concentrate among all the duties of an elder statesman. While still in office, he often retired to Lány, isolated from the rest of the world by a wall and a military guard, and came back with a largely finished text. Now he found he could not do the same in his office or in his villa. Before long he realized that he was the lone male in a household of women. There was Dáša's daughter Nina with her own daughter, Dáša's ageing mother and Dáša's two boxer dogs, Sugar and her daughter Madlenka.[6] Gradually, Havel vacated most of the huge villa he had bought with Olga to its growing number of female inhabitants and retired to a tiny first-floor bedroom resembling a monastery cell. Among friends he started to refer to his domicile as 'a house of horrors'.

The couple's house in Portugal was not very practical to go to on the spur of the moment. Bought with the dream of holding hands with Dáša while sipping red wine and watching the sunset over the ocean, it turned out to be a dreamer's folly. It was too far away by road and not easily accessible by air, the beach was windy, and the water too cold for most of the year. The only place where Havel knew he could do some writing in peace was Hrádeček. There was a problem even there, however. He did not like to go there alone, and Dáša did not enjoy being there as much and, after her return to the stage, could not stay as long as he did. She was also somewhat more demanding of his time and attention than the independent and self-reliant Olga. And she knew she was not nearly as loved and appreciated by Andrej Krob and Anna Freimanová, their next-door neighbours at Hrádeček, and the extensive circle of friends they shared with Václav.

For the umpteenth time, Havel was facing the problem of finding asylum. For rest and recuperation he could go to the house in Portugal or to the royal retreat in the Canary Islands that the king and queen of Spain repeatedly invited him to. For writing, he needed access to resources and libraries and people.

He found it equally difficult to reconcile the conflicting agendas and expectations of his own family. He was genuinely in love with his younger wife,

---

6   Havel had a habit of naming his dogs after politicians. The Alsatian-like mongrel he had in the late seventies and early eighties was named Golda after the Israeli prime minister Golda Meir, the occasionally biting Schnauzer dog in the second half of the eighties and early nineties was Djula after the Hungarian foreign minister Gyula Horn, while Madlenka was named . . . guess.

more romantically and sensually than he had ever been in love with Olga. On her own part, there is no need to doubt that her feelings were equally genuine. He was, as she used to say, the man of her life. But he was sixty-eight years old, tired and sickly after the exhaustions and punishments of a lifetime, and his agenda for the rest of his time was largely that of a writer and thinker, and a bit of an elder statesman. Dáša was eighteen years his junior, but what was even more important, she was a consummate actress, thriving on the limelight and the attentions of spectators and admirers. She apparently saw their future together as an integral part of a celebrity lifestyle, spent jetsetting between film festivals, beauty pageants and royal households, with some charitable activities thrown in. She also developed a taste for associating with the very rich. Soon billionaires vied for her favour and attention with mere millionaires, providing expensive gifts, foreign trips and rides in private jets. In return they could be seen with the presidential pair at theatre openings, concerts and film festivals. They also had the privilege of being the first to be asked for contributions for the new VIZE 97 Foundation and other charitable activities. Havel was no recluse, and he enjoyed partying as much as anyone else, but his needs were simultaneously simpler and intellectually more demanding. His deep devotion to Dáša nevertheless made him accept invitations, take trips abroad and hang around with people he would otherwise not have considered as essential. This in turn made him even more exhausted, depressed, confused and hung over in the aftermath of many a glittering social event.

His solution to this set of issues and its incompatible requirements turned out to be once again America. He had a standing invitation to be a visiting fellow in the Library of Congress in Washington. In the spring of 2005, after an attempt marred by an injury a year before, he finally set out. It was not a simple logistical operation. He was taking along not just his wife, and a bodyguard, but also the two boxer dogs. Since Dáša resolutely rejected the idea of her darlings travelling in the cargo hold of a commercial airliner, a prosperous friend had to be approached for private jet transport.

The couple and the dogs set up camp in a rented house in Georgetown. Madeleine Albright lived around the corner, and on a number of occasions served as the Havels' guide and escort to local bars and to the houses of assorted Washington socialites. The Library of Congress provided Havel with an office and a stipend. Otherwise, he was free to spend his time as he wished.

Havel made no pretence about the reasons he was going to America. His book *To the Castle and Back*,[7] large parts of which were written during his Washington stay, states these reasons in the very first paragraph: 'I've run away. I've run away to America . . . I've run away in the hope that I will find more time and focus to write something.'[8]

The book is a kind of presidential memoir, albeit as unusual and unique as its author was as a president. On the surface it is almost facetious, combining the author's reflections on his time in office in the form of an interview with the journalist Karel Hvížďala, with excerpts from his 'Instructions to the Castle', which became perhaps his main mode of communication with the office personnel in the years of his Czech presidency, and with impromptu scribblings about, for example, what to do with a bat that had settled down to roost in a cupboard, and how to prepare the pike he had been given as a present. At the same time, it is a diary of Havel's time in Washington and his impressions of America and of the period after his return home, which he spent largely at Hrádeček. Underneath it all, though, it is an existential meditation on the meaning of life, politics and love, for which the presidency is not much more than a backdrop.

Some of Havel's diary entries from Washington depict his meetings with a number of important Americans, including former President Clinton, his wife Hillary, Senator Kerry and many others at various dinners and functions. Some of them are amusing miniatures of life in America or rather of Havel's take on life in America: 'After several days in Washington it seems to me that people here are, on the whole, far kinder to one another than back home. They are long-suffering (the hours that they sit patiently behind the steering wheel during rush hour moving forward a couple of metres at a time!); they are considerate (you can tell the nature of a society by the way drivers behave towards pedestrians; I remember how in Moscow the drivers thought of pedestrians as insects who either had to get out of the way or get run over); they are cheerful, good-natured, understanding, they have smooth complexions, they have nice haircuts; it is obvious that they have time to look after themselves. They all say hello

---

7   The original Czech version (2006) is called *Prosím, stručně* (Briefly, please).
8   Ibid. 3.

to each other, and the main thing is – they're hardworking!'[9] Havel was not as naïve or uninformed as to confuse the streets of Georgetown with the whole of America; the subtle point he was trying to make here and elsewhere in the book was aimed back home.

It is clear from the book how much Havel enjoyed and appreciated America. Even his critical comments, about some of the 'Egyptian' architecture of the capital, American eating habits and the excesses of the consumer society, are treated in an understanding and humorous manner. The only thing Havel seriously objected to was the lack of salt in most meals, but even there he found a solution: 'I've gotten myself some salt and carry it around in my pocket. Now I'm one step ahead of everyone else!'[10]

On a second plane, in response to questions, not infrequently orchestrated by Havel himself, he revisits his presidency from the time of the revolution till the end, explaining, justifying and defending positions he took on various occasions. This part can be read as the 'accounting' he promised to his fellow citizens on departing the presidency.

On a third plane, he goes backstage, drawing on the notes, instructions and comments addressed to his staff in the ten years between 1993 and the end of his presidency. They include routine plans for the dramaturgy of various visits and trips, early concepts of various speeches, complaints about his own inability to meet deadlines and schedules, but also moments of amazement, wonder and exasperation: 'Dear V., all my documents, old and new, are printing out in some strange English Cyrillic. Your instructions for fixing it did not work. After half an hour, the normal letters came back. Please never exchange my old computer for a new one or put new programs on it.'[11] Sometimes the complaints border on the hilarious: 'As you all know I'm a pub person, I'm curious about everything, nothing can shock me. Therefore, when I walked down that famous avenue in Bangkok, which you all know, it deeply pained my heart to avoid the little lanes of the red-light district. How happy I would have been to see this just once in my life! But I knew that I was the guest of the King, that the King is informed of my every movement, and that I simply couldn't permit myself to do it. Why am I mentioning it? I consider it unfortunate that almost all my delegation,

---

9 *To the Castle and Back*, 25–6.
10 Ibid. 147–8.
11 Note of 2 November 2000, to private secretary Vladimír Hanzel, *To the Castle and Back*, 174.

with the minister of finance in the lead, ventured into these places (. . .) and that moreover they took pictures of each other there (. . .) What the Thai King thought about it I don't know.'[12] And some reflect Havel's sense of the contrast between the trappings of high office and the recurrent petty details of everyday life: 'In the closet where the vacuum cleaner is kept, there also lives a bat. How to get rid of it? The lightbulb has been unscrewed so as not to wake it up and upset it.'[13]

But there is also a darker plane to the book, reflecting the existential angst of the author. After all his triumphs and tribulations, he remains profoundly uncertain of his own worth, and of the meaning of the absurd comedy in which he had played the leading role for so long. Although he shows little regret and some satisfaction over the events in which he played a significant part, he is not very optimistic about the shape of Czech society or of the world at large. He also hints at an increasing alienation in his own marriage, which makes him retreat even further into himself, alone in the face of the signs of impending mortality. In the most haunting passage of the book, written back at Hrádeček on 5 December 2005, he returns to its opening theme: 'I'm running away. I'm running away more and more. (. . .) What I'm running away from is writing. But it's more than that. I'm running away from the public, from politics, from people. Perhaps I'm even running away from the woman who saved my life. Above all, I'm probably running away from myself.'[14]

What starts as a mere bout of existential angst soon develops into a full-blown eschatological exercise, demonstrating Havel's brilliant powers of introspection and his ability to combine the mundane with the sublime: 'What am I actually afraid of? Hard to say. What's interesting is that although I am here alone – and will continue to be here alone because no one that I know of has plans to visit – I keep the house tidy; I have everything in its place, everything has to be aligned with everything else, nothing can be left hanging over the edge of a table, or be crooked. At the same time the refrigerator must always be filled with a variety of food that I can scarcely eat myself, and there must be fresh flowers in the vases. In other words, it's as though I were constantly expecting someone to visit. But who? The

---

12 Note of 17 February 1994, *To the Castle and Back*, 19.
13 21 August 1999, *To the Castle and Back*, 348.
14 *To the Castle and Back*, 329.

unknown and unannounced guest? A strange and beautiful woman who admires me? My saviour, who likes to show up unannounced? Some old friends? Why is it that I don't want to see anyone, and at the same time I'm always expecting someone, someone who will really appreciate that everything is in its proper place and properly aligned?

'I have only one explanation: I am constantly preparing for the last judgement, for the highest court from which nothing can be hidden, which will appreciate everything that should be appreciated, and which will, of course, notice anything that is not in its place. I'm obviously assuming that the supreme judge is a stickler like me. But why does this final evaluation matter so much to me? After all, at that point I shouldn't care. But I do care because I'm convinced that my existence – like everything that has ever happened – has ruffled the surface of Being, and that after my little ripple, however marginal, insignificant, and ephemeral it may have been, Being is and always will be different from what it was before.'[15]

It may seem strange that someone capable of writing the above lines thinks of himself as running away from writing. What Havel means, and worries about at other places in the book, is his continuing inability to finish the work he had started to contemplate many years earlier and had meant to return to after he left the presidency. It is not the book he is writing; that is just a repayment of a debt. It is a play.

15 Ibid. 329–30.

LEAVING

You were silly like us; your gift survived it all:
The parish of rich women, physical decay,
Yourself . . .

> – W. H. Auden, 'In Memory of W. B. Yeats'

FOR HAVEL, writing *Leaving* had been a matter of delayed gratification for a long time. First conceived in 1987 as a variation on Shakespeare's *King Lear* in a milder Chekhovian tonality, he mentioned the *Lear* play occasionally in private conversations with friends, mostly bemoaning the fact that he could not seriously focus on it as long as he was in public office. At the end of the eighties he made copious notes and early drafts of dialogues, but for a time believed they had fallen victim to the revolutionary chaos. Now he rediscovered them at Hrádeček, six school notebooks and some pages printed on an obsolete dot-matrix printer.[1] Watching his wife Dagmar play Madame Ranevskaya in the Vinohrady theatre, he arrived at the idea to superimpose the *King Lear* theme on the layout of Chekhov's *The Cherry Orchard*.[2]

Obviously, his own experience as a statesman, now an elder statesman, gave him a unique perspective and a lot of comedy material for a meditation on the general dilemma of a public versus a private identity and on the generic process of ageing, decay and withdrawal. Some of the subplots,

---

1   Drafts and notes for *Leaving*, VHL ID6551.
2   Conversation with Dagmar Havlová, 11 July 2012.

such as Chancellor Rieger's agonizing over which of the thousands of gifts accumulated over the years rightfully belonged to the state and which were personal gifts to the statesman, are obviously drawn from personal experience.[3] So is the visceral revulsion to the tabloid press, a phenomenon yet unknown to Havel at the time the play was first conceived. The most striking thing, however, is the extent to which the play retained its original concept and the almost uncanny prescience of the author about a milieu so foreign to him in 1987.

The main character is a recently retired statesman (Chancellor Rieger), who is going through withdrawal symptoms over the loss of power. Step by step, he is being stripped of his support network, his perks and his memorabilia of office; he will finally be moved out of the government villa that for years he has considered home. All this with the smug help of Patrick Klein, his longtime political opponent and nemesis, along with the painful background of petty betrayals by people close to him and the ghoulish attention of the media.

The play is heavily peppered with quotes, paraphrases and allusions. Some of them come directly from *King Lear* and *The Cherry Orchard*. Lear's 'storm' monologue – 'Blow, winds, and crack your cheeks!' – gets recited in a cherry orchard, rather to the detriment of dramatic effect. A character named Old Yepichodov wanders around drunk somewhere in the wings. Other references, including quotes from Samuel Beckett and other dramatists, are not so obvious. Some are references to earlier Havel plays. Some are quotes from his famous speeches. And some, particularly those during an interview in which Rieger is desperately trying to sum up his political philosophy for posterity, are crude pastiches of Havel the politician: 'The government exists to serve the citizen; the citizen does not exist to serve the government... I placed great importance on human rights. In the name of freedom of expression, I imposed significant limits on censorship. I honoured the right of assembly, and during my terms as chancellor, fewer than half of all public demonstrations were broken up by the police.'[4]

Rieger, as should be obvious, is not entirely an admirable character. He is as vain and self-centred as any politician. He postures, he cheats on his

---

3 'But what does the law say in my case? What belongs to me and what belongs to the State?' Instructions to the Castle, 20 May 2001, VHL ID5663.
4 *Leaving*, translated from Czech by Paul Wilson (Prague: Aura-Pont script, 2008), Act I, 8.

wife, and he is perfectly incapable of weaning himself from power. When at the end he is offered the humiliating position of 'an adviser to an adviser to an adviser of an adviser,' he accepts it in a tragicomic rationalization, which Havel had widely used to illustrate the moral capitulations of his heroes in his plays from the Communist era: 'Either I will constantly reminisce about the past, returning to it over and over again, analysing it, explaining it, defending it, comparing it again and again to what exists now, in the present, persuading myself just how much better everything was back then. In other words, I could easily become completely obsessed with my own footprint in history, my past achievements, my legacy... Everyone would think I was just a vain and embittered old man who thumbed his nose at a generous offer to contribute his experience to the service of his country. But there is a second choice before me: to demonstrate clearly to everyone that serving my country is of greater importance to me than my personal position. I have been guided by that principle, sir, all my life and I don't see why I should back away from it now just because of the trivial concern that I would, officially, hold a somewhat inferior position to the one I have held for so long.'[5]

This is where a comedy of manners turns into a tragedy of identity. No matter how moral, humble and immune to the temptations of power you are, once you've had it, it's impossible ever to be free of it. It comes to define you as much in its absence as in its presence. The more you have achieved, the higher you have reached, the stronger its grip on you will be. You cannot keep it, at least not in a democracy, and yet psychologically you cannot entirely give it up. For the rest of your life, you are going to be defined not by what you do but by what you did. You are condemned to be an ex-chancellor, ex-secretary, ex-president.[6]

It is this that Havel was also trying to run away from. In the play itself, he manages to do it by exploiting the dramatist's licence to the full, playing with quotes and anachronisms, disrupting the flow of the play with *deus ex machina* voice-overs, reprimanding the actors, caricaturing himself and engaging in 'pure authorial whimsy'. Once again, he and he alone is in full control of his craft and his characters.

---

5 Ibid. Act 5, 57.
6 The above four paragraphs are an edited excerpt from the author's 'Tanned and Rested: Václav Havel Marks His Return with "Leaving"', *World Affairs Journal*, January/February 2011.

In real life, this was an impossible task. The outside world and its demands kept breaking through, and Havel's heightened sense of responsibility would not allow him to ignore it. There were more visitors to greet and more events to attend. Even the production of the play itself became strewn with problems of theatre politics, as treacherous and cruel as any party affairs. Like so often before, this time, too, Havel wrote a play with the leading actors in mind. Chancellor Rieger would be Havel's long-time friend, the wonderful actor Jan Tříska, who had left Czechoslovakia in the 1970s and settled in the United States. Rieger's long-time and long-suffering mistress and companion would be played by none other than Dáša.

Perhaps unwisely, Havel approached the National Theatre, whose management was not sure they could accommodate Dáša in an ensemble of scores of actors, most of whom had not seen a lead role for a long while. Her 'home' theatre Na Vinohradech objected in turn to Tříska and the choice of an external director.

In the end, the play was produced in the appropriate setting of Archa, the mainstay of Prague alternative theatre, under the direction of David Radok, the son of Havel's old mentor and friend. Radok Jr. who grew up in exile in Stockholm, and specialized mainly in operas, took a disciplined approach, trying to stage the play in faithful obedience to the author's intentions. The main protagonists had their own ideas. Tříska went for the dramatic gestures and declamations of a classical tragic actor, bordering on a caricature of Rieger, who is himself something of a caricature. Dáša would not be upstaged. Problems ensued, finally culminating in the departure of Dáša from the production and the hiring of Zuzana Stivínová, a versatile actress, comedienne and a formidable singer. When the play opened on 22 May 2008, it met with reactions ranging from wildly enthusiastic to respectfully admiring, despite the flurry of speculations about the parallels with the Havel–Klaus relationship. Havel himself was pleased with the result, but unhappy about his failure to see Dáša as a lead actress in one of his plays.

This may have been one, but certainly not the only one, of his motives in deciding to convert the play to screen. His lifelong ambition to be a film-maker was another. But once again, his deeply seated need to break out and be free of constraints and stereotypes may have played a role as well.

The play provided a straightforward, if rather unpromising base for the screenplay. Havel stuck to its single setting and shot the whole film, with the exception of the final departure scene, in the single location of a villa in Eastern Bohemia. To assist him, he had the *crème de la crème* of the Czech film industry. Jan Malíř, a leading cameraman, did the photography, Jiří Brožek did the editing and Jaroslav Bouček was the producer. Michal Pavlíček of Tribute to Freedom fame composed the music. Among the actors, Josef Abrhám of the Actors' Studio, perhaps the most popular Czech actor of his generation, played Vilém Rieger, Dáša Havlová was Irena, his consort, and Jaroslav Dušek, a popular comedian, played Patrick Klein. The grand dame of Czech theatre and a heroine of the resistance, Vlasta Chramostová, played the grandmother. A Who's Who of the A-list of Czech cinema made do with episodic roles. Pavel Landovský, the old bar-prowling buddy of the director, was the driver of the stagecoach (borrowed from John Ford's eponymous film of 1939), taking the disgraced chancellor away.

Rarely has a novice director been in a more enviable position, surrounded by a crew of friends who were consummate professionals, free from commercial pressures and able to act on his own whims. 'The director does not really do very much himself. Most of the time he waits,' commented Havel on his role. At the same time he obsessed over the film with the same single-minded focus and meticulous preparation he gave both his writing and his presidency. For some time it became difficult to have a conversation with Havel on any other subject. He stayed with the project at every phase of the post-production, and stage-managed many of the aspects of its premiere on 22 March 2011. Symbolically, it took place in the Lucerna cinema, which Havel's grandfather built a hundred years earlier, which the Communists confiscated, and which Havel's sister-in-law Dagmar Havlová, the wife of his brother Ivan, now owned.

Until the very last moment Havel was not sure he could even attend the premiere. Another bout of his regular spring respiratory ailment condemned him to a bed in the Central Military Hospital. He was only released on 20 March.

What awaited him was a barrage of previews and reviews, most of them harshly negative. The largely accurate observation that the film was basically the play on screen was the mildest of the criticism. The conclusion of many of the critics that the result of all this concentration of talent and creativity was a mediocre film was perhaps the most damning. The less charitable critics spoke of a self-serving trifle Havel had made for himself and his friends, and claimed that 'Havel's *Leaving* terrorizes with its absurdity'.[7]

Unlike the above condemnations, which stuck, some of them just, to the genre of film criticism, a number of people used the opportunity for an all-out attack. Vítězslav Jandák, the Social-Democratic ex-minister of culture and an actor known for his successful representations of various folksy characters, called the film 'a piece of junk', typical of the 'den of truth and love, which is flooding the country with its hypocritical pseudo-humanism and petty-Czech humour'.[8] Petr Hájek, the journalist-writer vice-chancellor of the office of President Klaus, who had created a stir a couple of years earlier by claiming that September 11, as it was shown and presented, never happened, seconded Jandák's opinion and pointed out that the film, which had cost 44 million CZK (around 2 million dollars), was in part financed by Czech public TV.[9] Much of the same followed.

Outwardly Havel seemed unperturbed by the criticism. 'I will leave it to the critics to determine where this film belongs,' he said at the premiere. But inside he was deeply hurt, not so much by the lack of appreciation for his film-making talents as by the unadulterated hatred that found its outlet in some of the reviews, and even more in the subsequent online discussions.

It had been simmering for a long time, in faint praise, snide remarks and attacks on surrogate targets, whether they were Havel's advisers, political supporters or his new wife. They were all fair game, but Havel himself had been spared the full brunt of the attacks as long as he was protected by the *lèse-majesté* of the quasi-monarchic presidency. Even after he retired, the residual respect for the office initially allowed only for criticism that was largely polite, respectful and issue-driven. But now the dam burst and the insults flooded in.

The psychological roots of this hatred are harder to explain. In small part it may have been the regrettable tendency of a nation with plebeian and petty bourgeois roots to cut anyone down to size. Masaryk in his own time was treated with very much the same disdain by a considerable number of Czech politicians and journalists, for whom 'The Castle' was not so much Kafka's impenetrable nightmare, as the den of elitists and

---

7 Kamil Filla, 16 March 2011, www.aktualne.cz.
8 'Jandák brutally trounced Havel's directing debut', 16 March 2011, www.parlamentnilisty.cz.
9 'Hájek laughed off Havel's film', 18 March 2011, www.parlamentnilisty.cz.

cosmopolitan intellectuals. But there was something else, something about the bohemian, liberal, outgoing Havel that irritated some people infinitely more than would have been the case with the scholarly, puritanical, almost stern Masaryk. The catchword was 'hypocritical'. What business had this man, who never denied inhaling, who had been unfaithful to his wife for years, even when she was ill and dying, who railed against mafia capitalists as he was pocketing the ill-gotten gains of his capitalist ancestors – what business had he preaching morals to others? And it was not just him, but all his hard-drinking, merry-cavorting, highfalutin friends, Mr Clean every one of them, the truth-and-lovers who would preach morals rather than just let us get along. Now there was a chance to get back at the cleanest of them all.

The wound would not heal. Havel, ill for a month before the premiere, now retreated back into the illness. Even before, friends had been noticing in him a sense of resignation, so foreign to the fighter he had been for most of his life. 'I am tired of fighting,' he complained to his assistant.[10] On occasion, when he made sure his wife was not around, he lit a cigarette. When friends protested, he dismissed their objections with a faint gesture.[11] 'It makes no difference now,' he would add sometimes.

But the torrent of abuse following the premiere was the last straw. For the next five months Havel cancelled almost all of his appointments, and spent most of his time at Hrádeček, alone. Never a heavy eater, he stopped taking in food. He became so weak that he could hardly move without assistance. Several Boromeian nuns were recruited to take turns tending to him. His friends were alerted it might be the time to say goodbye. Dáša, preoccupied with her acting duties and charity work, spent most of her time in Prague. Havel duly attended a rehearsal and the two first performances of the musical version of *Cyrano*, where she played Roxana, but then retired back to Hrádeček.

He saw very few people that summer. He met twice with his old fellow-prisoner and now Primate of the Czech Catholic Church and the Archbishop of Prague, soon to be a cardinal, Dominik Duka, whom he used to call by his given name Jaroslav. He went to see a film, *The Tree of Life*, in a local cinema in a village next to Hrádeček.

10 Conversation with Martin Vidlák, Prague, 28 February 2013.
11 Conversation with Jacques Rupnik, Prague, 17 September 2013.

There was another blow awaiting him at the end of that summer. A moderately popular Czech author, Irena Obermannová, published *The Secret Book*, purportedly the story of her love affair with the 'Greatest of Czechs', easily recognizable as the ageing ex-president. Havel angrily denied the allegations, and most reviewers and critics condemned the book as a gold-digging attempt to prey on his stature. The exact facts of the affair, which was supposed to have taken place in 2010, when Havel was working on the post-production of *Leaving*, could not be independently verified, but there is little doubt that Havel did develop a romantic crush on his fellow writer and met with her on a number of occasions. Dáša was beyond herself with anger, perhaps not so much because of her husband's apparent infidelity as because of the public humiliation. Once again Havel's enemies found proof of his hypocrisy in his feeble denials of the whole thing. The man who at one time deplored President Clinton's bad taste in women for making the cardinal mistake of befriending girls who would later talk about it in intimate detail was hoisted by his own petard. His wife would not speak to him, and his self-confessed girlfriend was bound to be mortally offended at not being acknowledged.

When Havel's health improved a little at the end of the summer, he went through the motions of opening his last Forum 2000 Conference. On 5 October he turned seventy-five. The Saturday before, many of his closest friends, and a few of the hangers-on, gathered to wish him well in the Prague DOX Centre for Contemporary Art. A few came from abroad, including Madeleine Albright, Adam Michnik and Tom Stoppard. Dáša came separately, with an entourage of her own family and relatives, and left early. This time there was no Helena Vondráčková and Karel Gott. The musical bill included the Plastic People of the Universe, a funky rock 'n' roll band, and folk and protest singers from the bygone dissident days. For most of the evening, Havel sat in the upper-floor gallery, receiving congratulations. He was traditionally polite and uncomplaining, but his jacket was two sizes too large, his face gaunt and haggard, his eyes watery. Whenever yet another friend came in, he gave a faint smile of recognition and appreciation. 'Michael,' he seemed to have cheered up, when I showed up, but would not pretend when asked how he was: 'I am a ruin.'

A week later, he once again met with Archbishop Duka. In fact, there were more meetings between the two former jail-mates in 2011 than in all the years since their release from prison. In November, they met in the archbishop's palace to record a TV talk about remembrance and hope. On 10 December, twenty-three years since the first officially sanctioned demonstration on Škroupovo Square, Havel received his friend Tenzin Gyatso, the 14th Dalai Lama of Tibet. The Dalai Lama took note of Havel's ill health and recommended some Tibetan medicine. 'I told him now I'm acting like a Tibetan physician to my long-time friend,' he said afterwards.[12] He wished Havel ten more years of life. The two men then spent half an hour in a mostly unspoken dialogue. At the end of the meeting they touched heads.

The trip in an ambulance from Hrádeček and back for the meeting left Havel totally exhausted, but it was one meeting he wanted to have. He spent the next week mostly in bed, often too weak and tired to get up. He nonetheless communicated with the nuns and took phone calls from friends. He spoke openly about the approaching end and was reconciled to it. On Saturday, 17 December, he felt a little better and wanted to discuss the upcoming Christmas holidays with Dáša who came earlier in the day. He wanted to spend it at Hrádeček and he wanted her to be there.

On Sunday morning, one of the nuns, Veritas Holíková, found him awake and encouraged him to get up for his morning hygiene. 'I'd like to sleep a little more, come back in an hour,' he said. When she came back an hour later, he kept sleeping and his breath was becoming shallower. Finally, some time between 9.45 and 9.50 a.m., the breathing stopped altogether. 'It was like a candle going out, so quiet.'[13]

12 Conversation with His Holiness the Dalai Lama, London, 18 June 2012.
13 Eliška Bártová, Interview with Veritas Holíková, 22 December 2013, http://aktualne.centrum.
   cz/domaci/spolecnost/clanek.phtml?id=726469.

Acknowledgements

MY ONLY WORRY in composing a list of people to whom I owe gratitude is that I might inadvertently leave someone out. If that happens, I beg his or her forgiveness.

Václav Havel is dead, but I still owe him a huge debt for being a constant presence, inspiration and an invisible guide in writing this book. His widow Dagmar has been supportive throughout the process, answered most of my questions, and imposed no limitations on what I was going to write despite knowing that some parts might be painful for her to read. His brother Ivan and his wife Dagmar Havlová-Ilkovičová have been friends for years, gave me generously of their time, memories and documents, and submitted to my immodest demands for more of the same.

I owe many thanks to all my interviewees and correspondents. Most of them have been friends to both Havel and me, which made my work also a pleasure. They include Madeleine Albright, Timothy Garton Ash, Joan Baez, Zdeněk and Michaela Bakala, Jiří Bartoška, Pavel Bratinka, Martin Bútora, Marián Čalfa, Věra Čáslavská, the late Oldřich Černý, Bill Clinton, David Dušek, Luboš Dobrovský, Jaroslav Dominik Duka, Mia Farrow, Miloš Forman, Anna Freimanová, Fedor Gál, Tomáš Halík, Vladimír Hanzel, Steven Heintz, the Hornosín gang, Petr Jančárek, František Janouch, Lenka Jungmannová, Ladislav Kantor, Helena Kašperová, Bill and Pamela Kiehl, Václav Klaus, Michael Kocáb, Pavel Kohout, Bessel Kok, Pavel Kolář, Eda Kriseová, Pavel and Petr Král, Andrej Krob, Daniel Kroupa, Pavel Landovský, Bill and Wendy Luers, Ivo Mathé, Vladimír Merta, Vladimír Mlynář, Martin Palouš, Petr Pithart, Jan Ruml, Jacques Rupnik, Carl Schmidt, Karel Schwarzenberg, Brent Scowcroft, Roger Scruton, Ladislav 'Agnes' Snopko,

Jan Sokol, Lise Stone, Tom Stoppard, Alois Strnad, Jiří Suk, Aung San Suu Kyi, Jiřina Šiklová, Tenzin Gyatso, Ladislav Špaček, Bára Štěpánová, Martin Vidlák, Jitka Vodňanská, Alexandr Vondra and Paul Wilson.

My immense gratitude goes to Marta Smolíková, Jan Hron, Jan Macháček, Ondřej Němec, Erika Zlámalová, and the whole team of the Václav Havel Library in Prague, without whose support and remote access to a huge number of digitized documents in their archives I would have found it impossible to work on the book from London. My thanks go also to Štěpán Gilar and the archives of the Czech Ministry of Foreign Affairs, the Museum of Czech Literature, the Institute for Contemporary History in Prague, Vít Smetana, and others. My former colleague and boss from Reuters, Colin McIntyre, along with archivist David Cutler, kindly reopened for me the Reuters morgue.

I have bothered more photographers for more pictures than I could use. They rewarded me with a chance to relive some of the memorable moments of Havel's life, and sometimes of mine. For this I have to thank Karel Cudlín, Bohdan Holomíček, Jaroslav Kořán, Tomki Němec, Tomáš Novák, Alan Pajer, Ivo Šilhavý, the late Oldřich Škácha, and others.

As a first-time author in English, I was immensely lucky to find a wholeheartedly supportive agent in Andrew Nurnberg and his brilliant team. I was equally lucky to find enthusiastic publishers in Toby Mundy of Atlantic Books and Morgan Entrekin of Grove Atlantic, and highly professional yet awfully kind editors in Margaret Stead and Corinna Barsan.

My special thanks go to my personal assistant Dana Pšenicová, who for the last quarter of a century has been my back-up memory, steadying influence and crisis manager.

Eric Ormsby, my favourite brother-in-law, was my first reader. I have been spared many blushes thanks to his mastery of English grammar and style.

Last but in the first place, my loving gratitude goes to my wife Jana for being the first to tell me what I was getting into, and standing by me regardless.

Select Bibliography

Havel's works cited

Havel, Václav, *Disturbing the Peace* [*Dákový výslech*], tr. Paul Wilson (New York: Alfred A. Knopf, 1990).

— *Letters to Olga*, tr. Paul Wilson (London, Boston: Faber and Faber, 1990).

— *Motomorfózy* [*Motomorphoses*] (Prague: Galén, 2011).

— *Open Letters, Selected prose 1965–1990*, ed. Paul Wilson (London: Faber and Faber, 1991).

— *Plays, 1970–1976* (Toronto: 68 Publishers, 1977).

— *Prase, or Václav Havel's Hunt for a Pig* (Prague: Gallery, 2010).

— *Selected Plays, 1963–83*, tr. Vera Blackwell (London: Faber & Faber, 1992).

— *Spisy 1* [*Works 1*], *Poems, Anticodes* (Prague: Torst, 1999).

— *Spisy 2* [*Works 2*], *Plays* (Prague: Torst, 1999).

— *Spisy 3* [*Works 3*], *Essays and other texts 1953–69* (Prague: Torst, 1999).

— *Spisy 4* [*Works 4*], *Essays and other texts 1970–89* (Prague: Torst, 1999).

— *Spisy 5* [*Works 5*], *Letters to Olga* (Prague: Torst, 1999).

— *Spisy 6* [*Works 6*], *Speeches 1990–2, Summer Meditations* (Prague: Torst, 1999).

— *Spisy 7* [*Works 7*], *Speeches and other texts 1992–99* (Prague: Torst, 1999).

— *Spisy 8* [*Works 8*], *Speeches and other texts 1999–2006, To the Castle and Back, Leaving* (Prague: Torst, 2007).

— *Summer Meditations*, tr. Paul Wilson (New York: Random House, 1993).
— *The Art of the Impossible, Politics and Morality in Practice*, tr. Paul Wilson and others (New York, Toronto: Alfred A. Knopf, 1997).
— *Three Vaněk Plays*, tr. Jan Novak and Vera Blackwell (London: Faber and Faber, 1990).
— *To the Castle and Back* [*Prosím Stručně*], tr. Paul Wilson (London: Portobello Books, 2008).
— *Toward a Civil Society*, tr. Paul Wilson and others (Prague: Lidové noviny Publishing House, 1995).

Other sources

Albright, Madeleine, *Madam Secretary* (New York: Hyperion, 2003).
— *Prague Winter* (New York: Harper Perennial, 2012).
Asmus, Ronald D., *Opening NATO's Door* (New York: Columbia University Press, 2002).
Bartuška, Václav, *Polojasno* [*Semi-clear*], *An Investigation of the Culprits of November 17, 1989* (Prague: Ex libris, 1990).
Benčík, Antonín, *Téma Alexander Dubček* (Prague: Christian Social Movement, 2012).
Blažek, Petr, and Bursík, Tomáš, *Pražský proces 1979* [*The Prague Trial 1979*], *The Investigation, Trial and Imprisonment of Members of the Committee for Defence of the Unjustly Persecuted* (Prague: Institute for Contemporary History, 2010).
Boučková, Tereza, *Indiánský běh* [*An Indian Run*] (Prague: Fragment K, 1991).
Bratinka, Pavel, et al., *Faustování s Havlem* [*Fausting with Havel*] (Prague: Václav Havel Library, 2010).
Bútora, Martin, *Odklínanie* [*Exorcism*] (Bratislava: Kaligram, 2004).
Císařovská, Blanka, and Prečan, Vilém, eds., *Charta 77: Dokumenty 1977–1989*, 3 vols (Prague: Institute for Contemporary History, 2007).
Dahrendorf, Ralf, *Reflections on the Revolutions in Europe: In a Letter Intended To Have Been Sent to a Gentleman in Warsaw* (New York: Random House, 1990).

Day, Barbara, *The Velvet Philosophers* (London: Claridge Press, 1999).

Forman, Miloš, and Novák, Jan, *Turnaround* [*Co já vím?*] (New York: Villard, 1994).

Freimanová, Anna, ed., *Příležitostný portrét Václava Havla* [*An Incidental Portrait of Václav Havel*] (Prague: Václav Havel Library, 2013).

— *Síla věcnosti Olgy Havlové* [*The Power of Matter-of-Factness of Olga Havel*] (Prague: Václav Havel Library, 2013).

— *Václav Havel o divadle* [*Václav Havel On Theatre*] (Prague: Václav Havel Library, 2012).

Garton Ash, Timothy, *The Magic Lantern: The Revolution of '89 Witnessed in Warsaw, Budapest, Berlin and Prague* (New York: Random House, 1990).

Gerová, Irena, *Vyhrabávačky* [*Scrappings*] (Prague, Litomyšl: Paseka, 2009).

Gjuričová, Adéla, et al., eds., *Rozděleni minulostí* [*Divided by the Past*], *The Emergence of Political Identities in Czechoslovkia After 1989* (Prague: Václav Havel Library, 2011).

Goldgeier, James M., *Not Whether But When: The U.S. Decision to Enlarge NATO* (Washington, DC: Brookings Institution Press, 1999).

Hanzel, Vladimír, ed., *Zrychlený tep dějin* [*A Quickened Pulse of History*] (Prague: Galén, 2006).

Havel, Ivan M., et al., *Dopisy od Olgy* [*Letters from Olga*] (Prague: Václav Havel Library, 2010).

Havel, Václav, *Citizen Vaněk/Občan Vaněk*, tr. Jan Novák (Prague: Levné knihy, 2009).

Havel, Václav, and Janouch, František, *Korespondence 1978–2001* (Prague: Akropolis, 2007).

Havel, Václav, and Prečan, Vilém, *Korespondence 1983–1989* (Prague: Czechoslovak Documentation Centre, 2011).

Havel, Václav, et al., *Circus Havel* (Brno: Větrné mlýny, 2008).

— *V hlavní roli Ferdinand Vaněk* [*Ferdinand Vaněk in the Title Role*] (Prague: Academia, 2006).

Havlová, Božena, *Didasko-Učím: Naučné obrázky Boženy Havlové* [*Didasko-I Teach: Didactic pictures of Božena Havlová*] (Prague: KANT, 2003).

Havlová-Ilkovičová, Dagmar, ed., *Podněcování a trest* [*Incitement and Punishment*] (Prague: Václav Havel Library, 2009).

Hejdánek, Ladislav, *Havel je uhlík* [*Havel is carbon*], *Philosopher and Political Responsibility* (Prague: Václav Havel Library, 2009).

Hiršal, Josef, and Grögerová Bohumila, *Let let* [*The Flight of Years*], *An Attempt at Recapitulation*, 3 vols (Prague: Mladá fronta, 1994).

Horáček, Michal, *Jak pukaly ledy* [*As the Ice was Breaking*] (Prague: Ex libris, 1990).

Hutchings, Robert L., *American Diplomacy and the End of the Cold War: An Insider's Account of U.S. Policy in Europe, 1989–1992* (Washington, DC: The Woodrow Wilson Center, 1997).

Institute of History of Czech Academy of Sciences, Historical Commission of the Coordination Centre of the Civic Forum, *Deset pražských dnů* [*Ten Prague Days*], *November 17–27, 1989, Documentation* (Prague: Academia, 1990).

Jirous, Ivan Martin, *Magorův zápisník* [*The Shithead's Diary*] (Prague: Torst, 1997).

— *Pravdivý příběh Plastic People* [*The True Story of the Plastic People*] (Prague: Torst, 2008).

Juráček, Pavel, *Deník* [*Diaries*] *1959–1974* (Prague: National Film Archives, 2003).

Kaiser, Daniel, *Disident, Václav Havel 1936–1989* (Prague: Paseka, 2009).

Kaplan, Karel, *Všechno jste prohráli* [*You Have Gambled Away Everything*] (Prague: Ivo Železný, 1997).

Keane, John, *Václav Havel, A Political Tragedy in Six Acts* (London: Bloomsbury, 1999).

Kipke, R., and Vodička, K., *Rozloučení s Československem* [*Parting with Czechoslovakia*] (Prague: Československý spisovatel, 1993).

Klíma, Ivan, *My Crazy Century, A Memoir*, tr. Craig Cravens (New York: Grove Atlantic, 2013).

Kohout, Pavel, *Kde je zakopán pes* [*Where the Dog is Buried*] (Brno: Atlantis, 1990).

— *Můj život s Hitlerem, Stalinem a Havlem* [My *Life with Hitler, Stalin and Havel*], 2 vols (Prague: Academia, 2011).

Komeda, Václav V., et al., eds., *Hnědá kniha o procesech s českým undergroundem* [*The Brown Book on the Trials with the Czech*

Underground] (Prague: Institute for the Study of Totalitarian Regimes, 2012).

Kosatík, Pavel, *Člověk má dělat to, nač má sílu* [*One Should Do What One Has The Strength to Do, The Life of Olga Havel*] (Prague: Mladá fronta, 2008).

— *Ústně více* [*More in Person*] (Brno: Host, 2006).

Kriseová, Eda, *Václav Havel, Životopis* [*Václav Havel, A Life*] (Brno: Atlantis, 1991).

Kroupa, Daniel, *Dějiny kampademie* [*The History of Kampademia*] (Prague: Václav Havel Library, 2011).

Landovský, Pavel, *Soukromá vzpoura* [*A Private Rebellion*], *A Conversation with Karel Hvížďala* (Prague: Galén, 2010).

Matějková, Jolana, *Děda se taky nebál* [*Grandpa was Not Afraid Either*], *An Interview with Alexandr Vondra* (Prague, Litomyšl: Paseka, 2012).

Müllerová, Alena, et al., *Albertov 16:00: Příběhy sametové revoluce* [*Albertov 4 p.m.: Stories of the Velvet Revolution*] (Prague: Czech Television, Lidové noviny Publishers, 2009).

Neubauer, Zdeněk, *Consolatio philosophiae hodierna* [*On Václav Havel's Sixteen Letters*] (Prague: Václav Havel Library, 2010).

Patočka, Jan, *Kacířské eseje o filosofii dějin* [*Heretical Essays on the Philosophy of History*] (Prague: Academia, 1990).

Pithart, Petr, *Devětaosmdesátý* [*The Eighty-ninth*] (Prague: Academia, 2010).

Prečan, Vilém, ed., *Charta 77 1977–1989: From a Moral to a Democratic Revolution* (Scheinfeld-Schwarzenberg, Bratislava: Czechoslovak Centre of Independent Literature, ARCHA, 1990).

— *Prague–Washington–Prague: Reports from the United States Embassy in Czechoslovakia, November–December 1989* (Prague: Václav Havel Library, 2004).

Pryce-Jones, David, *The Strange Death of the Soviet Empire* (New York: Henry Holt & Co., 1995).

Putna, Martin C., ed., *Měli jsme underground a máme prd* [*We Used to Have the Underground and Now We Have Bugger All*] (Prague: Václav Havel Library, 2009).

Putna, Martin C., *Václav Havel, duchovní portrét v rámu české kultury 20. století* [*A Spiritual Portrait in the Context of Twentieth-Century Czech Culture*] (Prague: Václav Havel Library, 2011).

Rakušanová, Lída, *Václav and Dagmar Havlovi, Dva osudy v jednom svazku* [*Two Lives in One Volume*] (Prague: Gallery, 1997).

Rocamora, Carol, *Acts of Courage: Václav Havel's Life in the Theater* (Hanover, NH: Smith and Kraus, 2004).

Rupnik, Jacques, *The Other Europe* (New York: Schocken, 1989).

Rychlík, Jan, *Rozdělení Česko-Slovenska 1989–1992* [*The Division of Czechoslovakia 1989–1992*] (Prague: Vyšehrad, 2012).

Scruton, Roger, *Notes from Underground* (New York: Beaufort Books, 2014).

Shawcross, William, *Dubcek* (New York: Simon and Schuster, 1990).

Simmons, Michael, *The Reluctant President: A Political Life of Vaclav Havel* (London: Methuen, 1991).

Škvorecký, Josef, *The Miracle Game* (Toronto: Knopf, 1991).

Smetana, Vít, ed., *Historie na rozcestí* [*History on the Crossroads*] (Brno: Barrister and Principal, 2013).

Špaček, Ladislav, *Deset let s Václavem Havlem* [*Ten Years with Václav Havel*] (Prague: Mladá fronta, 2012).

Stein, Eric, *Czecho/Slovakia: Ethnic Conflict, Constitutional Fissure, Negotiated Breakup* (Ann Arbor: University of Michigan Press, 2000).

Stoppard, Tom, *Rock 'n' Roll* (New York: Grove Press, 2006).

Suk, Jiří, ed., *Občanské forum II, listopad–prosinec 1989, Dokumenty* [*The Civic Forum II, November–December 1989, Documents*] (Brno: Doplněk, 1998).

Suk, Jiří, *Labyrintem revoluce* [*Through the Labyrinth of the Revolution*] (Prague: Prostor, 2003).

— *Občanské forum I, listopad–prosinec 1989, Události* [*The Civic Forum I, November–December 1989, Events*] (Brno: Doplněk, 1998).

— *Politika jako absurdní drama. Václav Havel v letech 1975–1989* [*Politics as Absurdist Drama. Václav Havel in the Years 1975–1989*] (Prague: Paseka, 2013).

Svora, Přemysl, *Sedm týdnů, které otřásly hradem* [*Seven Weeks that Shook the Castle*] (Prague: Svora s.r.o., 1998).

Tichý, Zdeněk A., and Ježek, Vlastimil, eds., *Šest z šedesátých* [*Six from the Sixties*] (Prague: Radioservis, 2003).

Tucker, Aviezer, *The Philosophy and Politics of Czech Dissidence from Patočka to Havel* (Pittsburgh: University of Pittsburgh Press, 2000).

Tůma, Oldřich, *Zítra zase tady* [*Tomorrow Here Again*]: *The Anti-regime Demonstrations in Pre-November Prague as a Political and Social phenomenon* (Prague: Maxdorf, 1994).

Uhl, Petr, and Pavelka, *Zdenko, Dělal jsem, co jsem považoval za správné* [*I Did What I Thought Was Right*] (Prague: Torst, 2013).

Urbánek, Zdeněk, *Stvořitelé světa* [*The Creators of the World*] (Prague: Václav Havel Library, 2012).

Vacek, Miroslav, *Proč bych měl mlčet* [*Why Should I Be Silent*] (Prague: NADAS, 1991).

Vaculík, Ludvík, *Český snář* [*Czech Dream Book*] (Brno: Atlantis, 1990).

Vladislav, Jan, *Otevřený deník* [*An Open Diary*] *1977–1981* (Prague: Torst, 2012).

Wilson, Paul, *Bohemian Rhapsodies* (Prague: Torst, 2012).

Zábrana, Jan, *Celý život* [*A Whole Life*]. *Selected Diaries*, 2 vols (Prague: Torst, 1992).

INDEX

ABOUT THE AUTHOR

Michael Žantovský is the current Czech Ambassador to the Court of St James. He was among the founding members of the movement that coordinated the overthrow of the communist regime. In January 1990 he became the spokesman, press secretary and adviser to his lifelong friend, President Václav Havel. He has combined a career in politics and the foreign service with work as an author and translator into Czech of many contemporary British and American writers.